The Jossey-Bass/AHA Press Series translates the latest ideas on health care management into practical and actionable terms. Together, Jossey-Bass and the American Hospital Association offer these essential resources for the health care leaders of today.

U.S.
HEALTH LAW
AND POLICY
2001

U.S. HEALTH LAW AND POLICY 2001

A GUIDE TO THE CURRENT LITERATURE

DONALD H. CALDWELL JR.

JOSSEY-BASS
A Wiley Company
San Francisco

Health Forum, Inc.
An American Hospital Association Company
CHICAGO

AHA
press

Published by

JOSSEY-BASS
A Wiley Company
350 Sansome St.
San Francisco, CA 94104-1342

www.josseybass.com

Copyright © 2001 by John Wiley & Sons, Inc.

This publication is designed to provide accurate and authoritative information in regard to the subject matter covered. It is sold with the understanding that the publisher is not engaged in rendering professional services. If professional advice or other expert assistance is required, the services of a competent professional person should be sought.

The views expressed in this book are strictly those of the author and do not represent the official positions of the American Hospital Association.

AHA is a service mark of the American Hospital Association used under license by AHA Press.

Jossey-Bass is a registered trademark of John Wiley & Sons, Inc.

Jossey-Bass books and products are available through most bookstores. To contact Jossey-Bass directly, call (888) 378-2537, fax to (800) 605-2665, or visit our website at www.josseybass.com.

Substantial discounts on bulk quantities of Jossey-Bass books are available to corporations, professional associations, and other organizations. For details and discount information, contact the special sales department at Jossey-Bass.

We at Jossey-Bass strive to use the most environmentally sensitive paper stocks available to us. Our publications are printed on acid-free recycled stock whenever possible, and our paper always meets or exceeds minimum GPO and EPA requirements.

Library of Congress Cataloging-in-Publication Data

Caldwell, Donald H. (Donald Harrison), 1959–
    U.S. health law and policy 2001 : a guide to the current literature / Donald H. Caldwell, Jr.
       p. cm. — (Jossey-Bass health series)
    Includes bibliographical references and indexes.
    ISBN 0-7879-5504-3 (hc : alk. paper)
    1. Medical care—Law and legislation—United States—Bibliography. 2. Medical laws and legislation—United States—Bibliography. 3. Medical policy—United States—Bibliography. I. Title: US health law and policy 2001. II. Title: United States health law and policy 2001. III. Title. IV. Series.

KF3821.A1 C35 2001
016.34473'041—dc21

FIRST EDITION
HB Printing   10 9 8 7 6 5 4 3 2 1

Brief Contents

Contents

The Author

Donald H. Caldwell, Jr., is an attorney in the private practice of corporate law in Charlotte, North Carolina. He received his A.B. in 1981 from Davidson College and his J.D. in 1987 from Vanderbilt University Law School, where he was editor-in-chief of the *Vanderbilt Journal of Transnational Law.* He is a member of the American Health Lawyers Association and the North Carolina Society of Health Care Attorneys and is coauthor (along with U.S. Magistrate Judge Carl Horn III and D. Christopher Osborn) of *Law for Physicians: An Overview of Medical Legal Issues* (Chicago: American Medical Association Press, 1999).

Foreword

Much has changed in the realm of health care law and policy since the first edition of this work was published. In enacting the Balanced Budget Act of 1997, Congress significantly tightened Medicare reimbursements to providers. Diminished federal payments, along with management turmoil, have contributed to a significant increase in bankruptcy filings nationwide by hospitals and managed care organizations. Rural hospitals and academic medical centers have experienced particular financial distress, given the distinctive character of their missions and patient populations. The federal government has continued its attempt to drive down costs by importing managed care into the Medicare program in the form of the Medicare+Choice initiative. It has also sharply increased enforcement of fraud and abuse statutes against targeted organizations, particularly home health agencies, for-profit hospitals, and physicians engaged in specialty practice.

Putting aside fears about tarnishing its image and professionalism, the American Medical Association in June 1999 voted to launch its own efforts to organize collective bargaining units for employed physicians and medical residents, who constitute from one-sixth to one-third of the nation's approximately 640,000 physicians. The move represents an effort by the AMA to strengthen physicians' hands in negotiating with managed care companies and to blunt inroads that the American Federation of State, County, and Municipal Employees and other traditional unions have made in organizing doctors. The Chicago-based AMA plans to establish a national office to help with the formation of local AMA bargaining units around the country. Physicians, with an average annual compensation of $164,000 as of this writing, have grown increasingly frustrated with what they feel is usurpation by large health plans and insurers of their once-unchallenged ability to order medical services and procedures for patients. Representing roughly one-third of American doctors, the AMA has forsworn, however, any intention of using the ultimate tool of organized labor: the strike.

With these and other changes in the landscape of health care in mind, I have made a number of alterations in the topics covered in this 2001 edition of *U.S. Health Law and Policy*. First, I have subdivided the coverage of hospitals by type of facility to make the materials presented more accessible to the researcher. Second, I have added or expanded sections on health insurance, reimbursement issues, insolvency of medical institutions, medical staff matters, and labor questions. Third, recognizing the increased acceptance of the Internet as a credible medium for disseminating information, I have added more than 140 new Websites relevant to health law and policy to Appendix C and have annotated each of them to aid researchers. Finally, and most significantly, I have added approximately six hundred citations to newly published sources that address the main issues of health care law and policy in order to bring this work up to date.

Charlotte, North Carolina
March 2001

To Barbara

Preface

No aspect of American law has undergone more revolutionary change during the past few years than health care law. Aside from malpractice litigation, health care law as a discipline scarcely existed prior to congressional enactment of Medicare and Medicaid in 1965. As health care costs began to soar ahead of inflation during the 1970s and 1980s, government at all levels—along with the insurance industry—revolted against these expenses, brandishing the swords of prospective payment, managed care, and global budgeting. Although the Clinton administration's attempt at broad-scale cost containment failed in 1994, piecemeal regulation of the industry is certain to continue in the years ahead as consolidation of health care providers into networks accelerates.

As I was researching a number of the topics contained in this book, it became clear to me that each law firm library, university collection, hospital, insurance company, HMO, or public library I examined contained a different set of materials, many that could be of great value to medical administrators, health insurance personnel, health care attorneys, and the general public. The existence and scope of these materials were often unknown, however, to the persons who might best make use of them. Nowhere did there exist an up-to-date, annotated bibliography embracing the vast outpouring of writing on health care law and policy that has been published in the last several years.

Two objections might reasonably be lodged against such a project. The first is that it would yield a text so broad as to be useless. I have attempted to respond to this concern by intentionally eliminating works that address clinical aspects of health care. I have focused my efforts on identifying books, journal articles, and significant government documents that are generally available through regional libraries and that have seen print, with few exceptions, since 1990. Admittedly, this date is arbitrary, but it ensures that the resources identified are relevant. Materials specific to the ill-starred Clinton health care plan are generally excluded here. Finally, resources specifically concerned with ethics, as opposed to law or policy issues, are excluded. Researchers seeking assistance on the latter topic are encouraged to consult the excellent *Bibliography of Bioethics,* edited by LeRoy Walters and Tamar Joy Kahn and published annually by the Kennedy Institute of Ethics at Georgetown University.

A second, and not insignificant, objection to the need for this work is the advent of the Internet. Although the Internet has ameliorated research problems, Internet search engines at this writing remain primitive. A key word search may yield fifty thousand vaguely connected "hits." Bias is rarely disclosed, erroneous factual information goes unchallenged, and it is often unclear when a Website's information was most recently updated—an issue of considerable importance in a field that changes as quickly as health law. Finally, the information provided in this new electronic medium is often sketchy and leaves the researcher uncertain as to the relevance or depth of the site being searched. In deference to this new medium, however, I have included an appendix of relevant, selected Internet Websites.

This guide to the literature of health care law offers health care administrators, corporate benefits managers, attorneys, economists, physicians, medical directors new to managed care, students, and the public at large a key to the door of health law and policy information. It focuses on evaluating available materials, many not widely disseminated, on health care facilities and evolving managed care organizations such as health care maintenance organizations, preferred provider organizations, and their numerous progeny. Furthermore, it examines the antitrust, tax, and reimbursement issues attendant to these new structures. It also addresses such topics as patient access to health care, environmental issues, and legal issues specifically arising in the context of AIDS.

Although I have attempted to focus primarily on books, articles, and other sources that are highly practical in nature, I have also included a selection of works concerning the broader debates surrounding health care that will influence future business trends and legislation. Every element of this book is designed to be practical and convenient. From the succinct summaries of works in print to its appendices, indexes, and convenient size, this work offers immediate access to the literature of health care law and policy. Periodic updates will ensure that the information in this work remains current.

A Note Regarding Comprehensiveness

One of the main objectives of this book is to be as comprehensive as possible, bearing in mind that the amount of material on health care law and policy is massive and constantly proliferating. The publisher and I have attempted to be thorough in determining which works belong in this guide, but we are aware that not all have been included.

Each reader is encouraged to contact the author at www.dcaldwellj@aol.com to bring to his attention any significant works that the reader believes should have been included. The author and publisher welcome any comments that the reader believes will improve this guide in subsequent editions, including correction of any omissions or errors, for which the author alone stands responsible. Readers should be aware that the next (third) edition of this work is scheduled for publication in 2004.

Acknowledgments

Many people deserve warm thanks for manning the ropes to bring this ship into port. First, I thank Chief U.S. Magistrate Judge Carl Horn III of Charlotte, North Carolina, for suggesting the original idea in 1996 and then encouraging me through this, the book's second edition. Second, I extend my gratitude to Professor Mark A. Hall of Wake Forest Law School, whose generous review of the first edition, in the *Journal of Legal Medicine,* provided me with sage guidance on how the book might be improved in subsequent editions (although I do not claim that this new edition does justice to his thoughtful suggestions). Additionally, I would like to thank Professor Timothy S. Jost of Ohio State University and Bruce John Shih Esq. of Latham and Watkins in Los Angeles for making me aware of additional materials that should be included in this edition. I also express gratitude to James Devereux, S.J., of Chapel Hill for conspiring to sneak me into various Jesuit-run libraries for research forays.

This book could not have been written without the willingness of so many institutions to open their library collections to me over the years. I therefore acknowledge the assistance of the E. H. Little Library at Davidson College in Davidson, North Carolina; the Edward Bennett Williams Law Library at the Georgetown University Law Center in Washington, D.C.; the Loyola University Law Library in Chicago; the Duke University Law Library in Durham; and the Wake Forest University Professional Center Library in Winston-Salem. I also acknowledge the Kathrine R. Everett Law Library at the University of North Carolina at Chapel Hill Law School, the J. Murrey Atkins Library at the University of North Carolina at Charlotte, the William Madison Randall Library at the University of North Carolina at Wilmington, the Emory University Law Library in Atlanta, the University of South Carolina Law Library in Columbia, the Charlotte Area Health Education Center Library, the Public Library of Charlotte and Mecklenburg County, and the Library of the Duke Endowment in Charlotte for their kindness.

To my receptionist, Tichina Thombs, I express thanks for keeping the phone at bay. I also thank Rick Hill and his staff at AHA Press, and Andy Pasternack and his staff at Jossey-Bass Publishers, for their skilled guidance. My friends at Shuford, Hunter and Brown supplied copious quantities of humor at various stages of this project, which were welcome. Once again, above all, I thank my parents and brothers Jeff and Steve for their encouragement, support, and patience.

U.S.
HEALTH LAW
AND POLICY
2001

Part One

Medical Facilities and Organizations

An Overview of Health Law

Scarcely a generation ago, health care law as we know it in its current baroque form did not exist in the United States. Medical malpractice law as it relates to physicians was at that time largely an uncodified branch of state common law. Hospitals operated under the umbrella of charitable tort immunity and almost invariably functioned as tax-exempt entities. To the extent that health insurance existed, it did so overwhelmingly in the form of indemnity coverage supplied by Blue Cross and Blue Shield. Competition among hospitals was viewed as incompatible with the eleemosynary aims of health care. Managed care existed only in embryonic form and in only a few communities. And when attorneys, physicians, and administrators encountered one another on a regular basis, it was more likely to be on a golf course than in a boardroom hammering out acquisitions, in a courthouse litigating malpractice allegations, or at a state certificate-of-need hearing haggling over equipment purchases.

What catalyzed these changes in the legal environment of health care, ones that have accelerated in recent years into what one commentator has described as a state of "permanent whitewater"?[1] The first factor is simply the steady enactment of federal legislation aimed at broadening access to health care. Beginning with the passage of the Medicare and Medicaid Acts in the mid-1960s up to and including the Health Insurance Portability and Accountability Act of 1996 (HIPAA) and the Balanced Budget Act of 1997 (BBA), Congress has responded to the public desire to expand the availability of health care services, although well short of universal coverage. Once the camel of government reimbursement stuck its nose into the health care tent, however, it became inevitable that the rest of the beast would follow. The consequence has been increased federal oversight of government dollars spent on health care and the imposition of both civil and criminal penalties upon physicians and health care organizations that fail to comply with often murky federal regulations. Sometimes, as with the enactment of the Employee Retirement Income Security Act of 1974 (ERISA), preemptive federal legislation targeted at protecting certain employee benefits has had the perverse effect of ultimately making private health insurance less accessible, at least to those with chronic illnesses.[2] Additionally, wide-ranging environmental statutes such as CERCLA (Comprehensive Environmental Response, Compensation, and Liability Act), RCRA (Resource Conservation and Recovery Act), TSCA (Toxic Substances Control Act), the Clean Water Act, the Clean Air Act, and the Emergency Planning and Community Right-to-Know Act have directly affected health care facilities by imposing new liabilities.

A second series of changes in the legal context of health care occurred during this period at the state level. Concerned with significant increases in malpractice premiums for providers such as physicians and hospitals, a number of states codified significant changes in their malpractice laws.[3] The states also enacted certificate-of-need statutes that for the first time limited the ability of hospitals and other health care organizations to add new facilities or capital equipment.[4] The states have additionally implemented a range of new regulatory approaches to Medicaid in an effort to lower costs and broaden access.[5]

Third, evolving judicial doctrine in a number of areas has altered the legal landscape of health care over the past thirty years. Reasoning that hospitals increasingly resembled commercial enterprises and that they could easily purchase malpractice insurance, courts across the country during the

1960s and 1970s, for example, struck down the doctrine of charitable immunity.[6] Health care organizations likewise encountered increasing governmental antitrust and tax scrutiny in the 1980s and 1990s as they became more complex and dynamic organizations.[7]

Underlying all of these statutory, regulatory, and judicial changes over the last three decades has been an explosion of new medical knowledge and related technology. Fueled by heavy federal and private financing, researchers have developed vaccines against a wide range of maladies; devised innovative therapies for cancer that have reduced its mortality; and devised and refined CT, MRI, and PET diagnostic radioscopy, among other achievements. These advances have, however, raised some health care costs. Restraining health care costs with an aging American population while accommodating technological change and broadening access remains the challenge facing health policy makers today and will remain so well into the future.

References and Notes

1. Peter B. Vaill. *Managing as Performance Art: New Ideas for a World of Chaotic Change.* San Francisco: Jossey-Bass, 1991.
2. See Chapter Fifteen.
3. See Chapter Twelve.
4. See Chapter Nine.
5. See Chapter Eight.
6. See Chapter Thirteen.
7. See Chapters Six and Seven.

ANNOTATIONS

American College of Legal Medicine. *Legal Medicine: Legal Dynamics of Medical Encounters.* (3rd ed.) Milwaukee, Wis.: American College of Legal Medicine, 1995, 700 pages.

This guide, edited by the ACLM, is targeted at physicians and contains advice from more than sixty attorneys and doctors. It includes twenty sample patient forms and provides a glossary. This new edition includes additional information on administrative hearings.

Judith Areen and others. *Law, Science and Medicine.* (3rd ed.) Westbury, N.Y.: Foundation Press, 1996, 1,445 pages.

This law school casebook's focus is on improving interdisciplinary understanding and cooperation among the three fields named in its title. The authors, all of whom hold faculty appointments in law schools, recognize that students in the fields of law, science, and medicine may come to their studies with differing backgrounds, experiences, working vocabularies, and perspectives. They examine science and technology and attempt to anticipate how changes in the scientific realm will cause changes in the social fabric that, ultimately, will call for changes in the law.

Scott Becker. *Health Care Law: A Practical Guide.* (2nd ed.) New York: Matthew Bender, 1998.

This one-volume loose-leaf treatise opens with an overall review of health care transactional activity and the increase in federal regulatory activity relating to health care. Topics covered in this text's twenty-two chapters include provider transactions, tax issues, Medicare-Medicaid fraud, the physician self-referral prohibitions of Stark Acts I and II, the False Claims Act, licensing, accreditation, medical malpractice, risk management, consent, patient information and confidentiality, and environmental concerns affecting health care facilities. The chapters on various transactional structures provide helpful checklists of issues for analysis and negotiation. The text is supplemented throughout with footnotes to case law and both statutory and regulatory authority.

Irwin M. Birnbaum, Alexander M. Capron, Robert M. Kaufman, and Michael G. MacDonald (eds.). *Treatise on Health Care Law.* New York: Matthew Bender, 1991.

This four-volume loose-leaf treatise, regularly updated, covers the entire gamut of legal issues subsumed under the rubric "health care law." Leading figures in their fields discuss the broad range of concerns of health care practice, including business aspects, relationship of individuals to health care organizations, financial issues, liability, and patient care. Includes a table of cases, detailed chapter synopses, and state-by-state charts on a variety of issues.

James F. Blumstein and Frank A. Sloan. "Health Care Reform Through Medicaid Managed Care: Tennessee (TennCare) as a Case Study and a Paradigm." *Vanderbilt Law Review,* 2000, *53*(1), 125.

Considers and analyzes elements of TennCare's design and implementation from a legal and policy perspective. It concludes that, in contrast to the contemporaneous Clinton Administration plan for improved access, TennCare's design demonstrated the triumph of pragmatism over ideology. It focuses on reform of Medicaid rather than comprehensively encompassing the entire health care market; it adopted a pluralistic rather than a unitary approach; and, at least nominally, it adopted a standard of adequacy rather than equality in defining the scope of the public's obligation to TennCare beneficiaries. Because the 1997 Balanced Budget Act allows states to adopt mandatory managed care for Medicaid, TennCare's managed care features can be replicated in other states without the need for a waiver. Finally, the article reports on empirical findings about such issues as quality of care, hospital profitability, and patient and physician satisfaction. It concludes that the quality of care, in general, has not suffered, that patient satisfaction has been good, that physician participation rates in the program exceed those of the preexisting Medicaid program, that hospital capacity has been decreasing at levels above the national average, and that hospital profitability overall has not suffered, but that levels of physician satisfaction are very low.

Bernadette M. Broccolo, Donald H. Caldwell, Jr., and others. *Fundamentals of Health Law.* (2nd ed.) Washington, D.C.: American Health Lawyers Association, 2000, 346 pages.

Written by and primarily for practicing attorneys, this book addresses the fundamental legal issues that need to be understood by a practicing health lawyer, regardless of the area of specialty in which he or she may practice. The book addresses not only the primary legal issues a lawyer may face but also the structural and operational issues affecting health care providers and payers. In addition, it provides a basic understanding of how health care is rendered. Some of the key topics discussed are tax and tax-exempt issues, federal and state fraud and abuse statutes, self-referral laws, false claims issues, antitrust, confidentiality, and Medicare and Medicaid reimbursement issues. Includes helpful charts, graphs, a glossary, and a list of relevant Internet sites.

California Medical Association. *California Physician's Legal Handbook.* 2 vols. San Francisco: California Medical Association, 1997, 1,800 pages.

Loose-leaf–bound text offering more than eighteen hundred pages of information on a wide range of topics. Chapters include AIDS and HIV, antitrust, organ donation/death, emergency transfer, fraud and abuse, medical records, Medicare and Medi-Cal, peer review, professional liability, and warning obligations. Regularly updated.

William J. Curran, Mark A. Hall, Mary Anne Bobinski, and David Orentlicher. *Health Care Law and Ethics.* (5th ed.) Gaithersburg, Md.: Aspen, 1998, 1,453 pages.

Textbook synthesizing the numerous conceptual strands that have come to be known as health care law. The authors organize the fundamental structural relationships that give rise to health care law into three primary themes: (1) the patient-physician relationship, which encompasses the duty to treat, confidentiality, informed consent, and malpractice; (2) government oversight of doctors and patients; and (3) the institutions that surround the treatment relationship, encompassing public and private insurance, hospitals, and health maintenance organizations (HMOs), along with more complex transactions and organization forms. The authors develop the traditional themes of quality, ethics, access, and cost throughout each of these three divisions. They also address such controversial topics as abortion, AIDS, genetics, managed care, and rationing. To update the text, the authors have created a dedicated Website to serve students and readers: php.iupui.edu/~healthlw.

Donald T. Dickson. *Law in the Health and Human Services: A Guide for Social Workers, Psychologists, Psychiatrists, and Related Professionals.* New York: Free Press, 1995, 640 pages.

Written for students in upperclass college or graduate courses and for professionals in the health services field, this books covers a wide range of topics, including privacy, personal autonomy, and records; confidential communications; informed consent; AIDS; and malpractice, among others.

Barry R. Furrow and others. *Health Law: Cases, Problems and Materials.* (3rd ed.) St. Paul, Minn.: West, 1997, 1,247 pages.

Law school casebook addressing many subjects not previously covered in depth in law and medicine texts: health care financing and cost control, organization and management of health care institutions, and antitrust. The authors also examine Medicare and Medicaid and the issue of access to health care. The text opens with the author's observation that health law is both broader and narrower than law and medicine as it has been traditionally taught in American law schools. Law and medicine has in the past focused on two topics: professional malpractice and forensic medicine. In recent years law and medicine courses have expanded to cover new issues that arise at the intersection of law and medicine. This text grows out of the author's belief that one semester-long course can no longer cover all the issues that now arise with the interaction of law and medicine and that any attempt to do so will be unfocused.

Barry R. Furrow and others. *Health Law.* 2 vols. St. Paul, Minn.: West, 1995, 1,524 pages.

The two volumes of this treatise provide a comprehensive overview of this field. It considers the law's response to quality and error both through institutional and professional regulation and through malpractice litigation against professionals, hospitals, and managed care organizations. It surveys tax, corporate, and organizational issues that arise in health care businesses. It explores efforts of the government to control costs and expand access through the Medicare and Medicaid programs and through private insurance regulation. It also examines government attempts to police anticompetitive activities and fraud and abuse. Finally, it considers legal and ethical issues involving death, reproduction, and medical research.

Barry R. Furrow, Daniel E. Johnson, Timothy S. Jost, and Stephen Schwarz. *Health Law: Cases, Problems and Materials,* 1999 Supplement. St. Paul, Minn.: West, 1999, 608 pages.

As the law of health care organizations and finance has evolved, law, medicine, public health, and health administration schools have responded by offering courses in this subject. This casebook is designed for such courses. It begins with an introduction to some fundamental concepts affecting law and policy, such as the definitions of illness, medical error, and rationing. The next chapter considers quality control in the health care setting, examining government regulation of the quality of care provided by professionals and institutions and oversight of professionals within institutions. The following four chapters examine issues central to structuring integrated systems and the organization of health care institutions. These chapters discuss such timely topics as corporate law and corporate structuring options, tax exempt status, staff privileging, contracting, regulation of financial relationships among providers (including fraud and abuse law and Stark law), and antitrust. The final chapters in the text examine health care access and cost control, with particular attention being paid to the ongoing debate about the proper role of government and the nation's responsibilities to provide health care for its indigent citizens.

Barry R. Furrow, Daniel E. Johnson, Timothy S. Jost, and Stephen Schwarz. *Liability & Quality Issues in Health Care.* St. Paul, Minn.: West Group, 1997, 496 pages.

This volume is devoted exclusively to the law of medical liability and quality control. It comprises Chapters One through Six and Twelve of the casebook *Health Law: Cases, Materials and Problems* (third edition) and is aimed at the specific content of an upper-level elective health law course. The books blends recent case law, statutory developments, and problems to maximize the flexibility of materials for teachers of health law. The notes are rich in detail and citations, allowing the instructor to spend more time on topics of particular interest.

Barry F. Furrow, Daniel E. Johnson, Timothy S. Jost, and Stephen Schwarz. *Bioethics: Health Care Law & Ethics.* St. Paul, Minn.: West Group, 1998.

This book is designed to provide a rigorous introduction to the discipline of bioethics and the intersection of bioethics and law for the serious beginning student in this area. Because the term *bioethics* is used idiosyncratically to describe a host of subjects that touch upon medicine, health policy, science, values, social and personal decision making, and law, these materials are unlikely to seem comprehensive. The book provides an introduction to the discipline of bioethics and a brief but thorough overview of the most significant theories of ethics, theories that anyone attempting bioethical analysis needs to be familiar with. It then provides a fuller discussion of two specific topics: human reproduction, human genetics and birth (in Chapters Two and Three) and death and dying (in Chapters Four and Five). The book concludes with a discussion of the distribution of health care resources, primarily in the context of organ transplantation and several subjects related to interdisciplinary health care decision making, including research upon human subjects and institutional ethics committees.

Group for the Advancement of Psychiatry. *The Mental Health Professional and the Legal System.* Washington, D.C.: American Psychiatric Press, 1991, 192 pages.

Forensic experts discuss confidentiality, patients' rights, duty to warn, civil commitment, and other issues at the intersection of psychiatry and the law.

Barbara A. Haley and Brian Deevey. *American Health Care in Transition: A Guide to the Literature.* Westport, Conn.: Greenwood Press, 1998, 337 pages.

This volume is an annotated bibliography targeted at readers who want to gain familiarity with the extensive academic and practice journal literature and with two little-known resources, the reports produced by the General Accounting Office, a congressional agency; and the Agency for Health Care Policy and Research, which is part of the U.S. Department of Health and Human Services. The 975 articles annotated are arranged into five chapters: (1) current challenges to the health care system, (2) health insurance, (3) health care providers, (4) future challenges to the health care system, and (5) discussions of policy and reform. This is an excellent resource for health care policy researchers.

Mark A. Hall and others. *Health Care Law and Ethics in a Nutshell.* St Paul, Minn.: West Group, 1998. 464 pages.

This book focuses on two areas of modern health law: the legal and financial structure of health care and bioethics. Law topics covered include contractual aspects of the doctor-patient relationship (duty to treat, termination of relationship), the legal nature of health care organizations, ERISA preemption, medical malpractice and informed consent, antitrust, and ethical considerations.

Clark C. Havighurst, James F. Blumstein, and Troyen Brennan. *Health Care Law and Policy.* (2nd ed.) St. Paul, Minn.: West Group, 1998, 1,472 pages.

This extensive revision of a widely praised 1988 text presents health care law in the context of an evolving industry trying to resolve the difficult trade-offs inherent in health care economics. The subject is unfolded by dramatizing the policy assumptions and paradigms underlying legal doctrine and statutory rules and by tracking the historic changes that have occurred in the organization and financing of health care services in recent years, and changes that are continuing today. Without sacrificing close attention to legal rules, the text challenges the student to view the legal environment of the health care sector as a totality and to understand how it advances or retards progress toward making the health care marketplace responsive to consumer needs and preferences and toward achieving efficiency in the allocation of resources to the health care enterprise.

Health Policy Tracking Service. *Major Health Care Policies: Fifty State Profiles.* Washington, D.C.: National Conference of State Legislatures, 1997, 295 pages.

Addresses current health care policies and legislation in all fifty states. This annual report, now in its fifth year of publication, provides a two-page summary of each state's activity along with a table of specific legislative activity on ten issues: ERISA, health workforce supply, HIPAA, insurer liability, MSAs, managed care, Medicaid, parity, pharmaceuticals, and the State Children's Health Insurance Program.

Regina Herzlinger. *Market Driven Health Care: Who Wins, Who Loses in the Transformation of America's Largest Service Industry.* Reading, Mass.: Addison-Wesley, 1997, 379 pages.

Argues that the free market system will correct many of the problems of the American health care system if it is consumer-controlled. The author, a professor at Harvard Business School, writes that consumer demand for information and convenience, along with technology and new organizational structures, are creating health care delivery systems that offer high quality and low costs. The text includes copious notes and an index.

Anthony R. Kovner (ed.). *Health Care Delivery in the United States.* (4th ed.) New York: Springer, 1990, 553 pages.

Consists of essays by fifteen prominent health care policy analysts. This introductory book is primarily descriptive, not prescriptive. Thus it serves the needs of both those who simply want to know what the U.S. health care delivery system is like and how it works and those who would take the descriptions provided and develop their own prescriptions for change. Its target audience is readers studying to be clinicians or managers.

Michael G. MacDonald and others (eds.). *Treatise on Health Care Law.* 4 vols. New York: Matthew Bender, 1995.

Covers in detail the entire spectrum of legal issues involved in health care practice and serves as a primary reference work and authority. This exhaustive treatise examines a broad array of topics and is the work product of almost thirty experts. Chapters One through Four examine the business aspects of health care, including corporate, organizational and tax issues, facility licensing, and contractual arrangements that involve the unique characteristics of the health care system. Chapters Five and Six cover the range of issues arising out of the relationship of individuals to health care organizations, from labor and employment issues to issues involving the medical staff, an area that remains dynamic.

Subsequent chapters examine reimbursement issues, utilization review, antitrust, medical waste disposal, access to care, medical malpractice, and informed consent. Each volume is extensively footnoted and regularly updated by the publisher. The final volume concludes with a table of cases and a topical index.

Jeffrey D. Mamorsky (ed.). *Health Care Handbook.* Boston: Warren Gorham & Lamont, 1991.

Practical guide written for personnel directors and administrators, management, and representatives of organized labor and government agencies grappling with complex legal constraints relating to health care benefits. Regularly updated by the publisher, it contains the work of experts in employee relations, finance, compliance, law, accounting, and plan design. It addresses the organizational implications that HMOs, PPOs, and other structures may have for employers.

Medical Group Management Association. *State Health Policy Reference.* Englewood, Colo.: MGMA, 1996, 120 pages.

Compendium of articles on state health policy published in 1995 and 1996. The book covers issues ranging from any-willing-provider laws to utilization review and provides analyses of major state health policy initiatives affecting medical groups.

Medical Group Management Association. *State Legislative Data Book.* Englewood, Colo.: MGMA, 1998.

Contains descriptions, analysis, charts, state summaries, and issue briefs on twenty-one state legislative and regulatory issues important to group practice management. Topics include integrated delivery systems, state regulation of managed care, state action antitrust immunity, and Medicaid. Also included is a listing of governors, legislatures, and legislative sessions. Regularly updated.

Robert D. Miller. *Problems in Health Care Law.* (7th ed.) Gaithersburg, Md.: Aspen, 1996, 612 pages.

Formerly known as *Problems in Hospital Law,* this guide has been expanded to address health care legal issues outside the realm of the hospital. It provides an excellent introduction to health care law, aimed primarily at nonlawyers. Core topics discussed include regulation and accreditation of institutions, payment, managed care, taxation, antitrust, reorganization, closure, and the relationship between the hospital and medical staff. Other issues examined are individual licensing and credentialing, staff relations, treatment authorization and refusal, medical records management and confidentiality, disclosure limitations, and reproductive issues. The text concludes with a glossary of relevant acronyms, a case index, an index to statutes and regulations, and a general index.

Jonathan Montgomery. *Health Care Law.* New York: Oxford University Press, 1997, 476 pages.

Examines the law that governs the delivery of health care in the United Kingdom. The first part of the book covers public health law and the workings of the National Health Service. The second part explores the general framework of regulating health care practice and malpractice law. The third part discusses the legal status of patients, including issues of confidentiality, consent, and access to records. The final section examines specific areas of practice that have particular legal and ethical problems, such as abortion, transplantation, and terminal care. This is a particularly valuable resource for the comparative law researcher.

Herman Nys (ed.). *International Encyclopaedia of Laws: Medical Law.* 2 vols. Boston: Kluwer Law International, 1994.

Covers national and international medical law. The national monographs contain a general introduction along with a description of the law relating to the medical profession such as access to care, illegal practice of medicine, and control over the practice of medicine; patient relationships, along with specific issues such as euthanasia and the abortion of children; and national law dealing with the physician in relation to colleagues, other health care providers, and the health care system. Part of Kluwer's International Encyclopedia of Laws series, this comprehensive work is updated by four to six supplements annually. This is a valuable tool for lawyers, law libraries, government agencies, and specialists in comparative law.

Peter A. Pavarini and others (eds.). *U.S. Health Care Law and Rules.* St. Paul, Minn.: West, 1997, 1,600 pages.

Contains the full text of the federal laws and rules referred to most often by health care attorneys, providers, administrators, and trustees. Prepared for the American Health Lawyers Association by

West, this book was edited by a distinguished panel of health care attorneys. The statute text includes section headings and legislative histories. Research aids include a user's guide and a detailed subject index, incorporating both legal and popular terminology for quick access to the materials. This compilation is an excellent resource.

Henry H. Perritt, Jr. *Health Care Legislation Update and Analysis.* New York: Wiley Law, 1995, 478 pages.

A guide to the changing legal environment of health care. Written by a professor at Villanova Law School and former deputy undersecretary of labor in the Ford administration, this work discusses how providers, patients, health care plans, and governments can protect their rights and manage risk in a reformed health care system. Chapter One examines the primary types of legal dispute that arise from the perspective of care recipients, municipal and state governments, the federal government, and employer-sponsored plans. Chapter Two reviews how health care reform affects subscribers and their dependents and discusses new legal theories that may be developed by individuals injured by inappropriate care, focusing on the possibility that the economic incentives created by managed care structures may compromise care quality. Chapter Three analyzes managed care arrangements and health care integration.

Chapter Four addresses the powers and duties of federal agencies, along with the Hill-Burton Act, Medicare, Medicaid, Armed Services Health Care, and the important topic of ERISA preemption. In the absence of comprehensive federal health care reform, state health care reform efforts are especially pertinent and are analyzed in Chapter Five. Chapter Six discusses health care plans in general, along with specific issues of plan modification, COBRA (Consolidated Omnibus Budget Reconciliation Act of 1985), and plan insolvency. Chapter Seven covers litigation issues, focusing on asserting claims to government benefits and the doctrine of the exhaustion of administrative remedies. In this context, the author supplies excellent case evaluation checklists for ERISA litigation, from both the plaintiff's and the defendant's perspectives. The final chapter is devoted to health information systems technology, focusing on privacy issues. Periodically updated, this is a helpful resource.

Ralph Reisner, Christopher Slobogin, and Arti Rai. *Law and the Mental Health System: Civil and Criminal Aspects.* (3rd ed.) St. Paul, Minn.: West Group, 1999, 1,218 pages.

This book is divided into three parts: (1) the relationship between the patient and the therapist, (2) state involvement with individuals who suffer from a mental disability, and (3) federal legislation intended to provide benefits to people with mental disabilities. The first part covers such topics as who mental health professionals are, how these professionals are licensed or otherwise regulated by the states, issues relating to malpractice and informed consent, and the requirements for protecting patient confidentiality and preserving testimonial privilege. The second part of the book covers issues regarding the expertise of mental health professionals, the relationship of mental disability to criminal law, civil commitment and postcommitment concerns, and determinations of competency and capacity. The third part addresses entitlement programs and antidiscrimination legislation.

Edward P. Richards III and Katherine C. Rathbun. *Law and the Physician: A Practical Guide.* Boston: Little, Brown, 1993, 571 pages.

Using a preventive law approach to medical practice, this book provides the information physicians need to avoid legal conflicts and better understand the delicate relationship between law and medicine. Topics explored include malpractice; consent to treatment; referral and consultation; disease control; AIDS; legal aspects of parental rights; genetic counseling and fertility treatment; institutional practice—teams, schools, and prisons; and OSHA rules on occupational medicine practice.

Richard Rognebaugh (ed.). *The Managed Health Care Dictionary.* (2nd ed.) Gaithersburg, Md.: Aspen, 1998, 288 pages.

With more than one thousand terms, this edition highlights new terminology, gives current definitions, and supplies an expanded listing of acronyms and abbreviations.

Rand Rosenblatt, Sylvia Law, and Sara Rosenbaum. *Law and the American Health Care System.* Westbury, N.Y.: Foundation Press, 1997, 1,343 pages.

This law school casebook examines the legal and policy issues implicated in creating and maintaining an equitable social system that can ensure adequate health care to all its citizens. The book's coverage is comprehensive and offers a balanced treatment of a wide range of health law issues, including federal health programs, health care reform, and long-term health issues. Rosenbaum was one of the architects of the Clinton administration health plan.

Michael H. Shapiro and Roy G. Spece, Jr. *Cases, Materials and Problems on Bioethics and Law.* St. Paul, Minn.: West, 1981.

For purposes of these materials, *bioethics* refers primarily to moral and legal analysis of the new biology—those biological technologies that permit a striking degree of influence over and knowledge about human characteristics and life processes, and in doing so generate or intensify serious value conflicts and problems. Topics discusses include behavior control, control of dying, and organ transplantation.

J. Stuart Showalter and others. *Southwick's the Law of Healthcare Administration.* (3rd ed.) Chicago: Health Administration Press. 1999, 569 pages.

Addresses basic law in health care administration and public health programs, antitrust, and intermediate sanction under the Internal Revenue Code. Revisions address the "anti-dumping" statute, rulings related to abortion. Also included is a chapter on health care fraud and abuse.

Vergil N. Slee. *Health Care Terms.* (3rd ed.) St. Paul, Minn.: Tringa Press, 1996, 655 pages.

Written to meet the needs of physicians, hospital administrators, and general readers, this dictionary contains terms drawn principally from health care management in the United States and includes acronyms and synonyms, usually as cross-references. Although technology advances medical progress, it has also caused information resources to increase; the chapter titled "Tracking Down Information" adds to the dictionary's value and usefulness by listing as sources physicians, librarians, and printed and electronic publications. Appendices include a chronology (1630–1996), an outline of health care reform, and a bibliography. Definitions provided are intended to be understood by general readers and health care providers alike.

Christopher Slobogin and Ralph Reisner. *Law and the Mental Health System: Civil and Criminal Aspects.* St. Paul, Minn.: West, 1998, 1,264 pages.

Covers the legal doctrine, as well as some of the most important clinical and empirical literature, relating to the mental health professions and to the relationship between society and the mentally disabled. It gives students a broad but clear picture of past, present, and possible future developments in the field and provides insight into how and to what degree the legal system can be used to implement desired social objectives.

Snoe's American Health Care Delivery System. St. Paul, Minn.: West, 1998, 896 pages.

This casebook surveys the core regulatory and financing issues affecting health care providers. The book is divided into parts covering individuals' access to health care (including HIPAA; COBRA continuation coverage; ERISA; the Americans with Disabilities Act, or ADA; and the Emergency Medical Treatment and Active Labor Act, or EMTALA), regulation of health care providers, managed care, tax exempt organizations, Medicare and Medicaid (including antikickback and self-referral prohibitions), and antitrust. Each chapter is a self-contained assignment to be covered in one or two class sessions; each chapter's overview provides the background necessary to understand the issues developed in the chapter; each chapter's materials section reproduces cases, statutes, and rulings relevant to the chapter's topic; and discussion questions facilitate discussions of practical and policy issues attorneys encounter in the health care sector.

Arthur F. Southwick. *The Law of Hospital and Health Care Administration.* (3rd ed.) Chicago: Health Administration Press, 1999. See the annotation above under J. Stuart Showalter.

This is a basic graduate text on health care law written by a veteran in the field.

Meg Wallace. *Health Care and the Law.* Sydney, Australia: Law Book, 1995, 471 pages.

Legal casebook examining a variety of health care legal issues—including consent to treatment, negligence, and medical records—through the prism of the federal laws of Australia, along with the laws of that nation's eight states and territories. Written by an Australian nurse who is also an attorney, this text is particularly valuable for the comparative law researcher.

Weissburg Aronson, Inc. staff. *Health Care Law Sourcebook: A Compendium of Federal Laws, Regulations and Documents Relating to Health Care.* New York: Matthew Bender, 1989.

This three-volume loose-leaf treatise covers (1) Medicare reimbursement and certification; (2) Medicaid reimbursements standards; (3) patient confidentiality and nondiscrimination; (4) approval of drugs and procedures; (5) antitrust and trade regulation; (6) environmental protection; (7) labor, employment, and occupational safety; and (8) other health care laws. Regularly updated with revisions, the sourcebook includes a Summary of Developments that highlights recent legislative and regulatory developments in the areas covered, and a regulatory alert that spotlights proposed changes involving Medicare and Medicaid. A final section of the sourcebook provides the full text of recent public laws affecting health care.

Kenneth R. Wing, Michael S. Jacobs, and Patricia C. Kuszler. *The Law and American Health Care.* Gaithersburg, Md.: Aspen, 1998, 1,250 pages.

This casebook is written as a basic text for a law school–based health law course surveying legal and political issues relating to health care delivery and financing in the United States. The authors write that they view this book primarily as the basis for a second-generation introductory health law course, one that could be offered as an elective in any legal curriculum. Their objectives are (1) to describe the structural elements of health care delivery and financing in the United States; the social, economic, political, and other forces that have shaped them into what they are today; and the trends that will affect them in the future; (2) to identify important issues and problems concerning cost, accessibility, and quality of health care; and (3) to analyze how the law will and should be applied to resolve these issues and problems. The text is supplemented by dozens of helpful charts, tables, exhibits, and sidebars.

2

Health Care Facilities and Settings

The term *health care facilities* would once have referred only to hospitals. Today, it has expanded to include nursing homes, hospices, ambulatory care centers, psychiatric institutions, drug and alcohol rehabilitation facilities, skilled nursing facilities, and others. As the fragmentation of the hospital has accelerated over recent years, the law governing these various facilities has expanded. Whereas hospital law once concerned itself primarily with liability issues, the broader field of health care facilities law also examines such issues as staff membership, clinical privileges, state licensing, federal certification, consumer protection, and patient rights.

The annotations that follow summarize recent examinations of a variety of health facilities law issues.

ANNOTATIONS

2.01   IN GENERAL

Annot. "Validity and Construction of Zoning Regulations Expressly Referring to Hospitals, Sanitariums, or Nursing Homes." *ALR3rd 27*, 1022.

This brief annotation collects and analyzes the cases discussing the construction or validity of zoning restrictions that, by their terms, expressly refer to hospitals, sanitariums, or nursing homes.

Anne M. Dellinger (ed.) *Healthcare Facilities Law: Critical Issues for Hospitals, HMOs, and Extended Care Facilities.* Boston: Little, Brown, 1991, 1,162 pages.

Describes the legal structure of facilities, discusses issues relating to the delivery of services, examines legal structures for health care facilities that were common at the time the book was written, and addresses such significant issues as AIDS and handling medical records. Although this text emphasizes the legal problems of hospitals, the distinctive features of care rendered by HMOs and extended care facilities also receive attention. This authoritative treatise represents a collective effort by eighteen leading attorneys with a range of experience in health law to assist both their colleagues who represent health care facilities and the individuals who administer them. Among the authors are teachers and writers on health as well as practicing attorneys who have served as staff and retained counsel for facilities. The editor is a professor of law and government at the University of North Carolina at Chapel Hill's Institute of Government.

Francis Gibbs and Christina A. Kasprisin (eds.) *Regulation and Accreditation: Surviving Inspections.* Bethesda, Md.: American Association of Blood Banks, 1989.

Guidebook intended for laboratory managers. Because blood banks and transfusion services are inspected and accredited by a variety of agencies, the laboratory manager must be familiar with the accreditation programs and be prepared to answer an assortment of questions pertaining to their operations. Representatives from the AABB (American Association of Blood Banks) Accreditation Program, FDA, OSHA, CLIA (Clinical Laboratory Improvement Amendments of 1988), and CAP discuss their accreditation programs, offer an overview of regulatory agencies, discuss some of the most common deficiencies, and explain the legal rights and responsibilities of the institutions.

Louis C. Grapenski. *Understanding Health Care Financial Management: Text, Cases, and Models.* Chicago: Health Administration Press, 1993, 761 pages.

Textbook intended for the health care financial management course required in graduate programs in health administration. Students will often have had some background in business topics such as financial and managerial accounting, probability and statistics, and corporate finance. However, the text contains a great deal of background information in these areas that is useful to the health care attorney.

Kenneth Kaufman and Mark A. Hall. *The Financially Competitive Healthcare Organization: The Executive's Guide to Strategic Financial Planning and Management.* Chicago: Probus, 1994, 201 pages.

Provides strategic planning tools to aid CFOs and other finance executives in strategic planning, with the view in mind that the long-term health of a hospital rests on its ability to remain financially competitive.

Anthony R. Kovner. *Really Managing: The Work of Effective CEOs in Large Health Organizations.* Chicago: Health Administration Press, 1988.

Examines the role of the chief executive officer in large health care organizations. The author suggests that we must better understand what CEOs do and their contribution to their organizations' effectiveness in order to evaluate their performance. The book presents interviews with four CEOs and their close associates and indicates the activities and episodes of work Kovner observed when following the CEOs. Finally, the author extracts from the data four themes common to managerial effectiveness in large health organizations, and he makes recommendations of action that managers can take relative to these themes.

Anthony R. Kovner and Duncan Neuhauser. *Health Services Management: Readings and Commentary.* (4th ed.) Chicago: Health Administration Press, 1990, 513 pages.

Offers twenty-seven essays on a range of issues, including the role of the manager, control, organizational design, professional integration, adaptation, and accountability. This is primarily a classroom text.

William J. Krowinski and Steven R. Steiber. *Measuring and Managing Patient Satisfaction.* (3rd ed.) Chicago: American Hospital Publishing, 1996, 280 pages.

Written for leaders in quality improvement, patient relations, planning, research, marketing, and operations, this work details how to plan and conduct patient satisfaction studies within the context of the current regulatory environment.

Charles R. McConnell (ed.). *The Healthcare Supervisor on Law.* Gaithersburg, Md.: Aspen, 1993, 227 pages.

Assembles eighteen articles intended to heighten the supervisor's awareness of the major areas of supervisory conduct or involvement that have undergone significant change because of legislative action. Topics discussed include liability and the supervisor, mandatory reporting laws, duties of health care providers regarding withdrawal of treatment, wrongful discharge, and managing a discrimination case.

Edited by a vice president for employee affairs at the Genesee Hospital in Rochester, New York, the book also focuses on AIDS issues. One essay concerns the conflict between the rights of individuals afflicted with the disease and the rights and concerns of health care workers who care for AIDS patients. Others address the obstacles to conducting HIV antibody testing within health care organizations while still protecting the health of the public and ensuring individual rights. The book concludes with a series of essays on organized (and organizing) labor.

Robert D. Miller. *Problems in Health Care Law*. (7th ed.) Gaithersburg, Md.: Aspen, 1996, 612 pages.

Identifies a broad range of issues, areas to explore, and applicable standards and principles without going into great depth on any one topic. Written for a general audience, it is particularly useful for the health care novice seeking to identify relevant issues in a given situation. Previously published under the title *Problems in Hospital Law,* the title change makes sense given the expansion of the book's coverage to include a range of issues beyond those encountered by hospitals. New topics include the ADA, corporate problems, and labor issues. The researcher seeking an explanation of the differences between medical device liability, pharmaceutical liability, and the theories of tort liability in general, for example, will also find helpful information here.

James E. Orlikoff and Mary K. Totten. *The Future of Health Care Governance: Redesigning Boards for a New Era.* Chicago: American Hospital Publishing, 1996, 120 pages.

Examines the forms and functions of governance. Written for boards and their members, it assists board members in understanding the circumstances propelling the need for change, in identifying barriers to change and methods of overcoming them, and assessing practical models for governing an integrated health care delivery system.

George D. Pozgar and Nina S. Pozgar. *Case Law in Health Care Administration.* Gaithersburg, Md.: Aspen, 1996, 215 pages.

In this text, the authors provide a companion to their *Legal Aspects of Health Care Administration,* sixth edition. This book supplies more than 175 recently decided cases from an array of jurisdictions covering important legal issues facing health care providers. Topics addressed include criminal aspects of health care, exclusive physician contracts, statutes of limitation, nursing and the law, and health care records. Other topics examined are patient consent, AIDS, and labor relations. The book concludes with a self-test with answers and answer sheet.

George D. Pozgar and Nina Santucci Pozgar. *Legal Aspects of Health Care Administration.* (6th ed.) Gaithersburg, Md.: Aspen, 1996, 738 pages.

The goal of this volume is to impart to health care professionals a working knowledge of basic health care law. Free of legal jargon, the book assumes no prior background in legal matters. Topics examined include how the legal system works, tort law, contracts, trial practice, corporate liability, and medical staff issues. Also discussed are nursing and the law, liability of professionals, information management and health care records, AIDS, labor relations, employment law, and malpractice issues. The book concludes with a chapter on managed care and organizational restructuring, along with a glossary of terms. This book could serve both as a reference for health care personnel as well as a text for the management curriculum of health care programs.

Uwe R. Reinhardt. "Spending More Through 'Cost Control': Our Obsessive Quest to Gut the Hospital." *Health Affairs,* 1996, *15,* 145.

Examines Congressional Budget Office data indicating that the growth of national health care spending has flattened. A noted health care economist, Reinhardt questions whether the centerpiece of this nation's cost control strategy—a push to reduce the number of hospital inpatient days per capita—may actually have been counterproductive. He posits the view that the nation's health care system is like a balloon: squeeze it in one place and it is likely to bulge out in another.

David W. Young. "Accounting and Financial Management for Health Care Facilities." In Mark A. Hall (ed.), *Health Care Corporate Law: Financing and Liability.* Boston: Little, Brown, 1994.

The focus in this ninety-five-page chapter is on financial and management accounting principles. As for other business clients, effective lawyering for health care clients requires some understanding of the principles of accounting and financial management. Accounting information falls into two general categories: financial accounting and management accounting. Financial accounting provides information to outside parties; management accounting provides information to managers in an organization. Financial accounting is the subject of the first half of the chapter. The discussion is divided into three broad sections: (1) financial accounting principles, (2) financial statement analysis, and (3) fundamental financing issues. Management accounting is discussed in the second half of the chapter. The major topics are full cost accounting, differential cost accounting, and responsibility accounting.

2.02   HOSPITALS

Michael W. Peregrine. "Advising a Health System Board on Fiduciary Duties." Washington, D.C.: American Health Lawyers Association [Report No. VHH99–0010], 1999, 36 pages.

Reviews the basic tenets of the fiduciary duties of oversight, care, and loyalty, and identifies current developments in the law of fiduciary duty and of charitable trust law as they apply to nonprofit health care corporations and their governing boards.

Stephen M. Shortell. *Effective Hospital-Physician Relationships.* Ann Arbor, Mich.: Health Administration Press, 1991.

Studies ten health care institutions that have cultures and policies that fully integrate physicians into all phases of institutional management. Topics discussed include managerial style, managing conflict, hospital-physician joint ventures, and nurse-physician relationships.

2.02(1)   In General

The AHA Guide to the Health Care Field. Chicago: Health InfoSource, 2000, 1,000 pages (approx.).

This annual guide supplies timely and comprehensive information about hospitals, networks, health care systems and alliances, and health organizations and providers. It is the result of a regular survey of hospitals conducted by Health InfoSource, Inc., a subsidiary of the American Hospital Association.

American College of Healthcare Executives. *Contracts for Healthcare Executives.* (3rd ed.) Chicago: Health Administration Press, 1995, 64 pages.

Focuses on changes in the health care delivery environment and the crucial role executive employment contracts play. Other issues addressed include the applicability of contracts under hospital merger or closure, as well as noncompete, confidentiality, and arbitration requirements. Appendices include model contracts for CEOs and vice presidents.

Aspen Health Law Center. *Hospital Law Manual.* Gaithersburg, Md.: Aspen, 1998.

Topics addressed include AIDS issues, antitrust, bankruptcy, environmental issues, financial management, immunity from liability, and labor. Other subjects are hospital licensure, medical records, and ad valorem taxation. It concludes with a table of cases and a topical index. This meticulously organized treatise consists of eight loose-leaf volumes, four administrator's volumes, and four volumes for attorneys. The wide range of subject matter is broken down into tabbed sections and six hundred subject references. Available in binders or in CD-ROM format, the set is kept up-to-date with four supplements and monthly newsletters mailed throughout the year. Thorough and authoritative, more than one-half of the hospitals in the nation subscribe to this work.

Atlantic Information Services. *The Business Book on 5 Top Hospital Corporations.* Washington, D.C.: Atlantic Information Services, 1997, 250 pages.

Provides information on purchasing procedures; information technology; strategic alliances; and pending litigation on Columbia/HCA Healthcare Corp., Tenet Healthcare Corp., Vencor, Health South Corp., and Magellan Health Services. In addition to the book, purchasers receive a disk with contact information and number of beds for each of the more than sixteen hundred hospitals owned by these companies.

Howard J. Berman and others (eds.). *The Financial Management of Hospitals.* (8th ed.) Chicago: Health Administration Press, 1994, 724 pages.

The editors of this now-standard volume draw an analogy between the HMO industry and the U.S. auto industry early in the century. At that time there were three hundred to four hundred manufacturers, many with imperfect products, some precariously underfinanced, with poor facilities and inexperienced management. Hundreds of companies were started but only the Big Three survived. The editors foresee that many HMOs will find it impossible to cope with such competitors as Blue Cross and Blue Shield, Kaiser Permanente, large insurance companies, and investor-owned chains. They further predict a shakedown in the capitation insurance business. The surviving companies will need to offer nationwide insurance coverage to satisfy the national corporations that have employees all across the country.

Robert E. Bloch and others. "The Long Island Hospital Merger Case." Washington, D.C.: American Health Lawyers Association [Report No. VHL-0034], 1998, 10 pages.

Reviews the elements of the litigation surrounding the Long Island Jewish Medical Center.

Walt Bogdanich. *The Great White Lie: How America's Hospitals Betray Our Trust and Endanger Our Lives.* New York: Simon & Schuster, 1991, 320 pages.

A Pulitzer Prize–winning journalist exposes what he terms medicine's "great white lie," a myth holding that doctors and hospitals are equally deserving of our complete, unquestioning trust. Bogdanich makes his case by detailing hospitals' use of temporary (and often inadequately trained) nurses, pharmacy department bungling, systematic overbilling of Medicare and Medicaid, business transactions with physicians that create conflicts of interest, dumping of uninsured patients, and institutional arrogance toward the public. The book is marred, however, by purple prose and its general lack of analysis of the topics it presents.

Charles Brecher and Sheila Spiezio. *Privatization and Public Hospitals.* Washington, D.C.: Brookings Institution, 1995, 96 pages.

Examines the evolution of the municipal hospital system and analyzes the role of the government-funded Health and Hospitals Corporation.

Joseph Burns and Martin Sipkoff. *Hospital Strategies in Managed Care: Survival Tactics and Success Strategies for the Age of Managed Care.* New York: Faulkner and Gray, 1997, 299 pages.

Collection of essays covering a range of issues of concern to hospital administrators. Chapter topics include (1) moving from physician-hospital organizations to integrated delivery systems, (2) converting from nonprofit status to for-profit status, (3) preparing to merge, (4) how capitation works in a hospital setting, and (5) survival strategies for rural hospitals and networks. The text is supplemented by appendices and a glossary.

J.R.G. Butler. *Hospital Cost Analysis.* Boston: Kluwer, 1995, 416 pages.

Provides an overview of theoretical developments in the economic analysis of hospital costs. Butler examines empirical results on the effect of case mix, scale and utilization, public or private owner-ship, and the centralized administration of hospital systems on hospital costs. He also analyzes the implications of hospital cost analysis for public policy regarding hospital payment methods, includ-ing those based on DRGs.

Peter J. Cunningham and others. "The Use of Hospital Emergency Departments for Non-Urgent Health Problems: A National Perspective." *Medical Care Research and Review,* 1995, *52,* 453.

Hospital emergency departments have been used as substitutes for doctors' offices and other out-patient settings by people who lack access to primary health care. The cost of a visit to an emer-gency department for nonurgent conditions is between 2.5 and 3.0 time times higher than a visit to an office-based physician. Contrary to the widely held notion that nonurgent users have few other options, the data show that most nonurgent users have private health insurance, have middle or high income, are white, and have a physician's office as their regular source of care. The authors conclude that policy makers should consider the potential risk of some persons' losing access to the emergency department as their major source of care in order to achieve a relatively modest sav-ings to the health care system.

Anne M. Dellinger (ed.). *Hospital Law in North Carolina.* Chapel Hill: University of North Carolina Institute of Government, 1985.

Discusses the state and federal statutes, regulations, and cases that affect the administration of hos-pitals in North Carolina. Faculty at the University of North Carolina's Institute of Government and distinguished attorneys in the field of hospital law write the respective chapters, which are indi-vidually issued for sale as they become available. The completed book will contain more than twenty chapters covering such topics as medical records, staff privileges, employer-employee mat-ters, medical records, antitrust law, and consent to treatment.

Kathryn Saenz Duke. "Hospitals in a Changing Health Care System." *Health Affairs,* 1996, *15,* 49.

Presents data from a 1995 study of fifteen diverse communities; sketches the broad economic and organizational forces affecting hospitals in these communities and the hospitals' responses. Health system change is happening locally, and hospitals are at the center of this change. Within the larger trends, however, local flavors and differences emerge. These appear to reflect variations in each community's employment base and health care purchasing experience, in the history and political strength of health system stakeholders, and in regional issues of culture or religious affiliation for some hospitals.

Mary Gabay and Sidney M. Wolfe. "Who Controls the Local Hospital? The Current Hospital Merger and Acquisition Craze and the Disturbing Trend of Not-for-Profit Hospital Conversions to For-Profit Status." Washington, D.C.: Public Citizen's Health Research Group, 1996, 33 pages.

Examines the causes and consequences of hospital consolidation. Part One considers merger and acquisition activity, the reasons hospitals have stepped up merger activity, and what the possible consequences of this activity are for health care consumers and for health care delivery. Part Two focuses on the conversion of not-for-profit hospitals to investor-owned, for-profit businesses. The authors recommend that states enact legislation to severely restrict, if not forbid, ownership of hospitals by investor-owned chains. They also recommend changes to state statutes that will, among other things, require public disclosure of hospital plans to convert, allow public hearings and comment, require an independent valuation of hospital assets, and ensure the independence of foundations created as a result of these conversions.

John R. Griffith. *The Well-Managed Community Hospital.* (3rd ed.) Chicago: Health Administration Press, 1992, 685 pages.

Focuses on how a hospital can be responsive to its community by making decisions that customers view as necessary and efficient, and as a result popular. Written in unusually clear prose, it is designed to help managers, trustees, doctors, and health care attorneys understand the complexity of the hospital, make well-informed and satisfactory decisions, and improve the management of their hospital. The author begins by noting that the community hospital, well managed or not, is usually the most visible single expression of the Samaritan motive, a theme that runs throughout the book. Commitment to such locally managed institutions, he maintains, is infinitely better than the detached cynicism that surrounds too many of the nation's other social organizations, public and private. Topics include governance and finance systems, planning and marketing, the medical staff, nursing services, human resources, and plant systems. The well-organized text is supplemented by a plethora of figures and tables, along with a glossary and index. Every hospital library should have a copy of this book, a winner of the James A. Hamilton Hospital Administrators' Book Award.

C. Craig Holden. "Government Corporate Integrity Agreements." Washington, D.C.: American Health Lawyers Association [Report No. VMM98–0003], 1998, 11 pages.

Summarizes corporate integrity agreements and corporate compliance plans, summarizes standard corporate integrity agreement provisions, reviews the provisions of the OIG model compliance plans for laboratories and hospitals, and examines key legal points relating to corporate integrity agreements, including negotiating points and issues of attorney-client privilege.

B. Jon Jaeger (ed.). *Hospitals in the Year 2000: Three Scenarios.* Durham, N.C.: Duke University, 1992, 174 pages.

Report of the 1991 National Forum on Hospital and Health Affairs held in Durham. It examines change under three possible future scenarios: continued incremental change, a universal mandated minimal set of services, and comprehensive national health insurance.

George O. Jernigan, Jr. "Hospital Within a Hospital." Washington, D.C.: American Health Lawyers Association [Report No. VLT98–0030], 1998, 38 pages.

Outlines issues related to the transitional hospital—the long-term care hospital, also known as a hospital within a hospital. Discusses federal requirements for certification and reimbursement, the BBA amendments affecting long-term care providers, Health Care Financing Administration (HCFA) scrutiny of this type of medical facility, and state licensure and certificate-of-need issues. Includes regulations, a memorandum from the deputy director of the Bureau of Policy Development-DHHS on the hospital-within-a-hospital concept and circumvention of Prospective Payment System (PPS) exclusion criteria, and memoranda from the Mississippi and Arkansas health departments on state licensure and certificate-of-need review.

Kathrin E. Kudner. "Public Hospitals." In Mark A. Hall and William S. Brewbaker III (eds.), *Health Care Corporate Law: Facilities and Transactions.* Boston: Little, Brown, 1996.

Discusses the special legal status of public hospitals. Kudner begins by providing an overview of the types of hospital operated by federal, state, and local government. The bulk of the chapter explains the tax status of public hospitals and examines the legal restrictions on the activities of public facilities, including the special obligations to which public hospitals are subject in dealing with medical staff members and employees. Finally, legal immunity issues affecting public hospitals are considered.

Samuel Levey (ed.). *Hospital Leadership and Accountability.* Chicago: Health Administration Press, 1992, 441 pages.

An anthology of twenty-four articles from the journal *Hospital and Health Services Administration.* Written primarily for hospital executives, it examines such topics as leadership and governance, management, financial strategies, quality management, human resource management, and leadership ethics. The articles are supplemented by numerous tables and graphs along with copious lists of references.

David E. Matyas and Elizabeth A. Lewis. "OIG Releases Compliance Program Guidance for Hospitals." *Health Law Digest,* Mar. 1998, *26,* 3–10.

Supplies an overview of the genesis of corporate compliance programs and a discussion of why they have become prevalent in the health care sector. Compares the 1998 guidelines for hospitals with those issued earlier for clinical laboratories. The article describes problems that an organization may face when attempting to integrate a compliance program into the organization's corporate culture, along with suggestions as to how to overcome these obstacles.

Robert W. McAdams (ed.). *Hospital Contracts Manual.* Gaithersburg, Md.: Aspen, 1998.

This three-volume, loose-leaf guide includes more than fourteen hundred pages of sample agreements, checklists, and forms divided into twenty-five tabbed sections. Topics addressed include contracts for professional services, management agreements, third-party payer considerations, federal and state agreements, facilities and equipment acquisition, and managed care. The manual is updated twice annually.

Richard A. McCormick, S.J. "The End of Catholic Hospitals?" *America,* July 4–11, 1998, 179(1), 5–12.

The Catholic Health Care System is the largest private not-for-profit system in the United States. It includes 10 percent of all nonfederal hospitals and 15 percent of hospital beds; it counts 542 hospitals in forty-eight states, hundreds of long-term facilities, sixty-one multi-institutional systems, and hundreds of thousands of employees. These institutions care for seventy million patients annually.

The author, a professor of Christian ethics at Notre Dame University, examines the current environment of managed care and asks whether the expected consolidation of Catholic and non-Catholic health care institutions in coming years will destroy the philosophy of giving hope through the example of Jesus that has animated Catholic health care for more than a century. In this article, he decries the metamorphosis of health care into a business, the depersonalization of treatment, and cuts in Medicare and Medicaid that constrain hospitals' ability to provide charity care. Furthermore, he attacks the merger mania that has characterized the hospital scene in recent years and the exponential rise in executive salaries while nursing staffs are reduced. Finally, he describes the threat to pastoral care that results from managed care.

Howard S. Rowland and Beatrice L. Rowland. *Hospital Legal Forms Checklists and Guidelines.* 2 vols. Gaithersburg, Md.: Aspen, 1998.

Provides a library of hospital law and administrative strategies in a loose-leaf format. Materials contained in this volume address consents, death and donors, the emergency department, malpractice, medical records, medical staff issues, medical staff appointment and credentialing procedures, personnel policies, quality assessment, tax issues, corporate structural issues, and managed care, among others. This work is supplemented semiannually.

Howard S. Rowland and Beatrice L. Rowland. *Hospital Management: A Guide to Departments.* Gaithersburg, Md.: Aspen, 1984, 471 pages.

Considers the medical staff, medical records, nursing services, the pharmacy, the emergency room, risk management, licensing, and certification.

Howard S. Rowland and Beatrice L. Rowland. *Manual of Hospital Administration.* 2 vols. Gaithersburg, Md.: Aspen, 1996.

Ring-bound treatise covering financial management, strategic planning, mergers and acquisitions, capital investment, human resources management, and working within a managed care environment. Exceptionally well written, the book is richly augmented by numerous charts, graphs, exhibits, and checklists.

In their introduction, the authors make a number of striking predictions about trends facing hospitals over the next ten years:

- Rising demand for hospital services and improved profitability
- Accelerated movement toward managed care
- Development of local networks of hospitals, medical office buildings, ambulatory, and long-term care facilities
- Development of practice guidelines to dictate standards of practice for every medical specialty
- Demand by major payers for real-time access to hospital and physician practice data as a condition for managed care contracts
- Loss of control of their confidential medical data on the part of hospitals and physicians, within only a few years

Stephen M. Shortell, Robin R. Gillies, and Kelly J. Devers. "Reinventing the American Hospital." *Milbank Quarterly,* 1995, *73*, 131.

Describes the major forces driving the reinvention of the hospital, highlighting the systemic structure within which hospitals exist. Then, drawing largely on existing research, the authors examine various approaches and methods for achieving reinvention as well as the associated problems and implications.

Stephen M. Shortell and others. *Strategic Choices for America's Hospitals: Managing Change in Turbulent Times.* San Francisco: Jossey-Bass, 1990, 397 pages.

Attempts to examine the conditions under which strategic change can occur in an organization, in this case the hospital. The authors examined the strategic adaptation processes of eight leading hospital systems from 1983 through 1987. Their goals were to advance knowledge of the basic processes of strategic adaptation, to advance the strategic thinking and behavior of executives in the hospital industry, and to suggest ways in which greater knowledge of how hospitals adapt strategically can contribute to more effective health care policies. Written for hospital executives, academics, and public policy writers, this text is supplemented by a large number of tables, charts, and graphs, an extensive bibliography, and an index.

J. Stuart Showalter, *Southwick's Law of Healthcare Administration.* (3rd ed.) Chicago: Health Administration Press, 2000, 569 pages.

Focuses on the interrelationship between the U.S. legal system and the structure and functions of health care institutions. Southwick includes information on the legal aspects of corporate reorganization and hospital mergers, antitrust laws, institutional liability in the wake of structural change, and peer review of professional practice.

J. Stuart Showalter and Bernard D. Reams, Jr. (eds.). *The Law of Hospital and Health Care Administration: Cases and Materials.* Chicago: Hospital Administration Press, 1993, 201 pages.

Companion to *The Law of Hospital and Health Care Administration,* supplying cases to help students apply the concepts in Southwick's book. Each case is followed by suggested discussion questions.

Toby G. Singer. "Hospital Advertising." Washington, D.C.: American Health Lawyers Association [Report No. VHH99–0035], 1999, 45 pages.

Discusses laws governing advertising by health care professionals, including consumer protection, antitrust and unfair competition laws, and practical implications of these laws.

I. Donald Snook, Jr. *Hospitals: What They Are and How They Work.* (3rd ed.) Gaithersburg, Md.: Aspen, 1992, 266 pages.

> Includes an introduction to the organization, internal operations, and functions of the community general hospital. Topics discussed are hospital management and governance, outpatient treatment, the emergency department, the medical staff, the nursing staff, hospital finance, medical records, quality assurance, risk management, accreditation and licensing, marketing, and planning. The author is the president of the Presbyterian Medical Center of Philadelphia.

Christine S. Spencer. "Do Uncompensated Care Pools Change the Distribution of Hospital Care to the Uninsured?" *Journal of Health Politics, Policy and Law,* Feb. 1998, *23,* 53.

> In 1983, New York State established an uncompensated care pool using the New York Prospective Hospital Reimbursement Methodology (NYPHRM). Two policy objectives of the NYPHRM were (1) to encourage more equitable distribution of uncompensated care across hospitals and (2) to increase access to hospital care for the uninsured. This article argues that the New York uncompensated care pool was only moderately successful in achieving these goals. The principal findings are that the NYPHRM did result in routine care being redistributed away from hospitals that traditionally provided care to the uninsured, while provision of highly technological care was not significantly redistributed. The article suggests that if the primary policy goal is to increase access to care for the uninsured by changing the distribution of hospitals willing to provide care, the uncompensated care pool approach is moderately successful.

John D. Stoeckle. "The Citadel Cannot Hold: Technologies Go Outside the Hospital, Patients and Doctors Too." *Milbank Quarterly,* 1995, *73,* 3.

> The hospital, our treatment institution for the care of the sick in bed, is being downsized. Many hospitals have closed, and many have reduced their beds as their admissions decrease. This exodus of care has transpired over the past twenty-five years. Meanwhile, ambulatory visits to physicians and the use of diagnostic and treatment technologies in out-of-hospital and home settings have increased. Although the expansion of prepaid practice plans and managed care has exerted organizational pressure on efficiency and costs, leading to a decrease in hospital use, the trends were evident long before. As diagnostic testing moved outside and practitioners depended less on observation and bed rest, treatment also moved as it, too, relied decreasingly on bed rest, the major historical rationale for hospital care. The shift to outside care might also be interpreted as a movement by practitioners who are interested in obtaining more control over decision making in their practices (and sometimes achieving more profits) than was possible in the hospital.

Matthew M. Strickler, Robert I. Field, and Sandra E. Bohn. "Basic Hospital Structure." In Mark A. Hall and William S. Brewbaker III (eds.), *Health Care Corporate Law: Facilities and Transactions.* Boston: Little, Brown, 1996.

> This 115-page chapter provides the introductory materials for this treatise volume. Topics covered include corporate structure, the hospital medical staff, medical staff membership criteria, leases and management services contracts, health care facilities leases, equipment leases, and medical office building leases. The chapter concludes with a lengthy examination of physician contracts and recruitment, including features of typical arrangements, fraud and abuse, exclusive arrangements with hospital-based physicians, common employment contract provisions, and common independent contractor agreement provisions.

Ron B. Thomson. "Review: Competition Among Hospitals in the US." *Health Policy,* 1994, *27,* 205.

> Competition between hospitals does not bring costs down, the author contends. Approximately 75 percent of American hospitals have a competitor within fifteen miles, but it doesn't reduce costs. To do well, hospitals must attract and keep doctors, give high-quality care, and offer more services.

These all push prices up. Even nearby hospitals are usually dissimilar enough that other characteristics besides price influence patients and doctors.

Robin Fretwell Wilson. "Hospital Ethics Committees as the Forum of Last Resort: An Idea Whose Time Has Not Come." *N.C. Law Review,* Jan. 1998, pp. 353–406.

Hospital ethics committees have become a fixture in American medicine and are poised to become a forum of last resort for end-of-life decisions as a result of state statutes giving committees immunity and privilege. The effect of such legislation is to transform ethics committees from an adjunct to the courts into a substitute for them, without giving patients any of the protections attendant to judicial decision making. The author provides a critical comparison of ethics committees to courts and concludes that contrary to the conventional wisdom of the ethics committee movement, it is unclear that hospital ethics committees are innately better suited to make end-of-life decisions than state and federal courts.

Gooloo S. Wunderlich, Frank A. Sloan, and Carolyne K. Davis (eds.). *Nursing Staff in Hospitals and Nursing Homes: Is It Adequate?* Washington, D.C.: National Academy Press, 1996, 542 pages.

Hospitals and nursing homes are responding to changes in the health care system by modifying staffing levels and the mix of nursing personnel. This study examines whether these personnel changes endanger the quality of patient care and whether nursing staff suffer increased rates of injury, illness, or stress because of workplace demands. The committee that prepared this report draws fundamental conclusions about the evolving role of nurses in hospitals and nursing homes and presents recommendations about staffing decisions, nursing homes, nursing training, quality measurement, reimbursement, and other areas. The volume also addresses work-related injuries, violence toward and abuse of nursing staffs, and stress among nursing personnel.

Kenneth Yood. "Managed Care Contracting." Washington, D.C.: American Health Lawyers Association [Report No. VHH99–0035], 1999, 22 pages.

Discusses key managed care risk contracting provisions from the provider's perspective relating to reimbursement and nonreimbursement issues, utilization review and provider liability, medical necessity in coverage determinations, confidentiality of patient records, and risk sharing arrangements with medical and physician groups.

2.02(2)   Rural Hospitals

Dan A. Ermann. "Rural Health Care: The Future of the Hospital." *Medical Care Review,* 1990, *47*, 33.

American rural hospitals are in trouble. Several hundred have closed over a period of fifteen years, and six hundred are in danger of closing. Their problems stem from their patients' poorer health, education, and income; less insurance coverage; and a preponderance of elderly patients needing long-term care. They have had trouble adjusting to the new Medicare of the Prospective Payment System. Some strategies they are using to survive: turning to nonacute care such as emergency care, preventive medicine, and elder care and rehabilitation; diversifying services; and affiliating with larger hospital systems.

David R. Melloh. "Rural Health Care Transactions." Washington, D.C.: American Health Lawyers Association [Report No. VHL98–0054], 1998, 76 pages.

Describes certain representative rural health care transactions, sets forth the law applicable to such transactions, and briefly assesses the implications of the laws to various types of rural transaction.

Penny E. Mohr and others. "Vulnerability of Rural Hospitals to Medicare Outpatient Payment Reform." *Health Care Financing Review,* Fall 1999, *21,* 1.

Because the Balanced Budget Act of 1997 requires implementation of a Medicare Prospective Payment System for hospital outpatient services, the authors evaluated the potential impact of outpatient PPS on rural hospitals. Among the areas examined: (1) How dependent are rural hospitals on outpatient revenue? (2) Are they more vulnerable than urban hospitals to payment reform? (3) What types of rural hospital will be most vulnerable to reform? Using Medicare cost report data, the authors found that small size and government ownership are more common among rural than urban hospitals and are the most important determinants of vulnerability to payment reform.

Margo L. Rosenbach and Debra A Dayhoff. "Access to Care in Rural America: Impact of Hospital Closures." *Health Care Financing Review,* 1995, *17,* 15.

Rural hospitals tend to be at higher risk of closure than urban hospitals because they are smaller, have low occupancy rates, high expenses relative to revenues, and a high proportion of debt. Data from eleven geographic areas where hospitals closed during 1986 and 1987 showed a significant drop in medical admissions in the year of closure, especially relative to areas with no hospital. Baseline utilization rates were higher in the closure areas than in comparison groups, with a considerable narrowing of the gap following the closure. More hospital admissions shifted to urban teaching hospitals following closures.

Washington Business Group on Health. *The Corporate Round Table on Rural Health Care: Improving the Delivery System in Rural and Non-Metropolitan Areas.* Washington, D.C.: WBGH, 1997.

Provides highlights of a 1996 WBGH meeting of employers, providers, public policy makers, and others concerned with health care cost, quality, and access in rural areas.

2.02(3)   Academic Medical Centers

M. Gregg Bloche. "Corporate Takeover of Teaching Hospitals." *Southern California Law Review,* 1992, *65,* 1035–1171.

Provides an extensive history of the financing of academic medical centers and then examines the needs and strategies of investor-owned hospital chains before analyzing specific objections to corporate acquisition of teaching hospitals. After surveying a range of practical legal considerations that could act as a bar to such acquisitions, it provides a list of issues for negotiation should the parties seek to proceed. The author concludes that sale and lease arrangements deserve a place in the quiver of strategies available to academic medical centers for coping with an austere economic environment.

David Blumenthal and Gregg S. Meyer. "Academic Health Centers in a Changing Environment." *Health Affairs,* 1996, *15,* 200.

Presents case studies of seven nationally prominent academic health centers (AHCs) conducted during 1994 to evaluate the potential problems facing AHCs as a result of market-driven health care reforms. Findings suggest that although AHCs were not yet feeling the predicted impact of competition on their financial health and ability to sustain their academic missions of teaching, research, and care of vulnerable populations, they were adopting a variety of strategies for responding to those perceived threats, especially networking and cost reduction. They were placing considerably less emphasis on restructuring their research and teaching missions to prepare for anticipated fiscal pressure. The authors' analysis suggests that even the most successful AHCs are likely to be fundamentally altered by the revolutionary changes occurring in health care markets.

Robert S. Bromberg. "Academic Medical Centers." Washington, D.C.: American Health Lawyers Association [Report No VTX98–0010], 1998, 14 pages.

Reviews specific tax issues for academic medical centers, including how to prepare for a CEP (Coordinated Examination Program) audit, compensating faculty members for clinical and educational services, and tax treatment of drug and medical device testing.

J. K. Inglehart. "Rapid Changes for Academic Medical Centers: First of Two Parts." *New England Journal of Medicine*, 1994, *331*, 1391–1395.

J. K. Inglehart. "Rapid Changes for Academic Medical Centers: Second of Two Parts." *New England Journal of Medicine*, 1995, *332*, 407–411.

Discusses changes in reimbursement along with the historical role of the academic medical center.

General Accounting Office. "Medicare: Concerns with Physicians at Teaching Hospitals (PATH) Audits." (GAO/HEHS-98–174.) July 23, 1998, 35 pages.

About twelve hundred hospitals in the United States have graduate medical educational programs to train doctors in medical specialties after they have completed medical school. In December 1995, the University of Pennsylvania, without admitting wrongdoing, entered into a voluntary settlement with the Justice Department, agreeing to pay about $30 million in disputed billings and damages for Medicare billings by teaching physicians. The settlement resulted in an audit done by the Department of Health and Human Services' Office of the Inspector General. Concerned that such problems might be widespread, the OIG, in cooperation with the Justice Department, launched a nationwide initiative—now commonly known as Physicians At Teaching Hospitals (PATH) audits—to review teaching physician compliance with Medicare billing rules. As of April 1998, five additional PATH audits had been resolved, resulting in settlements, in three of these cases, totaling more than $37 million.

The PATH initiative has generated considerable controversy. The academic medical community disagrees with the OIG about the billing and documentation standards that were in effect during the periods under review. The medical community also contends that the Justice Department is coercing settlements from teaching institutions through threats of federal lawsuits. This report determines (1) whether the DHHS OIG has a legal basis for conducting PATH audits, (2) whether the OIG has followed an acceptable approach and methodology in conducting the audits, and (3) the significance of the billing problems cited in selected audits.

Lee Goldman. "The Academic Health Care System: Preserving the Missions As the Paradigm Shifts." *Journal of the American Medical Association*, 1995, *273*, 1549.

A health care system that was previously based on solo practitioners and hospitals is now being led by HMOs, managed care, group practices, integrated health networks, and capitation. Increasingly, these managed care plans tend to compete with each other to enroll patients on the basis of price. The demise of the Clinton health plan accelerated the trend toward managed care and capitation, under the auspices of a primary care physician who shares in the financial risk with the insurer and other members of the health care system. New incentives encourage primary care physicians to limit unnecessary care, consultations, procedures, and admissions to keep prices low for insurers and to protect their own salaries.

Because of market pressures, the academic medical centers that have led in developing modern medicine are in jeopardy of losing their role. This has already been the case for the centers in geographic areas that are in the forefront of the evolution of managed care. In the 1990s, the growth of capitation put pressure on hospitals and physicians to increase efficiency and to control the volume of admissions and visits per patient. The side effects for the academic medical center were substantial: fewer admissions, fewer procedures, and fewer referrals to specialists. The patients who choose academic centers for their capitated care may be the sickest and neediest, which further disadvantages the academic medical institutions.

To maintain even a reasonable referral volume of tertiary and quaternary cases for their teaching and research missions, academic medical centers must obtain contracts with other primary care providers, build large integrated networks, or both. If they choose the former, competition is likely to be driven by price rather than by quality. If they choose the latter, the diversion of resources into these new endeavors threatens the maintenance of the teaching and research enterprise. Even if academic health care systems can harness technology and innovation to equal or exceed the cost efficiency of nonteaching systems, the true incremental cost of the teaching and research missions seems certain to consign them to being somewhat more expensive.

At the core academic hospitals, specialty faculty will have to adjust to a diminished number of trainees, and primary care training must increase dramatically. Some specialty faculty may consider the option of retraining or refocusing as primary care physicians. Shrinking income for clinical specialists will reduce or even eliminate the availability if excess clinical income to support otherwise unfunded research.

Richard L. Solit and David B. Nash. "Academic Health Centers and Managed Care." In Kongstvedt, *The Managed Health Care Handbook*. (3rd ed.) Gaithersburg, Md.: Aspen, 1996.

Topics discussed in this eighteen-page chapter include changes in market mechanisms, the increasing role of purchasers, the shift in financial risk allocation, medicine as a commodity, graduate medical education, barriers to organizational change, strategies for success, maintaining a patient base, network formation, primary care strategy, specialty care strategy, information sharing, and outcomes.

2.02(4) Religious Medical Institutions

Kathleen Boozang. "Deciding the Fate of Religious Hospitals in the Emerging Health Care Market." *Houston Law Review*, 1995, *31*(1), 429.

Suggests that looking at church-state relations as an example of legal pluralism provides a fresh and instructive perspective that aids policy makers and legal scholars in mediating the inevitable tension between the religious dictates of sectarian (usually, Catholic) and civil law. Boozang recommends that the state should acknowledge the current pluralistic system of health care delivery by considering sectarian facilities' limitations in health planning, encouraging joint ventures among sectarian and nonsectarian health care providers, and distinguishing between the duty to inform and the duty to provide treatment. Ultimately, she contends, in those instances in which an accommodation cannot be achieved between the religious precepts of the provider and patient access to health care, the state should either compel the religious institution to provide the desired care or license an alternative facility to render the service.

Catholic Health Association. *Renewing the Catholic Healthcare Ministry: A Handbook for Planning and Developing Integrated Delivery*. St. Louis: Catholic Health Association of the United States, 1993, 177 pages.

Designed to help Catholic health care organizations plan and develop integrated delivery of services. It helps them understand integrated delivery and build toward that vision in their local communities. Containing the experiences of many Catholic Health Association members, the handbook has been written to assist readers new to integrated delivery with basic concepts and to provide a review, checklists, and summaries of others' experiences for readers who are more advanced. This practical volume is well organized and is amply supplemented with twenty-five exhibits, a glossary, four appendices, and a bibliography.

Monte I. Dube, Eric B. Gordon, Nancy Rodkin Rotering, and Lawrence E. Singer. "Unique and Specialized Hospitals." In Mark A. Hall and William S. Brewbaker III (eds.), *Health Care Corporate Law: Facilities and Transactions.* Boston: Little, Brown, 1996.

Discusses the issues facing four unique types of hospital: teaching and research hospitals, rural hospitals, hospitals operated by religious organizations, and hospitals providing specialized or chronic care. All hospitals face a common set of regulatory and business problems. They operate in an environment of increasing competition, limited government funding, regulatory complexity, and technological change. Despite these common problems, different types of hospital have always faced special issues as a consequence of their location, their particular mission, their ownership, or the patients they serve. In each case, the discussion focuses on issues that are unique to the organization under discussion. Other, more general issues are explored elsewhere in the treatise.

Lawrence E. Singer and Elizabeth Johnson Lantz. "The Coming Millennium: Enduring Issues Confronting Catholic Health Care." *Annals of Health Law,* 1999, *8,* 299.

Excellent article presents an overview of Catholic health care in the United States and addresses in detail three key issues affecting Catholic health care in coming years: (1) clarity in canonical and ethical interpretation, (2) industry consolidation, and (3) "next generation" sponsorship. The authors conclude that successful Catholic health care organizations must maintain strong mission and business fundamentals in an increasingly competitive reimbursement and regulatory environment.

Lawrence E. Singer. "Realigning Catholic Healthcare: Bridging Legal and Church Control in a Consolidating Market." *Tulane Law Review,* 1997, *72,* 159.

Catholic health care is at a crossroads. Faced with increasing competition in the health care industry, the church must balance contemporary business realities and governmental regulation with its traditional mission of providing high-quality, spiritually based care, particularly to the poor. The article begins with an overview of Catholic health care and its role in the nation's health care delivery system. The author then examines the state and federal law governing Catholic health care providers, as well as the applicable church law. The author concludes that the law has failed to keep up with the rapidly changing world of religious-sponsored health care and suggests how sponsors, lawmakers, and affected communities can cooperate to ensure the future of Catholic health care in the United States.

2.03   NURSING HOMES

Omar N. Ahmad. "Medicaid Eligibility Rules for the Elderly Long-Term Care Applicant: History and Developments, 1965–1998." *Journal of Legal Medicine,* 1999, *20,* 251.

This lengthy commentary provides an overview of spousal impoverishment and related transfer-of-asset rules. It also includes a discussion of criminal sanctions for fraudulent transfer of assets to gain Medicaid eligibility.

James E. Allen. *Nursing Home Federal Requirements and Guidelines for Surveyors: A User-Friendly Rendering of the Health Care Financing Administration's State Operations Manual Provider Certification.* (3rd ed.) New York: Springer, 1995, 286 pages.

This handbook sets forth the regulations that are the technical basis for certifying, decertifying, issuing deficiencies, requiring plans of correction, and assessing fines. It also sets out the guidelines and procedures that are used by federal surveyors as the official understanding of how the regulations are to be interpreted.

James E. Allen. *Key Federal Requirements for Nursing Facilities: Medicare and Medicaid Requirements.* New York: Springer, 1992.

Contains the updated Medicare and Medicaid requirements for long-term care facilities and nurse's aide training. Topics include resident rights, admission, transfer and discharge rights, use of restraints, quality of life, physical environment, infection control, and administration. Written by a professor of health policy and administration at the University of North Carolina at Chapel Hill, this manual also contains the Department of Labor's *Final Rule on Bloodborne Pathogens,* covering exposure control, methods of compliance, Hepatitis B vaccination, and postexposure evaluation and follow-up, communication of hazards to employees, and record keeping.

James E. Allen. *Nursing Home Administration.* (3rd ed.) New York: Springer, 1997, 605 pages.

Covers a range of topics that relate to nursing home administration, including accounting, Medicare, Medicaid, labor laws and regulations, workplace safety, and accreditation.

James E. Allen. *Nursing Home Federal Requirements and Guidelines to Surveyors.* New York: Springer, 1997, 286 pages.

Describes the regulations, guidelines, and procedures used by federal surveyors in certifying facilities for participation in Medicare and Medicaid, issuing deficiencies, requiring plans of correction, or imposing fines. This book includes a table of contents and index.

American Association of Retired Persons. *Decision Making, Incapacity and the Elderly.* Washington, D.C.: AARP, 1997.

A guide for planning for extended periods of incapacity by surveying long-term financial and health care issues. This protective services manual for attorneys, paralegals, advocates, and others who represent the elderly includes chapters on powers of attorney, financial planning, multiple-party accounts, representative payee programs, guardianship, nursing home admission contracts, and planning for Medicare eligibility. It also supplies model forms, tables comparing model forms, charts identifying state law requirements for planning documents, checklists, and state summaries, with more than two hundred significant cases.

American Association of Retired Persons. *Disability Practice Manual: Social Security and SSI Programs.* 3 vols. Washington, D.C.: AARP, 1997.

Provides complete coverage of Social Security and SSI disability programs for the advocate. Thoroughly researched chapters include procedural matters such as medical evidence, hearings, appeals, judicial review, overpayments, acquiescence, and attorney fees. The special disability issues of AIDS, childhood disability, mental impairments, medical improvements, and pain receive particular attention. The manual includes extensive footnotes with the latest cases and regulations; useful practice tips; and an abundance of sample letters, forms, checklists, and charts. Each set includes computer software in WordPerfect with sample letters, forms, pleadings, and checklists ready for the practitioner's use. The 1997 update provides the most recent benefit figures. Modestly priced compared to similar publications, this is an excellent resource.

Annot. "Licensing and Regulation of Nursing or Rest Homes." *ALR4th 53,* 689.

Collects and analyzes the federal and state cases dealing with the validity, construction, and effect of state statutes, municipal ordinances, and administrative rules and regulations providing specifically for licensing and regulation—as contrasted with taxation, zoning, need certification, public reimbursement or remuneration for services to patients, or certification of eligibility—of institutions that provide shelter, nutrition, and care for sick, aged, or infirm persons, apart from hospitals and clinics.

Annot. "Right to Notice and Hearing Prior to Termination of Medicaid Payments to Nursing Homes under the Medicaid Provisions of the Social Security Act." *ALR Federal, 37,* 682.

Collects and analyzes the federal court cases that have considered a nursing home's right to notice and a hearing prior to termination of Medicaid payments to it under the Medicaid provisions of the Social Security Act. In some cases, this question arises in a situation involving actual removal of patients eligible for Medicaid benefits from the home itself.

Gordon J. Apple. "Corporate Compliance for Long Term Care." Washington, D.C.: American Health Lawyers Assn. [Report No. VLT99–0028], 1999, 40 pages.

Provides a basic outline for long-term care providers in how to develop and implement a corporate compliance program. Reviews the practical realities of compliance programs and identifies key elements from the OIG guidance documents that can be tailored to fit institutional needs. Discusses training ideas to move a program from the bookshelf to the workplace and strategies to address compliance exposures.

Gene Berk and Jeanne L. Vance. "Buying, Selling and Financing Long Term Care Facilities." Washington, D.C.: American Health Lawyers Assn. [Report No.VLT99–0008], 1999, 33 pages.

Highlights the issues that drive transactions involving long-term care facilities. Discusses (in the context of the letter of intent) due diligence, drafting of the purchase agreement and managing the closing, licensing, Medicare accounts receivable, fraud and abuse, Stark, covenants not to compete, physician arrangements, successor liability, nonprofit regulations, transfer of resident funds, and Medicare contracting. Attachments include a sample long-term care facility letter of intent, a health care due diligence document request, long-term care facility representations and warranties, licensure statutes and regulations, a covenant not to compete, and sample legal opinions for long-term care facilities.

Joseph L. Bianculli. "You Can Win Nursing Home Appeals!" Washington, D.C.: American Health Lawyers Association [Report No VLT 99–0027], 1999, 40 pages.

Outlines six steps to a successful appeal and injunctive relief against terminations in extraordinary cases. Includes presentation overheads.

Joseph L. Bianculli. "Long-Term Care Network Formation: The Attorney's Role." Washington, D.C.: American Health Lawyers Association [Report No. VLT98–0005], 1998, 30 pages.

Addresses the attorney's role in counseling long-term care providers who are considering forming a network, and also outlines significant antitrust, organizational, and operational issues presented by typical network arrangements.

Richard L. Butler and Mick Cowles. "Getting the Most Out of OSCAR." Washington, D.C.: American Health Lawyers Association [Report No. VLT99–0044], 1999, 26 pages.

Outlines how to read and interpret standard Online Survey Certification and Reporting (OSCAR) reports. Focuses on production of designed custom reports and data development as additional outside support for the facility's position. Attachments include sample OSCAR reports.

Eric Carlson. "Illegal Guarantees in Nursing Homes: A Nursing Facility Cannot Force a Resident's Family Members and Friends to Become Financially Responsible for Nursing Facility Expenses." *Clearinghouse Review,* May 1996, p. 33.

Discusses federal law regarding financial responsibility for nursing facility expenses. Federal law prohibits a nursing facility from requiring a third party to guarantee payment as a condition of a resident's admission. Nevertheless, nursing facilities across the country continue to obtain third-party guarantees by ignoring or evading federal law. This article, written by an attorney who is the director of the Nursing Home Advocacy Project at Bet Tzedek Legal Services in Los Angeles, explains the background and purpose of the statute, codified at 42 U.S.C. § 1396 r(a), and the regulations issued pursuant thereto at 42 C.F.R. § 483.12(d)(2).

Michael H. Cook. "Subacute Care: Issues and Opportunities." Washington, D.C.: American Health Lawyers Association [Report No. VMM99–0064], 1999, 30 pages.

Reviews subacute care reimbursement issues, including bed reserve agreements, management contracts, lease of a wing of a long-term facility to a hospital, and issues involving long-term care hospitals. Attachments include charts of various relationships between hospitals, long-term care facilities, and physicians.

Michael H. Cook. "Medicare SNF [Skilled Nursing Facility] Cost Limit Exceptions and Exemptions." Washington, D.C.: American Health Lawyers Association [Report No. VMM98–0044], 1998, 77 pages.

Outlines routine cost limits, including routine versus ancillary services; reasonable costs; establishing routine service cost limits; reclassification; exemptions and exceptions to routine cost limits; the new provider exemption; exception request procedures; atypical services exception; atypical direct cost (atypical nursing services); atypical employee health and welfare cost; atypical administrative and general cost; atypical nursing administration costs and other atypical cost exceptions with specific cost centers, extraordinary circumstances exception, and unusual labor cost exception; exception for providers in areas with fluctuating populations; and general strategy regarding exceptions.

Alan S. Dorn. "Issues and Decisions Relating to Nursing Home Certification." Washington, D.C.: American Health Lawyers Association [Report No. VLT98–00183], 1998, 19 pages.

Discusses issues and rulings regarding challenges to nursing home enforcement remedies imposed after finding noncompliance. Examines which determinations or issues can be appealed, requirements for appeal, civil money penalty determinations, the authority to impose remedies, burden of proof, and evidentiary issues concerning compliance.

Toby S. Edelman. "The Nursing Home Reform Law: Issues for Litigation." *Clearinghouse Review*, Oct. 1990, p. 545.

The nursing home reform law, as described in this article, sets a new standard of care for nursing facilities. This article describes standards for resident care as set forth in the legislation. The standard of resident care is expressed through Requirements of Participation. This article discusses some of the requirements and sets out litigation theories to enforce them.

Toby S. Edelman. "Discrimination by Nursing Homes Against Medicaid Recipients: Improving Access to Institutional Long-Term Care for Poor People." *Clearinghouse Review*, 1986, *20*, 339.

Examines such forms of discrimination as (1) informing a prospective patient that no beds are available; (2) asking for "voluntary" contributions to a building fund before admitting a resident; (3) including private-pay, duration-of-stay clauses in admission contracts, which require payment from private funds before accepting Medicaid funds; and (4) involuntary transfers from those facilities.

David M. English, Michael Gilfix, and Rebecca C. Morgan. *Tax, Estate and Financial Planning for the Elderly: Forms and Practice.* New York: Matthew Bender, 1991.

This one-volume loose-leaf practice guide, regularly updated, includes forms, checklists, and practice tips for health care, retirement, tax, and financial decisions. Divided by tabs, the subjects covered include planning for Medicaid and nursing home care, use of the durable power of attorney for both property management and health care decisions, income tax and estate planning, and securing government benefits such as Social Security and Medicare. Each tabbed section offers detailed checklists and client interview forms and sample letters, along with annotated and blank sample forms including wills, trusts benefits applications, powers of attorney, living wills, and tax forms.

Stephen A. Feldman. "Elder Law Issues: Medicaid Planning, Financial and Responsibility for Residents' Rights." Washington, D.C.: American Health Lawyers Association [Report No. VLT99–0046], 1999, 35 pages.

Examines the techniques used by estate planners and elder-law attorneys to address the special health concerns of clients who are incapacitated by acute or chronic illnesses or conditions, to assist their clients in qualifying for medical assistance. Discusses the spousal impoverishment provision of the Medicare Catastrophic Coverage Act and nursing home residents' rights in general.

Stephen A. Feldman. "Elder Law Issues: Medicaid Planning, Financial and Responsibility for Residents' Rights." Washington, D.C.: American Health Lawyers Association [Report No. VLT98–0003], 1998, 36 pages.

Discusses the techniques used by estate planners and elder-law attorneys to address the special health concerns of clients who are incapacitated by acute or chronic illnesses or conditions, to assist their clients in qualifying for medical assistance. Examines the eligibility rules under the Medical Assistance Act and the spousal impoverishment provision of the Medicare Catastrophic Coverage Act.

Robert J. Fogg. *Nursing Home Regulations Manual.* Washington, D.C.: Thompson, 1998.

Focuses on new HCFA initiatives and policies, as well as those spearheaded by the OIG, OSHA, the Centers for Disease Control (CDC), and other federal agencies with a voice in the quality of nursing home care. This loose-leaf manual, updated with monthly bulletins, examines such topics as survey procedures for assessing facility compliance, standards for determining deficiencies, procedures for investigating resident complaints, scope and severity scales, penalties for non-compliance, hearing and appeals procedures, nurse's aide certification and registry rules, pre-existing state and federal regulations, and updates to the State Operations Manual.

Julie Fralich and others. *Reducing the Cost of Institutional Care: Downsizing, Diversion, Closing and Conversion of Nursing Homes.* Portland, Maine: National Academy for State Health Policy, 1994.

Provides useful information and a summary of policy considerations for states trying to reduce the cost of institutional long-term care.

Gavin J. Gadberry. "State Certification and Licensing Appeals." Washington, D.C.: American Health Lawyers Association [Report No. VLT98–00193], 1998, 67 pages.

Identifies the procedural problems contained in the applicable regulations and the developing trends in administrative law judge and Department Appeals Board decisions for those representing providers in licensing and certification appeals. Also covers defense strategies for representing providers in the enforcement process and appeal strategies after remedies have been imposed. Includes a sample HCFA notice of adverse action letter, a model hearing request letter, DHHS Civil Remedies Division procedures, a sample subpoena duces tecum, and guidance to surveyors for long-term care facilities.

General Accounting Office. *California Nursing Homes: Care Problems Persist Despite Federal and State Oversight.* (GAO/HEHS-98-202.) July 27, 1998, 53 pages.

Overall, despite federal and state oversight, some California nursing homes are not being monitored closely enough to guarantee the safety and welfare of the residents. Unacceptable care continues to be a problem in many nursing homes. GAO found that nearly one in three California nursing homes was cited by state surveyors for serious or potentially life-threatening care problems. Moreover, GAO believes that the extent of serious care problems portrayed in federal and state data is likely to be understated. Nursing homes could generally predict when their annual on-site reviews would occur and, if inclined, could take steps to mask problems. GAO also found irregularities in homes' documentation of the care provided to their residents, such as missing pages of clinical notes needed to explain a resident's injury later observed by a physician. Finally, GAO found many cases in which California Department of Health Services surveyors did not identify serious care problems, including dramatic weight loss, failure to prevent bed sores, and poor management of incontinence. Even when the states identified serious shortcomings, HCFA enforcement policies have not ensured that the deficiencies are corrected and stay that way. For example, California state surveyors cited about one in eleven nursing homes in GAO's analysis—accounting for more than seventeen thousand resident beds—for violations in both of their last two surveys that resulted in harm to residents. Yet HCFA generally took a lenient stance toward many of these facilities. GAO recommends a less predictable schedule of inspections for all nursing homes and prompt imposition of sanctions when violations are found.

Daniel M. Gitner. "Nursing the Problem: Responding to Patient Abuse in New York State." *Columbia Journal of Law and Social Problems*, 1995, *28*, 559.

Surveys New York State's legal responses to nursing home patient abuse. Nearly 25 percent of U.S. citizens will someday be patients in a nursing home. Nonetheless, researchers have neglected the study of nursing home patient abuse by nursing home staff. Gitner argues that although the legal regime surrounding patient abuse aids those bringing patient abuse cases, it is incomplete. He concludes by suggesting measures to reform New York's patient abuse laws in order to better protect nursing home patients' rights.

Karen L. Goldsmith. "Legal Ethics in the Practice of Long Term Care." Washington, D.C.: American Health Lawyers Association [Report No. VLT99–0030], 1999, 37 pages.

Brief case study presents a hypothetical scenario raising ethical issues for an attorney appointed by an insurer to represent a nursing home. Includes selections from relevant ethics rules, federal statutes, and regulations.

Kathleen M. Griffin. "The Impact of the Survey Process on Providing Managed Care Subacute and Specialty Units." Washington, D.C.: American Health Lawyers Association [Report No VLT98–0010], 1998, 24 pages.

Most subacute care is provided in skilled nursing facilities. Discusses how subacute providers can comply with federal and state regulations for SNFs, particularly those related to covered services and admissions and discharges, and mitigate their risk while meeting the needs of managed care payers.

Robert A. Griffith and Heather L. Overholser. "White Collar Criminal Cases." Washington, D.C.: American Health Lawyers Association [Report No. VLT98–0014], 1998, 55 pages.

Highlights areas in which the long-term care sector is most susceptible to fraud and abuse prosecutions. Examines fraud alerts, OIG work plans and reports, and reported cases prosecuted by the government in recent years. This paper also offers suggestions on handling multiagency investigations where potential civil and criminal liability exist.

Joel M. Hamme and Harvey M. Tettlebaum. "Legal Developments for Long Term Care Providers." Washington, D.C.: American Health Lawyers Association [Report No VHL98–0024], 1998, 147 pages.

Surveys statutory, regulatory, and case law developments affecting long-term care providers after June 1, 1997. Attachments include answers to commonly asked questions about the long-term provisions of the BBA, and HCFA letters to state Medicaid directors on repeal of the Boren Amendment and Qualified Medicare Beneficiaries.

Malcolm J. Harkins III and Julia McMillen. "Uncharted Waters: Managed Care and Long-Term Care Provider Contracts." *Journal of Health and Hospital Law,* Fall 1997, *30*(3), 179–194.

Presents an overview of the contracting issues critical to long-term care providers and managed care organizations. First, it describes the special characteristics of managed care that affect long-term care. Next, it addresses the major areas of potential concern to long-term care providers—including risk, covered services, relationships of the parties, utilization review, and fraud and abuse. Finally, the authors conclude that despite growing pains, long-term care and managed care will necessarily become partners in an era of cost consciousness.

Donna Lind Infeld and John R. Kress. *Cases in Long-Term Care Management.* Chicago: Health Administration Press, 1989.

This text consists of fourteen case management studies set in a variety of long-term care settings.

Lisa Hathaway-Phillips. "Successful A-Z Legal Strategies for the Survey and Enforcement Process." Washington, D.C.: American Health Lawyers Association [Report No. VLT99–0038], 1999, 36 pages.

Supplies practical strategies and tips for avoiding deficiencies before and during nursing home surveys. Addresses how to remove or reduce deficiencies after exit and through the informal and formal appeal process. Also discusses specific high-risk areas, use of tactics, different state approaches and requirements, publicity, corporate compliance, and dealing with remedies and regulations.

Hugh F. Hill III. "Hospice in Nursing Homes." Washington, D.C.: American Health Lawyers Association [Report No. VLT98–0021], 1998, 26 pages.

Supplies a brief history of the hospice movement, the Medicare Hospice benefit, and the role of hospice in long-term care facilities. Provides a sample service agreement between a hospice and a nursing facility.

Marie C. Infante. "Litigation for the Elderly: The Fuel and the Explosion." Washington, D.C.: American Health Lawyers Association [Report No. VHL99–10019], 1999, 25 pages.

Examines legal actions against health care providers brought on behalf of elderly plaintiffs.

Jonathan M. Joseph. "Programs of All-Inclusive Care for the Elderly." Washington, D.C.: American Health Lawyers Association [Report No. VLT98–0028], 1998, 34 pages.

Outlines the 1997 federal statute governing Programs of All-Inclusive Care for the Elderly (PACE), including the legal issues related to the operation of a PACE program. Includes BBA sections 4801–4804, in which Congress authorized up to twenty-eight additional PACE sites during the year following enactment and twenty more additional sites each year thereafter.

Marshall B. Kapp. *Geriatrics and the Law: Patient Rights and Professional Responsibilities.* (3rd ed.) New York: Springer, 1992, 352 pages.

Written by one of the preeminent authorities in the field, this work offers an examination of the full spectrum of geriatrics practice from the legal viewpoint.

Marshall B. Kapp. *Key Words in Ethics, Law and Aging.* New York: Springer, 1995, 89 pages.

Assembles the contemporary meanings of more than a hundred terms and concepts in a clear and concise style. Entries include definitions as well as examples to illustrate key concepts. Recommended additional readings and references are also included for most terms.

Marshall B. Kapp. "Nursing Home Restraints and Legal Liability: Merging the Standard of Care and Industry Practice." *Journal of Legal Medicine,* 1992, *13,* 1–32; reprinted in Cyril H. Wecht (ed.), *Legal Medicine 1993.* Salem, N.H.: Butterworth, 1994.

Nursing home personnel often restrain patients because administrators fear they will be exposed to liability should a patient fall and injure herself. This article attempts to place in realistic perspective the risks of liability associated with failing to restrain, and imposing restraints on, nursing home residents. It then discusses contemporary social forces that reinforce and strengthen a legal presumption against restraint use. Finally, Kapp explores possible defenses and risk management strategies for dealing with the restraint problem.

Marshall B. Kapp. *Patient Self-Determination in Long-Term Care: Implementing the PSDA in Medical Decisions.* New York: Springer, 1994, 240 pages.

This volume supplies practical advice to long-term care providers regarding legal and ethical challenges brought about by medical issues that may arise in later life. It focuses primarily on the Patient Self-Determination Act of 1990, which requires all Medicare- and Medicaid-certified provider organizations to notify patients of their right to make decisions about their medical treatment and the right to formulate advance directives.

Mark Allen Kleiman. "Crime and Punishment—The Battle for Accountability in Long Term Care." Washington, D.C.: American Health Lawyers Association [Report No. VLT99–0021], 1999, 26 pages.

Examines fraud and abuse issues affecting long-term care providers, including the increase in false claims enforcement actions, common kickback problems in long-term care, cost reporting, medical necessity issues, and the effect of the PPS.

Kathleen Knepper. "Involuntary Transfers and Discharges of Nursing Home Residents under Federal and State Law." *Journal of Legal Medicine,* June 1996, pp. 215–275.

Examines the permissibility of involuntary transfers and discharges of nursing home residents under the joint federal and state involvement in overseeing nursing home operations. Although both Medicaid and Medicare have relevance in this area, the article focuses on the requirements of the Medicaid statute and regulations because Medicaid is the primary source of governmental funding for nursing home care. Knepper considers the nature of the rights that are protected under the federal statute and regulations and examines the federal structure that has been established to protect these rights. The article reviews the licensure and certification statutes and regulations of two midwestern states, Illinois and Missouri, and compares them with the requirements of federal law. Finally, Knepper draws inferences about how effective the application of the statutes and regulations of these states have been in protecting the rights of elderly individuals not to be transferred or discharged from nursing homes without their consent.

Kimber L. Latsha. "Legal Considerations in Management Contracts for Nursing Homes." Washington, D.C.: American Health Lawyers Association [Report No. VLT98–0017], 1998, 45 pages.

Examines compliance with IRS Private Activity Bond Regulations and Revenue Procedure 97–13 and structuring management fee arrangements by determining "reasonable compensation." Reviews typical contract provisions, including a board review of management contracts, as well as additional issues for management contracts between nonprofit and for-profit service providers. Also reviews Medicare/Medicaid reimbursement issues for management contracts between related parties and regulatory issues for management contracts. Attachments include the IRS Revenue Procedures 93–19 and 97–13 and the IRS Model Conflicts-of-Interest Policy with May 1977 revisions.

Kimber L. Latsha and Lawrence Wilson. "Reimbursement for Long Term Care Facilities." Washington, D.C.: American Health Lawyers Association [Report No. VMM98–0038], 1998, 80 pages.

Examines questions relating to PPS and consolidated billing regarding long-term care. Also examines Medicare risk HMOs and their impact on long-term care, and the requirements for Section 1115 and 1396(n)(b) and (d) waivers. Attachments include the final rule on residential assessments in long-term care facilities, HCFA program memorandum on consolidated billing, HCFA program memorandum on the BBA and out-patient rehabilitation services and brief summaries of the Arizona long-term care system and the Minnesota Senior Health Options Program.

Frank H. Marsh. "Physician Authority for Unilateral DNR Orders—Federal Patient Self-Determination Act." In Cyril H. Wecht (ed.), *Legal Medicine 1993*. Salem, N.H.: Butterworth, 1994.

Analyzes the decision-making process and the extent to which an individual patient is entitled to request administration of care that is futile and inappropriate. Examines the physician-patient relationship with emphasis placed on the obligations and rights of the respective parties and the manner in which these obligations and rights may be affected by the federal Patient Self-Determination Act.

Patricia M. McGillian. *Response to Allegations of Poor Care*. Washington, D.C.: American Health Lawyers Association [Report No VLT99–0020], 1999, 152 pages.

Examines case law and regulatory issues concerning quality of care problems in nursing homes and how to respond to allegations of poor care. Extensive attachments include White House and HCFA press releases announcing quality of care initiatives, a list of Websites of interest to wound care specialists, consent orders for *United States* v. *GMS Management-Tucker, Inc.* and *United States* v. *Chester Care Ctr.*, the settlement agreement for *United States* v. *City of Philadelphia* and the memorandum opinion issued in *Northern Health Facilities, Inc.* v. *United States.*

Frances Meehan. "Advance Directives: Cases and Trends." Washington, D.C.: American Health Lawyers Association [Report No. VLT98–0025], 1998, 9 pages.

Outlines issues regarding advance directives, physician-assisted suicides, and surrogacy, and examines state statutes governing health care advance directives, proxies and surrogates, and DNRs in the fifty states and the District of Columbia.

John R. Munich and Karen S. Rieger. "Neglect, Abuse and Exploitation: The Criminal Acts." Washington, D.C.: American Health Lawyers Association [Report No.VLT99–0041], 1999, 46 pages.

Discusses the potential criminal liability associated with acts of abuse, neglect, and exploitation in the long-term care setting. Summarizes case law on these issues and suggests ways to minimize exposure. Includes a list of citations to state elder abuse statutes and peer review laws.

Cornelius D. Murray and Harvey M. Tettlebaum. "Litigation and Regulatory Update." Washington, D.C.: American Health Lawyers Association [Report No. VLT98–0003], 1998, 56 pages.

Examines regulatory developments and proposals, Medicare and Medicaid rate issues and recent reimbursement case law, fraud and abuse issues affecting long-term care providers, managed care issues for long-term care facilities, labor management issues, and end-of-life issues.

Richard P. Nelson. "Jurisdictional Issues in Challenging the Surveying Process." Washington, D.C.: American Health Lawyers Association [Report No. VLT98–0027], 1998, 10 pages.

Examines the obstacles confronting providers in attempting to preserve and present litigable issues in challenging the survey process, and presents possible solutions.

Jody Ann Noon. "Corporate Compliance Plans for Long-Term Health Facilities." Washington, D.C.: American Health Lawyers Association [Report No. VLT98–0026], 1998, 42 pages.

Surveys the laws that impose Medicare and Medicaid compliance programs, the basic elements of a compliance program, the relationship between compliance programs and quality assurance, the use of attorney-client privilege to protect audit results, and a step-by-step approach to implementing a compliance program. Attachments include the following OIG documents: the February 1997 open letter to health care providers on model compliance programs; the June 17, 1996, notice of publication of a Special Fraud Alert on Fraud and Abuse in the provision of services in nursing facilities; the June 1995 review of improper payments made to hospitals and skilled nursing facilities for beneficiaries; and a list of projects from the Inspector General's 1998 work plan.

George D. Pozgar. *Long-Term Care and the Law: A Legal Guide for Health Care Professionals.* Gaithersburg, Md.: Aspen, 1992, 498 pages.

Seeks to provide health care professionals and students with a description of the legal aspects of long-term care. The author, an instructor in the graduate program in health care administration at the New School for Social Research in New York City, contends that increases in the complexity of treating long-term patients and incomplete awareness of their needs increases the probability of lawsuits. Early discharge of the elderly from acute-care facilities because of irrational reimbursement schemes, such as diagnosis-related groups (DRGs), has served to exacerbate the problem by affecting the admission of sicker patients to nursing facilities, he writes.

Topics discussed include the liability of long-term care facilities, the role of the medical staff, nursing and the law, nursing facility services, consent, resident rights and responsibilities, long-term care records, and legal reporting requirements. Other topics include euthanasia, death and dying, financing long-term care, malpractice insurance, labor relations, and medical malpractice. Information contained in the seven appendices at the book's conclusion includes a form for consent to use restraints, a residents' bill of rights, national practitioner data bank forms, living will forms, durable power of attorney forms, a health care proxy form, and a glossary.

Karen S. Rieger and Cori H. Loomis. "Credentialing Policies for Long-Term Care Facilities." Washington, D.C.: American Health Lawyers Association [Report No. VLT98–0029], 1998, 54 pages.

Discusses the legal, regulatory, and accreditation requirements applicable to long-term care facilities in the area of credentialing, including JCAHO (Joint Commission on the Accreditation of Healthcare Organizations) requirements for long-term health facilities and the Health Care Quality Improvements Act of 1986. Attachments include a sample preapplication form, a sample application for appointment or clinical privileges, and a sample biennial reappointment and clinical privileges application.

Dennis A. Robbins. *Ethical and Legal Issues in Home Health and Long-Term Care.* Gaithersburg, Md.: Aspen, 1996, 254 pages.

Although this book focuses primarily on ethical rather than legal issues, it does briefly trace the legal legacy surrounding consent and end-of-life decision making from the *Quinlan* to the *Cruzan* decisions.

Charles P. Sabatino. "Nursing Home Admission Contracts: Undermining Rights in the Old-Fashioned Way." *Clearinghouse Review,* Oct. 1990, p. 553.

Discusses common contractual provisions, litigation alternatives should problems arise, and litigation strategies. Sabatino writes that to evaluate fully the admission contract provisions in any state, one must be aware of (1) applicable Medicare and Medicaid law and regulations; (2) state licensure laws and regulations; and (3) state regulations specific to Medicare and Medicaid-certified facilities. If a facility does not participate in Medicare or Medicaid, then only state licensure laws and regulations apply.

William J. Scanlon. "Long-Term Care: Baby Boom Generation Presents Financing Challenges." (GAO/T-HEHS-98–107.) Mar. 9, 1997, 14 pages.

This testimony by the director of Health Financing and Systems Issues before the Senate Special Committee on Aging (1) provides an overview of current spending for long-term care for the elderly, (2) discusses the increased demand that the baby boomers will likely create for long-term care, (3) describes recent shifts in Medicaid and Medicare financing of long-term care, and (4) discusses the potential role of private long-term care insurance in helping to pay for this care.

James G. Sheehan. "Damages Under the False Claims Act for Denial of Care or Denial of Minimum Quality Care by Skilled Nursing Homes." Washington, D.C.: American Health Lawyers Association [Report No VLT99–0004], 1999, 9 pages.

Briefly highlights from the government's perspective the circumstances under which denial of care, or knowing failure to provide adequate care in skilled nursing facilities, results in false or fraudulent claim, and how the government's damages sustained from poor quality of care should be calculated under the False Claims Act.

Thomas D. Vaughn. "Acquisition and Sale of Long-Term Health Facilities." Washington, D.C.: American Health Lawyers Association [Report No. VLT98–0008], 1998, 39 pages.

Outlines acquisition and sale of long-term care facilities, including predeal requirements (letter of intent, confidentiality and nonuse agreements), due diligence review, Hart-Scott-Rodino antitrust analysis and filing, drafting and negotiation agreements with emphasis on representations and warranties, title insurance, license, Medicare and Medicaid issues, and closing and postclosing issues. Attachments include a health care compliance questionnaire, document request list, purchase of assets from seller checklist, buyer and seller corporation closing checklist, and Missouri regulation on filing of seller's final Medicaid cost report after a sale.

Jennifer L. Williamson. "The Siren Song of the Elderly: Florida's Nursing Homes and the Dark Side of Chapter 400." (Note.) *American Journal of Law & Medicine*, 1999, *25*, 423.

Examines nursing home liability in the context of Florida's expansive Residents' Rights Act, codified as Chapter 400 of the Florida Statutes. The author concludes that the current Florida statute is vague and counterproductive and will ultimately drive up the cost of medical care. She contends that even though any reform should maintain a patient's right to sue, some attempt should be made to shelter providers from excessive liability.

Peter M. Wright. "Long-Term Care Facilities." In Mark A. Hall and William S. Brewbaker III (eds.), *Health Care Corporate Law: Facilities and Transactions*. Boston: Little, Brown, 1996, 94 pages.

Provides an overview of the new permutations of institutional long-term care facilities—chiefly nursing homes, intermediate care facilities for the mentally retarded, continuing care retirement communities, and assisted living facilities—and the legal issues accompanying their formation and operation. Topics discussed include regulation of nursing homes, multifacility chains, acquisition, restructuring, and financing. It also examines Medicare and Medicaid reimbursement, types of state Medicaid plan, and capital cost reimbursement.

2.04   MEDICAL OFFICES

Alice Anne Andress. *Manual of Medical Office Management*. Philadelphia: Saunders, 1996, 360 pages.

Designed to provide a medical office manager with necessary information for immediate use. Especially helpful is the chapter on legal issues in health care. An appendix includes a sample office procedure and policy manual and a sample patient information handbook. The text concludes with an index and glossary.

Robert S. Bromberg. "Tax-Exempt Physician Clinics." Washington, D.C.: American Health Lawyers Association [Report No. TX97–0010], 1997, 34 pages.

Discusses exemption, conflict-of-interest policy, captive professional corporations, physician compensation, and physician review. Includes sample conflict-of-interest policy.

Richard B. Howington and Sally Nan Barber. "Physician Group Practices." In Mark A. Hall and William S. Brewbaker III (eds.), *Health Care Corporate Law: Facilities and Transactions.* Boston: Little, Brown, 1996.

Addresses the legal issues that are common to both small, single-specialty physician practices and larger multispecialty groups. This 104-page chapter, written by two attorneys in private practice in North Carolina, focuses primarily on the corporate and business law issues of forming and operating any physician practice. The chapter begins by surveying the basic corporate forms available for structuring a physician practice and their various advantages and disadvantages. It then examines the decisions that must be made concerning the group's governance, management, and control. Following an introduction to the group practice without walls, the chapter explores the various tax issues that affect forming operating a medical group, retirement plan issues, and federal regulation of physician compensation under the referral fee laws (Stark I and Stark II). The chapter concludes with a discussion of covenants not to compete and state licensing and regulation issues.

Marcia A. Lewis and Carol D. Tamparo. *Medical Law, Ethics and Bioethics in the Medical Office.* (3rd ed.) Philadelphia: F. A. Davis, 1993, 260 pages.

Written to educate medical office personnel about medical law, ethics, and bioethics. Topics discussed in this text include consent, collection practices, medical records, hiring practices, abortion, AIDS, and death and dying.

2.05   HOME HEALTH CARE

Cathy Bellehumeur. "Fraud and Abuse Issues for I.V. Companies, Home Health Agencies and Ancillary Service Providers." Washington, D.C.: American Health Lawyers Association [Report NoVHL98–0064], 1998, 32 pages.

Outlines issues involving medical director agreements for the home health care industry, agreements for medical advisory services, fraud and abuse problems in I.V./home health care agency arrangements with hospitals, and billing and reimbursement issues.

E. Michael Flanagan. "Fraud and Abuse Issues in the Home Health Industry." Washington, D.C.: American Health Lawyers Association [Report No.VHL98–0065], 1998, 32 pages.

Outlines risk areas confronted by home health agencies in complying with Medicare fraud and abuse laws.

General Accounting Office. "Medicare Home Health Agencies: Closures Continue, With Little Evidence Beneficiary Access Is Impaired." (GAO/HEHS-99–120.) May 26, 1999, 44 pages.

Until 1998, home health care was one of Medicare's fastest growing benefits. In response to concern about rising costs, fraud and abuse, and inadequate oversight, an interim payment system has been introduced that limits Medicare payments for home health care. Industry representatives claim that the cost limits are too stringent, causing some home health agencies to close. GAO found that prior to the widely publicized closures of agencies, both the number of agencies and the use of home health services had grown considerably. Although 14 percent of agencies closed between October 1997 and January 1999, beneficiaries are still served by more than nine thousand agencies—about the same number that were in business in 1996. Forty percent of the closures were concentrated in three states, with considerable growth in the number of agencies and utilization rates (visits per user as well as users per thousand fee-for-service beneficiaries) well above the national average. In addition, most closures occurred in urban areas that still have a large number of agencies offering services. The pattern of agency closures suggests a response to the interim payment system. Attention has focused on the number of Medicare-certified home health agencies available to provide care, but GAO believes that the more important question is whether beneficiaries continue to have access to Medicare-covered home health services. GAO interviews in thirty-four primarily rural counties with substantial closures indicate that beneficiaries continue to have access to services.

General Accounting Office. "Medicare Home Health Benefit: Impact of Interim Payment System and Agency Closures on Access to Services." (GAO/HEHS-98–238.) Sept. 9, 1998, 28 pages.

Until 1996, Medicare spending for home health care had been rising dramatically, consuming about $1 in every $11 of Medicare outlays in 1996, compared with $1 in every $40 in 1989. To control this rapid cost growth, the HCFA was required to implement a Prospective Payment System that sets fixed, predetermined payments for home health services. Until that system is developed, home health agencies will be under an interim payment system that imposes limits on the cost-based payments they receive. The limits provide incentives to control per-visit costs and the number and mix of visits for each user. Industry representatives claim that the system's new cost limits have caused some home health agencies to close or some beneficiaries, particularly those with high-cost needs, to have difficulty obtaining care. This report identifies the potential impact of the interim payment system on home health agencies; (2) determines the number, distribution, and effect of recent home health agency closures; and (3) assesses whether the interim payment system could be affecting beneficiaries' access to services, particularly beneficiaries who are expensive to serve.

John J. Meyer. "Fraud and Abuse Issues for Home Health Care." Washington, D.C.: American Health Lawyers Association [Report No. VLT99–0039], 1999, 14 pages.

Outlines current issues in health care fraud enforcement affecting home health agencies and reviews the OIG's proposed guidelines for home health agency compliance plans.

Martha Dale Nathanson. *Home Health Care Answer Book.* Gaithersburg, Md.: Aspen, 1995, 238 pages.

Written in a question-and-answer format, this handbook addresses the home health agency as a specialized health care provider, an employer, a billing entity, and as a business engaging in the normal range of contractual and operational activities. It addresses laws and regulations at the state and federal levels. As a general guide to the array of legal issues affecting the home health agency, it serves as a quick reference to give the reader working knowledge of the issues and directs the reader to sources that provide more detail about their problem.

Kevin P. O'Donnell and Elaine M. Sampson. "Home Health Care: The Pivotal Link in the Creation of a New Health Care Delivery System." *Journal of Health Care Finance,* 1994, *21,* 74.

Examines the six major types of home care and describes how, in an effort to maintain market share and control costs under prospective and capitated payment, hospitals entered the home health care market.

Connie A. Raffa. "Survey and Certification for Home Health Agencies and Hospices." Washington, D.C.: American Health Lawyers Association [Report No. VLT99–0032], 1999, 13 pages.

Discusses the Medicare Survey and Certification Process, Comprehensive Medical Reviews, and wedge audits and their respective appeal processes. Surveys the proposed Medicare COPs (conditions of participation) for home health agencies and the Outcome and Assessment Information Set (OASIS) program, and identifies inconsistencies with current activities under these requirements. Examines branch versus subunit status certification issues for home health agencies (HHAs), telemedicine issues in survey and certifications, hospice COP issues, vendor issues in survey and certification as a result of contracting for services, and confidentiality and access issues.

Deborah A. Randall. "Home Health Care: The Deluge." Washington, D.C.: American Health Lawyers Association [Report No. 98–0010], 1998, 40 pages.

Reviews legislative implementation of new Medicare payment systems—the regulatory interpretations and the legal challenges already made, new health system organizational models for home health, innovative techniques in disease management and telemedicine, and fraud and abuse actions and compliance strategies. Attachments include (1) 63 Fed Reg. 25590-25593, (2) model denial letter of noncoverage of services under Medicare, (3) HCFA transmittal No. A-98-13 requiring new inquiries by fiscal intermediaries of home health agencies entering the Medicare program concerning related parties and any bankruptcy or fraud activities with those related parties, and (4) HCFA transmittal AB-97-11 announcing a new reimbursement policy on counting non-Medicare home health visits and reporting the associated costs in determining the average costs per visit.

Deborah A. Randall. "Home Health Business and Corporate Issues." Washington, D.C.: American Health Lawyers Association [Report No. VLT99–0026], 1999, 51 pages.

Highlights issues affecting acquisition of home health agencies and the reimbursement challenges under the Interim Payment System (IPS). Outlines major due diligence areas and identifies questions arising with home health care network sanctions. Also discusses disease carve-out issues and examines new product lines for home health care businesses. Attached are a selection of draft regulations on the provider-based entities, published in a notice of proposed rule making on hospital outpatient services, 47 Fed. Reg. 47552 (Sept. 8, 1998) and HCFA Transmittal No. AB-97-11, to intermediaries and carriers on counting non-Medicare home health visits and reporting the associated costs in determining the average cost per visit for home health services.

Deborah A. Randall. "Home Health: A Year to Remember." Washington, D.C.: American Health Lawyers Association [Report No. VHL99–0013], 1999, 56 pages.

Detailed outline presents an overview of home health reimbursement developments in 1998–99, with references to relevant case law. Attachments include Donna Shalala's report to Congress, "Homebound: A Criterion for Eligibility for Medicare Home Health Care," OIG proposed guidelines for home health agency compliance plans, and an OIG Special Fraud Alert on physician liability for certification in providing for medical equipment, supplies, and home health services.

Fay A. Rozovsky. *Liability and Risk Management in Home Health Care.* Gaithersburg, Md.: Aspen, 1998.

Topics discussed in this ring-bound volume include regulation, liability, risk management, accreditation, and relevant forms.

S. Mitchell Weitzman. "Legal and Policy Aspects of Home Care Coverage." *Annals of Health Law,* 1992, *1,* 1.

Reviews home health coverage and reimbursement by public and private payers, with particular emphasis on the Medicare and Medicaid programs. Additionally, regulation of the service and product sectors of the home care industry is reviewed. Finally, Weitzman makes the case for a uniform and comprehensive home care system.

2.06 ASSISTED LIVING FACILITIES

General Accounting Office. "Assisted Living: Quality of Care and Consumer Protection Issues in Four States." (GAO/HEHS-99–27.) Apr. 26, 1999, 55 pages.

Assisted living facilities provide a growing number of Americans with an alternative to nursing homes. To make informed choices about various facilities, however, consumers need clear and complete information on services, costs, and policies. A GAO review of assisted living facilities in four states—California, Florida, Ohio, and Oregon—found that the facilities did not always give consumers enough information to determine whether a particular facility could meet their needs, for how long, and under what circumstances. Marketing materials, contracts, and other information provided by facilities are often incomplete and sometimes vague or misleading. Only about half of the facilities reported they provide residents with key information in writing, such as the amount of information that residents can expect to receive with medications, the circumstances under which the cost of services might change, or when residents might be required to leave if their health deteriorates. Consumers also need assurance that the facilities provide high-quality care and protect consumers' interests. All four states license assisted-living facilities and conduct periodic inspections and investigate complaints. Yet GAO found that more than one-fourth of the facilities it reviewed had been cited by state licensing, ombudsman, or other agencies for five or more quality-of-care or consumer protection deficiencies or violations during 1996 and 1997. Eleven percent of the facilities had been cited for ten or more deficiencies and violations during the same period. Frequently identified problems included facilities' (1) providing poor care to patients, such as inadequate medical attention following an accident; (2) having insufficient, unqualified, and untrained staff; (3) not providing residents with appropriate medications and not storing medications properly; and (4) not following admission and discharge policies required by state regulation.

Robert L. Mollica and Kimberly Irvin Snow. *Guide to State Assisted Living and State Policy.* (3rd ed.) Portland, Maine: National Academy of State Health Policy, 1996.

This report reviews the assisted living and board and care policies in each of the fifty states.

Robert A. Walker and Chad E. Turner. "Gold at the End of the Rainbow: Medical Expenses and Below-Market Rate Loans in Continuing Care Retirement Communities." *Virginia Tax Review,* 1998, *18,* 1.

Residents of continuing care retirement communities (CCRCs), or their children if the residents are the children's dependents, face significant tax consequences associated with the fees they pay to a CCRC. On the positive side, they can usually take a large tax deduction for the medical expense portion of their entrance fee and may also deduct the medical portion of their monthly fees. Negative consequences may occur, however, if the CCRC is obligated to refund some or all of the entrance fee. This article addresses these consequences and analyzes the methods CCRCs use in estimating the portions of the entrance and monthly fees allocable to medical care.

2.07 HOSPICES

Ellen H. Moskowitz and Edward S. Kornreich. "Free Care Provided by Hospices." *Journal of Health Law,* 1999, *32,* 475.

Many hospices have traditionally provided certain assistance and services to the community without charge through "pre-hospice" or "bridge" programs. Current regulatory pressures have raised questions about this practice. This article analyzes whether the provision of free pre-hospice care would run afoul of Medicare hospice conditions of participation, Medicare billing rules that deny payment for health care services ordinarily provided to patients without charge, or the federal anti-kickback law. It finds that adopting certain business structures should permit compliance with these laws. Drawing a distinction between "pre-hospice educational services and "pre-hospice therapeutic services," it also suggests that providing free pre-hospice therapeutic services that could be considered covered services under Medicare or Medicaid billing rules raises material regulatory risks.

3

Managed Care Organizations

Managed care refers to medical care that combines the functions of insurance with the management of delivery of health care services. As an insurer of medical services, the managed care entity is able to absorb the risk inherent in delivering and paying for these services. As a utilization manager of medical services, the entity sets up the vehicle through which the providers can render services to a large number of insureds. Through a series of contracts, the insured, or enrollee, is induced to seek medical services from the organization's contracted providers since the insureds will be charged less than the usual and customary fee ordinarily charged by these providers. The providers likewise have an incentive to engage in these contracts since providing medical services to the entity's enrollees will greatly increase the physician's patient base.

The method of payment these providers receive is not the traditional fee-for-service arrangement to which most physicians and insurers were long accustomed. In a fee-for-service reimbursement, the providers receive payment based on actual costs incurred. In managed care arrangements, the method of reimbursement is usually a fixed rate that is prospectively set based on various factors. These fixed rates may be disbursed based on a per-patient (capitated), per-diem, or per-diagnosis (DRG) basis, regardless of services actually rendered to the insured. Some managed care entities still employ a modified fee-for-service reimbursement rate whereby the provider receives payment for actual costs, less a percentage to cover the risk that costs will exceed the budget. These methods of reimbursement, therefore, provide the incentive for physicians to control costs.

Under the traditional fee-for-service reimbursement method, since providers were reimbursed based on the amount expended (plus markup), they assumed no risk and thus were immune to the effects of rising costs. The degree to which the provider is sensitive to medical costs under managed care varies with the nature of the arrangement. Managed care may take several forms where each system attempts to contain costs using different mechanisms and where each provides varying degrees of incentives for both the provider and the insured to enter into these contracts. In short, delivering high-quality health care at a reasonable price is one of the ultimate goals of all parties in any managed care system.

In an HMO, costs are contained primarily through strictly managing the delivery of health care services. The HMO controls not only the method of payment for all services the insured receives and for which the HMO is obligated to pay but also which physicians provide service to the insureds. In order for the insured to have medical services paid for by the HMO, the insured must receive these services only from a participating physician who has contracted with the HMO. Otherwise, the enrollee is responsible for 100 percent of the cost for those outside services (except in emergency situations). The consumer is essentially "locked in" to the providers with which the HMO has contracted; consequently, HMOs were labeled "closed delivery systems." When seeking services from a participating physician, although the insured is usually required to pay some amount toward the provider's fee, the enrollee always pays less than the usual and customary fee. The provider, then, is reimbursed on a prepaid basis that varies depending on the particular nature of the HMO.

There are four commonly used HMO types:

1. Staff model
2. Group model
3. Independent practice association (IPA) model
4. Contract model

In both the staff and group models, the providers are treated as salaried employees of either the HMO (in a staff model) or a medical group (in a group model) and deliver services at one location, usually owned by either the HMO or the medical group. The only real distinction between the staff and group models is in the existence of an intermediary in the group model. In a group model, the HMO pays a fixed fee to a medical group practice, which then pays the providers' salaries, whereas in a staff model the HMO pays the salaries directly.

The IPA model is similar to the group model in that the HMO contracts with an association, which then contracts with or employs the providers. The IPA model differs from the group model, however, in three ways. First, in the IPA model the HMO pays a fixed fee to the professional association; but instead of the association paying its providers as salaried employees as in the group model, it pays them on a fee-for-service basis less a percentage for the risk of overutilization. Second, because the participating physicians in the IPA model render services as independent contractors instead of on an employee-employer basis, the insureds receive all outpatient services at the private office of each individual provider instead of at one centralized location. Third, as a cost-containment measure, the IPA model (unlike the group model) requires that the insured receive a threshold consultation or examination by a primary care physician prior to receiving specialist services. Only if the insured receives the approval and referral of a participating primary care physician will any treatment by a specialist be covered.

This "gatekeeper" feature is also characteristic of the contract model. The only difference between the contract model and the IPA model is the "middleman" association; in the contract model, the HMO contracts directly with the private physician. The reimbursement method in a contract model may be on either a fixed-fee or a fee-for-service basis, just as in the IPA model.

The HMO itself may be a health insurer or a licensed carrier whose sole business purpose is to set up such managed care systems, in which case these plans would be subject to regulation by state law. The HMO may also be an employer's self-insured plan where the employer bears the insurance risk, in which case it would not be regulated by state law with regard to many provisions, most notably liability and insurance regulations. Instead, the self-insured plan would be considered an employee benefit plan and therefore governed by ERISA, preempting nearly all state regulation affecting the plan. Whether the plan is run by licensed carriers or is a self-insured plan entails in-depth analysis as to the possible state and federal regulation, which is discussed below. Although the self-insured plans are not paid for by private insurance carriers, they are often managed and administered by these carriers or HMOs. For those plans that are subject to state laws, most states have adopted HMO enabling acts outlining the requirements of such plans, which are much the same as the requirements for insurance carriers. Because HMOs take on liability and assume risks similar to those of insurance carriers, state regulation should come as no surprise.

Many states have a particular statutory provision, referred to as the "hold harmless" provision, that helps to contain costs by increasing physician sensitivity to the cost of providing medical services. Under this provision, a provider is prevented from seeking payment from the patient-insured in the event that the HMO fails to pay any amounts agreed upon. Because the provider's sole recourse for monies owed by the HMO is against the HMO, it forces the provider to share the insurance risks with the HMO, making the provider sensitive to such costs. This allows the HMO to serve the purpose for which it was intended—involving all parties in cost containment.

A preferred provider organization (PPO) is an arrangement similar to an HMO except the enrollees are not restricted only to the organization's contract physicians. The incentive for the insiders to seek treatment from the participating providers and for the providers to become participating physicians is the same as it is with an HMO. The fundamental difference is the flexibility of a PPO. Enrollees may seek services outside the group of contract providers and still have a portion of those services paid for by the plan. Insiders will have to pay, however, more than they would if they were receiving services from a participating provider, usually in the form of increased deductibles and/or copayments. In most states, statutes limit the percentage a plan may charge the insured for services outside the PPO contract. Usually, 20 percent over the amount the insured would normally be charged is the maximum a plan may force the enrollee to pay. Because of the increased flexibility of PPOs, the management entity has less control and therefore is less effective at cost containment than an HMO.

PPOs may be divided into four categories, depending upon the nature of the entity organizing the plan. PPOs can be organized by the providers themselves, insurance companies, brokers, or employers. In each form, the entity organizing the plan enlists the providers and markets the plan to health care purchasers, insurance companies, or employers. The employer-sponsored plan is merely a self-insured plan that the employer institutes for the benefit of its employees. The methods of reimbursement in PPO plans are the same as those for HMOs. Although PPOs do not ordinarily utilize a gatekeeper, most plans employ permission certifications, second opinions, and screening procedures to help contain costs.

Here are common, key characteristics of PPOs:

- *Select provider panel.* PPOs typically contract with selected providers in a community to provide health services for covered individuals. Most PPOs contract directly with hospitals, physicians, and other diagnostic facilities. Providers are selected to participate on the basis of their cost efficiency, community reputation, and scope of services. Some PPOs assemble massive databases of information about potential providers, including costs by diagnostic category, before they make their contracting decisions.
- *Negotiated payment rates.* Most PPO participation agreements require providers to accept the PPO's payments as payment in full for covered services (except for applicable coinsurance or deductibles). PPOs attempt to negotiate payment rates that provide them with a competitive cost advantage relative to charge-based payment systems. These negotiated payment rates usually take the form of discounts from charges, all-inclusive per diem rates, or payments based on DRGs. Some PPOs have established bundled pricing arrangements for certain services, including normal delivery, open heart surgery, and some types of oncology.
- *Rapid payment terms.* Some PPOs are willing to include prompt payment features in their contracts with participating providers in return for favorable payment rates. For example, a PPO may commit to pay all clean claims submitted by its providers within fifteen days of submittal in return for a larger discount from charges.
- *Utilization management.* Many PPOs implement utilization management programs to control the utilization and cost of health services provided to their covered beneficiaries. In the more sophisticated PPOs, these utilization management programs resemble those operated by HMOs. Unlike indemnity plans, where failure to comply with utilization management precertification programs increases the financial liability to the member (or covered insured), many PPOs impose the financial penalty for noncompliance on the participating provider, who may not bill the penalty to the member (of course, if the member uses a nonparticipating or out-of-network provider, the financial penalty for noncompliance falls back on the member).
- *Consumer choice.* Unlike traditional HMOs, PPOs generally allow covered beneficiaries to use non-PPO providers instead of PPO providers when they need health services. Higher levels of beneficiary cost sharing, often in the form of higher copayments, typically are imposed when PPO beneficiaries use non-PPO providers.[1]

Reference

1. Peter R. Kongstvedt (ed.). *The Managed Health Care Handbook.* (3rd ed.) Gaithersburg, Md.: Aspen, 1996; see also Marianne F. Fazen. *Managed Care Desk Reference.* Reston, Va.: St. Anthony, 1996, p. 228.

ANNOTATIONS

3.01   THE HEALTH MAINTENANCE ORGANIZATION (HMO) MODEL OF CARE

American Health Lawyers Association. *Critical Steps in Managed Care Contracting: A Loose-Leaf Guide, Vol. II.* Washington, D.C.: American Health Lawyers Association, 1995.

Includes sample provisions and agreements, specific contractual language, alternative contract provisions, and negotiating strategies. Topics covered in this manual include fundamentals of managed care contracting, organizational documents for integrated delivery systems, payer agreements, physician practice and employment agreements, drafting capitation contracts, indemnification and structuring contracts to prevent future liability, managed care provider agreements, and government contracts.

Aspen Health Law Center, with John P. Marren (consulting editor). *Managed Care Law Manual.* Gaithersburg, Md.: Aspen, 2001.

Discusses HMOs in general, HMO models, federal HMO law, relevant state laws, contracts with subscribers, rate regulation, marketing, business management reporting requirements, examination requirements, recourse for noncompliance, and health care operations. This manual provides the pros and cons of various types of managed care structure, how they operate, and the legal issues pertinent to each. This one-volume loose-leaf manual, supplemented twice annually, is available in binder form or on disk.

Aspen Health Care Group. *Managed Care Contracts Manual.* Gaithersburg, Md.: Aspen, 1998.

Focuses on the fundamentals of contracting. Written in practical, easy-to-understand language, the text addresses HMOs and other types of managed care structure. Topics covered include contract considerations, potential liabilities, negotiation tips and strategies, direct contracting, risk sharing, quality-based agreements, and antitrust issues. This loose-leaf manual, supplemented annually, is available in binder form or on diskette.

Lawrence C. Baker and Joel C. Cantor. "Physician Satisfaction Under Managed Care." *Health Affairs* (Supplement), 1993, *12*, 258.

Explores how managed care arrangements have affected physicians' perceptions of professional autonomy and satisfaction with their current practices and careers. Data are drawn from a 1991 representative survey of young, allopathic physicians, sponsored by the Robert Wood Johnson Foundation. The authors found that HMO employees are more likely to be female and members of racial and ethnic minorities than other employees of self-employed physicians. Employees typically have less experience and have been in practice fewer years than have their self-employed colleagues. HMO employees are more likely to be generalists and report spending a comparatively large portion of their time providing primary care. HMO employees seem to care for fewer complex patients, and their patient loads contain relatively few poor and uninsured patients, as compared to employees of government and other employers.

    Managed care exerts its strongest negative influence on the level of perceived autonomy in the areas of time management and patient selection. Among self-employed physicians and employees of other employers, exposure to managed care tends to result in the perception of less freedom for patients unable to pay. Self-employed physicians obtaining more than half of their revenues from managed care were significantly less likely to feel able to spend sufficient time with patients and to care for patients unable to pay. Physicians affiliated with managed care tend to feel freer to hospitalize patients and to order tests and procedures. Although HMO employees were significantly less likely than self-employed physicians to be satisfied with their current practice, they were only slightly less likely than employees of other employers to be satisfied. The authors conclude that the results hold out the hope that a large-scale move toward managed care would not cause the damage to physician morale that some observers have expected.

Steven J. Balla. "Markets, Governments, and HMO Development in the 1990s." *Journal of Health Politics, Policy and Law,* Apr. 1999, 24(2), 215.

This article examines the impact of population demographics, health market characteristics, and government purchasing and regulation on the development of the HMO industry in the 1990s. The author focuses on two facets of development: HMO market share and the number of HMOs in operation in metropolitan areas.

Joseph Cardinal Bernardin. *Managing Managed Care.* St. Louis: Catholic Health Association, May 1996.

In this pamphlet, the late Cardinal Archbishop of Chicago examines managed care through the prism of Catholic social teaching.

California Medical Association. *Physician's Managed Care Manual.* (3rd ed.) San Francisco: CMA, 1996.

Handbook examining capitation, financial incentives, contract negotiations and amendments, point-of-service plans, risk-sharing arrangements, and pertinent California managed care laws.

Bruce W. Clark. "Negotiating Successful Managed Care Contracts." *Healthcare Financial Management,* Aug, 1, 1995, p. 27.

This brief article, written by a practicing attorney, highlights several critical issues that arise in managed care contracting and offers several practical suggestions for resolving those issues. The goal of managed care contracting is to create a coherent framework for treatment and payment decisions that is as unintrusive, flexible, and cooperative as possible for both payers and providers. This goal is rarely achieved with a generic contract, the author writes, which ignores the circumstances and interests unique to a particular payer and provider.

Consumer's Checkbook Magazine Editors. *Consumers' Guide to Health Plans.* Washington, D.C.: Center for the Study of Services, 1995, 96 pages.

Describes types of HMO and PPO, and supplies—in the form of charts, diagrams, and lucid text—a company-by-company evaluation of overall quality, access, and choice in all fifty states. The guide concludes with a set of six appendices setting forth hospitals with the lowest death rates, how to interpret the 1994 survey of health plan members, health plans that chose not to have their members surveyed, state HMO regulators, state insurance counseling services, and state agencies on aging.

Sheryl Tarat Dacso and Clifford C. Dacso. *Managed Care Answer Book: Forms and Checklists.* Gaithersburg, Md.: Aspen, 1999, 400 pages.

Contains a guide to decision making, articles of incorporation and bylaws for providers, types of managed care arrangements including special language, funding alternatives and exculpatory arrangements, mergers and takeovers of providers and plan sponsors, window plans, and administrative considerations.

Karen Davis and others. *Health Care Cost Containment.* Baltimore: Johns Hopkins University Press, 1990, 266 pages.

Reviews the growth of HMOs over the past two decades, examines trends in the HMO market, assesses the data pertaining to the cost-saving effects of HMOs, and considers the role HMOs are likely to play in the U.S. health care system in the future. HMOs are discussed in seven sections. The first describes the various types of HMO. The second reviews federal policies that were implemented to encourage HMO development, the growth in HMOs that ensued, recent trends in the HMO market, and the demographic characteristics of HMO enrollees and disenrollees. The third section examines data pertaining to the extent to which HMOs provide care at less cost than the fee-for-service sector does. The fourth section—based in part on a case study of HMO development in Baltimore that provides insight into policy issues related to HMOs and the role HMOs are likely to play in the future—discusses expected future HMO growth and important issues that will need to be considered as that growth occurs. The fifth section examines various methods of paying HMOs. The sixth section presents a summary of the authors' analysis, while the final section sets forth recommendations regarding how to promote HMO growth without jeopardizing quality of care.

Ezekiel J. Emanuel and Lee Goldman. "Protecting Patient Welfare in Managed Care: Six Safeguards." *Journal of Health Politics, Policy and Law,* Aug. 1998, *23,* 635.

The public is suspicious that managed care threatens its health because of managed care's interest in reducing costs. Since physicians' decisions control 75 percent of all health care spending, managed care organizations are focusing their cost-cutting strategies on influencing physician decision making through financial incentives and guidelines. These two techniques have some important contributions, especially in enhancing efficiency and standardizing care to a high level. Nevertheless, they pose a threat—and are perceived by the public as posing a threat—to patients' health and well-being. The authors propose and analyze six safeguards that might mitigate the threats to patient welfare posed by financial incentives and guidelines: (1) disclosure, (2) professionalism, (3) competition, (4) limiting financial incentives, (5) guideline review boards, and (6) appeals boards.

Marianne F. Fazen. *Managed Care Desk Reference: The Complete Guide to Terminology and Resources.* Reston, Va.: St. Anthony Messenger Press & Franciscan Communications, 1997, two volumes.

This practical work is primarily a glossary of approximately twelve hundred terms covering the entire managed care industry. Indexed and extensively cross-referenced, this text offers quick access to current and past terminology, including acronyms and abbreviations. The books also include a list of trade associations, policy and research organizations, accrediting organizations, and pertinent government agencies, along with their addresses, phone numbers, and the name of a contact. This work supplies providers, purchasers, payers, and patients with a common language, allowing them to focus on issues rather than on semantics.

Allan Fine and Colleen E. Dowd. *Provider Sponsored Organizations.* Gaithersburg, Md.: Aspen, 1998, 200 pages.

Examines the legal, regulatory, and operational issues critical to forming a provider sponsored organization (PSO). Describes the advantages and pitfalls of PSO risk assumption. Specific topics addressed include differences between PSOs and MCOs, aspects of risk contracting, factors to consider before entering a Medicare risk contract, legal requirements of forming a PSO, operational requirements of a PSO, legislative issues that affect PSO structure and market entry, and regulatory issues for PSOs.

Madelon Lubin Finkel. *Health Care Cost Management: A Basic Guide.* (3rd ed.) Brookfield, Wis.: International Foundation of Employee Benefit Plans, 1996, 204 pages.

Supplies an introduction to major contemporary issues in health care. The manual includes a glossary of health care terms, a history of health reform efforts, and helpful appendices on ERISA and quality measurement organizations.

Michele M. Garvin. "Health Maintenance Organizations." In Mark A. Hall and William S. Brewbaker III (eds.), *Health Care Corporate Law: Managed Care.* Boston: Little, Brown, 1996.

Provides an excellent overview of the HMO model of health care delivery and the federal and state legal issues relating to HMO product development and operations. Unlike independent hospitals, physicians, and insurers, HMOs combine the financing and delivery of care into a single integrated system. As a result of its hybrid role, an HMO faces legal and regulatory issues relating both to its "insurance"—or financing—function and to its "provider"—or delivery—function.

Garvin, an attorney with Ropes and Gray in Boston, supplies perhaps the most comprehensive analysis of HMO regulation in print. After tracing the development of the HMO concept, she focuses on the current regulatory environment and on the evolution of HMO model types. She also examines in detail federal qualification guidelines and the variety of state HMO enabling acts, providing more than twenty-one pages of valuable information on state licensure requirements and on the National Association of Insurance Commissioners (NAIC) Model HMO Act.

Garvin further examines government reimbursement programs as they relate to HMOs, including Medicare, Medicaid, and the federal employees health benefit program. She discusses physician payment incentives along with HMO management and operational issues such as credentialing, provider contracts, and HMO liability for provider malpractice. She reviews issues concerning mergers, closures, and bankruptcy of HMOs. Finally, she supplies in appendix form the NAIC Model HMO Act, a list of jurisdictions that have enacted the Model Act and Related Rules, and a series of helpful charts and tables giving an overview of regulations in state HMO laws.

General Accounting Office. "Managed Care: Explicit Gag Clauses Not Found in HMO Contracts, But Physician Concerns Remain." (GAO/HEHS-97–175.) Aug. 29, 1997, 23 pages.

Assesses the extent to which HMO contracts limit physicians from discussing outside treatment options with patients. In recent years, some physician and consumer advocacy groups have contended that HMOs impose contractual limitations that restrict doctors from informing patients of all treatment options, including those available outside the HMO. As a result, some states have prohibited these clauses from managed care contracts. Of the 529 HMOs that GAO studied, none used contract clauses that specifically ban doctors from discussing all appropriate medical options with their patients. Two-thirds of responding plans did have a nondisparagement, nonsolicitation, or confidentiality clause that some doctors might interpret as limiting communication about all treatment options.

Yet it appears that such provisions are not likely to have a significant impact on physician behavior. Doctors told GAO that they often do not read carefully all of their contracts with HMOs. They maintain that they openly communicate with their patients because habit, professional ethics, and fear of medical liability are more powerful influences on their behavior than are contract requirements. However, this report cautions that the power of HMOs in the health care market is growing, and their ability to terminate physicians' contracts can exact a heavy price from doctors who refuse to modify their practice patterns.

Michael Higgins. "Second Opinions on HMOs." *ABA Journal,* Apr. 1999, pp. 60–65.

Trial lawyers are pursuing new theories of managed care liability. This article examines such battlegrounds as agency liability, negligence, fiduciary duty, the ADA, RICO (Racketeer Influenced and Corrupt Organizations), and potential new legislation.

Bruce A. Johnson and Gerald A. Niederman. *Managed Care Legal Issues: A Practical Guide for Health Care Decision-Makers.* Englewood, Colo.: MGMA, 1996, 260 pages.

Examines managed care products, antitrust problems, fraud and abuse prohibitions, tax issues, ERISA, organizational models, taxation, and risk management. This book, written by two attorneys, is intended for the layperson with no legal background.

Peter R. Kongstvedt (ed.). *The Managed Health Care Handbook.* (4th ed.) Gaithersburg, Md.: Aspen, 2000, 1,045 pages.

In this book, the editor, a board-certified internist and a consultant with Ernst & Young LLP, has produced the most comprehensive, detailed analysis of the topic available in one volume. The principal goal of the book is to present possible solutions and multiple approaches to problems as well as information needed by managers of managed care operations. This work is written for managers who are considering entering the field, for middle managers in the field who are trying to advance their careers, for senior executives in the industry with less experience than they would like, for medical directors new to managed care, and for doctors in group practice who are charged with managing their peers and colleagues in a risk arrangement with a managed care plan. It will also prove useful to hospital administrators sorting out the merits of various health care plans, corporate benefits managers charged with controlling health care costs for employees, and regulators who write the regulations for an ever-changing industry. The book is remarkable not only for its clear prose but also for its often sparkling wit.

Among the range of topics covered are the types of managed care organization, acquisition, joint venture, and partnership between providers and managed care organizations; physician compensation; negotiating and contracting with hospitals and institutions; operational management and marketing; state regulation of managed care federal qualification; and ERISA. The book supplies helpful contract clauses along with a sample agreement between an HMO and a physician and one between a hospital and an HMO. Every managed care organization should have a copy of this handbook.

Harold S. Luft. *Health Maintenance Organizations: Dimensions of Performance.* New Brunswick, N.J.: Transaction Books, 1987, 468 pages.

Examines the growth and development of HMOs in the 1980s. In this updated version of his 1981 text, the author—a researcher at the Institute of Health Policy Studies at the University of California, San Francisco—offers a comprehensive review of the relevant literature and impartial analysis of HMO performance. Specifically addressed are cost, utilization, preventive care, quality of service, and patient satisfaction.

Medical Group Management Association. *Federal Legislative and Regulatory Briefing Book.* Englewood, Colo.: MGMA, 1998.

Produced annually each spring, this book of approximately one hundred pages includes description, analysis, and, when appropriate, a position statement on twenty-one federal public policy issues that medical group practices will face. Topics include fraud and abuse reforms, physician self-referral, Medicare physician policies, direct contracting, antitrust problems, and liability reform.

Glen A. Reed. "Representing Provider Sponsored Managed Care Organizations." Washington, D.C.: American Health Lawyers Association [Report No. VHH99–0012], 1999, 17 pages.

Outlines the structural and functional design of provider-sponsored managed care organizations and discusses tax exemption, fraud and abuse, and antitrust considerations for lawyers organizing provider-sponsored MCOs. Also identifies the documents defining the legal infrastructure, as well as licensure, regulatory, and accreditation requirements in organizing MCOs.

Stephen M. Shortell and others. *Remaking Health Care in America: The Evolution of Organized Delivery Systems.* (2nd ed.) San Francisco: Jossey-Bass, 2000, 338 pages.

Written by one of the nation's leading health care management authorities and a team of experts, this book examines the progress of nine health care delivery systems that were analyzed in the book's first edition. On the basis of recent research, the authors scrutinize the successes, failures, and lessons learned and confront health care concerns such as the public backlash against managed care and the unmet need to provide care to people with chronic illness.

Alan Steinberg, M.D. *The Insider's Guide to HMOs: How to Navigate the Managed Care System.* New York: Plume, 1997, 231 pages.

Diagnoses perceived problems with HMOs, including the often perverse incentives associated with capitation; the difficulties in obtaining access to specialists; special problems of Medicare HMOs; the difficulty of choosing among competing health plans; cutting through the red tape; and special issues associated with the treatment of pregnant women, children, and those in need of psychiatric care. This consumer guide, written by an internist who practices medicine and is a part-time medical director of a managed care company, concludes with a helpful glossary, a list of sources of further information, and an index.

Barbara Tymann. *Primer on Assessing Managed Care Quality.* Washington, D.C.: National Governors Association 1998, 40 pages.

States are experimenting with how to collect, combine, present, and disseminate performance measurement data that are accurate and meaningful. The approaches that states are using to educate and empower consumers include developing and disseminating consumer guides, health plan comparison report cards, medical procedure report cards, and physician profiles. This report provides an overview of managed care quality assessment efforts at the national and state levels and highlights state quality measurement approaches.

Weiss Ratings. *HMO and Health Insurance Directory: A Guide to Health Insurers with Their Safety Ratings Including Blue Cross/Blue Shield Plans.* Palm Beach Gardens, Fla.: Weiss Ratings, 1996.

The purpose of this directory is to provide consumers with information on the financial strength and safety of health insurance companies. Included are commercial for-profit insurers, mutual insurers, Blue Cross and Blue Shield plans, and for-profit and nonprofit HMOs. The directory includes more than eleven hundred health insurers offering a variety of health insurance products. It provides an opinion regarding a company's ability to meet its commitments to its policyholders—not only under current business and economic conditions but also during a declining economy or in the event the company suffers a sharp increase in claims. An excellent resource, regularly updated.

Florence Wilson and Duncan Neuhauser. *Health Services in the United States.* (Rev. 2nd ed.) Cambridge, Mass.: Ballinger, 1987.

Provides a basic description of laws, personnel, institutions, and financing of health services.

3.02 HMO MODEL TYPES

Russell C. Coile, Jr. *The Five Stages of Managed Care: Strategies for Providers, HMOs, and Suppliers.* Chicago: Health Administration Press, 1997, 268 pages.

Examines strategies that providers and payers currently use to succeed and to prepare for the health care system's further evolution. Examples of delivery systems throughout the country illustrate which markets are at which stage and highlight successful strategies and potential pitfalls.

Donald K. Freeborn. *Promise and Performance in Managed Care: The Prepaid Group Practice Model.* Baltimore: Johns Hopkins University Press, 1994.

Examines the potential for HMOs of the group practice variety to deliver managed care and some of the consequences. Statements are supported by the data derived from special research projects, from the Kaiser Permanente Center for Health Research information database, and from observations by other researchers, including those prominently associated with health policy. The context is the long-term operation of a plan based on principles that are advanced by the author as incorporating desirable features of managed care. The scope of this book is broad, including an exploration of why people select alternative plans and why they stay with or move away from them, an examination of personal and systemic factors that influence the utilization of services, a comparison of individuals' satisfaction with various aspects of the HMO program and similar judgments regarding the fee-for-service source of care, and a study of physicians' attitudes and what physicians like and dislike about the HMO.

Karen A. Jordan. "Managed Competition and Limited Choice of Providers: Countering Negative Perceptions Through a Responsibility to Select Quality Network Physicians." *Arizona State Law Journal*, 1995, *27*, 875.

Describes how the relationship an HMO maintains with its physicians distinguishes one HMO model from another. In a staff model, the HMO owns and operates the facility in which the physicians work. It also directly employs physicians and retains them as salaried employees. The HMO has full responsibility for selecting participating physicians. Because these physicians are considered part of the HMO staff, a typical employer-employee relationship exists.

The group-model HMO markets its health plan as a total care package. It enables a patient to obtain a variety of services from a single source rather than from various independent providers. The group-model HMO is similar to the staff model in the sense that physicians in a group model usually work in facilities owned or operated by an HMO. The author points out that the difference between the two models is that a group-model HMO provides health care services to its members by contracting with an independent medical group rather than with individual physicians.

Thomas Palay. "Organizing an HMO by Contract: Some Transaction-Cost Considerations." *Nebraska Law Review*, 1986, *65*, 728.

Discusses the governance of HMOs and associated transaction costs.

Alan G. Raymond. *The HMO Health Care Companion: A Consumer's Guide to Managed Care Networks*. New York: HarperCollins, 1994, 254 pages.

Addresses such topics as the various types of HMO and managed care network, choosing among HMOs, emergency care, specialty care, and how to resolve disputes with an HMO. Written in clear, direct language, the text is supplemented by a helpful glossary that elucidates the alphabet soup of managed care terms. The book also includes a list of the names, addresses, and phone numbers of state HMO regulators.

Tracey Thompson Turner, Norman C. Payson, and Richard B. Salmon. "Health Maintenance Organizations in Rural Markets." In Peter R. Kongstvedt (ed.), *The Managed Health Care Handbook*. (3rd ed.) Gaithersburg, Md.: Aspen, 1996.

Surveys the barriers to rural HMOs, including physician supply, regulatory factors, and demographic characteristics. Managed care, the authors point out, is predicated on competition among providers. Such competition, however, is largely absent in rural areas of the nation. After examining a pilot program in Maine, the authors conclude that skilled HMO managers can overcome these hurdles and achieve success in underpenetrated markets if they add significant value to the existing rural health care infrastructure.

Eric R. Wagner and Valerie J. Hackenberg. *A Practical Guide to Physician Sponsored HMO Development*. Washington, D.C.: American Society of Internal Medicine, 1986, 63 pages.

Proposes a way to examine the feasibility of HMO development, reviews the organizational structures for HMOs, and discusses the steps that should be followed during development. This guide is intended to provide direction to physicians who are contemplating development of a physician-sponsored HMO. It is not intended to provide assistance with developing staff-model HMOs.

Jonathan P. Weiner and Gregory de Lissovoy. "Razing a Tower of Babel: A Taxonomy of Managed Care and Health Insurance Plans." *Journal of Health Politics, Policy and Law,* 1993, *18, 75.*

Elucidates managed care and health insurance terminology. To many, the U.S. health care system has become an unintelligible alphabet soup of three-letter health plans. There is little agreement about which characteristics distinguish one type of plan from another. The authors review past and current trends in the market for nontraditional health benefit plans and propose a taxonomy, or system of classification, to aid understanding how managed care plans differ from conventional health insurance and from one another. Also included is a comprehensive glossary of terms. Like the article itself, the glossary is written for a general health care audience.

3.03 STATE REGULATION OF HMOs

Howard A. Burde. "The Theory and Practice of Managed Care—How to Stop Worrying and Learn To Love Your Regulator." Washington, D.C.: American Health Lawyers Association [Report No. VMC98–0022], 1998, 24 pages.

Discusses what regulators consider when developing rules governing managed care. Examines the impact of national standards (such as Medicare rules; NAJC model rules; National Committee for Quality Assurance, or NCQA; and JCAHO) on development and applications of state rules; the theoretical basis for managed care regulation; and the aspects of managed care transactions that concern state regulators and why. Reviews what influences regulatory response; what regulators look for with respect to network development, quality assurance, utilization management, assignment of risk, medical management, consumer and provider appeals, and solvency and reserve requirements. Looks at the challenges facing state governments in regulating managed care, and how responses to them affect review of proposed managed care arrangements.

Patricia A. Butler. *Oversight of Managed Care Entities: Issues for State Policymakers.* Washington, D.C.: National Governors' Association, 1996, 31 pages.

Outlines the policy questions raised by government regulation of managed health plans and other managed care activities. Butler provides an overview of state issues raised by four relationships: between the enrollee and the plan, the plan and the provider, patients and providers, and public purchasers and their contractors. This framework will help policy makers grasp the variety of policy issues that can arise with each relationship.

California Medical Association. *Model Managed Care Contract.* San Francisco: CMA, 1995, 34 pages.

Discusses capitation provisions, termination provisions, fee-for-service provisions, risk withhold provisions, and hold harmless clauses.

Garry Carneal. "State Regulation of Managed Care." In Peter R. Kongstvedt (ed.), *The Managed Health Care Handbook.* (3rd ed.) Gaithersburg, Md.: Aspen, 1996.

This fourteen-page chapter includes a discussion of such topics as the regulatory process; anti–managed care legislation; insurance reform initiatives; and regulation by market segments.

Families USA. *Hit and Miss: State Managed Care Laws.* Washington, D.C.: Families USA, 1998, 45 pages.

This report surveys state legislation addressing common problems with managed care. The report analyzes, state by state, activity on thirteen illustrative consumer protections and demonstrates that many Americans are left unprotected. The spottiness of state consumer protections is compounded by ERISA, which preempts state laws for those in "self-insured" plans—one out of three people with employer-provided coverage.

Robert C. Feightner. "State Regulation of Capitated Reimbursement for Physician-Hospital Organizations." *Health Matrix*, 1997, *7*, 301.

This article addresses the issue of PHO regulations and advances the position that PHOs and other IDSs should be permitted to directly contract with self-funded employer groups and receive capitated compensation. It analyzes the positions of the National Association of Insurance Commissioners and state insurance commissioners regarding PHOs' accepting capitated risk. Further, he argues, these employer-employee relationships may be free of state interference because of the broad preemption provisions of ERISA.

Harkey and Associates. *Georgia Managed Care Compendium.* 4 vols. Nashville: Harkey and Associates, 1998.

This comprehensive guide focuses on providing detailed, local information for providers, insurers, and managed care organizations. Topics covered in Volume One include HMOs and PPOs, with company profiles, provider affiliations, contracting approaches, and financial information. Volume Two, which covers hospital-linked organizations, examines parent organizations, managed care contracting entities, board structures, PHO affiliations, MSO descriptions, and physician organization relationships. Volume Three supplies information on physician organizations, including primary care multispecialty, and single specialty, arrangements. It includes an organizational and board structure description, type of model, affiliations, reimbursement methods, and types of contract. Volume Four, which covers specialty provider networks, discusses home health care, dental care, mental health, pharmacies, vision coverage, hospice programs, chiropractics, and rehabilitation. Information includes structural description, numbers, and types of provider member and types of contract.

William W. Horton and F. Hampton McFadden, Jr. "Disclosure Obligations of the Newly Public Healthcare Company: Practical Strategies for the Company and Its Counsel." *Journal of Health Law,* Winter 1999, *32*, 1.

Founders of health care companies, like entrepreneurs in general, dream of the opportunity to take their companies public. The benefits flowing from access to public markets, however, carry with them additional responsibilities that are enforceable both by the regulatory authorities and the well-organized plaintiffs' securities bar. The authors of this article provide the newly public company and its counsel extensive guidance for navigating this regulatory maze.

Helen Leeds. "Health Care Cost Containment in the States: Strategies from the 1990s." Denver: National Conference of State Legislatures, 1996, 34 pages.

Written by an attorney, this report examines some of the key strategies that have emerged and are proving successful in states' efforts to contain rising health care costs.

Sara D. Mars. "The Corporate Practice of Medicine: A Call for Action." *Health Matrix: Journal of Law-Medicine,* 1997, *7*, 241.

Argues that state statutes should be amended to relax the corporate practice doctrine so as to allow corporations to enter into employment agreements with licensed medical practitioners. Mars outlines the origins and development of the doctrine and then elaborates on its flaws. After examining numerous legal safeguards available to aid in protecting against those evils that the corporate practice-of-medicine doctrine set out to prevent, the author illustrates the potential threat of the doctrine's staying power in light of recent federal and state legislation.

Edward P. Richards III. "The Police Power and the Regulation of Medical Practice: An Historical Review and Guide for Medical Board Regulation of Physicians in ERISA—Qualified Managed Care Organizations." *Annals of Health Law,* 2000, *8*, 201.

Reviews the use of state police power to regulate the medical profession. Also analyzes the role of physicians in managed care organizations, and describes how this role can be controlled through state police power regulation.

Stephen M. Shortell and Arnold D. Kaluzny. *Health Care Management: Organization, Design, and Behavior.* (4th ed.) Albany, N.Y.: Delmar Publishers, 2000.

This 493-page health services management text covers the study of health care organizations; internal organizational issues, performance issues related to organizational design; and strategic and legal issues. Updates from the 1994 edition primarily relate to environmental and technological changes that have occurred in recent years.

Molly Stauffer and others. *State by State Guide to Managed Care Law.* Gaithersburg, Md.: Aspen, 2000, 368 pages.

Supplies statutory and organizational definitions of HMOs, HMO penetration of the market, the HMO certification process, review by insurance and health departments, capital requirements, appeals processes, and managed care alternatives and variations. It reviews the range of contractual and statutory issues related to enrollees access to managed care providers, disclosure of financial information on providers and patient care, pharmaceuticals, and due process matters.

3.04 POINT-OF-SERVICE (POS) PRODUCT REGULATION

Peter R. Kongstvedt (ed.). *The Managed Health Care Handbook.* (4th ed.) Gaithersburg, Md.: Aspen, 2000, 1,045 pages.

Discusses the development of indemnity coverage to satisfy the demands of HMO members for out-of-plan service options. Many HMOs have recognized that the major impediment to enrolling additional members and expanding market share has been the reluctance of patients to completely give up their ability to receive reimbursement for using nonparticipating providers. These individuals fear that they or their families might unexpectedly need the services of a well-known specialist in a distant city to treat a rare disorder and believe the HMO would not refer them for care or reimburse their expenses.

To respond to this concern, an expanding number of HMOs have adopted a solution to this problem: they provide some level of indemnity insurance for their members. HMO members covered under this type of benefit plan may decide whether to use HMO benefits or indemnity-style benefits for each instance of care. In other words, the member is allowed to make a coverage choice at the point of service (POS) when medical care is needed.

The indemnity coverage provided under POS options from HMOs typically incorporates high deductibles and coinsurance to encourage members to use HMO services instead of out-of-plan services. Members who use the non-HMO benefit portion of the benefit plan may also be subject to utilization review (for example, preadmission certification and continued stay review).

3.05 OTHER STATE LAWS

American Association of Health Plans. *Guide to State PPO Laws and Regulations.* Annapolis Junction, Md.: American Association of Health Plans, 1995, 132 pages.

Provides a state-by-state analysis of laws and regulations applying to PPOs.

American Association of Health Plans. *State Managed Care Legislative Resource.* Annapolis Junction, Md.: American Association of Health Plans, 1996.

Provides more than 250 pages of useful information on state managed care laws and legislation, including any-willing-provider laws, utilization review, and PHO regulation.

3.05(1)   State Insurance Laws

American Health Lawyers Association. *Annual Report on State Health Issues: A Fifty State Survey.* Washington, D.C.: American Health Lawyers Association, 2001, 289 pages.

> Provides access to difficult-to-find information on how state legislatures are addressing initiatives on numerous health care topics. The fifty profiles describe the status of health policy efforts in each state, including legislation and studies expected to lead to legislative proposals. Innovative programs, areas of leadership, and special circumstances are all discussed. The book includes maps, narratives, and definitions of terms. Specific topics addressed include tax incentives, medical savings accounts, Medicaid, cost containment, data collection, regulation of physician practice, antitrust law, and managed care.

3.05(2)   Coordination of Benefits

Carol K. Lucas. "Multiple Payor Issues in Risk Contracting." Washington, D.C.: American Health Lawyers Association [Report No. VMC98–0020], 1998, 36 pages.

> Examines basic coordination of benefits rules, including commercial and Medicare rules, and application of the rules in the prepaid health plan context. Also reviews contract provisions and their fraud and abuse implications, and ERISA preemption issues.

3.05(3)   Certificate-of-Need Laws

[Reserved]

3.05(4)   State Rate-Setting Laws

[Reserved]

3.05(5)   Any-Willing-Provider Laws

F. Hellinger. "Any-Willing-Provider and Freedom-of-Choice Laws: An Economic Assessment." *Health Affairs*, Winter 1995, *14*, 297–302.

> Describes the evolution and implications of two laws that require managed care plans to accept qualified providers into their network and permit enrollees to obtain reimbursable health care from providers in their network. Hellinger addresses the laws' effects on administrative costs, practice, and prices paid to providers.

F. Hellinger. "The Expanding Scope of State Legislation." *Journal of the American Medical Association*, Oct. 2, 1996, *276*, 1065–1070.

> This article traces the growth of three types of state law that regulate managed care plans: laws limiting the ability of plans to direct patients to specific providers, those prohibiting exclusivity clauses, and laws mandating minimum length of stay for deliveries.

3.05(6)   Small-Group Insurance Reform

[Reserved]

3.06   FEDERAL QUALIFICATION

Christine C. Boesz. "Federal Qualification: A Foundation for the Future." In Peter R. Kongstvedt (ed.), *The Managed Health Care Handbook.* (4th ed.) Gaithersburg, Md.: Aspen, 2000, pp. 835–848.

Outlines "federal qualification," which is commonly used to describe HMOs and the health benefit plans they offer when both the benefits and the HMO meet federal requirements. Federal qualification status is important to HMOs for two reasons. First, it signifies to employers and other consumers of health care that an HMO meets the standards of fiscal soundness and consumer protection set forth in the HMO Act of 1973 (42 U.S.C. §§ 300-e et seq.). Second, it establishes the eligibility of an HMO to contract with the federal government to serve Medicare beneficiaries.

3.07   GOVERNMENT REIMBURSEMENT PROGRAMS

3.07(1)   Products for Medicare Beneficiaries

Michael H. Cook. "Managed Care Contracting." Washington, D.C.: American Health Lawyers Association [Report No. VLT99–0010], 1999, 75 pages.

Examines significant legal issues involved with integrating long-term care providers and where nursing facilities fit into the managed care process, including Medicare+Choice, Medicaid, and general managed care contracting concepts. Attachments include a chart illustrating examples of potential integrated networks, a checklist of legal issues in managed care contracting, and selections from the DHHS Negotiated Rulemaking Committee on the Shared Risk Exception's Jan. 22, 1998, recommendations on establishing standards for HIPAA Section 216, which exempts certain remuneration from the antikickback provisions of Section 1128B of the Social Security Act.

Department of Health and Human Services, Office of Inspector General. "Beneficiary Perspectives of Medicare Risk HMOs." Washington, D.C.: DHHS OIG [OE1-06-91-00730], 1995.

Reports survey findings on such topics as access to service and timeliness of care. Generally, beneficiary responses indicate Medicare risk HMOs provided adequate service access for most beneficiaries who had joined, according to this survey and report. The majority of enrollees and disenrollees reported medical access that maintained or improved their health; timely appointments for primary and specialty care; good access to Medicare-covered services and to hospital, specialty, and emergency care; and sympathetic personal treatment by their HMOs and HMO doctors. In some instances, however, enrollees and disenrollees differed markedly in reporting their HMO experiences. This report recommends that beneficiaries be better informed about their appeal rights. It also recommends that HCFA examine service-access problems reported by disabled persons. The report concludes with a lengthy bibliography.

Department of Health and Human Services, Office of Inspector General. "Medicare Risk HMOs: Beneficiary Enrollment and Service Access Problems." Washington, D.C.: DHHS OIG [OE1-06-91-00731], 1995, 11 pages.

Documents and analyzes problems with Medicare risk HMOs. These include the following:

1. Asking beneficiaries about their health problems during application was a fairly widespread and intensive problem.
2. Lack of awareness of appeal rights was the most widespread and intensive problem, while beneficiary misunderstanding of other requirements was common but less severe.

3. Beneficiaries complained that primary care HMO doctors failed to take their complaints seriously and that doctors appeared to believe that holding down the cost of medical care was more important than giving the best medical care.

General Accounting Office. "Medicare HMO Institutional Payments: Improved HCFA Oversight, More Recent Cost Data Could Reduce Overpayments." (GAO/HEHS-98-153.) Sept. 9, 1998, 23 pages.

A growing number of the elderly—about five million out of thirty-eight million Medicare beneficiaries—receive care through HMOs that participate in Medicare's risk contract program. Unlike fee-for-service providers, which are paid on a per-claim basis, these HMOs receive from Medicare a fixed monthly sum per enrolled beneficiary—a capitation rate—and assume the risk of providing beneficiary health care, regardless of the actual costs involved. The estimated 2.6 million beneficiaries in nursing homes and other long-term care facilities often incur greater-than-average Medicare-covered expenses. Consequently, the "institutional" risk adjuster generally raises capitation payments for Medicare HMO enrollees in such facilities. However, some of the facilities that GAO visited that HMOs had classified as institutional residences provided no medical services, but rather offered recreational activities for the elderly who are capable of living independently.

HCFA acted on this finding by narrowing the definition of eligible institutions. Even with more stringent criteria, however, HCFA relies on the HMOs to determine which beneficiaries qualify for institutional status. HCFA conducts only limited interviews, about every two years, to confirm the accuracy of HMO records. The task of ensuring accurate data may be further complicated by HCFA's policy of allowing HMOs three years to retroactively change institutional status data in beneficiary records. HCFA generally waits two years to verify that HMOs have corrected inaccurate record-keeping systems, even when serious errors have been identified. Moreover, HCFA continues to use twenty-year-old cost data to determine payment rates for institutionalized enrollees. As a result, HCFA overcompensates HMOs for their enrolled, institutionalized beneficiaries.

General Accounting Office. "Report to the Honorable John F. Kerry, U.S. Senate; Medicare HMOs: Rapid Enrollment Growth Concentrated in Selected States." (GAO/HEHS-96-63.) Jan. 18, 1996, 39 pages.

Discusses HMO enrollment of Medicare beneficiaries. Medicare, the nation's largest health care insurer, has traditionally provided health insurance coverage to its elderly and disabled beneficiaries on a fee-for-service basis. Although the option of receiving Medicare benefits through an HMO has existed for more than twenty years, Medicare beneficiaries have enrolled in HMOs to a much lesser degree than persons with private sector health insurance. Private sector insurers cite extensive use of HMOs and other managed care approaches as a key factor in slowing the growth of their insurance premiums. As a result, part of the current attention to controlling rising Medicare costs has focused on how to bring about greater use of HMOs.

This report identifies two key factors that could be influencing HMO decisions to offer services to Medicare beneficiaries. First, states with the highest concentration of HMOs offering services to Medicare beneficiaries tend to be ones with the highest level of HMO participation in the general population. Second, those counties with the highest monthly rates paid by the government for each Medicare beneficiary—over $500—also tend to have a higher level of HMO participation.

To attract Medicare beneficiaries, participating HMOs have increasingly turned to incentives for beneficiaries. One is to offer coverage with a low monthly premium, or none, that Medicare beneficiaries must pay. Another incentive is to provide services—such as outpatient drugs or dental benefits—beyond those required under Medicare. This report is amply supplemented by tables, graphs, and appendices.

Lisa A. Hathaway and Alan E. Schabes. "Avoiding Pitfalls in Managed Care Contracting." Washington, D.C.: American Health Lawyers Association [Report No. VLT98–0016], 1998, 42 pages.

Outlines points that an attorney must consider when negotiating payer agreements between managed care organizations and long-term care facilities. Contains samples of contract language that illustrate the legal issues from both payer and provider perspectives. Also discusses a number of issues that arise in managed care contracting for long-term care facilities, including resident rights, admission and discharge, bed-hold issues, fee discounts, and marketing.

Harold S. Luft (ed.). *HMOs and the Elderly.* Chicago: Health Administration Press, 1994, 348 pages.

Edited by a professor of health economics at the University of California, San Francisco, this book features new studies on the costs, utilization, satisfaction, and quality of care related to HMOs that serve Medicare beneficiaries. Written primarily for economists and health care policy makers, this book gives special emphasis to Medicare risk HMOs and social HMOs.

Raja M. G. Sekaran. "The Uneasy Union of Managed Care and Medicare." *Medical Trial Technique Quarterly,* 1997, *44,* 179.

Discusses the federal government's policy of encouraging Medicare participants to join a managed care entity for their health care. Managed care entities have as one of their goals financial austerity, resulting in a restriction and reduction of service. The author, an associate counsel to the Inspector General of the DHHS, analyzes the transition from fee-for-service to managed care.

Carlos Zarabozo and Jean D. LeMasurier. "Medicare and Managed Care." In Peter R. Kongstvedt (ed.), *The Managed Health Care Handbook.* (4th ed.) Gaithersburg, Md.: Aspen, 2000.

Examines the Tax Equity and Fiscal Responsibility Act of 1982 (TEFRA), which created the current body of law treating Medicare HMOs. This practical and witty chapter begins with an overview of the tangle of acronyms necessary to decipher managed care and then explains the requirements to obtain a TEFRA contract, the steps in the contracting process, and beneficiary rights and responsibilities.

3.07(2)   Medicaid Contracting

Joan L. Buchanan and others. "HMOs for Medicaid: The Road to Financial Independence Is Often Poorly Paved." *Journal of Health Politics,* 1992, *17,* 71.

Discusses financial difficulties encountered by HMOs participating in Medicaid. During the 1980s, both the federal government and the private sector articulated policies to encourage development and participation of HMOs in the Medicaid program. However, the policies—intended to save costs—limited the ability of new HMOs to achieve financial independence. New plans that emphasize Medicaid participation have few, if any, options on benefit design or in setting capitation rates. Relative to fee-for-service Medicaid programs, their costs to provide services may be quite high, as they have neither the buying power nor the ability to impose discounts. As a consequence, plans must focus their financial planning efforts on targeting and attaining a stable enrollment base and on controlling the amount of services provided, tasks that are difficult for all HMOs.

Achieving a stable enrollment base is particularly hard because Medicaid eligibles have few incentives to enroll and, once enrolled, often lose their Medicaid eligibility. Traditional HMOs control the amount of services provided through physician selection, financial incentives on physicians, and monitoring and utilization review. Lack of information and the difficulty inherent in attracting sufficient provider participation limit the first two strategies, so new plans often adopt organizational structures that rely heavily on monitoring activities. Unfortunately, management information systems for HMOs are often the weakest link. The authors discuss the challenges and present data on financial planning, on putting financial plans into operation, and on monitoring progress toward financial independence for a set of ten demonstration projects sponsored by the Robert Wood Johnson Foundation.

Robert E. Hurley, Deborah A. Freund, and John E. Paul. *Managed Care in Medicaid: Lessons for Policy and Program Design.* Chicago: Health Administration Press, 1993, 215 pages.

Examines a decade of Medicaid reform initiatives, specifically those relating to primary care case management. The authors evaluate three sets of managed care programs likely to be adopted. One set reimburses the provider on a fee-for-service basis, another uses networks of physicians at financial risk, and the third involves enrolling Medicaid beneficiaries in HMOs.

Robert E. Hurley, Leonard Kirschner, and Thomas W. Bone. "Medicaid Managed Care." In Peter R. Kongstvedt (ed.), *The Managed Health Care Handbook.* (4th ed.) Gaithersburg, Md.: Aspen, 2000.

Examines relevant background and history that explain the rapid expansion of Medicaid managed care. They then discuss distinctive characteristics of the Medicaid program and its beneficiaries, introducing principal models and reviewing experience they have gained from each of them. The authors focus on Arizona's and Virginia's Medicaid programs before turning to the impact of managed care, more specifically in terms of cost savings, utilization satisfaction, and quality. They conclude with a discussion of operational issues for the Medicaid product line and likely future trends.

Michael S. Sparer and Lawrence D. Brown. "Nothing Exceeds Like Success: Managed Care Comes to Medicaid in New York City." *Milbank Quarterly,* 1999, 77, 205.

Nearly every state is encouraging or requiring Medicaid beneficiaries to enroll in managed care delivery systems. In New York City, Medicaid officials began with an incremental, but not insignificant, managed care initiative. Buoyed by its success, New York policy makers tried, and failed, to accelerate the transition to managed care. The legacy of that failure still plagues them. A comparison of such initiatives in other states indicates that most state officials have remembered what New York's leaders temporarily forgot, namely, that Medicaid managed care is a complex exercise that demands consultation and consensus building.

3.07(3) The Federal Employees Health Benefit Program (FEHBP)

Joel L. Michaels and Christine C. Rinn. "The Federal Employees Health Benefit Program and Managed Care." In Peter R. Kongstvedt (ed.), *The Managed Health Care Handbook.* (4th ed.) Gaithersburg, Md.: Aspen, 2000.

This chapter includes a discussion of such topics as the application process, premium contribution and benefit design, premium rating, audits and appeals, false claims liability, and miscellaneous contracting issues.

3.07(4) State Government

[Reserved]

3.08 HMO MANAGEMENT AND OPERATIONAL ISSUES

3.08(1) Internal Organization and Controls

Martin P. Charns and Laura J. Smith Tewksbury. *Collaborative Management in Health Care.* San Francisco: Jossey-Bass, 1993, 321 pages.

Written for health care executives and clinical leaders who want to improve the functioning of their organizations. The general framework and specific examples provided can guide designing and implementing organizational innovations to improve productivity, quality of work life, and responsiveness to the needs of patients and their families. The authors clarify and define terms that are often misused, providing a common language for clinicians and managers to use in discussing integrative approaches to management and delivery of care.

Robert B. Fetter, John D. Thompson, and John R. Kimberly (eds.). *Cases in Health Policy and Management.* Homewood, Ill.: Irwin, 1985.

Topics covered include new roles for medical staff, ways of managing organizational change, mergers and control, product-line management, hospital efficiency and effectiveness, and management information systems. The first part of this casebook includes five cases focusing on institutions organized around a traditional structure. The second part includes six cases on DRGs and HMOs.

Douglas A. Hastings and others. *The Insider's Guide to Managed Care: A Legal and Operational Roadmap.* Washington, D.C.: American Health Lawyers Association, 1990, 276 pages.

Consists of ten essays, primarily written by health care attorneys, on a range of managed care issues. Topics addressed in this volume include utilization and quality management, self-insured employers, ERISA and managed care, bankruptcy and rehabilitation, antitrust concerns, and legal and regulatory issues in managed mental health care.

Arnold D. Kaluzny and Stephen M. Shortell. *Essentials of Health Care Management.* Albany, N.Y.: Delmar Publishers, 1996.

This undergraduate text blends current organizational theory with applications in health services management. Each section features a "debate time" focusing on controversial topics to stimulate discussion and critical thinking.

Phillip Kotler and Roberta N. Clarke. *Marketing for Health Care Organizations.* Upper Saddle River, N.J.: Prentice Hall, 1987.

This volume demonstrates the application of business techniques to health care organizations.

Anthony R. Kovner and Duncan Neuhauser (eds.). *Health Services Management: Readings and Commentary.* (6th ed.) Chicago: Health Administration Press, 2000, 512 pages.

Divides material into five sections: the role of the manager, control of health organizations, organizational design, professional integration, and adaptation and accountability.

Anthony R. Kovner and others. *Health Service Management: A Book of Cases.* (5th ed.) Chicago: Health Administration Press, 2000, 231 pages.

Prepared for graduate programs in health services management, this book provides descriptions of situations or problems actually faced by managers that require analysis, decision, and planning a course of action. The casebook specifically addresses cases relating to HMOs. It is divided into sections covering the role of the manager, control, organizational design, professional integration, adaptation, and accountability.

Jonathan Rakich, Beaufort B. Longest, Jr., and Kurt Darr. *Managing Health Services Organizations.* (3rd ed.) Philadelphia: Saunders, 1985, 532 pages.

This is a standard, if dated text containing case studies in health services management. The book is most beneficial to two types of readers: persons engaged in the formal study of health services management and current managers who wish to supplement their experience.

David B. Smith and Arnold D. Kaluzny. *The White Labyrinth: A Guide to the Health Care System.* (3rd ed.) Beard Books, 2000.

This 268-page paperback edition describes how various organizations in the health care sector work and discusses approaches to changing those organizations.

Barbara J. Youngberg. "Risk Management in Managed Care." In Peter R. Kongstvedt (ed.), *The Managed Health Care Handbook.* (4th ed.) Gaithersburg, Md.: Aspen, 2000.

Addresses such topics as changes in the health care organization related to managed care, operational risks under managed care, managing corporate negligence, credentialing, utilization management issues, and the convergence of financial and risk management. Written by a professor of law at Loyola University College of Law in Chicago, this chapter concludes with a checklist for risk managers for managing the process of providing health care in a managed care environment.

3.08(2)　Employer Agreements

Robert W. McAdams, Mary L. Gallagher, and Charles D. Weller. *Managed Care Contracts Manual.* Gaithersburg, Md.: Aspen, 1996.

This loose-leaf manual examines the comparative merits of different types of managed care structure along with contract considerations, potential liabilities, negotiation strategies, risk sharing, quality-based agreements, and antitrust.

Perry Moore. *Evaluating Health Maintenance Organizations: A Guide for Employee Benefits Managers.* New York: Quorum, 1991, 195 pages.

Examines the growth and development of HMOs since 1970, detailing the success they have had in controlling costs, and assesses the quality of care they provide to their enrollees. Topics examined include quality in HMOs; HMOs and employers; HMOs and providers; HMOs, Medicare, and Medicaid; HMOs in rural areas; HMOs and PPOs; and cost containment.

3.08(3)　Provider Relationships

David B. Nash, M.D. (ed.). *The Physician's Guide to Managed Care.* Gaithersburg, Md.: Aspen, 1994, 272 pages.

Written by a physician who is also the holder of an MBA, this practical volume shows physicians how they can prosper under managed care. Topics covered include the life of an HMO physician, the role of the physician-manager, and case-mix systems.

3.08(3)(a)　Provider Credentialing

Katherine Benesch. "Emerging Theories of Liability for Negligent Credentialing in HMOs, Integrated Delivery and Managed Care Systems." *Health Lawyer,* Fall 1996, 9, 14.

This article examines the liability of provider organizations and networks for the failure to exclude for cause or revoke the membership privileges of providers from HMOs, networks, and integrated delivery systems following a problem with the provider's individual professional conduct, competence, and credentials.

John D. Blum. "The Evolution of Physician Credentialing into Managed Care Selective Contracting." *American Journal of Law and Medicine,* 1996, 22, 173–203.

Focuses on managed care credentialing—the process of appointing, reappointing, and delineating clinical privileges—from a legal perspective. Although the article centers on the link between capitation and credentialing, it also provides a brief overview of capitation and credentialing and a discussion of trends that have altered hospital medical staff credentialing processes. The article then analyzes the regulation of managed care credentialing, organizational liability for inappropriate credentialing, including a consideration of the impacts of ERISA, and physician rights in the new environment of capitated plan credentialing.

Richard A. Feinstein. "Economic Credentialing and Exclusive Contracts." *Health Lawyer,* Fall 1996, 9, 1.

Focuses on developments in the law relating to challenges to using economic criteria in credentialing decisions, including indirect forms of economic credentialing such as exclusive contracts. It analyzes the few reported cases in the area along with legislative initiatives in a variety of states.

David E. Willett. "Centralized Credentialing." *Health Lawyer,* Fall 1996, 9, 12.

Asserts that integrated or centralized credentialing is a natural product of the integration of health care and is likely to proceed. Credentialing by payers and their delivery systems, on top of credentialing by hospitals and other facilities, gives rise to demands for information and the elimination of redundant efforts. Willett discusses concerns about and benefits of centralization.

3.08(3)(b)   Provider Contracts—Compensation Arrangements

American Psychiatric Association. *The Psychiatrist's Guide to Capitation and Risk-Based Contracting.* Washington, D.C.: American Psychiatric Press, 1997, 114 pages.

Provides instruction on how to calculate an equitable capitation rate, evaluate and negotiate a contract, minimize financial risks, and resolve a range of other issues that are crucial to a successful capitation contract. A demonstration disk developed to educate psychiatrists about the relationships among mental health utilization, mental health service cost, and managed care accompanies the book.

American Psychiatric Association. *The Psychiatrist's Guide to Managed Care Contracting.* Washington, D.C.: American Psychiatric Press, 1997, 96 pages.

Develops, in a step-by-step fashion, a framework and sets forth strategies a psychiatric practice can employ to shape a managed care contract in its favor. It examines standard contract issues and provisions involved to identify problems early in the negotiating process.

Kevin Outterson. "Physician Contracting." Washington, D.C.: American Health Lawyers Association [Report No. MC97–0028], 1997, 36 pages.

Analyzes important issues in managed care physician contracting, including contract negotiation, a model provider agreement, utilization management, provider manual issues, due process, credentialing and termination, continuation of coverage, managed care liability, and priority.

Jerry R. Peters. "Legal Issues in Integrated Delivery Systems." In Peter R. Kongstvedt (ed.), *The Managed Health Care Handbook.* (4th ed.) Gaithersburg, Md.: Aspen, 2000.

Written by a practicing health care attorney, this article examines the variety of integrated delivery system (IDS) models and focuses particular attention on governance, tax exemption, physician compensation, and antitrust issues.

Mark E. Rust. "Physician Managed Care Contracting." Washington, D.C.: American Health Lawyers Association [Report No. VPH99–0006], 1999, 32 pages.

Provides a sample managed care medical services agreement, including sections addressing delivery of services, compensation and related terms, medical services entity's obligation, company's obligation, records and confidentiality, insurance, term and termination, and dispute resolution. Also includes descriptive text that explains contract particulars.

Joseph A. Welfeld. *Contracting with Managed Care Organizations: A Guide for the Health Care Provider.* Chicago: AHA Press, 1996, 100 pages.

Offers guidance on how to evaluate and negotiate with managed care organizations to create strategic relationships and details the steps necessary to execute a strategic approach to managed care contracting. The author describes the key performance indicators for evaluating a managed care organization and offers insights into their contractor requirements and provider network strategy. He also discusses the essential operational and functional components in managed care agreements and ways for the health care provider to control or limit risk. Finally, the book supplies a clause-by-clause comparison between a desirable agreement and an undesirable one, each with a managed care organization.

3.08(3)(c)   Provider Contracts—Nonrate Issues

Anthea R. Daniels. "Contractual Delegation of Duties." Washington, D.C.: American Health Lawyers Association [Report No. VMC98–0033], 1998, 35 pages.

Addresses the operational and legal issues that need to be reviewed in agreements that contractually delegate duties between MCOs and providers. Reviews those types of service that are traditionally delegated (credentialing of health care providers, utilization review, collections) and the problems in assuming the delegation of such duties. Includes a sample delegation agreement.

William Gross and Mark E. Lutes. "Actuaries/Consultants and Lawyers: How the Professions Can Learn to Talk to Effectively Serve Clients with Managed Care Contracts." Washington, D.C.: American Health Lawyers Association [Report No. VMC98-0039], 1998, 34 pages.

Examines twenty-six fundamental managed care contracting issues in an easy reference format and provides a sample contract clause for each topic. Contrasts the relevant issues for providers and provider networks with an MCO's perspective. Also includes the business consultant's perspective so that the health care lawyer can learn to draft contracts to accomplish business goals.

Mark S. Joffe. "Legal Issues in Provider Contracting." In Peter R. Kongstvedt (ed.), *The Managed Health Care Handbook.* (4th ed.) Gaithersburg, Md.: Aspen, 2000.

Offers to the managed care plan and the provider a practical guide to reviewing and drafting a provider contract. The chapter sets forth common clauses, provisions, and negotiating points, including those relating to utilization review standards, confidentiality, hold harmless agreements, notification, insurance, indemnification, termination, and other clauses. Written by a practicing health care attorney, this chapter includes a sample physician agreement and a sample hospital agreement, both annotated with the author's helpful comments.

Ann Leopold Kaplan. "PPMC Contracts: Nuts and Bolts." Washington, D.C.: American Health Lawyers Association [Report No. VPH99–0003], 1999, 36 pages.

Provides an overview of legal issues in acquisition, management services, and employment agreements. Includes sample provisions and a summary of the due diligence process.

Bryan A. Liang. "An Overview and Analysis of Challenges to Medical Exclusive Contracts." *Journal of Legal Medicine,* Mar. 1997, *18,* 1–45.

Examines various challenges regarding medical exclusive contracts, including antitrust and due process approaches. After an extensive analysis of reported case law, the author concludes with a proposal that these contracts be equitably scrutinized and that alternate dispute resolution methods have a role in their interpretation.

Brooke S. Murphy and Cori H. Loomis. "Recent Developments Regarding Enforceability and Drafting of Arbitration Provisions in Managed Care Contracts." Washington, D.C.: American Health Lawyers Association [Report No. VMC98–0026], 1998, 39 pages.

Provides a general legal background for arbitration clauses, including the Federal Arbitration Act, the McCarran-Ferguson Act, and state laws. Also reviews recent developments regarding arbitration provisions in MCO agreements and problems encountered, and provides recommendations and advice on drafting arbitration provisions.

Francis J. Serbaroli. "Avoiding the Corporate Practice and Fee-Splitting Prohibitions in Structuring Physician Arrangements." Washington, D.C.: American Health Lawyers Association [Report No. VPH99–0008], 1999, 30 pages.

Explains the corporate practice and fee-splitting prohibitions, their origins in law and public policy, and how to avoid violating the prohibitions when structuring various types of medical service and managed care arrangement. Includes OIG advisory opinion 98-4 (whether a contract between a medical practice management company and a physician practice would constitute illegal remuneration).

Linda V. Tiano. "Managed Care Participating Provider Agreements." Washington, D.C.: American Health Lawyers Association [Report No. VPH99–0007], 1999, 28 pages.

Examines trends in provider contracting from the health plan's perspective. Also analyzes the AMA's model contract and compares it to a typical managed care plan contract and offers comments and alternative provisions.

3.08(3)(d) HMO Liability for Provider Malpractice

[Reserved]

3.08(3)(e) Rate Setting and Financial Strategy

Annot. "Payment for Services Provided by Health Maintenance Organizations." 70A *American Jurisprudence* 2d, Social Security and Medicare §§ 1192–1195.

Analyzes the state of the law regarding payment for services by HMOs, with voluminous annotations.

Montague Brown (ed.). *Managed Care: Strategies, Networks and Management.* Gaithersburg, Md.: Aspen, Health Care Management Review Series, 1993, 272 pages.

This book consists of twenty-five authoritative articles drawn from the journal *Health Care Management Review.* Written for the managers of provider, insurer, buyer, or government organizations, it deals with issues ranging from making existing product lines efficient to the policy logic of building comprehensive, integrated systems. Topics covered include strategies employed by HMOs to achieve hospital discounts, the growth and effects of hospital selective contracting, contracts between hospitals and HMOs, a hospital administrator's guide to successful HMO negotiations, critical factors in recruiting HMO physicians, determinants of HMO success, and controlling disenrollment in HMOs.

Charles W. Wrightson, Jr. *HMO Rate Setting and Financial Strategy.* Chicago: Health Administration Press Perspectives, 1990, 354 pages.

Focuses on HMO rating and underwriting, community rating, alternative rating methods, selection bias, and premium rate setting. Other topics include HMO competitive strategy and financial strategies. Generally quantitative in approach, the book has a helpful glossary of HMO actuarial terminology and an index, along with extensive figures, exhibits, and tables.

3.09   MERGERS AND CLOSURES

Gary Scott Davis. "Managed Care Considerations for M&A Transactions." Washington, D.C.: American Health Lawyers Association [Report No. VMA 98–0030], 1998, 15 pages.

Highlights considerations and structures for managed care mergers and acquisitions.

Ralph E. DeJong. "Executive Compensation: Protecting the Organization and Executive Management in Mergers and Acquisitions." Washington, D.C.: American Health Lawyers Association [Report No. VMA 98–0020], 1998, 54 pages.

Reviews the protection of the organization and executive management in mergers and acquisitions through using employment agreements, retention incentives, severance pay, deferred compensation, and release and waiver agreements. This seminar manuscript includes a sample release, a waiver and settlement agreement, a sample retention bonus agreement, and excerpts from a sample employment agreement.

Daniel G. Hale and Robert L. Johnson. "Deals That Could Not Close—or Shouldn't Have." Washington, D.C.: American Health Lawyers Association [Report No. VMA 98–0017], 1998, 12 pages.

Addresses four key issues in major transactions: cash, culture, control, and the CEO. It also discusses facilitating multiparty transactions, due diligence and the "smoking gun," board disclosure, conflict of interest, and retrospective adjustments.

Health Care Mergers and Acquisitions. Forum on Health Law of the American Bar Association, Chicago, Dec. 1995, 192 pages.

This monograph contains essays on such topics as structural options, due diligence, acquisition of tax-exempt hospitals by investor-owned companies, financing the development of an integrated delivery system, and Medicare reimbursement issues related to health care mergers and acquisitions. It also covers tax issues and the corporate practice of medicine prohibition.

Michael P. Kennedy. "Community Hospitals' Alternatives to Selling to or Merging with Larger Systems." Washington, D.C.: American Health Lawyers Association [Report No. VHH99–0023], 1999, 37 pages.

Provides a basic outline of the factors that enter into a community hospital's decision to merge or be acquired by larger health systems. Discusses alternative models of hospital ownership and operations and addresses the legal issues presented by each alternative organizational structure, including antitrust, governance, federal tax exemption, fraud and abuse, and charitable trust issues.

Karen S. Rieger and Eric S. Fisher. "Maneuvering the Mundane Minefield: A Practical Guide to Legal Opinions in Healthcare Transactions." *Journal of Health Law,* 1999, *32,* 173.

This article examines the variety of issues presented when attorneys prepare legal opinions for health law transactions. The authors analyze two major pieces of guidance for drafting such opinions, and offer practical advice and checklists for preparing them.

3.10   HMO GRIEVANCE PROCEDURES

Alan B. Bloom. "HMO Grievance Procedures and Liability from Denial of Claims." Washington, D.C.: American Health Lawyers Association [Report No. MC97–0026], 1997, 32 pages.

Reviews the issues and approaches to resolution of grievances, claims review, and other aspects of administration of the HMO contract that require joint decisions and quick responses in view of the division of decision making on patient care management and coverage among the HMO, the physician, and the provider entity.

Alfred J. Chiplin, Jr., and Patricia B. Nemore. "Due Process Considerations for Medicare and Medicaid Beneficiaries in Managed Care Systems." *Clearinghouse Review*, Oct. 1995, *29*, 629.

Discusses the specific requirements of Medicare and Medicaid law and proposes a framework to guide advocacy as these two programs change. This article does not discuss the substantial questions of whether and how managed care actually saves money in delivering health care, to whom any savings that are achieved accrue, and whether managing health care in fact results in greater access and better health. Rather, the article's premise is that managed care is a fact of life and that such delivery systems must include basic due-process rights.

Families USA. *The Best From the States II: The Text of Key State HMO Consumer Protection Provisions.* Washington, D.C.: Families USA, 1998, 49 pages.

This publication offers the text of relevant state laws and regulations addressing important managed care consumer protections, including emergency room services, access to providers, and liability.

R. Feldman, D. Wholey, and J. Christianson. "Economic and Organizational Determinants of HMO Mergers and Failures." *Inquiry*, 1996, *33*, 118.

The total number of HMOs peaked in 1986 and has been diminishing since then as a result of failures and mergers, even though a few new ones have started up. Between 1986 and 1993, 149 HMOs went out of business and 80 disappeared as a result of mergers. Those that survived had lower administrative costs, along with higher enrollments and profit margins. States that have anti-takeover regulation in place have fewer mergers but may have more failures.

Douglas A. Hastings and Wendy C. Goldstein. "Patient Rights Meets Managed Care: Understanding the Underlying Conflicts." Washington, D.C.: American Health Lawyers Association [Report No. VHL98–0005], 1998, 71 pages.

Analyzes and categorizes the key conflicts underlying the tensions embroiling managed care and the relationships among employers, health plans, providers, government regulators, and consumers. Seeks to predict the future direction of managed care legal issues and identifies solutions to these conflicts.

Eleanor D. Kinney. "Procedural Protections for Patients in Capitated Health Plans." *American Journal of Law and Medicine*, 1996, *22*(2 and 3), 301–330.

Addresses the procedural issues raised by the need to protect patients in public and private capitated health plans. It concludes with recommendations for appropriate procedural protections that should be required of capitated health plans with respect to rate setting, policy making, dispute resolution, and judicial review.

Harvey M. Shapiro. *Managed Care Beware: 5 Steps You Need to Know to Survive HMOs and Get the Care You Deserve.* West Hollywood, Calif.: Dove, 1997, 288 pages.

Consumer guide written by a California anesthesiologist. Shapiro begins by explaining managed care, setting forth its virtues and drawbacks, and then presents a format for the reader to determine individual health care needs. Next, the book presents a standardized method for selecting an HMO. The author then outlines procedures and precautions for obtaining quick, high-quality health care from the HMO. Finally, he supplies practical guidelines for solving problems, including when to talk with a lawyer. The book is well organized, engagingly written, and balanced in its approach. It concludes with a glossary and six appendices, which include such information as a list of health consumer publications, a list of health consumer agencies, and sample worksheets.

Susan J. Stayn. "Securing Access to Care in Health Maintenance Organizations: Toward a Uniform Model of Grievance and Appeal Procedures." (Note.) *Columbia Law Review*, 1994, *94*, 1674.

Uses the limited data that have been collected through the Medicare program to examine the types of access-to-care problems that occur in HMOs and the mechanisms available to help patients obtain covered, necessary health care services. Unfortunately, although the federal Medicare program and state regulations offer patients some hope of adequate care from HMOs, there is currently no uniform recourse system in place for protecting patients from undertreatment in a timely, effective manner. Well-structured grievance and appeal procedures would facilitate access to treatment by enabling HMO members to dispute denial of coverage and, if successful, secure needed services without prohibitive out-of-pocket costs. The existence of a uniform recourse system would also ensure the integrity of HMO decision-making processes. Holding HMOs directly accountable to their members and to government officials would encourage fair and accurate coverage determinations and inspire trust in these health care systems.

3.11   PREFERRED PROVIDER ORGANIZATIONS (PPOs)

James C. Dechene. "Preferred Provider Organization Structures and Agreements." *Annals of Health Law*, 1995, *4*, 35.

Written by a practicing lawyer, this thirty-four-page article addresses the nuts and bolts of creating a PPO, including a helpful checklist of items that a typical PPO/provider contract should address. The author concludes by arguing that PPOs are a necessary transitional structure as our health care delivery system evolves away from the unrestricted fee-for-service system toward one of managed care.

Robert G. Shouldice. *Introduction to Managed Care: Health Maintenance Organizations, Preferred Provider Organizations, and Competitive Medical Plans.* Arlington, Va.: Information Resources Press, 1991, 545 pages.

Discusses the organizational structure of HMOs, PPOs, financial management, marketing, and quality control. The product of a course in developing and managing HMOs conducted by the graduate program in health care administration at George Washington University, the book is shaped to meet the needs of students in the program, managers in the field, and government officials. The text is supplemented by abundant charts, graphs, tables, footnotes, and bibliographical references, along with an index, a glossary, and a list of acronyms.

4

Integrated Delivery Systems

An integrated delivery system (IDS) is a local or regional health care network that provides a full range of services for all aspects of health care for patients in a defined geographical area. Those services may include wellness programs, preventive care, ambulatory clinics, outpatient diagnostic and laboratory services, rehabilitation, long-term care, congregate living, psychiatric care, home health care, and hospice care. Typically, an IDS establishes strategic alliances and contractual relationships with other providers for those services not provided directly by the IDS. In theory, because the IDS offers many alternatives to inpatient care, it is better able to provide and coordinate high-quality, cost-effective care and also assume the financial risk involved in fixed-rate (capitated) contracts.[1]

Managed care has placed increasing pressure on health care providers to reduce costs and to maintain or improve quality, while at the same time protecting market share. The certainty of continuing reform of the American health care system, whether through legislative action or marketplace-driven reform, provides an impetus to accelerate change further. This has impelled care providers of various levels of health care, out of defensive motives, to align with one another. This alignment aims to permit greater economies of scale, the ability to deploy clinical resources most cost-effectively, a greater ability to control provider behavior, and greater negotiating strength. Whether these and other goals can be attained through integration is not always clear at the outset.[2]

IDSs fall into three broad categories: systems in which only the physicians are integrated, those in which the physicians are integrated with facilities (hospitals and ancillary sites), and those that include the insurance functions. Within the context of the first two categories, IDSs fall along a rough continuum. Figure 4.1 illustrates the common names used for such organizations. From one end of the continuum to the other, the degree of integration increases, as does the potential ability of the organization to operate effectively in a managed care environment. Also, the complexity of formation and operation, required capital investment, and political difficulties increase from one end of the continuum to the other.

Independent Practice Association (IPA)

The first type of IDS to be described is the independent practice association (IPA), a form that has been in existence for several decades and was even codified to some degree by the original HMO Act of 1973. The IPA is a legal entity, the members of which are independent physicians who contract with the IPA for the sole purpose of having the IPA contract with one or more HMOs. IPAs are usually not for profit, although that is not an absolute requirement. The term *IPA* is often used synonymously (and inaccurately) with terms for any type of open-panel HMO; although the use of IPA in this fashion is now widespread, it is not technically accurate. The true IPA is discussed here.

In its common form, the IPA negotiates with the HMO for a capitation rate inclusive of all physician services. The IPA in turn reimburses the member physicians, although not necessarily using capitation. The IPA and its member physicians are at risk for at least some portion of medical costs in that if the capitation payment is lower than the required reimbursement to the physicians,

FIGURE 4.1. Types of Integrated Health Care Organization.

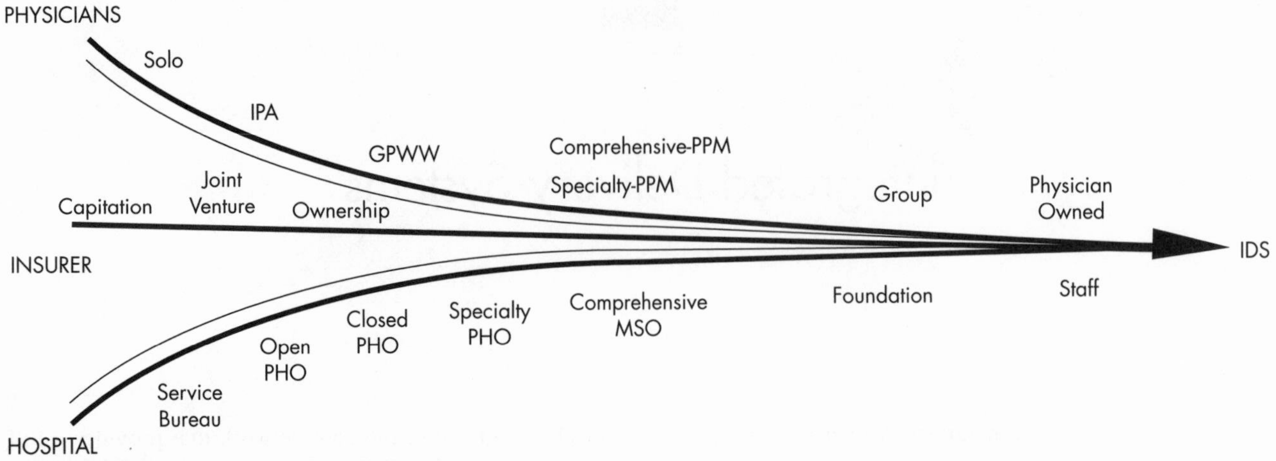

PHYSICIANS

Solo

IPA

GPWW

Comprehensive-PPM

Specialty-PPM

Joint Venture

Capitation

Ownership

Group

Physician Owned

INSURER

IDS

Foundation

Staff

Comprehensive MSO

Specialty PHO

Closed PHO

Open PHO

Service Bureau

HOSPITAL

Key:
IPA—independent practice association
GPWW—group practice without walls
PPM—physician practice management
PHO—physician-hospital organization
MSO—management services organization

Source: Reprinted with permission from Peter R. Kongstvedt (ed.). *The Managed Health Care Handbook.* (3rd ed.) Gaithersburg, Md.: Aspen, 1996, p. 47.

the member physicians must accept lower income. It is the presence of this risk sharing that stands the IPA apart from a negotiating vehicle that does not bear risk. It is also the reason that true IPAs generally are not subject to antitrust problems (unless the IPA was formed solely or primarily to keep out competition). The usual form of an IPA is as an umbrella organization for physicians in all specialties to participate in managed care. Recently, however, IPAs that represent only a single specialty have emerged.

The IPA may operate simply as a negotiating organization, with the HMO providing all administrative support, or it may take on some of the duties of the HMO, such as utilization management (UM), network development, and so forth. The IPA generally has stop-loss reinsurance, or the HMO provides such stop-loss coverage, to prevent the IPA from going bankrupt. The history of IPAs in the early years of HMOs was variable, and a number of IPAs did indeed go out of business. Recently, IPAs have been enjoying considerable success, especially in the western states. The hospital usually has no role in a traditional IPA, although some hospitals have begun sponsoring IPA development as an alternative to a physician-hospital organization (PHO) structure, which is discussed below.

Advantages of the IPA

Currently, there is a resurgence of interest in IPAs as a vehicle for private physicians to contract with managed care plans. It stops well short of full integration but has more ability to share risk and obtain HMO contracts than many PHOs. It is also a model that is more easily understood and accepted by many managed care executives, who may cast a wary eye on less-traditional models. The newly dominating IPAs are those that allow more convenient geographic access, have succeeded in bearing risk, and have limited specialist membership. They may be the only model available in nonurban areas, where one- or two-physician offices are the norm. Finally, in contrast to the staff model, IPAs require much less capital to start up and operate, and some managers feel that IPAs motivate their physicians more successfully than models that depend on salary.

Disadvantages of the IPA

The IPA is inherently unwieldy because it is usually made up of a large number of independent physicians whose only commonality is the contracting vehicle of the IPA. The IPA's ability to preserve private practice also means it is unable to leverage resources, achieve economies of scale, or change behavior to the greatest degree possible. An IPA that accepts a high degree of risk for medical costs may be found by the state insurance commissioner to be an HMO and be required to become licensed, with all the issues that go along with being a licensed health plan. Finally, many IPAs contain a surplus of specialists, resulting in upward pressure on characteristic resource consumption.

Physician Practice Management Organization (PPM)

Physician practice management (PPM) organizations are recent arrivals in the integration scene. PPMs may in some ways be viewed as variants of the management service organization (MSO), but unlike the MSO described below (in the discussion of physician-hospital vertical integration), PPMs are physician only. In other words, there is no involvement by the hospital. Some managed care taxonomists refer to these organizations as physician-only MSOs, but that convention is not the predominant one. The operations of a full MSO are described in a later section of this chapter.

Recently, some large PPMs have been branching into more activities than physician-only management. These activities include joint ventures in PHO development and even the purchase of insurance licenses. Thus PPMs, like everything else in managed care, continue to make classification a high challenge indeed.

For-Profit Comprehensive PPMs

In a melding of Wall Street and the physician's office, entrepreneurs have capitalized for-profit PPMs operating independently of hospitals. They have most often purchased physician practices, beginning with primary care groups but including certain large specialty groups as well, and have signed multiyear contracts with those physicians. The physicians may be given varying degrees of equity participation in the PPM (the equity model PPM) and a voice in governance. In some cases, the PPM may offer equity only to those physicians who are early participants, or it may offer equity in exchange for the value of the acquired practice, but not if it pays cash for the practice.

These entities may be attractive to some practitioners who, exasperated by the business pressures of practice, would prefer selling to an entity specializing in managing physician practices as opposed to a possibly distrusted hospital, or who feel that a PPM has more capability to manage a practice than a hospital. As these entities become publicly traded, a further attraction to physicians is seeing their equity grow.

In general, the PPM provides management for all support functions (billing and collections, purchasing, negotiating contracts, and so forth) but remains relatively uninvolved with the clinical aspects of the practice. In many cases, the physician remains an independent practitioner, although the PPM owns all the tangible assets of the practice. The PPM usually takes a percentage of the practice revenue, often at a rate equal to or slightly below what the physician was already paying for overhead. The physician agrees to a long-term commitment as well as noncompete covenants.

Although the early track record appears promising, it is far too soon to articulate clear advantages and disadvantages. Compared with hospitals and insurers acquiring practices, the PPM is theoretically more nimble and better able to give physicians an investment return. All practice acquisitions make the physician an employee (or employeelike) for many years, however, with all the attendant concerns about motivation. The guiding principle behind the early success of PPMs may be the virtue of an IDS that is physician-driven as opposed to hospital- or insurer-driven. This advantage derives in part from the fact that physicians control or direct 75–90 percent of health resources consumed.

Specialty PPMs

A variation on the comprehensive PPM theme, the specialty PPM has adopted most of the comprehensive PPM features to preserve or expand the market share of a single specialty. The most common specialties involved are oncology and cardiology, and multistate networks are now in place. Other specialties are ophthalmology, radiology, anesthesiology, and occupational medicine. The specialty PPM is a variant of a specialty network.

Advantages of the PPM

The primary advantage of a PPM is that its sole purpose is to manage physicians' practices. This means that it will either have or obtain expertise that does not usually reside in either a hospital or a payer (other than a group- or staff-model HMO). Also, the PPM has the ability to bring substantial purchasing power to bear through combining the purchasing needs of several hundred (or potentially more) physicians. The PPM can also provide a greater sense of ownership to the participating physicians in an equity model, thus helping align incentives and goals.

Disadvantages of the PPM

The primary disadvantage is that the PPM may not achieve sufficient mass in the market to influence events substantially or to negotiate favorable terms. Also, the physicians may chafe under the long terms usually required and may not change their practice habits sufficiently to be truly effective in managed care; this last issue becomes especially critical if the PPM is seen more as a vehicle to negotiate fees than as a system to lower costs and improve quality. These PPMs often lack strong physician leadership; business leadership comes from nonphysicians. Finally, investor-owned PPMs are businesses that are expected to return a substantial profit; they are not philanthropic institutions. If that profit is not forthcoming, it may be anticipated that the investors will begin to demand action, some of which may not be palatable to the participating physicians.

Group Practice Without Walls (GPWW)

The group practice without walls (GPWW), also known as the clinic without walls, is a significant step toward greater integration of physician services. The GPWW does not require the participation of a hospital; indeed, it is often formed as a vehicle for physicians to organize without being dependent on a hospital for services or support. In some cases, GPWW formation has occurred to leverage negotiating strength not only with MCOs but with hospitals as well.

The GPWW is composed of private practice physicians who agree to aggregate their practices into a single legal entity, but the physicians continue to practice medicine in their independent locations. In other words, the physicians appear to be independent from the view of the patient, but from the view of a contracting entity (usually an MCO) they are a single group. This is differentiated from the for-profit, physician-only MSOs described earlier by two salient features: first, the GPWW is owned solely by the member physicians and not by any outside investors, and second, the GPWW is a legal merging of all assets of the physicians' practices rather than the acquisition of only the tangible assets (as is often the case in an MSO).

To be considered a medical group, the personal income of the physicians must be affected by the performance of the group as a whole. Although an IPA will place a defined portion of a physician's income at risk (that portion related to the managed care contract held by the IPA), in a GPWW the group's income from any source has an effect on the physician's income and on profit sharing in the group; that being said, it is common in this model for an individual physician's income to be affected most by individual productivity.

The GPWW is owned by the member physicians, and governance is by the physicians. The GPWW may contract with an outside organization to provide business support services. Office support services are generally provided through the group, although as a practical matter the practicing physicians may notice little difference in what they are used to receiving.

Advantages of the GPWW

The GPWW enjoys an advantage over some other models in that it has the legal ability to negotiate and commit on behalf of all the members of the group. Unlike a PHO, where the physicians remain independent private practitioners, the GPWW is a legal group and can legitimately bargain with MSOs or other organizations. The GPWW also has the ability to achieve some modest economies of scale, similar to those enjoyed by MSOs. The most common subset of these services includes centralized billing, centralized scheduling, group purchasing, and data sharing. Less often, the GPWW centralizes recruiting and can help with employee leasing. The GPWW is free of hospital influence (at least theoretically) and therefore has greater flexibility.

Perhaps the key advantage of the GPWW is that income is affected by the performance of the group as a whole. Therefore, the GPWW has some ability to influence practice behavior. If a member physician is practicing in such a manner as to affect the group as a whole adversely, considerable peer pressure can be brought to bear. The group can even expel a physician member if the problems are serious and not rectified.

Disadvantages of the GPWW

The primary disadvantage of the GPWW is that the physicians essentially remain in independent practice. Except for obvious practice behavior, the physicians continue to practice in the manner to which they have become accustomed. The ability of the group actually to manage practice behavior is thus seriously limited to only those elements that are gross outliers (for example, exceptionally long lengths of stay). Thus optimal efficiencies are not achieved. Although there is some alignment of incentives, disparate goals still exist.

The ability of a GPWW to accept risk-based reimbursement (for example, capitation) is enhanced but not optimal. The GPWW is potentially capable of negotiating with MCOs for such contracts, but distribution of income and risk usually favors those methods used by IPAs.

The very feature that attracts many physicians to a GPWW, independence from a distrusted hospital, is also a source of weakness. That is, alternative sources of capital, information systems, and management expertise must be explored.

Finally, the GPWW structure generally does not have leadership as strong as in a true medical group. This, along with other disadvantages noted, may lead to relative structural instability. Some managers in the industry believe that the GPWW concept is transitional to a more traditional medical group. Furthermore, although sharing of certain administrative services lowers overhead, there are many more economies of scale to be found in a true, or consolidated, medical group practice.

Consolidated Medical Group

The term *consolidated medical group,* or *medical group practice,* refers to a traditional structure in which physicians have combined their resources to become a true medical group practice. Unlike the GPWW, in which the physicians combine certain assets and risks but remain in their own offices, practicing medicine as they always have, the true medical group is located in a few sites and functions in a group setting; in other words, the physicians occupy the same facility or facilities. This means a great deal of interaction among members of the group and common goals and objectives for group success.

Traditional medical groups are totally independent of the hospital. Even so, it is common for the group to identify strongly with one or more hospitals. Although this is good for the hospital so long as relations are good, it can be devastating to a hospital if relations sour or if the group is motivated to change hospitals for any reason. Some hospitals sponsor medical groups, but those operate more like other models discussed later in this chapter.

The group is usually a partnership or professional corporation, although other forms are possible. Usually the more senior members of the group enjoy more fruits of the group's success (higher income, better on-call schedules, and so forth). New members of an existing group who pass a probationary period are often required to pay a substantial contribution to the group's capital to join, which can create an entry barrier to growth. Other groups employ new physicians for a lengthy period to control the finances of the group as well as to give all parties the opportunity to see whether it is a good fit. In any event, it is common for the group to require physicians to agree to a noncompetition clause in their contract to protect the group from a physician defecting and taking patients away from the group.

Advantages of Medical Groups

Medical groups have the ability to achieve substantial economies of scale, strong negotiating leverage, and the ability to influence physician behavior. Groups are usually attractive to MCOs because they not only deliver a large block of physicians with one contract but also have the ability to manage their own resources. The group can also decide to make a change in resource use (for example, change hospitals) that can have a rapid and substantial positive effect on managed care.

Although the capital investment required of partners or group shareholders can be an entry barrier, it is also an exit barrier, promoting greater stability. An additional exit barrier exists in the form of a noncompetition clause required of member physicians, again promoting stability, which is desirable in the eyes of a managed care plan. Medical groups are often able to recruit new physicians more easily because they offer an improved lifestyle compared with solo practice, which allows them to grow along with a managed care plan. On the whole, medical groups are in a superior position to benefit from managed care compared to many other models, and certainly compared to independent private physicians.

Disadvantages of Medical Groups

Medical groups can certainly have serious problems, such as uncontrolled overhead or poor utilization patterns. If these problems are not rectified, the impact of failure is felt to a far higher degree than is the case if a single physician or small group fails. If the group has markedly disproportionate compensation or lifestyle differences between the senior members and the new physicians, the turnover of new members can be unacceptably high. Medical groups can also have inflated opinions of their worth, impeding effective contracting.

Medical groups can become calcified in their ways and less able to change than individual physicians. This is a serious problem if compounded by the group being top heavy with subspecialists and in turn treating primary care physicians (PCPs) as second-class members. If the group is unwilling to consider redistributing the rewards to the PCPs, it may suffer defections of those physicians, which will make the group less desirable from a managed care standpoint.

Physician-Hospital Organization (PHO)

The physician-hospital organization (PHO) is an entity that, at a minimum, allows a hospital and its physicians to negotiate with third-party payers. PHOs may do little more than provide such a negotiating vehicle, although this could raise the risk of violating antitrust laws. PHOs may actively manage the relationship between the providers and MCOs or they may provide more services, to the point where they may more aptly be considered MSOs, which are described below.

In its weakest form, the PHO is considered a messenger model. This means that the PHO analyzes the terms and conditions offered by an MCO and transmits its analysis and the contract to each physician, who then decides individually whether to participate.

In its simplest and common version, the participating physicians and the hospital develop model contract terms and reimbursement levels and use those terms to negotiate with MCOs. The PHO usually has a limited amount of time to negotiate the contract successfully (for example, ninety days). If the time limit passes, then the participating physicians are free to contract directly with the MCO; if the PHO successfully reaches an agreement with the MCO, then the physicians agree to be bound by those terms. The contract is still between the physician and the MCO and between the hospital and the MCO. In some cases, the contract between the physicians and the MCO is relatively brief and may refer to a contract between the PHO and the MCO.

PHOs are generally considered the first step on the evolutionary ladder in vertical integration with respect to practitioners and facilities. They often form as a reaction to market forces from managed care. PHOs are considered the easiest type of vertically integrated system to develop (although they are not actually that easy, at least if done well). They also are a vehicle to provide some integration while preserving the independence and autonomy of the physicians. For hospitals, PHOs offer opportunities to form a more unified medical staff, more effectively market medical services to payers, and enhance physician relationships overall.

By definition, a PHO requires the participation of a hospital and at least some portion of the admitting physicians. Often, the formation of the PHO is initiated by the hospital, but unless the leadership of the medical staff is also on board it is unlikely to get far. It is not uncommon for a PHO to be formed primarily as a defensive mechanism to deal with an increase in managed care contracting activity. It is also not uncommon for the same physicians who join the PHO to be under contract already with one or more managed care plans.

The PHO is usually a separate business entity, such as a for-profit corporation. This requires thorough legal analysis for the participating not-for-profit, tax-exempt (Internal Revenue Code § 501(c)(3)) hospital because it could lose tax-exempt status if access to tax-exempt financing confers an advantage to the PHO's balance sheet.

Initial capitalization and ownership occur with varying formulas, but most strive toward equal ownership between the physicians and the hospital. The hospital may put up the majority of the cash, however. For the sake of practitioner motivation, physician equity is a favorable feature.

Governance can evolve over time. That is, in its simplest form hospital administrators may run the entity. Most PHOs, however, are establishing formal governing boards. Board composition is usually equally divided between hospital administrators and physicians, with attention being given to primary care representation within the physician component.

PHOs fall into two broad categories: open and closed. These are described separately because MCOs often view them that way.

Open PHOs

The first type of PHO is open to virtually any member of the medical staff of the hospital. There will often be minimum credentialing requirements, but not always. Open PHOs are almost universally specialty-dominated; in other words, there are disproportionately more specialists in the PHO than there are PCPs. The creators of the open PHO are often the specialists themselves, who become concerned that MCOs are selectively contracting, thereby reducing the amount of business that the specialists collectively are doing. The medical staff then approach the hospital administration to form the PHO primarily to allow all the members of the medical staff to participate with MCOs. In this situation, PCPs are usually courted but may still be relegated to second-class citizenship, even if unintentionally.

Some open PHOs claim that although their genesis is an open format, the ultimate goal will be to manage the membership and remove those physicians who are unable to practice cost-effectively. MCOs view such claims with skepticism, although it is certainly possible. The political reality of an open PHO is that it is quite difficult to bring sufficient discipline to bear on medical staff members who wield a high level of influence. This is currently complicated by the continued dichotomy of payment mechanisms, in which a certain portion of reimbursement to the hospital rewards cost-effectiveness (for example, prospective payment, capitation, and package or bundled pricing), whereas other forms of reimbursement reward the opposite (fee-for-service, simple discounts on charges).

Closed PHOs

The primary difference between a closed PHO and an open one is the proactive decision to limit physician membership in the PHO. This is clearly more difficult politically than an open model, but it carries greater potential for success. The two general approaches to limiting membership are by specialty type and practice profiling.

Limitations by specialty type are more common and more easily done. The most common limitation is the number of specialists, to address the imbalance between PCPs and specialists found in an open PHO. In fact, it is not uncommon to find closed PHOs having a disproportionate number of PCPs on the governance board as well as in the membership of the PHO. Although an extreme instance of this concept is the primary care–only PHO that simply subcontracts with certain specialists, the PHO usually places limits on the number of specialists of any given specialty type beyond primary care for equity sharing and/or membership status. This limitation on the number of specialists is most often accomplished by projecting the enrollment (or covered lives) that the PHO is expected to cover over the next several years and then recruiting specialists according to predetermined ratios of specialists needed for that enrollment.

The second type of limitation involves practice profiling and is more difficult to carry out for technical reasons. This type of limitation requires the PHO to examine some objective form of practice analysis (it could be a subjective analysis, but that would probably raise a restraint-of-trade issue). Based on the analysis, physicians are invited to join the PHO or not. This is difficult to accomplish unless the PHO has access to adequate data, which is most uncommon. The closed PHO may be impeded in its quest to demonstrate selectivity by those states enacting any-willing-provider legislation and needs to be aware of any possible antitrust issues.

As part of ongoing recredentialing, the PHO also regularly reevaluates the number of physicians required for each specialty. If the PHO has the ability to capture and analyze data regarding practice behavior and clinical quality, those data may be used in managing the physician membership and, ultimately, ending the participation agreement with any physicians who repeatedly depart from the PHO's practice guidelines. Such analyses are difficult to perform properly. It is important for the PHO (or for any type of IDS, for that matter) that accepts full risk to negotiate the right to receive claims data on all members for whom the PHO has the full capitated risk; otherwise the PHO will not have sufficient data to analyze all medical costs.

Specialist PHOs

A variant of the PHO has emerged over the past few years. The specialist PHO has taken the general closed PHO concepts down to the level of a single specialty. Common specialties involved are cardiology and pediatrics; psychiatric PHOs have existed for many years. Their track record is too brief in most cases for analysis, but the value placed on them by the market should follow the logic described above under specialist PPMs, except that this entity brings with it an expensive facility.

Advantages of the PHO

The primary advantage of a PHO is its ability to negotiate on behalf of a large group of physicians allied with a hospital. This advantage can be ephemeral if no MCO wishes to negotiate (see below), but it may be very real if the hospital and key members of the medical staff are attractive to MCOs and are not already under contract. Closed PHOs are more attractive to MCOs than open ones. Of course, if the providers have already contracted with the MCO and threaten to pull out (that is, boycott the MCO) unless the MCO uses the PHO, a serious antitrust problem may arise. If the MCO has not already contracted with the providers, the PHO may be an expeditious route to developing a delivery system capability. Even in those situations where a contract already exists, contracting through the PHO may represent a sufficient improvement in terms such that an MCO will be willing to switch from direct contracting to using the PHO; for example, the PHO may be willing to provide performance guarantees. Finally, physicians may view the PHO as a facilitator in landing direct contracts with self-insured employers, with the HCFA for Medicare risk contracts, and with the state for managed Medicaid contracts.

A second advantage of a PHO is its theoretical ability to track and use data and to manage the delivery system, at least from the standpoints of UM and quality management. Once again, this advantage is more likely to be found in a closed PHO than in an open one, primarily because a closed PHO has a greater concentration of events over fewer physicians.

The third advantage of a PHO is that it is the first step to greater integration between a hospital and its medical staff. Although a PHO by itself may result in improved relations, those relations can quickly sour if the PHO consumes time, energy, and money but fails to yield results. If the PHO does result in better ability to contract or yields economic rewards, then its mission is successful, at least for the near term. If the PHO does not succeed, or if success appears to be short-lived, then the PHO may be the base from which a more integrated model is built.

Disadvantages of the PHO

The chief disadvantage of a typical PHO is that it often fails to result in any meaningful improvement in contracting ability. In many cases, MCOs already have provider contracts in place and see little value in going through the PHO. Even worse, an MCO may see the PHO as little more than a vehicle for providers to keep their reimbursement high.

Open PHOs are at a significant disadvantage if the MCO (or employer, in the event that the PHO chooses to contract directly with employers) does not want all the physicians in the PHO to be participating with the health plan. MCOs often want the right to select the providers and are unlikely to give it up. Even closed PHOs may suffer from this problem if the MCOs specifically wish to avoid contracting with certain physicians who are members of the PHO.

MCOs may view the PHO as a barrier to effective communication with the physicians and a hindrance to fully effective UM. Unless the PHO has a compelling story to tell regarding its ability to manage utilization, the MCO may believe that it can do a better job without the PHO's interference. Alternatively, if the health plan has relatively unsophisticated UM capabilities, or if the plan is too small to be able to devote adequate resources to UM, the PHO may represent an attractive alternative.

Because PHOs are relatively loosely structured and because the physicians may still be completely independent, the PHO's ability to affect provider behavior is rather limited. This can have an impact not only on UM but also on getting the entire organization to make necessary changes.

Management Service Organization (MSO)

An MSO represents the evolution of the PHO into an entity that provides more services to the physician. The MSO is a vehicle for negotiating with MCOs, and it also provides additional services to support the physician's practice. The physician, however, usually remains an independent private practitioner. The MSO is based around one or more hospitals. The reasons for the MSO's formation are generally the same as for the PHO, and ownership and governance issues are similar to those discussed earlier.

In its simplest form, the MSO operates as a service bureau, providing basic practice support services to member physicians. The activities include billing and collection, administrative support in certain areas, electronic data interchange (such as electronic billing), and other services.

The physician can remain an independent practitioner, under no legal obligation to use the services of the hospital exclusively. The MSO must receive compensation from the physician at fair market value, or the hospital and physician could incur legal problems. The MSO should, through economies of scale as well as good management, be able to provide those services at a reasonable rate.

The MSO may be considerably broader in scope. In addition to providing all the services described above, the MSO may actually purchase many of the assets of the physician's practice; for example, the MSO may purchase the physician's office space or office equipment (at fair market value). The MSO can employ the office support staff of the physician as well. MSOs can further incorporate functions such as quality management, UM, provider relations, member services, and even claims processing. This form of MSO is usually constructed as a unique business entity, separate from the PHO. Because the MSO is its own corporation, legal advisers are finding advantages in characterizing them as limited liability corporations, but alternatives exist.

The MSO does not always have direct contracts with MCOs for two reasons: many MCOs insist on having the provider be the contracting agent, and many states will not allow MCOs (especially HMOs) to have contracts with any entity that does not have the power to bind the provider. The physician may remain an independent private practitioner under no contractual obligation to use the hospital exclusively. It should be noted here that there are IDSs that operate under the label of MSO that actually do purchase the physician's entire practice (possibly including intangible values such as goodwill) and function much like a more fully integrated system, as discussed later in this chapter.

Advantages of the MSO

The primary advantage of an MSO over a PHO is the ability of the MSO to bind the physician closer to the hospital, although not as a contractual obligation to use the hospital on an exclusive basis. The MSO certainly has the ability to bring economies of scale and professional management to the physician's office services, thus potentially reducing overhead costs. The MSO may have the potential ability to capture data regarding practice behavior, which may be used to help the physicians practice more cost-effectively. This develops when the MSO contains more advanced functions, such as UM and claims processing.

Disadvantages of the MSO

The disadvantages of an MSO are similar to those of a PHO in that the physician may remain an independent practitioner with the ability to change allegiance with relative ease. Also, if the MSO does not employ the physician, it has somewhat limited ability to effect change or to redeploy resources in response to changing market needs.

Special problems arise with MSOs, problems that can be compounded by MSOs that purchase assets from a physician's practice. These are the problems of the transaction being perceived as inuring to the benefit of the physician in an illegal manner and of fraud and abuse for federally funded patients.

Foundation Model

A foundation-model IDS is one in which a hospital creates a not-for-profit foundation and actually purchases physicians' practices (both tangible and intangible assets) and puts those practices into the foundation. This model usually occurs when, for some legal reason (for example, the hospital is a not-for-profit entity that cannot own a for-profit subsidiary, or there is a state law against the corporate practice of medicine), the hospital cannot employ the physicians directly or use hospital funds to purchase the practices directly. It must be noted that to qualify for and maintain its not-for-profit status, the foundation must prove that it provides substantial community benefit.

A second form of foundation model does not involve a hospital. In this model, the foundation is an entity that exists on its own and contracts for services with a medical group and a hospital. On a historical note, in the early days of HMOs many open-panel types of plan that were not formed as IPAs were formed as foundations; the foundation held the HMO license and contracted with one or more IPAs and hospitals for services.

The foundation itself is governed by a board that is not dominated by either the hospital or the physicians (in fact, physicians may represent no more than 20 percent of the board) and includes lay members. The foundation owns and manages the practices, but the physicians become members of a medical group that, in turn, has an exclusive contract for services with the foundation; in other words, the foundation is the only source of revenue for the medical group. The physicians have contracts with the medical group that are long-term and contain noncompetition clauses.

Although the physicians are in an independent group and the foundation is also independent from the hospital, the relationship in fact is close among all members of the triad. The medical group, however, retains a significant measure of autonomy regarding its own business affairs, and the foundation has no control over certain aspects, such as individual physician compensation.

Advantages of the Foundation Model

The primary advantages of this model pertain to legal constraints that require the foundation's creation in the first place. Because the construction of this entity is rather unwieldy, it is best suited to those states in which it is required (for example, California, at the time this chapter is being written) so that a not-for-profit hospital can proceed with a fully integrated model. That said, the foundation model provides for a greater level of structural integration than any other model discussed to this point. A not-for-profit foundation may also be better able to access the bond market for capital in an advantageous manner.

Because the foundation clearly controls the revenue that the medical group will get, it has considerable influence over that group. The foundation also has the ability to rationalize the clinical and administrative resources required to meet obligations under managed care contracts (and fee-for-service, of course) and can achieve greater economies of scale. If the foundation consolidates medical office locations, these economies are improved, as is the foundation's ability to provide more comprehensive services to enrolled members. A foundation also has the ability to invest required capital to expand services, recruit PCPs, and so forth. For these reasons, a foundation model may be viewed quite favorably by a contracting MCO.

Disadvantages of the Foundation Model

The primary disadvantage of a foundation model is that the physicians in the medical group are linked only indirectly to the foundation and the business goals of that foundation. Although this indirect link is quite strong, the medical group remains an intermediate organization (vaguely analogous to an IPA) that can operate in ways that are potentially inconsistent with the overall goals of managed care. One example of this becoming a problem would be a medical group that is top heavy with specialists and in which PCPs are treated as second-class members. Another example would be a group that compensates member physicians based on fee-for-service or other measures that are easily gamed, leading to less-than-optimal control of utilization and quality.

Related to this issue is a built-in potential for conflict between the governance boards of the hospital and the medical group. If the goals and priorities of the two organizations are not completely aligned (and they rarely are), then it is possible for serious disputes to arise, which impede success.

The last main disadvantage is the not-for-profit status of the hospital and foundation. Because of it, the foundation must continuously prove that it provides a community benefit to maintain its status. The risk of private inurement (discussed below) is also heightened. To compete against foundation models, several not-for-profit hospitals have, as this book is being written, formed PHOs and MSOs (both for-profit and not-for-profit entities), allowing well over 20 percent board representation by physicians. These developments have been permitted by a favorable interpretation of regulatory requirements, although their ultimate corporate stability is still undetermined.

Staff Model

Not to be confused with the staff-model HMO, a staff model in the context of this chapter refers to an IDS owned by a health system rather than by an HMO. The distinction is whether the primary business organization is a licensed entity (for example, an HMO) or primarily a provider. This distinction is not always easy to observe, and in some cases the only way to make any distinction is to look at the genesis of the parent organization: Was it founded to be a health plan or founded to be a provider? If the distinction rests on history only, then it is meaningless.

The staff model is a health system that employs the physicians directly. Physicians are integrated into the system either through the purchase of their practices or by being hired directly. The system is often more than a hospital, being rather a larger, more comprehensive organization for delivering health care. Because the physicians are employees, the legal issues that attach to IDSs using private physicians are attenuated.

Advantages of the Staff Model

Staff-model IDSs are theoretically in a good position to be able to rationalize resources and to align goals of all the components of the delivery system. Physicians are almost always paid based on a salary, and incentive programs can be designed to reward the physicians in parallel with the goals and objectives of the system. Far greater economies of scale are achievable, and capital resources can be applied in a businesslike manner. Staff models also have a greater ability to recruit new physicians because there is no cost to the new physician and the income stream to the new physician begins immediately. The ability to manage the physicians in the system is also at least theoretically enhanced. The problems of taxable status, private inurement, and fraud and abuse are greatly diminished. MCOs generally consider staff-model IDSs as desirable business partners, assuming that cost, quality, and access are acceptable; the exception would be if the staff model chooses to pursue obtaining its own HMO license, thus becoming a direct competitor and threat to a contracting MCO.

Disadvantages of the Staff Model

One key problem with staff models is when management assumes that simply because the physicians are employees, they can be managed in a manner similar to that of other employees of the system; this is a false and unproductive assumption. Physicians are highly intelligent and highly trained professionals who must operate clinically with considerable autonomy. Any health system that does not recognize these qualities is bound to have difficulties with its medical staff.

Despite the previous statement, staff models often run into problems with physician productivity. Salaried physicians are obviously no longer motivated to see high volumes of patients, as they are under fee-for-service. Staff models may be most attractive to physicians who do not wish to practice full-time or who wish to limit their hours. Some staff-model HMOs have had such problems with low productivity that they have at least partially eroded the economies of scale that are available in tightly integrated systems. Physicians in staff models often feel little loyalty and are more easily recruited away than physicians who have an investment in a group.

The last disadvantage is the high capital requirement to build and operate the system. Once adequate patient volume is coming through, staff models can have excellent financial performance. Until then, however, they are heavily leveraged. Expansion of an existing system likewise requires a great deal of capital investment.

Physician Ownership Model

The physician ownership model refers to a vertically integrated system in which the physicians hold a significant portion of ownership (that is, equity) interest. In some cases, the physicians own the entire system; in other cases, the physicians own less than 100 percent, but more than 51 percent. The physicians' equity interest is through their medical group(s). Physicians holding equity as simple shareholders could raise problems with Medicare fraud and abuse.

The physician ownership model operates with features combining those of the staff model and MSO. Unlike the situation with the staff model, the medical groups have a strong role in the overall management of the system, and the physicians (at least those physicians who are partners in the group) have a clear vested interest in the system's success.

Advantages of the Physician Ownership Model

The advantages of the physician ownership model are similar to those enumerated for the staff model above. In contrast to the staff model, this model enjoys a powerful advantage by virtue of the physician ownership: total alignment of goals of the medical group and the health system. Because the physician-owners' success is tied directly to the overall success of the entire organization, there is far less of a problem with conflicting goals and objectives. As a consequence of this alignment, strong physician leadership is present, which is more effective in managing the medical groups. Finally, this model can choose either to contract with or to own the hospital rather than be dominated by the hospital.

Disadvantages of the Physician Ownership Model

The primary disadvantage of the physician ownership model is the high level of resources required to build and operate it. Large capital resources are required to acquire the personnel, facilities, and practices necessary to provide comprehensive medical services, an adequate level of managerial support, and the required infrastructure. The source of this capital is primarily the physicians' practices, although outside access to capital is certainly possible. Related to that issue is the generally high buy-in cost to new physician partners, which may be a barrier to some physicians joining the group other than as employees.

Virtual Integration

Goldsmith argues that it is possible, and even likely, that many of the structurally rigid vertical integration models are not going to succeed. He argues that success will be more probable with models of virtual integration, in which more or less independent parties come together for the purpose of behaving like an IDS under managed care but retain their own identities and mission. This virtual integration requires aligning the financial incentives among the parties as well as alignment of business purpose.

In a virtual integration, each of the major segments of the health care system—the physicians, the institutional providers, the payers/MCOs, and the ancillary providers (for example, a pharmacy)—act in concert for a common cause, but none is an employee or subdivision of another. This allows each party to manage its own affairs and meet its own financial goals without being managed by another segment of the industry. In this model, there is greater horizontal integration (between hospitals, between physicians, and so forth), with each horizontally integrated system then forming relationships with other parts of the health care system.

Global Capitation

Global capitation applies to IDSs that are capable of accepting full, or nearly full, risk for medical expenses, including all professional, all institutional, and many ancillary services as well. This differs from full capitation, which applies to primary care groups accepting full risk for all professional services but not for institutional or ancillary services. Global capitation includes institutional as well as professional services, and the party accepting the capitation payment is a large, vertically integrated organization with presumably greater resources. Even though the IDS has accepted global capitation, it often purchases reinsurance to protect it against catastrophic cases; the reinsurance is either provided by the HMO or purchased by the IDS from a reinsurer.

Many IDSs accept a percentage of premium revenue from an HMO rather than a fixed capitation. Although these forms of revenue are similar, they are not the same. A percentage of premium may be affected by underwriting and marketing issues (primarily in commercial enrollment; in Medicare and Medicaid, percentage of revenue and capitation are nearly the same). If underwriting is poor and there is a revenue shortfall from the standpoint of covered lives, the percentage of that shortfall passed on to the IDS will mirror the percentage of revenue it is receiving from the MCO.

Although the HMO may have capitated the IDS, the IDS still faces the issue of how to divide up the revenue and risk among the parties. In a sense, global capitation simply transfers the burden of payment and management from the HMO to the IDS, but the fundamental issues remain. If the IDS employs the physicians, then it is relatively easier to distribute income.

Many IDSs, however, are combinations of private and employed physicians. Even hospitals that employ physicians usually still rely on private physicians for at least some services, and often the genesis of the IDS was to allow the hospital and private physicians to remain competitive in a managed care environment. Therefore, the IDS that accepts global capitation must still figure out how to allocate risk and reward.

Providing the Insurance Function

Up to this point, this chapter has concentrated on vertical integration of practitioners and facilities. The MSO and PHO models are examples of delivery systems that can expand horizontally (by finding other PHO partners and forming a regional network—the super-PHO—with convenient geographic access) and then become independently capable of direct contracting with self-insured purchasers. This capability requires incorporating most of the typical insurance functions. These usually begin with claims processing but may extend to ownership of the insurance license itself.

There are several options for an IDS to converge with insurance functions: the insurer buys the hospital and physician groups, an integrated provider network buys or builds the insurance function, or the insurer and the integrated provider network form a joint venture with shared ownership (or perhaps a looser relationship). An integrated provider network may also rent an insurance function; for example, it may pay several dollars per subscriber per month for third-party administrator (TPA) functions and possible insurance licensure fronting services.

Clearly, when dealing with purchasers that are not self-insured, the IDS or MSO needs to incorporate all the classic insurance functions, including underwriting and actuarial rate development, as it takes on risk. The IDS also needs to have an insurance license. Many small insurance companies and TPAs are willing to price their role in this scheme competitively and are capable of avoiding the double-digit overhead associated with the largest insurance companies. One must be cognizant, however, that many of these TPAs are not capable of carrying out sophisticated managed care functions. It is also possible for an IDS to contract with an insurer to front the license—that is, to use the insurer's license to back up the IDS's activities.

Advantages

A joint venture between an IDS and an insurer or MCO has several advantages. Both parties bring assets to the venture (at least theoretically). The IDS brings a network, some medical management, the ability to accept some level of risk for medical expenses, and a framework for contracting. The insurer or MCO brings a license (and its ability to meet the attendant capital and regulatory needs); possibly an enrolled subscriber base; and expertise in functions such as claims processing, member services, and the like.

Disadvantages

The main disadvantage of an IDS assuming the insurance functions is that it may fail to carry them out competently, and failure would have far-reaching effects. The activities of an insurance company or MCO go well beyond medical management, and it would be naïve for the management of an IDS to believe that those functions do not require expertise or that they are not fraught with complexities.

Pursuing the insurance partner requires great caution. Too many insurance entities are configured as indemnity claims processors, incapable of understanding the subtleties associated with managing care. Significant capital may be required to structure the new entity. A large organization perceived to have deep pockets that has gotten closer to providing care will also need to evidence due diligence in credentialing providers to minimize the risk associated with negligent credentialing.

Governance and control of a joint venture may be a sensitive area. Although joint representation on the board is likely to be required, controlling representation may become a contentious issue.

References

1. Marianne F. Fazen. *Managed Care Desk Reference.* Reston, Va.: St. Anthony, 1996, p. 151.
2. Peter R. Kongstvedt (ed.). *The Managed Health Care Handbook.* (3rd ed.) Gaithersburg, Md.: Aspen, 1996, pp. 46–62.

ANNOTATIONS

4.01   IN GENERAL

Sam W. Barcus III. *Healthcare Controller's Manual.* Boston: Warren Gorham & Lamont, 1996.

The manual is divided into six parts. Section A reviews emerging issues and the forces of change affecting the health care industry. Chapters cover the changing health care system, the role of government in health care reform, the future of integrated health care delivery systems, and health information networks. Section B is devoted to the role of the health care controller, with chapters addressing financial responsibilities, information systems responsibilities, negotiation and collaborative decision-making skills, work redesign, and productivity. Section C provides practical guidance in the accounting and financial reporting aspects of the health care controller's role. Step-by-step advice is included on revenue and expense recognition, internal controls, and external reporting.

The purpose of section D is to help the health care controller prepare financial plans that balance short-term goals with long-term objectives, emphasizing the importance of strategic financial planning along with financial modeling and capital budgeting. Section E covers master planning for hospital assets and capital resources, debt, and real estate development and retrofit options. Asset management tools and techniques are included that can reduce interest costs, strengthen liquidity, and improve overall financial performance. Section F addresses legal, regulatory, and tax issues, providing information on the latest health care tax news; Medicare and Medicaid programs; contracting with other health care providers; and risk-based contracting with insurance companies, government agencies, and employer groups.

The manual contains a large number of practical forms and figures to guide the user. It is updated annually.

Paul R. DeMuro. "Provider Sponsored Organizations (PSOs)." Washington, D.C.: American Health Lawyers Association [Report No. VMC98–0025], 1998, 23 pages.

Outlines the fundamental organizational requirements for PSOs, licensing and interaction processes, waivers, solvency standards, and alternative PSO models.

Mark A. Hall. "Managed Competition and Integrated Health Care Delivery Systems." *Wake Forest Law Review,* 1994, *29,* 1.

Introduces a law school symposium on health care law and explains how two central concepts—managed competitive and integrated health care delivery systems—relate to each other. The first section sketches the basic structure of managed competition and explains why this concept is expected to lead to a dramatic increase in the role of HMOs and other managed care entities. The second section explains how hospitals, physicians, and insurers are responding to the anticipated growth in managed care by forming integrated delivery systems. The third section briefly summarizes the articles that compose the symposium and how they relate to these two themes.

James O. Hepner and others. *Case Studies on Health Administration.* 6 vols. Vols. 1 and 2 (St. Louis: C.V. Mosby, 1978–1980); vols. 3–9 (Chicago: Foundation of the American College of Healthcare Executives, 1983–1993).

These books consist of cases developed by health services professionals to meet requirements for the advancement process of the American College of Healthcare Executives. Volumes deal with the following subjects: (1) health planning for emerging multihospital systems, (2) hospital administrator–physician relationships, (3) strategic planning, (4) ethics for health services managers, (5) an economic approach to rationing health care resources, (6) hospital labor relations, (7) alternative delivery systems, (8) evolution of strategy, and (9) management of continuous quality improvement.

Regina E. Herzlinger. *Creating New Health Ventures: The Role of Management.* Gaithersburg, Md.: Aspen, 1992.

Twenty cases on market opportunities in health care written by a business school professor. Also includes text on opportunities for health care ventures. Case studies include Health Stop, Hospital Corporation of America, Humana, New England Critical Care, Shouldice Hospital Ltd., and U.S. Health Care.

Peter R. Kongstvedt and David W. Plocher. "Integrated Health Care Systems." In Peter R. Kongstvedt (ed.), *The Managed Health Care Handbook.* (4th ed.) Gaithersburg, Md.: Aspen, 2000.

Topics discussed in this eighteen-page chapter include independent practice associations, physician practice management organizations, group practice without walls, consolidated medical groups, PHOs, MSOs, the foundation model, the staff model, the physician ownership model, virtual integration, and global capitation.

Keith M. Korenchuk. *Transforming the Delivery of Health Care: The Integration Process.* (3rd ed.) Englewood, Colo.: Medical Group Management Association, 1994, 436 pages.

Describes the complete scope of integration processes that physicians and hospitals are currently undergoing. It covers such physician integration topics as physician organizations, contracting networks, clinics without walls, and medical group mergers. The book also covers the physician-hospital integration process and discusses in detail the formation of physician-hospital organizations, which provide managed care contracting networks to health care plans.

Also discussed is the creation of other levels of physician-hospital integration, including management service organizations, employment and medical division relationships, and foundation relationships. This text, written by an attorney with Davis, Wright & Tremain, P.A., in Charlotte, North Carolina, serves as a basic resource for the taxonomy and discussion of integrated delivery systems development.

Robert H. Miller. "Competition in the Health System: Good News and Bad News." *Health Affairs,* 1996, *15,* 107.

Assesses the impact of health care competition in fifteen markets. Competition among health plans, hospitals, and physicians has taken place in these markets primarily on the basis of price and secondarily on network breadth and style of care. In most markets, competition resulted in lower (or slowly growing) premium prices. Within a type of plan product, competition was leading to similar prices and networks and was reducing product differentiation among health plans. Competition was not taking place on the basis of measured and reported quality of care, which limited the capacity of employers and enrollees to make informed health plan choices. As a result, there was a substantial gap between competition as envisioned by the architects of the managed competition model and competition as it is evolving today, the author argues.

Robert H. Miller. "Health System Integration: A Means to an End." *Health Affairs*, 1996, *15*, 92.

Discusses the market impact of the creation of integrated health care firms and contractual networks. According to Miller, creating these entities is often a precondition for other forms of integration that could actually lower costs and improve quality of care. Although different types of integration activity are leading to innovation in production of services and the care of populations, the continued influence of the "old" indemnity insurance or fee-for-service system creates important obstacles to those integration activities, the author contends. If creation of integrated firms and contractual networks races ahead of other forms of integration, it could produce uncompetitive markets that reduce pressures to integrate in ways that can cut costs and improve quality of care. Purchasers' actions could play a major role in determining the future of various integration activities, he concludes.

Deborah A. Randall. *Legal Issues and the Integrated Delivery System: An Executive Guide.* Chicago: American Hospital Publishing, 1996, 93 pages.

Designed to assist nonattorneys at the highest levels of hospital management in forming and operating an IDS. To efficiently address managed care requirements, accept increased financial risks, and maintain high-quality care standards, hospitals are developing integrated delivery systems to coordinate the delivery of health care among hospitals, physicians, and other providers. The purpose of this concise book is to provide an overview of the key legal issues involved with a hospital-affiliated IDS. Topics examined include formation, legal issues affecting IDS formation and operation, antitrust issues, pricing, tax exemption, Stark issues, liability issues, and contracting questions.

Lisa K. Rolfe and Paul Wehner. *Making the Physician Network Work: Leadership, Design and Incentives.* Chicago: American Hospital Publishing, 1995, 101 pages.

A practical guide to developing a physician-driven health care system. Topics include issues to consider when planning the physician network, tangible steps toward implementing the network, and preparation for the next phases of health care delivery.

Elizabeth Olmsted Teisberg, Michael E. Porter, and Gregory B. Brown. "Making Competition in Health Care Work." *Harvard Business Review*, July–Aug. 1994.

Contends that innovation, driven by rigorous competition, is the key to successful health care reform. The authors note that in a variety of industries, competition compels companies to deliver constantly increasing value to consumers. The fundamental driver of this continuous quality improvement and cost reduction is innovation. Without incentives to sustain innovation in health care, short-term cost savings will soon be overwhelmed by the desire to widen access, the growing health needs of an aging population, and the unwillingness of Americans to settle for anything less than the best treatments available.

The authors argue that the assumption underlying much of the debate about health care is that technology is the enemy. By assuming that technology drives up costs, reformers neglect the central importance of innovation or, worse yet, attempt to slow its pace.

4.02   ADVANTAGES AND DISADVANTAGES OF INTEGRATION

4.02(1)   Potential Barriers to Integration

Carol Bayley. "Ethical and Religious Issues in Mergers Between Catholic and Non-Catholic Entities." Washington, D.C.: American Health Lawyers Association [Report No. VMA 98–0033], 1998, 38 pages.

> Discusses myths about Catholic hospital affiliations, considers how the worldviews of bishops and attorneys differ, and illustrates five lessons learned from successful mergers of Catholic and non-Catholic health care entities.

John J. Huber, Michael A. Bell, and John Turner. "Securities Issues." Washington, D.C.: American Health Lawyers Association [Report No. VMA 98–0032], 1998, 40 pages.

> Seminar manuscript on capital finance, providing an overview of the registration process for making an initial public offering and addressing a number of the disclosure, accounting, and regulatory issues that physician practice management companies should address prior to and during the initial public offering process.

4.02(2)   Financial Issues

Catholic Health Association. *A Workbook on Redesigning Care: Becoming the Values-Driven, Low-Cost Provider.* St. Louis: Catholic Health Association, 1995, 140 pages.

> Designed to assist members of the Catholic Health Association in assuming leadership roles and participation in networks by showing how ministry values support and guide efforts to redesign care and reduce costs.

Thomas C. Fox, Carol Colborn, Carl Krasik, and Joseph W. Metro. *Health Care Financial Transactions Manual.* St. Paul, Minn.: West Group, 1997.

> Designed primarily to guide financial officers, lenders, and investors in identifying health care regulatory issues that commonly arise in health care transactions. Highly practical and written by four attorneys, this loose-leaf treatise suggests transactional mechanisms that may be incorporated into the structure of a deal so that it complies with pertinent regulatory requirements. Unusually well organized, the volume is divided into four parts. Part One supplies a seven-step analysis that should be followed in identifying issues that may arise in a particular transaction. Part Two elaborates on how legal requirements affect various types of transactions involving health care companies, from acquisitions to bond financings. Part Three describes the health care entities commonly involved in transactions, their regulators, and the legal environment in which they conduct their business. Part Four analyzes proposed legislation and regulatory initiatives as well as congressionally mandated studies, which could influence the structure of health care transactions. The text is supplemented regularly by the publisher and includes a wealth of sample documents and letters, along with a table of cases, a table of statutes, and an index. This is a highly valuable reference work.

Louis C. Grapenski. *Understanding Health Care Financial Management: Text, Cases and Models.* (3rd ed.) Chicago: Health Administration Press, 1996, 856 pages.

> Designed to provide health administration students with an operational knowledge of basic financial management theory, principles, and concepts for a broad range of health service delivery settings. This new edition was written in response to the rapid changes occurring in health care since

the first edition appeared in 1992. New features in the second edition include expanded coverage on dealing with financial risk, new information on mergers and acquisitions (M&A), a new chapter on capitation, and additional focus on tax and reimbursement matters.

Kenneth Kaufman and Mark A. Hall. *The Financially Competitive Healthcare Organization: The Executive's Guide to Strategic Financial Planning and Management.* Chicago: Probus, 1994, 201 pages.

Written by two Chicago health care consultants, this book is aimed at financial and nonfinancial executives who wish to be more effective producers and consumers of financial data and analysis. The first three chapters provide a theoretical foundation making use of case studies. The last three chapters were developed to reinforce the concepts described in the first half of the book and apply them in an in-depth fashion to specific situations. Specific topics addressed include capital deployment, acquisitions analysis, analysis and sizing of project investments, and physician-hospital integration analysis.

Eldon L. Schafer, Dwight J. Zulaus, and Michael E. Gocke. *Management Accounting for Fee-for-Service/Prepaid Medical Groups.* Chicago: American Medical Association, 288 pages.

Takes a management accounting approach, detailing everything administrators need to know to better manage complex financial systems.

4.02(3)   Structure and Degree of Integration

Douglas Conrad, Robert Bonney, Michael Sachs, and Robert Smith. *Managed Care Contracting: Concepts and Applications for the Health Care Executive.* Chicago: Health Administration Press, 1996, 152 pages.

Provides a comprehensive model for how the provider organization can proactively respond to an evolving managed care environment. The authors contend that the survival of health care organizations, in managed care markets, will depend on their ability to become part of a vertically integrated, regional health care system. They further argue that only by attaining administrative efficiencies will health care organizations be able to invest in the management and information systems they will require to manage risk-based contracts. Topics include contract administration, information systems, contract negotiations, pricing services for managed care, and formulation of strategy. This is an excellent reference tool for midlevel or senior-level administrators implementing organizational change.

St. Anthony's Integrated Health Care 100 Directory. (3rd ed.) Reston, Va.: St. Anthony, 1997, 744 pages.

A comprehensive presentation of the top one hundred integrated delivery systems, as determined by the publisher's proprietary ranking formula. Listing each integrated system by size, the book offers evaluations based on business factors only; quality-of-care issues are not addressed in this directory or body of research.

Systems are ranked on a formula that includes revenue data, number of covered lives, number of provider arrangements, number of inpatient admissions and outpatient visits, number of beds, and number of physicians. The editors then assigned to each system a degree of integration code to denote how far along each system is in the integration process. The codes range from 1 to 5, with 1 indicating a barely integrated system and 5 indicating a fully integrated system.

Rich in charts, graphs, and tables, the book also contains a detailed introduction, a chapter on evaluating the financial performance of integrated delivery systems through the use of economic value-added analysis, a chapter on vendors and integrated delivery systems, and a variety of helpful indices and appendices. This is an excellent, up-to-date resource.

Latham Williams. "Integration Options." *Journal of Health and Hospital Law,* 1996, *29,* 88.

Reviews three models of integration: (1) management service organizations, (2) managed care joint ventures (including physician-hospital organizations), and (3) integrated delivery systems. For each model, the author, an attorney in private practice, examines choice of entity and governance issues; operations matters; tax considerations; political challenges; and a range of general legal considerations, including antitrust issues, Stark law compliance, and other matters. The article is supplemented by a three-page checklist of negotiating considerations and endnotes.

4.03   COMMON LEGAL ISSUES

American Health Lawyers Association. *A Loose-Leaf Guide to Mergers and Acquisitions: Contract Provisions and Transactional Models.* Washington, D.C.: American Health Lawyers Association, 1997.

This binder of approximately 450 pages supplies a variety of alternatives for documents and model arrangements. Like others in AHLA's loose-leaf series, this manual is designed to provide analysis of contractual language and specific provisions and practical negotiating strategies. It is written by about a dozen veteran health care attorneys. Topics include fundamental transactional considerations, limited liability companies, joint operating agreements, lease agreements, acquiring and merging IPAs, affiliations and acquisitions by physician practice management organizations, employee stock ownership plans, conversions of nonprofit organizations, affiliation agreements between nonprofits, and joint ventures between tax-exempt and proprietary organizations. Contractual language is also available on 3.5" PC–formatted disk.

Stephen W. Bernstein. "Complex Corporate Structures." In Mark A. Hall and William S. Brewbaker III (eds.), *Health Care Corporate Law: Facilities and Transactions.* Boston: Little, Brown, 1996.

Examines creation and operation of three of the most significant types of complex hospital corporate structure: (1) the "parent holding company" model of hospital ownership, (2) the "multi-facility chain," and (3) the shared service or group purchasing organization. For most of this century, hospitals were operated as single nonprofit organizations or perhaps as public corporations. As health care delivery has become more complex, however, so have the corporate structures of health care institutions. Complex corporate structures can sometimes help hospitals operate more efficiently, avoid regulation, increase reimbursement, and establish vital alliances with other health care providers.

This 103-page chapter, written by an attorney at Ropes and Gray in Boston, concludes with appendices setting forth a sample form plan of hospital reorganization, along with hospital bylaws providing for specific allocation of decision-making responsibilities between hospital and parent.

Andrew J. Demetriou. "Nonprofit–Nonprofit Affiliations." Washington, D.C.: American Health Lawyers Association [Report No. VMA 98–0005], 1998, 35 pages.

Outlines the key issues that arise in nonprofit affiliations, including strategic considerations, basic affiliation structures, governance options, Medicare certification and reimbursement consequences of corporate transactions, and drafting considerations. Attachments include diagrams of a joint operating company model, a revenue-sharing model, a confederation model, and a centralized model.

Christopher J. Evans, F. Gene DePorter, and Robert L. Wilson, Jr. *Integrated Community Healthcare: Next Generation Strategies for Developing Provider Networks.* Westchester, Ill.: Healthcare Financial Management Association, 1997.

Sets forth strategies for managing an IDS, whether a hospital, HMO, or physician organization. This manual of approximately three hundred pages also includes a detailed review of the legal and regulatory issues in the formation and operation of an IDS.

R. Todd Greenwalt. "Due Diligence and Closing Issues in Healthcare Transactions." Washington, D.C.: American Health Lawyers Association [Report No. TX97–0028], 1997, 26 pages.

Outlines the due diligence and closing process, including sample due diligence checklists.

James L. Hall Jr., Teresa A. Williams, and Eric S. Fisher. "Critically Important/Often Overlooked Provisions of a Definitive Agreement." Washington, D.C.: American Health Lawyers Association [Report No. VMA 98–0026], 1998, 95 pages.

Evaluates and compares the standard provisions of definitive written agreements. This seminar manuscript also identifies and analyzes the pitfalls and problems that practicing attorneys face when drafting definitive agreements. It contains several sample contractual provisions to illustrate the discussions, including a memorandum of understanding, a membership substitution agreement, a checklist of due diligence documents, and a sample legal opinion letter.

William W. Horton. "Big Deals: Stock Purchases, Mergers and Other Complex Corporate Transactions." Washington, D.C.: American Health Lawyers Association [Report No. VMA 98–0003], 1998, 46 pages.

Discusses the issues that arise in the context of negotiating, structuring, and documenting acquisitions involving larger companies and divisions encompassing operations in multiple locations and lines of business, with a particular emphasis on transactions involving public companies. This seminar manuscript lists and defines terms commonly used in acquisition transactions. It also includes a sample form of a confidentiality agreement and a form of exclusive agreement.

Hal S. Katz. "Physician Managed Care Contracting." Washington, D.C.: American Health Lawyers Association [Report No. VMC98–0015], 1998, 37 pages.

Outlines strategies for negotiating fee-for-service and risk-sharing managed care contracts, focusing on the various clauses that are required by law for accreditation purposes and for a successful business relationship.

Susan Smith Makos. "State Review of Merger and Acquisition Transactions." Washington, D.C.: American Health Lawyers Association [Report No. VMA 98–0028], 1998, 63 pages.

Reviews the state law implications of nonprofit-to-for-profit conversions and examines particular transactions. It also addresses the standards of care of trustees, the role of state attorneys general, and recent legislative initiatives enhancing state review requirements.

Marc S. Margulis. "Fairness Opinions." Washington, D.C.: American Health Lawyers Association [Report No. VMA 98–10012], 1998, 18 pages.

Highlights the role of fairness opinions in transactions, the fiduciary duties of the board of directors to the company and its shareholders, the role and duties of the opinion provider, and issues raised by judicial decisions. This seminar manuscript includes diagrams of value levels and the valuation implications of various business combinations.

Elizabeth M. Mills. "Fairness Opinions." Washington, D.C.: American Health Lawyers Association [Report No. VMA 98–0013], 1998, 11 pages.

Analyzes the role of fairness opinions in transactions and the roles and duties of the opinion provider. Mills also addresses current issues and controversies raised in judicial decisions, including state statutes regulating conversion of nonprofit hospitals to for-profit entities.

Mark G. Mishek. "Legal Issues in Operating a Vertical and Horizontal Integrated Company." Washington, D.C.: American Health Lawyers Association [Report No. VMA 98–0004], 1998, 11 pages.

Uses the Alina Health System as an example to outline the legal challenges and solutions arising out of forming and operating a vertically and horizontally integrated health system.

Jerry R. Peters. "Legal Issues in Integrated Delivery Systems." In Peter R. Kongstvedt (ed.), *The Managed Health Care Handbook.* (4th ed.) Gaithersburg, Md.: Aspen, 2000.

This nineteen-page chapter addresses such topics as IDS models, governance, delegated board authority, advisory committees, conflict of interest policy, tax exemption and charitable benefit, physician compensation, practice acquisitions and valuations, Medicare and Medicaid provider numbers, antitrust law, independent contractor status, and covenants not to compete.

G. Scott Rayson. "Covenants Not to Compete in Healthcare Merger and Acquisition Transactions." Washington, D.C.: American Health Lawyers Association [Report No. VMA 98–0024], 1998, 36 pages.

Summarizes covenants not to compete in the context of hospital acquisitions, hospital joint ventures, physician practice acquisitions, and physician joint ventures of health care facilities. It contains sample contract provisions for a hospital acquisition covenant not to compete, a joint venture transaction covenant not to compete, a physician practice acquisition covenant not to compete, and a surgery center physician syndication.

Chris Rossman. "Merger, Affiliation and Acquisitions Due Diligence: Managing the Process." Washington, D.C.: American Health Lawyers Association [Report No. VHL98–0006], 1998, 17 pages.

Summarizes both substantive and procedural issues that arise in performing due diligence. Emphasizes interaction between the due diligence process and negotiation of definitive legal agreements. Offers practical advice for streamlining the due diligence process.

Bruce John Shih. *Health Care M&A 1999: How to Structure the Transaction.* New York: Practicing Law Institute, 1999, 949 pages.

This compilation of essays and legal documents examines a range of topics, including for-profit and nonprofit hospital mergers, economic issues in antitrust policy toward mergers, practical advice in obtaining and negotiating the terms and conditions for equity capital in representing management in start-up health care companies, structuring and documenting deal issues, advantages of purchasing hospitals out of Chapter 11 bankruptcy, prepackaged Chapter 11 bankruptcy as a vehicle for acquisition, and disposition of health-care related businesses. The book also includes relevant DHHS documents.

Timothy P. Terrell. "Hospital and Health Facility Integration." Washington, D.C.: American Health Lawyers Association [Report No. VAT98–0034], 1998, 25 pages.

Spotlights two scenarios—a hospital and health facility integration and a physician contracting and network formation—as a backdrop for discussion of basic ethics rules.

4.04   PARTICULAR NETWORK ISSUES

American Medical Association. *Physician Practice Management Companies: What You Need to Know.* Chicago: American Medical Association, 1997, 100 pages.

Designed to help physicians make informed decisions about working with physician practice management companies. As the health care market continues to consolidate, more and more physicians are considering selling their practices to physician practice management companies. Written from the physician's perspective, this practical volume provides an overview of the industry, weighs the opportunities and challenges, and offers support in identifying likely candidates.

Dean C. Coddington and Barbara J. Bendrick. *Integrated Health Care: Case Studies.* Englewood, Colo.: Center for Research in Ambulatory Health Care Administration, 1994, 216 pages.

Presents case studies offering in-depth information about how nine health care organizations have progressed toward becoming more integrated, each in its own distinctive fashion. Every one of the nine case studies in this text addresses economic integration, financial arrangements, major accomplishments, lessons learned, issues for the future, and conclusions. Among the practical observations repeatedly made by persons interviewed are that (1) small negotiating teams (no more than four persons per side) work most successfully; (2) it is important to tackle the difficult issue of leadership of the new organization early in negotiations; (3) negotiators should attempt to move as quickly as possible, employing an outside facilitator if necessary; (4) any informal agreements should always be documented; and (5) the health care organization should hire an integrated group administrator as soon as possible. The book is amply supplemented by a wealth of charts, maps, graphs, tables, and exhibits.

Paul R. DeMuro and Cathy Jackson Lerman. "Physician Practice Management Companies." Washington, D.C.: National Health Lawyers Association [Report No. VMA 98–0009], 1998, 100 pages.

Outlines in detail various PPM models and the provisions of a model management services agreement, a medical practice asset purchase agreement, and a physician employment contract. This seminar manuscript also considers major business, financial, corporate, and legal considerations for PPMs.

Carl H. Hitchner and others. "Integrated Delivery Systems: A Survey of Organizational Models." *Wake Forest Law Review*, 1994, 29, 273.

Broadly examines various integrated delivery systems. Beginning with basic models, the authors explore the legal issues that arise in each system. As the models conceptually evolve, new and sometimes unique legal problems arise. Hitchner and his colleagues—all practicing attorneys—discuss several such problems, including fraud and abuse, tax exemption, licensing, and the corporate practice of medicine; they guide the reader through the evolution of integrated delivery systems, concluding with an outline of one of the most complex, the staff (or group) model HMO.

Thomas M. Susman and Timothy M. McCrystal. "Mergers, Acquisitions and Affiliations." In Mark A. Hall and William S. Brewbaker III (eds.), *Health Care Corporate Law: Facilities and Transactions.* Boston: Little, Brown, 1996.

Begins with a discussion of the principal advantages and disadvantages of each model of collaboration. This chapter reviews key issues often considered when selecting a partner and briefly outlines a proposed transaction structure for implementing a provider combination. It then addresses the major legal issues raised by health care provider combinations, concentrating in particular on the various antitrust and corporate law issues that typically arise in the context of a health care provider merger, acquisition, or affiliation transaction.

4.04(1)　Acquisition of Physician Practices

American Health Lawyers Association. *Critical Steps in Managed Care Contracting: A Loose-Leaf Guide.* Washington, D.C.: National Health Lawyers Association, 1994.

Provides guidance on a range of managed care topics. This manual, written by about a dozen veteran health care attorneys, covers such subjects as negotiating provider agreements, PHO and super-PHO organizational documents, payer-based agreements, government contracts in managed care, IDS implementing agreements, capitation and risk-sharing agreements, antitrust analysis of multiprovider and multipayer contracts, and managed care alternative-site provider agreements.

David W. Ball. "Hospital Acquisitions of Physician Practices." Washington, D.C.: American Health Lawyers Association [Report No. TX97–0006], 1997, 35 pages.

Analyzes (from the physician's perspective) options and considerations involved in counseling physicians considering a sale to a hospital system, typical issues that arise in negotiations, and the range of issues that physician counsel must consider in ensuring that the transaction is properly documented and complete.

Neil Baum, M.D., and Elaine Zablocki. *Take Charge of Your Medical Practice.* Gaithersburg, Md.: Aspen, 1996, 224 pages.

A practical hardcover volume written primarily for physicians, medical directors, group practice managers, and physician executives, this guide offers methods that will assist doctors in negotiating contracts.

California Medical Association. *Buying and Selling a Medical Practice.* (3rd ed.) San Francisco: California Medical Association, 1995, 96 pages.

Provides a discussion of such issues as valuation, handling medical records, and elements of the practice sale agreement.

Richard G. Cowart. "Physician Group Deals." Washington, D.C. American Health Lawyers Association [Report No. VMAT98–0007], 1998, 101 pages.

Outlines recent developments in the physician practice management company marketplace, in addition to state regulatory issues and accounting and tax matters relating to this industry. Examines the unwinding or restructuring of a physician management service agreement and the restructuring of tax exempt integrated delivery systems. Also provides the final order of the Florida Board of Medicine for *In re Petition for Declaratory Statement of Magan L. Bakarania, M.D.* (ruling that a management fee based on a percentage of a physician's net income, which was paid to a PPMC in return for referrals that the PPMC helped to generate, violates Florida's fee-splitting statute), and the final report of the Financial Accounting Standards Board Emerging Issues Task Force on Issue No 97–2, "The Application of Financial Accounting Standards Board Statement No 94, *Consolidation of All Majority Owned Subsidiaries,* and APB Opinion No. 16, *Business Combinations,* to Physician Practice Management Entities and Certain Other Entities with Contractual Management Arrangements."

Anthea R. Daniels. "Making Physician Transactions Viable." Washington, D.C.: American Health Lawyers Association [Report No. VMA 98–0021], 1998, 50 pages.

Examines key legal and business issues that arise when a hospital, an integrated delivery system, a physician group, or any type of health care entity decides to acquire a physician's practice. This seminar manuscript addresses how to make physician transactions viable from a legal and operational standpoint. It also discusses due diligence in order to know what is being acquired, staffing, billing and compensation issues, and closing and postclosing issues. It concludes with sample contract terms in the stock or asset purchase agreement.

Thomas J. Danzi (ed.). *Positioning Your Practice for the Managed Care Market.* Chicago: American Medical Association, 1997, 328 pages.

Describes the types of reimbursement and successful contracting strategies. Legal implications are included as well as an excellent section focusing on the financial assessment of a physician's practice.

Kenneth M. Heckman. *Buying, Selling and Merging a Medical Practice*. Englewood, Colo.: Medical Group Management Association, 1996, 194 pages.

Covers such topics as valuation of tangibles and intangibles, negotiations, tax considerations, and the diligence process. Written by a medical management consultant, this book contains appendices with relevant IRS revenue rulings and present value tables.

John R. Holdenreid. "Acquisition and Valuation of Physician Practices." Washington, D.C.: American Health Lawyers Association [Report No. TY97–0006], 1997, 43 pages.

Reviews valuation issues and resolution of tax, contract, and legal issues. Discusses major legal risks, acquisition models, antikickback issues, physician compensation, for-profit professional corporations, asset allocation, and conflicts-of-interest policies.

John R. Holdenreid. "Tax Planning in Physician Practice Transactions." Washington, D.C.: American Health Lawyers Association [Report No. VMA 98–0011], 1998, 45 pages.

Addresses tax issues in physician practice acquisitions from the standpoint of the hospital buyer and the physician seller. This seminar manuscript emphasizes valuation issues and resolution of tax, contract, and legal issues. It discusses major legal risks, acquisition models, antikickback issues, physician compensation, for-profit professional corporations, asset allocation, and conflicts-of-interest policies.

John R. Holdenreid. "Fair Market Value—What's Fair?" Washington, D.C.: American Health Lawyers Association [Report No.VTX98–0024], 1998, 39 pages.

Describes the major legal risks for providers in establishing that relationships are at fair market value under IRS, OIG, and HCFA standards, and applies these standards to specific transactions (leases, practice acquisitions, medical director services, physician support services, employment). Also provides suggestions for documentation of fair market value.

Bruce G. Krider. *Valuation of Physician Practices and Clinics*. Gaithersburg, Md.: Aspen, 1997, 200 pages.

Suggests the best methods of determining the correct value when considering selling or buying a particular practice.

4.04(2)   Types of Acquisition

Catholic Health Association. *A Workbook on Long Term Care in Integrated Delivery*. St. Louis: Catholic Health Association, 1995, 97 pages.

Provides Catholic and other not-for-profit health care leaders with thoughts on how to shape the movement toward integrated delivery rather than be shaped by it.

Paul R. DeMuro. "Complex Corporate Transactions." Washington, D.C.: American Health Lawyers Association [Report No.VMAT98–0004], 1998, 32 pages.

Addresses initial considerations and steps in complex corporate transactions, including use of transaction counsel; deal structure considerations; auctions; predefinitive document agreements; letters of intent, term sheets, and expressions of intent; exclusivity agreements; and due diligence. Also discusses transactional structure issues for mergers, stock purchases, and asset acquisitions; drafting and negotiating the agreements; representations and warranties; covenants; and directors' duties. Briefly discusses SEC, antitrust, and other regulatory issues; special considerations (such as acquisition of a division, physician practice management companies, and venture capital-backed enterprises); and coordination of work and players in the transaction.

Keith M. Korenchuk. *Series on Integration Document Design and Analysis: Medical Division/ Hospital Employment.* Englewood, Colo.: Medical Group Management Association, 1994, 179 pages.

Offers physicians, hospitals, and other health care organizations the critical information (including legal forms) necessary to evaluate, negotiate, and implement successful employed relationships with each other. Each day, physicians are making decisions regarding how, where, and under whose direction they will provide health care services to their patients. One of the more popular arrangements physicians are choosing is an employment model relationship with a hospital, large group practice, or publicly held parent organization. For many physicians, there has been a lack of information available to assist them through the decision-making process, including choosing a partner, reviewing the governance structure and operational systems, and valuing their practices for buyout. Highly recommended.

Keith M. Korenchuk. *Series on Integration Document Design and Analysis: Merging Medical Practices.* Englewood, Colo.: Medical Group Management Association, 1994, 147 pages.

Consists of forms useful to the health care attorney. Chapter One is particularly valuable reading for the principals of any entity contemplating a merger. It provides necessary thought processes and frameworks for any contemplated merger. The importance of the discussion pertaining to group culture and strategic plan cannot be overemphasized. A highly practical resource.

Keith M. Korenchuk. *Series on Integration Document Design and Analysis: Physician Equity Model.* Englewood, Colo.: Medical Group Management Association, 1994, 229 pages.

Consists of contract forms, interpretation, and commentary. One option being considered by many group practices and physicians is to create a new group practice jointly owned by physicians and a capital partner. This model has many names but is described in this book as the "physician equity model." In this model, physicians in group practice contribute the entire practice, including both hard assets and intangible value such as goodwill, to the new group practice. The new group practice also receives a capital contribution from the partner, which may be a hospital, health plan, venture capital organization, or physician management company. This capital partner contributes an amount that combines with the equity contribution of the physicians to the new organization.

Susan S. Makos. "Affiliation Agreements Between Nonprofits." Washington, D.C.: American Health Lawyers Association [Report No. VMAT98–0009], 1998, 19 pages.

Outlines legal considerations in nonprofit M&A transactions (mission, corporate, financing, and antitrust considerations), identifies nonprofit M&A structures, and lists key points for affiliation agreements between nonprofits.

Robert J. Moses and Neil F. Castaldo. "Health Plan Acquisitions and Spin-Offs." Washington, D.C.: National Health Lawyers Association [Report No. VMA 98–0014], 1998, 58 pages.

Discusses specific issues relating to acquisitions and spin-offs of health plans (particularly HMOs). This seminar manuscript focuses on factors influencing the decision to go forward—that is, the business risks and opportunities, as well as the legal exposure associated with the business of operating a health plan in the context of an acquisition or spin-off. It contains examples of contract language and also discusses the regulatory approval process.

4.04(3)   Structuring Payment

[Reserved]

4.04(4)   The Management Service Organization (MSO) Model

Keith M. Korenchuk. *Series on Integration Document Design and Analysis: Management Service Organizations.* Englewood, Colo.: Medical Group Management Association, 1994, 164 pages.

Designed to provide the depth of understanding necessary to comprehend the transformation of medical groups, hospitals, and physicians into complex, integrated organizations. Each monograph in the series contains sample legal documents that are necessary to form these relationships. By understanding these sample documents and the framework in which they are used, the parties can achieve a more collaborative effort. With this basic understanding, it will be possible to negotiate from a more knowledgeable perspective. The author hopes that this wider knowledge base will result in a fairer relationship among physicians, hospitals, and other parties. Highly practical in nature, this series of books provides lengthy sample contract language, followed by interpretation and commentary. This volume is an excellent resource that will be highly useful to any practicing health care attorney, administrator or physician/manager.

Bruce John Shih, Daniel K. Settelmayer, and L. Susan McGinnis. "Friendly Professional Corporations Complying with the Corporate Practice of Medicine Prohibition." *California Health Law News,* Spring 1998, *18*(1).

To avoid direct confrontation with the corporate practice of medicine prohibition, physician practice management companies and management service organizations often use an affiliated, captive, or "friendly" professional corporation as a vehicle to integrate the professional component of medical practices with the PPMC or MSO. This arrangement requires physicians who are friendly with the PPMC to establish, own, and control a professional corporation and to take direction from the PPMC or MSO as to certain of the operations of the professional corporation. As friendly shareholders of the professional corporation, the physicians align themselves with the PPMC/MSO, a lay entity, to effect its practical control to varying degrees over the medical enterprise.

This article explores the use of a friendly professional corporation under the corporate-practice-of-medicine prohibition. To determine the vulnerability of a friendly professional corporation model in California or another state that prohibits the corporate practice of medicine, two questions must be answered: How much authority needs to be delegated to make the friendly professional corporation relationship work from the PPMC or MSO perspective? Is such delegation of authority permitted under the corporate-practice-of-medicine prohibition? To answer these questions, the article analyzes (1) the genesis of friendly professional corporations, (2) the variety of mechanisms employed to maintain the friendly professional corporation's affiliation with the PPMC/MSO, and (3) the tensions involved in developing a friendly professional corporation model that complies with the restrictions imposed by the prohibition.

4.04(5)   The Physician Hospital Organization (PHO)

American Medical Association. *A Guide to Forming Physician-Directed Managed Care Networks.* Chicago: American Medical Association, 1997, 56 pages.

Written for physicians interested in exploring the formation of physician-directed managed care networks. This practical softbound book includes charts, graphs, and a resource list for capital-funding programs.

American Medical Association. *Implementing a Physician Organization.* Chicago: American Medical Association, 1997, 90 pages.

Offers a step-by-step guide to implementing physician organizations. Case studies are provided to show how the principles discussed can be applied in practice. Topics include organizational and human resource management, financial systems, selecting and implementing management information systems, and marketing.

Jerry A. Bell, Jr. "Hospital Affiliated Physician Organizations." Washington, D.C.: American Health Lawyers Association [Report No. VHH99–0017], 1999, 37 pages.

Discusses and analyzes hospital-affiliated physician organizations, including possible corporate organizational structures and key legal and business issues, such as those related to hospital-physician employment agreements and to managed care contracts.

Jerry A. Bell, Jr. "Issues Relating to Hospital Affiliated Physician Organizations." Washington, D.C. American Health Lawyers Association [Report No VHL98–0008], 1998, 14 pages.

Discusses corporate organizational models and structures, capitalization and financial issues, conflict of interest, governance, hospital-physician employment agreements, and managed care contracting issues.

Donald H. Caldwell, Jr. "Options for Structuring a Medical Practice." In Carl Horn III, Donald H. Caldwell, Jr., and D. Christopher Osborn, *Law for Physicians: An Overview of Medical Legal Issues.* Chicago: American Medical Association, 1999, 246 pages.

Discusses various physician-hospital organization models and their advantages and disadvantages, primarily from the point of view of the physician.

Paul R. DeMuro. "Physician Group Practice Formation." Washington, D.C.: American Health Lawyers Association [Report No VHL98–0009], 1998, 28 pages.

Discusses the different types of physician group, including independent practice associations, clinics without walls, integrated medical groups, and physician practice management companies. Addresses the alternatives and processes for group formation and forms of consolidation, along with governance alternatives. Also examines preliminary tax, compensation, valuation, and pension issues. Includes an outline of key terms in physician practice asset acquisitions.

Terry A. Jacobs and Phillip G. Royalty. "Taxation of Managed Care Plans." In Peter R. Kongstvedt (ed.), *The Managed Health Care Handbook.* (4th ed.) Gaithersburg, Md.: Aspen, 2000.

Presents a general discussion of the tax treatment of managed care plans. It begins with the tax treatment of HMOs before turning to the treatment of other types of managed care organization. The authors conclude that taxation of managed care plans is currently in a state of change. Tax-exemption requirements vary depending on the type of plan involved and are frequently revised and updated by the IRS. Furthermore, careful analysis of the plan's activities is required to determine whether the plan qualifies as an insurance company for tax purposes.

Jennings Ryan & Kolb, Inc. *Developing a Successful Physician-Hospital Organization.* (Peter F. Straley, ed.) Chicago: American Hospital Publishing, 1995.

A reference guide for managers and medical staff seeking to form a PHO. Physician-hospital organizations have existed for years but were often inactive and ineffective, created reactively (by design or inadvertence) to ward off managed care and to maintain the status quo. More recently, however, PHOs have been formed in response to fundamental changes in the health care marketplace. The first three chapters provide an overview of the PHO formation process and include a timetable and a means of assessing local market readiness to determine whether and how a PHO can help the hospital and physicians compete for health care funds in a managed care environment. Chapters Four through Nine present specific business, legal, and tax issues a task force must address, including perhaps the most ticklish of all: how physicians should be credentialed for the PHO provider panel and who can be excluded from membership.

This book was specifically written as a how-to manual. Consistent with this approach, the authors have included four appendices that summarize the Health Plan Employer Data and Information Set (HEDIS) 2.0, a sample request proposal, an example of a PHO application, and examples of addenda to a participating physician agreement. The text is richly supplemented with thirty-one diagrams and tables. Highly recommended.

David A. Kindig and Anthony R. Kovner (eds.). *The Role of the Physician Executive: Cases and Commentary.* Chicago: Health Administration Press, 1992.

Consists of nineteen case studies involving physician-managers. The cases are organized into five parts: emerging roles, control, organizational design, adaptation, and accountability.

Keith M. Korenchuk. *Series on Integration Document Design and Analysis: Physician-Hospital Organizations.* Englewood, Colo.: Medical Group Management Association, 1994, 206 pages.

Offers information and legal forms pertaining to formation of a PHO, a relative newcomer in the taxonomy of integrated delivery system models. PHO formation offers an opportunity to enter a highly competitive medical market with a minimum of risk and, because of the simplicity of a PHO, relatively quickly. For those physicians in medical groups, this more loosely formed organization allows significant autonomy. Physicians who prefer to control their own destiny find the PHO an ideal means to participate in the managed care landscape. This book and its accompanying legal forms are highly useful.

4.04(6) Foundation Models

[Reserved]

4.04(7) Capitation Issues

American Medical Association. *Capitation: The Physician's Guide.* Chicago: American Medical Association, 1995.

Discusses the essential features of capitated medical service payment arrangements. Written primarily for doctors seeking to learn how to negotiate better contracts and evaluate rates, to identify when an expert is needed, to isolate potential sources of risk, to understand the overall impact on Medicare and specialty procedures under capitation, and so on.

American Medical Association. *Physician Capitation Strategies.* Chicago: American Medical Association, 1997.

Based on real-life case studies, this work includes more than one hundred pages of physician case scenarios. Topics include transitioning to capitation, operational issues under capitation, special capitation issues, and specific medical specialties under capitation.

Catholic Health Association. *A Workbook on Understanding Capitation.* St. Louis: Catholic Health Association, 1994, 150 pages.

Presents practical and ethical guidelines for using a capitated payment system to transform health care delivery.

Andrew J. Demetriou. "Negotiating Capitation Contracts: Key Terms in Capitation Contracts." Washington, D.C.: American Health Lawyers Association [Report No. VMC98–0001], 1998, 23 pages.

Describes the legal and contractual issues that recur in negotiating capitation agreements and other managed care contracts, such as scope of services, payment methodologies, and risk pool arrangements.

Clark C. Havighurst. "Contract Failure in the Market for Health Services." *Wake Forest Law Review*, 1994, *29*, 47–70.

Argues that the market fails to offer consumers a full range of health care choices, particularly low-cost options. Here, Havighurst makes the novel claim that overspending on health care is attributable to the failure of private contracts to specify the precise character and scope of the health care services to be provided and the particular rights and obligations of the various parties to the transaction. This contract failure, he contends, is in large part the fault of a legal system that has effectively displaced private contract as the ultimate source of entitlements and rights. He argues for making an expanded role for contracts a cornerstone of health care reform.

St. Anthony's Capitation Reference Manual. Reston, Va.: St. Anthony, 1997.

This manual consists of hundreds of pages of sample capitation contracts and rate methodologies from a variety of health plans, health systems, and physician groups.

St. Anthony's Medicare Risk Contracting Manual. Reston, Va.: St. Anthony, 1997.

This manual presents Medicare risk contracts, per-member-per-month (PMPM) rate methodologies, real-life case studies, innovative approaches to common problems in Medicare risk contracting, and Medicare's official rules and regulations for risk contracting. Includes reference manual, monthly newsletter, and data file and rate-finding software.

4.04(8) Medical Practice Mergers

Irwin Birnbaum and others. *Health Care M&A: How to Structure the Transaction.* New York: Practising Law Institute, 1997, 384 pages.

Topics discussed in this collection of seminar materials include limited liability company issues, due diligence, transactions to convert nonprofit health care assets to for-profit status, antitrust, quality-of-care issues, and taking physician practice management companies public.

Richard G. Cowart. "Physician Mergers." Washington, D.C.: American Health Lawyers Association [Report No. VAT98–00017], 1998, 18 pages.

A summary of lessons learned from a federal district court decision declining to block the merger, challenged by a competitor, of the only two multispecialty hospitals in the Vicksburg, Mississippi, area in *HTI Health Servs.* v. *Quorum Health Group Inc.* (S.D. Miss. 1997), including the role of the U.S. Justice Department, plaintiff's antitrust standing, injunctive relief standards, and claims under the Sherman Act and the Clayton Act.

Thomas S. Crane. "Fraud and Abuse in Mergers and Acquisitions." Washington, D.C.: American Health Lawyers Association [Report No. VMM99–0030], 1999, 27 pages.

Reviews the significant fraud and abuse issues that arise in M&A, including transfer of ownership, successor liability, upstream liability, the law and the reality of deep pockets, regulatory due diligence, representations and warranties, securities law opinions, issues in valuing assets, and preclosing and postclosing identification of wrongdoing.

Paul R. DeMuro and Irwin Birnbaum (eds.). *Health Care M&A: Commercialization of the Medical Industry.* New York: Practising Law Institute, 1996, 841 pages.

Specific topics discussed include tax issues; Medicare and Medicaid fraud and abuse; antitrust issues relating to mergers, acquisitions, and networks in the health care industry; FTC antitrust actions; nursing home acquisitions; acquisition of ambulatory surgery centers or occupational medicine companies; and due diligence.

David W. Hilgers. "Acquisitions, Divestitures and LBOs of Physician Groups." Washington, D.C.: American Health Lawyers Association [Report No. VMA 98–0002], 1998, 31 pages.

Discusses some of the methods by which physician organizations seek to maintain and preserve their independence while developing effective organizations to deliver more efficient care that is competitive with the larger nonphysician-owned organizations. This seminar manuscript also examines efforts to reconstruct ownership of some of the failed consolidated organizations owned by hospitals and others.

William W. Horton. "Basic Mergers and Acquisitions." Washington, D.C.: American Health Lawyers Association [Report No. VMAT98–0001], 1998, 38 pages.

Outlines the basic types of acquisition structure and discusses issues and strategies in negotiating acquisitions from the buyer's and seller's perspectives. Includes sample contract provisions and related commentary.

Lloyd E. Oliver. "Economic Issues in Physician Mergers." Washington, D.C.: American Health Lawyers Association [Report No. VAT98–0018], 1998, 21 pages.

Analyzes the economic issues in physician merger matters, including product and geographic market definition, measurement and significance of market concentration, entry barriers, and likely competitive effects.

Bruce John Shih (ed.). *Health Care M&A: How to Structure the Transaction.* New York: Practising Law Institute, 1998, 1,296 pages.

Focuses on M&A activities and related topics. Specific topics discussed include hospital transactions, physician management companies, bankruptcy as a vehicle for acquisition and disposition of health care-related businesses, integrated delivery system development, OIG compliance, fraud and abuse control, and Stark I and II regulations.

Jeffrey M. Teske. "Physician Mergers." Washington, D.C.: American Health Lawyers Association [Report No. VAT98–0019], 1998, 8 pages.

Provides an overview of issues associated with physician mergers. Outlines an analytical framework for review under Justice Department and Federal Trade Commission merger guidelines, relevant case law, business review letters, and advisory opinions.

4.04(9)   Rural Hospital Networks

Michelle M. Casey, Anthony Wellever, and Ira Moscovice. "Rural Health Network Development: Public Policy Issues and State Initiatives." *Journal of Health Politics, Policy and Law,* 1997, *22,* 23.

Analyzes public policy issues related to integrated rural health network development, discusses current efforts to encourage network development in rural areas, and suggests actions that states may take if they desire to support rural health network development.

Rural health networks are a potential way for rural health care systems to improve access to care, reduce costs, and enhance quality of care. Networks provide a means for rural providers to contract with managed care organizations, develop their own managed care entities, share resources, and structure practice opportunities to support recruitment and retention of rural physicians and other health care professionals. The authors contend that the results of early network development initiatives indicate a need for state officials and others interested in encouraging network development to agree on common rural health network definitions, identify clearly the goals of network development programs, and document and analyze program outcomes. Future network development efforts need to be much more comprehensive if they are to have a significant impact on rural health care.

The suggested actions for states include adopting a formal rural health network definition; providing networks with alternatives to certain regulatory requirements; and providing such incentives as matching grants, loans, or technical assistance. Without public sector support for networks, managed care options may continue to be unavailable in many less densely populated rural areas of the country, and locally controlled rural health networks are unlikely to develop as an alternative to the dominant pattern of managed care expansion by large urban entities. Implementation of Medicare reform legislation could provide significant incentives for developing rural health networks, depending on the reimbursement provisions, financial solvency standards, and antitrust exemptions for provider-sponsored networks in the final legislation and federal regulations.

Arnold D. Kaluzny, Howard S. Zuckerman, and Thomas C. Ricketts III. *Partners for the Dance: Forming Strategic Alliances in Health Care.* Chicago: Health Care Administration Press, 1995, 235 pages.

Consists of a series of papers presented to the National Invitational Conference on Strategic Alliances in Chapel Hill, North Carolina, held Nov. 11–12, 1993. Topics include a discussion of the Charlotte-Mecklenburg Hospital Authority by its CEO, Harry A. Nurkin; alliances among rural hospital networks; and strategic alliances as a structure for integrated delivery systems.

Tracey M. Orloff and Barbara Tymann. *Rural Health: An Evolving System of Accessible Services.* Washington, D.C.: National Governors' Association, 1996, 293 pages.

Profiles state strategies designed to improve rural health access and delivery. Two case studies examine initiatives in West Virginia and Minnesota and describe how these states developed and implemented their rural health goals.

Bruce J. Toppin. "Direct Provider Contracting for Rural Healthcare Providers." Washington, D.C.: American Health Lawyers Association [Report No. VMC98–0027], 1998, 15 pages.

Outlines the challenges that rural health care providers face in direct contracting with employers, using Health Link, the North Mississippi-area PPO health care system, as an example. Reviews the rural health care provider exceptions from the Stark Law and the antikickback "safe harbor." Also examines issues involving antitrust law, insurance regulation, third-party administration licensure activities, utilization review agents, credentialing and deselection, ERISA, telephone triage, and contracts.

4.04(10)   Freestanding Outpatient Facilities and Services

J. Reginald Hill and Howard T. Wall III. "Freestanding Outpatient Facilities and Services." In Mark A. Hall and William S. Brewbaker III (eds.), *Health Care Corporate Law: Facilities and Transactions.* Boston: Little, Brown, 1996.

Discusses the operational and legal issues arising in connection with four types of freestanding outpatient facility and service: freestanding emergency or urgent care centers, diagnostic imaging centers, ambulatory surgery centers, and home health agencies and hospices. The focus of this chapter is on such facilities operated separately from hospitals. Topics discussed include corporate, tax, and financing issues; management issues; limitations on physician investment and referral incentives; certificates of need; licensing requirements; operational issues; and reimbursement.

4.04(11)   Joint Ventures

Jerry A. Bell, Jr. "Collaboration Without Integration: Non-Acquisition Strategies for Physician Alliances." Washington, D.C.: American Health Lawyers Association [Report No. VHL99–0004], 1999, 25 pages.

> Detailed outline analyzes the business and legal issues arising between hospitals and independent physician groups, including various legal relationships and arrangements. Discusses the problems of capitalization and funding of an affiliated physician organization by an exempt hospital, issues relating to managed care contracts, and key ancillary issues.

Robert J. Hill. "Governance Responsibilities and Ownership Rights in Health Care Joint Ventures." Washington, D.C.: National Health Lawyers Association [Report No. VMA 98–0015], 1998, 65 pages.

> Outlines some of the more significant issues associated with health care joint ventures, including various mechanisms used for governance of the venture and the ownership rights of the joint venture participants both during operation and upon occurrence of a deadlock. This seminar manuscript summarizes significant health care fraud and abuse provisions governing joint ventures, including fraud and abuse bailout provisions. Attachments include the OIG's Special Fraud Alert on Joint Venture Arrangements, OIG Advisory Opinion No. 97-5, and sample contractual provisions.

Mark J. Horoschak. "Physician Joint Ventures/Networks." Washington, D.C.: American Health Lawyers Association [Report No. VAT98–0014], 1998, 34 pages.

> Spotlights antitrust issues raised by physician networks and joint ventures, including the significance and sufficiency of economic integration, the doctrine of ancillary restraints, and the assessment of market power.

Douglas M. Mancino. "Joint Operating Agreements." Washington, D.C.: American Health Lawyers Association [Report No. TX97–0003], 1997, 20 pages.

> Outlines strategic reasons for selecting joint operating agreement (JOA) or joint operating company (JOC) approaches, which are often used as alternatives to more traditional integration forms. It examines basic structural approaches, fundamental tax principles affecting JOAs and JOCs, allocation of responsibilities between JOCs and operating companies, and a case study of IRS private letter rulings dealing with JOA and JOC affiliations.

Jean M. Mitchell and Elton Scott. "Evidence on Complex Structures of Physician Joint Ventures." *Yale Journal on Regulation*, 1992, 9, 489.

> Reviews the current debate and presents new empirical evidence based on a study of more than twenty-six hundred health care clinics in Florida. Physician ownership of health care facilities has become a controversial issue in the national debate over how to control rising health care costs. Proponents of physician ownership contend that investment by physicians in health care facilities broadens access to health care by increasing the financing available for such facilities. Critics of physician ownership contend that such ownership arrangements lead to higher prices for medical services and more frequent use of unnecessary medical procedures, without improving the quality of care.
>
> The evidence presented here indicates that physician investment in health care clinics is more widespread than previously believed. The evidence also indicates that physician investment tends to increase both the frequency of referrals to the clinics and the cost of the services provided by the clinics. In light of this evidence, the authors argue that current legislation that prohibits or restricts physician joint ventures is inadequate. They recommend that future legislation be strengthened to include stronger prohibitions and restrictions on indirect physician investment.

Jennifer Herndon Puryear. "The Physician as Entrepreneur: State and Federal Restrictions on Physician Joint Ventures." (Comment.) *North Carolina Law Review,* 1994, *73,* 293.

Examines physician ownership of facilities providing services such as magnetic resonance imaging (MRI) and clinical laboratory tests. Critics have feared that physicians who self-refer will, consciously or unconsciously, recommend more tests than are necessary. The author concludes that physician investment can benefit communities, especially rural ones, in which an insufficient number of outside investors can be found for needed facilities. Where there is little need for a facility, however, the evidence is strong to warrant restrictions on self-referral, particularly if the structure of a joint venture reveals a clear design to ensure a stream of referrals from physician-investors. This article also provides an overview of the Stark I and Stark II legislation of the early 1990s.

Joan Ragsdale. "Hospital and Medical Staff Joint Ventures." In Mark A. Hall and William S. Brewbaker III (eds.), *Health Care Corporate Law: Facilities and Transactions.* Boston: Little, Brown, 1996.

Maintains that despite sometimes formidable legal barriers, joint ventures remain an important tool for participants in the health care marketplace. The joint venture mechanism can no longer be used by health care businesses to induce referrals from physicians, but health care facilities (particularly hospitals) may find it advantageous to offer certain services in partnership with other providers, especially physicians. Topics discussed include common purposes of joint ventures, structural alternatives, contracting issues, referral fee and exemption laws, fraud, and abuse. Other issues analyzed include the Stark laws and their exceptions, tax exemption, and antitrust liability. Finally, the chapter includes a helpful checklist for specific joint venture arrangements, including outpatient facilities, real estate and equipment ventures, physician-hospital organizations, and management service organizations.

Latham Williams. "Structuring Managed Care Joint Ventures." *Healthcare Financial Management,* Aug. 1, 1995, p. 32.

Cautions that providers who undertake joint ventures to secure managed care contracts must understand the important governance, operational, legal, and political issues involved. Careful planning in all these areas, Williams writes, will ensure that the joint venture can meet its goals and avoid such problems as inappropriately negotiated contracts and legal violations.

4.04(12)   Unwinding Deals

Michael A. Cassidy. "Litigating PPMC/Physician Breakups." Washington, D.C.: American Health Lawyers Association [Report No. VPH99–0009], 1999, 25 pages.

Addresses the strategic planning and practical steps involved in terminating, breaching, or preparing for litigated issues involving physician practice management contracts. Discusses appropriately documenting the breach, observing notice requirements, protecting existing cash flow and accounts receivable, establishing new practice assignment accounts, and relating practical steps with the initial negotiating process and results. Also discusses the emerging theory and precedent asserting that volume-related physician practice management contracts are unenforceable because of their illegality.

Derek F. Covert and Alan S. Gassman. "The Honeymoon's Over: Divorcing, Separating or Restructuring the Troubled Physician Ownership Organization." Washington, D.C.: American Health Lawyers Association [Report No. VHL99–0028], 1999, 85 pages.

Detailed outline discusses the considerations of hospitals and health systems in negotiating the termination or restructuring of physician organization relationships. Attachments include a sample class action complaint for violations of the Securities and Exchange Act and a management agreement.

James R. Jones. "Tax Issues for Physician Disengagement." Washington, D.C.: American Health Lawyers Association [Report No. VPH99–0011], 1999, 11 pages.

Discusses federal tax considerations of disengagement by physicians from their relationship with a physician practice management company.

Daniel W. Krane and Carol G. Kroch. "Dis-integration: Disposing of Physician Practices and Unwinding Unprofitable Risk Deals." Washington, D.C.; American Health Lawyers Association [Report No.VTX98–0023], 1998, 63 pages.

Discusses tax, fraud and abuse, antitrust, charitable trust, and state insurance issues that are raised when a tax-exempt, nonprofit hospital unwinds a risk arrangement or sells a physician practice.

5

Utilization Review

Utilization review (UR) is a management technique whereby trained health care professionals evaluate the appropriateness, quality, and medical necessity of services provided to plan members. UR includes (1) prospective review, in which a proposed schedule of treatment—comprising patient care, discharge plans, policies, or procedures that specify how care will be provided—is evaluated; (2) concurrent review, in which routine medical procedures are monitored during the course of hospitalization or treatment to ensure that appropriate care is delivered; (3) retrospective review, in which audits of selected medical records help payers ensure that appropriate care was provided and billed; and (4) statistical utilization review, in which such claims data as pricing and utilization are analyzed to determine which providers offer the most efficient and cost-effective patient care.

Utilization review organizations (UROs) conduct these activities for managed care organizations. They determine whether a patient may be admitted to a medical facility, length of stay in the facility, and the provision of other health services. These organizations usually employ physicians part-time, often as consultants or advisers. Registered nurses are heavily involved in first-level decisions, but physicians become more involved during the second-level review and the appeals process. These organizations often use commercially developed review criteria when making their recommendations.[1]

Reference

1. Marianne F. Fazen. *Managed Care Desk Reference.* Reston, Va.: St. Anthony, 1996, p. 301.

ANNOTATIONS

5.01   IN GENERAL

American Accreditation Health Care Commission. *State Survey of Utilization Review Laws and Regulations.* Oct. 1998, 172 pages.

> This text contains the first state-by-state detailed comparison of UR laws and regulations. It outlines licensure and certification requirements for UR programs and provides trends and analysis on the UR industry.

American Accreditation Health Care Commission/URAC. *National Utilization Management Standards.* Washington, D.C.: American Accreditation Health Care Commission, June 1997.

> These standards for utilization review were developed and approved by the Utilization Review Accreditation Commission (URAC), which was established to encourage efficient and effective UR processes and to provide a method of evaluation and accreditation of utilization review programs.

The purpose of these standards is to encourage consistency in the procedures for interaction between UROs and providers, payers, and consumers of health care. The standards encourage consistency by establishing standards for the procedures used to certify health care services and to process appeals of UR determinations. The standards also promote consistency by providing an accreditation mechanism that can be applied nationwide for those states that choose to regulate URO activities. The standards govern such matters as confidentiality, staff qualifications, utilization management program qualifications, accessibility and on-site review procedures, information upon which UR is conducted, procedures for review determination, and appeals of determinations.

John Blum. "An Analysis of Legal Liability in Health Care Utilization Review and Case Management." *Houston Law Review,* 1989, *26,* 191.

Examines the legal liability involved in both utilization review and case management. Although government efforts in the UR area are briefly described, this article stresses liability in the context of private sector programs. The author's discussion of legal liabilities primarily concerns risks that are faced by corporate entities engaged in UR and case management. Also, the liability of individual professionals is of great importance. A large portion of this article is devoted to review of *Wickline* v. *California,* 138 Cal. App. 3d 1175, 228 Cal. Rptr. 661 (Cal. Ct. App. 1986).

Michael A. Dowell. "Avoiding HMO Liability for Utilization Review." *University of Toledo Law Review,* 1991, *23,* 117.

Describes the potential liability of HMOs for utilization review programs. If a doctor abstains from treatment because the HMO declines to pay for the treatment and the patient is harmed, the HMO may become the target of litigation. The author, a practicing attorney who specializes in representing HMOs, analyzes several recent cases and offers practical ideas for preventing and defending suits brought by HMOs for utilization review decisions. He notes that although no single action on the part of an HMO can effectively insulate it from liability related to utilization review, an HMO can significantly reduce its exposure to liability through prudent planning. The HMO must segregate utilization review, which is a financial reimbursement function, from the treatment or discharge decision, which is a clinical medical function made by attending physicians. Furthermore, all HMO utilization review determinations should clearly acknowledge that the physician is free to exercise his or her discretion whether to provide the proposed medical service to the member at the member's sole expense.

Peter Franks, Carolyn M. Clancy, and Paul A. Nutting. "Gatekeeping Revisited—Protecting Patients from Overtreatment." *New England Journal of Medicine,* 1992, *327,* 424–427.

Advances data supporting the role, albeit imperfectly realized, of the primary care physician as gatekeeper. The authors conclude that the gatekeeping activities of primary care physicians are critical to an optimal health care system and should be further developed to improve the health care of all patients.

Alice G. Gosfield. "Is Less Really More? Utilization Management in the 1990s." In Alice G. Gosfield (ed.), *Health Law Handbook.* Deerfield, Ill.: Clark, Boardman, Callaghan, 1996.

This article warns against the consequences of secrecy and gag orders on physicians, which only serve to undermine whatever valid arguments might be made about the intentionally different behavior MCOs seek to stimulate and provide.

Mark A. Hall and Gerard F. Anderson. "Health Insurers' Assessment of Medical Necessity." *University of Pennsylvania Law Review,* 1992, *140,* 1637.

Health insurance coverage disputes are subject to a complex interplay among courts, insurers, physicians, and patients. Out of deference to treating physicians, courts are refusing to respect the mechanism the parties have chosen to define the scope of coverage, forcing them to contract in ways they prefer not to, and even then refusing to enforce the provisions other courts have imposed. Two forms of market failure result: pricing purchasers out of the market altogether, or forcing them to buy more expensive insurance products than they desire. The authors propose a mechanism that they hope will resolve this impasse: to contract explicitly for a process of resolving disputes over medical appropriateness rather than to further define the substance of the criteria applied by the courts.

The authors do not assume that this process by itself can solve all the vexing allocation problems that confront our nation's policy makers. They also recognize that case-specific utilization review ultimately may not prove to be the most effective cost-containment tool. But the courts, they contend, are not the proper institution for deciding which type of managed care—utilization review, provider selectivity, financial incentives directed to patients and physicians, or a combination thereof—is best. The proper role of the courts is not to insert themselves into the center of this debate, but to stand on the sidelines to referee the processes that are followed, with an objective, nonresult-oriented view of what the parties have agreed to within prevailing ethical, social, and economic constraints.

Clark C. Havighurst. "Prospective Self-Denial: Can Consumers Contract Today to Accept Health Care Rationing Tomorrow?" *University of Pennsylvania Law Review,* 1992, *140,* 1755.

Explores whether "prospective self-denial"—that is, voluntary decisions by consumers to economize by accepting substantial restrictions on their freedom to draw upon a common fund for future medical needs—can be useful in rationalizing societal spending on health services. The article addresses practical questions having to do with writing and administering private contracts, legal questions concerning the enforceability of such contracts, and policy questions having to do with equity. An overriding question is whether the legal and political culture can tolerate such private economizing or would interfere with it so much that the only allocational mechanism remaining as a health policy option is explicit rationing by public authorities. At issue ultimately may be the long-run viability of a market-oriented health policy in the United States, because, the author contends, if consumers cannot effectively exercise choice concerning the level of their spending on health services, some public decision maker will have to step in and set priorities for them.

Paul J. Kenkel. *Report Cards: What Every Health Provider Needs to Know about HEDIS and Other Performance Measures.* Gaithersburg, Md.: Aspen, 1995, 182 pages.

Finds that because of widespread support by large private employers, HEDIS is likely to become the managed care industry standard for managing the performance of the nation's health plans. The author, an attorney, argues that the demands of preparing data for these report cards will cause providers to change the way they do business. Health care providers will have to ensure that they are able to collect and measure data accurately for performance measurement. This one-volume, loose-leaf resource, written primarily for providers, discusses the New England HEDIS coalition, Rush Prudential health plans, United Health Care Corporation, U.S. Healthcare, Kaiser Permanente, and Health Net, among others.

Eve A. Kerr and others. "Managed Care and Capitation in California: How Do Physicians at Financial Risk Control Their Own Utilization?" *Annals of Internal Medicine,* 1995, *123*(7), 500–504.

Examines the internally imposed utilization management techniques used by ninety-four physician groups in California, having the objective of describing the structure and range of utilization management methods initiated by physicians in response to capitation. This study concludes that physicians are responding to capitation by using utilization management techniques (some at early stages of development) that were previously used only by insurers. This physician-initiated management approach represents a fundamental transformation in the practice of medicine, the authors write.

Lawrence C. Kleinman and others. "Adherence to Prescribed Explicit Criteria During Utilization Review." *Journal of the American Medical Association,* Aug. 13, 1997, 497.

Investigates how well the UR process—which seeks to improve the quality and cost-efficiency of health care—works in practice. In this study, four medical school professors reviewed a retrospective analysis of transcripts of precertification reviews. The reviewers recommended 78 percent of cases for surgery, of which only 29 percent were supported by the criteria or had extenuating circumstances. The authors conclude that physician reviewers were more lenient than the explicit criteria that the reviews were designed to implement. In no cases did the reviewers depart from the criteria's recommendations in favor of surgery. These data, the authors write, may be sobering to those who anticipate rapid reduction in health care costs through implementing criteria to eliminate inappropriate care.

James W. Lytle. *Investigational and Experimental Treatments: An Overview of the Legal, Litigation and Legislative Issues.* Washington, D.C.: American Health Lawyers Association [Report No. VMC98–0005], 1998, 21 pages.

Outlines the legal, litigation, and legislative issues related to investigational and experimental treatments. For years, insurers have sought to exclude coverage for treatments regarded as unknown, dangerous, or useless. Looks at case law governing coverage disputes and explores approaches taken by state legislatures to resolve coverage issues.

Vernellia R. Randall. "Managed Care, Utilization Review, and Financial Risk Shifting: Compensating Patients for Health Care Cost Containment Injuries." *University of Puget Sound Law Review,* 1993, *17,* 1.

Focuses on the relationship of third-party payers to the delivery of health care. Randall begins her analysis by noting that third-party payers have not been held liable in the past for the actions of health care providers. This standard was developed because no contractual relationship existed between the third-party payers and the health care providers. Now, she observes, third-party payers have contractual relationships with health care providers that require the doctor to act as an agent for the third-party payer. These new contractual relationships obligate providers to supply care within the guidelines of managed care products. Thus, third-party payers, not providers, set the standard for care. Yet when patients are injured because of the standard of care, the third-party payers are insulated from liability by ERISA. The author concludes by calling for creation of a medical injury compensation fund to eliminate the risk of uncompensated medical injuries.

Cynthia Ransburg-Brown. "The Ultimate Jigsaw Puzzle: ERISA Preemption and Liability in the Utilization Review Process." (Comment.) *Cumberland Law Review,* 1998, *28,* 403.

This article explores ERISA preemption, the utilization review process as a cost control device, and the conflict between the purposes of each doctrine. It begins by discussing utilization review and its unique liability problems as a cost-containment device. It then reviews the congressional intent underlying ERISA's primarily purpose: "to protect the interests of participants in employee benefit [programs]." It then examines ERISA's preemption clause, congressional intent in enacting the clause, and the Supreme Court's interpretation of ERISA preemption. Next, the article discusses ERISA preemption and its application in several recent cases involving utilization review and the resulting split in state and federal authorities. Finally, the author proposes a balancing test for ERISA preemption problems and offers suggestions for congressional revision of the ERISA statute.

Marc A. Rodwin. "Conflicts in Managed Care." *New England Journal of Medicine,* Mar. 2, 1995, p. 604.

Focuses on such topics as fiduciary relations, patient choice, and informed consent in the context of utilization review. The author calls for public policies to encourage development of professional norms for case managers as well as codes of conduct. Such norms and codes would be a countervailing force to interests that favor managed care organizations over patients. Faced with pressure from employers to make decisions that are not in the patients' interest, case managers could point to these codes as their basis of refusal. Public policy could also create legal obligations for case managers as well as the means to enforce them. Independent review organizations could monitor the conduct of case managers to ensure that decisions follow norms. If the decisions of case managers were monitored, the author writes, it might also be possible to deny payment to managers who abuse their discretion.

Cheralyn E. Schessler. "Liability Implications of Utilization Review (UR) as a Cost Containment Mechanism." (Comment.) *Journal of Contemporary Health Law and Policy*, 1992, *8*, 407.

Examines the nature of health care cost-control strategies and discusses UR as a mechanism for cost containment. Schessler particularly emphasizes how UR applies to the Medicare and Medicaid DRG system of reimbursement and the HMO-form provider organization. Finally, she examines the liability implications of the UR process by analyzing case law and the ramifications of a cost-control defense. The focus of this comment is on prospective review of health care costs.

Martin F. Shapiro and Neil S. Wenger. "Rethinking Utilization Review." *New England Journal of Medicine*, 1995, *333*, 1353.

Argues that utilization review should consider outcomes before expenditures, check for underuse and overuse, and construct an ethically based structure in which consumption of medical services is reduced equitably. According to the authors, if utilization review programs are conducted without representation of the appropriate range of interest groups, they may increase disparity in care and harm health outcomes rather than improve them. A more defensible system that is explicit, representative, and based on solid medical evidence may transform utilization review from a sometimes embarrassing process that operates by hidden procedures into an activity conducted in the light of rational discourse, they write.

Jeffrey E. Shuren. "Legal Accountability for Utilization Review in ERISA Health Plans." *North Carolina Law Review*, 1999, *77*, 731.

This article addresses incongruities in ERISA and recommends that any reform efforts should be directed to the realization of the goal of U.S. health care policy to provide high-quality, economically efficient health care. The author proposes that ERISA be amended to hold utilization review organizations to the medical standard of care but with the ability to defend their actions if they demonstrate by reasonable scientific evidence that their decisions and guidelines furnish plan participants with a level of care of efficacy and safety comparable to the medical standard of care. As a result, participants would receive quality health care while holding utilization review organizations to a standard that permits them to implement cost-effective health care without necessarily incurring liability for unsuccessful treatment outcomes.

Linda V. Tiano. "Empire Blue Cross Blue Shield's External Review Program." Washington, D.C.: American Health Lawyers Association [Report No. VMC98–0006], 1998, 47 pages.

Describes Empire Blue Cross Blue Shield's external review program and its impact on Empire's medical decision-making process, dispute resolution, and litigation. Includes a copy of *Elsroth* v. *Consolidated Edison Co. of N.Y.*, 98 Civ. 4150 (S.D.N.Y. July 17, 1998), in which the court denied plaintiff's motion for a preliminary injunction compelling Empire to precertify an investigational cancer treatment.

James L. Touse. "Medical Management and Legal Obligations to Members." In Peter R. Kongstvedt (ed.), *The Managed Health Care Handbook.* (4th ed.) Gaithersburg, Md.: Aspen, 2000.

Discusses a variety of legal and regulatory obligations related to developing and operating the medical management programs of managed care plans. The author, general counsel for Blue Cross and Blue Shield of Tennessee, briefly discusses these obligations and plans' legal liability exposure if they fail to satisfy the obligations. The chapter also suggests what can be done to minimize that liability exposure while still accomplishing the organization's medical management objectives. Topics discussed include obligations to conduct medical management activities, contractual actions related to medical management activities, negligence actions related to medical management activities, and liability for the negligence of participating providers. The author concludes with a checklist of eighteen recommended actions that plans should take to comply with their medical management obligations and to minimize their liability related to medical management activities.

H. G. Welch and others. "Physician Profiling: An Analysis of Inpatient Practice Patterns in Florida and Oregon." *New England Journal of Medicine,* 1994, *330,* 607.

Offers discussion of physician profiling, a method of cost control that focuses on patterns of care instead of on specific clinical decisions. It is one cost-control method that takes into account physicians' desire to curb the intrusion of administrative mechanisms into the clinical encounter. To provide a concrete example of such profiling, the authors analyzed the inpatient practice patterns of physicians in Florida and Oregon, drawing from Medicare data compiled from 1991 through 1994. They conclude that Florida physicians used markedly more resources, on average, than did their colleagues in Oregon. The difference was apparent in all specialties and all types of service.

Thomas M. Wickizer. "Controlling Outpatient Medical Equipment Costs Through Utilization Management." *Medical Care,* 1995, *33,* 383.

In response to escalating health care costs, insurance carriers have developed cost-containment programs that rely on utilization management procedures that ensure that care provided is clinically appropriate and medically necessary. These programs have focused primarily on hospital inpatient care, using prospective review procedures to reduce inpatient utilization and expenditures, which can occur through either a sentinel (or volume) effect or increased denials resulting from the review and verification process. Reductions in expenditures associated with utilization management are about 10–15 percent, according to the author. He concludes that utilization management offers insurers and payers a tool for controlling costs when these costs result from high volume or service utilization, although it does increase paperwork.

Thomas M. Wickizer. "Effect of Utilization Reviews." *Medical Care Review,* 1990, *47,* 327.

Utilization review looks at hospital admissions to see if they are necessary, or if the number of days in the hospital was appropriate. It may be performed before, during, or after admission. Wickizer reviews the studies that have examined utilization review and finds most of them suffer from various defects.

5.02 JOINT COMMISSION FOR THE ACCREDITATION OF HEALTHCARE ORGANIZATIONS (JCAHO)

Michael J. Astrue. "Health Care Reform and the Constitutional Limits on Private Accreditation as an Alternative to Direct Government Regulation." *Law and Contemporary Problems,* Autumn 1994, 75.

Astrue, formerly general counsel of DHHS, begins with a witty and insightful discussion of federal health care regulators, explaining that the HCFA has historically viewed itself as a check-writing office that has not thought of itself as a regulatory agency and has stubbornly resisted congressional efforts to transform it into one. As a consequence, HCFA has attempted to minimize its regulatory role through use of private contractors and private accrediting agencies. By contrast, he writes, the FDA has eagerly sought to expand its jurisdiction at the same time it has been pleading poverty as the excuse for its failure to perform some of its most important duties, such as approving new drugs.

Lauren Dame and Sidney M. Wolfe. *The Failure of Private Hospital Regulation: An Analysis of the Joint Commission on Accreditation of Healthcare Organizations' Inadequate Oversight of Hospitals.* Washington, D.C.: Public Citizen Health Research Group, 1996, 42 pages.

This scathing report describes the workings of the JCAHO, a private, industry-dominated organization that inspects and accredits hospitals and related health care entities. Both federal and state laws accept accreditation by the Joint Commission as a substitute for certain government inspections and as evidence that government quality and safety standards are met, turning the JCAHO into a regulator—at least in theory. In practice, the authors write, the Joint Commission is a regulator so dominated by the industry being regulated that it cannot and does not do an adequate job of protecting the public. They contend that it views and treats hospitals not as entities to be regulated but as customers to be served and kept satisfied. This report is based, in part, on information not previously made public, including interviews with former Joint Commission employees, internal documents supplied to the authors by former employees, and information obtained from DHHS under the Freedom of Information Act.

The report reaches three conclusions: (1) the JCAHO is subject to inherent conflict of interest owing to its governance, funding, and multiple roles; (2) as a private entity, the Joint Commission is not bound by and does not voluntarily observe the same standards of accountability required of governments; and (3) although government reliance on private accreditation may appear to save public funds, it merely shifts costs between different budgets and payment sources. The authors recommend that DHHS propose and Congress enact legislation to repeal 42 U.S.C. §1395 bb, which "deems" Joint Commission–accredited hospitals to meet the conditions of participation in Medicare and Medicaid. They also recommend the HCFA should seek authorization and adequate funding to contract with state agencies to annually survey all participating hospitals to determine compliance with Medicare and Medicaid requirements.

Joint Commission on Accreditation of Healthcare Organizations. *Comprehensive Accreditation Manual for Hospitals: The Official Handbook.* Chicago: JCAHO, 1998.

Supplies accreditation policies, standards, scoring, aggregation rules, and decision rules.

Timothy S. Jost. "Medicare and the Joint Commission on Accreditation of Healthcare Organizations: A Healthy Relationship?" *Law and Contemporary Problems,* Autumn 1994, 15.

Examines the Joint Commission accreditation process. With JCAHO accreditation, a health care institution is deemed to meet the Medicare conditions of participation; Jost notes that more than five thousand hospitals nationwide are permitted to provide Medicare-financed services solely because they are so accredited. He concludes that because the Joint Commission must be responsive to so many constituencies, it is arguably better able to ensure the quality of health care than direct public regulation.

Eleanor D. Kinney. "Private Accreditation as a Substitute for Direct Government Regulation in Public Health Insurance Programs: Where Is It Appropriate?" *Law and Contemporary Problems,* Autumn 1994, 47.

Explores the appropriateness of using private accreditation in defining and regulating the quality of health care providers under government health insurance programs. First, the article describes the various functions of private accreditation in public health insurance programs. Second, it reviews the history and use of private accreditation in state license programs as well as in the Medicare and Medicaid programs. Third, it proposes a theory for deciding when private accreditation should be used by public health insurance programs for defining and regulating the quality of different types of health care institution.

Margaret E. O'Kane. "External Accreditation of Managed Care Plans." In Peter R. Kongstvedt (ed.), *The Managed Health Care Handbook.* (4th ed.) Gaithersburg, Md.: Aspen, 2000.

Presents a summary of the three primary commissions that currently accredit managed care organizations. Mirroring the organizations they review, the accrediting commissions vary in their goals and in their approach to external review. Although they diverge greatly in their approaches, they hold the potential for rationalizing and consolidating current external review processes for state, federal, and individual purchasers that are sometimes duplicative or contradictory in their requirements.

Peter H. Schuck. "Tort Liability to Those Injured by Negligent Accreditation Decisions." *Law and Contemporary Problems,* Autumn 1994, 185.

Examines the few reported court decisions in which consumers challenged accreditation decisions. The author writes that consumers' claims of negligent accreditation are likely to be barred at the threshold by a narrowly defined scope of legal duty for accreditors and by a requirement that consumers show detrimental reliance on, and increased risk from, the accrediting decision.

Part Two

Regulatory Matters

6

Tax Issues

From a financial perspective, tax law considerations are of primary importance to many health care organizations. Although for-profit hospitals are becoming more widespread, especially in the Sun Belt states, the majority of hospitals in the United States remain nonprofit organizations. For-profit (or proprietary) hospitals are subject to the general rules applicable to other business entities under federal tax law. Nonprofit hospitals, along with other nonprofit health care organizations, are generally entitled to important privileges under the Internal Revenue Code (IRC) and the regulations promulgated thereunder.

The following materials summarize the significant amount of recent writing on tax law and policy as it concerns health care in the United States.

ANNOTATIONS

6.01 THE SECTION 501(C) EXEMPT INSTITUTION: QUALIFYING FOR AND MAINTAINING THE EXEMPTION

Scott Becker and Linas Grikis. "Proposed Regulation on Taxation of Excess Benefit Transactions." *Health Care Law Monthly,* Oct. 1998, pp. 21–29.

This brief article (from a monthly publication of Matthew Bender & Co.) examines the August 1998 proposed regulations to the Excess Benefit Transactions sections of the Taxpayers Bill of Rights. The proposed regulations should prove helpful in their effort to define "disqualified persons" and their efforts to guide parties through appropriate exempt entity approval processes.

Katherine Benesch and others. *Medicolegal Aspects of Critical Care.* Gaithersburg, Md.: Aspen, 1986, 205 pages.

Contains essays providing guidance from various professional disciplines to the complex medical, legal, psychological, ethical, and economic problems that professionals, their patients, and relatives encounter with the critical care system. The volume is written as a resource for physicians and surgeons, nurses, respiratory therapists, health care attorneys, and health care administrators. The underlying assumption of the book is that critical care is a multidisciplinary specialty requiring the skills of a team of health care providers working with patients and their families for effective, timely decision making in the face of difficult treatment choices that often involve life and death.

John D. Colombo and Mark A. Hall. *The Charitable Tax Exemption.* Boulder, Colo.: Westview Press, 1995, 266 pages.

In this important addition to the theory of tax law, the authors develop an original "donative" theory that links the charitable tax exemption to the ability of an organization to derive donated support from the community. The tradition of tax-exempt status for nonprofit charitable organizations is well established. However, the tax-exempt sector of the economy is vast and rapidly growing, resulting in the loss of billions of dollars of tax revenue. At the same time, there exists no consensus on what constitutes a charity or what purpose the charitable exemption serves. The implications of the authors' theory would rationalize the charitable tax exemption, comport with legal precedent, and simplify administration of the law.

Dan Gottlieb and Cathy Traugott. "A Primer on the IRS Private Letter Ruling Process." *Health Care Law Monthly,* Oct. 1998, pp. 3–16.

Transactions and arrangements involving tax-exempt entities often raise concerns about such transactions' impact on the tax-exempt status of the entities and the characterization of income generated by the venture. To resolve the uncertainty about the tax implications, exempt organizations may request guidance from the IRS. The IRS provides guidance in the form of letter rulings, closing agreements, determination letters, opinion letters, notification letters, information letters, revenue rulings, and oral advice. In a private-letter ruling, the IRS applies the tax laws to the facts offered by the exempt organization and then rules on the effect of such facts or transaction on tax status. This helpful article explains the procedures and discusses the concerns when exempt health care organizations request private-letter rulings under Section 501(a) of the IRC. The article includes a sample form for a letter ruling request.

Thomas K. Hyatt and Bruce R. Hopkins. *The Law of Tax-Exempt Healthcare Organizations.* New York: Wiley, 1995, 680 pages.

Offers a comprehensive analysis of how the Internal Revenue Service has applied the tax code to the new and dynamic health care organizations that have evolved in recent years. In Part One, the authors—two Washington, D.C., tax attorneys—discuss the public policy reasons for granting tax exemption to health care organizations. In Part Two, they set forth the fundamental tax principles that apply to exempt organizations and examine how they are applied to health care organizations by the IRS and the courts. In Part Three, the authors discuss the tax-exempt status of each type of health care provider and supplier organization commonly in operation today. Part Four focuses on the tax status of health-related organizations such as for-profit subsidiaries.

Part Five discusses organizational issues such as reorganizations, mergers, and conversions. Part Six discusses operational issues such as tax treatment of unrelated business activities, physician recruitment, charity care, employee benefits, and executive compensation, along with Medicare and Medicaid fraud and abuse and its effect on exemption. Part Seven focuses on the nuts and bolts of obtaining and maintaining the exempt status of a health care organization, including the exemption recognition process, avoidance of penalties, and audits.

The text is supplemented by a series of seven helpful appendices regarding safe harbors, IRS hospital audit guidelines, and the consequences of physician recruitment incentives. They are followed by tables of cases, IRS revenue rulings and revenue procedures, IRS general counsel memoranda, IRS private-letter rulings, and technical advice memoranda.

Douglas M. Mancino. *Taxation of Hospitals and Health Care Organizations.* Boston: Warren Gorham & Lamont, 1996.

This loose-leaf treatise is written by a veteran health care tax attorney practicing in Los Angeles. The book is divided into five sections. The first section, Exemption Requirements, follows an introductory chapter and comprises Chapters Two through Ten. Chapter Two covers in detail the organizational and operational requirements that apply to section 501(c)(3) organizations generally, and Chapter Three discusses the procedural steps that an organization seeking exemption must follow.

Chapters Four through Seven cover the substantive requirements of exemption that apply to virtually all types of health care organization as well as those that are frequently associated with health care organizations. Chapter Four discusses the exemption rules for nonprofit and public hospitals, and Chapter Five covers the rules applicable to organizations that provide facilities and services to the elderly. Chapter Six examines managed care organizations, with primary emphasis on the rules applicable to prepaid health plans and health maintenance organizations. The chapter also covers the rules that apply to other types of managed care organization, including independent practice associations and physician-hospital organizations. Physicians are critical components of the health care delivery system, and the tax-exempt status of medical groups and faculty practice plans is discussed in detail in Chapter Seven.

Since the early 1990s, government payment changes and competitive market conditions have forced the various components of the health care delivery system to begin to restructure how they interrelate. The result has been the formation of various types of integrated delivery system. Chapter Eight covers in detail the developing tax-exemption rules that apply to the integrated delivery systems already in place or under development, whether they achieve partial or complete integration.

The health care industry is a large consumer of supplies, equipment, and human resources. To achieve economies of scale, cost savings, or other benefits, hospitals and health care organizations frequently form separate entities through which they collaborate to purchase supplies on a group basis, acquire centralized administrative and support services, and otherwise attempt to reduce their costs and improve efficiencies. Chapter Nine discusses the rules applicable to cooperative hospital service organizations, a tax-favored cooperative organization first authorized by Congress in 1968.

Finally, Chapter Ten is a catch-all chapter that discusses the exemption rules applicable to a significant number of organizations that often constitute important components of a vertically and horizontally integrated health care delivery system. These rules are significant because, with limited exceptions, the availability of tax-exempt status to an organization will depend on the organization's ability to demonstrate that it is formed and operated exclusively for a charitable or other exempt purpose.

The second section of the book, Special Transactions, covers significant transactional issues faced regularly by hospitals and health care organizations. Chapter Eleven discusses joint ventures and similar transactions between hospitals, health care organizations, and others, including members of their medical staffs and proprietary and investor-owned health care organizations. Chapter Twelve examines physician recruitment and retention activities and discusses the most recent revenue ruling proposed by the IRS.

The special rules governing lobbying and electioneering are discussed in Chapters Thirteen and Fourteen, respectively. These rules are significant because of the highly regulated nature of all hospitals and most health care organizations.

The third section of the book, Public Charity Status, focuses on the significant public charity and private foundation classification questions relevant to health care organizations. Chapter Fifteen describes in detail the procedural requirements that must be satisfied by an organization to obtain public charity status, as well as the substantive rules that apply to various public charity classifications. Chapter Sixteen discusses the rules applicable to health care organizations that operate as private foundations. This chapter approaches the private foundation rules using a functional rather than tax code section approach, since health care organizations operating as private foundations are usually complex operating companies that do not rely on grant making alone. This chapter also discusses the steps that must be taken if an organization wants to terminate its private foundation status.

The fourth section of the book, Unrelated Business Income, provides a comprehensive discussion of the unrelated business income tax (UBIT) rules that apply to hospitals and health care organizations. Chapter Seventeen deals with the general UBIT rules, and Chapter Eighteen covers the unrelated debt-financed income rules. According to data released by the IRS in 1995, an estimated 32,690 tax-exempt organizations reported more than $3.4 billion in gross unrelated business income.

The fifth section, Compliance, includes two chapters that discuss a variety of operational and audit issues. Chapter Nineteen covers the information retention and reporting requirements.

Chapter Twenty examines the IRS's audits of hospitals and health care organizations, including those conducted as part of the IRS's Coordinated Examination Program.

The book also contains seven appendices that are updated annually. They contain significant IRS forms as well as other key pronouncements and documents relating to hospitals and health care organizations. Finally, the book is updated with three supplements and newsletters each year. Additional coverage will reflect new legislative developments, such as proposals for intermediate sanctions applicable to public charities, and will expand specific topics, such as conversions to and from tax-exempt status.

Deborah Z. Read. "Taxable Subsidiaries and Limited Liability Companies." Washington, D.C.: American Health Lawyers Association [Report No. VTX98–0004], 1998, 65 pages.

Discusses the use of taxable subsidiaries by tax-exempt health care providers, including the basic concepts and new developments affecting taxable subsidiaries. Compares using a taxable subsidiary and a limited liability company when structuring arrangement with taxable organizations. Also discusses LLCs and their potential uses by health care providers, including general concepts applicable to an LLC, classification for income tax purposes, potential uses of LLCs by health care professionals and health care providers, and the LLC as an exempt organization.

T. J. Sullivan. "The Tax Status of Nonprofit HMOs after Section 501(m)." *Tax Notes*, Jan. 7, 1991, pp. 75, 79.

Traces the development of HMOs with the evolution of their tax treatment. Case law and IRS interpretations make it nearly impossible for most nonprofit HMOs to qualify for 501(c)(3) status. Qualification for 501(c)(4) status, although it involves a looser test, still poses problems for HMOs that resemble commercial businesses or are found to benefit someone other than a broad cross section of the community. The 1986 enactment of section 501(m), which eliminated the tax exemption of Blue Cross and Blue Shield on the ground that the Blues were acting like commercial health insurers, has thrown the tax-exempt status of nonprofit HMOs into question. As few HMOs have medical staffs and more are moving toward a managed care model that allows patients to consult doctors unaffiliated with the HMO, they may have difficulty arguing that insurance is "incidental" to providing health care under the HMO exception of section 501(m)(3)(B).

6.01(1) The 501(c) Exemption: Advantages and Disadvantages

Boris I. Bittker and Lawrence Lokken. *Federal Taxation of Income, Estates and Gifts.* (3rd ed.; paragraph 100.5.) Boston: Warren, Gorham, and Lamont, 1999; B. Hopkins. *The Law of Tax-Exempt Organizations.* 300–51 (6th ed. 1992); Treusch. *Tax-Exempt Charitable Organizations,* 263–329 (3rd ed., 1988).

Boris I. Bittker and George F. Rahdert. "The Exemption of Nonprofit Organizations from Federal Income Taxation." *Yale Law Journal,* 1976, *85,* 299.

A seminal work arguing that the exemption of nonprofit organizations from federal income taxation is neither a special privilege nor a hidden subsidy. Rather, it reflects the established principles of income taxation to organizations that, unlike the typical business corporation, do not seek profit.

Bernadette M. Broccolo. "Tax Exemption and Tax Issues." Washington, D.C.: American Health Lawyers Association [Report No. VFH98–0005], 1998, 225 pages.

Discusses in detail fundamental tax exemption issues for health care organizations. Examines qualification as a Section 501(c)(3) tax-exempt organization or a Section 501 (c)(4) social welfare organization. Also discusses unrelated business tax liability, intermediate sanctions, revocation and denial of exemption, restrictions on political activities and lobbying, compensation issues, integrated delivery systems, joint operating agreements, annual reporting requirements, and current IRS audit activity. Applies tax principles to present trends in the health sector, such as the sale and conversion of tax-exempt hospitals, hospital joint ventures, and physician recruitment and retention devices. Examines hospital audit guidelines, management contract and research agreement guidelines, regulations and revenue procedure on change in use of bond-financed facilities, repeal of the bond cap, and BBA provisions affecting provider-sponsored organizations. Includes sample articles of incorporation, a summary of the Section 4958 intermediate sanctions provision, application of the section 509(a) public support tests, the May 22, 1997, IRS Conflicts of Interest Policy, Revenue Ruling 97–21 and a checklist of factors considered in Revenue Ruling 98–15.

Bernadette M. Broccolo. "Tax Exemption and Tax Issues." Washington, D.C.: American Health Lawyers Association [Report No. FH97–0005], 1997), 219 pages.

Discusses in detail a variety of issues in tax exemption. This seminar paper examines qualifying as a section 501(c)(3) tax-exempt organization or as a section 501(c)(4) social welfare organization. Also covered is UBIT liability, intermediate sanctions, restrictions on political activities and lobbying, compensation issues, integrated delivery systems' tax issues, joint operating agreements, annual reporting requirements, and IRS audit trends. It applies tax principles to trends in the health industry, such as the sale and conversion of tax-exempt hospitals, hospital joint ventures, and physician recruitment and retention devices. It examines hospital audit guidelines, management contract and research agreement guidelines, regulations and revenue procedure on change in use of bond-financed facilities, repeal of the bond cap, and BBA provisions affecting PSOs.

Robert Charles Clark. "Does the Nonprofit Form Fit the Hospital Industry?" *Harvard Law Review*, 1980, *93*, 1417–1489.

Critically examines the basis for the favored legal status enjoyed by nonprofit hospitals. Clark begins by identifying endemic problems in the health care industry and then explores the relationship between nonprofit hospitals and these problems. He finds that the evidence does not persuasively establish that nonprofit hospitals serve as fiduciaries rather than exploiters and that nonprofits engage in much involuntary cross subsidization of medical services. He concludes that the legal favoritism for the nonprofit form is based not on sound reasoning and hard data but on intuition. Clark proposes that the legal rules affecting nonprofit hospitals reflect this reality by treating both nonprofits and for-profits neutrally, by controlling cross subsidization, and by strengthening consumers' information about control over health care decision making.

Kevin B. Fischer. "Tax Exemption and the Health Care Industry: Are the Challenges to Tax-Exempt Status Justified?" *Vanderbilt Law Review*, 1996, *49*, 161.

Focused discussion of challenges to tax-exempt status. At the present time, tax exemption has an uncertain future in the health care industry. Many states have attempted to revoke this benefit in order to tap into hospitals and other health care organizations as badly needed sources of reserve. Meanwhile, the IRS's challenge to the tax-exempt status of an HMO in *Geisinger Health Plan* v. *Commissioner*, 985 F.2d 1210 (3d Cir. 1993), and the IRS's application of the community benefit standard have made it increasingly difficult for health care organizations to maintain tax-exempt status.

Fischer concludes that there is a valid basis for distinguishing between the types of entity that merit tax exemption and those that do not. This basis is a properly defined community benefit standard, which must focus on both the organizational structure and the beneficial outcomes produced by nonprofit health care organizations. The principal benefits of the nonprofit structure will be eliminated if the courts and the IRS continue to narrow the definition of *community benefit* so as to preclude more efficient and innovative organizational structures within the health care industry. Implementation of a well-defined community benefit standard, which explicitly focuses on both organization and outcomes, would help to align our tax policy with the overall goals of our health care system.

Thomas K. Hyatt. "Current Governance Issues in Tax-Exempt Health Care Organizations." Washington, D.C.: American Health Lawyers Association [Report No. 97–0009]), 17 pages.

Outlines IRS guidance that raises issues of statutory and common law duties of officers and directors of business corporations, the IRS community board and conflict-of-interest policy, intermediate sanctions, physician recruitment, and regulatory approval of transactions.

Thomas K. Hyatt. "Introduction to Tax Issues." Washington, D.C.: American Health Lawyers Association [Report No. TX97–00291], 1997), 68 pages.

Describes relevant tax research resources, and then discusses in depth qualifying as a section 501(c)(3) exempt organization, a section 501(c)(4) social welfare organization (includes HMOs), a section 501(c)(6) association, a section 501(e) cooperative hospital service organization, a section 501(m) commercial-type insurance association, or a section 502 feeder organization. Also discusses unrelated business taxable income, charity care and community benefit, intermediate sanctions for excess benefit transactions, community board and conflict-of-interest policy, physician recruitment, and tax-exempt bond financing. The materials include excerpts from the IRS's *Exempt Organizations Examination Guidelines Handbook*.

Theodore R. Marmor, Mark Schlesinger, and Richard W. Smithey. "Nonprofit Organizations and Health Care." In Walter W. Powell (ed.), *The Nonprofit Sector: A Research Handbook*. New Haven, Conn.: Yale University Press, 1987.

Examines the history of the nonprofit form in American medicine and attempts to set that story in the broader context of American medical care. The chapter next sketches the then-current state of nonprofit health institutions. The following part addresses the role of nonprofits in an industry with a mix of nonprofits, for-profits, and government institutions, viewed through the prism of the expected differences among these forms. It analyzes in detail arguments about the merits and disadvantages of the nonprofit and for-profit forms, emphasizing the paradigmatic claims about cost, quality, and access among the opposing camps and significant commentators. The authors then conclude that the environment facing decision makers in medical institutions and the rules by which they operate are more significant than what institutions call themselves on their legal charters. The text is supplemented by seven tables and a detailed bibliography.

Julia McMillen. "Non Profit Hospitals: Is the Public Getting Its Money's Worth?" (Comment.) *Journal of Health and Hospital Law*, 1997, 30, 51.

Analyzes two recent empirical studies examining the justification for continued tax-exempt status for nonprofit hospitals.

Mark Schlesinger, Bradford Gray, and Elizabeth Bradley. "Charity and Community: The Role of Nonprofit Ownership in a Managed Health Care System." *Journal of Health Politics, Policy and Law*, 1996, 21, 697.

Identifies forms of community benefit associated with nonprofit managed care. As American medicine has been transformed by the growth of managed care, so too have questions about the appropriate role of nonprofit ownership in the health care system. The standards for community benefit that are increasingly applied to nonprofit hospitals are, at best, only partially relevant to expectations for nonprofit managed care plans. Drawing from historical interpretations of tax exemption in health care and from the theoretical literature on the implications of ownership for organizational behavior, the authors identify five forms of community benefit that might be associated with nonprofit forms of managed care. Using data from a national survey of firms providing third-party utilization review services in 1993, the authors test for ownership-related differences in these five dimensions.

Nonprofit utilization review firms generally provide more public goods, such as information dissemination, and are more "community oriented" than proprietary firms, but they are not distinguishable from their for-profit counterparts in addressing the implications of medical quality or the cost of the review process. However, a subgroup of nonprofit review organizations with medical origins are more likely to address quality issues than are either for-profit firms or other nonprofit agencies. Evidence on responses to information asymmetries is mixed but suggests that some ownership-related differences exist.

6.01(2) Charitable Purpose Defined

6.01(2)(a) Introduction

Laura B. Chisolm. "Politics and Charity: A Proposal for Peaceful Co-Existence." *George Washington Law Review*, 1990, *58*, 308.

Considers section 501(c)(3) of the IRC, which limits the charitable exemption to organizations that do "not participate in, or intervene in . . . any political campaign on behalf of (or in opposition to) any candidate for public office." This article concludes that as currently formulated and applied, this prohibition on campaign intervention is constitutionally questionable, incongruent with campaign finance regulation, inconsistent with the premises underlying the charitable tax exemption, and contrary to free speech values.

John D. Colombo. "Charitable Tax Exemption." In Mark A. Hall (gen. ed.), *Health Care Corporate Law: Formulation and Regulation*. Boston: Little Brown, 1993.

Covers such topics as exemption from federal income taxes, private benefit and inurement, limitations on lobbying and political activity, and unrelated business income issues. It also covers the distinction between public charity and private foundation status, state tax exemption, and the procedural aspects of exempt status.

Derek F. Covert and Gayl A. Westendorf. "Paying Physicians for Charity Care." *Healthcare Financial Management*, Dec. 1995, 46.

Explains that the IRS's Announcement 95-25 gives important legal support to the practice of compensating physicians for providing charity care. The announcement describes a situation in which tax-exempt hospitals may compensate nonemployee physicians who are members of their staffs for providing charity care—a practice that in the past has had only indirect legal support. Before creating arrangements to compensate physicians for charity care, however, health care executives must first establish guidelines that ensure the arrangements comply with IRS rules and federal antikickback laws. The guidelines should require the hospital to document the need for charity care, document any agreement to pay physicians for charity care, secure board approval for any such agreement, define charity care, and define reasonable compensation, among other actions. Careful planning on the part of health care executives can ensure that an important community service is provided without jeopardizing the hospital's tax-exempt status or exposing it to monetary penalties.

Seth Dewees. "Healthcare Organizations and 501(c)(3): Uncertainty in the Post-Geisinger World." (Comment.) *Health Matrix*, 1997, *7*, 351.

Analyzes the confusion that has surrounded the application of both the "community benefit" and "integral part" tests used by the IRS to newly developed health care providing organizations. It focuses on decisions by the IRS, then by the tax court, and ultimately by the Third Circuit Court of Appeals over the tax treatment of the Geisinger Health Plan, an HMO serving a large portion of northeastern Pennsylvania.

Gerald M. Griffith. "IRS Guidance on Physician Recruitment: From the Seeds of Hermann Hospital to the Proposed and Final Rulings and Beyond." *Journal of Health and Hospital Law*, 1997, *30*, 75.

Discusses physician recruitment guidelines released in final form by the IRS on Apr. 21, 1997, as Revenue Ruling 97-21. This article, written by a practicing attorney, explores the checklist-type guidance of Hermann Hospital, how the IRS shifted to a more flexible analysis in the proposed ruling, and how the IRS took that flexibility a step further and resolved some past ambiguities in the final ruling. In addition, the article notes how, with that increased flexibility, the final ruling likely foreshadows key points of guidance on establishing a rebuttable presumption of fair market value to avoid intermediate sanctions.

Shane T. Hamilton. "The Need for Guidance on the Use of Physician Recruitment Incentives by Nonprofit Hospitals." (Note.) *Virginia Tax Review*, 1996, *15, 739.*

Discusses physician recruitment incentives, which are subject to IRS scrutiny because they potentially violate the prohibitions against private inurement and private benefit found in section 501(c)(3) of the IRC and the corresponding U.S. Treasury regulations. The IRS's approach to the use of physician recruitment incentives by nonprofit hospitals is confusing; moreover, the author argues, the approach is inconsistent with prior developments in the law of exempt organizations relating to private benefit and private inurement issues.

This comment begins by providing a legal background against which the IRS's approach to physician recruitment must be analyzed. It then provides a general description of the prohibitions against private inurement and private benefit. Next, the article defines physician recruitment incentives and explains how the IRS fits them into this existing legal background. The article concludes with an analysis of a proposed IRS revenue ruling on the subject.

Michael W. Peregrine. "Charitable Trust Laws and the Evolving Nature of the Nonprofit Hospital Corporation." *Journal of Health and Hospital Law*, 1997, *30,* 11.

Reviews the basic principles of charitable trust law as they apply to nonprofit hospitals and the relevant case law. This article, written by a practicing attorney, also discusses recent state investigations, challenges and related activities, and proposed legislation. Finally, the article offers an "action plan" to assist nonprofit boards in responding to these problems.

Beth Schermer and Lawrence Foust. "Assumption of Risk: Federal Regulation of Physician Incentive Plans." *Journal of Health and Hospital Law*, 1997, *30,* 1.

Reviews the federal statutes and regulations governing payment arrangements that can result in a provider limiting or reducing services. These statutes address incentive programs intended for physicians and operated by hospitals and, directly or indirectly, by Medicare and Medicaid managed care organizations. The article first discusses statutes that outright prohibit payments by hospitals and managed care organizations to induce reduction or limitation of services to patients under certain circumstances. The second part, making up the bulk of the article, discusses a more sophisticated approach that regulates, rather than prohibits, physician incentive plans.

6.01(2)(b) Charitable Hospitals

Edward J. Buchholz. "The IRS's Whole Hospital Joint Venture Ruling: Guidance or Confusion?" *Taxes: The Tax Magazine*, June 1998, at 11.

The author examines whole hospital joint ventures in light of Revenue Ruling 98–15. Using two distinct factual situations, the ruling concludes that if the joint venture does not allow the contributing tax-exempt hospital to continue to meet the community benefit standard to the exclusion of meeting the other venturer's profit-making goals, the hospital will not be treated as continuing to operate exclusively for exempt purposes. Hence, the hospital would lose its exempt status. Although the ruling is helpful in the two narrowly circumscribed situations it addresses, because of the multiple factors in both situations it remains unclear (1) under what circumstances a tax-exempt hospital participating in a whole hospital joint venture could lose its tax-exempt status, (2) whether the issue is resolved merely by creative drafting that places the community benefit standard ahead of profit-making goals, (3) whether the appropriate governance provisions will in all circumstances preserve the hospital's status, and (4) whether limiting exposure to liabilities and equalizing the proportion in which capital is contributed and profits are shared remain unclear. The author concludes that the ruling will only create confusion for the far more common ancillary services joint venture.

Cyril F. Chang and Howard P. Tuckman. "Do Higher Property Tax Rates Increase the Market Share of Nonprofit Hospitals?" *National Tax Journal*, June 1990, 175–187.

Theorizes that property tax exemptions increase the market share of nonprofit hospitals. Analyzing data from Tennessee, the authors find that nonprofit market share is not increased by the property tax exemption. They then hypothesize that high property tax rates predict a single hospital in a county and affect the probability that this hospital will be a nonprofit. The analysis shows that although higher tax rates increase the probability that a county will have only one hospital, they do not add to the probability that the hospital will be nonprofit. This casts doubt on the proposition that property tax rates affect nonprofit market share.

John Copeland and Gabriel Rudney. "Federal Tax Subsidies for Not-for-Profit Hospitals." *Tax Notes*, 1990, 46, 1559–1576.

Not-for-profit hospitals benefit from four major tax subsidies: the property tax exemption and the corporate income tax exemption at the state and local levels, and the corporate income tax exemption and tax-exempt bond financing at the federal level. This article focuses on the two federal subsidies.

The authors, both tax analysts formerly with the Treasury's Office of Tax Policy, conclude that although tax subsidies have spurred hospital construction and equipment acquisitions by reducing their net cost to hospitals and increasing rates of return, the issues of cost escalation and inadequate coverage for the medically indigent have not been resolved.

They find that the tax subsidies contribute to overexpansion. Also, the subsidies provide not-for-profits with the ability to outbid taxable entities in the capital markets. In addition, some assert that the subsidies are wasted in increased doctor and hospital staff incomes rather than on improving medical care or enlarging charitable care. Further, the tax subsidies are inequitable and inefficient, providing benefits to the financially strongest not-for-profit hospitals and assisting them in their competition with both taxable and not-for-profit hospitals that are not financially strong.

Although the subsidy for income tax exemption is traditional in the not-for-profit sector, the erosion of traditional mission and the move toward competitive market behavior warrants reconsideration of the exemption by Congress, as it did with respect to commercial insurance activities by not-for-profit organizations. Similarly, reconsideration of unlimited subsidization of borrowing costs in tax-exempt bond financing is warranted, even though such financing has aided not-for-profit hospital construction, they write.

Mark A. Hall and John D. Colombo. "The Charitable Status of Non-Profit Hospitals: Toward a Donative Theory of Tax Exemption," *Washington L. Review*, 1991, 66, 307.

Examines the controversy over the multibillion-dollar charitable tax exemption enjoyed by nonprofit hospitals. This article begins by articulating four criteria for evaluating a rationale of the charitable exemption: (1) deservedness, incorporating the elements of worth and need; (2) proportionality; (3) universality; and (4) historical consistency. The article then employs these criteria to refute three conventional explanations of why nonprofit hospitals are exempt: because health care is a per se charitable activity, because the treatment of indigent patients relieves a government burden, and because nonprofit hospitals provide community benefits. The article also uses these criteria to refute two academic theories: Boris Bittker's income measurement rationale and Henry Hansmann's capital subsidy theory.

This article proposes a "donative theory" as an alternative rationale for the charitable exemption. The donative theory posits that *charity* describes an entity capable of attracting a substantial level of philanthropic support from the public at large. Donations exist where there is a combined failure of private markets and direct public funding to supply a shared public benefit at the optimally desired level. Donative institutions deserve a tax subsidy because the public signals their worth, and the free-rider tendency that affects all giving ensures the need for an additional, shadow subsidy. The article further demonstrates that the donative theory provides the only explanation of the tax law's otherwise unjustifiable reliance on the law of charitable trusts.

David A. Hyman. "The Conundrum of Charitability: Reassessing Tax Exemption for Hospitals." *American Journal of Law and Medicine,* 1990, *16,* 327.

Assesses the appropriateness of tax-exempt status for hospitals in the context of current changes in the health care industry. Tax exemption is an ancient, honorable, and expensive tradition, the author writes. Tax exemption for hospitals is all of these three, but it also places in sharp focus a fundamental problem with tax exemption in general. Organizations can retain their tax exemption while changing circumstances or expectations undermine the rationale that led to the exemption in the first place. Hospitals are perhaps the best example of this problem, the author writes. The dramatic changes in the health care environment have eliminated most of the characteristics of a hospital that originally persuaded the citizenry to grant it an exemption. Hospitals have entered into competition with tax-paying businesses and have increasingly behaved like competitive actors. Such conduct may well be beneficial, but it does not follow that tax exemption is appropriate. Rather than an undifferentiated subsidy, a shift to focused goals will provide charitable hospitals with the opportunity and incentive to do the right thing.

G. Scott Rayson. "Hospital Joint Venture Transactions Between Tax Exempt and Proprietary Organizations." Washington, D.C.: American Health Lawyers Association [Report No. VMA 98–0008], 1998, 23 pages.

Outlines the material issues that routinely arise in negotiating joint venture transactions between tax-exempt health care organizations and proprietary health care organizations. This seminar manuscript discusses the reasons and purposes for entering into hospital joint ventures, formation of the joint venture—including determining the appropriate type of entity to use as the joint venture entity—structuring the partners' capital contributions and certain related tax and antitrust issues, preservation of the tax-exempt status of the section 501(c)(3) venture partner, unwinding the joint venture, and scrutiny of the transaction by the state attorney general.

Helena G. Rubenstein. "Nonprofit Hospitals and the Federal Tax Exemption: A Fresh Prescription." (Comment.) *Health Matrix,* 1997, *7,* 381.

Explores the continued viability of the prevailing definition of *community benefit,* the IRS's current measuring stick for a nonprofit hospital's expression of its charitable purpose. As currently interpreted, the community benefit standard is an inadequate measure of the benefits the community derives from a special class of hospitals, which by the very nature of what they do, provide a benefit not calculated in numbers of indigents treated nor easily measured against the value of the exemption. The author proposes that a different measure be taken to define community benefit, reflecting both the wider scope of the community and the greater and more diverse scope of the benefit. For such hospitals, whose research and innovation reach well beyond local boundaries, the community benefit standard, as currently defined by the IRS, she writes, is too narrow to encompass the many ways in which medicine, as practiced in these hospitals, has become nationalized. Finally, the author suggests criteria against which the IRS can determine which hospitals can qualify for this treatment.

Bruce John Shih and Daniel K. Settelmayer. "Joint Ventures Rev. Rul. 98–15: Don't Apply Blindly." *Health Lawyer,* May 1998, *10*(5).

In March 1998, the IRS released the long-awaited revenue ruling on whole hospital joint ventures, Revenue Ruling 98-15. This ruling establishes two fact patterns: one that permits a tax-exempt nonprofit hospital entity to participate in a whole hospital joint venture and maintain its tax-exempt and public charity status, and one that does not. Although the ruling emphasizes the IRS position on the importance of control by a tax exempt entity in the whole hospital joint venture, the factual standards in Revenue Ruling 98-15 should not be applied blindly to all joint ventures between tax-exempt nonprofit entities and for-profit entities, the authors write. In this article, they summarize the facts of the ruling, review and examine tax-exempt joint venture analysis, and examine the factual elements in the two situations that the ruling highlights.

Bruce John Shih and Daniel K. Settelmeyer. "IRS Revenue Ruling Released on Physician Recruitment: Still Plenty of Leeway." *Health Lawyer*, 1997, 9(6), 1–11.

Discusses Revenue Ruling 97-21, which analyzes whether five hypothetical physician recruitment arrangements by a tax-exempt hospital are permissible under Section 501(c)(3) of the IRC.

James B. Simpson and Sarah D. Strum. "How Good a Samaritan? Federal Income Tax Exemption for Charitable Hospitals Reconsidered." *University of Puget Sound Law Review*, 1991, *14*, 633.

Argues that a review of cases decided over the past fifty years indicates that in the majority of states, charity care continues to be a determinative issue in granting state tax exemption.

6.01(2)(c)   Charitable Nursing Homes

Annot. "Nursing Homes as Exempt from Property Taxation." *ALR5th 34*, 529.

Collects and analyzes those cases wherein it was determined under the pertinent constitutional and statutory provisions whether real property actually employed in connection with operation of nursing homes and like institutions was entitled to exemption from property taxation. In many jurisdictions, the property of charitable institutions is exempted from taxation by statutory or constitutional authority.

Generally, the ground upon which the exemption is based is the benefit conferred upon the public by such institutions and the consequent relief of the burden imposed on the state to care for and advance the interest of its citizens. The court's determination as to exemption, in a specific case, depends upon whether the organization claiming the exemption is in fact a charitable one and whether the property on which the exemption is claimed is being devoted to charitable purposes. The issue certainly arises as to whether nursing homes, or similar institutions, are exempt as charitable institutions from property taxation. In *St. Margaret Seneca Place* v. *Board of Property Assessment, Appeals & Review* (Pa. 1994) 640 A.2d 380, 34 *ALR5th* 845, for example, the court held that the subject nursing home qualified as a "purely public charity" and, as such, was entitled to a property tax exemption; the court particularly stressed that the institution advanced a charitable purpose, donated gratuitously a substantial portion of its services, benefited a substantial and indefinite class of persons who were legitimate subjects of charity, relieved the government of some of its burden, and operated entirely free from private profit motive.

6.01(2)(d)   Charitable Professional Standards Review Organizations

[Reserved]

6.01(2)(e)   Charitable Share Service Organizations

[Reserved]

6.01(2)(f)   Individual Practice Associations

Bernadette M. Broccolo. "Tax Issues for Managed Care Organizations." Washington, D.C.: American Health Lawyers Association [Report No. VMC98–0024], 1998, 67 pages.

Discusses tax-exemption aspects of HMOs, individual practice associations, physician-hospital organizations, medical service organizations, and provider sponsored organizations. Also discusses the tax implications of allocation of provider and payer risk in managed care arrangements, allocation of ownership and control interest in jointly sponsored MCOs, and conversion from nonprofit to for-profit status.

John D. Colombo. "Are Associations of Doctors Tax-Exempt? Analyzing Inconsistencies in the Tax Exemption of Health Care Providers." *Virginia Tax Review*, 1990, *9*, 469.

Argues that the IRS's doctrine that promoting health is in itself a charitable activity eligible for a federal tax exemption, whether or not the entity provides free or subsidized care (the per se rule), has been arbitrarily enforced. This arbitrary enforcement, Colombo contends, is evident from fundamental inconsistencies in the IRS's application of the private benefit and inurement doctrine to health care cases, in the relationship between this doctrine and enforcement of the federal UBIT, and in the IRS's approach to applying the exemption standard to nonprofit pharmacies and nursing homes. The result has been an enforcement morass: traditional nonprofit hospitals receive virtually automatic exemption, while HMOs and other nontraditional health care providers must struggle to establish their eligibility for exemption.

The author believes there is no legal justification for these disparities in treatment. He would expand the eligibility of nontraditional health care providers for tax-exempt status. This expansion, however, is consistent with the per se view that promoting health is a charitable purpose. Proper enforcement of the per se standard will intensify the debate concerning the propriety of that standard for tax exemption—but until the standard is changed, it will ensure fair treatment of all types of health care provider under the current exemption standards.

6.01(2)(g) Faculty Group Practice Plans

[Reserved]

6.01(2)(h) Integrated Delivery Systems

Terry A. Jacobs and Phillip G. Royalty. "Taxation of Managed Health Care Plans." In Peter R. Kongstvedt (ed.), *The Managed Health Care Handbook*. (4th ed.) Gaithersburg, Md.: Aspen, 2000.

This brief chapter includes discussion of both tax-exempt HMOs and taxable HMOs. It also discusses a range of other managed care organizations and the state and federal tax rules applicable to them.

Kenneth L. Levine. "Obtaining 501(c)(3) Status for Professional Medical Corporations." *DePaul Journal of Health Care Law*, Winter 1998, *2*, 231.

This article examines how corporations have obtained tax-exempt status under Section 501(c)(3) as the physician component of an integrated delivery system by being organized and operated as nonprofit organizations or the equivalent of nonprofit organizations, subjecting themselves to the control of another tax-exempt entity, either providing sufficient community benefits or serving as an integral part of the other tax-exempt entity.

Douglas M. Mancino. "Tax Exemption Standards for HMOs." Washington, D.C.: American Health Lawyers Association [Report No. VHL99–0001], 1999, 49 pages.

This seminar paper provides extensive discussion of HMO tax exemption standards.

6.01(2)(i) Physician Hospital Organizations

T. J. Sullivan. "Managed Care Tax Issues." Washington, D.C.: American Health Lawyers Association [Report No VTX-0008], 1998, 16 pages.

Discusses current IRS views on tax treatment of HMOs, PPOs, IPAs, PHOs, MSOs, and PSOs, as well as certain issues involving taxable HMOs.

6.01(2)(j)   Other Charitable Organizations

Sandra Greiner. "Tax-Exempt Status of Health Maintenance Organizations: Geisinger Health Plan v. Commissioner." (Note.) *Tax Lawyer,* Winter 1994, p. 513.

Presents the facts and holding of the Third Circuit's decision in *Geisinger Health Plan* v. *Commissioner,* 985 F.2d 1210 (3d Cir. 1993), and discusses the IRC standards for HMOs seeking tax exemption. Greiner then compares *Geisinger* with the only other case to date addressing the issue of section 501(c)(3) status of HMOs, *Sound Health Assoc.* v. *Commissioners,* 71 T.C. 158 (1978), acq., 1981–2 C.B. 2.

Gerald M. Griffith. "HMO Exemption Revocation Signals New Approach to Section 501 (m) Enforcement." *Journal of Taxation of Exempt Organizations,* July–Aug. 1999, *11,* 12.

In December 1998, the IRS issued a technical advice memorandum regarding the tax-exempt status of IHC Health Plans, a subsidiary of Intermountain Health Care. In this memo, the IRS ruled that a typical nonstaff-model HMO is substantially engaged in commercial-type insurance unless it shifts a significant portion of the risk it has assumed. This article examines the memo in detail.

Gerald M. Griffith. "Revenue Ruling 98–15: Dimming the Future of All Nonprofit Joint Ventures?" *Journal of Health and Hospital Law,* June 1998, *31,* 71.

Whole hospital joint ventures between nonprofit and for-profit hospitals have proliferated in the 1990s. At the same time, various state legislatures and attorneys general have entered into the fray by challenging a number of whole hospital joint ventures and enacting statutory restrictions on sales and joint ventures of nonprofit hospitals. In each case, these state initiatives have generally restricted and arguably slowed the growth of such joint ventures. Now the IRS has joined in by issuing Revenue Ruling 98-15. This ruling does not necessarily sound the death knell for whole hospital joint ventures, although it may put them on the critical list. Moreover, nonprofit hospitals may find that the consequences of the ruling are even more far reaching and place an array of hospital-physician joint ventures (including physician hospital joint organizations) and management service organizations in serious jeopardy.

Kenneth L. Levine. "Obtaining 501(c)(3) Status for Professional Medical Corporations." *DePaul Journal of Health Care Law,* 1998, *2,* 231.

This article describes the steps to be followed to obtain tax-exempt status from the IRS.

Philip S. Neal. "IRS Perpetuates Confusion over the Tax Status of Health Maintenance Organizations." *Taxes,* Feb. 1991, 90.

Argues that the IRS's reliance on General Counsel's Memorandum (GCM) 39829 will have adverse tax consequences for HMOs in that it will result in unwarranted reliance on section 501(m)(1) to deny exemption to some nonprofit HMOs and reinforce the IRS's inclination to deprive for-profit HMOs of the right to be taxed as insurance companies under Subchapter L. In reaching his conclusion, the author, a practicing attorney, examines the ambiguous statutory language of IRC section 501(m), the legislative history, and relevant case law.

6.01(2)(k)   Intermediate Sanctions

Susan R. Bills. "How to Set Physician Compensation Under the Intermediate Sanctions." *Journal of Taxation of Exempt Organizations,* July–Aug. 1999, *11,* 21.

This article discusses the statutory background, IRS Guidelines on Reasonable Compensation (including Revenue Ruling 97–21), and the impact of intermediate sanctions.

Boris I. Bittker and Lawrence Lokken. *Federal Taxation of Income, Estates and Gifts.* (3rd ed.; paragraph 100.5.) Boston: Warren, Gorham, and Lamont, 1999; B. Hopkins. *The Law of Tax-Exempt Organizations.* 300–51 (6th ed., 1992); Treusch. *Tax-Exempt Charitable Organizations.* 263–329 (3rd ed., 1988).

Bonnie S. Brier. "Physician Compensation: Exempt Organization Creativity Without IRS Problems." Washington, D.C.: American Health Lawyers Association [Report No. VTX98–0015], 1998, 47 pages.

Reviews tax issues involving physician compensation, including intermediate sanctions, incentive compensation, and gain sharing. Discusses payments by for-profit affiliates, tax-exempt financing issues, physician recruitment and retention incentives, and reporting issues. Also provides planning suggestions.

Bernadette M. Broccolo. "Tax Exemption Update." Washington, D.C.: American Health Lawyers Association, [Report No. VHL98–0052], 1998, 74 pages.

Discusses developments in IRS regulations, including IRS CEP audits, exemption and denial of exemption, intermediate sanctions, participation by tax-exempt organizations in partnerships with individuals or taxable entities, horizontal IDS developments, joint operating agreements, revised IRS model conflicts of interest policy, stand-alone exemption for captive PSOs, incentive compensation issues, unrelated business income, political activities, tax-exempt financing developments, new PSO tax rules, and rulings on Pennsylvania property tax revocation issues.

Gerald M. Griffith. "Hospital-Physician Relationships: Compensation and Recruitment." Washington, D.C.: American Health Lawyers Association [Report No. TX97–0014], 1997, 52 pages.

Examines tax issues involved in hospital-physician compensation (base salary and incentives) and recruitment relationships of relevance for planning and audits. Also covers exempt status; intermediate sanctions; and the interplay among tax, fraud and abuse, and Stark law issues. Includes employed physicians chart, physician professional service agreement (nonemployee), and physician recruitment charts, all of which compare Stark laws, antikickback statutes, and section 501(c)(3) issues.

Thomas K. Hyatt. "IRS Intermediate Sanctions for Hospitals and Health Systems: Applying the New Proposed Regulations." Washington, D.C.: American Health Lawyers Association [Report No. VHH99–0030], 1999, 32 pages.

Reviews and analyzes the new IRS proposed regulations implementing intermediate sanctions that impose tax penalties on individuals who receive excessive private benefit from their transactions with tax-exempt organizations.

Thomas J. Hyatt. "Healthcare Joint Ventures and Tax Exemption: Current Issues." Washington, D.C.: American Health Lawyers Association [Item No. WM990002], 1999, 92 pages.

This spiral-bound monograph examines IRS treatment of joint ventures between tax-exempt health care organizations and nonexempt individuals and organizations such as physicians and investor-owned systems. The author focuses on developments in the IRS position on "whole hospital" joint ventures in Revenue Ruling 98-15 and on ancillary joint ventures in the *Redlands Surgical Services* case. Topics discussed include governance issues, management contracts, unrelated business income, tax-exempt bond financing, valuation, intermediate sanctions, and drafting tips; also reviewed are prior IRS guidance and case law in this area and a synopsis of IRS joint venture private letter rulings.

Thomas K. Hyatt. "IRS Intermediate Sanctions: Applying the Regulations." Washington, D.C.: American Health Lawyers Association [Report No. VHL 99–0017], 1999, 38 pages.

Detailed outline explores application of the IRS intermediate sanctions for failing to comply with the obligations of tax-exempt status under Section 501(c). Includes in-depth review of statutory provisions and definitions.

Thomas K. Hyatt. "Intermediate Sanctions for Tax-Exempt Healthcare Organizations: The Proposed Regulations." Washington, D.C.: American Health Lawyers Association [Report No. VTX98–0002], 1998, 32 pages.

Describes existing IRS sanctions for failure to comply with obligations of IRC Section 501(c)(3) status, intermediate sanctions (the "new weapon" to enforce compliance), the statutory scheme and the proposed regulations, reasonableness and fair market value, first-tier and second-tier excise taxes and their effect on existing sanctions, open questions on percentage of revenue transactions and excessive private benefit that does not involve disqualified persons, and the real-world impact of intermediate sanctions.

Internal Revenue Service. *Continuing Professional Education Exempt Organizations Technical Instruction Program Textbook.* (1996 ed.) Washington, D.C.: IRS, 1995.

Includes valuable tax materials relevant to hospital-affiliated integrated delivery systems. In this textbook, for example, the IRS modified the 20 percent rule to exclude IDSs and hospital administrative employees (and former employees). It also sets forth a detailed checklist of items that the IRS looks for in determining whether, for purposes of favorable tax treatment, an IDS benefits the community.

Internal Revenue Service. *Exempt Organizations Guidelines Handbook.* Washington, D.C.: IRS, 1996.

This is a valuable resource for attorneys, accountants, and administrators who work for tax-exempt hospitals and other tax-exempt health organizations.

Joseph C. Mandarino. "Intermediate Sanctions Flow Charts." *Journal of Health Law,* Winter 1999, *32,* 169.

These two highly detailed flowcharts describe the operation of Section 4958 of the IRC, the so-called "intermediate sanctions" legislation. The flowcharts assume that the proposed regulations will be adopted as final in their current form.

6.02   UNRELATED BUSINESS INCOME TAX (UBIT)

Bonnie S. Brier. "Tax Considerations in Managed Care Affiliations with Nonprofit Health Care Organizations." Washington, D.C.: American Health Lawyers Association [Report No. TX97–0013], 1997, 14 pages.

Discusses qualifications for exemption of various managed care organizations, impact on exemption or possibility of intermediate sanctions when a tax-exempt organization owns an interest in or otherwise participates in a managed care organization, and the unrelated taxable business income consequences resulting from amounts received or imputed to the managed care organization.

Bonnie Brier and Gerald M. Griffith. "Impact of Taxable PHOs and MSOs on Hospital Tax Exemption." Washington, D.C.: American Health Lawyers Association [Report No. VHL98–0027], 1998, 54 pages.

Analyzes the impact on a hospital's tax-exempt status of establishing a taxable physician hospital organization or management services organization. Looks at physician control, disproportionate capitalization, loans and preferred stock arrangements, allocation of revenues from third-party payers, acquisition issues, and service and lease arrangements. Also provides an overview of related commercial-type insurance and UBIT issues. Discusses *Redlands Surgical Services,* Revenue Ruling 98-15, and *United Cancer Council.*

D. Louis Glaser. "Unrelated Trade or Business Income and Hospitals: Reconciling Operating Losses and Charity Care." (Comment.) *Loyola University (Chicago) Law Journal,* 1988, *19,* 1307.

Justifies the tax exemption of unrelated business income for tax-exempt hospitals. The IRS and the courts have recognized that peculiar circumstances merit exempting from taxation unrelated business activities carried on by hospitals. The financial difficulty faced by many hospitals and the need for providing indigent care are two such circumstances. For hospitals to be able to continue in operation and treat charity patients, sufficient operating revenues must be available. One method of making increased revenues available is to exempt unrelated business income from taxation to the extent of business losses. By permitting this exemption, tax-exempt hospitals do not gain a competitive advantage over nonexempt hospitals. Rather, the author contends, the exemption merely permits hospitals to continue to benefit their communities by continued operation and service.

Lisa Hayes. "Hospitals and Unrelated Business Taxable Income." *Medical Trial Technique Quarterly,* 1993, *39,* 513.

Suggests that hospitals must be increasingly careful in tax planning of new business ventures. Owing to economic and social pressures, hospitals feel compelled to investigate new business opportunities that will stabilize their financial position. The author writes that jurisprudence on the issue of unrelated business income and hospitals has not resulted in clear and concise rules. The majority of the cases depend on whether the activity in question is substantially related to the exempt function of the hospital. This determination necessitates examining whether the activity contributes importantly to accomplishing those purposes and depends, in each case, on the facts and circumstances involved. Consequently, the author notes, to ensure that an activity is not an unrelated business, a hospital might want to submit a request to the IRS for a private ruling. This is especially important, for example, if the activity is considered to be commercial in nature or is financed by tax-exempt bonds. Although the private ruling might be expensive, if the venture involves a significant investment, it will be necessary to obtain an understanding of the particular tax consequences.

LaVerne Woods. "Unrelated Business Income Tax: Current Developments." Washington, D.C.: American Health Lawyers Association [Report No. VTX98–0001], 1998, 29 pages.

Reviews pertinent tax legislation and IRS releases affecting unrelated business income, including taxation of payments from controlled entities, ownership of S Corporation stock, corporate sponsorship payments, laboratory services, health club facilities, and pitfalls of unrelated income in tax-exempt bond financing.

6.03   APPLICATION OF FEDERAL TAX LAWS TO CORPORATE RESTRUCTURING AND JOINT VENTURING

Patricia Butler. *Profit and Public Interest: A State Policymaker's Guide to Non-Profit Hospital and Health Plan Conversion.* Portland, Maine: National Academy for State Health Policy, 1996.

Examines why state officials have such keen interest in the complex issues of conversion of nonprofits to for-profits (such as Blue Cross plans considering for-profit status) and provides guidance about what actions they might consider to ensure appropriate public oversight of health care conversion activities.

Richard G. Cowart. "Mergers and Acquisitions: For-Profit Tax Strategies." Washington, D.C.: American Health Lawyers Association [Report No. TX97–0012], 1997, 35 pages.

Summarizes buyers' and sellers' points of view, taxable acquisitions, tax-free acquisitions, hybrid transactions, miscellaneous tax considerations, tax due diligence, and accounting issues. Includes taxable stock purchases chart, taxable asset purchases chart, and two charts examining tax-free organizations.

John A. Good. "Contracting with PPMCs." Washington, D.C.: American Health Lawyers Association [Report No VTX98–0017], 1998, 42 pages.

Identifies key business, legal, and tax considerations in structuring a physician practice acquisition. Analyzes the tax impact of various acquisition and transaction structures and reviews certain financial accounting treatment considerations.

R. Todd Greenwalt. "Mergers and Acquisitions: Tax Exempt Financing Issues." Washington, D.C.: American Health Lawyers Association [Report No. VTX-98–0016], 1998, 30 pages.

Outlines changes in use and acquisition financing provisions applicable to tax-exempt bonds as those provisions pertain to merger and acquisition transactions.

Gerald M. Griffith. "Joint Operating Agreements: Current Issues." (Washington, D.C. American Health Lawyers Association [Report No VTX-0009], 1998, 53 pages.

Analyzes corporate structural and tax issues for nonprofit joint operating agreements. Discusses the IRS approach to three key tax issues for nonprofit hospital JOAs: (1) private use of bond-financed facilities, (2) unrelated business income, and (3) tax-exempt status of the participants and the joint operating company. Also reviews issues related to the former $150 million cap on non-hospital bonds, and special issues for holding companies and Catholic hospitals. Includes a checklist for JOA board authority (structural integration), a detailed list of IRS private letter rulings on approved reserved powers over JOCs (as entities), approved reserved powers over hospital operations, and approved delegation to hospital boards.

Gail P. Heagen. "Nonprofit Mergers and Acquisitions." Washington, D.C.: American Health Lawyers Association [Report No. VMA 98–0006], 1998, 29 pages.

Outlines the advantages and disadvantages of the forms of merger and acquisition that most likely will be used to achieve integrated health care, including asset mergers, asset purchases, lease of facilities, management contracts, virtual mergers or revenue mergers, partial ownership, sale or exchange of stock, and limited liability corporations. It also describes some of the components of the business plan for the three most common types of transaction: hospital mergers, managed care, and physician practices.

David I. Kempler. "Mergers and Acquisitions: For Profit Tax Issues." Washington, D.C., American Health Lawyers Association [Report No. VTX98–0005], 1998, 34 pages.

Discusses the federal income tax implications of various types of merger and acquisition, including taxable acquisition of a corporate business, asset acquisitions, stock acquisitions, sales and distributions of a subsidiary's stock, allocation of purchase price and basis, tax-free reorganizations, acquisitive reorganizations, stock-for-assets and stock-for-stock acquisitions, forward and reverse triangular mergers, treatment of the parties to an acquisitive reorganization, failed reorganizations, net operating losses, and operation of IRC Section 381.

Richard M. Lipton. "IRS Attacks Hospital Joint Ventures." *Taxes*, Feb. 1992, p. 59.

States that in GCM 39862 the IRS threw into turmoil a type of relationship that had developed between many physicians and tax-exempt hospitals. Until the release of GCM 39862, hospitals had increasingly been entering into joint ventures with physicians to provide a financial inducement for the physicians to use the hospital's facilities. In certain situations, the hospital would attempt to transfer to a joint venture the future revenues from a portion of the hospital's operations. GCM

39862 raises the question of whether such hospital service joint ventures will jeopardize the hospital's tax-exempt status.

Douglas M. Mancino. "Whole Hospital Joint Ventures after Revenue Ruling 98–15." Washington, D.C.: American Health Lawyers Association [Report No. VTX98–0003], 1998, 38 pages.

Discusses general issues involved in structuring joint ventures between tax-exempt and for-profit entities, joint ventures and maintaining Section 501(c)(3) tax-exempt status, planning whole hospital joint ventures in the aftermath of Revenue Ruling 98-15, and joint ventures and intermediate sanctions. Includes a selection of the IRS FY 1999 CPE (Continuing Professional Education) text for exempt organizations, discussing whole hospital joint ventures.

Douglas M. Mancino. "Following the Money." *Health Systems Review*, May–June 1997, p. 10.

Addresses what a nonprofit entity may do with the proceeds of selling its operating assets. In his analysis the author, a practicing attorney, examines both federal and California law.

Joseph C. Mandarino. "Recent Changes to the Internal Revenue Code May Require Tax-Exempt Hospitals to Restructure Ownership of Certain Activities." *Annals of Health Law*, 1998, *7*, 159.

Explores the implications of a 1997 change in the IRC affecting tax-exempt hospitals that run or operate for-profit businesses. The author examines the application of prior law to hospital ownership of for-profit ventures and then reviews the implications of the 1997 amendment, particularly on existing structures. The article concludes with suggestions to avoid applications of the amended section.

William S. Painter and Jody B. Martin. "Tax Issues." Washington, D.C.: American Health Lawyers Association [Report No VMAT98–0019], 1998, 36 pages.

Outlines tax issues in transactions from the seller's and buyer's points of view, taxable and tax-free acquisitions, hybrid transactions, tax-free spin-offs, joint venture arrangements, miscellaneous tax considerations, tax due diligence, and accounting issues.

Michael W. Peregrine. "Mergers and Acquisitions: Tax Exempt Issues." Washington, D.C.: American Health Lawyers Association [Report No. VTX98–0011], 1998, 57 pages.

Examines the relevant IRS rulings and judicial decisions relating to the various forms of merger and acquisition structure that tax-exempt organizations may participate in. Also discusses the relationship between the prohibitions against private benefit and private inurement and the intermediate sanction regulations and M&A activity, and offers suggestions on a process by which these issues may be addressed. Includes several charts illustrating tax-planning processes.

Michael W. Peregrine. "Transactions between Nonprofit and For-Profit Organizations." Washington, D.C.: American Health Lawyers Association [Report No. VMA 98–0007], 1998, 43 pages.

Examines the numerous legal issues presented when nonprofit and for-profit health care entities combine in any of a number of transactional models, such as asset purchase, sale, joint venture, and whole hospital venture. This seminar manuscript also reviews application of the relevant legal issues from the perspective of the nonprofit entity, including federal as well as state statutory considerations. It summarizes litigation in the area and includes a copy of the Texas attorney general's letter regarding the sale of Baylor University Medical Center and Baylor Health Care System to a for-profit entity, a California attorney general's press release regarding the Good Samaritan settlement, a client memorandum regarding IRS regulations and revenue procedure regarding change in use of bond-financed facilities, and sample contract language regarding IRC section 501(c)(3) factors.

Deborah Z. Read. "Taxable Subsidiaries and Limited Liability Companies." Washington, D.C.: American Health Lawyers Association [Report No. TX97–0004], 1997), 63 pages.

Examines using taxable subsidiaries by tax-exempt health care providers, including the basic concepts and new developments affecting taxable subsidiaries, and compares using a taxable subsidiary versus a limited liability company in structuring arrangements with taxable organizations. Also discusses LLCs and their potential use by health care providers, including general concepts applicable to an LLC, classification for income tax purposes, conversion of an existing entity to an LLC, potential use of LLCs by health care professionals and health care providers, and the LLC as an exempt organization.

T. J. Sullivan and Michael W. Peregrine. "Revenue Ruling 98–15: Is Control Now the 'Name of the Joint Venture Game'?" *Health Law Digest*, Apr. 1998, pp. 3–9.

With the Mar. 23, 1998, publication of Revenue Ruling 98-15, the IRS provided long-awaited, precedent-setting guidance on tax-exemption issues associated with formation of whole hospital joint ventures between nonprofit tax-exempt hospitals and for-profit companies. The ruling also provides useful clarification of the IRS position with respect to a tax-exempt hospital's participation in the more traditional ancillary joint venture model. The authors conclude that the ruling is consistent with controlling case law governing the exemption aspects of joint ventures.

6.04   STATE AND LOCAL TAXES

N. Keith Emge, Jr. "Nonprofit Hospitals and the State Tax Exemption: An Analysis of the Issues Since Utah County v. Intermountain Health Care, Inc." (Note.) *Virginia Tax Review*, 1990, *9*, 599.

Focuses on the challenges that have been made to the tax-exempt status of nonprofit hospitals in state courts since 1985. Emge provides background for the issue of tax-exempt status by discussing the history of and rationale for the tax exemption for nonprofit hospitals, the importance of this exemption for these hospitals, and the activities at the federal level that have shaped the current controversy.

O. David Gulley and Rexford E. Santerre. "The Effect of Tax Exemption on the Market Share of Nonprofit Hospitals." *National Tax Journal*, Dec. 1993, 477–486.

Reexamines the correlation between high property tax rates and nonprofit market share. It has been hypothesized that higher tax rates lead to a larger market share for nonprofit hospitals, given their tax-exempt status. However, existing cross-sectional studies offer little empirical support for the hypothesis. The authors find that higher state corporate income and local property tax rates do lead to greater market share for nonprofit hospitals. The results also indicate that a higher corporate tax rate leads to lower for-profit hospital market share, while a higher property tax rate is associated with lower public hospital market share.

Margaret A. Potter and Beaufort B. Longest, Jr. "The Divergence of Federal and State Policies on the Charitable Tax Exemption of Nonprofit Hospitals." *Journal of Health Politics, Policy and Law*, 1994, *19*, 393.

Focuses on the charitable exemption from real estate taxes that has traditionally been enjoyed by nonprofit hospitals because they provide specific social benefits. However, in the past three decades, major health policy changes at the federal level—most significantly, implementation of the Medicare and Medicaid programs—have weakened this rationale, the authors write. Federal tax regulations during this period have changed in ways that complement these federal health programs and the accompanying federal interests in encouraging efficiency and performance uniformity among hospitals. States and local governments, however, have different interests, which may favor a strict set of tax-exemption standards that disregard efficiency and elevate the importance of a measurable level of charitable service. Their divergent policies rest on a fundamental value judgment about whether nonprofit hospital care is intrinsically charitable or not. Increasingly, this judgment may be forced upon state courts and legislation by local governments seeking new tax revenues through elimination of hospital exemption from real estate taxes, the authors observe.

6.05 TAX-EXEMPT FINANCING

Daniel W. Coyne. "Minefields and Opportunities—Tax Exempt Financing in the M&A World." Washington, D.C.: American Health Lawyers Association [Report No. VMA 98–0019], 1998, 50 pages.

Reviews issues involved in outstanding tax-exempt financings relevant to a merger or acquisition and explores the possibilities for acquisition financing. This seminar manuscript also explores issues related to tax-exempt bonds. Appendices include IRS Revenue Procedure 97-13 on tax-exempt bonds and private activity bonds, a sample resolution declaring official intent to reimburse certain expenditures from proceeds of indebtedness, and a due diligence review list.

Robert C. Louthian III and Elizabeth M. Mills. "Physician Recruitment after Hermann Hospital." *Annals of Health Law,* 1995, 4, 1.

Discusses how physician recruitment changed after the IRS required Hermann Hospital in Houston to publish its tax-exempt bond closing agreement. This 560-bed tertiary care hospital was planning to issue the bonds when concerns arose internally as to certain physician recruitment and other practices. Presumably to receive an opinion of bond counsel, Hermann voluntarily approached the IRS to clear any possible blight on its tax-exempt status. As a result, the IRS made public its guidelines for physician recruitment. This article discusses the evils the guidelines are designed to prevent, summarizes previous guidance on this issue, and addresses certain specific provisions of the guidelines.

Robert W. McCann. "Capital Financing and Capital Cost Reimbursement." In Mark A. Hall (ed.), *Health Care Corporate Law: Financing and Liability.* Boston: Little, Brown, 1994.

Examines the basic alternatives for raising capital and the associated tax and securities law issues. Over the last two decades, debt financing has far and away supplanted other sources of capital financing for health care entities, particularly in the not-for-profit sector. Consequently a significant portion of this seventy-one-page chapter is devoted to tax-exempt debt financing. Other topics addressed include sources and forms of equity financing, private placements, venture capital, Medicare reimbursement of capital costs, lease expenses, and issues unique to nonprofit versus investor status.

Robert M. McNair, Jr., and Charles B. Congdon. "Selected Issues in Tax-Exempt Financing for Health Care Providers." Washington, D.C.: American Health Lawyers Association [Report No. VTX98–0026] 1998) 50 pages.

Describes the overall structure of tax-exempt financing requirements, with a particular focus on management contracts in the context of private business use restrictions. Summarizes Revenue Procedure 97-13 and provides hypothetical fact patterns applying 97-13.

Michael W. Peregrine. "Mergers and Acquisitions: Tax-Exempt Issues." Washington, D.C.: American Health Lawyers Association [Report No. TX97–0017], 1997), 50 pages.

This seminar paper reviews relevant law concerning asset sales, mergers and consolidations, joint ventures between exempt and nonexempt entities, affiliations between nonprofit health care providers, joint operating companies, limited liability companies, leases, and tax-exempt bond questions.

Therese L. Wareham and James E. Luebchow. "Finance 101." Washington, D.C.: American Health Lawyers Association [Report No. VIH99–0010], 1999, 63 pages.

Provides an overview of innovative financing options available to health care borrowers, with suggestions on how to select and implement the best financing vehicle. Includes outline of a debt issuance transaction. Attachments include an outline describing tasks to be completed with the issuance of bonds, and a form letter requesting documents for review with respect to tax-exempt bonds.

6.06   TAXATION OF HEALTH BENEFITS

J. L. Landry. "Preserving the Tax Advantages of Medical Savings Accounts." *Journal of Taxation*, 1999, *90*, 161.

P. J. Schneider. "Final Regs Under COBRA—Long Overdue Clarifications on Group Health Coverage." (Part 1) *Journal of Taxation*, August 1999, *91*, 102; (Part 2) *Journal of Taxation*, Sept. 1999, *91*, 172.

Provides full text of the COBRA regulations.

Jay A. Soled. "Taxation of Employer-Provided Health Coverage: Inclusion, Timing and Policy Issues." *Virginia Tax Review*, 1996, *15*, 447.

Explores three independent arguments in favor of excluding the cost of employer-provided health care coverage from taxation. Many tax theorists argue that the fair market value of all employer-provided health coverage must be included in the tax base. Anything less than full inclusion, they contend, constitutes a deviation from the ideal tax base and represents a tax expenditure. Similarly, many economists suggest that receiving tax-free health care coverage functions as a subsidy that artificially inflates demand. They postulate that repealing section 106 of the IRC would bring cost consciousness back into provision of health care, resulting in a corresponding reduction in overall demand, which would decrease medical care costs.

6.07   AUDIT ISSUES

Bonnie S. Brier. "Tax Issues—Staying Out of Trouble with the Regulators." Washington, D.C.: American Health Lawyers Association [Report No. AM97–0006], 1997, 64 pages.

Explores tax issues involving exempt health care providers, including general tax principles, acquisition of physician practices, physician compensation issues, physician recruitment and retention incentives, integrated delivery systems exemption, "virtual mergers" and joint operating agreement affiliations, tax exemption for PHOs and MSOs, joint ventures, and tax-exempt financing issues.

Diane Cornwell. "IRS Enforcement Case Studies." Washington, D.C.: American Health Lawyers Association [Report No VTX98–0013], 1998, 39 pages.

Discusses the implications and historical context of IRS and tax court determinations in 1997–98, such as *Redlands Surgical Servs., Anclote Psychiatric Ctr., Baptist Health Sys.* and *Great Plains Health Alliance,* regarding the activities of certain tax-exempt health care organizations, including whole hospital joint ventures and valuation of medical practices. Includes an excerpt from the IRS FY 1999 CPE text for exempt organizations for evaluating whether a partnership furthers charitable purposes and whether private benefit to the for-profit partners or manager is greater than incidental.

Derek F. Covert. "IRS Coordinated Examination Procedure: 'Surviving an IRS CEP Audit.'" Washington, D.C.: American Health Lawyers Association [Report No. VTX98–0006], 1998, 9 pages.

Summarizes a comprehensive approach toward managing an IRS CEP audit of a large, complex, tax-exempt health system.

Alan S. Goldberg. "Legal Ethics: Healthcare Law Challenges." Washington, D.C.: American Health Lawyers Association [Report No. VTX98–0014], 1998, 64 pages.

Identifies legal ethical issues that arise in counseling providers and suppliers, whether for profit or nonprofit, or individuals or corporations, when involved in health care transactions, relationships, affiliations, and contracts. Includes a sample form acknowledging and consenting to counsel's conflict of interest, a model procedure for analyzing ethical considerations in multiple representations, and legislative information on IRC Section 7525, the Taxpayer Confidentiality Act of 1988, which extends the federal attorney-client confidentiality privilege to tax advice from a tax practitioner to a taxpayer if the advice would be privileged between an attorney and a client.

R. Todd Greenwalt. "Planning for and Surviving a CEP Audit." Washington, D.C.: American Health Lawyers Association [Report No. VHL99–0021], 1999, 27 pages.

Discusses steps to take to reduce the amount of disruption and cost that accompany an IRS CEP audit. Includes practical tips on preparing for and managing an audit, including document control and interviewing hospital personnel.

Internal Revenue Service. *Introduction to the Healthcare Industry.* Washington, D.C.: IRS Corporate Education Section, 1995, 500 pages.

Written by the IRS's technical and health care examination experts, this audit training textbook provides a comprehensive presentation of the IRS position in health care issues. Topics analyzed include employment tax, fringe benefits, exemption issues, hospital system parents and other supporting organizations, clinics and integrated delivery systems, managed care organizations, UBIT, and deferred compensation. In view of its 1995 publication date, the text serves as an updated and more comprehensive presentation of the 1992 audit guidelines.

One especially significant chapter sets forth audit techniques for taxable health care entities; it is followed by initial interview questions for physicians, clinics, and laboratories. These questions relate to accounting systems, records, and internal controls. This book was designed for training purposes only, and the contents consequently may not be cited as authority for setting or sustaining a technical position. The book does, however, provide an excellent window into the IRS and its likely position on technical issues.

Internal Revenue Service. *IRS Audit Guidelines for Hospitals.* Washington, D.C.: Internal Revenue Service. www.irs.gov (updated continually).

This valuable manual supplies a range of tax information and technical guidance for hospitals.

Kenneth L. Levine. "The New Hospital Audit Hit List: An Analysis of the Revised Tax-Exempt Hospital Audit Guidelines." *Taxes,* June 1992, 399.

Examines the IRS's Audit Guidelines for Tax-Exempt Hospitals, issued Apr. 1, 1992. These guidelines focus on the following topics: (1) the community benefits standard; (2) the private inurement and benefit prohibitions; (3) the political activity prohibition; (4) IRS rules on hospital participation in joint ventures; (5) IRS tests for determining the proper employment relationship between physicians and hospitals; (6) the proper reporting of unrelated trade or business income; (7) antitrust laws; and (8) specific health care laws, including EMTALA.

The author, a practicing attorney, writes that a hospital audit may result in revocation of the tax exemption if the hospital is found to have violated the community benefit standard, the private inurement or benefit prohibition, the political activity prohibition, or the patient-dumping or fraud and abuse law. If the exemption is revoked, the hospital would have to pay income taxes. Also, the hospital's income tax liability could be retroactive to the date of the violation triggering the revocation and could entail penalties and interest. In addition, the revocation may subject the hospital to state and local sales and property taxes. Finally, the revocation would cause the hospital to default on its tax-exempt bond covenants, with the result that bondholders (1) would lose their federal income tax exemption on the bond interest; (2) may be subject to back taxes, penalties, and interest; and (3) may have a legal right to sue the hospital to recover these payments.

James J. McGovern. "The IRS Compliance Program for Nonprofit Hospitals." *Health Lawyer,* Winter 1996, p. 1.

Discusses such topics as the reasons for the IRS's hospital tax compliance program, available IRS documents that provide insight to the IRS position on audit issues, hospital examination guidelines, *The Healthcare Textbook for Agents, Tax-Exempt Bond Guidelines, and Fringe Benefits.* The author, a principal with KPMG Peat Marwick, was formerly assistant commissioner of employee plans and exempt organizations at the IRS.

Martin D. Moll. "Surviving a CEP Audit." Washington, D.C.: American Health Lawyers Association [Report No. VTX98–0007], 1998, 5 pages.

Brief outline provides practical advice on how to prepare for an IRS CEP audit. Reviews IRS and health care organization agendas for the first meeting with the IRS, CEP audit flow overview, dos and don'ts for IRS examinations, and what the IRS looks for during a CEP examination of a health care organization.

Gerald R. Peters. "An Examination of the Internal Revenue Service's Fiscal Years 1995, 1996 and 1997 Exempt Organization Continuing Professional Education Technical Instruction Program Textbook." Washington, D.C.: American Health Lawyers Association [Report No. TX97–0022], 1997, 51 pages.

Summarizes major issues that the IRS discussed in its *Continuing Professional Education Textbook* for three successive years, including integrated delivery systems, MSOs, valuation of medical practices, board of directors and conflict policy, joint operating agreements, partnerships, and joint ventures.

Cynthia F. Reaves and Derek F. Covert. "Developing and Implementing an In-House Compliance Program for Tax-Exempt Health Organizations." Washington, D.C.: American Health Lawyers Association Report No. TX97–0016], 1997), 71 pages.

IRS audits indicate that compliance problems exist for exempt health care organizations. This work outlines those areas that should be included in a comprehensive tax compliance program, and provides a framework for understanding the issues that must be monitored through such programs. Includes sample corporate policy on physician practice acquisitions, U.S. Sentencing Commission guidelines for organizations, a chart on Justice Department health care settlements, and the Clinical Practices of the University of Pennsylvania and Department of Justice settlement agreement.

6.08   FOR-PROFIT CONVERSION ISSUES

Gerald B. Curington. "Review of Proposed Not-for-Profit Hospital Transactions." Washington, D.C.: American Health Lawyers Association [Report No. VMA 98–0029], 1998, 8 pages.

Seminar manuscript providing a checklist of the types of document and the required provisions and explanations that an attorney general reviews in evaluating the conversion of a nonprofit hospital. It contains citations of Florida statutes and case law.

Kevin F. Donohue. "Crossroads in Hospital Conversions—A Survey of Nonprofit Hospital Conversion Legislation." *Annals of Health Law,* 1999, vol. 8.

Discusses the history of nonprofit hospital conversions in the United States and analyzes the National Association of Attorneys General Model Conversion Act. Additionally, surveys conversion related legislation in seventeen states plus the District of Columbia. Finally, recommends implementing adequate safeguards to ensure that nonprofit hospital assets are maximized and to ensure that subsequent use of conversion proceeds continues to fulfill the original charitable mission of the nonprofit hospital.

Joel Ferber and Jo Anna King. "A Cure for the Blues: Resolving Nonprofit Blue Cross Conversions." *Journal of Health Law,* Winter 1999, *32, 75.*

Analyzes the issues involved in converting nonprofit Blue Cross organizations to for-profit status. These issues have arisen in the context of litigation regarding the "reorganization" of Blue Cross and Blue Shield of Missouri (BCBSMo). BCBSMo had reorganized by creating and transferring a majority of its business to a new for-profit subsidiary. Missouri consumer groups and state regulators characterized the reorganization as a conversion, requiring BCBSMo to transfer its assets to a foundation dedicated to charitable health purposes. BCBSMo, however, denied that it had any obligation to leave behind its assets in the nonprofit sector. The BCBSMo litigation raises issues common to most conversions of nonprofit Blue Cross plans. This article provides a road map for state regulators and the public to follow in ensuring that the public interest is fully protected in such conversions.

General Accounting Office. "Not-for-Profit Hospitals: Conversion Issues Prompt Increased State Oversight." (Letter Report. GAO/HEHS-98–24.) Dec. 16, 1997.

Pursuant to a congressional report, GAO reviewed the process that some not-for-profit hospitals have used in converting to for-profit status, focusing on (1) the method used to value assets; (2) the process used to solicit interest and obtain bids; (3) the terms negotiated as part of the sales agreement, including provisions for continued charity care; (4) the extent of community involvement in the process; (5) how the proceeds from the sale were used to fulfill charitable missions; and (6) the role that state and federal governments play in regulating and monitoring hospital conversions.

GAO noted that (1) the process of converting from a not-for-profit hospital to a for-profit hospital was similar among the transactions GAO reviewed; (2) most transactions were carried out between boards and executives of the selling hospitals and representatives of the for-profit purchasers, and not routinely subject to public disclosure; (3) standard industry methodologies were used to estimate the value of the fourteen not-for-profit hospitals GAO reviewed; (4) eight of the fourteen hospitals received multiple bids, and almost all of the hospitals reported accepting a purchase price greater than the valuation estimate; (5) in negotiating conversion terms, most hospitals included provisions for continued charity care and services in the agreement; (6) the for-profit hospital or joint venture boards resulting from the conversions are responsible for monitoring compliance with these agreements and ensuring that they are enforced; (7) except for members of the boards of directors, community involvement in conversion decisions was limited; (8) net proceeds reported from the conversions totaled about $950 million; (9) of the fourteen transactions, twelve directed net proceeds to charitable foundations; (10) in most states, attorneys general have authority to monitor and oversee hospital conversions through common law and not-for-profit corporation law; (11) for nine of the conversions reviewed, five state attorneys general exercised their authority to review the conversion process; (12) states are beginning to increase the authority of attorneys general through specific conversion legislation allowing a state official to review the terms of the deal and direction of the charitable proceeds; (13) the federal government's role in monitoring hospital conversions is carried out mostly by the IRS and the FTC, which oversee tax and antitrust issues; (14) IRS officials stated that the operation of the joint venture may result in more-than-incidental benefit to the for-profit partner, thereby creating a basis for denying or revoking the tax status of the charitable entity; (15) another issue related to joint ventures involves the participation of individuals on both not-for-profit and for-profit boards, creating a potential conflict of interest; and (16) FTC officials reported that antitrust issues related to hospital conversions do not differ from other mergers and acquisitions, and the agency's involvement has generally been limited to a routine oversight role.

Eleanor Hamburger, Jeanne Finberg, and Leticia Alcantar. "The Pot of Gold: Monitoring Health Care Conversions Can Yield Billions of Dollars for Health Care." *Clearinghouse Review,* Aug.-Sept. 1995, 475–504.

This article, written from the perspective of a nonprofit consumer organization, summarizes Blue Cross of California's troubled effort to enter the for-profit arena.

Jeffrey Heidt. "Conversion of Status and Facility Closure." In Mark A. Hall and William S. Brewbaker III (eds.), *Health Care Corporate Law: Facilities and Transactions.* Boston: Little, Brown, 1996.

Addresses certain legal issues prompted by two important trends in the health care sector: the declining use of hospitals and the rise of their for-profit ownership and management. The particular transactions prompted by these trends that are the focus of this chapter are closure or bankruptcy of a hospital or other health care facility, conversion of a facility from one health care use to another, and conversion of a facility from nonprofit to for-profit status. After a brief discussion of these trends, this chapter focuses first on regulatory and corporate issues relating to facility closure and conversion to other uses and then on concerns that are unique to nonprofit facilities, particularly when they convert or are sold to for-profit ownership. Finally, issues that arise in bankruptcy and insolvency proceedings, including bankruptcy issues specific to health care, are discussed.

Thomas K. Hyatt. "Conversions of Nonprofit Health Organizations to For-Profit Status." Washington, D.C.: American Health Lawyers Association [Report No. VHL98–0015], 1998, 27 pages.

Reviews the state and federal law regarding conversions of tax-exempt health care organizations. Includes analysis of the IRS revenue ruling on whole hospital joint ventures.

Daniel W. Krane. "Conversion of Blue Cross/Blue Shield Plans and Other Non-Profit Insurers." Washington, D.C.: American Health Lawyers Association [Report No. MC97–0041], 1997), 37 pages.

Addresses various issues surrounding conversions of nonprofit health plans to for-profit form, including definitions of conversion, state and model legislation, and the rules of the various players interested in the conversion process. This report includes a review of conversion legislation and relevant legal issues such as charitable status, *cy près,* and fiduciary obligations.

Carol G. Kroch. "Non-Profit Conversions in the Health Care Industry." Washington, D.C.: American Health Lawyers Association [Report No. TX97–0020], 1997), 62 pages.

Outlines nonprofit conversions in the health care sector from the perspective of an exempt organization's federal income tax. Also addresses state charitable trust law issues that are intertwined with federal income tax when a nonprofit corporation undergoes a conversion.

Howard S. Levy. "Ronald J. Thompson v. Midwest Fnd'n Phy. Assn. (Choice Care): The Conversion of Nonprofit Health Maintenance Organizations to For Profit Status." *Northern Kentucky Law Review,* 1988, 16, 361.

Presents an overview of the conversion process, which entails analysis of the more controversial conversions as of the date this article was published. Levy then presents an analysis of *Thompson*

v. *Midwest Foundation Independent Physicians' Ass'n. (Choice Care)* (S.D. Ohio 1988), focusing on the problems of insider dealing, valuing the nonprofit HMO, and distribution of the nonprofit HMO's assets.

Pamela Kessler Lieber. "When 'Other Nonprofits' Convert." *Health Care Law Monthly,* June 1999, at 30.

Conversion, the process by which charitable organizations change from nonprofit to for-profit status, is now reaching beyond the health care sector and into other service areas of the nonprofit community. This article discusses catalysts for this change, stages of change, and implementing change.

Theresa McMahon. "Fair Value? The Conversion of Nonprofit HMOs." *University of San Francisco Law Review,* 1996, *30,* 355.

Reviews the background of HMO conversions, discusses the conversion process of one HMO as a paradigm of the California HMO conversion process, and critically analyzes the economic interpretation of "fair value" relied upon by the California Department of Corporations in assessing the value of nonprofit HMOs. The article concludes that the department's limited and erroneous interpretation of fair value lies at the heart of the undervaluation problem. Finally, the author offers suggestions about how the valuation process for nonprofit HMOs might be improved for future conversions.

Damien M. Prather. "Private Ruling Provides Template for Conversion to For-Profit Status." *Journal of Taxation of Exempt Organizations,* May–June 1999, *10,* 235.

This article provides a detailed, practical discussion of Private Letter Ruling 9853034, in which the IRS ruled that several exempt operating entities of an exempt health care system could convert to for-profit status without jeopardizing the exempt status of the parent organization or its remaining exempt affiliates.

John C. Sawyer. "When the Party's Over: Hospital Conversion Issues and Strategies." *Exempt Organization Tax Review,* Aug. 1999, *25,* 203.

Discusses five groups of conversion issues facing a hospital board that are unrelated to previous hospital operations: (1) state regulation, (2) policy, (3) governance, (4) management and administration, and (5) taxes.

Natalie Seto, Kathy Collins, and Bess Karger Weiskopf. "Protecting Health, Preserving Assets: Laws Governing Conversions, Mergers and Acquisitions Among Health Care Entities." *Clearinghouse Review,* Mar.-Apr. 1998.

When nonprofit health care corporations and insurers convert to for-profit status, billions in charitable assets are transferred into organized philanthropy. Issues about valuation and conflict of interest remain unresolved in many states, however, and threaten a lifeline for persons who increasingly face barriers to adequate health care. This article examines twenty-one state laws that address restructuring nonprofit entities.

Lawrence E. Singer. "The Conversion Conundrum: The State and Federal Response to Hospitals' Changes in Charitable Status." *American Journal of Law and Medicine,* 1997, *23,* 221.

Examines the reasons hospitals are exploring conversion to for-profit status and presents an overview of the kinds of conversion that are occurring. Singer explores relevant corporate law principles surrounding the fiduciary duties of those involved in conversion decisions, as well as charitable trust laws governing the assets of the not-for-profit entity as it goes through a conversion (each implicating the state attorney general's enforcement authority). The next section of the article reviews state laws governing conversion, which display a spectrum of views ranging from outright banning to seeming disinterest in these transactions. After examining the federal role in conversions, the article concludes with analysis of the policy implications of what has become the "largest redeployment of charitable assets in the history of the United States."

James D. Standish. "Hospital Conversion Revenue: A Critical Analysis of Present Law and Future Proposals to Reform the Manner in Which Revenue Generated from Hospital Conversions Is Employed." *Journal of Contemporary Health Law and Policy,* 1998, *15,* 131.

This article focuses on the use of revenue generated through conversion of nonprofit hospitals to for-profit status. It begins by outlining the concept of conversion, explaining the mechanics and detailing concerns over the historical uses of conversion revenue. It then surveys legislation covering the use of conversion revenue and discusses three proposals for future regulation of the use of conversion revenue. Next, it critically evaluates the three proposals, concluding with a model statute that attempts to build on the best of the three proposals and present legislation.

Nichole J. Starr. "The Conversion and Settlement of Georgia Blue: Are Consumer Groups Still Singing the Blues?" *Journal of Health Law,* Winter 1999, *32,* 115.

As more Blue Cross and Blue Shield organizations employ various means to convert to for-profit status, numerous issues arise concerning the proper treatment of assets that were accumulated during their not-for-profit years. Moreover, state officials face pressure from all sides to ensure that the conversion process is fair. The author examines the conversion of Blue Cross and Blue Shield in Georgia to demonstrate the various conversion issues that arise under the traditional legal principles—as well as the means by which that Blue employed newly enacted legislation to avoid many of the requirements that otherwise would have attended its conversion.

Aaron S. Wilkins and Peter D. Jacobson. "Fiduciary Responsibilities in Nonprofit Health Care Conversions." *Health Care Management Review,* Winter 1998, 77–90.

Examines key issues surrounding conversion of nonprofit hospitals to for-profit status. Such conversions have been controversial because of concerns that community interests are not represented at the bargaining table. As a result, several states have either enacted or are considering conversion legislation. However, there remains significant variation among the states in approaching conversion, including the extent of attorney general intervention. Federal or state legislation could standardize rules for nonprofit conversions, but such comprehensive legislation is unlikely, the authors write. Instead, CEOs and trustees of nonprofit organizations undergoing conversion must honor their fiduciary duties to ensure that a conversion represents community interests.

Antitrust Issues

The antitrust laws have as their central purpose to protect and foster competition. As recently as the 1970s, the antitrust statutes and their considerable judicial gloss were given little attention in terms of application to health care. Today, however, with health care accounting for more than 15 percent of U.S. GDP, with its growth exceeding that of inflation, and with the increasingly proprietary ownership of many facilities, the Federal Trade Commission and the U.S. Justice Department's Antitrust Division have begun to focus their enforcement efforts more intensively on this sector of the economy. As a consequence, an eye toward antitrust considerations is necessary in a variety of corporate planning situations, including whether to expand an existing facility or to share or merge facilities and services with other institutions; granting, denial, and limiting medical staff privileges; contracting with physicians on an exclusive basis; participation in hospital association and other coalition activities; and relationships with government, private business, and insurance companies.[1]

However, because he application of antitrust goals to health care is recent, reported judicial opinions display considerable uncertainty as to the extent to which the health care market is susceptible to antitrust principles developed over a number of decades in the framework of other commercial markets.[2] This chapter annotates a range of books, journal articles, and other materials that have seen print during the past decade and that explore how and whether antitrust rules can apply to health care.

References

1. George Heitler, Steven A. Hirsch, and Jocelyn Shaw. "Antitrust and Health Care." Reprinted in Michael G. Macdonald and others (eds.), *Health Care Law: A Practical Guide.* New York: Matthew Bender, 1997, § 9.01.
2. Heitler, Hirsch, and Shaw (1997).

ANNOTATIONS

7.01   GENERAL APPLICATION OF ANTITRUST PRINCIPLES TO HEALTH CARE

American Bar Association. *The Antitrust Healthcare Handbook II.* Chicago: ABA, 1993, 100 pages.

Designed for antitrust and health care lawyers and for health care administrators. Discusses the antitrust issues facing the health care industry, including an overview of federal antitrust laws, with emphasis on developments since the 1988 edition.

American Bar Association (Antitrust Law Section). *Developments in Antitrust Health Care Law.* Chicago: ABA, 1990, 208 pages.

Intended for both health care and antitrust attorneys, this book discusses and analyzes major antitrust issues and problems now facing health care providers and counsel.

American Bar Association. *Managed Care and Antitrust: The PPO Experience.* Chicago: ABA, 1990, 132 pages.

A practical guide to applying antitrust law to the activities of preferred provider organizations.

Aspen Health Law Center. *Health Care Antitrust.* Gaithersburg, Md.: Aspen, 1998, 160 pages.

Provides a practical overview of the principal legal issues relating to health care antitrust. It also promotes general understanding of antitrust analysis as applied to contractual relationships and business strategies that present antitrust risks in a managed care environment.

James F. Blumstein. "The Application of Antitrust Doctrine to the Healthcare Industry: The Interweaving of Empirical and Normative Issues." *Indiana Law Review,* 1998, *31*, 91.

This article opens with discussion of professional and market paradigms as they apply to medical care and then describes the contributions of antitrust laws to the evolution of the health care marketplace toward a more market-oriented focus. Antitrust focuses on promoting competition and evaluates conduct according to considerations of economic efficiency and consumer welfare. Because so much policy in the health care arena has been driven by concern for equity regarding access to quality medical care, enforcement of antitrust in the health care arena raises inevitable tension. Market efficiency may result in more appropriate use of resources, and improved competition and efficiency may result in economies that benefit consumers who might otherwise not be able to afford those services. However, even with an efficient system, there will be persons whose income is just too low to pay for medical care.

Traditionally, the health care system has used cross subsidies to achieve "worthy purposes," such as financing services for those without the resources to pay for medical care on their own. The funds for this cross subsidization have stemmed from receipt (typically by hospitals) of supracompetitive returns in some areas; those supracompetitive returns reflect the ability of hospitals to exert a form of monopoly control in certain market niches, allowing receipt of revenues beyond a competitive return. By focusing on promoting competition and economic efficiency, and by barring anticompetitive conduct that leads to earning supracompetitive returns, antitrust laws constrain the ability of providers and provider institutions to achieve supracompetitive returns. This in turn compromises the ability of health care institutions such as hospitals to cross-subsidize.

The competing away of supracompetitive returns is a natural result of introducing competition; also because antitrust circumscribes anticompetitive collusive or monopolistic conduct, it limits the ability of providers and provider institutions to restore their ability to cross-subsidize by earning supracompetitive returns. Many of the steps necessary to achieve supracompetitive returns will subject an institution to antitrust enforcement scrutiny.

Edward J. Buchholz and Stacey L. Murphy. "Internal Revenue Service Approval of Two Gain Sharing Programs—The Rulings and Their Implications." *Journal of Health Law,* 1999, *32*, 417.

Gain sharing is a mechanism by which hospitals can encourage physicians to participate in cost-saving programs by allowing the physicians to share in a percentage of the savings generated by the programs. Two recent IRS revenue rulings have held that gain sharing will not per se cause a hospital to lose its nonprofit status. However, in order for a nonprofit hospital to maintain its nonprofit status, the hospital must include safeguards in its gain-sharing plan to ensure that (1) quality care is maintained, (2) physicians are not overcompensated for their participation, and (3) all other applicable legal hurdles are cleared.

Howard Feller (ed.). *Antitrust Developments in Evolving Healthcare Markets.* Chicago: Section of Antitrust Law, American Bar Association, 1996, 429 pages.

This compilation of seminar papers covers a range of topics, including analysis of damages, interaction between antitrust laws and fraud and abuse laws, hospital staff privileges, peer review, antitrust implications of information sharing between competitors, state action immunity as a defense in the health care context, provider exclusion issues raised by integrated delivery systems, and the FTC's enforcement policy for health care markets.

Howard Feller and Neil P. Motenko. "Antitrust Compliance Programs for the Healthcare Industry." Washington, D.C.: American Health Lawyers Association [Report No. VAT98–0012], 1998, 27 pages.

Examines why antitrust compliance programs are necessary, the preliminary steps in establishing a compliance program, and the actual implementation of such programs.

Thomas L. Greaney. "Regulating for Efficiency in Health Care Through the Antitrust Laws." *1996 Utah Law Review,* 1995, 465.

Discusses the Health Care Policy Statements issued in 1994 by the Justice Department and the FTC, which attempt to illuminate the shadowy line between beneficial and harmful cooperation among rivals. These statements—which cover a range of combinations and joint activities involving physicians, hospitals, and third-party payers—seek to provide guidance regarding the antitrust implications of the extensive vertical and horizontal integration that is occurring in the health care sector. The policy statements, the author writes, embody the view that decision makers can and should evaluate the procompetitive potential of even the most suspect agreements among rivals.

Greaney finds that there exists a "startling absence of consensus in the antitrust community concerning the meaning of efficiency and the serious methodological problems associated with performing a trade-off analysis."

Thomas L. Greaney. "Antitrust and the Healthcare Industry: The View from the Three Branches." *Journal of Health Law,* 1999, *32,* 391.

This article provides a critical appraisal of three major health care antitrust events. The *California Dental Association* case, the Aetna-Prudential merger challenge, and the proposed Quality Health Care Coalition Act of 1999 are likely to provide tremendous influence in coming years, the author writes. The reasoning of these precedents suffers from too much reaction to the managed care bogeyman, he concludes. Consequently, their impact is unlikely to be for the good.

Clark C. Havighurst and Peter M. Brady. "Accrediting and the Sherman Act." *Law and Contemporary Problems,* Autumn 1994, 197.

Seeks to demonstrate and correct doctrinal and analytical shortcomings in antitrust law as it applies to private accrediting. This article argues that antitrust law, as currently applied, does not effectively protect consumers against private accrediting that distorts the options available to consumers in the marketplace. On the premise that information and opinion concerning goods and services offered in the marketplace should be produced under competitive conditions to the extent that competition is feasible, the article argues that private accrediting should be subject to antitrust enforcement targeted at artificial restrictions on the output of such information.

Michael S. Jacobs. "Rural Health Care and State Antitrust Reform." *Mercer Law Review,* 1996, *47,* 1045.

Argues that state reform laws represent an ineffectual response to the serious problems of rural poverty and an ill-conceived solution to "problems" with federal antitrust law that are more imagined than real. Federal antitrust laws have helped open health care markets to competition and are still crucial to continue that improvement.

David Marx Jr. and James H. Sneed. *Antitrust and Healthcare: Meeting the Challenge.* (2nd ed.) Washington, D.C.: American Health Lawyers Association, 1998 [Book No. WB98–0002].

Competition continues to drive providers and payers into nontraditional business relationships—increasing exposure to antitrust liability. Challenges from the Justice Department and the FTC have attempted to expand the reach of the Sherman Act and the McCarran-Ferguson Act. Meanwhile, Supreme Court decisions continue to define new concerns for health care providers, payers, and allied professionals. Written by two attorneys in private practice, this book addresses nine areas of potential liability: (1) price fixing, market allocation, and boycotts among competitors; (2) mergers, affiliations, and acquisitions; (3) provider networks and managed care contracting; (4) specialized joint ventures involving equipment or clinical services; (5) trade associations and group purchasing organizations; (6) medical staff privileges and peer review; (7) hospital diversification; (8) health insurance and purchasers of health care services; and (9) price discrimination.

Catherine Mazanec. "The Efficiency Study." Washington, D.C.: American Health Lawyers Association [Report No. VAT99–0010], 1999, 10 pages.

Although the DOJ and FTC guidelines on merger were revised in 1997 to emphasize the importance of efficiencies in determining whether a merger's benefits exceed its potential anticompetitive effects, there are still a number of problems and misconceptions associated with these analyses. Specific features and characteristics of efficiency studies that address identified concerns outlined in this paper should increase their acceptance to the DOJ and FTC while enhancing the value of the study to the merging organizations.

David L. Meyer and Charles F. Rule. "Antitrust Liability." In Mark A. Hall (gen. ed.), *Health Care Corporate Law: Financing and Liability.* Boston: Little, Brown, 1994.

Surveys the basic principles of antitrust as they relate to the health care field, with primary focus on federal antitrust laws. Part A of this chapter provides an overview of the history of federal antitrust laws and their expansion into the health care field during the past generation, as well as an overview of the purpose and basic structure of the law. It also summarizes the core statutory provisions that, together with their considerable judicial gloss, define the scope of potential antitrust liability. Part B describes the manner in which antitrust laws are enforced by private litigants and federal and state government agencies.

Part C addresses in more detail the standards of liability under Section One of the Sherman Act, which is the core antitrust prohibition against joint conduct having an unreasonable effect on competition. It first addresses the basic requirement of joint action embodied in Section One. It then describes the basic analytical framework used to determine whether joint conduct poses an unreasonable threat to competition and the specific categories of conduct deemed so likely to cause harm to competition that they are unlawful per se. The application of the analytic framework known as the rule of reason is illustrated with several types of conduct in the health care field that have recently received (or likely soon will receive) a high degree of scrutiny from courts and antitrust enforcers.

Part D addresses other aspects of the federal antitrust laws that are most relevant to health care institutions. The major topics are the legality of mergers and acquisitions, the application of antitrust laws to unilateral conduct, and the Robinson-Patman Act prohibition of certain forms of price discrimination in the sale of commodities. Finally, Part E addresses a variety of defenses to or exclusions from antitrust liability having particular application to the health care field.

John J. Miles. "Antitrust Fundamentals." Washington, D.C.: American Health Lawyers Association [Report No. FH97–0006], 1997, 95 pages.

Provides a thorough overview of the history of antitrust laws and their application to the health care sector. This seminar paper includes extensive footnotes citing leading cases and an antitrust bibliography.

John J. Miles. *Health Care and Antitrust Law: Principles and Practice.* St. Paul, Minn.: West Group, 1998.

This two-volume treatise, written by a practicing attorney, is addressed to both the attorney and the nonattorney. Part One presents a basic overview of generally applicable antitrust statutes along with their ample judicial gloss, without special emphasis on the health sector. It outlines those materials' substantive and procedural applications. Part Two takes the principles set forth earlier and applies them to specific situations frequently faced by participants in the health care sector. This section will be helpful for attorneys as well as hospital administrators, health care association executives, physicians, payer executives, and others who understand health care but who are not familiar with antitrust principles and how they apply to the health care sector.

The book identifies the types of practice that have led to antitrust litigation thus far (along with some that likely will lead to litigation in the future) and explains how antitrust principles apply to them. It incorporates practice changes resulting from the 1996 Antitrust Enforcement Policy in Healthcare. It also supplies some practical pointers to minimize the probability of the problem arising from the start. Written in laudably clear prose, this treatise concludes with an index, table of cases, and extensive appendices setting forth pertinent Justice Department and FTC documents. This loose-leaf treatise is regularly updated.

John J. Miles and Douglas C. Ross. "Antitrust Compliance." Washington, D.C.: American Health Lawyers Association [Report No VAT99–0021], 1999, 14 pages.

Discusses reasons for a compliance program, contents of a good program, potential antitrust problems against which a compliance program should guard, elements of a program, and how to implement and coordinate antitrust compliance within a broader health care compliance program.

William McD. Miller III. "Distribution/Pricing Issues in Health Care." Washington, D.C.: American Health Lawyers Association [Report No. VAT98–0020], 1998, 40 pages.

Examines in detail antitrust statutes and pricing issues in various health care arrangements, nonprice joint conduct by health care providers, and special antitrust issues in distribution of medical goods.

Robin Remis. "Health Care and the Federal Antitrust Laws: The Likelihood of a Harmonious Existence." *Journal of Contemporary Health Law and Policy,* 1996, *13,* 113.

Discusses the conflict between the federal antitrust laws and the structure of the U.S. health care industry. Advocates for reform of antitrust law argue that the only method of resolving the conflict entails reexamination of the application of the current antitrust laws. This position, however, fails to acknowledge the importance and the underlying purpose of federal antitrust laws. Reformation of antitrust laws is unnecessary to respond to the changes occurring in the health care industry, the author contends. Federal antitrust laws, as presently written and enforced, provide a great degree of flexibility for private collaborative efforts aimed at achieving more efficient and less costly delivery of health care services and thus should be applied to safeguard economic competition in the health care industry. The flexibility of federal antitrust laws, coupled with the ability of states to replace competition with state regulation under the state action doctrine, support the thesis that there should not be blanket immunity from federal antitrust laws for the health care industry, as proposed by many economists and health care professionals.

Douglas C. Ross. *Antitrust and Health Care: New Approaches and Challenges.* Chicago: American Bar Association, 1998, 399 pages.

This book is a collection of eighteen articles presented at a 1996 seminar sponsored by the ABA Section on Antitrust Law and the ABA Section on Health Law.

Douglas C. Ross. "CHINs/Information Alliances." Washington, D.C.: American Health Lawyers Association [Report No. VAT98–0016], 1998, 14 pages.

Community Health Information Networks (CHINs) collect information gathered from providers, payers, and consumers. This work examines antitrust issues that arise because information is gathered from providers and payers who otherwise are competitors, pertaining to membership, pricing, and the kind of information exchanged among participants.

William M. Sage. "Judge Posner's RFP: Antitrust Law and Managed Care." *Health Affairs,* 1997, *16*(6), 144–161.

Asserts that the emergence of a competitive market in health care portends an increasingly important role for antitrust law. It is even more difficult to analyze managed care in the quantitative, economic terms required by modern principles of antitrust law than it is fee-for-service practice. This article examines a decision authored by a prominent judge and antitrust scholar, *Blue Cross and Blue Shield United of Wisconsin* v. *Marshfield Clinic,* 65 F.3d 1,406 (7th Cir. 1995), cert. denied, 116 S. Ct. 1288 (1996). In this article, the author attempts to illustrate the assumptions and gaps in understanding that can occur when courts are asked to evaluate this complex and rapidly changing industry without the benefit of sound empirical research.

John J. Smith. "The Specialty Boards and Antitrust: A Legal Perspective." *Journal of Contemporary Health Law and Policy,* 1994, *10*, 195.

Describes the twenty-four specialty boards recognized by the American Board of Medical Specialties and the process and consequences of certification for physicians. After briefly examining basic antitrust doctrine, Smith, who holds degrees in both law and medicine, applies the doctrine to medical specialty boards; despite the absence of extensive case law addressing the application of antitrust law to specialty boards, he perceives a number of trends emerging from the few reported cases. He concludes that it is highly likely that any antitrust challenge to the specialty boards would be evaluated under a deferential rule-of-reason analysis, which does not pose a serious threat of liability.

Mary Lou Steptoe and Francis M. Fryscak. "Review of Traditional Defenses: Noerr-Pennington, Efficiencies and Not-For-Profit Status." Washington, D.C.: American Health Lawyers Association [Report No. VAT98–0022], 1998, 15 pages.

Assesses traditional and evolving defenses to antitrust challenges of hospital mergers and collective actions by physicians, including the Noerr-Pennington doctrine, not-for-profit defense, efficiencies, and postmerger conduct agreements.

Michael E. Vita and others. "Economic Analysis in Health Care Antitrust." *Journal of Contemporary Health Law and Policy,* 1991, *7,* 73.

Written by four staff members of the FTC's Bureau of Economics, this article focuses on health care mergers and acquisitions and anticompetitive agreements among competitors.

Jacqueline S. Zinn. "Market Competition and the Quality of Nursing Care." *Journal of Health Politics, Policy and Law,* 1994, *19,* 555.

Identifies factors influencing the degree of competition in the nursing home market. Using data obtained from the 1987 Medicare and Medicaid Automated Certification Survey, the relationship between competition and structural and process measures of quality (registered nurse staffing and resident care management practices) is estimated. Results suggest that the quality effects of indicators of competition vary and that market concentration may not diminish quality-based competition. The authors evaluate proposals for nursing home reimbursement reform with respect to their incentives for enhancing quality, particularly in the Medicaid market segment.

Jack Zwanziger and others. "Hospitals and Antitrust: Defining Markets, Setting Standards." *Journal of Health Politics, Policy and Law,* 1994, *19,* 423.

The definition of geographic and product markets is a critical aspect of any antitrust analysis. This paper argues for a different approach to market definition in areas where insurance plans that contract selectively are a significant market presence. Such a proposed approach is described, and some policy implications are drawn.

7.02 ANTITRUST ISSUES RAISED BY PROVIDER ACTIVITIES

American Bar Association (Antitrust Law Section). *Antitrust Aspects of Joint Health Care Provider Activities Affecting Price.* Chicago: ABA, 1989, 112 pages.

Suggests how hospitals, physicians, and insurers can cooperate to improve efficiency within the existing antitrust regulations on price fixing.

American Bar Association. *Information Sharing among Health Care Providers: Antitrust Analysis and Practical Guide.* Chicago: ABA, 1994, 48 pages.

A guide to the antitrust laws of information sharing in the health care industry and methods of reducing the risk of antitrust challenge.

American Bar Association. *Practical Implications of the Health Care Quality Improvement Act: Antitrust Analysis.* Chicago: ABA, 1994, 80 pages.

Written for health care attorneys and their clients, this text addresses the antitrust impact of the Health Care Quality Improvement Act of 1986 on peer review proceedings. It examines the provisions of the act and its judicial gloss, which provide immunities and protections from antitrust liability to providers who participate in peer review.

James F. Blumstein. "Assessing Hospital Cooperation Laws." *Loyola Consumer Law Reporter,* 1996, *8,* 248–268.

Examines the nature of the health care market and its evolution, explains the legal basis for state conferral of antitrust immunity for hospital cooperative conduct, reviews federal antitrust hospital industry enforcement guidelines, and summarizes the state hospital cooperation laws. Blumstein concludes with a discussion of the likely impact of hospital cooperation laws on the consumer.

James F. Blumstein. "Health Care Reform and Competing Visions of Medical Care: Antitrust and State Provider Cooperation Legislation." *Cornell Law Review,* 1994, *79,* 1459.

Argues that certain aspects of antifraud and abuse laws are premised on a philosophical and institutional regime hostile to market-based principles, yet they coexist with other doctrines, such as antitrust, that are based on traditional market assumptions. As the reality of the health care sector changes, leftover legal land mines impede economically rational behavior.

The state hospital cooperation laws, Blumstein contends, represent a "potentially revanchist attempt by the industry to restore professional and provider dominance by reestablishing a more comfortable regime conducive to cross subsidization." Experience with such planning and regulatory efforts, he writes, has not been reassuring. "Pro-market advocates are rightly skeptical of initiatives that eliminate antitrust law's assurance of a pro-competitive environment."

William S. Brewbaker III. "Antitrust Conspiracy Doctrine and the Hospital Enterprise." *Boston University Law Review,* 1994, *74,* 67.

Evaluates antitrust conspiracy doctrine in litigation surrounding medical staff privileges. The thesis of this article is that given the typical economic and managerial independence of physicians from hospitals, courts are usually wrong to view hospital decision making regarding medical staff privileges as the equivalent of decision making within a single integrated firm. Except in the unusual case of staff physicians' medical practices and hospital operations being significantly integrated, traditional hospital governing structures create the risk of anticompetitive physician conduct. In the typical case, hospital decisions involving medical staff participation should escape scrutiny under Section One of the Sherman Act only if it can be demonstrated that the medical staff acted in a purely advisory role, Brewbaker contends.

Anthony J. Dennis. "Potential Anticompetitive Effects of Most Favored Nation Contract Clauses in Managed Care and Health Insurance Contracts." *Annals of Health Law,* 1995, 4, 71.

Considers the anticompetitive effects of MFN contract clauses as well as the arguments in their favor. An MFN contract clause consists of a promise by a seller of products or services (in the health care context, a medical provider) to a purchaser of those products or services (an insurer), pursuant to which the seller agrees to give the purchaser as favorable a price as that seller is giving to any other purchaser. Although there are procompetitive justifications for using such clauses, MFN provisions appear to tend to force competitors from the health care market and set an artificial price floor in the health care marketplace.

Alice G. Gosfield and Brian M. Peters. "Hospital/Physician Relationships." Washington, D.C.: American Health Lawyers Association Report No. VAT98–0033], 1998, 31 pages.

Examines the reasons for competition between hospitals and physicians and the forms of hospital-physician relationship, provides an overview of the antitrust laws, and analyzes direct competition between physicians and hospitals. Discusses hospital credentialing criteria and the litigation risks of underinclusion and overinclusion in provider networks.

A. Everette James and others. "Legal Considerations of Medical Imaging." In Cyril H. Wecht (ed.), *Legal Medicine 1993.* Salem, N.H.: Butterworth, 1994.

This article examines, among other issues, application of antitrust principles to radiologists functioning in a hospital setting.

William G. Kopit and Alexandre B. Bouton. "Antitrust Implications of Provider Exclusion." In Peter R. Kongstvedt (ed.), *The Managed Health Care Handbook.* (4th ed.) Gaithersburg, Md.: Aspen, 2000.

Subjects addressed in this twenty-four-page chapter include the importance of market power, the relevant market, exclusive dealing arrangements, the importance of efficiencies, antitrust standing, group boycotts, and state any-willing-provider legislation.

Robert F. Leibenluft. "Antitrust Issues for Long Term Care Providers." Washington, D.C.: American Health Lawyers Association [Report No. VLT99–0037], 1999, 14 pages.

Describes in outline form the antitrust analysis of joint ventures generally, and then considers antitrust issues raised by long-term care provider joint ventures to contract with managed care. Also addresses the providers' collective provision of information to payers, joint purchasing arrangements, "captive referral," tie-in and leveraging cases, and mergers of long-term care providers.

Robert F. Leibenluft. "Antitrust Issues for Physicians." Washington, D.C.: American Health Lawyers Association [Report No. VPH99–0013], 1999, 23 pages.

Describes the principal antitrust issues raised by health care provider networks and discusses antitrust issues raised by joint contracting with managed care, including application of the 1996 DOJ/FTC Statements of Antitrust Enforcement Policy in Health Care. Also addresses providing information to payers, physician unions, joint purchasing arrangements, captive referral cases, and physician mergers.

Howard Feller and Robert F. Leibenluft. "Antitrust Issues Involving Allied Health Providers." Washington, D.C.: American Health Lawyers Association [Report No. VAT99–0020], 1999, 37 pages.

> Discusses the various antitrust issues and recent court decisions that apply to nonphysician health care providers. Specifically addresses the antitrust challenges that have been raised to arrangements that exclude allied health providers, including restraints of trade under Section One of the Sherman Act, monopolization, attempts to monopolize and challenges of conspiracy to monopolize, and corresponding defenses and immunities. Also discusses joint ventures among health care providers.

Arthur N. Lerner. "Payor Relationships with Providers—Comments from the Government and Private Perspective." Washington, D.C.: American Health Lawyers Association [Report No. VAT99–0023], 1999, 25 pages.

> Discusses selected areas of antitrust regarding provider network arrangements, problems specific to markets with a dominant provider, most-favored-nation (also known as most-favored-customer) clauses, erection of barriers by managed care organizations, and provider network exclusions.

Arthur N. Lerner. "Antitrust Issues in Long-Term Care." Washington, D.C.: American Health Lawyers Association [Report No. VLT98–0034], 1998, 33 pages.

> Assesses how antitrust issues affect long-term care by reviewing managed care contracting, tie-ins and captive referrals, mergers, and boycotts. Reviews antitrust principles and laws, and looks at case law developments in long-term care.

Robert N. Meals. "Slim and Next to None: A Physician Advocate's Evaluation of the Current Chances of Success for Federal Antitrust Claims Based on the Denial or Loss of Medical Staff Privileges." Washington, D.C.: American Health Lawyers Association [Report No. VAT99–0025], 1999, 30 pages.

> Supplies a physician advocate's perspective on the chances of success for federal antitrust claims based on denial or loss of medical staff privileges. Includes digests of relevant case law, and analyzes the impact of the Health Care Quality Improvement Act on antitrust claims in medical staff privilege cases since 1990.

Jeff Miles. "Hospitals, Hospital Systems and Antitrust." Washington, D.C.: American Health Lawyers Association [Report No. VHH99–0033], 1999, 65 pages.

> An overview of the most important antitrust issues affecting hospitals and hospital systems today, including antitrust analysis of hospital mergers, virtual mergers, joint ventures, and contrasting networks, with particular emphasis on premerger behavior, relevant geographic market definition, efficiencies analysis, nonprofit status, and customer testimony.

William McD. Miller III. "Antitrust Issues in Rural Markets: Antitrust Analyses of Hospital Conduct in Rural Areas." Washington, D.C.: American Health Lawyers Association [Report No. VAT99–0019], 1999, 34 pages.

> Analyzes the unique nature of rural hospital markets and the impact of antitrust laws upon them. Discusses the antitrust laws that most often affect rural hospital markets. Examines several governmental approaches that restrict application of antitrust laws in rural settings. Also analyzes federal antitrust agencies' recognition of the special status of rural markets.

Neil P. Motenko. "Provider and Payor Collaboration on Clinical Standards: The Antitrust Implications." Washington, D.C.: American Health Lawyers Association [Report No. VHL99–0011], 1999, 29 pages.

Examines how conventional antitrust principles apply to provider and payer collaboration on issues of quality of care. Topics include joint ventures, information sharing, standard setting, and marketplace opportunities for providers.

John J. Smith. "The Specialty Boards and Antitrust: A Legal Perspective." *Journal of Contemporary Health Law and Policy*, 1995, *10*, 195.

At the time this article was written, there were no major cases addressing substantive federal antitrust issues in the context of board certification, thus making definitive analysis impossible. Decisions addressing organizations and issues similar to those found in board certification do, however, give respectable insight into possible treatment of the specialty boards, the author writes.

Emerging from this case law are several trends. Initially, courts appear to favor application of the rule of reason to legitimate professional standards promulgated by private organizations. The availability of this treatment, and the deference afforded by the courts in actually applying it, appear to depend heavily on one and perhaps two factors. The key consideration is whether the record suggests that the standard at issue was promulgated primarily for economic reasons. If such a motive is apparent, courts will either apply a per se rule or quickly find liability while ostensibly applying the rule of reason. Another qualification may exist where the privilege or benefit denied by application of private standards effectively prevents an individual from engaging in an economic activity—that is, the privilege or benefit is of paramount commercial significance. Should neither condition exist, there is strong evidence of significant judicial deference under the rule of reason to medical or academic standard decisions.

The specialty boards as they presently exist promulgate certification standards based on the medical knowledge deemed necessary to practice high-quality specialty medicine; economics plays no explicit role in this decision-making process. In addition, certification is not essential to practice medicine, nor is there any concerted effort on the part of the boards or organized medicine to enforce a particular use of certification standards. These realities make the commercial significance of board certification activities tenuous at best. Given the lack of both an underlying economic motive and commercial impact, it is highly likely that any antitrust challenge to the specialty boards would be evaluated under a deferential rule-of-reason analysis, one that does not pose a serious threat of liability.

James H. Sneed. "Staff Privileges Cases: Are Antitrust Claims Viable?" Washington, D.C.: American Health Lawyers Association [Report No. VAT99–0026], 1999, 9 pages.

Presents the defendant's outlook on why physicians' challenges to denial, termination, or limitation of medical staff privileges under the antitrust laws fail, and analyzes the typical issues raised in cases of this type.

Mark J. Swearingen. "Applying Antitrust Law to Nonprofit Healthcare Entities: Arguments for a Greater Attention to Detail." *Journal of Health Law*, 2000, *33*, 57.

This article begins with an antitrust primer and then analyzes appropriate application of antitrust principles to nonprofit health care providers. In light of the inherent charitable character of nonprofit health care providers, the author contends that the government and the courts should accord some deference to nonprofit hospitals when they are seeking approval of mergers. To date this has not generally been the case, although some recent court decisions have rested their approval of mergers in part upon the nonprofit character of the merging entities. The author, in particular, believes the paradigmatic local nonprofit hospital with a community board is less likely than a for-profit hospital to abuse any market power it may obtain through a merger; consequently any such merger should not be analyzed solely under the traditional presumptions of antitrust jurisprudence. Rather, the premerger analysis should involve meaningful consideration of the hospital's charitable character.

Sarah S. Vance. "Immunity for State-Sanctioned Provider Collaboration after Ticor." *Antitrust Law Journal,* 1994, *62,* 409.

Discusses the policy debate behind new state legislation and considers the viability of some enacted provider immunity laws under the antitrust principles announced in *Federal Trade Commission* v. *Ticor Title Insurance Co.* Health care providers often point to antitrust laws as a significant barrier to collaborative activities that could reduce health care costs and improve access to quality health care. As a consequence, they have pressured Congress and state legislatures to create exemptions from federal and state antitrust laws for various forms of provider collaboration. At the national level, the FTC and the Justice Department have issued joint policy statements creating antitrust safety zones exempting some hospital cooperation ventures from antitrust scrutiny, and a number of states have passed legislation to that end as well. In 1992, however, the U.S. Supreme Court, in *Federal Trade Commission* v. *Ticor Title Insurance Co.,* 112 S. Ct. 2169 (1992), made it more difficult for the states to cloak private actors with antitrust immunity.

Peter C. Ward. "State Action Antitrust Immunity for Public Hospitals: It Depends on What You Mean By 'Foreseeable.'" *Journal of Health Law,* 2000, *33,* 1.

The Supreme Court's refusal to hear an appeal from the Fifth Circuit's ruling on applying state action antitrust immunity doctrine leaves a split in the circuits as to the proper test to apply to determine antitrust immunity for public hospitals. The circuits have either adopted a "foreseeable conduct from state policy" approach or a "policy from foreseeable conduct" approach. This article analyzes the approaches and demonstrates that the former is the better approach.

7.03   MERGER AND JOINT VENTURE DEVELOPMENTS

Gloria J. Bazzoli and others. "Federal Antitrust Merger Enforcement Standards: A Good Fit for the Hospital Industry?" *Journal of Health Politics, Policy and Law,* 1995, *20,* 137.

Examines the implications of the 1992 Horizontal Merger Guidelines for the hospital industry and subsequent policy statements that were developed for health care providers. Application of antitrust policy to hospitals has raised several concerns, mainly because many communities have few hospitals and economic forces in the industry are accelerating interest in intramarket mergers and provider network development. The authors address several issues, including the standing of hospitals relative to the market concentration thresholds of the merger guidelines, market concentration compared among challenged and unchallenged mergers of the 1980s, findings of previous research about the relationship between market concentration and competition in hospital markets, and differences in characteristics other than market concentration that are relevant to the merger guidelines among challenged and unchallenged mergers.

The authors found that (1) the specific standards articulated in the merger guidelines do not provide good predictability of when a hospital merger challenge would occur, and (2) comparisons of challenged and unchallenged mergers in similarly structured markets suggest that enforcement actions may deviate in practice from the enforcement principles of the merger guidelines. The authors consider several options for refining antitrust enforcement policy.

Erwin A. Blackstone and Joseph P. Fuhr, Jr. "Hospital Mergers: The Shift from Federal Antitrust Enforcement to State Regulation." *Journal of Health Law,* 2000, *33,* 103.

The authors examine and analyze the burgeoning merger activity in the hospital arena, as well as the nonfederal attempts made to regulate that activity. They conclude that the present, ad hoc system of state regulation is sorely wanting and that it would be preferable if stronger antitrust enforcement and judicial decisions prevented competition-reducing mergers. If a merger results in a true monopoly (but nonetheless passes antitrust scrutiny), its regulation should be the responsibility of the permanent state public utility board, which, unlike the courts and state attorneys general, has sufficient expertise to adequately regulate the merged entities. Otherwise, the faults of the present system, which is easily manipulated by hospitals seeking political and legal cover for their activities, are likely to be perpetuated.

Robert E. Bloch and Scott P. Perlman. "Antitrust Analysis of Physician Practice Mergers." Washington, D.C.: American Health Lawyers Association [Report No. VAT99–0027], 1999, 26 pages.

Analyzes judicial decisions, DOJ business review letters, and state enforcement actions regarding antitrust issues raised by physician practice mergers.

Mark J. Botti. "Virtual Mergers of Hospitals: When Does the Per Se Rule Apply?" Washington, D.C.: American Health Lawyers Association [Report No. VAT99–0007], 1999, 25 pages.

Comments on the antitrust analysis of whether joint negotiation with managed care plans and other cooperative activities of competing hospitals following such virtual mergers are per se illegal or otherwise can be condemned without an extensive inquiry into market power or anticompetitive effects in the relevant markets. Provides background on general antitrust principles and reviews the Long Island Jewish Medical Center case.

Mark J. Botti. "Comments on the Antitrust Aspects of 'Virtual Mergers' and Affiliations." Washington, D.C.: American Health Lawyers Association, [Report No. VHL98–0057], 1998, 23 pages.

Discusses whether joint negotiation with managed care plans and other cooperative activities of competing hospitals are per se illegal or otherwise can be condemned without an extensive inquiry into market power or anticompetitive effects in the relevant markets. Provides background on general antitrust principles and reviews the *Long Island Jewish Medical Center* case.

Roxanne C. Busey. "Hospital Merger Hypothetical." Washington, D.C.: American Health Lawyers Association [Report No. VAT99–0005], 1999, 60 pages.

Presents hypothetical documents for the merger of two hospitals in the same region, illustrating the antitrust concerns with respect to both the structure of the transaction and its competitive effects in light of recent enforcement actions in Long Island, Poplar Bluff, and Poughkeepsie. Includes hypothetical and assumptions, a map, a letter of intent-joint operating agreement, the hospitals' affiliations, three documents required under 4(c) of the Improvements Act Notification and Report Form for Certain Mergers and Acquisitions, a feasibility study, a preliminary efficiency study, a preliminary economic analysis, and payer letters.

Roxane C. Busey. "Antitrust Aspects of 'Virtual Mergers' and Affiliations." Washington, D.C.: American Health Lawyers Association [Report No. VHL98–0056], 1998, 28 pages.

Discusses the relevant antitrust principles applicable to "virtual mergers," joint operating agreements, and other affiliations among providers and applies them to the basic models that are typically used in these arrangements.

Roxanne C. Busey. "Antitrust Aspects of 'Virtual Mergers' and Affiliations." Washington, D.C.: American Health Lawyers Association [Report No. VAT99–0006], 1999, 28 pages.

Discusses the relevant antitrust principles applicable to "virtual mergers," joint operating agreements, and other affiliations among providers and applies these principles to the basic models that are typically used in these arrangements. Attachments include diagrams of various merger models.

James A. Cherney. "Antitrust Issues in Health Care Mergers and Acquisitions." Washington, D.C.: American Health Lawyers Association [Report No. VMAT98–0016], 1998, 37 pages.

Discusses current issues in antitrust enforcement and counseling on antitrust issues in mergers and acquisitions, including statutory requirements and Hart-Scott-Rodino, definition of relevant product market, geographic market issues, physician mergers, collaborative ventures that are less than full mergers, and practical considerations for navigating through antitrust problems. Also contains the Department of Justice business review letters issued to CVT Surgical Center and Vascular Surgery Associates of Baton Rouge, Louisiana, and to Allentown, Pennsylvania, gastroenterologists.

Jonathan Choslovsky. "Agency Review of Health Care Industry Mergers: Proper Procedure or Unnecessary Burden?" (Comment.) *Administrative Law Journal of American University*, 1996, *10, 291*.

Analyzes attempts by the FTC and the Justice Department to apply antitrust laws to mergers and acquisitions in the health care industry. It concludes that substantive antitrust reform is not the best way to reduce the burden on the health care industry while still protecting the consumer. A more promising avenue, the author writes, is procedural reform. The author argues that pre-merger notification rules should be modified to create more filing exemptions for health care industry mergers.

Claudia Hastings Dulmage. "Physician Practice Mergers: 1997 Business Review Advice." Washington, D.C.: American Health Lawyers Association [Report No. VAT98–0006], 1998, 39 pages.

Outlines the standards for Justice Department business review of physician practice mergers, the steps in the inquiry, and the difference that caused opposite results in two mergers. Includes summaries of business review letters issued between September 1993 and November 1997. Also contains the business review letters issued to CVT Surgical Center and Vascular Surgery Associates of Baton Rouge, Louisiana, and to Allentown, Pennsylvania, gastroenterologists.

Robert J. Enders. "An Introduction to Special Antitrust Issues in Health Care Provider Joint Ventures." *Antitrust Law Journal*, 1993, *61, 805*.

Argues that in structuring a joint venture to avoid an antitrust challenge as a naked restraint of trade, prudent antitrust planning would usually involve creating significant financial integration among the participants. In simple terms, the participants must share opportunities for profit as well as possible loss from operations, in order to pass the U.S. Supreme Court's litmus test for a bona fide joint venture set forth in *Arizona* v. *Maricopa County Medical Society,* 457 U.S. 322, 356 (1982).

Frederic J. Entin and others. "Hospital Collaboration: The Need for an Appropriate Antitrust Policy." *Wake Forest Law Review*, 1994, *29, 107*.

Examines federal antitrust statutes, court decisions, and federal merger guidelines to highlight the conflict between current antitrust enforcement policy and collaborative solutions to national health policy concerns. The hospital field is engaged in a search for strategies that will reduce costs and improve the rationality of resource allocation. The American Hospital Association, whose office of general counsel prepared this article, has urged hospitals to collaborate with each other and with other health care providers to improve access and quality and to constrain costs. Many such collaborative arrangements, however, have run into significant barriers—both perceived and real—under federal antitrust laws. The AHA calls for policy makers to reexamine enforcement policies to ensure that they encourage health care institutions to provide the highest-quality care at the lowest possible cost. According to the AHA, for collaboration to successfully address the problems of overcapacity and irrationally allocated resources, hospitals must be able to determine with some degree of precision which forms of collaboration are permissible. The AHA concludes that, at present, the basis for such understanding is lacking.

David A. Ettinger. "Substantive Approaches to Antitrust Analysis of Hospital Mergers." Washington, D.C.: American Health Lawyers Association [Report No. VMA 98–0016], 1998, 41 pages.

Addresses substantive antitrust issues relevant to planning health care mergers and issues relating to the timing and effects of antitrust concerns. It reviews litigation and federal oversight regarding physician mergers, including successful antitrust defenses and federal authorities challenging mergers under new theories.

David A. Ettinger. "Physician Practice Acquisitions: Can They Survive Antitrust?" *Health Lawyer*, Winter 1995, 14.

Outlines some of the basic criteria to use in determining which physician mergers will and will not raise antitrust concerns and some of the most important practical steps to be taken to minimize those concerns when they occur. As more and more health care institutions consolidate, mergers of physician practices and acquisitions of physician practices by hospitals or managed care plans are becoming increasingly common. Most of these mergers should not lead to antitrust problems, Ettinger writes, but some can raise serious issues.

David A. Ettinger and Howard B. Iwrey. "Practical Issues Relating to Antitrust Exposure for Joint Operating Agreements." Washington, D.C.: American Health Lawyers Association [Report No. VAT98–0009], 1998, 14 pages.

Delineates the practical antitrust issues surrounding formation and operation of joint operating agreements, including issues relating to integration, postmerger conduct, and Hart-Scott-Rodino filing requirements. Includes sample requests for informal interpretation from the FTC Bureau of Competition concerning a joint operating agreement.

Kathryn M. Fenton. "Antitrust Implications of Joint Efforts by Third Party Payers to Reduce Costs and Improve the Quality of Health Care." *Antitrust Law Journal*, 1992, 61, 17.

Attempts to identify the antitrust concerns posed by the efforts of third-party payers, contemplating joint cost control, to collect and synthesize the guidance offered by related areas of antitrust law, and to provide a perspective on these issues. After briefly describing some of the current collaborative efforts promoting cost containment and quality improvement, the author summarizes the possible antitrust challenges that might be asserted against joint action. She then reviews the defenses and antitrust immunities available to respond to these challenges and discusses possible means of limiting antitrust risk.

John F. Fischer. "Physician Practice Mergers: Defining Relevant Markets." Washington, D.C.: American Health Lawyers Association [Report No. VAT99–0028], 1999, 62 pages.

Provides an overview of the legal and evidentiary issues involved in defining relevant markets for physician practice mergers. Discusses the 1992 Horizontal Merger Guidelines issued by the DOJ and the FTC, and the Elzinga-Hogarty approach to market definition. Also reviews the informal agency advice concerning physician practice mergers and the *Vicksburg* opinion. Contains copies of the DOJ's business review letters issued on physician practice mergers issued since 1987.

David L. Glazer. "Clayton Act Scrutiny of Nonprofit Hospital Mergers: The Wrong Rx for Ailing Institutions." (Comment.) *Washington Law Review*, 1991, 66, 1041.

Focuses on the Clayton and Sherman antitrust laws, which have long been used to challenge anticompetitive mergers between for-profit entities. Recently, the federal government began challenging mergers between nonprofit hospitals under the Clayton Act. Two federal circuit courts have split on whether nonprofit mergers are subject to Clayton Act scrutiny. This comment reviews the statutory interpretations and the policy arguments suggested by the two cases and concludes that the Clayton Act does not, and should not, apply to nonprofit hospital mergers.

Kevin E. Grady. "A Framework for Antitrust Analysis of Health Care Joint Ventures." *Antitrust Law Journal*, 1993, *61*, 765.

Examines some of the primary antitrust issues in forming joint ventures, such as the definition of joint venture, the importance of the purposes of the joint venture, the concept of "integration efficiencies," and the issue of market power created by the venture. Grady suggests that the fundamental threshold issue that the joint venturers must address is their purpose for entering into a joint venture. If the goal is simply to save costs by jointly purchasing expensive equipment, or to offer a service jointly that otherwise could not be offered, there is probably little risk of antitrust liability. If, however, the joint venture principally seeks to enhance bargaining power over price with third-party payers or excluding competitors from the market, such actions will always raise significant antitrust liability issues.

Concerning joint ventures that seem on face legitimate, issues of integration, efficiencies, and market power will then be determinative in surviving a rule-of-reason inquiry. No one factor will necessarily be controlling, but the joint venture should reflect some of the traditional indicia of cooperative activities that signal more than a cartel: (1) contribution of more than nominal capital, (2) potential of risk of loss by investors, (3) common marketing and administrative functions carried out independently from the venturers' other business activities, (4) a procompetitive justification for the joint venture, (5) membership criteria that would not prevent formation of competing entities, and (6) a reasonable relationship between the procompetitive goal of the venture and the restriction in question. The author concludes that in this area of antitrust analysis, there is little black-letter law, only common sense.

Kevin E. Grady and Suzanne Smith. "Antitrust Issues: Handling the Difficult Case." Washington, D.C.: American Health Lawyers Association [Report No. VMA 98–0025], 1998, 38 pages.

Analyzes issues involved in recent court decisions denying the government's attempt to enjoin several hospital mergers. It discusses strategy decisions in defending mergers, as well as applying antitrust principles to other merger types, such as physician groups, managed care entities, and loose affiliations of providers.

Thomas L. Greaney. "Night Landings on an Aircraft Carrier: Hospital Mergers and Antitrust Law." *American Journal of Law and Medicine*, 1997, *23*, 191.

Argues that those concerned about the drift in antitrust law toward standardless inquiries in merger cases may find their worst fears realized in the hospital merger cases. The author traces the somewhat surprising outcomes of recent hospital merger cases and concludes that they may reflect the political or social preferences of particular judges rather than a reasoned parsing of the facts before them.

Barry C. Harris. "Analyzing Hospital-Merger Efficiencies under the Revised Merger Guidelines." Washington, D.C.: American Health Lawyers Association [Report No. VAT98–0026], 1998, 23 pages.

Assesses the standards set forth in the 1997 revisions to federal merger guidelines, and examines the reduced impact of efficiencies in hospital merger review under the revised standards.

William G. Kopit. "Can the Nonprofit Status of the Merging Facilities Change the Proper Analysis of a Hospital Merger Under the Antitrust Laws?" Washington, D.C.: American Health Lawyers Association [Report No VAT99–0009], 1999, 22 pages.

Shows why evidence distinguishing a particular nonprofit entity from a profit-maximizing for-profit entity should be considered in evaluating the probable impact of a merger. Focuses on *FTC* v. *Butterworth Health Corp.* as demonstrating that the economic incentives and marketplace behavior of the merging nonprofit hospitals were different from what one would expect from for-profit entities.

William G. Kopit and Neil N. Rosenbaum. "Rethinking the Significance of Merging Hospitals' Nonprofit Status under the Sherman and Clayton Acts," Washington, D.C.: American Health Lawyers Association [Report No. VAT98–0013], 1998, 56 pages.

Examines the principles of antitrust analysis that can be used in determining the likely anti-competitive effects of nonprofit hospital mergers by focusing on *FTC* v. *Butterworth Health Corp.* Also discusses the argument that Section 7 of the Clayton Act does not extend to non-profit organizations. Redacted versions of the Justice Department's posttrial brief submitted in *U.S.* v. *Long Island Jewish Medical Center and North Shore Health System* is attached.

Robert F. Leibenluft. "Antitrust Enforcement and Hospital Mergers: A Closer Look." Washington, D.C.: American Health Lawyers Association [Report No. VHL98–0036], 1998, 21 pages.

Describes the nature of hospital competition, gives an overview of the steps used to analyze mergers generally, and discusses seven issues often raised concerning federal antitrust agency review of hospital mergers.

James E. Magleby. "Hospital Mergers and Antitrust Policy: Arguments against a Modification of Current Antitrust Law." *Antitrust Bulletin*, 1996, *41*, 137.

Maintains that it would be unwise to revise antitrust statutes for the benefit of the health care industry. Both the hospitals and the enforcement agencies should, instead, continue to explore innovative approaches under current law.

David Marx Jr. and Mercedes A. Laing. "The State Action Doctrine—Can It Be Applied to a Private Hospital's Acquisition of a Public Hospital?" *Health Lawyer*, Summer 1995, 1.

Provides a brief overview of the state action doctrine in antitrust law, and examines an unsuccessful challenge by the FTC to a Florida county hospital board's acquisition of a private hospital, in *FTC* v. *Hospital Board of Directors of Lee County,* 1994–2 Trade Cas. ¶ 70, 803 (11th Cir. 1994), aff'g 1994–1 Trade Cas. ¶ 70, 593 (M.D. Fla.). Although the authors write that the question posed in the article's title has not been settled, authority exists that arguably would extend the doctrine to such conduct by private parties.

Dayna B. Matthew. "Doing What Comes Naturally: Antitrust Law and Hospital Mergers." *Houston Law Review*, 1994, *31*, 813.

Examines policy approaches to hospital mergers that will be most likely to contain costs. Matthew presents evidence that a solution must occur on a national scale. She suggests further that the role of the judiciary in this problem must be greatly simplified in order to be effective.

David L. Meyer and Charles F. Rule. "Health Care Collaboration Does Not Require Substantive Antitrust Reform." *Wake Forest Law Review*, 1994, *29*, 169.

Disagrees with antitrust critics who maintain that if this country wants to cut health care costs, we must start by either exempting the industry from the antitrust laws or reforming the existing enforcement regime in significant ways. The authors, practicing attorneys who formerly served with the Justice Department's Antitrust Division, maintain that federal antitrust laws, as presently written and sensibly enforced, provide a great degree of flexibility for private collaborative efforts aimed at achieving more efficient and less costly delivery of health care services. They conclude that antitrust immunities are not necessary to achieve these goals; nor is it necessary to create a bureaucracy to oversee the formation or operation of joint ventures or competing networks of providers to shield them from antitrust risk. Indeed, the authors conclude that sound antitrust policy, and the system of free-enterprise competition it reflects, provide the most reliable means to ensure the emergence of the sort of marketplace innovations, including those involving collaboration, that can minimize health care costs.

Kevin J. O'Connor. "Federal and State Merger Review Process." Washington, D.C.: American Health Lawyers Association [Report No. VAT99–0011], 1999, 11 pages.

Provides an overview of federal and state merger enforcement actions, the filing requirements and procedures under the Hart-Scott-Rodino Antitrust Improvements Act of 1976, post-filing procedures, and application of horizontal merger analysis under the Horizontal Merger Guidelines issued by the FTC and the DOJ Antitrust Division in 1992.

Phillip A. Proger. "Mergers, Virtual Mergers and Consolidation: Hot Business and Transactional Issues." Washington, D.C.: American Health Lawyers Association [Report No. VHL98–0037], 1998, 48 pages.

Discusses antitrust considerations in mergers and joint ventures. Begins with a brief background description of antitrust law and policy and concludes with a description of the FTC/DOJ Health Care Antitrust Guidelines.

Richard D. Raskin. "Telling the Efficiencies Story: Ten Practical Suggestions for Hospital Counsel." Washington, D.C.: American Health Lawyers Association [Report No. VAT98–0027], 1998, 7 pages.

Contains ideas for counsel in the process of coordinating an efficiencies analysis in a hospital merger. Topics include engaging experts, guiding internal and external communications, and advocating before the agencies and courts.

Joe Sims. "A New Approach to the Analysis of Hospital Mergers." *Antitrust Law Journal,* 1996, *64,* 633.

Contends that the current approach to hospital mergers is not working. A new approach, Sims contends, should incorporate the following principles: (1) deemphasize assumptions based on market structure; (2) give at least as much weight to community support and objectives as to opposition; (3) give proper weight to the present and likely future condition of the merging facilities—taking into account distress as well as likely failure; (4) give proper weight to the fact, if it exists, of community control or influence over the operation of the merged facility; and (5) give great weight—perhaps determinative if the hospitals are truly distressed—to significant potential efficiencies.

Toby G. Singer. "Antitrust Issues." Washington, D.C.: American Health Lawyers Association [Report No. VAT99–0012], 1999, 33 pages.

Outlines recent case law involving antitrust challenges to hospital mergers, acquisitions, and affiliations.

James H. Sneed. "Antitrust Issues in Hospital Joint Operating Arrangements." Washington, D.C.: American Health Lawyers Association [Report No. VAT98–0010], 1998, 15 pages.

Highlights some of the more common joint operating agreements, and sketches the applicable antitrust principles and the factors that distinguish legitimate cooperative ventures from per se illegal cartels.

Oscar M. Voss. "Assorted Thoughts about Hospital Merger Efficiency Defenses." Washington, D.C.: American Health Lawyers Association [Report No. VAT98–0028], 1998, 13 pages.

Focuses on hospital merger efficiency defenses from the standpoint of a government staff attorney, with particular emphasis on how efficiencies fit into the competitive-effects analysis of the 1997 merger guidelines.

Christine L. White. "Presenting Efficiencies Claims under the 1997 Merger Guidelines." Washington, D.C.: American Health Lawyers Association [Report No. VAT98–0029], 1998, 7 pages.

> The revised 1997 merger guidelines recognize that mergers can create significant efficiencies that benefit competition and the economy, and that efficiencies therefore should be evaluated in assessing the likely competitive effects of a merger. Describes cognizable merger-specific efficiencies and strategies for anticipating the agencies' review of an efficiencies study.

Dennis A. Yao. "The Analysis of Hospital Mergers and Joint Ventures: What May Change?" *Utah Law Review*, 1995, 381.

> Argues that antitrust laws are sufficiently flexible to accommodate any special characteristics of the health care industry and that enforcers and courts do consider the peculiar characteristics of this industry. To depart from the Horizontal Merger Guidelines announced by the Justice Department and the FTC would mean abandoning a carefully crafted and tested framework distilled from years of antitrust experience. Such a departure, Yao argues, is not warranted.

7.04   ANTITRUST IMPLICATIONS OF INTEGRATED DELIVERY SYSTEMS

Jonathan B. Baker. "Vertical Restraints with Horizontal Consequences: Competitive Effects of 'Most-Favored-Customer Clauses.'" *Antitrust Law Journal*, 1996, 64, 517.

> Describes three ways in which vertical restraints can harm competition by having horizontal effects, here termed "facilitating practices," "raising rivals' costs," and "dampening competition." The three anticompetitive effects are illustrated with examples from most-favored-customer (also known as most-favored-nation, or nondiscrimination) clauses in the health care context.

Robert E. Bloch and Scott P. Perlman. "Most Favored Nation Clauses in Contracts Between Healthcare Networks and Providers: The Search for Practical Antitrust Guidance." *Health Law Digest*, May 1997, p. 3.

> Examines relevant court decisions and enforcement actions and attempts to identify grounds for reconciling the differing judicial views of most-favored-nation clauses. The authors focus specifically on *U.S.* v. *Delta Dental of R.I.*, Div. No. 96–113/B (D.R.I. Feb. 29, 1996). They conclude that although *Delta Dental* leaves unsettled a number of issues regarding the legality of MFNs between health plans and health care providers, the decision is significant because it indicates that courts now may be more receptive to the government's view that MFNs imposed by health plans with market powers can have serious anticompetitive effects.

Arnold Celnicker. "A Competitive Analysis of Most Favored Nation Clauses in Contracts between Health Care Providers and Insurers." *North Carolina Law Review*, 1991, 69, 863.

> Argues that MFN clauses have significant anticompetitive potential. An MFN clause is a contractual agreement between a buyer and a seller stating that the price paid by the buyer will be at least as low as the price paid by other buyers who purchase the same commodities from the seller. During the past decade, the anticompetitive impact of MFN clauses in the health care sector has been challenged under federal antitrust laws. The cases have considered MFN clauses included in contracts between large third-party payers, specifically Blue Cross and Blue Shield (BCBS) plans, and providers of health care. The clauses prohibit providers from selling their medical services to BCBS's competitors at a price lower than the price at which they sell to BCBS. The cases have challenged these clauses on the grounds that they limit selective discounting to the competitors, thereby making it difficult for the competitors to attract subscribers from dominant BCBS plans by lowering premiums.

Celnicker examines the competitive consequences of MFN clauses used in the health care industry, in an analysis that draws heavily on economic criticisms of the Robinson-Patman Act, which prohibits a seller from discriminating in price between customers in certain circumstances. The article concludes that, depending on the circumstances, MFN clauses discourage discounting, facilitate oligopolistic pricing, and deter entry or expansion by more efficient distribution systems.

Robert J. Enders. "Strategic Alliances for Hospitals and Managed Care Organizations." Washington, D.C.: American Health Lawyers Association [Report No. VAT-0031], 1998, 33 pages.

Highlights actions that can be taken to understand the business goals of strategic alliances, explores vertical restraints, and analyzes the joint FTC/Justice Department Statements of Antitrust Enforcement Policy in Health Care. Examines the First Priority Health and NEPPO Ltd. joint venture as an example of a provider-payer strategic alliance.

David A. Ettinger and Stanford P. Berenbaum. "Antitrust Issues Facing Multiprovider Networks." *Journal of Health and Hospital Law,* 1996, *29,* 30.

Outlines the antitrust considerations that are likely to be applicable to forming and operating multiple physician and multiple hospital networks. These networks, including most networks with high market shares, will likely avoid significant antitrust problems so long as they take certain basic steps, the authors write. However, the activities of some networks may raise issues comparable to those presented by a hospital merger in a very small market. Indeed, they may raise the risk of substantial treble damage actions. Providers planning to enter into such networks need to plan their activities carefully so that they can be aware of, and minimize, the risks of antitrust litigation. Written by two attorneys in private practice, the article is supplemented by copious and helpful endnotes.

Mark L. Glassman. "Can HMOs Wield Market Power? Assessing Antitrust Liability in the Imperfect Market for Health Care Financing." *American University Law Review,* 1996, *46,* 91.

Contends that market evolution, coupled with recent Supreme Court decisions determining antitrust liability in sophisticated but imperfect markets, threatens to increase the ease with which HMOs can obtain market power. The result will be increased HMO exposure to antitrust liability. This comment describes traditional methods for determining market power and examines how lower courts have assessed HMO antitrust liability and applied principles of market definition and market power. It then analyzes how market imperfections in health care financing, along with current trends in HMO enrollment and provider contracting, could reduce elasticity of supply and demand for HMOs, causing the HMO market to diverge from the health care financing market under traditional principles of market definition. The author concludes by recommending a hybrid legal analysis that would reduce both the ability of HMOs to obtain market power illegally and the threat that antitrust enforcement will undo the efficiencies that HMOs have introduced to the health care financing marketplace.

Thomas L. Greaney. "Managed Competition, Integrated Delivery Systems and Antitrust." *Cornell Law Review,* 1994, *79,* 1507.

Analyzes two key determinants of the competitive consequences of integrated delivery systems: the design of health care reform legislation and the antitrust principles applicable to the composition and activities of these networks. It proposes that to promote effective managed competition, both Congress and the judiciary should decide health care issues with a keen appreciation for the peculiar nature of health care markets, including such factors as information and agency problems, adverse selection, moral hazard, heterogeneity of services, monopoly barriers, cartelization, free riders, and fragmentation.

Clark C. Havighurst. "Antitrust Issues in the Joint Purchasing of Health Care." *Utah Law Review,* 1995, 409.

Focuses on antitrust questions that might be raised in connection with joint purchasing of health coverage. This article offers a more speculative line of defense for joint purchasers that exercise a degree of market power in ways not readily defensible under traditional doctrine. The author concludes that few employer coalitions or purchaser cooperatives are likely to cross the lines laid down by antitrust law. Indeed, he contends, entities following the guidelines in this article should be reasonably confident of their ability to win summary judgment against antitrust claims. A coalition or cooperative could reasonably expect to prevail if it can show either that it lacked market power in purchasing services or that its members' practices in conjunction with joint purchasing were such as to obviate concern about buying power abuse.

Mark J. Horoschak. "Antitrust and Rural Health Care Networks." Washington, D.C.: American Health Lawyers Association [Report No. VAT99–0018], 1999, 18 pages.

Addresses antitrust issues posed by rural provider networks. Focuses on how the antitrust concepts of clinical integration and market power are properly applied to provider collaboration in rural markets.

Joseph Kattan and Scott A. Stempel. "Antitrust Enforcement and Most Favored Nation Clauses." *Antitrust,* Summer 1996, p. 20.

Examines potential competitive effects of MFN clauses and other price protection devices in the context of FTC and Justice Department challenges in the 1990s, especially as they relate to managed care contracts.

William G. Kopit and Alexandre B. Bouton. "Antitrust Implications of Provider Exclusion." In Peter R. Kongstvedt (ed.), *The Managed Health Care Handbook.* (4th ed.) Gaithersburg, Md.: Aspen, 2000.

Written by two practicing attorneys, this chapter surveys and provides a framework for analyzing the antitrust issues raised by provider exclusion by MCOs. In addition, the chapter discusses the impact of state any-willing-provider laws on the ability of MCOs to limit physician participation. Topics discussed include the importance of market power, exclusive dealing arrangements, standing, and group boycotts. The article is extensively annotated.

Robert F. Leibenluft. "Antitrust Issues Involving Health Care Provider Networks." Washington, D.C.: American Health Lawyers Association [Report No.VMM99–0034], 1999, 20 pages.

Describes the principal antitrust issues raised by health care provider networks. Gives a brief introduction to antitrust analysis of joint ventures generally and then discusses antitrust issues raised by joint contracting with managed care organizations, including application of the 1996 DOJ/FTC Statements of Antitrust Enforcement Policy in Health Care. Other issues addressed including providing information to payers, joint purchasing agreements, captive referral cases, and physician mergers.

Arthur N. Lerner. "Insurance and Managed Care Organization Relationships with Providers." Washington, D.C.: American Health Lawyers Association [Report No. VAT98–0030], 1998, 28 pages.

Scrutinizes selected areas of antitrust law with a focus on managed care relationships with providers. Topics include provider network arrangements, pitfalls of the "messenger model," how much integration is enough, problems specific to dealing with physician-hospital joint ventures, most-favored-nation clauses, managed care organizations, barriers to competing plans, and provider network exclusions. Includes the Justice Department's proposed final judgment and competitive impact statement in *U.S.* v. *Delta Dental of Rhode Island,* eliminating Delta Dental's most-favored-nation clause, as it appeared in the Mar. 4, 1997, *Federal Register.*

Natalie Marjancik. "Risky Business: Proposed Reform of the Antitrust Laws as Applied to Health Care Provider Networks." (Note.) *American Journal of Law and Medicine,* 1998, *24,* 59.

This note addresses the degree to which network providers must be economically and financially integrated to legally collaborate and set prices. It then discusses relevant statutory and case law applicable to health care provider networks, the Antitrust Health Care Advancement Act of 1997, and the federal antitrust enforcement agencies' 1996 policy statements. Finally, it examines the ramifications of easing antitrust scrutiny of the formation and collaborative activities of nonfinancially integrated provider networks.

David Marx, Jr. "Antitrust Issues Raised by Networks." Washington, D.C.: American Health Lawyers Association [Report No. VAT99–0016], 1999, 37 pages.

Discusses the analytical framework that federal antitrust agencies have articulated to evaluate the antitrust issues associated with forming and operating networks consisting of competing health care providers.

Frances H. Miller. "Health Insurance Purchasing Alliances: Monopsony Threat or Procompetitive Rx for Health Sector Ills?" *Cornell Law Review,* 1994, *79,* 1546–1572.

Focuses specifically on antitrust issues involving alliances collaborating with respect to health insurance purchasing, rather than on the broader issue of group purchases from the health industry generally. This article emphasizes the special antitrust problems presented when buyers behave jointly with respect to the health insurance product, either spontaneously or as a result of government prodding. This article concludes that short of unlikely single-payer reform, Americans will be better off in the long run with competing alliance structures springing up spontaneously than they would have been with the huge mandatory alliances envisioned by President Clinton's White House Task Force on Health Care Reform.

Susan Barnhizer Rivas and Karen Ann P. Lloyd. "Antitrust Analysis of Strategic Alliances among Hospitals." Washington, D.C.: American Health Lawyers Association [Report No. VAT98–0032], 1998, 33 pages.

Examines strategic alliances among hospitals, summarizes the law regarding horizontal restraints and joint ventures, and applies the law to various types of strategic alliance entered into by hospitals. Includes an extensive bibliography of articles and speeches on related topics.

Douglas C. Ross. "A Practical Approach for Analyzing Antitrust Issues Faced by Provider Networks." *Journal of Health and Hospital Law,* Fall 1997, *30*(3), 133–145.

Analyzes the antitrust issues posed by networks, with specific emphasis on the underlying nature of their risk allocation arrangements, which are often crucial to the outcome of an antitrust analysis. This article does not attempt to review the law applicable to provider networks, nor to review agency enforcement standards.

Amy L. Woodhall. "An Antitrust Analysis of Physician Specialty Networks under Changing Market Conditions." *Journal of Legal Medicine,* 1996, *17,* 383.

As a consequence of confusion among the courts over the applicable legal standard applied to horizontal restraints purporting to provide procompetitive efficiencies, and because agency enforcement guidelines will not protect all networks or network activities, specialty network developers must engage in a risk-based approach to physician network development. The most important factors affecting the risk of antitrust challenges are the level of integration, the network and physicians' market power, whether network participation is exclusive or nonexclusive, and whether the pricing and membership restraints are necessary to provide the network's competitive benefits. This forty-page article provides an excellent analysis of the topic.

7.05   GOVERNMENT ENFORCEMENT ACTIVITIES

American Bar Association. *Compendium of Informal Enforcement Agency Advice in Health Care.* Chicago: ABA, 1991, 188 pages.

Contains approximately one hundred public speeches by Justice Department and FTC officials during the decade of the 1980s that addressed in substantial part the application of antitrust law to the health care field. This volume provides important insight into the government's evolving enforcement policies in this area.

American Bar Association. *Compendium of Antitrust Enforcement Agency Advice in Health Care 2: April 1991-August 1996.* Chicago: ABA, 1997, 446 pages.

This volume continues where the preceding one left off, digesting approximately seventy-five additional letters and speeches dated through December 1995. Contains text of FTC/DOJ Statements of Enforcement and Analytical Principles Relating to Health Care and Antitrust.

American Bar Association, Section of Antitrust Law. *Compendium of Informal Antitrust Enforcement Agency Advice in Health Care. April 1991-August 1996.* Chicago: ABA, 1997, 415 pages.

This compilation of advisory letters and speeches updates the original compendium published by the ABA in 1991. It presents summaries of informal advice and statements of policy in the health care field by federal antitrust enforcement agencies. This volume makes a contribution to practitioners in the antitrust and health care fields as an indication of the positions taken by the antitrust enforcement agencies in particular areas, as to the agencies' views and interpretations of their formal Statements of Antitrust Enforcement Policy in Health Care, released in 1993, and revised in 1994 and 1996. Topics addressed include health care provider networks and other provider joint ventures, exchange of information, group purchasing arrangements, peer and fee review, price discrimination, agreements on price, and mergers.

William Berlin. "Antitrust Issues Arising From Certification Requirements." Washington, D.C.: American Health Lawyers Association [Report No. VAT99–0014], 1999, 49 pages.

Collection of documents from antitrust cases involving certification requirements, including the DOJ press release announcing filing of a civil suit against the Association of Family Practice Residency Directors for restricting competition among its members for family practice medical residents; DOJ's Competitive Impact Statement relating to the proposed final judgment in that same action; and DOJ's amicus brief filed in *Massachusetts Sch. of Law* v. *American Bar Assn.*, No. 96–1792 (3d Cir.), which challenges the ABA's accreditation rules as violating the Sherman Act, 15 U.S.C. Sections One and Two.

Robert E. Bloch and Scott P. Perlman. "Analyzing and Defending Managed Care Mergers under the Antitrust Laws." Washington, D.C.: American Health Lawyers Association [Report No. VAT98–0024], 1998, 26 pages.

Scrutinizes issues raised by managed care mergers and discusses practical guidance for defense counsel. Also summarizes state enforcement investigations of ten transactions.

Mark J. Botti. "Sample Request for Additional Information and Documentary Material Issued to a Managed Care Organization." Washington, D.C.: American Health Lawyers Association [Report No. VAT98–0025], 1998, 15 pages.

Sample Justice Department form asking a managed care organization for additional information and documentary material regarding a proposed merger.

Richard A. Feinstein. "FTC Antitrust Actions Involving Health Care Services and Products." Washington, D.C.: American Health Lawyers Association [Report No. VAT99–0001], 1999, 61 pages.

Provides a comprehensive summary of FTC antitrust actions involving health care services and products, including agreements on price or price-related terms, agreements to obstruct innovative forms of health care delivery or financing, restraints on advertising and other forms of solicitation, illegal tying and other arrangements, restrictions on access to hospitals, and mergers of health care providers. Also reviews the FTC's antitrust enforcement policy statements and advisory opinions. Includes an alphabetical table of cases and FTC advisory opinions that the text of the paper refers to.

Kevin E. Grady and others. "[Antitrust] Litigation." Washington, D.C.: American Health Lawyers Association [Report No VAT99–0013], 1999, 65 pages.

Hypothetical scenario of the litigation following a nonprofit hospital's challenge to a joint operating agreement, or affiliation, entered into by another nonprofit hospital and a for-profit hospital under which both would operate under a parent entity. Accompanying documents include the complaint for preliminary injunctive relief; defendants' answer; a sample consulting agreement for defendants' expert witness; defendants' memorandum of law in opposition to motion for temporary restraining order; defendants' sample jury instructions on the issue of conspiracy to monopolize; and letter from plaintiff's attorney to plaintiff, setting forth the terms and conditions of the attorney's representations of plaintiff.

Gail Kursh. "Antitrust Division Health Care Task Force Recent Enforcement Actions." Washington, D.C.: American Health Lawyers Association [Report No. VAT99–0002], 1999, 21 pages.

Examines the Department of Justice Antitrust Division's 1998–99 health care enforcement activities involving hospital mergers, criminal price fixing, and civil nonmerger health care activities. Also reviews DOJ's revised guidelines for the health care industry and business review letters issued to players in the industry.

Gail Kursh. "Report from Federal Enforcement Officials." Washington, D.C.: American Health Lawyers Association [Report No. VAT98–0001], 1998, 43 pages.

Summarizes the DOJ Antitrust Division's health care civil cases and matters (from August 1983 through June 1997), criminal cases (from February 1990 to December 1995), and health care business review letters (through June 1997).

Robert M. Langer. "Advisory Opinions and Business Reviews: A Private Bar Perspective." Washington, D.C.: American Health Lawyers Association [Report No. VAT98–0007], 1998, 58 pages.

Weighs the risks and benefits associated with seeking advice from federal and state antitrust enforcement agencies. Discusses under what circumstances it is prudent to recommend to a client to pursue seeking an advisory opinion or business review, the risk of seeking such a review, when a request may be withdrawn, and when it is better to seek advice from the DOJ's Antitrust Division or the FTC and/or a state attorney general in addition to federal agencies. Attachments include correspondence with the Antitrust Division of the Justice Department concerning a request for the business review letter for Vermont Physicians Clinic and a request for an advisory opinion from the FTC for William W. Backus Hospital.

Robert F. Leibenluft and David R. Pender. "FTC Antitrust Actions Involving Health Care Services." (Washington; DC: American Health Lawyers Association [Report No. VAT98–0002], 1998, 53 pages.

Assesses Federal Trade Commission antitrust cases involving health care services. Includes summaries of consent orders, complaints, consent agreements, and briefs relating to conduct involving health care providers (price fixing, obstruction of innovative delivery systems and financing, advertising restraints, tying, and restrictions on access to hospitals) and mergers of health care providers. Also describes safety zones created by the DOJ/FTC Joint Statements of Antitrust Enforcement Policy in Health Care and amicus briefs filed by the FTC in a variety of cases. Concludes with a table of cases and a table of briefs for cross-referencing.

Mark E. Lutes. "Legal Ethics." Washington, D.C.: American Health Lawyers Association [Report No. VAT99–0024]), 1999, 23 pages.

Discusses the ethical problems typical in antitrust counseling, such as adherence to the duty of loyalty and avoidance of conflict. Explores areas where there is doubt as to what the law is, and examines the distinction between unsuggestive advice and encouragement of illegal acts. Includes excerpts from the superseding indictment in *U.S.* v. *Anderson.*

Judith A. Moreland. "Overview of the Advisory Opinion Process at the Federal Trade Commission." Washington, D.C.: American Health Lawyers Association [Report No. VAT98–0008], 1998, 36 pages.

Describes the FTC's advisory opinion process. Outlines the availability and effects of opinion letters and the type of information that should be submitted, and offers practical advice. Includes the FTC Bureau of Competition's January 1998 *Topic and Yearly Indices of Healthcare Antitrust Advisory Opinions by Commission and by Staff.*

Kevin J. O'Connor. "Antitrust Enforcement in Imperfect Healthcare Markets: A State Perspective." Washington, D.C.: American Health Lawyers Association [Report No. VAT98–0011], 1998, 22 pages.

Focuses on state health care antitrust enforcement from the point of view of state attorneys general. Describes the evolution of state antitrust enforcement in health care markets, discusses the concomitant lessening of state regulation of the health care sector, and examines how antitrust enforcement in health care is conducted.

Toby G. Singer. "Dealing with the Agencies." Washington, D.C.: American Health Lawyers Association [Report No. VAT98–0023], 1998, 7 pages.

Outlines the process of dealing with government antitrust enforcers on health care matters. Also sets forth some of the strategic issues associated with government investigations.

Martin J. Thompson. "Certification and Accreditation." Washington, D.C.: American Health Lawyers Association [Report No. VAT99–0015], 1999, 25 pages.

Addresses certain antitrust issues that have resulted historically from private standard-setting activity, including certain certification and accreditation programs. Includes FTC's *Staff Advisory Letter re Foundation for the Accreditation of Hematopoietic Cell Therapy* (Federal Trade Commission, Apr. 18, 1997).

U.S. Department of Justice and Federal Trade Commission. *Horizontal Merger Guidelines.* 1992. [Reprinted in Trade Reg. Rep. 4 (CCH), 1992, 13, 104.]

A significant number of staff members at the FTC and the Justice Department's Antitrust Division specialize in health care matters. In recent years, both agencies have devoted substantial efforts to publicizing and clarifying standards that apply in deciding whether to challenge conduct of doctors, hospitals, insurers, and others in the health care field. The most formal mechanism has been the publication of guidelines setting forth the analytical process the agencies employ in their enforcement efforts. The most significant of these by far is this set of joint horizontal merger guidelines.

U.S. Department of Justice and Federal Trade Commission. "Statements of Antitrust Enforcement Policy in Health Care." Washington, D.C.: American Health Lawyers Association [Document No. VAT98–0015], 1998, 46 pages.

Contains excerpts from the Statements of Antitrust Enforcement Policy in Health Care issued by the FTC and the Justice Department in August 1996 relating to physician network joint ventures.

Nancy K. Whittemore. "Antitrust Enforcement and Health Care Reform." (Comment.) *Houston Law Review,* 1996, *32,* 1493.

Examines the federal antitrust laws applicable to the health care industry. Whittemore argues that the history of antitrust enforcement in the health care field demonstrates that competition is a significant factor in containing costs and ensuring quality and that antitrust enforcement is sufficiently flexible to prevent harmful conduct without interfering with joint conduct beneficial to consumers. She concludes that the federal antitrust laws, as enacted, allow great flexibility in private cooperative efforts aimed at achieving more efficient and lower-cost health care services.

8

Provider Reimbursement Issues

Reimbursement mechanisms affect health care in terms of quality of care, use of new technology and services, and incentives or disincentives for utilization. For example, a change in a hospital-based reimbursement system from cost-based to a prospective payment system by diagnosis-related groups significantly changes hospital attitudes regarding issues such as length of stay. Specifically, under a prospective DRG system, hospitals are motivated to reduce rather than to prolong lengths of stay. To an increasing extent, reimbursement systems have become instruments of cost containment and mechanisms to implement health care policy. In the Medicare and Medicaid programs, total budgets are increasingly fixed in advance, and the payment mechanisms constitute the means by which budgeted funds are distributed.[1]

Most reimbursement systems specify in great detail the services covered and eligibility requirements for beneficiaries, prescribe basic service levels, contain mechanisms for monitoring the quality of care and utilization, and establish specific payment mechanisms. Furthermore, there are usually (1) procedures by which reimbursement disputes are resolved, (2) proscriptions on certain practices considered abusive, and (3) audit mechanisms.

Reimbursement systems distinguish generally between payment for "facility charge" and payment for professional services. Hospitals, skilled nursing facilities, long-term nursing facilities, and home health agencies are examples of institutional providers that receive facility charges. Doctors, by contrast, receive professional fees. To receive Medicare or Medicaid reimbursement as a facility, a provider usually must be licensed as such under state licensing laws.

Types of Reimbursement System

Under a charge-based system, a health care provider (individual or facility) computes a fee for the services rendered and charges that fee to the patient or the patient's insurance carrier. The charge will usually include the direct and indirect costs of providing the service plus a reasonable profit margin. Because the provider is reimbursed based on charges, an incentive is built into the system to perform more rather than fewer services. Third-party payers have moved to fee schedules and capitation to limit payments on the basis of charges and in many areas have sharply limited charge-based reimbursement. Because of the varying manner in which payers reimburse for services, it is common for providers to receive different types of reimbursement for different payers.

Physicians' services have traditionally been paid on a fee-for-service or charge basis. In the case of physicians, the federal government under Medicare and the state governments under Medicaid made efforts to impose limits on physician charges. These efforts culminated in replacement of physician set-charge reimbursement with fee schedules based on relative value scales, implemented over a five-year period beginning in 1992.[2]

Fee-for-service reimbursement has traditionally been very heavily oriented toward procedures and visits. Because of the linkage between services performed and compensation, performance of procedures is encouraged.[3]

Using relative value scales, which are resource-based, also affects this relationship. If the services are performed in the physician's office, the physician's fee will include a reasonable amount for overhead, known as "site-of-service differential." If services are performed in a facility with a facility charge being paid, the physician's fee will not include a site-of-service differential. In certain situations, HCFA has used the differential to motivate physicians to practice in alternative or less expensive settings such as their offices or outpatient surgery centers.

Because of the competition among providers and the demand for lower health care costs, providers often discount charges to maintain their share of the patient market. They have often done so through PPOs. There are a number of PPO and PPO product types. Typically, individuals are not required to use the services of the PPO, but if PPO services are chosen, they are provided at a discount. Payers are not required to pay in advance, and the services are paid case by case as in a fee-for-service arrangement.

Finally, as discussed below, major efforts have been undertaken nationally to control utilization.

Cost-Based Reimbursement

Cost-based reimbursement was almost uniformly the method of reimbursing health care facilities for their services during the late 1960s and for most of the 1970s. It is still the prevailing methodology for many facilities under Medicare and, despite introduction of DRGs for hospitals, remains the basis for reimbursement for many hospital costs. It is clearly, however, in decline as a reimbursement scheme.

Under a cost-based methodology, health care facilities are reimbursed for the actual "reasonable" costs they incur in providing their services. Cost reimbursement contributed sharply to the dramatic rise in health care expenditures because it provided a system under which one was reimbursed for development regardless of the actual need for services. As health care expenditures began to consume an increasing share of available resources, the states and the federal government placed limits on the costs they would pay for. Thus, ceilings were imposed on various types of costs, such as routine and ancillary costs, and costs that exceed the ceilings are now disallowed. Almost all cost-based reimbursement systems have been modified to impose such ceilings.

Cost-based reimbursement schemes contain detailed rules with respect to "cost finding" and apportionment of the provider's costs among various third-party payers.

Prospective Reimbursement

Prospective reimbursement methodologies were developed in response to the rise in health care costs under cost-based reimbursement systems. A prospective reimbursement system sets a provider's rate of compensation for its services in advance of the services being rendered. This causes the facility to budget and manage its resources per reimbursed item or service. Prospective methodologies provide an incentive to keep expenditures within the budget of the health care facility and to reduce expenditures so as to generate profits. However, because prospective methodologies also pay on a fee-for-service basis, they too tend to encourage utilization. This is a major disincentive in prospective reimbursement methodologies, including the DRG system for Medicare.

A major shift to prospective reimbursement occurred in 1992 with the shift of Medicare to a DRG-based payment system for hospital costs. Medicare's efforts to control capital costs by bringing them within the prospective rate methodology established for noncapital costs is being closely watched by third-party payers, many of which still reimburse per diem.

Prospective rates are usually determined by starting with a provider's historical noncapital operating costs. These costs are then "trended" forward from an historical base year to the rate year by various economic indices that attempt to reflect appropriate increases in the cost of goods and supplies and other expenses. In the case of per diem systems, once total allowable costs have been calculated they typically are divided by the total number of days of care provided to all patients cared for by the facility during the year, which results in an average per diem payment rate. This per diem rate is then multiplied by the number of days for which the third party is responsible, to yield aggregate annual revenues.

Most prospective methodologies start with the individual health care facility's costs, subject to various ceilings. For example, a health care facility might be grouped with similar facilities and reimbursement might be limited to the lower of the facility's actual rate produced by the calculation or the average rate of members of the group. Similarly, a provider's base-year costs might be limited by various ceilings based on such factors as average length of stay and routine and ancillary cost limitations.

In some prospective payment systems, the historical base year from which costs are trended forward to the prospective rate year changes with each new rate year. In the lexicon of reimbursement, the base year "rolls" forward. This produces the anomaly that a health care facility with high base-year costs will generally benefit under a prospective system, whereas a facility with reduced base-year costs will suffer. In addition, some states (New York being one) lock in base-year costs by using a single base year for a longer period of time. Thus, once the initial prospective payment rate is fixed, subsequent rates are determined by calculating appropriate increases based on the preceding year's rate, and not on the new base-year costs. Systems that freeze base-year costs can exert stringent control on the growth of health care facilities, since reimbursement relates directly to the size of the institution and the scope of its services at the time the initial base year is selected.

Obviously, prospective payment systems give tremendous discretion to the entity setting the rates. The government or other third-party payers have significant power to set rates, by selecting appropriate indices (for example, the labor index, which accounts for the majority of a health care facility's costs), imposing and calculating ceilings, determining peer groupings, and controlling the appeals process by which adjustments are made in individual situations.

Diagnosis-Related Groups

Reimbursement methodologies based on charges and on reasonable costs focus principally on the costs incurred by a health care facility in providing care without defining the unit of output to which the costs relate. DRGs attempt to define appropriate units of output and to assign an appropriate price to them. Thus, they permit comparison of the actual services or "products" produced by health care facilities. The DRG system applies the concept that similar services should be compensated identically, no matter who the provider of those services is (or what the costs are). DRGs have now become the basic reimbursement methodology for the operating costs of hospitals under Medicare and the principal methodology for reimbursement to hospitals in many states.

There are two basic types of DRG system. One system sets general DRG payment rates that are the same for all facilities, on the theory that similar units of output should be priced evenly, subject only to the most general sort of adjustment, such as for area wage differences; Medicare, for example, has implemented a DRG system for reimbursing hospital inpatient expenses that uses national rates. A second system uses the data from each health care facility and produces DRGs specific to that facility. In many ways, this is similar to the approach followed in prospective payment systems that use the provider's costs as the data baseline.

DRGs are often viewed as a crude measure of the quantity and quality of medical services needed to treat what would appear on the surface to be similar cases. Patients who are classified in the same DRG may require quite different levels of care, yet the reimbursement for each case is the same. Although DRG classifications attempt to solve this problem by taking into account the clearly atypical cases (sometimes called "outliers"), DRGs still represent a classification system based on a statistical average. These problems are arguably manifest in the present Medicare DRG system, which, according to some studies, does not adequately recognize the severity of a patient's illness.[4] Second, DRGs fail to recognize differences in the skills of individual providers. If the rate is the same for all providers, the most skilled doctors and health care facilities, together with those providers who are willing to cut corners, all receive the same payments.

The system also creates the incentive to maximize reimbursement by increasing utilization or by classifying patients into higher-paying DRGs. As with all prospective reimbursement methodologies, regulations on utilization usually are part of DRG payment mechanisms.

Finally, although DRG-based reimbursement can help control health care costs, issues regarding quality, content of the health care product, and introduction of technology remain. These issues have been identified as major concerns by Congress[5] and by the Prospective Payment Assessment Commission established by Congress to review implementation of DRGs under Medicare.[6]

Capitation

In a capitation system, a health care facility or physician agrees to provide all or nearly all of the health care needs of a defined patient population for a flat amount that is fixed in advance—generally, a per-member, per-month (PMPM) charge. By fixing total revenues in relation to the total health care needs of a specific group of beneficiaries, the facility has an economic incentive to limit utilization. This is a fundamental difference from all other systems (such as prospective payment systems and DRGs) that reimburse on the basis of episodic utilization. As noted, in cost-based and prospective systems, including DRG methodologies, utilization is typically controlled through regulation.

Because of capitation's strong incentives to control utilization and costs, a special study of the Medicaid program has recommended that Medicaid be converted to a capitation system.[7] In New York, the state legislature has mandated that the state's Medicaid program shift to a managed care system that contains many of the features of capitation.

In a capitation system, reimbursement is usually derived from premiums collected by providers directly from subscribers, or it is based on negotiations with the particular third-party payer whose beneficiaries will be using the services of the health care facility or physician. Contract negotiations with payers fix in advance the total funds or budget needed to take care of the health care needs of the particular patient population. This fixing of costs provides a strong incentive to control utilization but is defeated if all costs are guaranteed and the facility or physician is not "at risk."

Capitation programs are usually identified with HMOs. With increased pressure to limit health care expenditures, the number of HMOs has grown steadily in recent years. Since the physicians and other providers of service may be capitated by the HMO or employees of the HMO—that is, they are salaried—HMOs remove the financial incentive for increased utilization inherent in fee-for-service arrangements. In fact, HMOs generate profits by controlling utilization.

The annotations that follow examine issues related to reimbursement of health care costs, with particular emphasis on fraud and abuse issues.

References and Notes

1. Parts of these introductory chapter materials were excerpted, with minor alterations, from a chapter by attorney Scott Becker of Chicago, titled "Reimbursement and Related Issues" and reprinted in Michael G. Macdonald and others. *Health Care Law: A Practical Guide.* New York: Matthew Bender, 1997.

2. Omnibus Budget Reconciliation Act of 1989, Pub. L. No. 101–239, § 6102, 103 Stat. 2106 [hereinafter OBRA 1989] (adding § 1848 to the Social Security Act, ch. 531, 49 Stat. 620 (1935) [hereinafter Social Security Act] (codified as amended at 42 U.S.C. § 1395w-4 (Supp. II 1990). Congress had previously authorized development of relative value scales, with the enactment of the Consolidated Omnibus Budget Reconciliation Act of 1985, Pub. L. No. 99–272, 100 Stat. 82 (1986) [hereinafter COBRA].

3. Harold S. Luft. "Economic Decisions and Clinical Decisions." In Institute of Medicine. *The New Health Care for Profit: Doctors and Hospitals in a Competitive Environment.* (Bradford H. Gray, ed.) Washington, D.C.: National Academy Press, 1983.

4. "Interhospital Differences in Severity of Illness: Problems for Prospective Payment Based on Diagnosis-Related Groups (DRGs)." *New England Journal of Medicine,* 1985, *313,* 20, where the authors found, based on a study of patient charts, substantial differences in the distribution of severity within each DRG. They concluded: "An explicit assumption that . . . [the Health Care Financing Administration] has made in designing the present prospective payment system is that

DRGs will account for the major differences in the costs of treatment among patients due to severity of illness." To our knowledge, there is no published study that supports this assumption, and the findings reported here are in direct conflict with it." See also Alan M. Garber, Victor R. Fuchs, and James F. Silverman. "Case Mix, Costs, and Outcomes: Differences Between Faculty and Community Services in a University Hospital." *New England Journal of Medicine*, 1984, *310*(19), 1231–1237.

5. Extensive quality-of-care provisions were enacted by Congress in the Omnibus Budget Reconciliation Act of 1986, Pub. L. No. 99–509, § 9305, 100 Stat. 1874, 1988 [hereinafter OBRA 1986].

6. The Prospective Payment Assessment Commission, like the Physician Payment Review Commission, issues extensive reports concerning Medicare and related issues, which include excellent background materials and analyses of current issues.

7. National Study Group on State Medicaid Strategies. *Restructuring Medicaid: An Agenda for Change* (1983) [hereinafter *Restructuring Medicaid*].

ANNOTATIONS

8.01   IN GENERAL

Annot. "What Services, Equipment, or Supplies Are 'Medically Necessary' for Purposes of Coverage under Medical Insurance?" *ALR4th*, 1998, *75*, 763.

Collects and analyzes the cases in which courts have considered what treatment, services, equipment, or supplies are "medically necessary" or the equivalent, or, conversely, whether such services or equipment are excluded from coverage as "not necessary" or "unnecessary," for purposes of coverage under medical insurance other than that provided under governmental entitlement programs.

Robert J. Buchanan and James D. Minor. *Legal Aspects of Health Care Reimbursement.* Gaithersburg, Md.: Aspen, 1985, 291 pages.

Provides an overview of reimbursement under Medicare and Medicaid laws. Topics examined in detail include inpatient hospital reimbursement, long-term care reimbursement, hospice care, and fraud and abuse.

Lynn E. Burnsed. "Coverage and Reimbursement of Psychiatric Services." Washington, D.C.: American Health Lawyers Association [Report No. VMM99–0040], 1999, 27 pages.

Examines coverage and reimbursement for mental health services to include the outpatient mental health services limitation, hospital reimbursement and partial hospitalization benefit, and the changes proposed under the outpatient PPS system. Also discusses fraud and abuse issues in this area.

Terry S. Coleman. *Legal Aspects of Medicare and Medicaid Reimbursement: Payment for Hospital and Physician Services.* Washington, D.C.: American Health Lawyers Association, 1997, 197 pages.

Offers an introduction to the laws governing Medicare and Medicaid reimbursement for hospital and physician services. This book is intended for both lawyers and health care professionals who seek understanding of the basic principles of the complex Medicare and Medicaid payment systems. Although the book touches on many aspects of the two programs, it concentrates on the rules governing payments and does not detail the policies governing such topics as eligibility, quality of services, coverage, or prohibited arrangements.

Commerce Clearing House. *Medicare & Medicaid Laws and Regulations.* Chicago: CCH, 1997, 2,625 pages.

This two-volume set is compiled from the CCH Medicare and Medicaid Guide and supplies statutory and regulatory provisions governing these two programs. Volume One (Medicare and Medicaid Laws) contains the full text of the two titles of the Social Security Act enacting and implementing Medicare and Medicaid, as well as selected provisions from related Social Security Act titles. Volume Two includes the full text of Title 42 Chapter IV of the Code of Federal Regulations, the chapter containing Medicare and Medicaid regulations promulgated by the Health Care Financing Administration.

James C. Dechene. "Public Health Care Reimbursement Programs." In Mark A. Hall (gen. ed.), *Health Care Corporate Law: Financing and Liability.* Boston: Little, Brown, 1994.

This eighty-four-page chapter is divided into discussions of Medicare Part A, Medicare Part B, Medicaid, CHAMPUS, fraud and abuse, and exclusion provisions. Subtopics include strategies for coping with DRGs, administrative and judicial procedures, and the future directions of federal health care programs. This is a concise, highly structured presentation.

Mark A. Hall and others. "Judicial Protection of Managed Care Consumers: An Empirical Study of Insurance Coverage Disputes." *Seton Hall Law Review,* 1996, *26,* 1055.

Analyzes court decisions resulting from coverage disputes. After compiling a list of all health care coverage disputes involving issues of medical appropriateness that resulted in published federal and state court decisions from 1960 to mid-1994, the authors analyzed the data and conclude that courts appear to be receptive to patients' complaints that insurers have incorrectly denied them coverage. Patients win more than half the time; even specific exclusions are frequently not enforced, and courts appear to be sympathetic to patients in a serious condition. Patients, however, prevail less frequently in federal appellate courts, and insurers gain a great advantage by writing their contracts to give them discretion over the meaning of general coverage language.

The most troubling finding for patient protection in managed care settings is that very few disputes arising from this setting make their way to the courts. Either patients are not made aware of the coverage decisions that are implicitly being enforced, or they find it too expensive or too difficult to pursue their objections through the costly and time-consuming judicial process. Accordingly, calls for alternative dispute resolution mechanisms that are speedy and easy to access appear to be well founded.

Timothy S. Jost. "Public Financing of Pain Management: Leaky Umbrellas and Ragged Safety Nets." *Journal of Law, Medicine and Ethics,* 1998, *26,* 290.

Although many people in pain depend on public health care programs for aid, these programs cover pain relief only fragmentarily. Jost examines the gaps and deficiencies in Medicare and Medicaid funding of pain relief and explores the effects of Medicare and Medicaid fraud enforcement on pain management.

Robert T. Kauer, J. B. Silvers, and Jill Teplensky. "The Effect of Fixed Payment on Hospital Costs." *Journal of Health Politics, Policy and Law,* 1995, *20,* 303.

Considers the impact of new Medicare regulations that have replaced the cost-based system of reimbursement of capital expenditures by hospitals with a fixed payment per case based on assigned DRGs. For the first time, hospitals must pay the governmental share of their capital costs. At the same time, overall reform points toward more capitation or fixed payments from all payers. This article discusses possible responses to legislative and competitive reforms by hospital management and the resulting effectiveness of the changes. To identify the potential effect of capital payment reform, the authors examine some of the key provisions and assumptions of the new regulations, discuss the management implications of a changed capital payment system, and explore alternative models of hospital investment behavior in a world where one price for services for all buyers is a probable scenario.

Kimber L. Latsha. "Reimbursement for Long Term Care Facilities." Washington, D.C.: American Health Lawyers Association [Report No. VMM99–0067], 1999, 48 pages.

Provides an overview of Medicare PPS for long-term care facilities and addresses developing implementation issues, including admission policies for high-cost residents, possible metropolitan statistical area reclassification wage adjustments, bundling or unbundling of services within the PPS rate, automatic Medicare RUGS classifications, therapy caps, consolidated billing, other design issues, and post-Boren Medicaid rate setting issues. Includes a memorandum on the legal implications of excluding high-acuity Medicare eligible beneficiaries under PPS and OIG Advisory Opinion 99-2 on discounted ambulance services provided to SNF residents.

Harvey L. McCormick. *Medicare and Medicaid Claims and Procedures.* 2 vols. (3rd ed.) St. Paul, Minn.: West, 1998.

This regularly updated treatise is an effort to simplify a vast and complex body of law by first describing the most commonly used sections of the Medicare and Medicaid Acts, and then proceeding to organize the laws, regulations, and a massive gloss of judicial opinions in such a way that attorneys, judges, health care providers, and other interested providers will be able to effectively handle Medicare and Medicaid claims and appeals from claim denials.

Volume One examines inpatient hospital services, extended care services, and home health services, along with eligibility, enrollment procedures, benefit categories, and administrative procedures. Volume Two discusses the topics of judicial review and Medicaid in general. The treatise concludes with four appendices, including a directory of peer review organizations, an application and administrative procedure forms, a list of Medicaid state agencies, and a prospective payment plan for Medicare patients. It also features a table of statutes, a table of rules and regulations, and indexes to Medicare and Medicaid.

Julie Nelson. "Investigation and Monitoring Systems for Health System Reimbursement." Washington, D.C.: American Health Lawyers Association [Report No. VHH99–0020], 1999, 27 pages.

Examines investigation and monitoring systems for provider reimbursement issues; provides recommendations on establishing investigation and monitoring systems, and addresses documentation issues related to those systems. Also briefly discusses confidentiality of the investigation and monitoring system and self-reporting obligations.

Deborah A. Randall. "Home Health Ventures and Reimbursement." Washington, D.C.: American Health Lawyers Association [Report No. VMM99–0039], 1999, 71 pages.

Discusses reimbursement issues involving home health agencies and corporate structures for them. Attachments include HCFA responses to frequently asked questions for home health claims to sequential billing requirements and the limitation of fifty-six detail lines per claim; HCFA Transmittal No. A-98-13 on review of HHA-related (home health agency) businesses; information on OASIS; and an HCFA chart comparing SOC (start-of-care), follow-up, transfer, and discharge versions of OASIS-B1.

8.02   MEDICARE

Commerce Clearing House. *Medicare and Medicaid Guide.* Chicago: Commerce Clearing House, 1998.

This is an authoritative five-volume loose-leaf series. A practical guide to cases, statutes, regulations, and case law regarding Medicare and Medicaid, it includes a section on new developments and current agency proposals. It is recommended by Medicare advocates as one of the most comprehensive sources of up-to-date information on the topic.

Gail D. Edson. "Annotated Bibliography: Medicare and Managed Care." *Kansas Law Review,* 1996, *44,* 793.

This is an informative thirteen-page guide to the Medicare managed care program and its appeals process. The bibliography includes information on the Medicare appeals process in general, with some specific references to the managed care appeals process. The author focuses on materials that are relevant to the health care attorney and that are easily obtained from law libraries or academic research libraries. She intentionally excluded materials published prior to 1990.

J. D. Epstein and Leonard C. Homer. "Fundamentals of Medicare Part A and Part B Payment." Washington, D.C.: American Health Lawyers Association [Report No. VMM 98–0001], 1998, 86 pages.

Examines the fundamentals of Medicare Parts A and B, including the history of the government's involvement in health insurance, a reimbursement overview, administration of the Medicare program, eligibility, coverage, certification, payment of hospital and postacute care, assignment and reassignment, and selected Medicare appeal processes.

Laurence A. Frolik and Melissa C. Brown. *Advising the Elderly or Disabled Client: Legal, Health Care, Financial and Estate Planning.* Englewood, N.J.: Rosenfeld Launer, 1992.

This desktop reference work for attorneys and advocates is regularly supplemented. It contains a chapter on general Medicare advocacy and a short segment on Medicare HMOs.

Health Care Financing Administration. *HCFA Rulings on Medicare, Medicaid, Professional Standards Review and Related Matters.* Baltimore, Md.: Health Care Financing Administration.

Supplies current program regulations, manuals, instructions, rulings, and decisions along with illustrative case decisions.

Health Care Financing Administration. *HMO/CMP Manual.* Baltimore, Md.: Health Care Financing Administration, 1998.

Agency publication designed as a guide for participating managed care groups in a variety of cities.

"Medicare: GAO Views on Medicare Payments to Health Maintenance Organizations." (GAO/T-HRD-90–27.) 1990.

Statement of Janet L. Shikles, director of health financing and policy issues for HCFA, before the Committee on Ways and Means, Subcommittee on Health, House of Representatives.

"Medicare: HCFA Needs to Take Stronger Action against HMOs Violating Federal Standards." (GAO/T-HRD-92–11.) 1991.

Statement from Janet L. Shikles, director of health financing and policy issues for HCFA, before the Committee on Energy and Commerce, Subcommittee on Health and the Environment, House of Representatives.

"Medicare Managed Care: Enrollment Growth Underscores Need to Revamp HMO Payment Methods." (GAO/T-HEHS-95–207.) July 1995.

Statement of Jonathan B. Ratner, associate director of health financing and policy issues for HCFA, before the House Committee on Commerce, Subcommittee on Health and Environment, House of Representatives.

Wayne J. Miller. *Health Care Law Sourcebook: A Compendium of Federal Laws, Regulations and Documents Relating to Health Law.* New York: Matthew Bender, 1991.

This two-volume work provides the text of federal law, regulations, and other government documents relevant to the delivery of health care services. Intended for attorneys and health care practitioners, it includes extensive information on Medicare reimbursement and certification. Other parts are devoted to a range of topics that include managed care laws and recent legislation. Periodically updated.

Robert D. Reischauer, Stuart Butler, Judith Lave, and Michael Gluck (eds.). *Medicare: Preparing for the Challenges of the 21st Century.* Washington, D.C.: Brookings Institution, 1998.

This book of approximately two hundred pages begins with consideration of the underlying social contract between Medicare's beneficiaries and workers. Noting that Medicare historically has had particular significance for civil rights and women's economic security, the authors debate the appropriate social contract for the future. The book also distills the issues in financing Medicare as health care costs rise and the population ages. A number of authors explore how the growth in managed care is likely to affect Medicare beneficiaries, with special emphasis on beneficiaries with chronic illness.

8.02(1)   General Framework

American Association of Retired Persons. *Medicare Practice Manual.* Washington, D.C.: AARP, 1997.

Written by attorneys for attorneys, this manual contains a comprehensive summary of the Medicare program with emphasis on Part A coverage and issues. Its legal analysis and practical applications are based on successful advocacy tactics.

Timothy P. Blanchard. "Medical Necessity Denials, Overpayments and False Claims." Washington, D.C.: American Health Lawyers Association [Report No. VMM99–0012], 1999, 31 pages.

Examines in detail Medicare medical necessity determinations, criteria, and processes for determining medical necessity and substandard medical care, and resulting overpayment and false claims exposure.

George S. Chulis and others. "Health Insurance and the Elderly." *Health Affairs,* 1993, *12,* 111.

The interconnection of Medicare benefits with other forms of insurance makes reform of the Medicare system a tricky proposition. The two main types of private insurance that cover expenses not covered by Medicare are employer-sponsored retiree insurance and individually purchased Medigap policies. On the public side, Medicaid benefits for the elderly poor can be partial (covering only Medicare premiums, deductibles, and coinsurance) or complete (providing full coverage of service). This study examines survey data to estimate the extent of supplementary insurance held by Medicare enrollees.

Thomas W. Coons and J. D. Epstein. "Fundamentals of Medicare Part A and Part B Payment." Washington, D.C. American Health Lawyers Association [Report No.VMM99–00001], 1999, 105 pages.

Examines the evolution of Medicare policy and law and gives an overview of the Medicare program and sources of law. Looks at Medicare Part A eligibility, coverage certification, payment, assignment and reassignment, and appeals. Also discusses Medicare Part B eligibility, coverage, payment methods and policy, billing documentation rules and requirements, and appeals.

Families USA. *Shortchanged: Billions Withheld from Medicare Beneficiaries.* Washington, D.C.: Families USA, 1998, 29 pages.

Four million low-income Medicare beneficiaries are entitled to, but not receiving, subsidies to help cover their Medicare premiums and, for some, their deductibles and copayments. This report provides state-by-state numbers of low-income elderly or disabled persons who should be receiving qualified Medicare beneficiary, SLMB, or Ql-1 benefits and the dollar amounts they have lost, with recommendations for government action.

General Accounting Office. "Medicare Billing: Commercial System Could Save Hundreds of Millions Annually." (GAO/AIMD-98-91.) Apr. 15, 1998, 20 pages.

More than three years after GAO recommended that Medicare acquire commercial software to detect inappropriate billings—which could save hundreds of millions of dollars each year—the HCFA has tested the software and plans to install it. Incorrect billings, fraudulent or otherwise, cost Medicare about $1.7 billion in improper payments in 1997. This report analyzes HCFA's progress in testing and acquiring a commercial system for identifying inappropriate Medicare bills, the consequences of HCFA's initial management decisions, and its plans for implementation.

Alice G. Gosfield. "Private Contracting by Medicare Physicians: 'The Pit and the Pendulum.'" *Health Law Digest,* Jan. 1998, *26,* 3–9.

Throughout the history of Medicare physician payment, potential government intrusion in private financial relationships between doctors and patients has been at issue. Congressional action on this topic has moved from an affirmative avoidance policy to one of increasing involvement in private activity, and now back in the other direction. The Balanced Budget Act of 1997 (BBA) enacted a provision to liberalize the restrictions imposed by Medicare law on private financial arrangements between doctors and their Medicare patients by eliminating imposition of limited charges in certain situations. But as a result of a controversial conference committee modification, Gosfield writes, the statute is confusing at best, internally inconsistent, and in the final analysis eviscerates the whole point of the provision.

Institute of Medicine. *Improving the Medicare Market.* Washington, D.C.: National Academy Press, 1996, 368 pages.

Analyzes how to provide Medicare beneficiaries the same choice of health plan options available in the private sector, while protecting them as patients and consumers. This report by the Institute's Committee on Choice and Managed Care recommends approaches to ensuring informed purchasing and accountability for Medicare beneficiaries in an environment of managed care. It addresses how the government should evaluate and approve plans; how to assist the elderly in understanding and comparing their options; what role the traditional Medicare program should play; and how to develop the necessary guidelines concerning enrollment, marketing, and grievance procedures.

Timothy S. Jost. "Governing Medicare." *Administrative Law Review,* 1999, *51,* 39.

This article offers a comprehensive overview of the governance of Medicare. It begins by examining each of the dozen cases that the Supreme Court has decided involving Medicare, as well as a sampling of lower court cases spanning the history of the program. It concludes that the courts have become extraordinarily deferential to the bureaucracy that administers the program. This deference is both procedural (the courts refuse to intervene in Medicare disputes until an extensive series of administrative remedies have been exhausted) and substantive (the courts rarely challenge the bureaucracy's interpretation of Medicare statutes or regulations). Second, the article examines the role of Congress, which, by contrast, has taken an active role in governing Medicare, constantly tinkering with the Medicare statute and redirecting the program. Third, it studies HCFA, the Medicare bureaucracy, which, perpetually struggling to keep up with Congress, governs the program largely through a massive body of subregulatory issuances, while the courts benignly look the other way. The author concludes that Americans ought to look at European corporatist structures for models for organizing interest group input into the administrative governance of Medicare.

"Medicare: PRO Review Does Not Assure Quality of Care Provided by Risk HMOs." (GAO/T-HRD-91–48.) 1991.

This is an evaluation of PRO (peer review organization) effectiveness in assessing HMO quality and access. It concludes that these organizations fail to assure quality care to Medicare beneficiaries.

James B. Wieland. "Billing Company Issues." Washington, D.C.: American Health Lawyers Association [Report No. VPH99–0015], 1999, 23 pages.

Reviews Medicare reassignment issues relating to billing companies including "lock box" and "sweep account" requirements and analyzes antikickback and false claims implications of percentage fee arrangements. Also discusses issues in contracting with physician billing companies and billing company compliance plans; contains a sample billing company contract.

8.02(2)   Part A: Inpatient Services Related to Acute Hospital Inpatient Care

David M. Frankford. "The Complexity of Medicare's Hospital Reimbursement System: Paradoxes of Averaging." *Iowa Law Review*, 1993, *78*, 517.

In this 151-page article, the author examines the structure of Medicare's inpatient hospital reimbursement system from its inception to the present. He concludes that the United States should abandon per-case payment and move to a system with a federal budgetary cap to protect overall fiscal integrity and the use of hospital budgeting, administered locally, to allocate these funds.

Chris Rossman. "Reimbursement in the Provider-Based Setting." Washington, D.C.: American Health Lawyers Association [Report No. VHH99–0031], 1999, 20 pages.

Analyzes the Medicare proposed rules for prospective payment systems for hospital outpatient services. Includes HCFA Transmittal No A-98–15 (May 1998) clarifying HCFA's policy regarding provider-based and freestanding designation decisions.

8.02(2)(a)   Diagnosis-Related Groups

Judith R. Lave. "The Impact of the Medicare Prospective Payment System and Recommendations for Change." *Yale Journal on Regulation*, 1990, *7*, 499.

Examines the prospective payment system established for hospitals under the Medicare program with the passage of the Social Security Reform Act in 1983. PPS represents an approach to paying for care that differs radically from the retrospective cost-based reimbursement system it replaced. The program pays hospitals a prospectively determined amount for each Medicare patient treated, depending on the patient's diagnosis. Although not the only hospital prospective payment system in operation, the Medicare PPS has had the greatest impact on our health care delivery system since it covers approximately 33.2 million people and accounts for nearly 27 percent of all expenditures on hospital care in the United States. The Medicare PPS has influenced where program beneficiaries receive health care services, how long they stay in hospitals, and the kinds of care they receive.

This article, written by the former director of the research office of the HCFA, argues that the evidence to date indicates implementation of PPS has not been accompanied by a decrease in quality of care or by discrimination against more seriously ill patients. However, since the general financial condition of hospitals has deteriorated significantly in the past few years, further shortfalls may seriously threaten quality of care. Since the national rate now in effect under PPS does not adequately adjust for the factors that influence the level of costs in specific hospitals, changes to the structure of PPS would make the system more sensitive to the costs of individual institutions.

Some evidence suggests that PPS has influenced diffusion of new technologies into the health care system since certain technologies would have been used more widely if hospitals were still being paid on the basis of retrospective costs. Thus, PPS has made a small inroad into curtailing the growth of service intensity. However, control of medical inflation will require more work on this problem. Research and policy must focus on determining the effectiveness of particular medical practices and the usefulness of old and new technologies so that informed choices can be made. According to Lave, the challenge of the future is to recognize our medical limits and to develop policies to ensure that wise decisions are made within them.

8.02(2)(b) Special Payment Rules for Certain Costs

Darryl E. Bueker and Samuel D. Orbovich. "Lingering Issues in Cost-Based Retrospective Reimbursement." Washington, D.C.: American Health Lawyers Association [Report No. VLT99–0006], 1999, 30 pages.

Focuses on key issues still remaining in cost-based retrospective reimbursement after enactment of the BBA and implementation of prospective rates, such as Medicare-reimbursable bad debts, routine operating cost limit exemptions and exceptions, owner's compensation, prudent buyer, salary equivalency, and others. Attached are an example of computing a comparison of peer group per diem amounts and an HCFA provider questionnaire for Medicare cost reporting requesting information on owner or management personnel compensation.

Families USA. *Monitoring Medicare HMOs: A Guide to Collecting and Interpreting Available Data.* Washington, D.C.: Families USA, 1998, 86 pages.

Targeted chiefly at groups working with Medicare beneficiaries, this guide provides step-by-step instructions for gathering and making sense of Medicare HMO data from federal agencies, state governments, and other sources. Parts of the guide will be useful to those interested in Medicaid or commercial HMOs.

Joel M. Hamme and others. "Medicare Skilled Nursing Facilities: Prospective Payment, Consolidated Billing and Contracting with Ancillary Suppliers." Washington, D.C.; American Health Lawyers Association [Report No. VLT99–0016], 1999, 69 pages.

Addresses legal issues for long-term care providers and suppliers under the BBA's provisions relating to a PPS and consolidated billing for Medicare SNFs.

Joel M. Hamme and Joseph M. Lubarsky. "Medicare Prospective Payment and Consolidated Billing for SNFs: Financial and Legal Perspectives." Washington, D.C.: American Health Lawyers Association [Report No. VLT99–0015], 1999, 69 pages.

Highlights major provisions and most recent developments relating to Medicare PPS and consolidated billing for SNFs such as problem areas in implementation and major reimbursement issues and legal pitfalls for SNFs; gives strategies for financial survival and success.

John R. Hellow and others. "Procedural Issues at the Provider Reimbursement Review Board." (Washington, D.C. American Health Lawyers Association [Report No. VMM99–0002], 1999, 58 pages.

Reviews procedural issues that arise in dealing with the PRRB, including prospective payment system, capital appeals, direct graduate medical education appeals, revised notices of program reimbursement, and wage index disputes under the prospective payment system. Discusses selected Medicare jurisdiction and procedural cases.

Michael D. Intriligator. "Challenging the Use of Statistical Procedures in Overpayment Determinations." Washington, D.C.: American Health Lawyers Association [Report No. VMM99–00007], 1999, 20 pages.

Examines use of statistical sampling and extrapolation in provider audits under Medicare and Medicaid. It covers the statistical and legal requirements for valid sampling and extrapolation and discusses eight areas in which intermediates go wrong in sampling and extrapolation.

Kenneth R. Marcus. "Payment Principles Applicable to Mergers and Acquisitions." Washington, D.C.: American Health Lawyers Association [Report No. VMM99–0004], 1999, 53 pages.

Discusses procedural and substantive Medicare payment principles to be addressed when providers enter into merger or acquisition transactions, including change of ownership, successor liability, and various hospital-specific payment parameters.

"Medicare Dialysis Patients: Widely Varying Lab Test Rates Suggest Need for Greater HCFA Scrutiny." (GAO/HEHS-97–202.) Sept. 26, 1997, 23 pages.

Medicare is the leading payer for dialysis and other medical treatments for end-stage renal disease. Medicare enrollment by kidney patients more than doubled between 1984 and 1994, while expenditures more than tripled, to $8.4 billion. Medicare does not scrutinize the level of laboratory tests for dialysis patients, and GAO found that similar patients received laboratory tests at widely differing rates. At one extreme, Medicare may be paying for excessive tests, while at the other patients may not be receiving the tests needed to monitor their condition. Fee-for-service reimbursement does not give physicians adequate incentive to order tests judiciously, and neither Medicare nor its claims-processing contractors routinely analyze the kind of claims data that GAO reviewed when it found anomalies. GAO recommends that Medicare profile doctors ordering laboratory tests for Medicare dialysis patients and notify contractors of unusual test rates. In addition, Congress should consider holding physicians liable when they order excessive tests.

"Medigap Insurance: Compliance with Federal Standards Has Increased." (GAO/HEHS-98–66.) Mar. 6, 1998, 36 pages.

Millions of Medicare beneficiaries depend on private "Medigap" insurance to cover Medicare's deductibles and coinsurance. This GAO report examines Medigap insurance's loss ratios—the percentage of premiums returned to policyholders as benefits—and finds that federal incentives to meet these loss ratio standards have been successful.

National Health Law Program and Families USA. *A Guide to Meeting the Needs of People with Chronic and Disabling Conditions in Medicaid Managed Care*. Washington, D.C.: Families USA, 1998), 44 pages.

This handbook examines the issues confronting states as they move toward mandating managed care for people with chronic and disabling conditions. It discusses problems experienced when either populations or services are carved out, looks at steps that states have taken to ensure quality care, and provides advocates with information about where to make their voices heard.

Virginia Peabody and Paul Sullivan. *The Medicare as a Secondary Payer Guide*. Brookfield, Wis.: International Foundation of Employee Benefit Plans, 1996, 194 pages.

Focuses on Medicare as a secondary payer. It also covers the rules affecting group health plans, including those concerning the working aged, disabled, and individuals with end-stage renal disease. It also covers rules affecting workers compensation and recovery of Medicare payments.

Lester J. Perling. "Challenging the Use of Statistical Procedures in Overpayment Determinations." Washington, D.C.: American Health Lawyers Association [Report No. VMM99–0008], 1999, 22 pages.

Summarizes the federal, state, and administrative cases addressing the issues of statistical sampling in the Medicare and Medicaid context. Also includes summary descriptions of materials prepared by HCFA and the DHHS Office of the Inspector General regarding statistical sampling. Addresses some strategies for challenging the use of statistical sampling.

Jacqueline R. Vaughn. "Provider Reimbursement Review Board Appeals and Administrator's Review." Washington, D.C.: American Health Lawyers Association [Report No. VMM99–0011], 1999, 9 pages.

Discusses the HCFA administrator's review of PRRB decisions and the regulations governing appeal and review.

8.02(3) Part B: Outpatient and Physician Services

Ann E. Berriman. "DME, Orthotics and Prosthetics." Washington, D.C.: American Health Lawyers Association [Report No. VMM99–0068], 1999, 43 pages.

Discusses coverage, reimbursement, and claims processing for Part B nonphysician claims and includes supplier standards and fraud and abuse initiatives in this area as well as the OIG's compliance guidance for DME (durable medical equipment), O&P (orthotic and prosthetic), and supplies.

Irwin Cohen. "Part B Billing Issues in Hospital/Physician Integration." Washington, D.C.: American Health Lawyers Association [Report No. VMM99–0016], 1999, 16 pages.

Briefly examines hospital-physician integration structures, reassignment, physician billing issues under Stark and antikickback rules, and assessing Part B billing issues in hospital-physician integration.

Thomas W. Coons and Howard L. Sollins. "New Medicare Payment Approaches for Outpatient and Post-Acute Care Providers." Washington, D.C.: American Health Lawyers Association [Report No. VHL98–0023], 1998, 46 pages.

Discusses the payment approaches for services furnished by home health agencies, skilled nursing facilities, hospital outpatient departments, and specialty providers, all of which were reimbursed in whole or in part under the reasonable cost system but which will be reimbursed under various prospective payment approaches as the result of the BBA's Medicare payment reforms.

Dennis K. Grindle. "Non-Physician Practitioner Issues: Medicare Part B Billing Reference Guide." Washington, D.C.: American Health Lawyers Association [Report No VMM99–0055], 1999, 73 pages.

Outlines and examines Medicare billing statutes, regulations, and rules for physician assistants, nurse practitioners, clinical nurse specialists, certified nurse midwives, clinical psychologists, clinical social workers, physical and occupational therapists, and speech pathologists. Includes a chart showing highlights of Medicare billing rules for nonphysician practitioner services.

Janet K. Horan. "Compliance Guidelines for the Physician's Office." Washington, D.C.: American Health Lawyers Association [Report No. VMM99–0063], 1999, 43 pages.

Presents guidelines to assist the physician or the physician's attorney in establishing a proactive program to monitor and audit such office practices as billing, coding, and contracting. Also assists in identifying activities in a physician's office that could potentially be considered fraud.

"Medicare Home Health: Differences in Service Use by HMO and Fee-for-Service Providers." (GAO/HEHS-98–8.) Oct. 21, 1997, 28 pages.

HMOs manage Medicare-provided home health care more actively than do fee-for-service providers, emphasizing short-term recuperation and rehabilitation goals. Differences between

HMO and fee-for-service providers are most apparent in use of home health aides. In the fee-for-service programs, using home health aides to provide long-term care for patients with chronic conditions is growing, whereas the six HMOs that GAO visited do not provide such services on a long-term basis. Although fee-for-service providers have less-effective controls for preventing unnecessary services, the Medicare program lacks the data needed to determine if the chronically ill are adequately served by HMOs.

"Medicare: Home Oxygen Program Warrants Continued HCFA Attention." (GAO/HEHS-98–17.) Nov. 7, 1997, 24 pages.

In fiscal year 1996, nearly 480,000 Medicare beneficiaries received supplemental oxygen at home, at a cost of about $1.7 billion. GAO found that Medicare pays about 38 percent more for home oxygen supplies than the competitive marketplace rates paid by the Department of Veterans Affairs (VA). In some cases, Medicare obtains even fewer oxygen benefits despite paying higher prices. The Balanced Budget Act of 1997 includes provisions that should bring Medicare's reimbursement rates more in line with the competitive marketplace rates paid by VA. The act also requires developing service standards for home oxygen suppliers that serve Medicare patients, as well as monitoring patient access to home oxygen equipment. However, concerns have been raised that these rate reductions could reduce Medicare beneficiaries' access to portable units, which do not offer suppliers the attractive profit margins associated with lower-cost oxygen concentrators.

Mark V. Pauley and others. *Paying Physicians: Options for Controlling Cost, Volume and Intensity of Services.* Chicago: Health Administration Press, 1992, 223 pages.

Offers discussion of payment for Medicare physician services, and models of physician behavior, an analysis of the controls on Medicare fees, and the impact of the Resource-Based Relative Value Scale (RBRVS).

James B. Wieland. "Carrier Payment Issues for Physicians." Washington, D.C.: American Health Lawyers Association [Report No. VMM99–0050], 1999, 32 pages.

Part One of this paper examines developments in Medicare Part B payment for physician services. Looks at Medicare physician payment; Medicare Part B reimbursement under the RBRVS and Physician Payment Reform; the RBRVS scale; adjustments to RVRVS amounts, physicians, and other practitioners affected by the RBRVS; and specialty-specific considerations. Part Two examines the role and authority of Medicare carriers, and Medicare carriers under physician payment reform.

8.02(4)   Medicare+Choice Program

Robert P. Charrow, David C. Main, and Joseph N. Onek. "Retooling Medicine through PSOs and Medicare+Choice Plans: Can Providers Catch the Brass Ring?" *Health Law Digest* 25(10), Oct. 1997, 3–12.

Summarizes the Medicare+Choice Program enacted into law by the Balanced Budget Act of 1997, which adds a new Part C to the Medicare system. The authors highlight some of the various regulatory actions that must be taken before implementation and analyze the new Part C from the provider's and the beneficiary's perspectives.

Paul R. DeMuro. "Medicare+Choice." Washington, D.C.: American Health Lawyers Association [Report No. VMM99–0037], 1999, 54 pages.

Examines the Medicare+Choice (M+C) program, including the M+C process; eligibility, election, and enrollment; benefits and beneficiary protections; quality assurance; relationships with providers; payments to M+C organizations, premium, and cost sharing; PSOs, preemption, and contracts with M+C organizations; grievances, organization determinations, and appeals; fundamental organizational requirements for PSOs; the licensing and certification process; waiver of the state licensure requirement; solvency standards for Medicare managed care organizations; and solvency standards for PSOs.

Gary W. Eiland. "The Medicare+Choice Program." Washington, D.C.: American Health Lawyers Association [Report No. VHL98–0044], 1998, 42 pages.

Describes the Medicare+Choice program's implementation rules, including organizational requirements for participating entities regarding eligibility, licensure, waiver, and application; beneficiary eligibility, election, and enrollment; and sanctions and other user fees. Features a table of contents for the Medicare+Choice Final Rule, 63 Fed. Reg. 34968.

Lynn Etheredge. "The Medicare Reforms of 1997: Headlines You Didn't Read." *Journal of Health Politics, Policy and Law,* June 1998, *23,* 573.

The 1997 Medicare reforms were among the most important social and health policy legislation of the past three decades, the author writes. The legislation was notable in reestablishing a viable health policy process; in disproving predictions that government-run insurance would restrict consumer freedoms more than employer-based health insurance; and in ratifying market-oriented approaches as a national health paradigm. Most important, the legislation achieved an historic philosophical compromise between advocates of government health insurance on the one hand and of private health insurance on the other. The author concludes that political agreements came at the expense of greater regulatory capture of the Medicare program by health provider and health plan interests and at the expense of deficient consumer protection.

General Accounting Office. "Medicare+Choice: New Standards Could Improve Accuracy and Usefulness of Plan Literature." (GAO/HEHS-99–92.) Apr. 12, 1999, 30 pages.

GAO found that sixteen managed care organizations participating in the Medicare+Choice program (Medicare's alternative to fee-for-service) gave beneficiaries materials containing inaccurate or incomplete beneficiary information. For example, materials from five organizations said that annual screening mammograms required a physician's referral, even though Medicare explicitly prohibits this. One organization provided an outpatient prescription drug benefit that was substantially less generous than that agreed to in its Medicare contract. Each organization used its own format and terms to describe the plan benefit package, making it difficult for beneficiaries to compare available options. GAO concludes that beneficiaries would be helped by (1) full implementation of HCFA's new contract form describing a plan's benefit coverage; (2) new standards for terminology, formats, and distribution of key member literature; (3) standard forms for routine administrative functions; (4) standard marketing procedures to review material; and (5) a requirement that organizations provide beneficiaries with a single standard brochure like that distributed to members of the Federal Employees Health Benefits Program.

Jennifer E. Gladieux. "Medicare+Choice Appeal Procedures: Reconciling Due Process Rights and Cost Containment." *American Journal of Law and Medicine,* 1999, *25,* 61.

This article outlines the historical approach to Medicare risk contractor appeal rights, which was based primarily on the traditional model developed in the fee-for-service context. The author then describes in detail the current regulatory structure for grievance and appeals procedures from the managed care perspective. She discusses the National Association of Insurance Commissioners' model grievance and appeals procedures and the National Committee for Quality Assurance accreditation and performance measurement standards. Gladieux argues that if a relatively uniform system of government regulation can be established to monitor Medicare+Choice options through the Quality Improvement System for Managed Care, along with providing consumers useful information about grievance and appeal procedures, Medicare beneficiaries' fears concerning service denials will likely be mollified. The resulting regulatory structure should encourage, rather than hinder, the switch to Medicare+Choice. This approach, she contends, is advantageous in that it is cost-efficient and can evolve organically to protect Medicare beneficiaries' due process rights as new delivery systems emerge in the marketplace.

Mark S. Joffe. "Medicare+Choice and Medigap Programs." Washington, D.C.: American Health Lawyers Association [Report No. VMM98–0017], 1998, 77 pages.

Provides an overview of the Medicare+Choice program as established by the Balanced Budget Act of 1997. Focuses on the coordinated care plans options and changes to the Medigap program. Includes a chart comparing the Medicare Risk program and the Medicare+Choice program, and relevant time lines for risk contractors along with a flowchart for determining whether an organization qualifies as a provider-sponsored organization.

Jonathan M. Joseph. "Patient Rights and Remedies in Managed Care." Washington, D.C.: American Health Lawyers Association [Report No VLT99–0008], 1999, 52 pages.

Discusses the rights and remedies enrollees in managed care plans have regarding decisions made by the plan. Provides in-depth discussion of Medicare+Choice requirements for managed care plans in handling appeals of determinations and grievances. Also covers Medicaid proposed regulations for managed care plans and discusses state laws governing grievances. Attachments include *Grijalva* v. *Shalala,* 152 F.3d 1115 (9th Cir. 1998) (mandating better monitoring and enforcement of appeals rights of Medicare beneficiaries enrolled in HMOs), selected patient protection language from the proposed federal Patient Protection Act (H.R. 425), and a copy of New York's Managed Care Act.

Donald G. Kosin. "Medicare+Choice: An Overview." Washington, D.C.: American Health Lawyers Association [Report No.VMM99–0038], 1999, 31 pages.

Gives an overview of the requirements and protections of the M+C law as created by the Balanced Budget Act of 1997, including new options and expanded availability of options; information dissemination, coordinated enrollment, and lock-in; payment changes and risk adjustment; announcement of rates and adjusted community rate proposal requirements; access issues and consumer and provider protections; member appeals; state-federal relations; and contracting standards. Includes a chart of provider subcontracting requirements showing statutory and regulatory requirements that M+C organizations must meet in the area of contracts and subcontracts, and listing ways they can show compliance, as well as HCFA Revised OPL 98.077 on M+C contracting requirements for provider and administrative services.

Wendy L. Krasner. "Developing a Provider Sponsored Organization and Qualifying for Medicare+Choice." Washington, D.C.: American Health Lawyers Association [Report No. VHL98–0046], 1998, 25 pages.

Addresses the applicability of state and federal laws to PSO operations once the organization has been established and received a contract under Part C of the Medicare program, known as Medicare+Choice.

Joel L. Michaels. "Balanced Budget Act (BBA) and Implementing Regulations." Washington, D.C.: American Health Lawyers Association [Report No. VMC98–0014], 1998, 30 pages.

Reviews the key changes brought about by the BBA and how they are being interpreted by HCFA's interim regulations, with a particular focus on the Medicare+Choice program. Addresses the steps for participating in M+C, including marketing and enrollment, new rating requirements and assorted certifications, provider issues in terms of contract arrangements, expansion of beneficiary access and appeal rights, and the new emphasis on improvement in quality management programs.

Cynthia F. Reaves. "Tax-Exempt Organization Participation in Provider Sponsored Organizations (PSOs)." Washington, D.C.: American Health Lawyers Association [Report NoVTX98–0022], 1998, 66 pages.

Outlines the statutory requirements for organizing PSOs for participation in the Medicare+Choice program. Applies these structural requirements to identify issues that arise for tax-exempt entities in their organization and participation in PSOs with for-profit parties. Attachment compares state solvency standards for HMOs with the federal solvency standards for Medicare PSOs.

Dan Settelmayer. "Provider-Sponsored Organizations Under the Medicare+Choice Program." Washington, D.C.: American Health Lawyers Association [Report No. VHL98–0047], 1998, 24 pages.

Focuses on the BBA's PSO authorizing legislation and implementing regulations, state licensing and federal certification process, comparison of context with discussion of IDS and PHO development, legal considerations in formation (antitrust, tax status, choice of entity, fraud and abuse laws) and practical considerations, market analysis, and feasibility studies.

Bruce John Shih and Julianne Chun. "Basics of Medicare+Choice, Including Provider Sponsored Organizations." *California Health Law News*, Winter 1998–99, *18*(3), 82–89.

Summarizes the primary provisions of the Medicare+Choice program.

Bruce John Shih and Daniel K. Settelmayer. "Knox-Keene Licensed Provider Plans: New Global Capitation Vehicle for Providers." *California Health Law News*, Fall 1996.

This article analyzes the California Department of Corporations decision to grant limited licenses under that state's Knox-Keene Health Care Service Act of 1975. The department took this action following several years of government agency and industry study of the legal ramifications of health plan and provider full risk sharing or global capitation arrangements, inaction on the issue by the California legislature, and continued provider evolution as full risk sharing or global capitation arrangements.

Bruce John Shih and Daniel K. Settelmayer. "New Global Capitation Opportunities for Providers: Provider Sponsored Organizations and Knox-Keene Licensed Provider Plans." *California HFMA*, Winter 1998, 33–36.

The BBA expanded beneficiaries' choice of programs under Medicare in a new Medicare+Choice Part C, including provider sponsored organizations. PSOs will contract directly with Medicare on a global-capitation or full-risk basis to provide hospital and physician services. As PSOs must comply with the applicable state's risk-bearing licensing laws, providers in California are well situated to take advantage of PSOs because of changes adopted by the California Department of Corporations, which regulates HMOs (known in California as health care service plans) under the state's Knox-Keene Act. This article explores the options that providers in California can choose to control their own long-term destiny under Medicare+Choice and California law.

8.02(5)   Home Health Care

Brooks E. Allen. "The Price of Reform: Cost-Sharing Proposals for the Medicare Home Health Benefit." (Note.) *Yale Journal on Regulation*, 2000, *17*, 137.

This note examines beneficiary cost sharing as a means of reducing expenditures in the Medicare home health program. The author concludes that cost sharing likely would be ineffective or inequitable. In contrast, alternative reform proposals are likely to generate cost savings without the limitations of cost sharing. She urges abandoning attempts to extend cost sharing to the home health benefit and calls for further exploration of alternative methods to ensure the program's long-term solvency.

R. Brown and others. "The Effects of Predetermined Payment Rates for Medicare Home Health-care." *Health Services Research,* Oct. 1997, 397.

Contends that there is little incentive for cost efficiencies under the current cost-based method of reimbursement for Medicare home health services. A novel three-year experiment with prospective rate setting for home health care found that such a program is unlikely to generate large cost savings. Under an experimental program begun in 1990 and involving forty-seven home health care agencies that volunteered to participate, the "treatment" agencies were paid prospectively for each of six types of home health visit—nursing, physician, occupational, speech therapy, home health aide, and medical social worker—with adjustments made for changes to the volume of services provided. The demonstration program had no discernible effect on the cost of any type of home health visit, the authors conclude.

"Medicare: Improper Activities by Mid-Delta Home Health." (GAO/OSI-98–5.) Mar. 12, 1998, 24 pages.

This report details improperly claimed payroll costs—and questions such matters as this home health company paying a $65,000 bonus to the owner's daughter even though she was in school full-time in the year it was awarded. It also examines reports that staff visited Medicare beneficiaries whose eligibility or need for nurse visits was doubtful.

William J. Scanlon. "Medicare Home Health: Success of Balanced Budget Act Cost Controls Depends on Effective and Timely Implementation." (GAO/T-HEHS-98–41.) Oct. 29, 1997, 14 pages.

Speech by the director of health financing and systems issues at DHHS, before the Subcommittee on Oversight and Investigations, House Committee on Commerce. This testimony examines how the BBA has addressed rapid cost growth in Medicare's home health benefit. This benefit is important to many beneficiaries recovering from illness or injury following hospitalization—the original purpose of the benefit. Of late, however, increasing numbers of beneficiaries have used the benefit for custodial-type care for chronic conditions. This change has helped to fuel growth in Medicare home health costs, which soared from about $2 billion in 1989 to nearly $18 billion in 1996. GAO's remarks focus on the following four areas: the reasons for the rapid growth of Medicare home health care costs in the 1990s, the interim changes to Medicare's current payment system under the act, establishment of a prospective payment system for home health care, and efforts by Congress and the administration to strengthen program safeguards to prevent fraud and abuse in home health services.

8.03 MEDICAID

8.03(1) General Framework

O. N. Ahmad. "Medicaid Eligibility Rules for the Elderly Long-Term Care Applicant: History and Developments." *Journal of Legal Medicine,* 1999, *20,* 251.

Provides a chronology and analysis of Medicaid eligibility rules.

John A. Flippen. "The Early and Periodic Screening, Diagnostic and Treatment Program and Managed Medicaid Mental Health Care: The Need to Reevaluate the EPSDT in the Managed Care Era." (Note.) *Vanderbilt Law Review,* 1997, *50,* 683.

Examines how the Early and Periodic Screening, Diagnosis, and Treatment program (EPSDT), as a broad mandate enacted before managed care, has the potential to diminish the cost-effectiveness of managed care, particularly in the area of managed mental health care. For a majority of Medicaid recipients, managed health care is fast becoming a reality. One major tool of cost containment has been privatizing delivery of Medicaid coverage into managed care organizations. This shift to managed care means that services will be rationed. Medicaid, however, originated in an era when the government was not as concerned about controlling health care costs. Flippen discusses the need to reevaluate the EPSDT in the context of current changes in the industry.

General Accounting Office. "Health Care Reform: Potential Difficulties in Determining Eligibility for Low-Income People." (GAO/HEHS-94–176.) 1994.

In three states studied—Georgia, Illinois, and Massachusetts—nearly one-half of the applications for Medicaid that were denied were turned down for procedural reasons. These applicants did not or could not provide the basic documentation needed to verify their eligibility or did not appear for eligibility interviews. GAO recommends that Congress determine the appropriate balance between increasing access to care and maintaining program integrity.

General Accounting Office. "Medicaid Long Term Care: Successful State Efforts to Expand Home Services While Limiting Costs." (GAO/HEHS-94–167.) 1994.

The federal government would like to bring down the cost of its Medicaid expenditures, so GAO explored the efforts of three states that have tried to shift care from institutions to home or community care, which is less expensive. Oregon, Washington, and Wisconsin have expanded their home and community care and are serving more beneficiaries with fewer dollars than other states. They have also put caps on how much they will spend, so access to some services is blocked for some beneficiaries. The three states have used Medicaid waivers, which limit enrollment and expenditures, and placed additional controls on provider fees.

Health Program Staff. *Medicaid Survival Kit.* Denver: National Conference of State Legislatures, 1996.

Explains the existing Medicaid program, impending changes, and issues that legislators face in reforming the system. Topics discussed in this notebook, written for state legislators, include federal changes, major Medicaid populations, public providers, and cost-containment strategies.

Valerie Lewis. "Medicaid Waivers: California's Use of a Federal Option." Oakland, Calif.: Medi-Cal Policy Institute, Mar. 2000, 27 pages.

Topics examined in this report include (1) the relevance of Medicaid waivers for California policy makers, (2) the history and purpose of Medicaid waivers, (3) Section 1915 program waivers, (4) Section 1115 research and demonstration waivers, (5) the waiver process, (6) the impact of the Balanced Budget Act of 1997, (7) additional waiver opportunities in California, and (8) key policy and research questions. The text includes helpful tables and flowcharts.

Medi-Cal Policy Institute. *Medi-Cal County Data Book.* Oakland, Calif.: Medi-Cal Policy Institute, 1999, 138 pages.

This book compiles and organizes information county by county for Medi-Cal, California's Medicaid agency. Chock full of graphs and charts, this text is a gold mine for researchers on Medicaid policy.

Medi-Cal Policy Institute. "Speaking Out: What Beneficiaries Say about the Medi-Cal Program." Oakland, Calif.: Medi-Cal Policy Institute, Mar. 2000, 31 pages.

This report, prepared by the institute and Lake Snell, Perry & Associates, a public opinion research firm in Washington, D.C., finds that most beneficiaries think Medi-Cal "is a good program and worth the hassle because of what you get in return." Most also are pleased with the services Medi-Cal covers. However, many beneficiaries indicate that coverage for dental care and certain other benefits needs improvement, and people are confused about their coverage despite a variety of sources of information. Most beneficiaries believe the quality of Medi-Cal is high but also that quality and access need to be improved. A significant majority say the locations for signing up for Medi-Cal are unpleasant, and the hours inconvenient. The report is bolstered by thirty-three charts and graphs and two appendices.

Claudia Page and Susan Ruiz. "The Guide to Medi-Cal Programs." Oakland, Calif.: Medi-Cal Policy Institute, 1999, 42 pages.

Policy makers, legislators, and health care experts often ask, "Who qualifies for Medi-Cal?" Unfortunately, there is rarely an easy answer. Medi-Cal was established in 1965. Although California operates its own Medicaid program, the federal government continues to establish new requirements and to monitor issues such as delivery and quality of services, funding, and eligibility standards. Medicaid is overseen at the federal level by the HCFA and at the state level by the California Department of Health Services (DHS). In addition, each of California's fifty-eight counties plays an enormous role in administering and implementing Medi-Cal. This well-organized, easy-to-use reference is aimed at helping individuals understand the basic Medi-Cal eligibility categories and the distinctions among coverage groups. The information in the guide is derived from the eight-hundred-plus-page state Medi-Cal Eligibility Policies and Procedures Manual, the California Code of Regulations (Title XXII), the Aid Code Quick Reference, and various county manuals. The text is organized into tabbed subsections for quick reference and is supplemented with diagrams, flow-charts, and a glossary.

Michele Prestowitz. "A History of Medi-Cal Physician Payment Rates." Oakland, Calif.: Medi-Cal Policy Institute, Mar. 2000, 21 pages.

This report concludes that California provides more services to more Medicaid beneficiaries at a lower per-recipient cost than any other state. It does so in part by paying physicians far less than Medicare and commercial rates. Debate has begun to focus on the economic disadvantage facing physicians who choose to treat Medi-Cal patients. However, policy makers must consider whether rate increase will be effective in achieving real improvement in quality and access. Further, some policy makers are concerned that a rate increase might result in spiraling program costs when the booming economy turns and Medi-Cal enrollment begins to grow. As the Medi-Cal program moves into a new century, it will continue to grapple with these questions and with balancing the competing goals of cost-containment, provision of effective and efficient care, and the need to attract and retain the physicians required to treat beneficiaries in the future.

Rosemary H. Ratcliff. "The Mistakes of Medicaid: Provider Payment during the Past Decade and Lessons for Health Care Reform in the 21st Century." *Boston College Law Review*, 1990, *35*, 141.

Addresses some of the fundamental issues of the Medicaid provider payment system. This article begins by describing the statutory framework governing payment to Medicaid providers. It then describes the conflicting case law involving whether providers can seek Medicaid payments under 42 U.S.C. § 1983. The author concludes that the current Medicaid provider payment system suffers from overly general statutory and regulatory language and excessive judicial interpretation. The result is a complex and confusing body of law governing provider rates, one that should not be incrementally revised but instead substantially reformed.

A reformed health care system, Ratcliff writes, should avoid vague delegation of authority over determination of rates by expressly delegating authority to federal and state agencies, with reasonable limits on appeals and judicial review. A new system should also require negotiated rule making and reasonable appeal procedures to ensure that those beneficiaries and providers who are affected by the rates have a meaningful opportunity to ensure that payment to providers is fair and appropriate. Finally, a reformed Medicaid system should ensure that judicial review is limited to review of rates and remand to agencies, where a more careful and appropriate decision can be made by agency experts and representatives of recipients and providers.

Lynn Shapiro Snyder. "Medicaid Overview." Washington, D.C.: American Health Lawyers Association [Report No. VMM-0004], 1998, 75 pages.

Summarizes federal-state financial arrangements, general Medicaid coverage groups, eligibility conditions, benefits, reimbursement, prescription drug benefit, disproportionate share hospitals, state tax and donation programs, and other Medicaid issues and trends. It includes a chart of the organizational structure of HCFA and the Center for Medicaid and State Operations.

8.03(2) Reimbursement Principles

Atlantic Information Services. *Managed Medicare and Medicaid: Facts, Trends and Data.* Washington, D.C.: Atlantic Information Services, 1997, 459 pages.

Analyzes strategies for managed care, state contracting opportunities, and Medicare contract designs, among other issues.

Families USA. "A Guide to Complaints, Grievances and Hearings Under Medicaid Managed Care." Washington, D.C.: Families USA, 1998, 43 pages.

This guide provides an overview of the legal rights of Medicaid managed care enrollees, a look at common problems that prevent beneficiaries from receiving an impartial review, examples of what states have done to protect the rights of the beneficiary, and suggestions for ways advocates can help ensure an adequate complaint process is in place.

Faulkner and Gray. *1998 Medicaid Managed Behavioral Care Sourcebook: Strategies and Opportunities in a Fast-Changing Regulatory Environment.* New York: Faulkner and Gray, 1998.

Written for providers, state Medicaid officials, and managed care plan personnel, this book indicates which services states are searching for. With the help of sample requests for proposals, providers and plans can learn how to write effective responses to an RFP that opens the door to state business. For state agencies moving into managed care, the book sets forth in practical terms how to comply with the HCFA's waiver process. Other topics include designing successful Medicaid behavioral programs, public-private partnerships, and measuring quality. The text is supplemented by five helpful appendices, including a directory of organizations, a list of Internet resources, a bibliography, a list of sources, and a glossary.

Lynn Shapiro Snyder. "Medicaid Overview." Washington, D.C.: American Health Lawyers Association [Report No. VMM99–0003], 1999, 63 pages.

Supplies an overview of the Medicaid program, including coverage of payment groups, eligibility rules, reimbursement rules, disproportionate share hospitals, state and tax donation programs, Medicaid managed care, and Section 1115 waivers. Attachments include HCFA correspondence on Medicaid managed care and Section 1115 waivers, and a chart that provides an overview of the status of Section 1115 waivers of various states.

Thomas G. Smith and Jeffrey Golland. "Medicaid Rate Litigation after Boren." Washington, D.C.: American Health Lawyers Association [Report No. VLT-0015], 1998, 47 pages.

Discusses what legal recourse hospitals and nursing homes may still have under state and federal law to ensure that they are fairly compensated for providing care to the government-sponsored poor in the wake of repeal of the Boren amendment. These materials include guidance by Sally K. Richardson, director of HCFA's Center for Medicaid and State Operations, offered to state Medicaid directors.

8.03(3)   Recent Reforms

Atlantic Information Services. *State Medicaid Marketing Guidelines and Restrictions.* Washington, D.C.: Atlantic Information Services, 1997.

> Marketing guidelines for Medicaid health plans have shifted substantially in recent years as more states move Medicaid beneficiaries into managed care. This book includes copies of restrictions imposed by forty states and the District of Columbia.

Jennifer Blackburn and Ingrid Aguirre Happoldt. "Medi-Cal Outstationing in California: Findings from a Statewide Survey." Oakland, Calif.: Medi-Cal Policy Institute, June 1999, 38 pages.

> Outstationing—placing trained individuals at sites other than county welfare departments to assist consumers in applying for Medi-Cal—increases the convenience of applying for Medi-Cal and generates financial savings by reducing the incidence of uncompensated care. This study concludes that locating outstations at sites that people regularly visit, such as clinics and schools, increases the convenience of applying for Medi-Cal and generates financial savings by reducing the incidence of uncompensated care.

Gordon Bonnyman, Jr., and Michele M. Johnson. "Unseen Peril: Inadequate Enrollee Grievance Protection in Public Managed Care Programs." *Tennessee Law Review,* 1998, *65,* 359.

> This article focuses on those managed care arrangements that involve "risk contracting" by managed care organizations. Specifically, it examines due process protections in fee-for-service Medicare and Medicaid, beneficiary appeal procedures under managed care, and constitutional analysis of Medicaid and Medicare managed care beneficiary appeal procedures.

Jeffrey A. Buck and Mark S. Kamlet. "Problems with Expending Medicaid for the Uninsured." *Journal of Health Politics, Policy and Law,* 1993, *18,* 1.

> Expanding the Medicaid program is often viewed as the chief means of extending public health insurance coverage to the uninsured poor. The program's administrative structure is in place, and all of the states participate in the program. Despite all this, serious problems remain to be addressed if it is to be successful. One concern is the financial impact that Medicaid expansion would have on the states. Establishing a national, noncategorical income standard of 100 percent of poverty and standardizing benefits at the median level would be expensive. States also differ in their inclusion of optional eligibility groups, so a national standard of 100 percent of the poverty line would require a much bigger change in some states than in others. Also, the percentage of a state's population that falls below the poverty line varies widely, and states have different costs of medical services and utilization. Medicaid's share of individual state budgets varies by a factor of as much as seven. The authors conclude that a general goal for Medicaid expansion proposals should be to reduce the differences between the Medicaid program and private sector plans.

Kenneth L. Burgess. "Medicaid Managed Care." Washington, D.C.: American Health Lawyers Association [Report No. VLT-0021], 1998, 161 pages.

> Examines some of the issues implicated in delivering long-term care through state Medicaid managed care programs, primarily through examining the experience of providers in California. Discusses issues faced by states, managed care organizations, and providers, as a result of state decisions to "subcontract" and delegate portions of their Medicaid service obligations to managed care. Includes selected portions of California's statutory and regulatory requirements.

Lisa W. Clark. "The Demise of the Boren Amendment: What Comes Next in the Struggle over Hospital Payment Standards under the Medicaid Act?" *Health Law Digest,* Jan. 1998, *26,* 11–18.

Examines consequences of the 1997 congressional repeal of the Boren amendment. Concludes that repeal of this provision eliminated a critical payment protection for hospitals, initiating an era in which states are expected to exert more control over their Medicaid programs.

Mary Crossley. "Medicaid Managed Care and Disability Discrimination Issues." *Tennessee Law Review,* 1998, *65,* 419.

This article examines issues potentially raised under the Americans with Disabilities Act by state decisions whether and how to include disabled Medicaid recipients in the massive shift toward Medicaid managed care. It examines the special issues that disabled Medicaid recipients pose with respect to managed care enrollment: cost, quality, access, and program design and implementation. It describes various approaches that state programs have taken or are proposing to take with respect to enrolling disabled Medicaid recipients in managed care. The approaches range from simply excluding the Social Security population from managed care enrollment to developing specialized managed care plans for Medicaid recipients with special needs and enrolling disabled recipients in mainstream Medicaid managed care plans. It concludes with suggestions regarding how state Medicaid officials can avoid ADA liability in developing Medicaid managed care programs.

Patricia DeMichele and Vicki Gottlich. "Medicare Managed Care: Has Its Time Come?" *Clearinghouse Review,* Oct. 1996, *30,* 569.

Examines issues for low-income Medicare beneficiaries in the shift in Medicare from traditional fee-for-service to managed care. Medicare meets an array of acute care needs but covers relatively few long-term care services, either in the home or in a nursing facility. Yet Medicare beneficiaries, whether their eligibility is based on age or disability, are among those most at risk for needing long-term care. Medicaid is the primary source of public funding for long-term care, with Medicare, the Social Services Block Grant, the Older Americans Act programs, the Department of Veterans Affairs, other state programs, and consumer out-of-pocket spending helping to pay for these services. This fractured funding stream, the authors write, leads to fragmentation of services between acute and long-term care as well as between home and community-based and nursing facility care. It also leads to discontinuity of administration. Moreover, care often lacks coordination among the various acute care and long-term care components.

Tony Dreyfus and Carol Tobias. *Financing Managed Care for Children in Foster Care.* Portland, Maine: National Academy of State Health Policy, 1998, 40 pages plus appendix.

This paper explores issues related to setting appropriate capitation rates for enrolling children in foster care in Medicaid managed care and analyzes potential payment strategies. In doing so, it addresses how these strategies can create incentives to improve the quality of health care services to this vulnerable population.

Joel D. Ferber. "Medicaid Advocacy and Managed Care: The Missouri Experience." *Clearinghouse Review,* Mar.–Apr. 1998, *31,* 601.

This article describes the statewide advocacy effort to influence Missouri's Section 1115 Medicaid managed care waiver. The primary focus here is on the role of consumer advocacy in developing a state's Medicaid managed care program. Specifically, this article focuses on the efforts involved in securing consumer protections for Medicaid recipients. The Missouri experience may be useful to advocates in other states that seek to replace Medicaid fee-for-service with managed care systems, whether through Section 1115 waivers, expansion of existing managed care waivers, or the new flexibility of implementing managed care without a waiver. The article also describes advocacy approaches that may be useful to groups or individuals working on a variety of health care issues.

Suzanne Felt-Lisk and Sara Yang. "Changes in Health Plans Serving Medicaid, 1993–1996." *Health Affairs,* 1997, *16,* 125.

To better understand the Medicaid managed care market, the authors developed a new data set that links Medicaid enrollment data with HMO industry data for 1993–1996 to analyze Medicaid enrollment in full-risk plans. Almost half of the Medicaid enrollees in a fully capitated managed care arrangement were in plans in which Medicaid makes up at least 75 percent of the total enrollment. Furthermore, the number of Medicaid-only plans has more than doubled since 1993. Commercial-based plans participated increasingly in Medicaid managed care during the period, but more than half of the plans entering the Medicaid market were newly formed. The article closes with discussion of the policy implications of these data.

Larry S. Gage and William H. E. von Oehsen. *Managed Care Manual: Medicaid, Medicare and State Health Reform*. St. Paul, Minn.: West Group, 1997.

Covers state regulation of managed care and how it interacts with federal Medicaid requirements; summarizes state health reform initiatives to date and discusses potential problems and abuses in Medicaid managed care. This resource includes an enormous amount of reference material in its appendices, including regulations governing HMOs, competitive medical plans, health care pre-payment plans, Medicaid managed care, and fraud and abuse compliance.

Caitlin J. Halligan. "'Just What the Doctor Ordered': Oregon's Medicaid Rationing Process and Public Participation in Risk Regulation." (Note.) *Georgetown Law Review*, 1995, *83*, 2697.

Discusses the debate over whether laypersons can and should participate in risk assessment and regulation. This note focuses on Oregon's Medicaid program, which explicitly rations health care by making particular services completely unavailable to Medicaid recipients, rather than following the usual cost-containment practice of excluding certain segments of the poor from Medicaid coverage. The state obtained cost and effectiveness data from health care providers; it calculated quality-of-life values based on the relative values assigned to various states of health by Oregon citizens who participated in a public survey. Halligan explains the process of ranking health care services—the central element of the rationing plan—and concludes with what lessons the Oregon experience offers to other states.

Jane Horvath. "Medicaid Financing Eligibility for Aged, Blind and Disabled: Survey of State Use of Selected Options." Portland, Maine: National Academy for State Health Policy, 1997, 21 pages.

Essentially a compendium of state Medicaid financial eligibility standards for aged, blind, and disabled optional eligibility categories. This report includes information from all fifty states and the District of Columbia.

Jane Horvath. "State Interagency Collaboration: Assuring Quality Care for Mothers and Children in Medicaid Risk-Based Managed Care." Portland, Maine: National Academy for State Health Policy, 1995, 21 pages.

Medicaid, insurance departments, and public health all play roles in assuring the quality of Medicaid managed care. This report describes the sometimes overlapping functions of various state agencies and programs and proposes a strategy to minimize duplication and increase collaboration.

Jane Horvath and Neva Kaye. *Snapshot of Medicaid Managed Care Ombudsman and Grievance Procedures*. Portland, Maine: National Academy for State Health Policy, 1996.

Examines how Medicaid agencies in five states (Delaware, Minnesota, Missouri, Oregon, and Tennessee) handle Medicaid managed care enrollee complaints. This report focuses on how ombudsman and grievance systems operate in these states and how the systems link with each other and the fair hearing process. It also examines how each state used information from these systems in contract management, quality assurance, and quality improvement efforts.

Jane Horvath and Lorrie Lutz. "Health Care for Children in Foster Care: Who's Keeping Track?" Portland, Maine: National Academy of State Health Policy, 1997, 21 pages with appendix.

This paper looks at systems of tracking health care services and providers of care for children in foster care. It builds on a National Academy survey of health passport activity around the country and highlights innovative approaches. The paper analyzes the barriers to successful implementation and the implications of Medicaid HMO contracting on health passport systems.

Jane Horvath and Kimberly Irvin Snow. "Emerging Challenges in State Regulation of Managed Care: Report on a Survey of Agency Regulations of Prepaid Managed Care Entities." Portland, Maine: National Academy for State Health Policy, 1996.

Using data collected in 1996, this report describes the authority and role of insurance, public health, and Medicaid agencies across the states that regulate and monitor prepaid managed care entities.

Dana C. Hughes and others. "Medicaid Managed Care: Can It Work for Children?" *Pediatrics,* 1995, *95,* 591.

This article documents the increase in states' total enrollment in Medicaid beneficiaries into managed care plans. The authors recommend that states design their programs to involve providers who traditionally serve low-income families, that managed care contracts contain language requiring plans to demonstrate the availability of providers capable of providing the services that children need, that fees and other incentives be high enough to encourage providers to furnish preventive care, and that providers offer a minimum of one year continuous coverage.

Deborah Lewis-Idema. "Monitoring Medicaid Provider Participation and Access to Care." Washington, D.C.: National Governors' Association, 1992, 42 pages.

Provides a framework to help states develop a system to monitor rates of provider participation in their Medicaid programs and to determine where problems result in gaps in available services or insufficient care.

John K. Inglehart. "Health Policy Report: Medicaid and Managed Care." *New England Journal of Medicine,* 1995, *332,* 1727.

Examines the implementation of Medicaid managed care programs in California, Arizona, and Tennessee, among others.

Mark S. Joffe. "Medicaid Managed Care and Children's Health Insurance Programs." Washington, D.C.: American Health Lawyers Association [Report No. VMM99–0045], 1999, 29 pages.

Provides an overview of Medicaid managed care contracting issues; discusses statutory and proposed regulatory amendments to medical managed care and their implications for provider and MCO contracting.

Mark S. Joffe. "Medicaid Managed Care and Children's Health Insurance Programs." Washington, D.C.: American Health Lawyers Association [Report No. VMC98–0041], 1998, 32 pages.

Examines current regulatory developments in the Medicaid managed care program, as well as the Children's Health Insurance Program (CHIP), and discusses its progress.

N. Kaye and C. Pernice. *Medicaid Managed Care: A Guide for States.* 4 vols. (4th ed.) Portland, Maine: National Academy of State Health Policy, 1999.

Based on a comprehensive survey of all fifty states and the District of Columbia, the first of this guide's four volumes provides a detailed summary of the current scope and operations of Medicaid managed care programs and offers a comprehensive analysis of trends in Medicaid managed care. The second volume examines risk-based Medicaid managed care programs serving the elderly and people with disabilities. Volume Three offers an in-depth look at trends in managed care programs serving SSI and aged populations, and Volume Four combines survey and case study information to examine innovations in payment strategies to improve plan performance.

Neva Kaye and others. "Monitoring the Quality of Health Care Provided to Children in Foster Care." Portland, Maine: National Academy of State Health Policy, 1998, 35 pages plus appendices.

This paper provides an overview of quality oversight systems and how such a system might be developed for the health care provided to children in foster care. It also identifies the issues that affect child welfare and Medicaid agencies' ability to deliver care to this population and discusses how some agencies have worked to address these issues.

Tamsen Douglass Love. "Toward a Fair and Practical Definition of 'Willfully' in the Medicare/Medicaid Anti-Kickback Statute." *Vanderbilt Law Review,* May 1997, *50,* 1029–1059.

The antikickback statute prohibits offering, paying, soliciting, or receiving any remuneration in exchange for future referrals or future use of a particular good, use, service, or facility. This paper examines case law applying this statute, whose broad reach has caused considerable anxiety in the health care industry.

Michael J. McCue and others. "Reversal of Fortune: Commercial HMOs in the Medicaid Market." *Health Affairs,* Jan.–Feb. 1999, *18*(1), 223.

Between 1992 and 1996 the number of health maintenance organizations entering the Medicaid market grew at an average annual rate of approximately 22 percent. Participation among all ownership segments grew, resulting in a broad distribution of beneficiaries across the HMO industry. However, recent declines in financial performance within the industry appear to be more dramatic for plans with many Medicaid members. In addition, concerns about rate adequacy and volatility as well as expanding administrative demands raise questions about the long-term commitment of commercial HMOs to Medicaid participation. This paper analyzes operating characteristics and financial performance of licensed commercial HMOs from 1992 through 1996, drawing on in-depth interviews with health plan executives and managed care stock analysts.

"Medicaid: Early Implications of Welfare Reform for Beneficiaries and States." (GAO/HEHS-98–62.) Feb. 24, 1998, 32 pages.

During the first year of welfare reform, the nine states GAO reviewed chose welfare reform options that generally sustained Medicaid coverage for their previously eligible populations, according to this GAO report. The options available to states included establishing different income and resource standards for their Medicaid and cash assistance programs, running the two programs separately, imposing Medicaid-related penalties on welfare recipients not complying with state work rules, and discontinuing Medicaid coverage for aliens. Four of the nine states had separate income or resource standards for their Medicaid and cash assistance programs. To foster administrative efficiencies, all nine states chose to continue using a common application for their welfare and Medicaid programs, and eight chose to continue using a single agency at the local level to determine applicant eligibility. No state chose to withhold Medicaid as a sanction for noncompliance with state work rules or to discontinue Medicaid coverage for most aliens.

"Medicaid Managed Care: Delays and Difficulties in Implementing California's New Mandatory Program." (GAO/HEHS-98–2.) Oct. 1, 1997, 31 pages.

Considers issues related to expanding Medi-Cal. In fiscal year 1996, it served 5.2 million beneficiaries—almost one-seventh of Medicaid beneficiaries nationwide—at a cost of nearly $18 billion in federal, state, and local funds. Medi-Cal has increasingly turned to managed care to improve the quality of care and reduce program costs. In 1992, California began planning a major expansion of its Medi-Cal managed care program, one that would eventually require more than 2.2 million beneficiaries in twelve counties to enroll in one of two managed care plans. A 1995 GAO report (GAO/HEHS-95–87) questioned California's ability to successfully carry out such an expansion because of several weaknesses in the Medi-Cal managed care program, including the state's potential inability to effectively monitor its contracts with managed care plans and to ensure that the plans actually delivered promised services.

This report follows up on GAO's earlier study. It (1) discusses the status of California's managed care expansion, including the leading causes of delays; (2) assesses the degree to which state efforts to educate beneficiaries about their managed care options and enroll them in managed care have encouraged beneficiaries to choose a plan; (3) evaluates the management of the state's education and enrollment process for the new program, including state and federal oversight of enrollment brokers that the state had contracted with to carry out these duties; and (4) makes an initial assessment of the managed care expansion regarding current safety-net providers, such as community health centers, that serve low-income beneficiaries.

Medi-Cal Policy Institute. "Baseline 1997: A Survey of Medi-Cal Managed Care Plans in County Organized Health System and Two-Plan Counties." Oakland, Calif.: Medi-Cal Policy Institute, June 1999, 27 pages.

This report presents baseline findings on the status of Medi-Cal managed care plan operations as of Dec. 31, 1997. Presented in this report are findings in the areas of data, quality, audits, provider payments, communicating with providers, communicating with consumers, health promotion and public health, and problems and barriers to improving health outcomes. The report is supplemented by twenty-three charts and two appendices.

Charles J. Milligan, Jr. "Checklist to Implement Managed Medicaid: State Agency Perspective." Washington, D.C.: American Health Lawyers Association [Report No. VMC98–0003], 1998, 27 pages.

Provides a brief checklist for implementing managed Medicaid, followed by selections from proposed DHHS regulations amending the Medicaid managed care requirements to allow states to require Medicaid recipients to enroll in managed care entities without obtaining waivers, and establishing greater beneficiary protections (63 Fed. Reg. 52022, Sept. 29, 1998).

David M. Mirvis and others. "TennCare: Health System Reform for Tennessee." *Journal of the American Medical Association*, 1995, *274*, 1235.

Prior to Tennecare, which was implemented in Tennessee in January 1994, only 5.9 percent of that state's population and only 2.7 percent of the state's Medicaid patients were enrolled in managed care plans. As a result of this program, virtually all Medicaid recipients and one-fourth of the total state population are enrolled. Although the program's goals included extending health insurance coverage to most residents as well as enrolling costs, at the end of the first year the program incurred a $99 million deficit. Physicians have attempted to block the program, and managed care organizations and hospitals have reported major financial problems.

Elizabeth Mitchell. *A Legislator's Guide to Medicaid Waivers: Tools for Medicaid Reform.* Portland, Maine: National Academy for State Health Policy, 1996.

Summarizes what states can and cannot do with waivers (1915b freedom of choice, 1915c home and community care, and 1115 research and demonstration) and explains how the federal waiver process works and under what timetables waivers are processed.

Robert L. Mollica and Trish Riley. *Managed Care, Medicaid and the Elderly: 5 State Case Studies.* Portland, Maine: National Academy of State Health Policy, 1996, 143 pages.

Features case studies of Arizona, Oregon, Utah, Minnesota, and Florida actively enrolling low-income seniors into managed care under each state's Medicaid program. A summary of key issues and common practices among the five states is included.

Robert L. Mollica and Trish Riley. "Managed Care of Low Income Elders: A Snapshot of State and Federal Activity." Portland, Maine: National Academy for State Health Policy, 1997, 41 pages.

Describes the many state and federal initiatives to serve dually eligible beneficiaries through managed care. A brief summary of activity is included, and state policies on dual eligibles in Medicare HMOs are also summarized.

Robert L. Mollica and others. *Protecting Low Income Beneficiaries of Medicare and Medicaid in Managed Care.* Portland, Maine: National Academy for State Health Policy, 1997.

Based on site visits to four states, these papers address contracting arrangements, choice, enrollment and disenrollment, coordination of benefits, payment mechanisms, and quality management in managed care programs serving dual eligibles.

National Health Law Program. "Making the Consumers' Voice Heard in Medicaid Managed Care: Increasing Participation, Protection and Satisfaction." Los Angeles: National Health Law Program, Dec. 1996.

This report presents the results of the National Health Law Program's study of the legally required and voluntarily initiated consumer involvement activities under way in the states, including advisory boards, ombudsprograms, grievance processes, member advocates, focus groups, consumer surveying, and consumer education. The report includes a review of federal and state laws, model Medicaid managed care contracts, RFPs, and interviews with more than 150 key informants. The interviewees reflect a range of state administrators, plan personnel, consumers, and consumer advocates. A bibliography of the consumer involvement literature, prepared by the Cecil G. Sheps Center for Health Services Research and the National Health Law Program, is included. This report provides suggestions for improving consumer involvement. It is available from the program's Los Angeles office at (800) 656-4533.

Thomas R. Oliver. "The Collision of Economics and Politics in Medicaid Managed Care: Reflections on the Course of Reform in Maryland." *Milbank Quarterly*, 1998, 76(1), 59.

One of the most dynamic areas of health policy is the transition of Medicaid programs to managed care and market competition. Maryland has been a leader in this trend, initiating three systems of managed care for the Medicaid population during the 1990s as it searched for the ideal plans. The Maryland experience illuminates the complex new demands that policy makers are facing. Health plans are expected not only to delivery budgetary savings but also to improve the quality of services and guarantee a place for safety-net providers in their delivery systems. As a result, there is a sizable gap between the original savings projected for the new Maryland system and its actual capacity for cost containment. The apparent collision between economic assumptions and political realities, however, may point the way toward a constructive synthesis—a form of managed care that balances economy with important community, personal, and professional values.

Jane Perkins. *Advocate's Medicaid EPSDT Reference Manual.* Los Angeles: National Health Law Program, 1993.

Part One steps through the necessary components of the EPSDT program, while Part Two provides a road map for getting advocates started with EPSDT advocacy.

Jane Perkins. "Resolving Complaints in Medicaid Managed Care: The 'Brutal Need' for Consumer Protections." Washington, D.C.: American Health Lawyers Association [Report No. VMC98–0004], 1998, 20 pages.

Describes the constitutional and statutory requirements for due process in Medicaid managed care settings. Also discusses recent Medicaid managed care regulations promulgated by DHHS and provides recommendations for complying with these laws and regulations.

Jane Perkins and Michele Melden. *Section 1115 Medicaid Waivers: An Advocate's Primer.* Los Angeles: National Health Law Program, 1994.

Assists advocates who are, or want to become, involved in the rapidly evolving Medicaid 1115 waiver process on behalf of clients.

Jane Perkins and Kristi Olson. "An Advocate's Primer on Medicaid Managed Care Contracting." *Clearinghouse Review,* May–June 1997, *31,* 19.

Medicaid managed care contracts are a significant Medicaid document, building on the existing array of legal requirements that protect beneficiaries: federal and state statutes, regulations, guidelines, case law, federal Medicaid Section 1115 waivers, federal Medicaid section 1915(b) waivers, and the standards of such voluntary accreditation organizations as the NCQA and the JCAHO. This practical article, written by two staff attorneys at the National Health Law Program in Chapel Hill, North Carolina, provides a lengthy, detailed checklist for analysis of managed care contracts, along with a large number of citations, tables, and other helpful resources. It also includes model provisions that can be included in Medicaid managed care contracts to ensure that they are consumer-oriented.

Jane Perkins and Kristi Olson. "Issue Brief: Due Process in Publicly-Funded Managed Care." Los Angeles: National Health Law Program, 1997.

Focuses on due process protections for members of publicly purchased managed care—Medicaid and Medicare. The authors highlight information garnered from an NHeLP survey of federal and state Medicaid requirements, from interviews with key figures from states, health plans, providers, and consumer organizations; and from focus groups of Medicaid beneficiaries.

Jane Perkins, Kristi Olson, Lourdes Rivera, and Julie Skatrud. *Making the Consumer's Voice Heard in Medicaid Managed Care: Increasing Participation, Protection and Satisfaction.* Los Angeles: National Health Law Program, 1996.

Presents the results of a national study of the legally required and voluntarily initiated consumer involvement activities under way in the states, including advisory boards, grievance processes, member advocates, consumer surveying, and consumer education.

Jane Perkins and Susan Zinn. *Toward a Healthy Future: Early and Periodic Screening, Diagnosis and Treatment for Poor Children.* Los Angeles: National Health Law Program, May 1995.

Offers extensive analysis of Medicaid's EPSDT program, Medicaid managed care and preventive care, and state-funded preventive care programs for children and adolescents.

Vernellia Randall and others. "Section 1115 Medicaid Waivers: Critiquing the State Applications." *Seton Hall Law Review,* 1996, *26,* 1069.

Section 1115 Medicaid demonstration waivers are granted by the HCFA to a petitioning state that seeks to test a program improvement in the health care delivery system. This article assesses seven state waivers—those of Florida, Hawaii, Illinois, Missouri, New York, Oregon, and Tennessee—to determine whether they have the potential of harming Medicaid beneficiaries.

St. Anthony's Medicaid Managed Care and Capitation Manual. Reston, Va.: St. Anthony, 1997.

This manual begins with a detailed seventy-one-page report prepared by the National Institute for Health Care Management, containing information on the proportion of Medicaid dollars paid through capitation and recent statistics on enrollment in Medicaid managed care plans. The balance of the manual presents, in tabular form, state-by-state information on rates, utilization, costs, and resources. Through quarterly updates, the manual brings readers additional documents—on paper and computer disk—that focus on Medicaid managed care as they are uncovered and rendered into an easy-to-use format. Based on this information, readers will be able to decide if contract offers are realistic by examining rates paid to other providers and health plans.

Joanne Rawlings-Sekunda and others. *The Lay of the Land: What Program Managers Need to Know to Serve People with HIV/AIDS.* Portland, Maine: National Academy for State Health Policy, 1997, 100 pages.

Designed to help state officials, advocates, and consumers implement Medicaid managed care programs that meet the health care needs of people with HIV/AIDS in a cost-effective way. This report raises significant issues regarding HIV/AIDS treatment in a managed care environment. It also describes the practices of thirty-five states enrolling people with HIV/AIDS in their managed care programs. Finally, it summarizes the federally funded programs serving these persons to assist program coordination efforts.

Trish Riley and others. "Transitioning to Managed Care: Medicaid Managed Care in Mental Health." Portland, Maine: National Academy for State Health Policy, 1997, 20 pages.

Provides a synthesis of selected state practices and a practical list of lessons learned to help other states and further advance innovative approaches to serving the mental health needs of Medicaid beneficiaries in managed care.

Judith M. Rosenberg and David T. Zaring. "Managing Medicaid Waivers: Section 1115 and State Health Care Reform." *Harvard Journal on Legislation,* 1995, *32,* 545.

Examines states' resort to Section 1115 waivers. With the collapse of federal health care reform in 1994, attention has turned to innovation at the state level, and many state health reform goals include reforms of the federal Medicaid programs that they administer. These attempts at reform, however, are often blocked by the complex requirements of the federal Medicaid statute, dealing with the methods by which health care may be delivered to the poor. Accordingly, states may apply for Section 1115 waivers that allow them to institute "demonstration projects" that are thereafter exempt from otherwise problematic federal Medicaid strictures. This brief article discusses the rise of Section 1115 waivers to the forefront of health care reform and then considers some of their strengths and weaknesses as a vehicle for government involvement in medicine.

Paul Saucier. "Federal Barriers to Managed Care for Dually Eligible." Portland, Maine: National Academy for State Health Policy, 1995, 16 pages.

Explains differences between federal Medicare and Medicaid policies that make it difficult to establish managed care for dually eligible persons.

A. Schneider and K. Fennel. "Medicaid Eligibility Policy for Children in Foster Care." Portland, Maine: National Academy of State Health Policy, 1999, 15 pages plus appendices.

States have more flexibility than is generally recognized in drawing down federal Medicaid matching dollars to provide Medicaid coverage to foster children. This paper explores these options and provides guidance to states on how to ensure improved access to health care for children in foster care.

S. A. Somers, K. Brodsky, and V. Harr. "The Coverage of Chronic Populations under Medicaid Managed Care: An Essay on Emerging Challenges." *Tennessee Law Review*, 1998, *65*, 649.

Although the commercial market has had the experience and infrastructure to deliver managed care services to employed individuals and their dependents, few, if any, plans have enrolled low-income people with disabilities. The authors, who are affiliated with the Center for Health Care Strategies, hold the position that capitated managed care is nearly inevitable for these populations, so we should take maximum advantage of its promise for individuals with chronic health problems.

Michael S. Sparer. *Medicaid and the Limits of State Health Reform.* Philadelphia: Temple University Press, 1996, 235 pages.

Examines the history and status of Medicaid programs in New York and California to try to understand interstate variation in Medicaid eligibility, reimbursement, and benefit policy, and to analyze the implications of these disparities. Drawing on the history of these states, Sparer argues that variation in Medicaid spending results in large measure from variation in bureaucratic discretion. The author makes the case that California officials have significant discretion to implement a cost-control agenda. By contrast, the political environment in New York is fragmented, decentralized, and pluralistic. These differing political cultures have allowed California to provide Medicaid recipients in that state with the most generous benefit package of all fifty states, at a cost per beneficiary that is two and one-half times less than that in New York.

Michael S. Sparer. "Medicaid Managed Care and the Health Reform Debate: Lessons from New York and California." *Journal of Health Politics, Policy and Law*, 1996, *21*, 433.

Examines the managed care initiatives of two states, New York and California. Nearly every state now encourages (or requires) its Medicaid beneficiaries to enroll in managed care. There is, however, extraordinary variation in all aspects of state managed care policy. In this article, the author focuses on variation in state policy making environments and on the influence of such variation on efforts to protect the medical safety net. He concludes that California's managed care initiative is less decentralized and pluralistic than New York's, and that California has used its discretion to adopt a strategy designed in part to protect safety-net hospitals. The author ends with a plea for greater federal control of managed care initiatives, a policy proposal that is at odds with the current trend to increase state authority.

Frank J. Thompson and John J. Dilulio Jr. (eds.). *The New Medicaid: Issues and Prospects.* Washington, D.C.: Brookings Institution, 1997.

In this text of approximately 140 pages, scholars and state health care officials analyze the policy and management implications of various options for Medicaid devolution.

8.04 REIMBURSEMENT REVIEW ACTIVITIES: PEER REVIEW ORGANIZATIONS

[Reserved]

8.05 FRAUD AND ABUSE STATUTES: PROSCRIBED CONDUCT

Ted Acosta and Howard J. Young. "The Health Insurance Portability and Accountability Act of 1996 and the Evolution of the Government's Anti-Fraud and Abuse Agenda." *Journal of Health and Hospital Law*, 1997, *30*, 37.

Analyzes the most salient features of the fraud and abuse amendments contained in HIPAA from the perspective of recent trends in the government's fraud prevention, detection, and enforcement efforts. This article, written by two practicing attorneys, traces the broadening of governmental powers in dealing with fraud in the health care sector and discusses how these forces have affected the incentives of private parties facing investigation and potentially catastrophic penalties. The authors contend that HIPAA's legislative "compromise" may have so dramatically shifted the balance of power in favor of the government as to embolden further the government's use of the informal, nonjudicial processes by which fraud and abuse law has been made in the past.

Cary M. Adams and Jeanne L. Vance. "Fraud and Abuse Advisory Opinions: The Gray Area Will Never Be the Same." *Health Law Digest*, Sept. 1997, *25*(9), 3, 201–300.

Examines the advisory opinion letter process implemented by the OIG on Feb. 21, 1997. Through this process, a health care provider can determine whether the government interprets its activities and proposed activities to constitute a legitimate means of doing business or a violation of the federal Medicare and Medicaid antikickback prohibitions. Advisory opinions contain a recitation of the facts that give rise to the opinion's basis; they are public documents, posted on the DHHS/OIG Website (www.sbaonline.sba.gov/ignet/internal/hhs/aolist.html).

Gordon J. Apple. "Operation Restore Trust and Voluntary Disclosure." Washington, D.C.: American Health Lawyers Association [Report No. VLT-0021], 1998, 27 pages.

Describes the expansion of Operation Restore Trust, and assesses compliance plan efforts of the OIG that are a tangible result of this initiative. Examines the issues surrounding voluntary disclosure of wrongdoing. Includes OIG's model compliance plan for clinical laboratories.

Aspen Health Law Center. *Health Care Fraud and Abuse Compliance Manual*. Gaithersburg, Md.: Aspen, 1997.

Written by a panel of practicing attorneys, this practical one-volume treatise is divided into seven chapters: (1) an overview of health care fraud and abuse, (2) false claims and fraudulent billing, (3) fraud and abuse prohibitions under the antikickback statute, (4) federal physician self-referral prohibitions (the Stark laws), (5) corporate compliance programs, (6) the anatomy of an investigation, and (7) an analysis of state fraud and abuse investigations and enforcement. The text is supplemented by a table of acronyms, glossary, table of cases, and index. Regularly updated.

Leon Aussprung. "Fraud and Abuse: Federal Civil Health Care Litigation and Settlement." *Journal of Legal Medicine*, 1998, *19*, 1–62.

Focuses on civil health care litigation and settlements involving the U.S. Justice Department. It specifically addresses settlement agreements between the federal government and private parties (individuals and institutions). These settlement agreements are significant because they illuminate much of the experience of the Justice Department in prosecuting health care fraud and abuse cases. Furthermore, the author writes, they have created a de facto body of health care fraud and abuse law. This detailed article is supplemented by copious footnotes and case citations.

Paul P. Cacioppo. *Health Care Fraud and Abuse: A Guide to Federal Sanctions*. 2 vols. St. Paul, Minn.: West Group, 1997.

Exhumes the text of fraud and abuse law buried in hundreds of pages of Titles V, XI, XVIII, XIX, and XX of the Social Security Act and thousands of pages of federal regulations and then reorganizes it in a more accessible fashion. Written by a practicing attorney, this comprehensive treatise explains which federal sanctions apply to which acts or omissions, provides substantial extracts from relevant statutes, and directs the reader to federal regulations that are on point. Each section also includes relevant cross-references. Each statutory section is explained in an introductory paragraph that precedes the statute. The text is supplemented by fifteen appendices.

Paul R. DeMuro. *Fraud and Abuse by and Against HMOs.* Washington, D.C.: American Health Lawyers Association [Document No. FA97–0010], 1997.

Addresses fraud and abuse by HMOs and health plans, including defrauding the government, subscribers, and providers; illegal incentives; failure to authorize or provide medically necessary care; inducements for referrals; and marketing issues. It considers fraud and abuse by provider-based managed care organizations that accept risk, including referral restrictions, risk pools, withholds, physician incentives, and Stark II considerations. It also discusses fraud and abuse against HMOs, health plans, and MCOs, including billing fraud, failure to provide contractual services, quality of services and care, reporting issues, and denial of services.

John J. Farley. "The Medicare Antifraud Statute and Safe Harbor Regulations: Suggestions for Change." (Note.) *Georgetown Law Journal,* 1992, *81,* 167.

Argues that the Medicare antifraud statute is generally an appropriate means of deterring exploitative conduct, especially when a physician's reimbursement is based on the number of services performed (fee-for-service). However, when reimbursement levels are limited under prospective payment or managed care arrangements, the risk that providers will exploit their financial interests in health care facilities is diminished because providers do not receive more money merely for performing or referring additional services. The author contends that safe-harbor regulations should be modified to protect financial arrangements where the reimbursement system itself provides incentives and controls that limit the risk of exploitative behavior by physicians.

David M. Frankford. "Creating and Dividing the Fruits of Collective Economic Activity: Referrals among Health Care Providers." *Columbia Law Review,* 1989, *89,* 1866.

Argues that regulatory initiatives such as the Medicare and Medicaid antifraud and abuse provisions will have the unintended effect of distributing wealth away from individual health care providers and increasing the overall amount of health care spending. They will favor development of fully integrated, hierarchical institutions, he contends, that are adept at coopting the professional labor they employ. The result will be still higher health care expenditures with diminished patient autonomy and fewer voices to frame our society's choices concerning just allocation of the wealth that is generated through health care.

Health Insurance Association of America. *Fraud: The Hidden Cost of Health Care.* Annapolis, Md.: Health Insurance Association of America, 1996, 286 pages.

Examines various types of fraud, as well as antifraud detection, and reviews relevant legislation and legal issues.

Leonard C. Homer. "Avoiding Fraud and Abuse in Medicare Part A and Part B Billing." Washington, D.C.: American Health Lawyers Association [Report No. VMM98–0026], 1998, 28 pages.

Examines prosecutorial tools used to define and eradicate practices leading to false claims exposure. Provides background, actions available to U.S. attorneys for false claims and statements as defined in HIPAA and the BBA, issues relating to prospective payment systems payment, cost reporting issues, noncovered items and services, and billing issues in the case of hospital labs acting as reference labs for physicians and other providers.

Jerry L. Mashaw and Theodore R. Marmor. "Conceptualizing, Estimating, and Reforming Fraud, Waste and Abuse in Healthcare Spending." *Yale Journal on Regulation,* 1994, *11,* 455.

Maintains that eliminating "waste, fraud, and abuse" from American medicine is not a quick or easy solution to the challenge of rising medical care costs. Although there are clearly some savings available, particularly in the area of administration, they likely amount to far less than many policy makers hope.

Many of the policy options available for reducing excesses face significant political hurdles or involve value judgments about nonquantifiable issues related to quality of care. Other alternatives seem as likely to bar necessary medical care as to eliminate abuses. In some instances, particularly those involving consumer fraud, a crackdown may merely shift costs without saving any money. Finally, a number of the suggestions for trimming waste and abuse involve ethical and moral judgments that Americans have yet to acknowledge and, in any event, may not wish to sign over to the government or any other third party.

Sanford V. Teplitzky. "Medicare and Medicaid Fraud and Abuse Issues." Washington, D.C.: American Health Lawyers Association [Report No. TK97–0011], 1997, 27 pages.

Examines general issues and governmental concerns, types of governmental liability, sources of liability, Medicare and Medicaid fraud and abuse laws, and federal self-referral prohibitions (Stark I and Stark II). Discusses the additional health care fraud and abuse measures contained in the 1997 BBA. Also details fraud and abuse sections of HIPAA (1996).

8.05(1) False Statements or Claims

American Health Lawyers Association. "Fraud and Abuse: Do Current Laws Protect the Public Interest?" Washington, D.C.: AHLA, 1999, 46 pages.

This report of the AHLA's public interest colloquium examines health care fraud and abuse in the context of four core legal questions: (1) What are the history and politics of fraud and abuse laws? (2) What are the goals of fraud and abuse laws? (3) What are the advantages and disadvantages of fraud and abuse laws as they are interpreted and applied by regulatory agencies and enforcement entities? (4) What workable alternatives to current fraud and abuse laws exist, or in what ways can the enforcement of current laws be improved? The report summarizes in readable form the results of this two-day discussion.

American Medical Association. *Health Care Fraud and Abuse: A Physician's Guide to Compliance.* Chicago: AMA, 1999, approx. 200 pages.

Aimed at physicians, this book seeks to help physicians understand recent legislation and identifies concrete steps that should be taken to create and implement compliance plans.

Annot. "Criminal Prosecution or Disciplinary Action Against a Medical Practitioner for Fraud in Connection with Claims under Medicaid, Medicare or Similar Welfare Program for Providing Medical Services." *ALR3rd*, 1998, 50, 549.

Collects and analyzes those cases involving disciplinary action or criminal prosecution arising out of fraudulent claims filed by medical practitioners under the Medicaid program, the Medicare program, or similar "welfare" or Social Security programs for providing these services.

Neville M. Bilimoria. "Lawyers Beware of Criminal Health Care Fraud: What Attorneys Can Learn from the Kansas City Health Care Attorney Indictments." *Health Care Law Monthly*, May 1999, at 1.

This article focuses on the current fraud and abuse climate and the possible dangers of attorney indictment for federal criminal penalties for counseling clients on fraud and abuse issues. It specifically discusses the indictment of two Kansas City attorneys, which may put to rest any doubts about the severity of federal fraud and abuse enforcement. It also discusses how attorneys in health care can limit their own personal liability when counseling clients on health care fraud and abuse: (1) being skeptical and aware of client activities, (2) reaching an understanding at the outset that the client will remedy situations of fraud and abuse violations should the attorney find noncompliance, and (3) request advisory opinions from the OIG to test the legality of proposed transactions.

Timothy P. Blanchard and Gary W. Eiland. "Keeping the Feds at Bay: A Provider's Perspective on Government Investigation and Enforcement Initiatives." Washington, D.C.: American Health Lawyers Association [Report No. VHH99–0004], 1999, 135 pages.

> Reviews the complex and continuously evolving body of federal law, including an update on recent fraud and abuse legislative and regulatory developments affecting hospitals and health systems, status of pending federal investigations, and current enforcement actions and targeted priorities by DHHS OIG, the DOJ, and the FBI. Offers tactics for dealing with investigative agencies and ways to minimize the risk of *qui tam* actions.

John T. Boese. "When Angry Patients Become Angry Prosecutors: Medical Necessity Determinations, Quality of Care and the *Qui Tam* Law." *Saint Louis University Law Journal,* 1999, *43,* 53–80.

> Written by a veteran litigator who represents defendants in federal fraud investigations, this article addresses the phenomenon of the patient aggrieved by real or perceived deficiencies in quality or access to managed care who, armed with the False Claims Act, files suit alleging fraud against the federal government. The author concludes that the costs of *qui tam* enforcement are disproportionate to any gain that may result from private enforcement of federal laws and regulations.

John T. Boese. "The Dark Side of *Qui Tam* Enforcement." *Health Law Litigation,* Summer 1996, *4,* 12–22.

> This article argues that the amounts that have been collected by private *qui tam* enforcement of the False Claims Act, 31 U.S.C. §§ 3729–3733, have been minuscule, and that such cases have spawned enormous inefficiency, bad law, and public cynicism over clear abuses by some relators. The author argues that in almost every circuit, there has developed a new body of law interpreting the False Claims Act adversely to the government (almost all of which was litigated by private *qui tam* attorneys) that is regularly cited against the government in arguably legitimate fraud cases. The long-term effect of these rulings will almost certainly be to reduce the amount of money the government recovers.

John T. Boese. "The New Florida False Claims Act: Florida Borrows a Powerful Federal Anti-Fraud Weapon." *Florida Bar Journal,* Mar. 1995, *69*(3), 24–30.

> This article summarizes the Florida statute and compares it to the federal act. It also sets forth a list of other states that have enacted similar statutes.

John T. Boese. *Civil False Claims and Qui Tam Actions.* Gaithersburg, Md.: Aspen, 1993, 796 pages.

> This one-volume loose-leaf manual, annually updated, provides a comprehensive analysis of the False Claims Act. Written by the cochair of the *Qui Tam* subcommittee of the American Bar Association's Health Law Litigation Committee, this book begins with an historical overview of the act before moving to an extensive discussion of liability under it. The author then discusses damages and penalties under the act, along with practice and procedure. He concludes with an analysis of state civil false claims acts. The text is supplemented with seventeen appendices setting forth statutes discussed in the manual, along with a table of statutes, regulations, and rules; a table of cases; and an index.

John T. Boese and Shannon L. Haralson. "Private Enforcement of State Fraud Laws: A Comparative Analysis of State *Qui Tam* Provisions." *Journal of Health and Hospital Law,* Winter 1998, *31*(1), 34–48.

> This article compares state and federal false claims acts and concludes with helpful charts that allow easy comparative analysis of *qui tam* provisions enacted in six states and the District of

Columbia on such specific topics as liability, damages, penalties costs, attorneys' fees, consequences of voluntary disclosure and cooperation, attorney general enforcement, bars to recovery, protective rules, statutes of limitation, standards of proof, and consequences of criminal conviction.

John T. Boese and Beth C. McClain. "Why *Thompson* Is Wrong: Misuse of the False Claims Act to Enforce the Anti-Kickback Act." *Alabama Law Review,* Fall 1999, *51*(1), 1–55.

This article examines *United States ex rel. Thompson* v. *Columbia/HCA Healthcare Corp.,* a case in which plaintiff alleged that claims for medically necessary goods and properly administered health care services are rendered "false" solely because of allegedly inaccurate certifications of compliance with health care laws and regulations, including the Anti-Kickback Act.

John T. Brennan. "General Overview of Federal Fraud and Abuse Law: Where to Find the Law." Washington, D.C.: American Health Lawyers Association [Report No. VMM99–0014], 1999, 35 pages.

Provides a survey of health care fraud and abuse law, including the False Claims Act, the Anti-Kickback Statute, and the physician self-referral (Stark) statutes. Gives the reader basic understanding of these statutes and how they are practically applied.

Pamela H. Bucy. *Health Care Fraud: Criminal, Civil and Administrative Law.* New York: Law Journal Seminars Press, 1998.

Chapters in this one-volume treatise address the following topics: an overview of health care fraud, types of fraud by health care providers, criminal causes of action, civil causes of action, collateral consequences, pretrial strategies in health care fraud cases, evidence and trial strategies in health care fraud cases, internal investigations when fraud is suspected, and corporate compliance plans. The author is a professor of law at the University of Alabama and a former assistant U.S. attorney in the Criminal Division, Eastern District of Missouri.

Pamela Bucy. "Growing Pains: Using the False Claims Act to Combat Health Care Fraud." *Alabama Law Review,* 1999, *51,* 57.

This article is part of a symposium issue devoted to health care fraud. It reviews the False Claims Act by discussing its role in the fight against health care fraud, the elements of such a case, and the *qui tam* provisions—the most complex and heavily litigated aspect of the act.

Michael A. Cassidy. "Third Party Billing Service Liability for False Claims Act Violations." *Health Care Law Monthly,* Apr. 1999, at 9.

This brief article discusses *United States* v. *Emergency Physicians Billing Services, Inc.,* 31 F. Supp.2d 1308 (1998), which held that liability for False Claims Act violation exists regardless of whether the actor is the ultimate recipient of the reimbursement stream.

Troy D. Chandler. "Lawyer Turned Plaintiff: Law Firms and Lawyers as Relators under the False Claims Act." *Houston Law Review,* Summer 1998, *35,* 541.

Argues that allowing lawyers and law firms to pursue an action under the *qui tam* provisions of the federal False Claims Act is consistent with the legislative intent of the 1986 amendments to the act. Although arguing that such actions are wholly consistent with the act, the author contends that professional ethics dictate strict rules to which attorneys must adhere when filing claims under the act.

Gary W. Eiland. "A Call for Balancing Agency Sentinel Priorities." *Journal of Health Law,* 1999, *32,* 503.

This article suggests that budget and time allocations for issuing regulations and guidelines to interpret the law in this area have been disproportionately set when compared to the budget and time allocations supporting these enforcement initiatives. As a result, HCFA and OIG have been seriously delinquent in providing the industry with needed regulatory guidance and workable instructions. Using enforcement initiatives in lieu of formal rule making to regulate the industry accords little respect to the legitimate health care providers who constitute the vast majority of the industry. The author calls for reexamination of enforcement agencies' priorities to provide regulatory guidance through formal rule making, rather than through coercive enforcement initiatives.

Gary W. Eiland. "Fraud and Abuse Involving Hospitals and Physicians." Washington, D.C.: American Health Lawyers Association [Report No. VMM99–0043], 1999], 76 pages.

Discusses the False Claims Act; OIG and DOJ initiatives focusing on specific areas of fraud and abuse associated with hospitals, physicians, and hospital-physician relationships; fraud and abuse risk areas, and targeted enforcement actions.

Gary W. Eiland. "Medicare Fraud and Abuse." Washington, D.C.: American Health Lawyers Association [Report No. VMC98–0011], 1998, 127 pages.

Discusses judicial, legislative, and regulatory developments in Medicare fraud and abuse laws affecting managed care providers. Looks at the potential impact of the M+C program; relevant judicial, administrative, and settlement decisions relating to quality, access to medical care, and similar issues; status of pending federal investigations and current enforcement actions; and targeted priorities by the OIG, Department of Justice, and FBI.

Stephen R. Geisler. "Voluntary Disclosures of Corporate Violations of Federal Law." *Alabama Law Review*, 1999, *51*, 375.

This article is based on hypothetical billing errors by a physician, the civil and criminal consequences of those errors, and options for action.

General Accounting Office. "Medicare: Application of the False Claims Act to Hospital Billing Practices." (GAO/HEHS-98–195.) July 10, 1998, 20 pages.

The Justice Department is using the False Claims Act, originally enacted during the Civil War to combat contract fraud, to deal with cases in which hospitals improperly bill Medicare. Justice's use of the False Claims Act includes two major multistate initiatives involving hospitals: the 72-Hour Window Project and the Lab Unbundling Project. The former investigates whether hospitals have separately billed Medicare for outpatient services covered by the Medicare inpatient payment, the eponymous example being preadmission tests done within seventy-two hours of admission. Hospitals that do so are, in effect, double-billing Medicare. The Lab-Unbundling Project investigates whether hospitals have billed Medicare separately for each blood test done concurrently on automated equipment, or for medically unnecessary tests. Under the former project, about three thousand hospitals received demand letters for recovery of overpayments, and about $58 million had been recovered as of April 1998.

Deborah L. Gersh and Karen K. Harris. "Healthcare and Franchising: The Regulatory Maze." Washington, D.C.: American Health Lawyers Association [Item No. WM990001], 1999, 38 pages.

The authors address the increasing convergence between new and innovative health care delivery systems and the complexities of franchising law. They discuss some of the similarities and differences between the FTC's and the various states' definitions of a franchise and examine some of the corresponding state business opportunity laws. By exploring franchising within the context of health care rules and regulations, the authors provide a better understanding of the impact that federal and state franchise laws and regulations have on delivering a variety of health care services.

Alice G. Gosfield. "Avoiding the Pitfalls in False Claims Liability under Part B." Washington, D.C.: American Health Lawyers Association [Report No. VPH99–0012], 1999, 39 pages.

Alice G. Gosfield. "Avoiding the Pitfalls in False Claims Liability under Part B." Washington, D.C.: American Health Lawyers Association [Report No. VMM99–0033], 1999, 42 pages.

These two reports consider reimbursement rules for physician practices, with particular attention to distinguishing between incident-to and the other uses of nonphysician practitioners. In addition, they explore relationships with billing agents and pitfalls creating false claims liability.

Douglas A. Hastings and others. "The Legal Implications of Patients' Rights Initiatives: Quality Improvement or the End of Managed Care?" Washington, D.C.: American Health Lawyers Association [Report No. VMC98–0013], 1998, 61 pages.

Analyzes and describes several key initiatives triggered by recent activity concerning patients' rights. Assesses these initiatives in the context of the challenge to the U.S. health care delivery system in balancing the dual demands for cost control and quality assurance. Illustrates the various initiatives with samples of federal and state legislation and regulations, case law, and voluntary efforts. Includes a chart comparing patients' rights provisions of several current and recently proposed federal and state efforts.

Leonard C. Homer. "Billing and Documentation Issues That Become the Basis for False Claims." Washington, D.C.: American Health Lawyers Association [Report No. VMM99–0042], 1999, 20 pages.

Looks at the false claims enforcement framework, typical billing and documentation areas of exposure, and agency initiatives directed toward minimizing erroneous and false claims.

Patric Hooper. "Strategies for Defending False Claims Suits." Washington, D.C.: American Health Lawyers Association [Report No. VMM99–0046]), 42 pages.

Discusses the history of the False Claims Act and gives an overview of the act; discusses avoiding *qui tam* actions, the investigation process and parallel proceedings, and legal and practical defenses. Includes the DOJ memo "Guidance on the Use of the False Claims Act in Civil Health Care Matters" and DHHS OIG memo "National Protocol Projects—Best Practices Guidelines."

Patric Hooper and Gabriel L. Imperato. "Strategies in Defending False Claims Suits." Washington, D.C.: American Health Lawyers Association [Report No. VMM98–0037], 1998, 81 pages.

Reviews the elements and issues involved in defending false claims suits, including, but not limited to, jurisdictional and substantive issues, as well as strategies for negotiation, settlement, and defense. Includes sections of the False Claims Act and two cases decided under that act: *United States ex rel. Aranda* v. *Community Psychiatric Centers of Oklahoma, Inc.* and *United States ex rel. Riley* v. *St. Luke's Episcopal Hospital.*

Carl Horn III. "Health Care Fraud and Abuse: Enhanced Civil and Criminal Penalties Place Honest Physicians and Providers at Genuine Risk." In Carl Horn III, Donald H. Caldwell, Jr., and D. Christopher Osborn, *Law for Physicians: An Overview of Medical Legal Issues.* Chicago: American Medical Association, 1999, 246 pages.

This chapter discusses the relevant criminal statutes, civil remedies, the False Claims Act, asset forfeiture, exclusion from Federal Health Care Programs, and how to develop an effective compliance plan.

David A. Hyman and Joel V. Williamson. "Fraud and Abuse: Regulatory Alternatives in a 'Competitive' Health Care Era." *Loyola University of Chicago Law Journal,* 1988, 19, 113.

Argues that the Medicare and Medicaid fraud and abuse statute (42 U.S.C. § 1395nn(b)) was sensible when Medicare and Medicaid used retrospective fee-for-service reimbursement. Minimal review meant that false claims were easily filed and overutilization was unchecked. But now that managed care has become the norm, the statute appears to prohibit many arrangements that pose little risk to the integrity of the programs or quality of care. Efforts to ensure a referral base or to reward efficiently rendered care, for example, are blocked unless one wishes to run the risk of criminal prosecution. The authors conclude that the statute is a superannuated remnant of regulatory control.

Gabriel L. Imperato. "Internal Investigations and Voluntary Disclosures." Washington, D.C.: American Health Lawyers Association [Report No. VMM99–0027], 1999, 15 pages.

Discusses the scope, accountability, and reporting requirements of an internal investigation; application of attorney-client, work product, and self-evaluative privileges; consideration of parallel criminal or civil litigation and disclosure and waiver of privilege; management and methodology for the internal investigation and expectations of the client; and risks and rewards of voluntary disclosure upon conclusion of the internal investigation.

Timothy S. Jost and Sharon L. Davies. *Medicare and Medicaid Fraud and Abuse.* St. Paul, Minn.: West Group, 1998, approx. 500 pages.

Contents include topics such as false claims; antikickback laws; self-referrals: federal and state prohibitions; administrative penalties and exclusions; the Civil False Claims Act and *qui tam* actions; investigations; and sentencing considerations for health care fraud offenders.

Peter M. Kazon. "Compliance and Reimbursement Issues for Laboratories." Washington, D.C.: American Health Lawyers Association [Report No. VMM99–0047]), 22 pages.

Discusses key regulatory and compliance issues facing laboratories, including the results of laboratory-negotiated rule making.

Denis M. King and Alan S. Goldberg. "Long Term Care Antifraud and Abuse Compliance Program Manual." Washington, D.C.: American Health Lawyers Association [Item No. WM990004], 1999, 127 pages.

In this spiral-bound text, the authors examine the government's increased use of aggressive investigative tactics to eliminate fraud in the health care industry, highlight some of the particular areas targeted in the long-term care industry, address the benefits of voluntarily implementing compliance programs in long-term care facilities, and outline suggestions for designing and implementing a program.

Mary DuBois Krohn. "The False Claims Act and Managed Care: Blowing the Whistle on Underutilization." (Comment.) *Cumberland Law Review,* 1998, *28,* 443.

Argues that the False Claims Act, traditionally invoked to uncover and attack overutilization, presents the government with a powerful tool to deter underutilization in managed care settings. It explores the incentives that managed care creates and the problem of underutilization in federal managed care programs. It argues that current mechanisms for deterring underutilization are not effective in managed care settings.

Gregory M. Luce. "Healthcare Fraud and Abuse: Compliance and Enforcement Programs." Washington, D.C.: American Health Lawyers Association [Document No. FA97–0004], 1997.

Outlines the current enforcement climate, specific enforcement programs, and recent statutory enforcement enhancements in the health care industry. This paper also examines voluntary compliance initiatives within the hospital industry and government-sponsored compliance efforts, such as model compliance plans and mandated corporate integrity provisions.

Gregory M. Luce. "Second Generation Compliance Programs." Washington, D.C.: American Health Lawyers Association [Report No.VHH99—0013], 1999, 24 pages.

Addresses the ongoing operations of establishing and maintaining a compliance program, including integrating the compliance function and developing and improving audits and internal reviews. Also discusses disclosing compliance issues to the government and making repayments, and the role of the compliance program during government investigations and *qui tam* litigation. Summarizes DOJ health care fraud investigations (for example, the outpatient lab and the pneumonia upcoding investigations) as well as the DOJ's announcement of increased focus on long-term care providers.

Patricia Meador and Elizabeth S. Warren. "The False Claims Act: A Civil War Relic Evolves into a Modern Weapon." *Tennessee Law Review*, 1998, *65*, 455.

Discusses the history of the False Claims Act and analyzes the provisions of the law, including provisions particular to *qui tam* actions. It then discusses how the False Claims Act has been applied to health care transactions and the results of those cases. The authors examine the disappointing result in the U.S. Supreme Court case *Hughes Aircraft Co.* v. *United States ex. rel. Schumer,* 117 S.Ct. 293 (1997), and the continuing split in the circuits over provisions of the False Claims Act. In conclusion, the article calls on the Supreme Court to analyze fully the False Claims Act and give practitioners, as well as health care providers, much needed guidance.

Joel L. Michaels. "Identification of Fraud and Abuse Issues: The Managed Care Payor's Perspective." Washington, D.C.: American Health Lawyers Association [Document No. FA97–0006], 1997).

Addresses fraud and abuse issues in managed care with specific focus on rate submissions, marketing and enrollment, and denial of medically necessary services.

Robert J. Milligan. "Risk Management for Physician Fraud and Abuse Liability: Internal Investigations and Voluntary Disclosure." Washington, D.C.: American Health Lawyers Association [Report No. VPH99–0010], 1999, 76 pages.

Examines the practical and legal issues that arise when physician practices discover potential health care fraud and abuse problems. Issues addressed include the scope of the attorney-client privilege and the work product doctrine; multiple representation and conflict of interest; joint defense agreements; and suggestions on client counseling regarding potential fraud and abuse liability.

J. E. Mitchem. "Parallel Proceedings: Concurrent *Qui Tam* and Grand Jury Litigation." *Alabama Law Review*, 1999, *51*, 391.

This article is based on a hypothetical situation in which a federal search warrant is executed on a hospital's business office premises.

L. Morris and G. W. Thompson. "Reflections on the Government's Stick and Carrot Approach to Fighting Health Care Fraud." *Alabama Law Review*, 1999, *51*, 319.

Written by two officials of the DHHS Office of the Inspector General, this article explores the background of the current fight against health care fraud; the enhanced enforcement authorities, resources, and initiatives available to the government; and collaborative efforts undertaken with the industry to strengthen the integrity of the government's health care programs.

John R. Munich. "State Initiatives in Prosecuting Abuse and Neglect in Long Term Care Facilities." Washington, D.C.: American Health Lawyers Association [Document No. FA97–0007], 1997).

Addresses state prosecution initiatives in the long-term care industry and provides illustrative examples of state statutory and case law activities. This paper also provides guidance on how nursing home owners and administrators may avoid criminal prosecution in abuse or neglect cases.

Jan E. Murray. "Disclosure of Medicare Billing Errors or Misconduct." Washington, D.C.: American Health Lawyers Association [Report No. VMM99–0028], 1999, 16 pages.

Examines the legal obligation to disclose errors or fraud as well as the distinction between errors and fraud, which has become controversial owing to use of the False Claims Act by the government. Finally, it considers whether a provider should voluntarily disclose errors or fraud.

Thomas F. O'Neil III and others. "The Buck Stops Here: Preemption of Third-Party Claims by the False Claims Act." *Journal of Contemporary Health Law and Policy*, 1995, *12*, 41.

Explains the origins of the False Claims Act before providing a detailed, highly practical analysis of the statute, its substantial judicial gloss, a preemption analysis, and alternative strategies to defeat third-party claims. The increasing frequency of litigation under this statute, particularly after the 1986 amendments, coupled with zealous reliance on the act by the government, make it more likely that a company depending on federal payments for its products will be named as a third-party defendant in a false claims action filed against another person or entity. This is a highly useful article.

Charles Pereyra-Suarez and Carole A. Klove. "Ring Around the White Collar: Defending Fraud and Abuse." *Whittier Law Review*, 1996, *18*, 31.

This highly practical article sets forth ways health care providers can defend themselves when faced with government investigations. It is partially written in a question-and-answer format. Topics addressed include what a health care provider should do when presented with a search warrant, obstruction of justice issues, abuse of process, determining the scope of the search warrant, and notifying employees of their rights.

David D. Queen and Elizabeth E. Frasher. *Designing a Health Care Corporate Compliance Program.* (3rd ed.) Washington, D.C.: Atlantic Information Services, 1997.

Sets forth a range of precautions—such as anonymous hotlines, ethics rules, and employee training—that can prevent violations from occurring and limit their impact. The Justice Department and OIG have placed great emphasis on compliance plans and have required that they be a nonnegotiable component of all settlement agreements.

Greg Radinsky. "Making Sense of the Federal Sentencing Guidelines: How Health Care Corporations Can Manage Risk by Adopting Corporate Compliance Programs." *Journal of Health and Hospital Law*, 1997, *30*, 113.

Analyzes and discusses the benefits and requirements of adopting a corporate compliance program. Proceeding from the analysis, this article (written by a practicing attorney) proposes a detailed model compliance plan for clinical laboratories that would likely meet government requirements. The proposed plan is based on provisions of several corporate integrity agreements and the model compliance plan issued by the Office of Inspector General of the Department of Health and Human Services.

Paul Reidinger. "Fraud Doctors." *ABA Journal*, May 1996, *82*, 50.

The *qui tam* provision of the False Claims Act enables employees of companies that do business with the U.S. government to bring suit (as relators) on behalf of the United States as redress for fraud. This brief article explores the uses of the statute in recent years as a weapon against Medicare and Medicaid fraud.

Daniel R. Roach and Cori MacDonneil. "The Compliance Conundrum." *Journal of Health Law*, 1999, *32*, 565.

Complex regulations and statutes, murky guidance from governmental agencies, and overly zealous enforcement initiatives make the legal questions in the health care arena a veritable minefield.

This article examines some of the issues that arise in the health care legal setting, explains why compliance programs are difficult to establish, and analyzes the issues that arise when providers attempt to establish them. Finally, the authors suggest changes in the governing legal framework that would facilitate achievement of the government's goals in a more efficient and just manner.

Robert L. Roth. "Credit Balance Enforcement Actions and Compliance Issues." Washington, D.C.: American Health Lawyers Association [Report No. VMM99–0024], 1999, 68 pages.

Explains the statutory and regulatory background of credit balances and overpayments, discusses potential sources of credit balance liability, and analyzes the requirements imposed by the government in settling False Claim Act credit balance cases, including the $5.6 million settlement with the Yale School of Medicine. Also provides suggestions about how to address credit balance and overpayment issues as part of provider compliance issues. The Yale University settlement agreement, corrective action plan, billing compliance plan, and excluded person policy are attached.

John C. Ruhnka and others. "Qui Tam Claims: Threat to Voluntary Compliance Programs in Health Care Organizations." Journal of Health Politics, Policy and Law, June 2000, 25, 283.

The Department of Justice reports that health care fraud is the department's second highest priority (after violent crime). The number of health care fraud investigations pending at the DOJ increased from 270 cases in 1992 to more than 4,000 in 1997. The DOJ's primary weapon in prosecuting health care fraud is the federal False Claims Act of 1863. Almost unique among federal antifraud provisions, the act may be used by "private prosecutors" to file lawsuits on behalf of the federal government charging organizations with submitting false claims to the government. The authors conclude that the act needs to provide more positive incentives for organizations to use voluntary compliance and audit programs.

John C. Ruhnka, Edward J. Gac, and Heidi Boerstler. "Qui Tam Claims: Threat to Voluntary Compliance Programs in Health Care Organizations." Journal of Health Politics, Policy and Law, 2000, 25, 283.

Almost unique among federal antifraud provisions, the False Claims Act of 1863 may be used by "private prosecutors" to file lawsuits on behalf of the federal government charging organizations with submitting false claims to the government. The act rewards such whistle-blowers with a share of any resulting recovery as a bounty and protects them from discharge for filing false claims lawsuits against their employers. It also requires defendants to pay the costs and attorney's fees of successful claimants. Following 1986 amendments by Congress, and paralleling the rapid increase in federal reimbursements for health care costs, private qui tam claims have far expanded beyond their traditional purview of defense contracts, into the area of health care. By 1997, health care providers were the target of 54 percent of the 530 private qui tam lawsuits filed that year.

David J. Ryan. "The False Claims Act: An Old Weapon with New Firepower Is Aimed at Health Care Fraud." Annals of Health Law, 1995, 4, 127.

Considers the value of the False Claims Act in deterring health care fraud. As managed care is increasingly the setting in which health care is provided, capitated payments can be expected to remove the incentive to overuse services and, perhaps, reduce the incidence of kickbacks and self-referrals. However, as payment systems shift, so too will the incentives. Providers who are compensated with capitated payments may be tempted to curtail treatment, or even fail to perform necessary services, since providing those services will yield no additional compensation. If a provider accepts capitated payments from the federal government without performing required services, a False Claims Act violation would occur.

Robert Salcido. False Claims Act & The Healthcare Industry: Counseling and Litigation. Washington, D.C.: American Health Lawyers Association [Item No. WB990002], 1999, 438 pages.

In this book, the author provides a section-by-section summary and analysis of each provision of the False Claims Act. Among the issues covered in the text are the history of the False Claims Act; definitions; the *qui tam* prosecutorial actions of the federal government (what it is enforcing and why, rights of the parties involved, expenses and fees, basis for determining damages and civil penalties, jurisdiction, and potential liabilities for both the corporation and certain individuals who work for the corporation); benefits and risks of voluntarily disclosing; and whistle-blower protection provisions.

Michael M. Schmidt. "Neither Aider Nor Abettor Be: Attorneys Become Prosecutorial Targets for Healthcare Crimes." *Journal of Health Law,* 1999, *32,* 251.

Attorneys representing health care entities are not immune to federal criminal prosecution for the assistance that they give their clients. This article focuses on the potential attorney liability for aiding and abetting a client's violation of the law. The author examines the fields of securities, tax, and white-collar crime for guidance regarding interpretation and application of the federal aid and abetting statute to attorneys practicing in the health care field. Based on these analogous areas, and on the federal criminal statutes applicable in the health care field, he recommends steps that can be taken to minimize the possibility of aiding and abetting liability. In addition, he recommends that the courts require a prosecutorial showing of both actual knowledge of wrongdoing and wrongful intent before imposing aider and abettor liability upon health law practitioners.

Paul W. Shaw and Kathleen McDermott. "Use of Non-Traditional Sanctions." Washington, D.C.: American Health Lawyers Association [Document No. FA97–0009], 1997.

Discusses "nontraditional" sanctions and new enforcement tools provided by HIPAA to investigate and prosecute health care fraud and abuse: injunctive relief, freezing and seizure of assets obtained as part of a fraudulent scheme, and forfeiture of property derived from committing health care offenses.

Malcom K. Sparrow. *License to Steal: Why Fraud Plagues America's Health Care System.* Boulder, Colo.: Westview Press, 1996, 240 pages.

Focuses on criminal fraud, as opposed to abuse, all the while accepting the difficulty of drawing a clear line between the two. After examining the characteristics of the fraud-control challenge, the author, a lecturer in public policy at the John F. Kennedy School of Government at Harvard, dismisses popular misconceptions about computer fraud and rejects the notion that using electronic media creates significant prosecutorial difficulties. He argues that managed care will not provide a structural solution to the fraud problem, and he suggests that the criminal justice system will become ever less relevant to fraud control. At the same time, the new forms of fraud—involving diversion of capitation fees and resulting in inadequate medical care—may be more dangerous to human health than the types of fraud familiar under traditional fee-for-service arrangements. Finally, the author focuses on detection tools currently used within the industry and identifies the most critical areas for developing new analytic and technological capabilities.

Sanford V. Teplitzky. "Balanced Budget Act of 1997: More Health Care Fraud and Abuse Measures." Washington, D.C.: American Health Lawyers Association [Document No. FA97–0001], 1997.

Discusses the fraud and abuse provisions of the BBA, including permanent exclusion of those convicted of three health care–related offenses, authority to refuse to contract with those convicted of felonies, imposition of civil monetary penalties, provision of identification numbers, new Medicare Part B fee schedule, and the nondiscrimination requirement for posthospital referrals to home health agencies.

Sanford V. Teplitzky. "Medicare and Medicaid Fraud and Abuse Issues." Washington, D.C.: American Health Lawyers Association [Report No. VLT98–0009], 1998, 37 pages.

Examines federal laws that concern fraud and abuse as they relate to the long-term care sector, including the civil portion of the False Claims Act and the federal self-referral prohibitions (Stark I and Stark II). Also reviews administrative and enforcement initiatives.

Donna K. Thiel. "Long Term Care Fraud Issues." Washington, D.C.: American Health Lawyers Association [Document No. FA97–0008], 1997.

Discusses fraud issues affecting the long-term care industry, including payment methodologies applicable to providers and suppliers, issues identified by HCFA and OIG, and practical advice regarding new areas of enforcement activity.

D. McCarty Thornton. " 'Sentinel Effect' Shows Fraud Control Effort Works." *Journal of Health Law,* 1999, *32,* 493.

The author, the chief counsel to the inspector general of the Department of Health and Human Services, analyzes the fraud-and-abuse track record of his agency and discusses why that effort has had beneficial effects for the health care sector and the federal budget. The benefits of this enforcement effect flow directly from the specific enforcement actions, and indirectly from the response of others in the industry to the standards set forth in those actions. The author disputes assertions by some that the enforcement actions are unfair, arbitrary, or draconian. Rather, he contends, they are an appropriate response to a documented problem with which the government is justifiably concerned.

Carrie Valiant. "Non-Institutional Providers Focus." Washington, D.C.: American Health Lawyers Association [Document No. FA97–0005], 1997.

Identifies and discusses fraud and abuse issues for laboratories, home care organizations, nursing home suppliers, and other noninstitutional providers, and also discusses fraud alert and advisory opinion issues, updated laboratory settlements, OIG audits of DME-pharmacy relationships, and model compliance programs.

Carrie Valiant and David E. Matyas. *Legal Issues in Healthcare Fraud and Abuse: Navigating the Uncertainties.* (3rd ed.) Washington, D.C.: American Health Lawyers Association, 1997), 403 pages.

Written by two health care attorneys, this text provides the reader with an updated and broader examination of relevant issues since the first edition was published. Chapter One gives an overview of the federal, state, and private agencies having oversight authority or responsibility for fraud and abuse issues; Chapter Two covers federal antikickback law; Chapter Three examines federal physician self-referral restrictions; Chapter Four discusses false claims, fraudulent billing, civil money penalties, and program exclusion; Chapter Five focuses on fraud and abuse issues affecting managed care; Chapter Six reviews nonfederal health care fraud initiatives; Chapter Seven is devoted to patient transfers, including EMTALA violations; Chapter Eight examines procedural issues, including representation concerns; and Chapter Nine anticipates future issues, enforcement priorities, and legislative activities. This timely resource is comprehensive, modestly priced, and highly recommended.

James B. Wieland. "Physician Focus: Fraud and Abuse." Washington, D.C.: American Health Lawyers Association [Document No. FA97–0003], 1997).

Reviews emerging fraud and abuse issues relevant to physicians. This paper, written by an attorney, details Medicare billing issues and other specific matters incident to billing, reassignment, and proper procedure and visit codes.

8.05(2)   Illegal Remuneration (Stark I and II)

American Bar Association. *Healthcare Exclusions: A Comprehensive Guide.* Chicago: ABA, 1997, 200 pages.

> Discusses the sanction of exclusion from participation in Medicare and Medicaid programs imposed on health care providers and suppliers who are found guilty of fraud, patient abuse, or other similar conduct.

Dennis M. Barry. "STARK-Considerations in Financial Relationships." Washington, D.C.: American Health Lawyers Association [Report No. VMM99–0032], 1999, 22 pages.

> Looks at self-referral issues that arise in business relationships under the Stark law, selected exceptions to the self-referral prohibitions, and reporting requirements.

Douglas A. Blair. "The 'Knowingly and Willfully' Continuum of the Anti-Kickback Statute's Scienter Requirement: Its Origins, Complexities and Most Recent Judicial Developments." *Annals of Health Law,* 1999, *8, 1.*

> Analyzes the evolution of the antikickback statute's scienter requirement. Includes an historical review of the statute and in-depth discussion of three notable cases in this area: *U.S.* v. *Greber, Hanlester Network* v. *Shalala,* and *U.S.* v. *Davis.* Concludes that without further guidance from either Congress or DHHS, the split among the circuits as to a proper definition of the statute's scienter requirement makes the matter ripe for Supreme Court review.

Timothy P. Blanchard. "New Developments in Fraud and Abuse and False Claims." Washington, D.C.: American Health Lawyers Association [Report No. VHL98–0051], 1998, 18 pages.

> Focuses on developments in the areas of fraud and abuse enforcement and claims litigation that involve kickbacks and inducements, OIG advisory opinions 97–1 through 98–7, health care compliance programs, national government initiatives, and the False Claims Act. Includes the guidance issued on June 3, 1998, by DOJ Deputy Attorney General Eric H. Holder to all U.S. attorneys, and Inspector General June Gibbs Brown's "best practice guidelines" for her staff in pursuing fraud initiatives.

James F. Blumstein. "The Fraud and Abuse Statute in an Evolving Health Care Marketplace: Life in the Health Care Speakeasy." *American Journal of Law and Medicine,* 1996, *22* (2 and 3), 205–230.

> Discusses the antikickback provisions of the fraud and abuse statute, its safe-harbor regulations, the implications for capitated payment arrangements, and formation of organizations to provide capitated care.

Donna Schmerin Clark. "Stark II." Washington, D.C.: American Health Lawyers Association [Report No. VPH00–0004], 1999, 27 pages.

> Examines key issues identified in the published proposal of Stark II rules, including basic concepts such as financial relationships, entities, designated health services, and referrals; exceptions to compensation arrangements with outside entities; group practice issues; reporting; and the advisory opinion process.

Thomas S. Crane and others. "Stark II Proposed Regulations." *Health Law Digest,* Feb. 1998, *26,* 3–16.

> Assesses HCFA's proposed Stark II regulations, issued Jan. 9, 1998.

Sharon L. Davies and Timothy S. Jost. "Managed Care: Placebo or Wonder Drug for Health Care Fraud and Abuse?" *Georgia Law Review,* 1997, *31, 373.*

Examines the changing nature of fraud and abuse under managed care. It defines the terms *fraud*, *abuse*, and *managed care* and identifies the parties who commit fraud and abuse and their victims, delineating their respective roles in traditional fee-for-service medicine and under managed care. It also surveys the manifestations of fraud and abuse and the limitations of those approaches in the managed care setting. The authors conclude by suggesting how both law and investigative techniques might be altered to better address fraud and abuse in managed care.

Gary Scott Davis and Robert J. Moses. "Negotiating a Risk-Based Managed Care Contract." Washington, D.C.: American Health Lawyers Association [Report No. VHL98–0022], 1998, 31 pages.

Hypothetical correspondence between attorneys negotiating a risk-sharing contract between an HMO and a provider group. Addresses product lines, compensation, credentialing, utilization management, quality improvement, information access, termination, and risk sharing.

James C. Dechene and Karen P. O'Neill. "Stark II and State Self-Referral Restrictions." *Journal of Health and Hospital Law*, 1996, 29, 65.

Written by two practicing attorneys, this article concludes with a helpful state-by-state summary of physician self-referral restrictions. Unlike other fraud and abuse laws, Stark II and various state self-referral laws largely prohibit all ventures within their sweep unless a specific exception applies. Although a transaction that may not fall within one of the safe harbors under the federal antikickback statute could nevertheless be perfectly legal, a financial arrangement involving physicians and any of the designated health services will be illegal under Stark II unless all of the requirements of a specific exception are satisfied. Moreover, because the sweep of Stark II is so broad, virtually every transaction involving any of the designated health services should be carefully reviewed to ensure it falls safely within an applicable Stark II exception.

J. M. Eades. "Life After *Bryan*: Intent Under the Antikickback Law." *Journal of Health Law*, 1999, 32, 633.

Examines *Bryan* v. *U.S.*, 118 S.Ct. 1939 (1998). Discusses the proper standard of *willfulness* necessary to violate the antikickback law.

J. D. Epstein and Leonard Homer. "HCFA and the OIG/DOJ: Where Does Payment Policy End and Enforcement Begin?" Washington, D.C.: American Health Lawyers Association [Report No. VHL98–0011], 1998, 44 pages.

Supplies an overview of the principal agencies involved in setting health care fraud and abuse control policies; identifies agency cooperation projects implemented in the 1990s. Reviews the jurisdictional issues and the development of new theories of prosecution dealing with fraud and reimbursement.

Alice G. Gosfield. "Avoiding the Pitfalls in False Claims Liability under Part B." Washington, D.C.: American Health Lawyers Association [Report No VMM98–0019], 1998, 18 pages.

Outlines issues under HIPAA for Medicare Part B reimbursement and examines the special rules for teaching physicians in the context of overall requirements for physician billing, including degrees of supervision, billing for evaluation in management services, billing agent arrangements, and general false claim liability.

Gary W. Eiland. "Fraud and Abuse Involving Hospitals and Integrated Delivery Systems." Washington, D.C.: American Health Lawyers Association [Report NO. VMM98–0022], 1998, 97 pages.

Examines judicial, legislative, and regulatory developments in Medicare fraud and abuse law (including HIPAA, BBA, antikickback, and Stark Laws), the government's crackdown on health care fraud, and the OIG's model compliance plans for clinical laboratories and hospitals.

Tamsen Douglass Love. "Toward a Fair and Practical Definition of 'Willfully' in the Medicare/ Medicaid Anti-Kickback Statute." (Note.) *Vanderbilt Law Review,* 1997, *50,* 1029–1059.

> Provides background, including the legislative history of the antikickback statute and case law interpreting it. This paper explores some of the issues raised by the breadth of the law and by the general notion of criminalizing this type of behavior. It concludes that defining *willfully* as requiring a corrupt intent, but not necessarily a specific intent to violate the law, is a rational and practical response to the difficulties posed by the breadth of the antikickback statute.

Douglas M. Mancino and others. *Navigating Your Way Through the Federal Physician Self-Referral Law.* (2nd ed.) Washington, D.C.: Atlantic Information Services, 1997.

> This guidebook is aimed at assisting health care organizations in complying with the federal physician self-referral ban, known as Stark I and Stark II.

Robert W. McAdams and Mary L. Gallagher. *State and Federal Prohibitions on Physician Referrals: A Guide to Compliance.* Gaithersburg, Md.: Aspen, 1998.

> This one-volume loose-leaf treatise, updated annually, is divided into two parts. The first part discusses federal prohibitions on physician referrals, specifically focusing on Stark I and Stark II. It includes an overview of the Stark Advisory Opinions, the text of the opinions, and extensive Stark compliance checklists. The second part discusses state prohibitions on physician referrals, with a state-by-state breakdown of the most significant characteristics of state self-referral laws, in addition to reproducing the full text of the laws and regulations of each state.

Kathy Nino. "OIG Advisory Opinion 99–6 Waiving Co-Payments." *Health Care Law Monthly,* May 1999, at 19.

> In its Advisory Opinion 99-6, the Office of the Inspector General of DHHS discussed the potential implications, under the federal antikickback statute, of the policy at St. Jude Children's Research Hospital of not billing pediatric oncology patients for coinsurance and deductible amounts. Although the OIG concluded that the billing policies could violate the statute if the requisite intent to induce referrals were present, the OIG determined that it would not subject St. Jude to sanctions under the statute. The OIG based its conclusion on many factors that, taken together, suggested that the billing policy was unlikely to result in overutilization or in provision of unnecessary services.

Charles B. Oppenheim. "Stark II Regulations: A Comprehensive Analysis." Washington, D.C.: American Health Lawyers Association, 1998, 40 pages.

> In this monograph, the author provides an analysis of new questions and ambiguities arising from the proposed Stark II regulations. The text identifies key themes of the proposed regulation changes; analyzes a number of the significant problem areas and offers interpretive guidance for navigating them, including the proposed changes to the "group practice" exception; explores the structuring of certain standard compensation arrangements to comply with the proposed regulations; and discusses the consequences and impact of the proposed regulations and potential future directions the Stark statute may take.

Philip L. Pomerance. "A Good Offense Is the Best Defense (Usually): Strategies for Defending Health Care Fraud and Abuse Cases." Washington, D.C.: American Health Lawyers Association [Report No VHL98–0042], 1998, 42 pages.

> Examines the issues faced by an organization or individual that is the subject of a health care fraud and abuse investigation; presents a summary of the law, practical advice regarding defense strategies, and an outline of settlement issues. Includes memoranda on responding to a corporate criminal investigation and a sample settlement agreement and plea agreement.

Glen A. Reed and Robert E. DeWitt. "Referral Fee Prohibitions." In Mark A. Hall (ed.), *Health Care Corporate Law: Financing and Liability.* Boston: Little, Brown, 1994.

This forty-two-page chapter sets forth the basic conceptual definition of a referral fee and examines the major sources of regulatory and prohibitory law. The chapter begins by explaining the rationale for referral fee prohibitions in the health care industry and why referral fees are unethical in many circumstances. It continues with detailed analysis of the Medicare fraud and abuse statute and the Stark bill, concluding with state antikickback statutes.

Albert Shay and Gary Francesconi. "Proposed Stark II Rules: Clarification or More Confusion?" *Journal of Health and Hospital Law,* June 1998, *31,* 95.

Outlines HCFA's attempt to clarify its interpretation and intended application of Stark II as it relates to designated health services. Despite the attempted clarifications, significant issues remain open to debate. This article discusses several of these issues, along with the authors' suggestions for HCFA to incorporate into the final Stark II rules.

Bruce John Shih and Barton A. Carter. "The Hidden Pitfalls of Marketing by Healthcare Providers." *Health Lawyer,* Sept. 1997, *10*(1).

The authors, practicing health care attorneys in Los Angeles, discuss the effects of (1) the federal antikickback statutes; (2) the physician self-referral law (Stark); and (3) the Civil Monetary Penalties Law as amended by HIPAA, on marketing.

Sanford V. Teplizky and William Mathias. "1998 OIG Advisory Opinions." Washington, D.C.; American Health Lawyers Association [Report No. VTX98–0018], 1998, 93 pages.

Reviews financial relationships in regard to federal antikickback statutes at issue in DHHS OIG Advisory Opinions No. 98–1 through 98–11. Includes a February 1998 Members Briefing on the Stark II proposed rule and Stark advisory opinions final rule prepared by the AHLA's Stark II Working Group, which reviews in detail the rules and their effect on various services and providers; and the DHHS OIG Provider Self-Disclosure Protocol, which gives guidance to hospitals and other health care entities that decide voluntarily to disclose irregularities in their dealings with federal health care programs.

Larry D. Thompson and Kristen L. Wood. "Healthcare Investigations: Compliance Issues and Parallel Investigations." Washington, D.C.: American Health Lawyers Association [Report No. VHL98–0043], 1998, 45 pages.

Discusses issues that arise for defendants involved in parallel proceedings, including whether to voluntarily disclose to the government inadvertent waiver of the attorney-client privilege or Fifth Amendment privilege, potential consequences of invoking the Fifth Amendment privilege, and potential for collateral estoppel. Contains a motion to stay proceedings pending termination of criminal litigation and supporting brief, and an agreement relating to confidential matter and protective order.

Thomas D. Vaughn. "Long Term Care and Hospital Contracts under the Prospective Payment System." Washington, D.C.: American Health Lawyers Association [Report No. VHL99–0009], 1999, 43 pages.

Provides an overview of long-term care hospital contracts under the prospective payment and consolidated billing systems. Exhibits include analysis of a draft services agreement under the personal services safe-harbor regulation, a comparison of personal services under the antikickback statute and Stark II, and an OIG Advisory Opinion concluding that arrangements for discounted ambulance services for residents of Medicare skilled nursing facilities might constitute prohibited remuneration under the antikickback statute.

Andrew B. Wachler and Phyllis A. Avery. "Federal Fraud and Abuse Laws Strengthened But Stark Self-Referral Prohibitions Untouched." *Health Lawyer,* Winter 1996, *9,* 8.

Examines the Health Insurance Portability and Accountability Act of 1996. Topics discussed include creation of a data collection program, privatization of fraud and abuse control, beneficiary incentive programs, amendments to fraud and abuse laws, Medicare HMOs, and criminalization of federal health care offenses.

Andrew B. Wachler, Mark S. Kopson, and Phyllis A. Avery. "Stark I Final Regulations: Implications for Health Care Providers and Suppliers." *Health Lawyer,* Aug. 1995, *8,* Special Edition, 1.

Elucidates the long-awaited final regulations for the antireferral legislation known as Stark I by the HCFA. This article analyzes the final rule in relation to Stark I and Stark II, contrasting its provisions with those of the earlier Stark I proposed rule and interim final rule. Where applicable, it also clarifies differences between Stark I and Stark II and how the new regulations bridge that statutory gap.

Ronald J. Waldheger. "Formation and Operation of Physician Networks." Washington, D.C.: American Health Lawyers Association [Report No. VHL98–0019], 1998, 12 pages.

Outlines the reasons for forming a physician network, the types of physician network, the best legal structure for such networks, antitrust considerations, fraud and abuse and Stark II issues, and Medicare reassignment rules.

8.05(3) Other Illegal Acts

Daniel R. Anderson and Rick Matarante. "Effective Fraud Control Tactics for Insurers and Managed Care Plans." Washington, D.C.: Atlantic Information Services, 1996.

Written by a former Maryland assistant attorney general and the manager of the Special Investigations Unit at Oxford Health Plans, this book supplies a blueprint for initiating a special investigative unit or improving an existing unit. Topics discussed include reasons to start the unit, setting up and marketing the unit, education, deterrence, and preparing cases.

H. Lee Barfield II and Randall E. Bruce. "Personal Liability for Health Lawyers: *U.S.* v. *Dan Anderson* and Beyond." Washington, D.C.: American Health Lawyers Association [Report No.VHH99–0037], 1999, 28 pages.

Gives an overview of federal fraud and abuse enforcement activities and the relevant federal laws that impose potential civil and criminal liability on health care attorneys. Summarizes recent civil and criminal actions brought against health care attorneys in *U.S.* v. *Dan Anderson* and *Mruz* v. *Caring, Inc.,* as well as actions against attorneys representing clients in other industries. Highlights the relevant provisions of ethics rules for the practicing health care attorney and offers practical strategies for avoiding liability in advising clients.

Lee W. Doty and Mark A. Lieberman. "A Practical Approach to Due Diligence and Related Activities in Hospital Mergers and Affiliations." Washington, D.C.: American Health Lawyers Association [Report No. VHH99–0029], 1999, 60 pages.

Discusses what to put in a term sheet or letter of intent and what to save for the definitive agreements; binding versus nonbinding agreements; how to rank and structure phased production information about a merger or affiliation; protecting sensitive information and avoiding antitrust violations; how to integrate the results of due diligence into representations, warranties, and indemnifications in the definitive agreements; how to organize and work with clients to produce schedules, exhibits, and attachments keyed to the definitive agreements, without disrupting clients' operations; and using checklists and preclosing and postclosing meetings to ensure that the deal is done.

Lawrence L. Foust and Beth Schermer. "Downstream Risk Issues." Washington, D.C.: American Health Lawyers Association [Report No. VMC98–0016], 1998, 33 pages.

Discusses the laws concerning providers who accept risk and highlights some of the new trends in regulating provider groups that accept risk from licensed insurers. Includes a selected bibliography and a list of state "undercare" laws. Also includes the August 1998 consent order from the Texas Commissioners of Insurance in *Harris Methodist Health Plan, Inc.* and the Texas Department of Insurance proposed Financial Incentive Guidelines for determining whether a financial incentive arrangement induces physicians to limit medically necessary services in violation of Texas law.

Ankur J. Goel. "The Lawyer As Witness or Target: Ethical and Strategic Issues." Washington, D.C.: American Health Lawyers Association [Report No. VHH99–0028], 1999, 10 pages.

Outlines actions against lawyers; discusses how lawyer conduct comes under scrutiny; ethical and legal restrictions on assisting client fraud; the relevance of the advice of counsel defense; special issues for in-house counsel; and breaches of privilege and confidentiality obligations. Includes two sample case studies.

Michael J. Holston. "Fraud and Abuse Risk in Structuring Transactions." Washington, D.C.: American Health Lawyers Association [Report No. VMA 98–0022], 1998, 16 pages.

Reviews the federal and state statutes and regulations under which authorities generally proceed when considering merger approval. Holston also discusses conduct that is prohibited, administrative sanctions, civil and criminal penalties, the due diligence process, and how to respond to problems uncovered in due diligence.

Richard O. Jacobs and Elizabeth Goodman. "Splitting Fees or Splitting Hairs? Fee Splitting and Health Care—The Florida Experience." *Annals of Health Law,* 1999, *8,* 239.

Reviews the prohibitions against fee splitting under Florida law; argues that Florida and other states need a clear statutory definition of prohibited activities. In addition, argues that the Florida Board of Medicine has applied the prohibition against fee splitting arbitrarily and in contrast to legal precedent set by the Second District Court of Appeals. Finally, suggests that Minnesota provides clear legislative guidance on the issue of fee splitting and that the approach adopted by Minnesota is more practical.

Gregory D. Jones. "Primum Non Nocere: The Expanding 'Honest Services' Mail Fraud Statute and the Physician-Patient Fiduciary Relationship." (Note.) *Vanderbilt Law Review,* Jan. 1998, *51,* 139–182.

Congress and the federal judiciary have steadily expanded the scope of the "honest services" mail fraud statute to criminalize an undisclosed breach of public or private fiduciary duty. Given the fiduciary relationship that exists between the physician and the patient, a physician's breaching her fiduciary duty by failing to disclose a referral fee or other financial kickback appears to be subject to mail fraud prosecution, the author writes. Likewise, in a managed care setting, a physician's failure to disclose financial incentives to limit a patient's care and the resulting breach of fiduciary duty would logically come within the purview of the mail fraud statute, he concludes.

Joan H. Krause. "The Role of the States in Combatting Managed Care Fraud and Abuse." *Annals of Health Law,* 1999, *8,* 179.

Describes the weapons available to state regulators to address managed care fraud. Argues that the states, through using a number of existing legal theories, have the flexibility to combat fraudulent managed care practices. By using these targeted state-based efforts (in contrast to broader federal provisions), state regulators may be able to resolve problems more efficiently and with greater patient benefits.

Gregory M. Luce. "Fraud and Abuse Risks in Structuring Transactions." Washington, D.C.: American Health Lawyers Association [Report No. VMA 98–0023], 1998, 24 pages.

Addresses the problems that arise from allocating liability between buyers and sellers. Luce discusses steps for avoiding and minimizing successor liability in transactions, uncovering kickback and false billing issues in the due diligence process; he also addresses fraud and abuse issues in the closing documents.

Theodore N. McDowell. "The Medicare-Medicaid Anti-Fraud and Abuse Amendments: Their Impact on the Present Health Care System." (Comment.) *Emory Law Journal,* 1987, *36,* 691–754.

Contends that the antifraud and antiabuse statute authorizing Medicare and Medicaid should be repealed because of the chilling effect on legitimate business arrangements.

John J. Meyer. "Fraud and Abuse Issues for Home Health Care." Washington, D.C.: American Health Lawyers Association [Report No. VMM99–0053], 1999, 15 pages.

Examines current issues in health care fraud enforcement affecting home health agencies, including OIG reports and alerts, GAO reports, and OIG compliance guidance and its requirements.

Normand F. Pizza. "Qui Tam Actions." Washington, D.C.: American Health Lawyers Association [Report No. VLT99–0005], 1999, 56 pages.

Discusses claims for medically unnecessary services and false certificates, the significance of involvement by the Department of Justice or the assistant U.S. attorney, government requirements for health care *qui tam* settlements, matters influencing settlements, relator opposition, multiple relators and the first-to-file rule, and multiple relator issues. Attachments include selected regulations and the June 3, 1998, DOJ memo from Deputy Attorney General Eric Holder to U.S. attorneys giving guidance on using the act in civil health care matters.

Philip L. Pomerance. "Selected Ethical Issues to Consider in Counseling Health Care Clients." Washington, D.C.: American Health Lawyers Association [Report No. VMM99–0029], 1999, 43 pages.

Discusses ethical issues for health care attorneys, including the standards that control a lawyer's conduct, who the client is, which communications are privileged, and what to do if an attorney is being investigated for assisting a client's allegedly bad acts.

Edward P. Richards III and Thomas R. McLean. "Physicians in Managed Care: A Multidimensional Analysis of New Trends in Liability and Business Risk." *Journal of Legal Medicine,* Dec. 1997, *18,* 443–473.

The objectives of this article are threefold: (1) to introduce physicians to new areas of liability, such as self-referral, unbundling, and fraud and abuse; (2) to illustrate how the potential risk of commercial crime infractions is much higher than traditional medical negligence; and (3) to provide some practical guidance as to how to mitigate the risk.

William J. Scanlon. "Medicare: Recent Legislation to Minimize Fraud and Abuse Requires Effective Implementation." (GAO/T-HEHS-98-9.) Oct. 9, 1997, 9 pages.

Testimony by the director of health financing and systems issues before the House Ways and Means Subcommittee on Health. With enactment of HIPAA in 1996 and the BBA in 1997, Congress has provided significant opportunities to strengthen areas in the Medicare program at high risk for fraud and abuse. How Medicare will use this legislation to improve its oversight of program expenditures remains to be seen, however. The outcome depends largely on how promptly and effectively the HCFA implements the various provisions. Its past efforts to implement regulations, oversee Medicare managed care plans, and acquire major computer systems have often been slow or ineffective. Now that many more demands have been placed on HCFA, GAO is concerned that the promise of the new legislation to combat health care fraud and abuse could be delayed or not realized at all.

James G. Sheehan. "Fraud and Abuse in Pharmacy Benefit Management." Washington, D.C.: American Health Lawyers Association [Report No. VMC98–0023], 1998, 8 pages.

Briefly identifies the issues that result in increased attention to prescription drug fraud issues, and discusses why pharmacy benefit management programs are attracting increased federal and state enforcement attention.

Sanford V. Teplitzky. "Legal Ethics in Representing Clients in Fraud and Abuse Cases." Washington, D.C.: American Health Lawyers Association [Report No. VLT98–0037], 1998, 31 pages.

Examines the professional standards of ethics applicable when counseling clients on fraud and abuse issues with respect to structuring business relationships and defending investigative and enforcement activities.

8.06 CIVIL MONETARY PENALTIES LAW

Pamela H. Bucy. "Civil Prosecution of Health Care Fraud." *Wake Forest Law Review*, 1995, *30*, 693.

Provides a comprehensive analysis of the civil and administrative remedies that are available in prosecuting medical practitioners for health care fraud. Careful consideration is given to the False Claims Act, the exclusion remedy, civil monetary penalties, the suspension remedy, professional licensure discipline, and rescission or denial of hospital staff privileges. Bucy also provides an assessment of the effectiveness of the existing enforcement hierarchy.

8.06(1) Proscribed Conduct

Annot. "Imposition of Civil Penalties, under State Statute, upon Medical Practitioner for Fraud in Connection with Claims under Medicaid, Medicare, or Similar Welfare Programs for Providing Medical Services." *ALR4th 32, 671.*

Collects and analyzes those cases, both state and federal, in which the courts considered imposing civil penalties, under state statutes, upon a medical practitioner for fraud in connection with claims under Medicaid, Medicare, and analogous programs.

Elizabeth M. Apisson. "Double Jeopardy and the Civil Monetary Penalties Dilemma: Is *Hudson* the Cure for Health Care Fraud and Abuse?" (Comment.) *Administrative Law Review,* 1999, *51*, 283.

In *Hudson* v. *United States,* 118 S.Ct. 488 (1997), the Supreme Court unanimously held that imposing civil monetary penalties prior to criminal prosecution for the same conduct fails to implicate the double jeopardy clause of the Constitution. The author discusses how this decision will widen the prosecutorial floodgates for mass civil penalties and exclusions from federally funded programs for many health care providers.

Lowell C. Brown and Hema R. Anwar. "Et Tu Counselor: May an In-House Attorney File a *Qui Tam* Action Against the Attorney's Employer?" *Journal of Health Law*, 1999, *32*, 621.

In general, there is no prohibition on attorneys who wish to bring *qui tam* actions. Nevertheless, a corporation can take preventive steps to eliminate the likelihood of attorney *qui tam* actions, according to the authors. In addition, the corporation can take advantage of state professional ethics laws to mount a defensive action against the attorney who files any such action.

8.06(2) Civil Monetary Act Procedures

[Reserved]

8.07 AUDITS

American Institute of Certified Public Accountants. *Health Care Organizations.* Jersey City, N.J.: American Institute of Certified Public Accountants, 1997, 236 pages.

A detailed auditing and accounting guide to the health care industry.

Jack R. Bierig. "Methodological Challenges to Government Sampling Techniques in Civil Fraud and Abuse Cases." *Journal of Health Law*, 1999, *32*, 339.

This article discusses the use of statistical sampling in Medicare and Medicaid fraud and abuse audits. The author reviews cases in which the government sampling methodologies have been challenged. Finally, the author describes the various alternatives available for challenging the validity of the statistical sampling used by the government in its audits.

G. L. Imperato. "Internal Investigations, Government Investigations, Whistleblower Concerns: Techniques to Protect Your Healthcare Organization." *Alabama Law Review*, 1999, *51*, 205.

Written by two practicing attorneys, this practical article discusses management of an internal investigation, whistle-blower concerns, and what to do when the government knocks.

Timothy S. Jost and Sharon L. Davies. "The Empire Strikes Back: A Critique of the Backlash Against Fraud and Abuse Enforcement." *Alabama Law Review*, 1999, *51*, 239.

The authors begin with a brief overview of the fraud and abuse laws to illustrate the breadth and depth of sanctions available to fraud and abuse enforcers. Second, they examine the types of conduct currently addressed by fraud and abuse enforcement. Next, they introduce and evaluate provider criticisms of fraud and abuse enforcement, concluding with their own recommendations as to how the issues raised by providers might be addressed without compromising the essential role of fraud and abuse enforcement.

Gregory M. Luce. "Internal Compliance Investigations, Audits and Actions." Washington, D.C.: American Health Lawyers Association [Report No. VHL-99–0003], 1999, 28 pages.

Examines internal investigations as a crucial component of a successful compliance program, including practical tips on developing an investigation strategy. Footnotes list relevant cases. Includes a sample consultant engagement letter with an appendix defining the scope of consultant's services.

G. E. Rountree, Jr. "Heath Care Providers and Fraud Investigations: What Can You Do When the Government Changes the Rules in the Middle of the Game?" *Annals of Health Law*, 1999, *8*, 97.

Addresses the federal government's multipronged attack on health care fraud, focusing on the options available to health care providers who are under investigation by the government. The article proposes three potential responses to fraud investigations: (1) lobbying the government for relief, (2) suing the government, or (3) waiting to defend or settle the fraud action. After analyzing each method, the author concludes that an aggressive lobbying campaign is likely to be the most successful of the three possible provider responses.

8.08   PRIVATE INSURANCE

Thomas Bodenheimer. "Should We Abolish the Private Health Insurance Industry?" *International Journal of Health Services,* 1990, *20,* 199.

A right to health care means that all people have equal access to a reasonable level of health services, regardless of income. This implies that financial barriers to health care are not greater for people who need more care or have lower incomes than for relatively healthy or well-off people. The alternative principle for financing health care is the insurance principle, whereby certain people and groups are classified as preferred risks, standard risks, and substandard risks, with costs varying accordingly. The insurance principle is unfair, for private insurers cannot insure 100 percent of the population. The health insurance industry also wastes billions in administrative and marketing costs and has undermined the positive features of health maintenance organization reform.

Robert Cunningham III and Robert M. Cunningham, Jr. *The Blues: A History of the Blue Cross and Blue Shield System.* Northern Illinois University Press, 1997, 328 pages.

Drawing on extensive company archives, this book traces the history of the nation's oldest and largest health insurer, a system that insures roughly one in four Americans.

Michael A. Dowell. "Legal Audits and Investigations: A Key Component of Healthcare Corporate Compliance Programs." *Journal of Health Law,* 1999, *32,* 229.

Health care organizations are increasingly implementing voluntary compliance programs as a means of avoiding severe penalties for violations of the law. The OIG has identified legal audits and investigations as key components of effective compliance programs. The author also examines the role of attorneys in legal audits and investigations, as well as explaining how information communicated from the health care organization to its attorneys can be protected from disclosure. As the article demonstrates, the monetary and human resource costs of such compliance audits and investigations are insignificant when compared to the potential costs of defending a legal action or paying monetary penalties.

General Accounting Office. "Health Insurance for Children: Private Individual Coverage Available, But Choices Can Be Limited and Costs Vary." (GAO/HEHS-98-201.) Aug. 5, 1998, 16 pages.

In 1996, nearly 10.6 million children in America lacked health insurance. Most of them were from poor, working families. In some cases, the children were ineligible for Medicaid or other public programs, or their parents did not receive health insurance coverage from their jobs. In response to congressional interest in the availability of private sector health coverage for children in the individual insurance market, GAO reviewed the availability and characteristics of these products. GAO found that private health insurance is available for almost all children, but sales of these policies account for only a small share of individual insurance policy sales (just 1–20 percent among insurance carriers GAO contacted).

Moreover, because many carriers tend to avoid states with certain regulatory requirements, consumers may have a limited choice of benefit plans and carriers in those states. Costs vary widely, as with adult policies, and children can be denied coverage, or charged higher rates, for existing conditions. Two carriers that market specifically to children do not cover babies because of the high cost of early preventive care and the lack of information about a child's possible future health problems.

Mark A. Hall. "Private Health Insurance." In Mark A. Hall (gen. ed.), *Health Care Corporate Law: Financing and Liability.* Boston: Little, Brown, 1994.

In this fifty-one-page chapter, Hall maps out in detail principles of reimbursement for acute care treatment as they relate to private health carriers. Extensively footnoted, this chapter reviews the deference insurers have traditionally shown to physicians in determining what is medically necessary and nonexperimental care. He also covers general public policy limits on exclusions, preexisting conditions, prospective utilization review, judicial enforcement of prospective review, estoppel to deny coverage, and restitution of erroneous payments. Finally, the chapter discusses usual and customary charges, deductibles and copayments, collection disputes, and the validity and effectiveness of assignments of claims.

Mark A. Hall. *Reforming Private Health Insurance.* Washington, D.C.: American Enterprise Institute for Public Policy Research, 1994, 111 pages.

Begins by explaining why insurance of any sort exists and what social benefits are to be expected from private health insurance. It then surveys the causes of the disintegration of the private insurance market. Hall articulates what benefits society can derive from a properly functioning market in health insurance. The bulk of his analysis then explores various proposals to reform the private insurance market, distinguishing between reforms to the existing voluntary system, in which purchasing insurance is optional, and insurance market reform under a system of mandatory universal coverage.

E. Paul Herrington III. "Experimental Healthcare Reimbursement: A Case Survey." *Health Lawyer,* Winter/Spring 1993, 6(4), 1.

Notes that denials of experimental treatment claims have come under increased scrutiny by the federal courts, specifically employer-sponsored insurance plans examined with respect to application of ERISA. ERISA has played an expanding role in defending experimental claims denials by preempting state law claims, permitting federal court bench trials, and establishing the standard of review. The author, an attorney for Humana, analyzes a range of cases decided at the federal level, emphasizing the importance for both the plan administrator and the court of reviewing the specific protocol and insurance policy language in question before rendering a decision. As treatment protocols change and policy language becomes more specific, he writes, attention to detail becomes more crucial.

Donald W. Light. "Life, Death and the Insurance Companies." *New England Journal of Medicine,* 1994, *330,* 498.

Only in the United States do private insurance companies run the health insurance system, handling claims and making determinations about coverage. The author argues that assuming that national health insurance reform will stop such practices as excluding coverage for persons with preexisting conditions is naïve.

Marc Rodwin. *Medicine, Money and Morals: Physicians' Conflict of Interest.* New York: Oxford University Press, 1993, 471 pages.

Examines the economic conflicts facing American physicians. Rodwin describes the numerous ways in which conflicts arise and how they affect the behavior of physicians and the welfare of patients. He discusses how medical professional organizations have dealt with this problem over the years and compares their responses with those of other professions that have also faced conflict of interest. He explains why this issue is of such great social importance, and he considers various ways it might be resolved through political and legal action.

Paul W. Shaw and Jerome B. Tichner. "Tips for Challenging an Audit Based on Statistical Sampling." *Journal of Health Law,* 1999, *32,* 649.

This is a brief introduction to statistical sampling and practical suggestions for how to confront a statistical sampling study.

James G. Sheehan. "Public/Private Information Sharing in Healthcare Fraud Investigations." *Journal of Health Law,* 1999, *32, 593.*

Private insurers have good reason, both in their private interest and in the public interest, for pursuing and rooting out fraud in the health care system; moreover, they often have sophisticated data systems, substantial investigative information, and management expertise that can be useful to prosecutors. It makes sense as a public policy matter to undertake steps that encourage insurers to be aggressive in pursuing legitimate fraud cases, and to provide a framework for effective cooperation and information sharing with law enforcement. At the same time, prosecutors are responsible for enforcing equal justice under the law; thus many such relationships must be handled in an appropriate manner, with safeguards to protect privacy and the reputation of investigative subjects.

Although the courts have not yet explored many of the relevant legal and factual issues in this area, the author, an assistant U.S. attorney, surveys existing guidance under governing laws and policies applicable to state and federal prosecutors, and suggests techniques to prevent inappropriate communication or use of such information. The article concludes with a four-page "Statement of Principles for the Sharing of Health Care Fraud Information between the Department of Justice and Private Health Plans."

9

Bankruptcy and Insolvency

The U.S. health care system finds itself in a chaotic sea change that first manifested itself during the middle and late 1990s in the rapid consolidation of a previously fragmented industry into large integrated delivery systems. The fear of exclusion from these systems and concerns over who would eventually dominate the managed care market produced a massive increase in affiliations among doctors, hospitals, and insurers, not all of which have proved to be financially successful. Many hospital networks found that they overpaid for physicians' practices and that wringing excessive costs from their newly created empires was not as easy as they had hoped. Compounding these difficulties is the use to which borrowed money has been put by some systems, with many physician management companies spending more on acquisitions than on improving physicians' efficiency or capital performance. In lieu of boosting internal long-range growth by investing in information systems, medical equipment, or expansion of medical services, the typical large system has relied on acquisitions to sustain revenue growth. Finally, and not least important, Congress slashed Medicare reimbursements to hospitals and physicians with passage of the Balanced Budget Act of 1997. The result of all of these actions has been the breathtaking slide of many nationally known institutions into insolvency and bankruptcy.

ANNOTATIONS

9.01   IN GENERAL

John L. Akula. "Insolvency Risk in Health Carriers: Innovation, Competition and Public Protection." *Health Affairs*, 1997, *16*(1), 9–33.

Reviews the framework of regulatory and managerial devices that have evolved in response to the special dangers to the public posed by insolvency of health carriers. These devices include prudential measures designed to decrease the likelihood of insolvency and measures to protect enrollees in the event that insolvency occurs nevertheless. It also reviews the debate over how this framework should be adapted to new forms of risk-bearing entities, especially provider-sponsored networks engaged in direct contracting with purchasers of coverage. Finally, the author explores parallels to the banking crisis in the United States in the late 1980s.

Sarah Robinson Borders and Rebecca Cole Moore. "Purchasing Medicare Provider Agreements in Bankruptcy: The Case Against Successor Liability for Prepetition Overpayments." *California Bankruptcy Journal*, 1998, *24*, 253.

The potential for successor liability poses serious problems for health care facilities wishing to acquire an existing Medicare provider agreement. The Bankruptcy Code may nonetheless protect debtor providers and their purchasers from these consequences. When characterized as a license to participate in a statutory and regulatory program rather than an agreement between arms-length contracting parties, a Medicare provider agreement may be transferred with the rest of a debtor provider's assets unencumbered by any HHS claim for reimbursement of past overpayments made to the debtor. Such protection is consistent not only with the noncontractual nature of the provider agreement but also with the policies underlying the Bankruptcy Code and the Medicare program as well.

Christopher W. Frost. "Healthcare Financing in Bankruptcy: Sales or Liens? Where You Stand Depends on Where You Sit." *California Bankruptcy Journal*, 1998, *24*, 185.

Examines the intersection of the growing trend of asset securitization and the anti-assignment provisions of the Social Security Act of 1972, the Medicare/Medicaid Antifraud Act of 1977, and state statutes enacted in response to these acts. These provisions prohibit paying Medicare and Medicaid reimbursement to any person other than the provider. Although some courts have held that these provisions do not preclude granting a security interest in the accounts, the courts have not addressed the effect of the anti-assignment rules in the context of an asset securitization transaction. In addition, the complexity of Medicare payment rules coupled with the Department of Health and Human Services' rights of set-off and recoupment create a serious risk that participants in securitizations and lenders with security interests in receivables will see a substantial erosion of the value of the receivables they have financed.

Robert A. Klyman. "Bankruptcy Opportunities and Pitfalls in the Healthcare Arena." Washington, D.C.: American Health Lawyers Association [Report No. VHL 99–0018], 1999, 53 pages.

Briefly examines and explains the bankruptcy process, its applicability to an integrated delivery system, and strategies for dealing with the process. Discusses the impact of bankruptcy on board members and shareholders. Includes practice tips for providers in anticipation of and during an integrated delivery system bankruptcy. Includes substantial endnotes citing relevant case law and articles.

Samuel R. Maizel and Judith A. Waltz. "Injunctive Relief in Health Care Insolvencies." *California Bankruptcy Journal*, 1998, *24*, 215.

In most bankruptcy cases, when the debtor has a need for cash following the petition, it can obtain postpetition financing. However, where the government is the debtor's largest (or only) source of funds for services rendered, such financing is likely to be unavailable unless continued payments from the government are ensured. After the government threatens continuity of payments, the debtor has to take immediate steps to remedy the situation. This usually takes the form of a demand for injunctive relief, seeking to compel the government to continue paying for postpetition services. In other cases, the injunctive relief may seek to forestall termination of Medicare or Medicaid contracts. This article discusses the arguments for and against injunctive relief in health care insolvencies.

Gary W. Marsh (ed.). "Health Care Insolvency Manual: The Basics of Business Bankruptcy for the Health Care Professional and the Basics of Health Care Law for the Bankruptcy Professional." Washington, D.C.: American Bankruptcy Institute, 1997, 80 pages.

Topics examined in this resource include health care providers' eligibility for bankruptcy; leases, executory contracts, and other agreements; treatment of provider agreements in bankruptcy; acquisition of financially distressed health care providers; health care financing; fraud and abuse; and treatment of Medicare and Medicaid disputes. Health care bankruptcy cases raise many unique issues, often stemming from the role of the state and federal government in subsidizing and regulating the health care process, the role of private insurance companies, and the public interests served by the health care industry. A product of the ABI's Health Care Insolvency Committee, this publication is addressed to bankruptcy and health care attorneys, workout officers, health care management and finance professionals, health care lenders, and buyers and owners of health care businesses. The text concludes with a glossary of health care terms and a glossary of bankruptcy terms.

Allison Overbay and Mark A. Hall. "Insurance Regulation of Providers That Bear Risk." *American Journal of Law and Medicine*, 1996, 22(23), 361–387.

Explores whether risk-bearing provider groups (RBPGs) should be regulated by the financial accounting standards governing traditional insurers and HMOs or by a unique set of standards. RBPGs pose a significant potential for financial insolvency that could leave subscribers without a source of medical care. This article first outlines the competing interests in consumer protection and market restructuring and articulates the conflicting positions of insurers and providers. After examining whether RBPGs should be regulated as insurers or HMOs, the authors describe and advocate an approach being developed by the National Association of Insurance Commissioners.

Michael W. Peregrine. "Workouts." Washington, D.C.: American Health Lawyers Association [Report No. VMAT98–0002], 1998, 27 pages.

The process by which an investment is converted to stronger fiscal underpinnings is known as a reorganization or workout. This paper examines tax exemption and fraud and abuse laws that have a direct bearing on the structure of a workout and identifies typical workout vehicles (for example, corporate or security vehicles and bankruptcy). Includes several charts illustrating some types of workout.

Elizabeth Swinton Schoen and Christopher Posey. "Health Care Corporate Compliance Considerations in the Bankruptcy Arena: What Debtors and Purchasers Need to Know." *California Bankruptcy Journal*, 1998, 24, 279.

In a bankruptcy context, as federal and state scrutiny of the health care industry increases, it is essential for debtors and purchasers to recognize the complex corporate compliance issues in a Chapter 11 reorganization. This article explores some of those issues, which are an evolving area of the law. It also discusses corporate compliance from the perspectives of the government and the health care industry and reconciles the two in the context of bankruptcy. It focuses on why and how compliance issues play a role in bankruptcy, both before and after petition.

Jonathan E. Tesar and Thomas A. Willoughby. "Dealing with the Financially Troubled Long-Term Care Facility." Washington, D.C.: American Health Lawyers Association [Report No. VLT98–0035], 1998, 55 pages.

Outlines basic creditors' and debtors' rights, and remedies that arise under state commercial and creditors' rights laws and the federal Bankruptcy Code, as well as some of the unique issues that arise when the creditor in question is the HCFA, which administers the Medicare program and the federal portion of the state Medicaid program. Attachment includes a trustee/receiver checklist for a health care facility.

Stephen H. Warren and William M. Sage. "Feasting in a Flak Jacket: Bankruptcy Risks and Opportunities for Solvent Health Care Organizations." In Alice G. Gosfield (ed.), *Health Law Handbook*. St. Paul, Minn.: West, 1998. (Formerly published by Clark, Boardman, Callaghan in earlier editions.)

This article highlights important issues presented by federal bankruptcy and state insolvency laws for health care organizations. These include key risks created by bankruptcy law when a managed care organization or other health care business fails, as well as possible countermeasures available to surviving companies and executives. In addition, the article seeks to help health care lawyers understand the potential for using bankruptcy law to further strategic business objectives.

P. K. Webster. "The Malpractice of Health Care Bankruptcy Reform." *Loyola (Los Angeles) Law Review*, 1999, *32*, 1045.

Concludes that health care cases should not be subject to special bankruptcy restrictions.

9.02 HOSPITALS

[Reserved]

9.03 MANAGED CARE ORGANIZATIONS

Joseph C. Branch and Kevin G. Fitzgerald. "HMO Insolvency: Implications of the Maxicare Decisions." *Tort and Insurance Law Journal*, 1990, *25, 766.*

Discusses the bankruptcy of the Maxicare chain of HMOs; compares rehabilitation or liquidation of an HMO under the Bankruptcy Code and pursuant to state insurance company insolvency laws.

Howard A. Burde. "Allegheny: What Happened and Why." Washington, D.C.: American Health Lawyers Association [Report No. VHL99–0027], 1999, 31 pages.

Detailed outline examines the history of the Allegheny Health, Education, and Research Foundation (AHERF) bankruptcy, including a detailed time line of events and the legal effect on the providers, facilities, and institutions involved in the bankruptcy. Discusses the legal issues involved in the bankruptcy, including fiduciary responsibility, securities and tax issues, and charitable reporting.

Lawton R. Burns and others. "The Allegheny System Debacle." *Health Affairs*, 2000, *19, 7.*

The $1.3 billion bankruptcy of AHERF in July 1998 was the nation's largest nonprofit health care failure. Many actors and factors were responsible for AHERF's demise. The system embarked on an ambitious strategy of horizontal and vertical integration just as reimbursement from major payers dramatically contracted, leaving AHERF overly exposed. Hospital and physician acquisitions increased the system's debt and competed for capital, which sapped the stronger institutions and led to massive internal cash transfers. Management failed to exercise due diligence in many of these acquisitions. Several external oversight mechanisms, ranging from AHERF's board to its accountants and auditors to the bond market, also failed to protect these community assets.

Jon B. Christianson and others. "State Responses to HMO Failures." *Health Affairs*, Winter 1991, 78–92.

Focuses on several policy issues relating to state-level HMO regulation. Does the frequency of HMO failures justify increased regulatory attention? Are the added costs that generally accompany HMO regulations justified, or will they negate the cost-savings advantages that HMOs offer? After examining in detail one HMO failure, the authors discuss the frequency of HMO failures and the evolution of state regulation. They conclude that additional research is necessary to determine whether existing regulations have attained their stated purposes before implementing further regulation.

Steven H. Felderstein and Cary M. Adams. "Bankruptcy and Financial Distress for Managed Care Organizations." Washington, D.C.: American Health Lawyers Association [Report No. MC97–0039], 1997, 50 pages.

Outlines creditors' rights and bankruptcy procedures, with an emphasis on cases involving insolvent managed care organizations and health care providers.

Gayle L. Holland. "Health Maintenance Organizations: Member Physicians Assuming the Risk of Loss under State and Federal Bankruptcy Laws." *Journal of Legal Medicine*, 1994, *15*, 445.

Highlights the controversy that exists over whether an HMO is entitled to federal bankruptcy protection. Historically, insurance companies have been regulated and liquidated under state law. State insurance regulators argue that HMOs cannot seek protection under federal law because they contain the same characteristics as insurance companies. HMOs, by contrast, contend that they are substantially different from insurance companies. After analyzing the pertinent case law, the author concludes that through adoption of the Uniform Insurers Liquidation Act, a majority of the states have created an equitable system of distribution of assets across state lines. State liquidation in the hands of a third-party conservator, Holland finds, is superior to bankruptcy court liquidation.

Jay M. Howard. "The Aftermath of HMO Insolvency: Considerations for Providers." *Annals of Health Law*, 1995, *4*, 87.

Discusses key issues surrounding federal bankruptcy protection for HMOs. As health care markets have become more competitive and managed care systems are forced to become more efficient, some HMOs will face insolvency. However, an HMO that petitions for federal bankruptcy protection faces dismissal based on the Bankruptcy Code's procedural exclusion for domestic insurance companies.

The author points out that courts have erratically applied the "state classification," "independent classification," and "alternative relief" tests to determine whether an entity is excluded from bankruptcy protection under the Bankruptcy Code (§ 109(b)(2)). In *Estate of Medcare HMO*, 998 F.2d 436 (7th Cir. 1993), the court proposed that the state classification test is controlling. In states where the statutory and regulatory classification is ambiguous, however, this analysis will not produce consistent conclusions. Additionally, in multistate insolvencies, it remains a practical truth that state law classifications may yield inefficient and disparate treatment of claims. Finally, it is not clear that Congress intended to delegate discretion to the states to control which entities will receive federal bankruptcy protection. The author concludes that as courts increasingly confront insolvencies of alternate delivery systems that eviscerate traditional insurance and HMO concept distinctions, the state classification test will likely prove inadequate.

Robert A. Klyman. "Bankruptcy Opportunities and Pitfalls: Strategies for Restructuring and Unwinding Integrated Delivery Systems." *Journal of Health Law*, Fall 1998, *31*, 163.

Many organizations in the health care field are facing issues regarding the dis-integration of previously assembled integrated delivery systems. In many situations, bankruptcy is the most effective means for pursuing this course of action. This article examines and explains the bankruptcy process, its applicability to an IDS, and strategies for dealing with the process.

Robert A. Klyman. "Disintegrating the Integrated Health System." Washington, D.C.: American Health Lawyers Association [Report No. VHL98–0025], 1998, 48 pages.

Examines activities around the country with regard to restructuring and reconfiguration of integrated health delivery systems or integrated health organizations (IHOs) and related unwinding issues. Provides a general bankruptcy overview, benefits of a bankruptcy unwind, impact of IHO bankruptcy on a hospital, strategies for doctors in anticipation of and during IHO bankruptcy, consideration of the IHO as a limited liability company, and prepackaged bankruptcy as an expedited strategy for unwinding an IHO.

James A Lebovitz. "Bankruptcy and the PPMC: Legal, Practical and Operational Issues." Washington, D.C.: American Health Lawyers Association [Report No. VPH99–0021], 1999, 14 pages.

Reviews the operations of physician practice management companies and developments in the PPMC industry. Also discusses general bankruptcy principles and their application to payers, providers, regulators, and patients in the bankruptcy context.

Samuel R. Maizel. "Bankruptcy's Impact on Healthcare Fraud Issues." Washington, D.C.: American Health Lawyers Association [Report No. FA97–0035], 1997, 53 pages.

Examines how the availability of bankruptcy court protection alters the normal relationship between health care providers and the government in health care fraud cases. It discusses the rights of providers facing exclusions or suspensions for fraud or collection of overpayments, and injunctive relief in bankruptcy.

Barry S. Scheur and others. "Bankruptcy and Rehabilitation." In Douglas A. Hastings and others (eds.), *The Insider's Guide to Managed Care: A Legal and Operational Roadmap.* Washington, D.C.: American Health Lawyers Association, 1990.

This thirty-page article first examines the state receivership statutes under which a state insurance department may take control of the assets of an HMO and attempt to bring it to a healthier financial condition or liquidate it. Under this rubric, the authors point out specific danger signals of impairment and examine the operational mechanics of rehabilitation. The authors, four practicing health care attorneys, then review the legal and operational aspects of bankruptcy and the circumstances under which an HMO may be an eligible debtor in a Chapter 11 proceeding. The discussion includes analysis of existing case law, followed by helpful appendices.

Brett A. Schlossberg. "The Bankruptcy of the Allegheny Health System and Its Consequences." *Journal of Health Law,* Winter 1999, *32*, 155.

In the midst of the health care consolidation of the past decade, many have overlooked the inevitable: some of the consolidated systems are bound to fail. This commentary provides the reader with a close look at the rapid decline of one such system, the Allegheny Health System, and how that failure, the "rescue" of the system's facilities, and the system's ongoing bankruptcy have affected delivery of health care in the Philadelphia area.

Michael O. Spivey and Jeffrey G. Miklos. "Developing Provider-Sponsored Organization Solvency Standards Through Negotiated Rulemaking." *Administrative Law Review,* 1999, *55*, 261.

Discusses negotiated rule making in the context of PSO solvency rule making. The authors conclude that negotiated rule making in this case brought valuable technical expertise to HHS in a forum where such expertise could be efficiently and productively used, resulting in a rule that does no damage to the public interest.

Carol Steven. "Will More Blue Plans Break Down?" *Medical Economics,* 1991, *68*, 127.

In 1990, Blue Cross and Blue Shield of West Virginia was the first Blues plan to go bankrupt, leaving patients, doctors, and hospitals with $53 million in unpaid claims. This article examines the filing and resulting litigation.

Health Care Planning

Health care planning is a regulatory, as opposed to competitive, approach to allocating health care costs. Health care planning statutes require government approval of capital expenditures and modifications in the content and scope of services.[1] The federal government's first major foray into health planning was the Hospital Survey and Construction Act (the Hill-Burton Act), passed in 1946, which distributed health care funds according to population and need.[2] As governments at all levels became significant payers in the 1960s and 1970s through such programs as Medicare and Medicaid, they sought a direct means of ensuring that allocation of health care resources was consistent with the health care needs of the population and governmental budget limitations. This approach was compatible with the redistributionist economic views that animated all of the Great Society programs, along with those that followed well into the Nixon, Ford, and Carter administrations.

With the enactment of the National Health Planning and Resources Development Act of 1974 (the Health Planning Act)[3] and creation of reimbursement controls on capital expenditures, Congress adopted a regulatory approach to allocating health care resources and containing health care costs. This statute was consonant with the efforts of numerous state governments that had adopted strict controls on capital costs through certificate-of-need programs and regulatory limitations on operating expenses.[4] In essence, the federal legislation established the framework within which participating states must regulate health resources. Its goals were (1) to provide the population with access to health care, (2) to contain health care costs, and (3) to ensure the quality of health care.[5]

The Health Planning Act did not, however, prove to be a durable solution to the problem of escalating costs. Hospitals and other providers that chafed under the requirements of the Health Planning Act found a receptive ear in the Reagan administration and the Republican-dominated Congress, which repealed the Health Planning Act in 1986.[6] Despite the repeal of the Health Planning Act, a number of states continue to have planning laws that follow the now-defunct federal model. Other states have developed modified regulatory approaches to controlling and allocating health care resources, while others have eliminated their health planning laws altogether.

The annotations that follow examine the merits of the regulatory and competitive approaches to allocating health care resources. They also analyze particular state statutes and their effectiveness.

The National Health Planning Act

Until Congress repealed it in 1986, the National Health Planning and Resources Development Act of 1974 (the Health Planning Act)[7] provided an elaborate system of health care economic regulation involving interaction at the federal, state, and local levels. The Health Planning Act was predicated on the idea that competition would not allocate health care resources efficiently, and thus "command-and-control" regulation of entry into markets was necessary to prevent further overinvestment and maldistribution of resources in institutional health care sector industries, especially the hospital industry. By focusing primarily on regulating the supply of resources devoted to health care, the Health Planning Act was supposed to lower health care costs by preventing and eliminating duplicative and unnecessary, but costly, institutional facilities and services.[8]

The keystone of the Health Planning Act was the strong financial incentives it provided states to adopt certificate-of-need (CON) programs under which certain levels of capital investment and addition of institutional services had to be approved by the state before implementation. In addition, the act encouraged cooperative efforts among area health care providers and local health planning agencies to implement plans to reduce already existing facilities. Not infrequently, these led to understandings among competitors about the services each would offer.

Notwithstanding that the Health Planning Act was repealed in 1986, its effects are still felt. The CON laws of many states remain in effect, although often in a loosened form compared to their predecessors. The Health Planning Act did not dry up excess capacity, which seems to be decreasing today through hospital mergers and closures. Indeed, cost-based reimbursement and health planning (in addition to the Hill-Burton Act, which financed hospital expansion after World War II) were probably the two largest contributors to the excess capacity in the hospital industry existing today.

The repeal of the Health Planning Act together with prospective payment reimbursement methodologies and the growth of managed care have deregulated the hospital industry to a significant extent and have forced a competitive environment. Regulation often results in excess capacity, which then must be dissipated over time after deregulation through competition, and this appears to be occurring in the hospital industry today.[9]

The health planning environment was one of cooperation among competitors and thus fraught with potential antitrust problems. Practices that seemed permissible—even encouraged—in the environment of health planning are strictly taboo under antitrust laws. Thus, health care industries, especially the hospital industry, had to readjust basic thinking almost 180 degrees and formulate business strategies in an environment somewhat foreign to them. This adjustment process has not been easy and continues today, as hospitals see the antitrust laws applied to their activities and learn to live with them.[10]

References and Notes

1. Michael G. Macdonald and others. *Health Care Law: A Practical Guide.* New York: Matthew Bender, 1997, § 8.1.
2. 42 U.S.C. § 291 (1982).
3. Pub. L. 93–641, 42 U.S.C. §§ 300k-300t.
4. Macdonald and others (1997).
5. Macdonald and others (1997).
6. 42 U.S.C. §§ 11001 *et seq.,* Pub. L. 99–660 § 701 (enacted Nov. 14, 1986).
7. Pub. L. 93–641, 88 Stat. 2225 (1975) (codified at 42 U.S.C. §§ 300k-300n-5), repealed by Pub. L. 99–660, § 701, 100 Stat. 3799 (1986).
8. John J. Miles. *Health Care and Antitrust Law: Principles and Practice.* St. Paul, Minn.: West Group, 1998, § 16.1.
9. Miles (1998).
10. "Any antitrust enforcer will tell you that industries undergoing significant change are always good sources of enforcement business, because some in those industries are always intent on maintaining the old ways." Charles A. James, deputy assistant attorney general, Antitrust Division. "Antitrust in the Health Care Field." Text of remarks before the National Health Lawyers Association, Jan. 31, 1992; Appendix E20.

ANNOTATIONS

10.01   THE NATIONAL HEALTH PLANNING ACT

Richard G. McAlee and Dina L. Michels. "Rate Regulation." In Mark A. Hall (gen. ed.), *Health Care Corporate Law: Financing and Liability.* Boston: Little, Brown, 1994.

Examines the history and purpose of rate regulation along with its most common structures, including regulation methodologies. This sixty-one-page chapter, written by practicing attorneys in Baltimore, concludes with case studies of rate regulation in Connecticut, Florida, Maine, Maryland, Massachusetts, New Jersey, and New York.

10.02 PLANNING ACTIVITIES

Annot. "Validity and Construction of Statutes Requiring Establishment of 'Need' as a Precondition to the Operation of Hospitals or Other Facilities for the Care of Sick People." *ALR3rd,* 1998, *61,* 278.

Collects those reported cases in which a court has been called upon to construe or determine the validity of statutory provisions requiring, as a prerequisite to operating a hospital or other facility for the care of ill persons, that there be established to the satisfaction of the appropriate authority the existence of a "need" for the facility in question. This annotation is regularly updated by the publisher.

Ellen S. Campbell and Gary M. Fournier. "Certificate-of-Need Deregulation and Indigent Hospital Care." *Journal of Health Politics, Policy and Law,* 1993, *18,* 905.

Since they were implemented in the early 1970s, certificate-of-need laws and regulations have served as the regulatory lever of choice to protect existing hospitals from unrestricted competition in services. In essence, these regulations have sought to control hospital costs by intervening in investment decisions by hospitals that would create buildup of excessive patient service capacity. Although the explicit purpose of CON regulation was to prevent hospitals from duplicating services and investing in unnecessary beds and equipment, it has been unsuccessful in accomplishing this goal, and its failure has been amply documented in several studies. However, the authors suggest that CON policies have also been pursued with the implicit aim of "cross-subsidization"; that is, regulators have used their power to issue licenses and restrict competition in order to create a powerful incentive for hospitals to provide high levels of care to the indigent population. Posner (1971) noted that to achieve cross-subsidization, entry into specific, lucrative services must be restricted. The authors present evidence that CON licenses have been used to promote internal subsidization of indigent care in probit analysis, based on data from Florida spanning the period of 1983 to 1989. Although this method of financing indigent care may be preferred by legislators who do not want to face the political consequences of raising taxes to pay for the service, it has troubling implications for hospital provision of indigent care, especially in an era of CON deregulation. The authors conclude that promotion of indigent care was hidden from the public's scrutiny and that, in a more competitive environment, the feasibility of cross-subsidization is substantially weakened. The authors elaborate on how the incentive for hospitals to provide indigent care will be compromised in the deregulated marketplace for medical services that appears on the horizon for the 1990s and into the next century.

Christopher J. Conover and Frank A. Sloan. "Does Removing Certificate of Need Regulations Lead to a Surge in Health Care Spending?" *Journal of Health Politics, Policy and Law,* June 1998, *23,* 455.

This study assesses the impact of certificate of need regulation for hospitals on various measures of health spending per capita, hospital supply, diffusion of technology, and hospital industry organization. Using a time-series, cross-sectional methodology, the authors estimate the net impact of CON policies on costs, supply, technology diffusion, and industry organization, controlling for area characteristics, the presence of other forms of regulation (such as hospital rate setting), and competition. Mature CON programs are associated with only a modest (5 percent) long-term reduction in acute care spending per capita, but now with a significant reduction in total per capita spending. They find that there is no evidence of a surge in acquisition of facilities or in costs following removal of CON regulations. They report also that mature CON programs also result in a slight (2 percent) reduction in bed supply but higher costs per day and per admission, along with higher hospital profits. CON regulations generally have no detectable effect on diffusion of various hospital-based technologies. The authors conclude that it is doubtful CON regulations have had much effect on quality of care, positive or negative. Such regulations may have improved access, but there is little empirical evidence to document this, they find.

Elena Salerno Flash, Hillary T. Fraser, and Sally T. True. "Certificate of Need Regulation." In Mark A. Hall (gen. ed.), *Health Care Corporate Law: Formation and Regulation.* Boston: Little, Brown, 1993.

Discusses approvals that a health care facility must obtain prior to purchasing major equipment, undertaking construction of or renovating physical plants, or offering new health-related services. State health planning agencies issue CONs pursuant to a state statutory scheme patterned after a now-defunct federal statute. Despite repeal in some states, CON regulation will continue to be a major factor in health planning for the foreseeable future and, the authors contend, may even become more rigorous as the nation gropes for a more effective means to control health care spending than the market-oriented thinking that dominated public policy discussions during the 1980s.

Topics addressed in this 119-page article include facilities that are covered, expenditure thresholds, coverage of outpatient facilities, HMOs, the criteria for determining need, and qualitative and judicial review. The text is supplemented by a helpful appendix setting forth a state-by-state compendium of requirements.

Robert B. Hackey. "New Wine in Old Bottles: Certificate of Need Enters the 1990s." *Journal of Health Politics, Policy and Law,* 1993, *18,* 927.

Contends that although state CON programs have been the subject of intense criticism over the past decade, evidence suggests that CON programs may be more effective than commonly believed. Many state programs have yielded disappointing results, but the CON process can also be used to achieve other important policy objectives, such as increasing access to care for the uninsured and increasing lay participation in health policy planning, the author argues. In sum, rather than fading away after federal support for health planning was terminated in 1986, state CON programs are poised to assume new roles during the 1990s.

Mark E. Kaplan. "An Economic Analysis of Florida's Hospital Certificate of Need Program and Recommendations for Change." (Comment.) *Florida State University Law Review,* 1991, *19, 475.*

The certificate-of-need program, as initially conceived and implemented at the time this article was written, has as its goals containing costs and ensuring adequate indigent care. The first goal has not been achieved, while the second has not been efficiently or adequately achieved, in the author's view. Kaplan contends that the state should abandon its CON program as a tool of cost containment. By giving indigent care providers the property rights to exercise or sell CONs, and by permitting continued free transfer of CONs, market forces will help determine how best to provide compensation for providers of indigent care, he concludes.

Scott D. Makar. "Antitrust Immunity under Florida's Certificate of Need Programs." *Florida State University Law Review,* 1991, *19,* 149.

Antitrust concerns may arise when health care companies that compete for certificates of need enter into agreements among themselves that limit such competition. A critical issue is whether Florida's certificate-of-need program immunizes such agreements from application of the federal and state antitrust laws under the state action doctrine or the First Amendment Noerr-Pennington doctrine. This article concludes that Florida's CON program satisfies the state action immunity test only for particular types of state-authorized and state-controlled conduct, thereby subjecting certain other unauthorized anticompetition agreements to antitrust liability. First Amendment petition clause immunity under the Noerr-Pennington doctrine, however, is much broader than state action immunity and may be available for legitimate "petitioning" activities in legislative, administrative, and judicial forums.

Patrick John McGinley. "Beyond Health Care Reform: Reconsidering Certificate of Need Laws in a 'Managed Competition' System." (Comment.) *Florida State University Law Review*, 1995, *23*, 143.

Provides a detailed history of federal and state CON laws and the conditions that led to their enactment (and, in the case of the federal statute, to repeal). McGinley notes that CON laws remain in effect in more than thirty states. CON, he argues, has historically failed to control health care costs; perpetuating CON statutes threatens the likelihood that managed care will succeed in controlling health care costs.

Thaddeus J. Nodzenski. "Regulating Managed Care Coverage: A New Direction for Health-Planning Agencies." *Annals of Health Law*, 1998, *7*, 1.

This article focuses on the role of health planning agencies in the context of managed care. The author argues that health planning agencies can be redirected toward assessment of managed care plans. Planning entities can be used to evaluate the viability of managed care markets taking into account societal, financial, and medical considerations.

Regulation of Private Health Care Financing

Although a range of federal statutes affects medical insurance, none has so pervasive an influence as the Employee Retirement Income Security Act of 1974, as amended (ERISA).[1] This complex statute was enacted following the bankruptcy of the Studebaker automobile company, which left thousands of workers without their pensions. ERISA regulates most employer-sponsored employee benefit plans. It affects the nature, design, and administration of such plans. In addition, it will determine which state laws can be applied to such products, as well as what legal challenges can be made to administering those products.[2]

A plan maintained by a nongovernmental employer that provides health care or health care benefits to employees generally constitutes an employee benefit plan subject to ERISA. These plans must meet the reporting, documentation, and disclosure requirements set forth in ERISA. The U.S. Department of Labor prescribes the specific items of information that must be disclosed to covered employees in a booklet known as a summary plan description.[3]

ERISA broadly preempts all state law and state law causes of action that relate to ERISA plans.[4] Although specific exemptions exist for state laws that regulate insurance, ERISA's preemptive scope provides plan sponsors with great flexibility regarding design of their benefit programs, because ERISA generally will preempt state law attempts to regulate the terms and conditions of ERISA plans.[5]

References and Notes

1. 29 U.S.C. §§ 1001 *et seq.*
2. Jacqueline M. Saue and Gregg H. Dooge. "ERISA and Managed Care." In Peter R. Kongstvedt (ed.), *The Managed Health Care Handbook,* (3rd ed.). Gaithersburg, Md.: Aspen, 1996; see also "The Employee Retirement Income Security Act of 1974 ('ERISA') and Its Impact on Liability Exposures." In Christopher Kearns and others, *Health Care Liability Deskbook.* Deerfield, Ill.: Clark, Boardman, Callaghan, 1996.
3. 29 U.S.C. § 1022, 29 C.F.R. § 2520.104(b)-2.
4. 29 U.S.C. § 1144.
5. Saue and Dooge (1996), p. 946. See generally American Bar Association Section of Labor and Employment Law. *Employee Benefits Law.* (2nd ed. with 2000 supplement.) Washington, D.C.: BNA Books.

ANNOTATIONS

Edward J. Krill. "Legal Issues Affecting Health and Disability Coverage by Employers." *Health Lawyer,* Early Spring 1996, *8,* 16.

Sets forth specific circumstances under which an employer can face liability for providing misleading advice to its employees regarding future health and other employment benefits on grounds that the employer is serving as a plan fiduciary.

11.01   REGULATION OF PRIVATE INSURANCE

Annot. "What Services, Equipment or Supplies are 'Medically Necessary' for Purposes of Coverage under Medical Insurance?" *ALR4th*, 1990, *75*, 763.

Collects and analyzes the cases in which the courts have considered what treatment, services, equipment, or supplies are "medically necessary" or the equivalent, or, conversely, whether such services or equipment are excluded from coverage as "not necessary" or "unnecessary" medically, for purposes of coverage under medical insurance other than that provided under governmental entitlement programs.

Bryan Ford. "The Uncertain Case for Market Pricing of Health Insurance." *Boston University L. Review*, 1994, *74*, 109.

Explores some of the dysfunctional effects that arise from the inherent conflicts between market-based health insurance and Blue Cross and Blue Shield plans that ensure collective payment of medical costs. Ford considers why and in what sense competition in health insurance must be managed if it is to contribute to, and not corrode, quality of life. To that end, the essay (1) reviews the origins of the current health insurance system, (2) describes a simple model for pricing insurance in a properly functioning market, (3) explores the dynamics of the market for health insurance over time, (4) contrasts the results of market forces with the underlying goal of ensuring payment for health care, and (5) suggests changes to the health insurance system that might price health care coverage in the manner needed by American consumers.

I. M. Golub and Cynthia M. Combe. *COBRA Handbook.* (3rd ed.) Brookfield, Wis.: International Foundation of Employee Benefit Plans, 1997, 712 pages.

Complex requirements and conflicting court decisions have made COBRA one of the most significant statutes in the employee benefits area. This guidebook is written for benefits attorneys, plan administrators, and human resource personnel.

Health Insurance Association of America. *Fundamentals of Health Insurance: Part A.* Annapolis, Md.: Health Insurance Association of America, 1997, 257 pages.

The first of a two-volume set, this modestly priced book introduces the basic concepts underlying group and individual health insurance, both the technical and socioeconomic aspects. Topics include an overview of the industry, the coverage it provides, and the insurance contract.

Health Insurance Association of America. *Fundamentals of Health Insurance: Part B.* Annapolis, Md.: Health Insurance Association of America, 1997, 273 pages.

The second of a two-volume set, this modestly priced book examines such topics as health care cost management, claims administration, product pricing, fraud and abuse, and other subjects.

Health Insurance Association of America. *Health Insurance Terminology: A Glossary of Health Insurance Terms.* Annapolis, Md.: Health Insurance Association of America, 1992, 111 pages.

Provides a compilation of working definitions of important industry terms. This extensive glossary is primarily an edited compilation and synthesis of the glossaries and key terms appearing in the textbooks of HIAA's Insurance Education Program.

Health Insurance Association of America. *Long-Term Care: Knowing the Risk, Paying the Price.* Annapolis, Md.: Health Insurance Association of America, 1997, 248 pages.

Analyzes the fundamentals of long-term care insurance: what it is, who needs it, who provides it, and traditional ways of financing it.

Health Insurance Association of America. *Medical Expense Insurance.* Annapolis, Md.: Health Insurance Association of America, 1997, 309 pages.

Discusses issues related to coverage that reimburses policyholders for medical expenses. It also addresses various group and individual policies available, benefits payable, and reimbursement issues.

Health Insurance Association of America. *Source Book of Health Insurance Data.* Annapolis, Md.: Health Insurance Association of America, 1996, 211 pages.

Examines the history and role of health insurance, comprehensive statistics on health insurance (including managed care), public health care coverage (enrollment and expenditures), national medical care costs, utilization of health services, and disability. It includes a glossary and list of acronyms.

Health Insurance Association of America. *Supplemental Health Insurance* Annapolis, Md.: Health Insurance Association of America, 1998.

This modestly priced text explores administration of supplemental coverages such as vision, dental, and specified disease and cancer insurance; Medicare supplement; and hospital indemnity insurance.

International Foundation of Employee Benefit Plans. *Employee Benefit Plans: A Glossary of Terms.* (8th ed.) Brookfield, Wis.: IFEBP, 1993, 202 pages.

Covers all aspects of employee benefit terminology for the United States and Canada. It defines more than three thousand terms in such areas as actuarial science, employee benefits testing, government regulations and legislation, health care and health care cost-containment strategies, insurance, business law, and labor relations. Particularly helpful is a list of almost nine hundred acronyms and abbreviations covering a range of benefits-related topics.

Eleanor D. Kinney and Suzanne K. Steinmetz. "Notes from the Insurance Underground: How the Chronically Ill Cope." *Journal of Health Politics, Policy and Law,* 1994, 19, 633.

Describes the experience of individuals with multiple sclerosis (MS) in Indiana in getting and keeping private health insurance. The report presents the findings of a telephone survey of individuals with MS in Indiana. Survey respondents were generally able to obtain health insurance through the Medicare program or employer-based private health insurance plans, but many experienced formidable barriers to adequate and affordable health insurance, such as preexisting exclusions, cancellations, high premiums, and coinsurance. Respondents adopted a variety of strategies to keep private health insurance, including selectivity in submitting claims, which worked to reduce their health insurance coverage. The authors write that their findings raise two crucial questions: To what extent are the chronically ill forced to take extraordinary measures to get and keep health insurance? To what extent do insurer practices in pricing insurance and determining coverage of benefits actually make health insurance even more inadequate and unaffordable for the chronically ill? These two questions are critical in understanding the full dimensions of the health insurance crisis in the United States today, they write.

Margaret E. Lynch (ed.). *Health Insurance.* Washington, D.C.: Health Insurance Association of America, 1992, 112 pages.

Defines many of the most frequently used terms in the health insurance industry. Written primarily for the nonspecialist.

National Association of Insurance Commissioners. *Compendium of State Laws on Insurance Topics.* Kansas City, Mo.: NAIC, 1998.

Gives researchers the most current and comprehensive compilation of legislative and regulatory data available. When completed, the series will comprise more than two hundred charts setting forth clear, concise information, updated quarterly, in indexed, loose-leaf binders.

National Association of Insurance Commissioners. *Federalism and Insurance Regulation.* Kansas City, Mo.: NAIC, 1995.

This casebook examines how U.S. insurance regulation is structured. It includes a historical overview of the development of insurance regulation and the extent to which the courts have qualified and limited the powers of the states in interpreting the text of the McCarran-Ferguson Act.

National Association of Insurance Commissioners. *Insurance Department Directory.* Kansas City, Mo.: NAIC, 1998, 200 pages.

Lists the fifty-five insurance departments that make up the NAIC. Compiled in binder form, this publication identifies and provides contact information about each department and commissioner. It also includes key department personnel, titles, and phone numbers. Updated twice annually.

National Association of Insurance Commissioners. *Insurance Department Resources Report.* Kansas City, Mo.: NAIC, 1998, 64 pages.

Provides an in-depth look at the resources of each of the fifty-five NAIC insurance departments. This state-by-state comparative analysis includes a variety of information and is updated twice annually.

National Association of Insurance Commissioners. *Interpretive Manual for Rating Compliance under NAIC Model Acts Concerning Small Employer Health Insurance.* Kansas City, Mo.: NAIC, 1998, 120 pages.

This manual attempts to assist states in their rate review activities and to provide guidance as to reasonable interpretations of the model act and regulation.

National Association of Insurance Commissioners. *Model Laws, Regulations and Guidelines.* Kansas City, Mo.: NAIC, 1998.

This loose-leaf service provides access to every NAIC model law, regulation, and guideline ever published. The models are coded and consolidated into four tabbed binders, including more than two thousand pages of regulatory information affecting almost all facets of the insurance business. In addition to the laws themselves, a legislative history explains why the model was adopted and why certain provisions were included. Special sections devoted to each state cite the enacted model or similar (or related) legislation and indicate whether it is pending or adopted. Case law annotations present court interpretations on major subjects covered by the NAIC model laws. This service provides quarterly updates.

National Association of Insurance Commissioners. *Omnibus Budget Reconciliation Act of 1990.* Kansas City, Mo.: NAIC, 1991, 118 pages.

A section containing answers to frequently asked questions about the effect of OBRA 1990 on state regulatory programs for Medicare supplement insurance makes this report particularly useful. Seven other sections offer analysis of the Medicare Supplement Insurance Minimum Standards Model Act and Regulation, a cross-referencing of OBRA 1990 to the NAIC Model Act and Regulation, a list of exclusions allowed by Medicare pertinent to Section 6 of the NAIC Model Regulation, sample disclosures for the outline of coverage, and sample replacement notices. A helpful list of contacts in state insurance regulatory departments is also included in this reference work.

Joshua M. Weiner, Laurel Hixon Illston, and Raymond J. Hanley. *Sharing the Burden: Strategies for Public and Private Long-Term Care Insurance.* Washington, D.C.: Brookings Institution, 1994.

This is valuable reading for those seeking to understand the effects of proposals for reforming the financing of long-term care.

11.02 THE EMPLOYEE RETIREMENT INCOME SECURITY ACT OF 1974 (ERISA)

Henry J. Aaron. *Serious and Unstable Condition: Financing America's Health Care.* Washington, D.C.: Brookings Institution, 1991, 158 pages.

This text is a well-argued guide to the U.S. health care debate.

Henry J. Aaron (ed.). *The Problem That Won't Go Away: Reforming U.S. Health Care Financing.* Washington, D.C.: Brookings Institution, 1996, 298 pages.

Provides a cogent analysis by a variety of health care specialists regarding the health care reform process.

Karla S. Bartholomew. "ERISA Preemption of Medical Malpractice Claims in Managed Care: Asserting a New Statutory Interpretation." (Note.) *Vanderbilt Law Review,* 1999, *52,* 1131.

Provides an overview of ERISA, including statutory text and structure, congressional intent, and legislative history. It explores the Supreme Court's attempts to define "employee welfare benefit plan" and its jurisprudence of ERISA preemption, from the earlier broad interpretation to the arguably narrower recent interpretation. It also explores the current division among lower courts in deciding ERISA preemption of medical malpractice claims, before developing an alternative interpretation of ERISA's employee welfare benefit plan that views an ERISA plan as the employer's administrative plan providing for employee health coverage.

Katherine Benesch. "The Evolution of Managed Care Liability: ERISA and Consumer Protection Laws." Washington, D.C.: American Health Lawyers Association [Report No. VMC98–0040], 1998, 25 pages.

Provides an overview of the principles of managed care liability and the key ERISA preemption arguments. Also discusses the types of claim preempted by ERISA and presents a detailed discussion of plaintiffs' claims for breach of fiduciary duty. Concludes with an outline of key ERISA preemption of provisions of consumer protection statutes and detailed discussion of the impact of *Corporate Health Ins., Inc.,* v. *Texas Dep't of Ins.*

Judith C. Bronstron. "The Conflict of Interest Standard in ERISA Cases: Can It Be Avoided in the Denial of High Dose Chemotherapy Treatment for Breast Cancer?" *DePaul Journal of Health Care Law,* 1999, *3.*

Examines the financial interest of insurance companies in denying claims for expensive and controversial treatments for chronic illness.

Jesselyn Alicia Brown. "ERISA and State Health Care Reform: Roadblock or Scapegoat?" *Yale Law and Policy Review,* 1995, *13,* 339.

A number of states have enacted health care reforms that are conditioned upon receiving an exemption from ERISA. The author argues that although amending ERISA on a case-by-case basis may have some advantages, it is possible for states to enact and implement a range of financing, cost-containment, and administrative strategies for health care reform without making any changes to ERISA. This is particularly true in light of the U.S. Supreme Court's decision in *New York State Conference of Blue Cross & Blue Shield Plans* v. *Travelers Ins. Co.*, 115 S. Ct. 1671 (1995), which the author analyzes in depth.

James R. Bruner. "AIDS and ERISA Preemption: The Double Threat." (Note.) *Duke Law Journal,* 1992, *41*, 1115.

Examines the Supreme Court's opinion in *FMC Corp.* v. *Holliday*, 111 S. Ct. 403 (1990), which solidified the legal distinction between the effect of ERISA preemption with respect to self-insured health plans and purchased health plans. The author contends that the distinction drawn by the Court and its corresponding result are not required by the language of ERISA or by the legislative history. Further, it creates an anomaly by leaving millions of Americans with no substantive health insurance law protection. Also, Bruner writes, Congress never intended to preempt state insurance law from covering the leading source of private insurance. Finally, because of employers' efforts to exploit this legislative void and circumvent state law through self-insuring, courts and Congress should restore the original effect and protection afforded by state regulation of health insurance.

L. Edward Bryan, Jr. "Responsibilities of Directors of Not-for-Profit Corporations Faced with Sharing Control with Other Nonprofit Organizations in Health Industry Affiliations: A Commentary on Legal and Practical Realities." *Annals of Health Law,* 1998, *7*, 139.

This article considers three sets of legal duties board members have when faced with proposed affiliations that both threaten and ensure substantial change in the way long-standing nonprofit community institutions will relate to and serve the public in the future. Topics discussed include ancillary contractual obligations, mandatory statutory procedural laws, conflict of interest, and duality of interest.

Patricia A. Butler. "Policy Implications of Recent ERISA Court Decisions." Washington, D.C.: National Governors Association, 1998, 32 pages.

A state's ability to oversee the development of health care systems is significantly hindered by ERISA. The federal courts are the major interpreters of ERISA's effects on state health policy. This report addresses ERISA implications for state authority to regulate managed care organizations by examining ERISA court cases and suggesting ways states can craft laws to minimize ERISA preemption.

L. Frank Coan, Jr. "You Can't Get There from Here: Questioning Erosion of ERISA Preemption in Medical Malpractice Actions against HMOs." *Georgia Law Review,* 1996, *30*, 1023–1060.

Congress enacted ERISA to provide comprehensive federal regulation over employer-provided benefit plans. A prescribed component of such plans is delivery of medical services. Today, HMOs stand as the dominant provider of such services. ERISA therefore represents a formidable shield by which HMOs can protect themselves from imposition of tort liability in cases concerning the quality of care that a plan member receives.

Courts that have addressed the question of preemption in the medical malpractice context reach divergent conclusions. More troubling than this split in views are the respective paths taken to reach these end points. Courts finding that ERISA preempts such state law actions have done so by way of an analysis that is no longer wholly consistent with Supreme Court jurisprudence, the author finds. Moreover, courts reaching the conclusion that medical malpractice claims escape preemption have either relied too much on apparent limitations of the act's preemption clause or simply ignored Supreme Court guidance and interpreted section 514 in their own particular manner.

To correct the situation, courts must look to the analytical framework that the Supreme Court has developed. In doing so, they will construe ERISA's preemption clause in a manner consistent with established precedent and congressional intent. Under this paradigm, medical malpractice claims brought against HMOs should escape preemption because they do not fall within section 514.

Torin A. Dorros and T. Howard Stone. "Implications of Negligent Selection and Retention of Physicians in the Age of ERISA." *American Journal of Law and Medicine,* 1995, *21,* 383.

Under ERISA, federal law regulates the management and administration of employee benefit plans. With few exceptions, ERISA also specifically preempts any state laws that "relate to" employee benefit plans. Guided by the U.S. Supreme Court's ruling in *New York State Conference of Blue Cross & Blue Shield Plans* v. *Travelers Ins. Co.,* 115 S. Ct. 1671 (1995), ERISA may operate to preempt state law claims for a managed care organization's negligent selection and retention of physicians where the MCO administers an employee benefit plan regulated by ERISA. Consequently, state law claims for negligent selection and retention against MCOs that manage or administer employee benefit plans may not have the same effect of promoting high-quality care among MCOs that such laws have had in promoting high-quality care among hospitals.

The Supreme Court's decision in *Travelers,* the authors contend, essentially validates the decisions of those lower courts finding that ERISA did not preempt state law claims for negligent selection and retention. The authors write that the absence of ERISA preemption of negligent selection and retention claims indicates that employee benefit plan members have an important means of ensuring access to remedies in the event their physician has been improperly investigated or evaluated for medical competence. Thus, as MCOs—which administer employee benefit plans—undertake the responsibility to credential physicians, it may be more likely that MCOs are held liable for negligent selection and retention of physicians whose conduct falls below the requisite standard of care.

Margaret G. Farrell. "ERISA Preemption and Regulation of Managed Health Care: The Case for Managed Federalism." *American Journal of Law and Medicine,* 1997, *23,* 251.

In this article, Farrell discusses the Supreme Court's interpretive approach in applying ERISA's preemption provision broadly and contends that the Court's textual analysis produces unforeseen, nonsensical results. Instead, she argues, the Court's interpretation of vague, express preemption provisions should be informed by basic constitutional principles of federalism. The author next examines and decries the consequences of the Court's literal interpretive approach for aspiring state and federal regulators. After criticizing the competence of courts to formulate national health policy in the absence of effective legislation, she concludes that only a comprehensive legislative scheme for "managed federalism"—shared federal and state legislative authority based on the functions each can perform effectively—can make order out of the current confusion.

Catherine L. Fisk. "The Last Article About the Language of ERISA Preemption? A Case Study of the Failure of Contextualism." *Harvard Journal on Legislation,* 1996, *23,* 35–103.

ERISA has been held to preempt an array of state statutes and common law, ranging from family leave programs to health care finance reforms. In this article, the author argues that the Supreme Court's misguided faith in textualist methods of interpreting ERISA's preemption provisions has produced doctrinal confusion and unintended public policy. Although she endorses the Court's move to a more pragmatic approach to ERISA preemption, Fisk's account of the developments of ERISA preemption doctrine helps to explain how textualist methods of statutory interpretation may have significant—and oftentimes unintended—effects on the development of law and public policy.

Lawrence O. Gostin and Alan I. Widiss. "What's Wrong with the ERISA Vacuum? Employers' Freedom to Limit Health Care Coverage Provided by Risk Retention Plans." *Journal of the American Medical Association,* 1993, *269,* 2527.

Examines *McGann* v. *H & H Music Co.,* 946 F.2d 401 (5th Cir. 1991), cert. denied sub nom. *Greenberg* v. *H & H Music Co.,* 113 S. Ct. 482 (1992). The article then uses the case to illustrate the limitations of ERISA and its effects on equitable access to health care coverage in the United States. The authors propose several legislative actions that would afford greater protection for those whose health care is currently provided by employer-sponsored plans: (1) vesting rights in health care benefits; (2) broadening antidiscrimination prohibitions; and (3) restoring the authority of states to regulate coverage features in employer risk retention plans.

Colleen Grogan. "Hope in Federalism? What Can the States Do and What Are They Likely to Do?" *Journal of Health Politics, Policy, and Law*, 1995, *20, 477.*

Although some states have passed major health care reform legislation, chances are slim that states will enact major system reforms, or reforms that guarantee access to health insurance to every person in the state. The states argue that ERISA prohibits them from regulating or taxing health plans of self-insured companies (which use their own assets, rather than policies, to pay employee medical claims) and presents the true barrier to health care reform. The author argues that ERISA is not the principal hurdle facing state governments, and lifting its provisions will probably not be the panacea that state governments portray it to be.

Devon P. Groves. "ERISA Waivers and State Health Care Reform." (Comment.) *Columbia Journal of Law and Social Problems*, 1995, *28, 609.*

Examines the impact of ERISA on state health care reform legislation and the various proposals in Congress to grant states a waiver to ERISA's preemptive effect. These waivers are important for the long-term financial viability of significant state reform, and many states have requested exemptions from the preemptive effect of ERISA. This article focuses on the three main clauses in ERISA and how the courts have interpreted these clauses in relation to various state regulations of health benefits and health insurance. After examining the political roadblocks to reform, the author offers a recommendation as to what might be included in an ERISA waiver to maximize the flexibility afforded to states and the possibility of actual passage into law.

Timothy F. Kennedy. "Summary of the New Proposed Regulations for ERISA Claims Procedures." *Health Care Law Monthly*, June 1999, at 26.

Examines proposed regulations revising benefit claims procedures for all ERISA benefit plans. The proposed regulations are based on comments received by the Department of Labor in response to their request for information sent out in September 1997. The proposals also take into account the report of the President's Advisory Commission on Consumer Protection and Quality in the Health Care Industry recommending a "Consumer Bill of Rights."

Jeffrey G. Lenhart. "ERISA Preemption: The Effect of Stop-Loss Insurance on Self-Insured Plans." *Virginia Tax Review*, 1995, *14, 615.*

ERISA was enacted in 1974 to provide broad federal preemption of diverse state regulation of certain employee benefit plans. Never viewed as a model of legislative drafting, ERISA fails to define the scope of federal preemption of state attempts to regulate self-insured plans with stop-loss coverage. Consequently, courts have been called upon to resolve the inevitable conflicts between state and federal law and have labored in their analysis. This article supplies a comprehensive summary of judicial interpretation of ERISA's preemption provisions as they relate to self-insured welfare benefit plans that reinsure with stop-loss coverage. Concluding that there is a paucity of statutory guidance and little consensus to be derived from the existing case law on the issue, this article ends with a call for legislative reform or, absent congressional willingness to act, guidance from the Supreme Court on the issue.

Dianne McCarthy. "Narrowing Provider Choices: Any Willing Provider Laws After *New York Blue Cross* v. *Travelers*." *American Journal of Law and Medicine*, 1997, *23, 97.*

Argues that "any willing provider" laws survive an ERISA challenge at both steps of the analysis: (1) the laws do not "relate to" employee benefit plans, and (2) they are exempt from preemption as laws that regulate insurance. Courts (for example, *Cigna Healthplan of Louisiana Inc.* v. *State*, 883 F. Supp. 94 (M.D. La. 1995)) and some commentators who dismissed the first step of the analysis and moved quickly to step two, miss a critical analysis in step one (as demonstrated in *New York Blue Cross Plans* v. *Travelers Ins. Co.*, 115 S. Ct. 1671 (1995)) and incorrectly analyze step two. Furthermore, the author argues, they wrongly ignore or minimize the critical policy consideration of consumer freedom of provider choice while focusing on the need to reduce health care costs.

E. Haavi Morreim. "Benefits Decisions in ERISA Plans: Diminishing Deference to Fiduciaries and an Emerging Problem for Provider-Sponsored Organizations." *Tennessee Law Review,* 1998, *65,* 511.

Over the years, ERISA has greatly stabilized pension plans, but it has also produced a number of unanticipated consequences in health care, particularly in three major areas: tort litigation, health care reform, and contract litigation. The author begins his argument by noting that typical ERISA plans are administered by fiduciaries whose central duty is to manage the plan for the good of its beneficiaries. These fiduciaries must exercise discretion in interpreting contractual ambiguities and making benefits determinations. At the same time, courts have noticed that fiduciaries' loyalty is sometimes tainted. This article reviews case law to understand the courts' struggle between their obligation to defer to fiduciaries' decisions and their contrasting duty to ensure that health plan subscribers are not illegitimately denied benefits. The author concludes by proposing ways in which conflict of interest can be managed by ERISA plans, including PSOs, so that fiduciaries can exercise the discretion that is essential if they are to maintain the balance between keeping plans solvent and serving all beneficiaries equitably.

Troy Paredes. "Stop Loss Insurance, State Regulation, and ERISA: Defining the Scope of Federal Preemption." *Harvard Journal on Legislation,* 1997, *34,* 233.

ERISA preempts state laws relating to employee welfare benefit plans. It does not, however, preempt state laws regulating insurance. Stop-loss insurance, by which an employer that self-funds its benefit plan insures against the risk of excessive payouts, does not fit neatly into ERISA's regulatory framework. As a result, the circuit courts of appeal have split over how to treat stop-loss plans for preemption purposes. In this note, the author argues that ERISA's dual regulatory scheme, precedent, basic insurance principles, and the legislative history of the act suggest that it should not be construed to preempt states from enforcing their insurance laws against a stop-loss plan's insurer.

Larry J. Pittman. "ERISA's Preemption Clause and the Health Care Industry: An Abdication of Judicial Law-Creating Authority." *University of Florida Law Review,* 1994, *46,* 355.

Suggests that the courts should create a federal substantive common-law cause of action to provide relief for injured patients.

Lee T. Polk. *ERISA Practice & Litigation.* Deerfield, Ill.: Clark, Boardman, Callaghan, 1997.

This two-volume treatise examines the broad range of issues encompassed by ERISA and devotes attention to health care law issues as they are preempted by it.

Christine C. Rinn. "ERISA and Managed Care: The Impact of Travelers." *Health Lawyer,* Early Spring 1996, *8,* 19.

Analyzes a U.S. Supreme Court case, *State Conference of Blue Cross & Blue Shield Plans* v. *Travelers Insurance Company,* 115 S. Ct. 1671 (1991), which narrowed the scope of ERISA preemption of state law by excluding from its scope those state laws that have an indirect economic influence on an employee benefit plan. The author contends that the ruling could lead to indirect regulation of employee benefit plans by the states through imposing direct obligations on the health care providers to those plans.

Curtis D. Rooney. "The States, Congress, or the Courts: Who Will Be First to Reform ERISA Remedies?" *Annals of Health Law,* 1998, *7,* 73.

The author reviews ERISA and its relationship to managed care. The article discusses relevant preemption provisions and extensively covers related U.S. Supreme Court decisions, before concluding with a discussion of reform initiatives directed toward the ERISA preemption and damage provisions.

Robert L. Roth. "Recent Developments Concerning the Effect of ERISA Preemption on Tort Claims Against Employers, Insurers, Health Plan Administrators, Managed Care Entities, and Utilization Review Agents." *Health Lawyer,* Early Spring 1996, *2.*

This highly useful article includes a succinct summary of ERISA and its preemption provisions and provides an overview of the unsettled state of the law that has resulted from congressional refusal to define the scope of the statute and the Supreme Court's reluctance to enter into the fray. This is an excellent overview of a complicated subject.

Jacqueline M. Saue and Gregg H. Dooge. "ERISA and Managed Care." In Peter R. Kongstvedt, *The Managed Health Care Handbook.* (4th ed.) Gaithersburg, Md.: Aspen, 2000.

Provides a working knowledge of the provisions of ERISA that are likely to affect their operations. Topics addressed include ERISA's documentation, reporting, and disclosure requirements; benefit plan design considerations; amendment of benefit plans; the duties of ERISA fiduciaries, which may include MCOs; challenges to benefit denials; ERISA's civil enforcement scheme and remedies; and the effect of ERISA preemption of state laws and causes of actions on MCO operations. This is a helpful summation of a complex area of the law.

David Henry Sculnick. "Liability and ERISA Preemption for Medical Malpractice." *Health Lawyer,* Early Spring 1996, *8,* 8.

Explores the impact of ERISA on medical negligence claims against HMOs and focuses on circumstances where the claims have been allowed to proceed. A sufficient body of decisional law now exists from which we can fairly conclude that a plaintiff's claim for medical negligence against an HMO for inadequate care, as opposed to a claim against a physician or hospital, can be pursued and not preempted by ERISA. To survive, the claim generally must rest on a theory of vicarious liability for the acts of the health care deliverer. HMOs can and must, the author writes, expect to face malpractice exposure as their involvement and control of service delivery systems increases.

There is, however, a definite split of judicial authority on the issue of whether or not ERISA preempts tort actions against HMOs. The author sets forth the rationale for each side of the debate, making reference to more than thirty cases on point.

Seema R. Shah. "Loosening ERISA's Preemptive Grip on HMO Medical Malpractice Claims: A Response to *PacifiCare of Oklahoma v. Burrage.*" (Comment.) *Minnesota Law Review,* 1996, *80,* 1545.

Medical malpractice claims against HMOs based on vicarious liability theories are the latest state common-law malpractice claims encountering ERISA's formidable preemptive structure. Courts already hold that ERISA preempts direct liability claims against HMOs for corporate negligence in selecting and retaining physicians and negligence involving utilization review. By preserving vicarious liability claims, *PacifiCare* restrains ERISA preemption. Because *PacifiCare* is a case of first impression among the federal circuit courts, future courts will undoubtedly rely on it for guidance on how to loosen state common-law medical malpractice claims from ERISA's grip.

This article contends that courts should not follow *PacifiCare*'s approach in future HMO medical malpractice cases. The author argues that although the court correctly held that ERISA did not preempt HMO malpractice claims based on a vicarious liability theory, the court offered a weak approach that compounds the inconsistency and frustration already plaguing courts faced with increasing ERISA preemption litigation.

William Tucker. "The Health Insurance Mess: How We Got in, How We Get out." *Weekly Standard*, Jan. 27, 1997, 2, 26.

This is an excellent layperson's introduction to access to health care and the impact of ERISA on insurance availability. The author writes that there is no reason private carriers cannot provide health coverage to the entire nation through basic risk-based commercial policies. He then advocates (1) allowing all individuals to buy health coverage with tax-free dollars; (2) avoiding mandated benefits at either the state or federal level; (3) continuing actuarial regulation of insurance companies, at either level; (4) assigning individuals who are uninsurable to subsidized high-risk pools; and (5) leveling the playing field by making ERISA all inclusive, or abolishing it entirely.

Lawrence Allen Vranka, Jr. "Defining the Contours of ERISA Preemption of State Insurance Regulation: Making Employee Benefit Plan Regulation an Exclusively Federal Concern." (Comment.) *Vanderbilt Law Review*, 1989, 42, 607.

Despite congressional attempts to elucidate an ERISA preemption standard, it is the courts that have been called upon to interpret ERISA's preemption provision. This has resulted in debate regarding the intent of its drafters, the underlying purpose of the legislation, and ultimately the essence of federalism. This comment explores the scope of ERISA preemption as it conflicts with state attempts to regulate insurance, especially in light of *Pilot Life Insurance Co.* v. *Dedeaux*, 481 U.S. 41 (1987) and *Metropolitan Life Insurance Co.* v. *Massachusetts*, 471 U.S. 724 (1985). The author concludes that to bring uniformity and certainty to the field of employee benefit plan regulation, courts should not find a state insurance regulation saved from preemption unless it is directed at the insurance industry and regulates the activities of insurance companies acting uniquely as insurance companies—not as administrators or underwriters of ERISA plans.

11.03   REGULATION OF MANAGED CARE

Health Insurance Association of America. *Managed Care: Integrating the Delivery and Financing of Health Care: Part B*. Annapolis, Md.: Health Insurance Association of America, 1996, 226 pages.

This modestly priced text provides discussion of operational and administrative aspects of managed care.

Part Three

Licensure, Liability, and Labor Issues

12

Licensure of Health Care Professionals

All fifty states and the District of Columbia mandate licensure of allopathic physicians (M.D.s), osteopathic physicians (D.O.s), dentists, registered nurses, practical nurses, dental hygienists, pharmacists, optometrists, physical therapists, podiatrists, chiropractors, and administrators of nursing homes.[1] Physicians' assistants, midwives, psychologists, social workers, opticians, physical therapy assistants, audiologists, speech pathologists, and others are frequently regulated by licensure laws. These state laws specify the minimum qualifications an individual must possess to practice a profession. They also prescribe penalties for those who practice without appropriate licensure and define the circumstances under which a license to practice may be revoked, suspended, or limited in some way. Health care facilities are often required by state law to ensure that professionals practicing there are properly licensed.[2]

Compulsory licensure laws mandate that any individual who seeks to practice a regulated profession first obtain a license. These licensed persons alone may legitimately use the professional title. Failure to adhere to state licensing requirements can result in fines or prohibition on future practice by the state licensing board or criminal penalties.[3]

Alongside state licensure statutes, a number of professional associations have also created their own voluntary systems for credentialing. The systems are often based on a set of minimum standards for educational attainment, success on examinations, and practical work experience. Although these private associations cannot bar an individual from professional practice, as can a state licensure agency, certification by a professional organization can significantly brighten career prospects. As an example, the American Board of Medical Specialties certifies physicians in more than twenty areas of professional practice. Hospitals and other health service providers view "board certification" as an indicator of competence when they find it necessary to evaluate a doctor's expertise.[4]

The primary public policy rationale advanced in support of state licensure laws is the need to protect the health and welfare of patients. This argument asserts that laypersons are at a disadvantage in accurately evaluating the expertise of medical personnel or determining the risks of substandard care. Furthermore, patient care often occurs on short notice, when any inquiry into a professional's qualifications is impossible. A patient arriving in a coma in the back of an ambulance is in a poor position to negotiate over his treatment options. Additional economic costs incurred by licensing procedures, the argument continues, are more than offset by the costs of poor health care at the hands of unqualified—and perhaps dangerous—practitioners.

That this licensing requirement has an undeniable tendency to raise the compensation of regulated health care professionals has not gone unnoticed by economists and other observers. In granting a monopoly over the practice of a profession to those persons who satisfy state-defined standards, the state prohibits competition by other persons who might also deliver satisfactory medical care although they cannot meet the criteria required for licensure.[5] As a consequence, licensure has often been coveted by professionals themselves, who, some economists contend, use the licensing requirement to exclude competitors from their field of practice,[6] such that an important result of licensure is that it contributes to higher health care costs and reduces consumer choice.

Critics of professional licensure have contended that the motive to restrict competition, rather than an interest in protecting the patient, is the driving force behind the enactment and maintenance of licensing laws.[7] State licensing boards have also faced accusations of being slow to accept alternative treatment methodologies, dilatory in adapting to technological change, and prone to establishing professional practice standards that are unrelated to a person's ability to care for patients.[8] Critics also attack these boards for coddling licensed professionals who fail to practice competently or who practice unethically, and for stifling innovation.[9]

In spite of these criticisms, no state has eliminated licensure.[10] Indeed, several factors augur continuation of state regulation. The most important of these is the high rate of technological change affecting medical practice and the public's desire to be assured that practitioners are abreast of new technologies and procedures. A second factor is the convenient leverage regulation furnished to state officials in making certain that public health crises are met. New Jersey's Board of Medical Examiners, for example, has issued a policy barring physicians with appropriate skills and experience from refusing to treat HIV-positive patients.[11] Failure to treat an HIV-positive individual because of HIV status could result in disciplinary action by the board, including suspension or revocation of a physician's license to practice.[12] In New York, as a condition of their initial licensure or relicensure physicians (including psychiatrists), chiropractors, dentists, registered nurses, podiatrists, optometrists, psychologists, and dental hygienists are required to complete two hours of state-approved training in identifying and reporting child abuse.[13] These health professionals are informed of the circumstances in which child abuse reports must be made, what follow-up actions they are required or permitted to take after reporting suspected child abuse, pertinent legal immunities protecting health professionals when making mandatory reports, and penalties for failing to report abuse.[14]

References and Notes

1. Michael G. Macdonald, Kathryn C. Meyer, and Beth Essig. *Health Care Law: A Practical Guide.* New York: Matthew Bender, 1998, § 16.01[1].
2. Macdonald, Meyer, and Essig (1998).
3. Macdonald, Meyer, and Essig (1998). See generally Paul Starr. *The Social Transformation of American Medicine.* New York: Basic Books, 1982, p. 44.
4. Macdonald, Meyer, and Essig (1998).
5. Macdonald, Meyer, and Essig (1998), § 16.01[3].
6. Macdonald, Meyer, and Essig (1998). For a detailed discussion of private credentialing mechanisms and the implications for health care professionals, see Havighurst and King. "Private Credentialing of Health Care Personnel: An Antitrust Perspective." (Parts 1 and 2.) *American Journal of Law & Medicine,* 1983, 9, 131, 263.
7. Macdonald, Meyer, and Essig (1998), § 16.01[2]. See generally Baron. "Licensure of Health Care Professionals: The Consumer's Case for Abolition." *American Journal of Law & Medicine,* 1983, 9, 335–336.
8. Macdonald, Meyer, and Essig (1998), § 16.01[2].
9. Macdonald, Meyer, and Essig (1998).
10. Macdonald, Meyer, and Essig (1998), § 16.01[3].
11. Macdonald, Meyer, and Essig (1998), § 16.02[2][B]. *See also* George Annas. "Legal Risks and Responsibilities of Physicians in the AIDS Epidemic." *Hastings Center Report,* Apr.–May 1988, 30.
12. Macdonald, Meyer, and Essig (1998), § 16.02[2][B]. Other states have enacted statutes requiring licensed health care practitioners, as a condition of licensure, to learn about transmission, treatment, and prevention of AIDS. See, for example, Fla. Stat. Ann. § 455.2226 (West Supp. 1990); Wash. Rev. Code Ann. § 70.24.270 (Supp. 1990); Iowa Code Ann. § 141.3(2)(b) (West 1989); N.J. Stat. Ann. § 26:5C-3(b) (West 1987).
13. Macdonald, Meyer, and Essig (1998), § 16.02[2][B]. See also N.Y. Educ. Law § 6507(3)(a) (McKinney Supp. 1990).
14. Macdonald, Meyer, and Essig (1998), § 16.02[2][B]. See also N.Y. Admin. Code tit. 8, § 52.2(c)(12) (1990).

ANNOTATIONS

12.01   PHYSICIANS

Carl F. Ameringer. *State Medical Boards and the Politics of Public Protection*. Baltimore: Johns Hopkins University Press, 1999, 188 pages.

Examines the socialization of physician regulation and discipline; traces the evolution of state medical boards within the context of the struggles for control over the health care industry waged by organized medicine, the state and federal governments, and corporate medical interests. It also gives readers insight into the ideological battles these groups fought as medicine moved from a system dominated by physicians to one largely shaped by corporations. This is a comprehensive, well-written examination of the political, public, and economic forces that have shaped state medical boards.

Annot. "False or Fraudulent Statements or Nondisclosures in Application for Issuance or Renewal of License to Practice as Ground for Disciplinary Action Against, or Refusal to License, Medical Practitioner." *ALR5th*, 1998, *32*, 57.

The broad power of a state to regulate the practice of medicine through licensure requirements is undisputed. The state may determine the grounds for revocation, suspension, or refusal to grant or renew a license to practice. Allegedly false or fraudulent statements or nondisclosure by an applicant regarding such matters as professional education, licensure, or disciplinary proceedings in other jurisdictions, and conduct implicating moral qualifications, have been asserted as grounds for disciplinary action or denial of licensure or renewal. In *In re Wolfe* (Ohio Ct. App.), 612 N.E.2d 1,307, 32 *ALR5th* 759, for example, the court determined that an applicant should not have been denied an Ohio license where her statements regarding the conclusion of West Virginia disciplinary proceedings, although perhaps technically inaccurate, were found not to have been made with an intent to mislead the licensing board. All such cases are collected and discussed in this annotation.

Annot. "Filing of False Insurance Claims for Medical Services as Ground for Disciplinary Action Against Dentist, Physician or Other Medical Practitioner." *ALR4th*, 1998, *70*, 132.

Addresses the propriety of state disciplinary action, such as suspension or revocation of a license to practice in the state, or suspension (under state law) from participation in a particular program such as Medicaid. It does not address criminal sanctions, monetary civil penalties, or discipline imposed under federal laws.

Annot. "Rights as to Notice and Hearing in Proceeding to Revoke or Suspend License to Practice Medicine." *ALR5th*, 1998, *10*, 1.

A license to practice medicine has been considered a property right by the courts; as with other forms of property, the possessor of the right cannot be deprived of it without due process of law. Therefore, in proceedings instituted by an administrative agency to determine whether a medical practitioner's license to practice should be suspended or revoked, the practitioner is entitled to a notice and hearing on the matter. The question whether notice or hearing in a particular case satisfied due process requirements is often an issue faced by the courts. In *In re Yemmanur* (S.D. 1989), 447 N.W.2d 525, 10 *ALR5th* 920, for example, a common objection to notices in revocation or suspension hearings was raised that the notice was not sufficiently clear to inform the practitioner of the charges against him. Equally formidable issues—such as the effect of errors in the notice, waiver of objections to notices or hearings, and entitlement to a closed hearing—have been considered by the courts. This annotation collects these cases, as well as all others, in which the courts have discussed the extent of a medical practitioner's rights to notice and hearing in a license revocation or suspension proceeding.

Timothy S. Jost (ed.). *Regulation of the Healthcare Professions*. Chicago: Health Administration Press, 1997, 220 pages.

Discusses the issue of regulating and certifying a health care provider's qualifications and skills. This book examines these topics in the context of managed care, cost containment, and outcomes measurement.

12.02   NURSES

Linda H. Aiken. "Transformation of the Nursing Workforce." *Nursing Outlook*, 1995, *43*, 201.

Nurses are underused throughout the entire health care system. The nursing workforce is adequate with regard to the aggregate supply of nurses, but the mix of nurses by education is not correct to meet the nation's changing health care needs. The United States has an excess supply of nurses trained in two-year community college programs and an insufficient number trained at the baccalaureate and graduate levels. The relative surplus of nurses is due to the restructuring of the hospital industry, and the demand for nurses is not keeping up with supply.

The author argues that having more than half of all new nurses trained outside the educational infrastructure of universities and their teaching hospitals and associated practices is not acceptable. The highest priority for nurses must be to move all nursing education to a university base. Medicare funding for nursing education should be retargeted to graduate level training of expert clinicians, making nursing education comparable to Medicare's policies for medical education.

American Association of Nurse Anesthetists. *Professional Practice Manual*. Park Ridge, Ill.: American Association of Nurse Anesthetists, 1997.

This text covers such topics as scope and standards of practice, guidelines for clinical privileges, guidelines for expert witnesses, legal issues in nurse anesthesia practice, informed consent in anesthesia, and management of waste anesthetic gases.

American Nurses Association. *ANA Model Practice Act*. Washington, D.C.: American Nurses Association, 1996, 64 pages.

Sets forth a state nursing practice act that incorporates ANA policy and regulatory positions, builds upon successful provisions in existing state practice acts, and incorporates new language to address anticompetitive barriers to practice.

American Nurses Association. *Legislative and Regulatory Initiatives for the 105th Congress*. Washington, D.C.: American Nurses Association, 1997.

Presents more than thirty-five legislative initiatives. Topics covered in this guide include managed care, Medicare and Medicaid, employee rights, federal health budget appropriations, third-party reimbursement, and domestic violence. The manual includes a comprehensive appendix on Congress and its committees, health-related federal agencies, and helpful phone numbers.

Annot. "Revocation of a Nurse's License to Practice [His or Her] Profession." *ALR3rd*, 1998, *55*, 1141.

Collects and analyzes the cases in which the courts have considered the circumstances under which a nurse's license to practice his or her profession may be revoked. This annotation is regularly updated by the publisher.

Nancy J. Brent. *Nurses and the Law: A Guide to Principles and Applications*. Philadelphia: Saunders, 1997, 586 pages.

Topics covered in this text include professional negligence and liability, risk management, licensure, employment issues, and informed consent. The book concludes with four appendices, a glossary, and an index.

Committee on Military Nursing Research. *The Program for Research on Military Nursing: Progress and Future Direction.* Washington, D.C.: Institute of Medicine 1996, 128 pages.

This volume reviews the military nursing research program of the TriService Nursing Research Program in terms of its management, funding, allocation of resources, and identification of program goals. The book also contains the results of that study and the committee's recommendations.

Helen Creighton. *Law Every Nurse Should Know.* (5th ed.) Philadelphia: Saunders, 1986, 335 pages.

This work is particularly valuable for the list of topics it addresses, among them nurse licensure, discrimination against nurses, the nurse's legal status and hospital liability, the nurse's rights and liabilities, negligence, malpractice, wills, and gifts.

Maureen Cushing. *Nursing Jurisprudence.* Old Tappan, N.J.: Appleton & Lange, 1988, 534 pages.

Discusses standards of care, nursing judgment, documentation, and the impact of the law on nursing practice. Unusually well written, this book also includes a helpful chapter entitled "Anatomy of a Suit."

Janine Fiesta. *20 Legal Pitfalls for Nurses to Avoid.* Albany, N.Y.: Delmar, 1994, 192 pages.

Designed to help nurses avoid legal problems in a range of areas, including medication administration, informed consent, whistle-blowing negligent supervision, and improper procedure. The author, a practicing attorney and nurse, has written the guide with admirable wit and clarity.

Janine Fiesta. *The Law and Liability: A Guide for Nurses.* (3rd ed.) New York: Wiley, 1988, 319 pages.

Designed to provide nurses with an introduction to the legal issues they are likely to encounter in their profession. The author emphasizes malpractice issues along with criminal actions, contracts, and wills.

Lois Friss. "Nursing Studies Laid End to End Form a Circle." *Journal of Health Politics, Policy and Law,* 1994, *19,* 597.

Examines reasons for the continuing cycle of growth and decline in the nursing profession. As early as 1915, leaders in the nursing profession were concerned with the "image problem of nurses," which they saw as needing improvement. Since then, countless studies, reports, and commissions have attempted to explain and solve alleged shortages of registered nurses, which have occurred regularly after brief periods of quiescence or oversupply. Usually, their recommendations have hinged on nurses' changing their image. In fact, few of these studies have dealt with the real issues of nursing work: narrow pay range, little extra pay for working on undesirable shifts, disincentives for full-time work, pay unrelated to education, and education unconnected to job level. The multiple studies and commissions do nothing more than recycle data, and in the process they obscure fundamental problems. Educational funding has been no more successful. The ineffectiveness suggests the need for less "image enhancement" and more support from physicians and employers to bring about systemic reform. This includes licensing nurses according to their education, assigning them in relation to their competency and education, and paying accordingly. These measures, and only these, will eventually curtail the cycles of nursing "shortages."

Ginny Wacker Guido. *Legal Issues in Nursing.* (3rd ed.) Old Tappan, N.J.: Appleton & Lange, 1997, 412 pages.

Intended to educate the beginning nurse about legal issues and the functions of laws, offer a ready source of information for practicing nurses, and provide a means for preventing malpractice suits.

Charlene Harrington and Carroll L. Estes. *Health Policy and Nursing: Crisis and Reform in the U.S. Health Care Delivery System.* Boston, Mass.: Jones and Bartlett, 1994, 535 pages.

This volume of forty-one essays grew out of the editors' experience teaching health care policy and financing to graduate students in nursing and sociology at the University of California at San Francisco. Topics examined include health care financing; private insurance and managed care; the structure of the U.S. health care delivery system, access to health care, and women's care; quality issues; and reform of the U.S. health delivery system.

Keith M. Korenchuk and Darlene M. Trandel. *Nursing and the Law.* (5th ed.) Gaithersburg, Md.: Aspen, 1996.

Examines a range of issues in health care law as they affect nurses. Topics addressed in this book of approximately four hundred pages include nursing licensure and certification; business aspects of health care, including utilization review and quality assurance; treatment authorization; disclosure of patient information; and professional liability.

Nurse's Legal Handbook. (3rd ed.) Springhouse, Pa.: Springhouse, 1996, 420 pages.

Contains a wealth of up-to-date information presented in a practical format. Numerous case studies in the text provide vivid examples of a nurse's legal and ethical responsibilities. Topics addressed include state nurse practice acts and the role of state boards of nursing, standards of care and their relevance in malpractice litigation, the patient's right to refuse treatment, potential legal problems posed by understaffing, legal risks when providing off-duty nursing services, documentation requirements, and employee rights. The text concludes with a glossary; general index; index of legal cases; and three appendices describing types of law, the judicial process, and interpretation of legal citations.

Barbara J. Safriet. "Health Care Dollars and Regulatory Sense: The Role of Advanced Practice Nursing." *Yale Journal on Regulation,* 1992, 9, 149.

The author concludes that the restraints on advanced practical nurses that may result from both ignorance of their abilities and bias based on rigid notions of professional role and turf protection suggest that physicians and other health care providers should not be included on regulatory boards that define these practitioners' scope of practice. Instead, consistent with other professional licensing systems, the regulation of nursing in all its aspects should be carried out by each state's board of nursing. Full interdisciplinary practice should surely be the norm in health care, but in defining the legal contours of each discipline legislatures should rely principally upon those who are educated and practice in that discipline.

12.03   PHYSICIAN ASSISTANTS

Aspen Health Law Center. *Physician Assistant Legal Handbook.* Gaithersburg, Md.: Aspen, 1997, 416 pages.

Focuses on such topics as licensure and scope of practice, prescribing and dispensing liability, quality review and risk management, medical records, credentialing and peer review, employment laws, third-party reimbursement, and participation in government affairs.

James W. Gilliam. "A Contemporary Analysis of Medicolegal Concerns for Physician Assistants and Nurse Practitioners." In Cyril H. Wecht (ed.), *Legal Medicine 1994.* Salem, N.H.: Butterworth, 1995.

The literature addressing physician assistants and nurse practitioners is sparse, fragmented, and often outdated. This significant article identifies one point of origin of the concept, in medical aid personnel in the Army Special Forces during the Vietnam era, and then traces it to the current period. It specifically addresses such medicolegal topics as supervision, transcribing of physician orders as a delegated medical act, national certification, state licensure, hospital privileges, and prescriptive practices.

Chris L. Gore. "A Physician's Liability for Mistakes of a Physician Assistant." *Journal of Legal Medicine*, 2000, *21*, 125.

Examines the qualifications and prerequisites necessary to become a PA, the history and role of PAs in the health care arena, and the statutory regulations from various states showing a legislative trend to reduce and limit liability for physicians who supervise PAs. Also discusses the standard of care applicable to PAs. The author then explores the elements of each cause of action used to hold supervising physicians liable for the mistakes of PAs. Finally, Gore outlines recommendations for minimizing a physician's liability for PAs' mistakes.

Ronald W. Scott. *Promoting Legal Awareness in Physical and Occupational Therapy.* St. Louis: Mosby, 1997, 310 pages.

Written by a physical therapist who is also an attorney, this book is intended to provide a basic overview of health care legal issues for clinicians, clinical managers, health care facility administrators, educators, and professional and postprofessional students. Although the material presented focuses on two specific disciplines—physical and occupational therapy—the concepts and issues are applicable to all other health care disciplines whose member-providers care for patients and engage in business pursuits.

Daniel B. Vukmer. "Non-Physician Practitioner Issues." Washington, D.C.: American Health Lawyers Association [Report No VMM99–0056], 1999, 33 pages.

Discusses legal issues involving use of nonphysician practitioners such as physician assistants and nurses, including liability for medical malpractice, scope of practice, professional corporations, insurance, credentialing, and Medicare fraud. Also contains reference sources.

13

Professional Relationships in the Health Care Enterprise

When Congress enacted the Hospital Survey and Construction Act of 1946 (the Hill-Burton Act), its primary aim was to subsidize hospital construction.[1] A secondary aim, however, was to require that each state receiving funds have a hospital licensure law. To that end, the federal government provided a model statute, derived from standards set by the American College of Surgeons (ACS) earlier in the century. In response, most states passed laws mandating an organized medical staff and formal medical staff bylaws. Appointment procedures were required to be based on professional qualifications. The statutes called for different categories of medical staff membership, departmentalization of medical staff, election of medical staff leaders, and periodic meetings of the medical staff to review clinical work.[2] In 1952, the ACS, the American College of Physicians, the American Medical Association, the American Hospital Association, and the Canadian Medical Association formed the Joint Commission for the Accreditation of Hospitals. It is now known as the Joint Commission for the Accreditation of Healthcare Organizations (JCAHO).[3]

The responsibility of a hospital's medical staff is to protect patients by monitoring the quality of medical services provided within that facility. In discharging this responsibility, the medical staff must interact with the hospital's governing body and its administration. The governing body assumes ultimate responsibility for the survival and existence of the organization. It is the repository of legal authority over the institution.[4] Although it delegates matters of quality of care to the medical staff, it retains the right, and has the obligation, to review and approve the exercise of that delegated power.[5] The hospital administration is responsible for the decisions that make up the day-to-day operations of the facility. Both groups must depend on the physicians who make up the medical staff to achieve the goal of high-quality medical care at the institution. Likewise, although the medical staff advocates high-quality care at the institution, it remains dependent on administration and the board to provide the resources to accomplish this aim.[6]

Although the Joint Commission requires that medical staffs be organized, it affords substantial latitude to them in forming committees to address issues such as patient care evaluation, surgical case review, drug usage evaluation, medical records review, blood usage review, pharmacy and therapeutics evaluation, risk management, disaster planning, safety, utilization review, and infection control.[7] The Joint Commission does, however, require that an executive committee of the medical staff, whose majority is composed of physicians, be charged with carrying out medical staff policy and coordinating medical staff activities.[8] The Joint Commission also requires that appropriate officers be elected from the medical staff membership and that there be an appropriate mechanism to ensure effective communication among the medical staff, the governing body, and administration.[9]

It is the medical staff that is charged with the task of credentialing applicants to practice. This involves verification of the applicant's training, degrees, and any certifications from specialty societies.[10] Separate from this general credentialing that precedes medical staff membership is privileging, which is a process of limiting a physician's activities at the institution to those for which he or she is trained.[11] The Joint Commission has established guidelines that govern credentialing[12] and privileging.[13]

References and Notes

1. Tom Curtis. "The Medical Staff." In Michael G. Macdonald and others (eds.). *Treatise on Health Care Law.* New York: Matthew Bender, 1995, § 6.01.
2. Curtis (1995). See also K. Taylor and D. Donald. *A Comparative Study of Hospital Licensure Regulations.* 1957.
3. Curtis (1995).
4. Curtis (1995).
5. Curtis (1995).
6. Curtis (1995).
7. Joint Commission for the Accreditation of Healthcare Organizations. *Accreditation Manual for Hospitals.* 1994, MS 1.
8. JCAHO (1994), at MS 3.3.6.
9. JCAHO (1994).
10. Curtis (1995), § 6.01[2].
11. Curtis (1995).
12. Curtis (1995).
13. Curtis (1995), § 6.01[2][b].

ANNOTATIONS

13.01 MEDICAL STAFF ISSUES

Aspen Health Law Center Staff. *Physician Organizations and Medical Staff: Contracts, Rights and Liabilities.* Gaithersburg, Md.: Aspen, 1998.

This comprehensive manual details the rights and liabilities of physicians and focuses on the contractual issues that are critical to health care relationships among physicians, providers, and plan managers. Topics covered include business and health care organizations, medical staff organization, documents governing physician relationships, credentialing, peer review, liability, contract and antitrust issues, fraud and abuse, and tax exemption.

Donald H. Caldwell, Jr. "Hospital Medical Staff Privileges." In Carl Horn III, Donald H. Caldwell, Jr., and D. Christopher Osborn, *Law for Physicians: An Overview of Medical Legal Issues.* Chicago: American Medical Association, 1999, 246 pages.

Discusses the organization of the medical staff, denial of medical staff privileges, due process, justifiable exclusions, and peer review as it relates to medical staff privileges.

John F. Horty and Daniel M. Mulholland. "The Legal Status of the Hospital Medical Staff." *St. Louis University Law Journal,* 1978, 22, 485.

The authors, both practicing attorneys, write that a medical staff is not a corporation since it possesses no charter and has not filed articles of incorporation. It also lacks the four key attributes of a corporation: centralization of management, continuity of life, free transferability of interests, and limited liability. Consequently, a medical staff has no legal life of its own and is merely one component of the hospital corporation. However important it may be as a component, the staff cannot sue or be sued as a body, they argue.

Daniel A. Lang. *Managing Medical Staff Change Through Bylaws and Other Strategies.* Chicago: American Hospital Publishing, 1995, 147 pages.

Provides a detailed road map for transforming the traditional medical staff organization as hospitals adapt to organized delivery systems. Beginning with a brief discussion of the changing health care delivery system, the author, a consultant to hospital medical staffs and governing boards, sets forth the primary reasons for reexamining hospital–medical staff relationships now. His thesis is that integrated systems must place greater value on group, rather than individual, performance to appeal to third-party payers to make pricing decisions and maintain corporate profit margins. The traditional medical staff—which rules by consensus, focuses on the individual doctor, and values fairness over results—paralyzes the smooth functioning of integrated systems, he writes. In short, it is a relic of the fee-for-service era and must be discarded.

Lang's proposals will doubtless be controversial. He argues that because the purpose of a medical staff is to support the common good by improving hospital performance, medical staff bylaws should be rewritten to hold doctors accountable for serving the needs of the integrated system. Hospitals should use their access to systemwide patient populations to obtain this new obligation, Lang contends, and he provides sample bylaw language to effect the changes he advocates.

Lewis M. Levin. *Medical Staff Privileges: A Practical Guide to Obtaining and Keeping Hospital Staff Privileges.* Los Angeles: Practice Management Information, 1991, 220 pages.

Written for practicing physicians, this handbook discusses such topics as the hospital power structure, competition among physicians, the credentialing process, administrative procedure under medical staff bylaws, representation by an attorney, and the Health Care Quality Improvement Act (HCQIA).

Brooke S. Murphy and others. "Medical Staff Issues." Washington, D.C.: American Health Lawyers Association [Report No. VPH98–0004], 1998, 45 pages.

Discusses emerging trends and difficult issues in credentialing, recredentialing, and disciplining physicians; and approaches and procedures to address those issues. Includes several scenarios that address use of economic credentialing and geographic proximity requirements by hospitals, the disruptive physician, initial appointment and reappointment issues, deselection by managed care plans, and credentialing issues faced by multiple provider systems. Supplies sample provisions from medical staff bylaws, policies, and procedures.

Marcia J. Pollard and Grace J. Wigal. *Hospital Staff Privileges: What Every Health Care Practitioner and Lawyer Needs to Know.* Chicago: Hospital Administration Press, 1996, 207 pages.

Surveys the history of hospital staff privileges in the 1990s. Covers areas including hospital liability for negligent selection, retention or supervision of a staff member, the Health Care Quality Improvement Act and its data bank reporting requirements, and antitrust claims related to hospital privilege decisions. Notes that rising health care costs, changing legal precedent, and emphasis on quality patient care are affecting how hospital staff privileges are determined in the 1990s. This guide will help the reader understand how to balance these competing interests, implement decision-making procedures designed to avoid liability, improve competency screening, and ensure institutional responsibility to patients. Includes a glossary, the text of the act, and related regulations.

Karen S. Rieger and Eric S. Fisher. "Medical Staff Bylaws: Related Documents and Advanced Issues." Washington, D.C.: American Health Lawyers Association [Report No. VHH99–0039]), 1999, 62 pages.

A comprehensive analysis of statutory, regulatory, and accreditation requirements applicable to medical staff bylaws and related documents. Discusses current issues in medical staff credentialing and provides specific recommendations and sample provisions for inclusion in medical staff bylaws and related documents.

Jack Spalding Schroder, Jr., and Michelle A. Williams. "Critical Revisions in Medical Staff Bylaws." *Health Lawyer* (Spring and Fall 1994), vol. 7.

Suggests specific changes that should be incorporated into a health care institution's bylaws. The rationale for making these changes is that the medical staff as constructed today is experiencing a transformation. Health care reform, judicial evasion of independent contractor status, and increased regulation of hospital-physician transactions (such as fraud and abuse and antireferral legislation) are accelerating this development. Specific provisions analyzed include definitions, qualifications for membership, notice requirements, antidumping and indigent care requirements, exclusive contract providers, nondiscrimination clauses, peer review, and suspension.

Sandra D. Van der Vaart. "Managed Care and Medical Staff Issues." Washington, D.C.: National Health Lawyers Association [Report No. MC97–0034], 1997, 29 pages.

Discusses medical staff issues arising from managed care, including medical staff self-governance, bylaws, criteria for membership, credentialing, exclusive contracting, contracting for hospital-based physicians, and mediating hospital-medical staff disputes.

June D. Zellers and Michael R. Poulin. "Termination of Hospital Medical Staff Privileges for Economic Reasons: An Appeal for Consistency." *Maine Law Review*, 1994, 46, 67.

Analyzes cases arising from the loss of medical staff privileges in private hospitals due to changes in the contractual relationship between the hospital and the physician. It identifies four kinds of economic relationship between hospital and physician. Using these classifications, the authors posit that courts have reached inconsistent results for two reasons. First, the parties neglected to set forth clearly their agreement with respect to privileges, creating ambiguity. Second, when faced with conflicting evidence, the courts have often overlooked the economic relationship between the physician and the hospital.

13.02   QUALITY

Mary M. Bearden. "cvo.com.plications?" Washington, D.C.: American Health Lawyers Association [Report No. VMC98–0029], 1998, 32 pages.

Addresses organizational structures for credentials verification organizations (CVOs). Examines confidentiality and other legal issues, NCQA accreditation, agreements between CVOs and their users, and how to minimize exposure to liability.

Donald M. Berwick. "Payment by Capitation and the Quality of Care." *New England Journal of Medicine*, 1996, 335, 1227.

Reviews the existing evidence and theories bearing on the relation of capitation to quality and suggests ways to ensure that the effect of capitation on the quality of care is a positive one. Berwick, a physician, concludes that capitation is growing in health care at a time of legitimate concern over threatened values and shortsighted cost reductions, and that capitation has been tarred unfairly by the association.

John D. Blum (ed.). *Achieving Quality in Managed Care: The Role of Law*. Chicago: Health Law Section, American Bar Association, 1997, 182 pages.

Prepared in conjunction with Loyola University Chicago's Institute for Health Law, this book contains nine essays on such topics as whether epidemiological issues affect quality in managed care, consumer protection options in managed care network breakups, significance of risk in direct contracts with health providers, mandatory public disclosure in managed care, the comparative institutional case against an antitrust exemption for Medical self-regulatory entities, and pharmaceutical pricing policies and their quality implications.

Troyen A. Brennan. "Improving the Quality of Medical Care: A Critical Evaluation of the Major Proposals." *Yale Law and Policy Review*, 1992, *10*, 431.

Reviews the evidence of the incidence of medical injuries and the manner in which they are compensated; concludes that traditional tort reform, which decreases the number of malpractice suits, is intellectually indefensible. Brennan, a professor of law and a physician, writes that among the more radical alternatives to tort law is a no-fault method of compensation for medical injuries, linked to experience-rated institutional liability; it holds the greatest promise of significant improvement in health care. A no-fault compensation system would not reduce overall costs, but it would reduce spending on administration of claims and distribute compensation for injuries over a much wider group of patients. The system would not require a large bureaucracy constantly vulnerable to budget cuts. Most important, such a system would force hospitals to adopt a systemic approach to quality assurance, thus bringing about significant improvements in the quality of care provided by the medical establishment.

Toby S. Edelman. "Health Care Financing Administration Retreats from Regulatory Role." *Clearinghouse Review*, Sept.-Oct. 1997.

The concept of total quality management has preoccupied the manufacturing and service industries, especially in the early 1990s when the United States was forced to compete more fiercely in world markets. Various players have been attempting to apply it to health care. This article examines the Health Care Quality Improvement Project, a collaboration between the HCFA and health care providers designed to incorporate procedures for improving quality of care. The article determines that quality assurance initiatives have been in the health care industry for quite a while and asks advocates to examine the *processes* of care, not just outcomes.

Barry R. Furrow. "Broadcasting Clinical Guidelines on the Internet: Will Physicians Tune In?" *American Journal of Law & Medicine*, 1999, *25*, 403.

The author looks at the Internet as a vehicle to improve the quality of medical care. He sees the Internet as a medium through which clinical practice guidelines can be made instantly available to physicians as they treat patients. Given the proliferation of medical information and the difficulties doctors experience in keeping up with current standards of care, Furrow believes that Internet access to guidelines will enhance the quality of care. He also investigates the implications of such technologies for malpractice suits against physicians.

Alice G. Gosfield. "Quality and Clinical Culture: The Critical Role of Physicians in Accountable Health Care Organizations." Washington, D.C.: American Health Lawyers Association [Report No. VPH99–0001], 1999, 27 pages.

Discusses how physicians are essential to the management of any health care organization. Lays out a continuum of issues to which physicians should direct their attention, articulates principles of engagement for effective collaboration between business and clinical leaders, and describes how physicians have in the past undermined their effectiveness in these undertakings.

Alice G. Gosfield. *Guide to Key Legal Issues in Managed Care Quality, Vol. II*. New York: Faulkner and Gray, 1996, 253 pages.

This work is designed to be a focused guide, primarily for nonlawyers, to the essential features of the law directly influencing quality in managed care programs. The author begins with a survey of the case law to date that characterizes who is currently held liable when things go wrong in delivering care. The text then moves to the fundamental federal controls on managed care quality through regulatory mechanisms imposed on the programs to which older people (Medicare) and poor people (Medicaid) are increasingly shifting. The next segment of the book focuses on the substance and desired influence of the federal antifraud and abuse laws as they regulate managed care behavior—and confuse those who are trying to change their ways. Other topics discussed include accreditation, state patient protection statutes, and provider contracts. The book concludes with a glossary, brief bibliography, and table of cases.

Timothy S. Jost. "Oversight of the Quality of Medical Care: Regulation, Management, or the Market?" *Arizona Law Review,* 1995, *37,* 825.

The deficiencies of the market ensure the existence of a continuing legitimate role for quality regulation, the author argues. The costs of government intervention point, however, to a limited rather than expansive government role. The task of professional regulation needs to be refocused on ensuring initial and ongoing competency and the professionalism that supports it. Prevention of error should by and large be left to management, and accountability to consumers should be ensured through the market and through an independent ombudsperson's office responsible for investigating consumer complaints. All the resources of modern technology must then be brought to bear on the residual tasks of regulation.

David Marx, Jr., and Sandra Muhlenbeck. "Review of Traditional Defenses: The Healthcare Quality Improvement Act and State Action Immunity." Washington, D.C.: American Health Lawyers Association [Report No. VAT98–0021], 1998, 49 pages.

Examines the state action immunity doctrine and its application to both public and private health care providers, with the focus on state hospital cooperation acts. Also reviews the HCQIA and cases applying immunity under the act. Attachments include a table of statutory citations to state cooperative health care legislation initiatives for twenty-one states.

Michael L. Millenson. *Demanding Medical Excellence: Doctors and Accountability in the Information Age.* Chicago: University of Chicago Press, 1997, 433 pages.

Written by a *Chicago Tribune* reporter, this book examines how doctors make treatment decisions. It looks at both the choice of the most appropriate treatment and how this treatment is provided. It asserts that errors in treatment have grown into a serious problem, with 180,000 treatment-related deaths in hospitals each year. Illustrating his case with a series of vignettes, the author examines how researchers go about gathering scientific evidence on which procedures work best and then putting them into practice. Millenson then previews the coming "era of the patient" in which the accelerated availability of clinical information on the Internet alters the relationship between physicians and the people they treat.

Christopher S. Morter. "The Health Care Quality Improvement Act of 1986: Will Physicians Find Peer Review More Inviting." (Note.) *Virginia Law Review,* 1988, *74,* 1115.

Part One of this article provides background information regarding the peer review process and presents some of the apprehensions of physicians who have refused to participate in peer review activities. Part Two examines the provisions of the act, with special emphasis on how it may encourage peer review. Part Three outlines some of the remaining concerns of physicians that the act does not govern. The greatest of these is the issue of confidentiality of peer review records and proceedings, which has typically been addressed at the state level. Finally, Part Four concludes that although the act is a step in the right direction to encourage good faith peer review, its scope is too narrow to meet this goal completely.

Mark A. Schuster, Elizabeth A. McGlynn, and Robert H. Brook. *Why the Quality of U.S. Health Care Must Be Improved.* Santa Monica, Calif.: RAND, 1997, 57 pages.

This report, funded by the bipartisan National Coalition on Health Care, is intended to provide information and guidance to the Advisory Commission on Consumer Protection and Quality in the Health Care Industry, appointed by President Clinton in September 1996. Topics addressed include why it is important to measure quality of care, how it is measured, the quality of care currently provided in the United States, how an organization can use information on quality to improve the care it provides, systems that are being used for external quality monitoring in the United States, and factors that are important for an effective quality monitoring and assessment system. The report concludes that the United States has only a patchwork of systems that measure quality, with little uniformity, breadth, or ability to produce rapid results. Furthermore, these systems do not yet assess most providers of health care in the nation. Supplemental material at the end of the report includes a list of references and tables setting forth examples of quality of preventive, acute, and chronic health care in the United States; and examples of quality of health care outside the United States.

Susan M. Wolf. "Quality Assessment of Ethics in Health Care: The Accountability Revolution." *American Journal of Law and Medicine*, 1994, *20*, 105.

Quality assessment and quality improvement techniques occupy a central place in what the author terms the current "Era of Assessment and Accountability." Wolf writes that "the notion is that if we can specify what constitutes good quality in health care, we can assess how closely current practice approximates that ideal and then convey those data to all concerned. This 'feedback loop' then has the potential to move practice closer to the ideal or to catalyze interventions to do so." This article is unusually well researched and well written.

13.03   PROFESSIONAL PEER REVIEW

Aspen Health Law Center. *Medical Group Practice: Legal and Administrative Guide*. Gaithersburg, Md.: Aspen, 1998.

This one-volume loose-leaf guide examines a range of topics relating to medical group practice, including formation, physician compensation, managed care contracting, credentialing and peer review, personnel issues, environmental compliance, reimbursement, billing and collections, patient care records, liability, insurance, marketing, and corporate compliance. It will be supplemented annually. Its format—which features abundant charts, checklists, graphs, flowcharts, figures, and legal forms—significantly enhances its value to the practicing attorney.

Aspen Health Law Center. *Physician Credentialing and Peer Review Answer Book*. Gaithersburg, Md.: Aspen, 1995, 274 pages.

Contains an introduction to credentialing and peer review; participants in the process; criteria for medical staff membership; termination, suspension, or restriction of privileges; special issues for managed care organizations; validation of clinical procedures; and clinical practice guidelines.

Michael J. Baxter. "A Potent Weapon: Federal Peer Review Immunity under HCQIA." *Defense Counsel Journal*, 1997, *64*, 364.

Examines the Health Care Quality Improvement Act of 1986, 42 U.S.C. §§ 11101–11152. As the stakes surrounding physician credentialing have risen, the providers' responses to adverse credentialing actions escalate. These responses—usually in the form of claims of antitrust violations, intentional torts, and discrimination—have focused attention on federal and state peer review immunity laws. When properly applied, the author argues, peer review immunity is a powerful defense for credentialing entities, and an almost insurmountable hurdle to individual health care providers.

Enacted by Congress to encourage the health care industry to conduct meaningful peer review, HCQIA's immunity provisions have been expansively interpreted and applied by the courts. This article reviews more than twenty cases construing the act and concludes that the immunity provisions it contains provide a formidable shield, assuming the credentialing entity acts reasonably in its peer review process.

Barbara A. Blackmond. "Current Issues—The National Practitioner Data Bank and Hospital Peer Review." *Health Lawyer*, Fall 1993, p. 1.

Examines the HCQIA and the National Practitioner Data Bank (NPDB). Topics discussed include which actions are reportable, which are not, sanctions for noncompliance, temporary privileges, definition of investigations, and precautionary suspensions.

Elise Dunitz Brennan. "Peer Review Confidentiality." Washington, D.C.: American Health Lawyers Association [Report No. VHL98–0053], 1998, 39 pages.

Explores the laws governing confidentiality of peer review records and considers evolving health care delivery system forces that affect the protection under existing laws. Includes the Credentialing and Peer Review Substantive Law Committee's fifty-state survey on the impact on the JCAHO sentinel event policy on peer review statutes.

Lowell C. Brown. "When Worlds Collide: Coping with Peer Review Law and Labor Law in Emerging Health Care Delivery Systems." Washington, D.C.: American Health Lawyers Association [Report No. MC97–0031], 1997, 28 pages.

Examines issues relating to how peer review law affects provider organizations as employee physicians become more prevalent (which traditionally applied only in independent contractor relationships) and employment law (which is new to most peer review bodies).

John T. Burroughs. "Peer Review, Disciplining, Hearings and Appeals." In *Legal Medicine.* (3rd ed.) St. Louis: Mosby-Year Book, 1995, pp. 105–117.

This article reviews case law on peer review, economic credentialing, and judicial review. It also discusses bias, violation of hospital bylaws, and sufficiency of evidence.

California Medical Association. *Peer Review Law.* (3rd ed.) San Francisco: CMA, 1993.

This guide of approximately two hundred pages discusses liability concerns and statutory protections. Topics include immunities, fair hearing requirements, peer review activities, confidentiality and record protection, notice requirements, and credentialing issues.

Bonnie Faherty. "Medical Malpractice and Adverse Actions Against Nurses: Five Years of Information from the National Practitioner Data Bank." *Journal of Nursing Law,* 1998, *5,* 17.

Discusses what data from the NPDB reveal about the involvement of nurses and other selected health care providers in malpractice and adverse actions.

Mark A. Kadzielski and Jack Spaulding Schroder, Jr. "Peer Review: Recent Developments and Future Trends." Washington, D.C.: American Health Lawyers Association [Report No. VHH99–0024], 1999, 30 pages.

Discusses new theories of liability in suits against hospitals over adverse peer review actions, despite the immunity afforded by HCQIA and centralization of the credentialing process and other sharing of information in health care organizations. Provides a capsule summary of recent judicial decisions involving peer review issues.

Daniel A. Lang. *Medical Staff Peer Review: Motivation and Performance in the Era of Managed Care.* (Rev. ed.) Chicago: AHA Press, 1999, 292 pages.

This book takes on a topic that could in other hands be a complete bore and brings it alive with insightful vignettes of peer relationships in the medical community, the problems that often result, and how they can be resolved. The author, an expert in medical staff management, writes both succinctly and authoritatively. Topics discussed include credentialing, measurement of professional performance, improving individual performance, and physician health.

Medical Group Management Practice Legal and Administrative Guide. Gaithersburg, Md.: Aspen, and Medical Group Management Association, 1998.

This one-volume loose-leaf treatise discusses formation of group practice; designing physician compensation systems; managing personnel and human resource issues; maximizing reimbursement; avoiding patient care liability; initiating a corporate compliance program; contracting with managed care companies; and starting a credentialing and peer review program, among other topics.

Bernard D. Reams, Jr. *The Health Care Quality Improvement Act of 1986: A Legislative History of Pub. L. No. 99–660.* Buffalo, N.Y.: Hein, 1990.

Before 1986 a physician disciplined by a state licensing board, hospital, or medical society was often able to resume practicing medicine by voluntarily resigning in return for the hospital's silence regarding the sanction or by the threat of legal action if the hospital attempted to sanction the physician or if a colleague attempted to report the malfeasance. To encourage doctors and hospitals to more strictly review their peers and to shield reporting doctors and institutions from retaliatory lawsuits, Congress enacted the Health Care Quality Improvement Act of 1986, S. 1774, Title IV. Congress intended the act to reduce the incidence of medical malpractice and to erect barriers to the movement of incompetent or negligent doctors from state to state without their prior conduct being disclosed. The act created a reporting system requiring state licensing boards to report disciplinary action to DHHS, for collection and dissemination to hospitals. The act, moreover, extends limited immunity to doctors and hospitals involved in good faith peer review and reporting from damages sought by censured doctors.

This book of approximately five hundred pages contains the text of the law as enacted, along with relevant reports, hearings, and congressional commentary. The materials are set forth in chronological order. The book also includes a helpful bibliography of journal articles. The author, a professor of law and director of the law library at Washington University in St. Louis, has produced a valuable, authoritative resource.

Susan O. Scheutzow. "State Medical Peer Review: High Cost But No Benefit—Is It Time for a Change?" *American Journal of Law and Medicine,* 1999, *25,* 7.

This article, through analysis of data available from the National Practitioner Data Bank, suggests that peer review protection statutes do not encourage peer review. As such, legislatures committed to enhancing the quality of health care through peer review must find additional means of promoting effective peer review. If legislatures keep their protection statutes in place, lawmakers should tailor such laws to minimize the laws' negative effect on the judicial process. Additionally, legislatures should guarantee that hospitals do not use these laws to protect themselves for failing to engage in effective peer review. Data from this study also reveal that the NPDB receives more adverse peer review actions in states that impose significant penalties on hospitals failing to report peer review actions to state licensing boards. This indicates that hospitals are failing to report certain peer review actions that, under state law, must be transmitted to the appropriate government agencies, suggesting that stronger peer review statutes are needed.

Charity Scott. "Medical Peer Review, Antitrust, and the Effect of Statutory Reform." *Maryland Law Review,* 1991, *50,* 316.

Analyzes whether the HCQIA will effect any real change in peer review litigation under the antitrust laws or whether it is what the author describes as just another round of "cosmetic surgery." Although HCQIA's protection from legal liability is not limited to antitrust cases, the threat of antitrust liability associated with peer review provided the primary impetus for enacting the immunity provision; thus this article focuses on the act's impact on antitrust litigation only. It contends that the statutory reform effected by the act falls short of that heralded by its supporters and concludes that because the act does not change the substantive rules governing antitrust liability in peer-review cases, its "immunity" is more imaginary than real.

Kenneth G. Starling. "Antitrust Defenses in Physician Peer Review Cases." *Antitrust Law Journal,* 1995, *63,* 399.

Physician peer review programs seek to enlist those professionals with sufficient training and qualifications to monitor the quality of patient care provided by their peers and to restrict or remove those doctors who do not satisfy applicable standards of competence. In recent years, a substantial number of physicians who have been subject to this discipline have filed antitrust suits against the peer review participants, who are often their professional competitors. In 1986 Congress passed the HCQIA to shield physician and hospital participants in peer review from damage liability under the antitrust laws, as well as under most other federal and state laws. The author concludes that the defenses available to physicians taken altogether—with or without the Health Care Quality Improvement Act—have been quite effective.

13.04 PHYSICIAN DESELECTION

Joanne P. Hopkins and Mark A. Kadzielski. "Managed Care Credentialing and Deselection of Providers." Washington, D.C.: American Health Lawyers Association [Report No. VHL98–0016], 1998, 35 pages.

Covers a range of credentialing and deselection issues that affect managed care organizations and their practitioners: accreditation organizations and standards, delegated credentialing, potential liability for such actions as negligent credentialing, termination or deselection without affording due process rights, and others being contested in the courts.

Bryan A. Liang. "Deselection under *Harper v. Healthsource:* A Blow for Maintaining Physician-Patient Relationships in an Era of Managed Care." *Notre Dame Law Review,* 1997, *72,* 799.

In a managed care environment, the author writes, excess capacity of physicians, hospitals, and other services must be pared to maximize profits. This process, particularly for physicians, is accomplished through deselection. Deselection is a process whereby providers have their contracts with managed care organizations terminated. Many physicians have been deselected under a termination-without-cause clause; the few who have challenged these terminations have generally been denied relief. Indeed, the terminated physician has usually sought some form of due process before termination rather than questioning the right to terminate itself.

In *Harper v. Healthsource,* 674 A2d 962 (N.H. 1996), the New Hampshire Supreme Court held that aside from due process considerations, the decision for termination itself is reviewable on the basis of good faith and public policy, and not simply the procedure by which it is accomplished. This article examines the court's reasoning and argues that the court correctly understands the new role of the physician under managed care. The author concludes by proposing a health policy that would protect vulnerable patients from the consequences of deselection.

Bryan A. Liang. "An Overview and Analysis of Challenges to Medical Exclusive Contracts." *Journal of Legal Medicine,* 1997, *18,* 1.

Exclusive contracts have been used and accepted by the courts in an attempt to fulfill the goals of decreased costs and high-quality medical care in the U.S. health delivery system. Future reform efforts may also result in substantial increases in the use of exclusive contracts. However, courts have not recognized important implications for the reputations of physicians who have had privileges denied, limited, or terminated because of exclusive contract arrangements. Exclusive contract challenge denials by courts have also relied on statements by potentially biased parties in the contracting relationship as well as on a medical business judgment rule in validating privilege termination actions. Further, either through extension of the medical business judgment rule or through decision-making precedent, courts have denied challenges to exclusive contracts when physician care is deemed to potentially affect patient welfare or the public interest.

John A. Rizzo and John H. Goddeeris. "The Economic Returns to Hospital Admitting Privileges." *Journal of Health Politics, Policy and Law,* June 1998, *23,* 483.

Legal suits contesting denial or termination of hospital staff privileges are the most common antitrust cases involving medical markets. There is, however, little evidence about the economic implications, for the physicians, of having staff privileges. Using a nationally representative sample of self-employed physicians from 1992, this article presents estimates of the effects of hospital admitting privileges on physician earnings. The results indicate that for nonprimary care specialists with few admitting privileges, gaining an additional privilege increases earnings. This effect diminishes as the number of admitting privileges increases, however, and there are no economic gains in earnings beyond having three or four admitting privileges. With the growing emphasis on managed care, physicians are being scrutinized both in terms of the quality of care they deliver and their impact on the economic performance of hospitals and managed care organizations. The authors conclude that this suggests the frequency of lawsuits involving denial or rescission of medical staff privileges may assume even greater importance.

Michael D. Roth. "Managed Care Organization (MCO): Credentialing and Deselection." Washington, D.C.: American Health Lawyers Association [Report No. VMC98–0021], 1998, 23 pages.

Examines the duty of MCOs to credential physicians employed by the MCO, under contract with the MCO, or otherwise participating in the MCO's provider network. Reviews case law and statutory law concerning due process relative to denial or termination of a provider. Also looks at economic credentialing considerations and HCQIA immunity and confidentiality issues.

14

Labor Issues

One of the hottest topics of conversation among physicians today is the formation of labor unions. That this debate is even occurring would have stunned many of their predecessors only a generation ago, when the profession was an autonomous, self-regulating guild at the apex of its institutional power. What has catalyzed this debate?

A number of developments beginning in the latter part of 1996 spurred physician interest in forming unions. The first was the August 1996 announcement by the American Podiatric Medical Association that it was working with the Office Professionals Employees International Union (OPEIU) to form a union for podiatrists. This was covered by the *New York Times* and received widespread attention elsewhere in the press. Another development, also reported in the general press, was the Nov. 8, 1996, ruling of the regional director of the National Labor Relations Board (NLRB) that physicians employed by the Thomas-Davis Medical Centers, P.C., in Tucson, Arizona, could form a bargaining unit and engage in collective negotiations with their employer. Next, the Service Employees International announced their intention in 1999 to actively recruit physicians as members of the SEIU. Texas lawmakers then introduced legislation that would give self-employed physicians the right to bargain collectively.

Needless to say, these developments attracted considerable attention among physicians. Union formation quickly became a topic of discussion at many county and state medical societies and other groups of doctors. As a result, the AMA and other professional organizations received and handled many inquiries about the law of union formation, what activities unions are allowed to engage in on behalf of physicians, the activities of existing physician unions, whether medical societies can organize unions, and what activities medical societies can engage in to assist physicians other than starting a union. Many state, county, and specialty medical societies heard presentations from the main physicians' unions advocating that medical societies affiliate with a union. Some of these societies are considering such affiliation.

This debate culminated in the 1999 vote by the AMA to develop an affiliated national labor organization to represent employed physicians and (where allowed by law) residents. Further, the AMA's House of Delegates vowed to seek antitrust relief for physicians and medical groups, as well as creation of a national organization to support development and operation of local negotiating units. These units would provide an option for self-employed physicians and medical groups. Finally, the organization acted to expand its advocacy programs by initiating litigation and stepping up lobbying efforts to augment physician bargaining power with payers. In taking these actions, however, the AMA forswore any use of a union's ultimate weapon: the strike.

ANNOTATIONS

14.01   IN GENERAL

Gene G. Abel. "Addressing Sexual Harassment by Medical Staff Members." Washington, D.C.: American Health Lawyers Association [Report No. VHH99–0015]. 1999, 22 pages.

Discusses dealing with sexual harassment in the context of medical staff membership and privileges; understanding the clinical aspects of sexual harassment; and identifying what evaluation is needed to assess a staff member who is engaged in sexually harassing conduct. Also highlights the range of treatment options needed to address sexual harassment by a physician, and when and under what conditions a physician should be permitted to retain privileges after engaging in harassing behavior.

Bruce R. Alper and Shawn O. Miller. "Unions, Nurses, and the Health Care Industry: Recent Administrative and Judicial Developments." *Journal of Health and Hospital Law*, 1995, 28(2), 65–72.

Summarizes recent NLRB and court decisions that may affect labor relations within the health care sector.

Stuart I. Cohen. "Labor Law Update." Washington, D.C.: American Health Lawyers Association [Report No. VLT99–0013], 1999, 49 pages.

Reviews relevant labor law issues for long-term care providers, including the continuing battle over the status of charge nurses as employees or supervisors, employees' right to organize at facilities other than those in which they are employed, a union's unilateral extension of its ten-day strike notice, WARN (Worker Adjustment and Retraining Notification) Act obligations after a strike is belatedly canceled, and curing incorrect treatment of an exempt employee under the Fair Labor Standards Act.

Henry E. Farber and Carol Scott. "Negotiating the Labor Law Mine Field: Selected Topics." *Whittier Law Review*, 1995, 16, 1051–1068.

Examines employment issues in the health care sector, and relevant federal and California statutes and case law.

John C. Gilliland II. "Minimum Wage and Overtime Pay Issues." Washington, D.C.: American Health Lawyers Association [Report No. VLT99–0031], 1999, 35 pages.

Outlines the basic concepts involved in complying with minimum wage and overtime pay laws. Identifies and examines many of the common problems encountered in wage and hour compliance by long-term care facilities and home health agencies.

Virginia A. Hackney. "Addressing Sexual Harassment by Medical Staff Members." Washington, D.C.: American Health Lawyers Association [Report No. VHH99–0016], 1999, 20 pages.

Summarizes U.S. Supreme Court decisions and current laws addressing sexual harassment in the workplace. Also discusses practical issues to consider when dealing with complaints of sexual harassment involving a physician or health care professional, such as preserving privilege and confidentiality of the disciplinary proceedings. Contains a sample excerpt from medical staff bylaws discussing the governing body's authority to take certain actions against medical staff members whose actions constitute sexual harassment, and a sample physician surveillance form.

Charles R. McConnell (ed.). *The Health Care Supervisor on Law*. Gaithersburg, Md.: Aspen, 1993, 238 pages.

The focus of this collection of articles from the *Health Care Supervisor* is legislation and other legal matters as they may affect the working health care supervisor. Topics include mandatory reporting laws; withdrawal of treatment, employment documentation, sexual harassment, wrongful discharge, privacy rights, and HIV in the hospital setting; health care union organizing; strike issues; grievances; and arbitration.

J. Bruce Mulligan. "Employment Law Issues." Washington, D.C., American Health Lawyers Association [Report No. VIH99–0009], 1999, 37 pages.

Detailed overview of all federal employment laws affecting health care. Examines Title VII, the early Civil Rights Act, the ADEA (Age Discrimination in Employment Act of 1967), the Older Workers Benefit Protection Act, the ADA, the Equal Pay Act, and other laws, with citations to relevant cases. Provides update on sexual harassment, criminal background checks, and other issues.

D. Christopher Osborn. "A Primer on Employment Discrimination Law: What You Don't Know Can Hurt You." In Carl Horn III, Donald H. Caldwell, Jr., and D. Christopher Osborn. *Law for Physicians: An Overview of Medical Legal Issues.* Chicago: American Medical Association, 1999, 246 pages.

Examines federal civil liability for race or gender discrimination, religious discrimination, age discrimination, discrimination against persons with disabilities, the Family and Medical Leave Act of 1993, retaliation claims, litigation of federal employment discrimination claims, state employment discrimination statutes, and practical suggestions for reducing exposure to employment discrimination claims.

Courtney Price. *The Group Practice Personnel Policies Manual.* Englewood, Colo.: Medical Group Management Association, 1997.

This updated edition covers such standard personnel issues as selection, compensation, and evaluation, but also adds policies related to such newly enacted legislation as the ADA and the Family and Medical Leave Act. Other topics include workplace violence, electronic communications, and employee committees. The manual also includes a disk with files of generic policies that can be used as is or modified as necessary.

Mark A. Rothstein. "Labor and Employment Law Issues in Hospital Closure and Downsizing." *Journal of Health and Hospital Law,* 1995, 28(6), 336–343.

Examines some of the labor and employment law implications of hospital downsizing or closure. This article discusses the National Labor Relations Act (NLRA) and the special issues associated with unionized workplaces subject to collective bargaining agreements. Next, the author considers law designed specifically for economically distressed companies, the WARN Act, the Bankruptcy Act and unemployment compensation, the Age Discrimination in Employment Act, Title VII of the Civil Rights Act of 1964, and common law.

William P. Schurgin. "Employment Law Issues for the Health Care Industry." Washington, D.C.: American Health Lawyers Association [Report No. VHL98–0030], 1998, 82 pages.

A review of employment law issues facing health care employers under select provisions of the ADA, Title VII, the NLRA, and the Family and Medical Leave Act. Also briefly reviews independent contractor and leased employee issues.

William P. Schurgin. "Labor and Employment Law in the Healthcare Setting." Washington, D.C.: National Health Lawyers Association [Report No. FH-970007], 1997, 49 pages.

Examines a range of issues in labor and employment law, including the Family and Medical Leave Act, the ADA, the 1991 Civil Rights Act, and other issues.

Scotty Shively. "Preventive Measures for Employers in the Healthcare Arena." Washington, D.C.: American Health Lawyers Association [Report No. VHH99–0013], 1999, 35 pages.

Provides guidelines and measures to minimize or prevent employer liability in the context of federal wage and hour labor laws.

Richard J. Simmons. *Wage and Hour Manual for California Employers.* (5th ed.) Sacramento: California Healthcare Association, 1997.

This handbook covers state and federal wage and hour laws, the Fair Labor Standards Act, Industrial Welfare Commission wage orders, and Labor Commission policies.

Skoler, Abbott & Presser, P.C. *Health Care Labor Manual.* Gaithersburg, Md.: Aspen, 1999.

This three-volume loose-leaf text surveys the entire range of labor law as it relates to health care. Contents include an overview of labor and personnel problems in the health care field; an overview of the NLRA; the organizing campaign; elections; negotiating the collective bargaining agreement; administering the collective bargaining agreement; strikes, picketing, and job actions; federal wage and hour laws; equal employment opportunity laws; fair employment practices; safety, health, and related issues; employee benefits; personnel administration in the health care field; wrongful discharge; employment relationships with physicians; text of laws and regulations; organizing materials; selected contract provisions; grievance and arbitration materials; personnel administration guides; employee handbooks; directories of labor agencies; selected bibliographical materials; table of cases; topical index; NLRB Advice Memoranda; and a glossary.

James Walsh. *Rightful Termination: Defensive Strategies for Hiring and Firing in the Lawsuit-Happy '90s.* Santa Monica, Calif.: Merritt, 1994, 362 pages.

Highlights such key workplace issues as job applicant testing, at-will employment, civil rights claims, and termination methods. This text includes checklists, case studies, and standard forms.

14.02   PHYSICIAN UNIONIZATION

Robert E. Bloch and Scott P. Perlman. "Collective Bargaining by Physicians and the Antitrust Laws." Washington, D.C.: American Health Lawyers Association [Report No. VHL98–0032], 1998, 20 pages.

Reviews collective bargaining by physicians and the relationships of labor and antitrust laws.

Donald H. Caldwell, Jr. "Physicians Unions: Developing Strength in Numbers." In Carl Horn III, Donald H. Caldwell, Jr., and D. Christopher Osborn. *Law for Physicians: An Overview of Medical Legal Issues.* Chicago: American Medical Association, 1999, 246 pages.

Explores why physicians are interested in forming unions, the costs of organizing a union, and the laws governing union formation. Also provides information about specific unions and addresses what medical societies can do to meet the needs of self-employed physicians interested in forming a union.

John J. Deis. "The Unionization of Independent Contracting Physicians: A Comedy of Errors." *Houston Law Review,* 1999, *36,* 952.

Explores the purported consumer benefits of allowing independent physicians to form labor unions and collectively bargain with managed care organizations. Concludes that (1) allowing independently contracting physicians to collectively bargain would be a drastic departure from current labor law, (2) labor law is not amenable to protecting consumers' interests, and (3) the regulatory board overseeing labor relations is relatively powerless to protect patient interests.

Edward B. Hirshfeld. "Physicians, Unions, and Antitrust." *Journal of Health Law,* Winter 1999, *32,* 43.

Increasing consolidation of health care delivery systems and the concomitant push for perceived efficiencies, speed, and profits has laid the foundation for renewed interest in unionization by many physicians. This article analyzes the barriers that are posed by the antitrust laws; it provides analysis of how to proceed with unionization without violating those laws. The article also analyzes the status of physicians' ability to unionize and surveys the status of physician unions. The author was associate general counsel and vice president for private sector advocacy at the AMA at the time of his death in August 1998.

Edward B. Hirshfeld. "Physicians, Unions and Antitrust." Washington, D.C.: American Health Lawyers Association [Report No. VAT98–0004], 1998, 18 pages.

Explores why physicians are interested in forming unions, the status of physician unions, information about specific unions that are seeking to organize physicians, the AMA's evolving position regarding unions, the laws governing union formation, and pertinent NLRB rulings. Addresses what medical societies and advocacy groups can do to meet the needs of self-employed physicians interested in forming a union.

Forrest W. Hunter. *"Physician Unionization: Current Legal Constraints and Future Trends."* Washington, D.C.: American Health Lawyers Association [Report No. VHH99–0021], 1999, 13 pages.

Briefly examines the current legal constraints on physician unionization imposed by the NLRA. Highlights recent and pending cases and discusses trends surrounding physician unionization issues.

Ellen L. Luepke. "White Coat, Blue Collar: Physician Unionization and Managed Care." *Annals of Health Law,* 1999, *8,* 275.

Provides an historical overview of the rise of the physician unionization movement in the United States. Also examines the barriers faced by employed and independent physicians that prevent or limit their collective bargaining, and reviews the responses of the various organized medical societies to the physician unionization movement.

Jeremy Lutsky. "Is Your Physician Becoming a Teamster: The Rising Trend of Physicians Joining Labor Unions in the Late 1990s." *DePaul Journal of Health Care Law,* Fall 1997, *2,* 55.

Presents examples of physician unionization along with underlying reasons for the trend.

National Labor Relations Board. "NLRB Petition Re AmeriHealth, Inc./AmeriHealth HMO." Washington, D.C.: American Health Lawyers Association [Document No. VAT98–0005], 1998, 7 pages.

Letter from Dorothy Moore-Duncan, regional director of NLRB Region Four, rejecting a request to certify a New Jersey union under the NLRA as the bargaining representative of physicians participating in AmeriHealth HMO network, based on its conclusion that the physicians are independent contractors, not employees.

Chris Phan. "Physician Unionization: The Impact on the Medical Profession." *Journal of Legal Medicine,* Mar. 1999, *20*(1), 115–140.

This commentary begins with a description of how unionization may adversely affect the physician-patient relationship, thus corroding the core of the medical profession. It then documents how decisions and resolutions from authoritative sources in the legislature and the courts may affect development of physician unions. Next, the article comments on the evolution of the physician union movement and the medical associations' positions on this issue. Finally, the author analyzes the situations that may arise if physicians unionize, as well as the pros and cons of unionization.

J. A. Shorb. "Working Without Rights: Recognizing Housestaff Unionization." *Vanderbilt Law Review,* May 1999, *52,* 1051.

This note advocates reversal of the NLRB's decisions in *Cedars-Sinai Med. Center,* 223 NLRB 251, 260–262 (1976), and *St. Clare's Hospital and Medical Center,* 229 NLRB 1000 (1977), in which it held that house officers working in private nonprofit hospitals do not have the right to organize and bargain collectively.

15

Liability of Health Care Professionals

Since the early 1970s, when many of the problems associated with medical malpractice came to be labeled a "crisis," there have been constant, vigorous efforts to reform the present system of injury compensation or to revise it completely. Most state legislatures have enacted legislation modifying existing rules in some way. Although some of these changes have not been substantial, others have implemented such reforms as imposing limitations on the amount of damages that can be recovered and controlling the contingency fees that plaintiffs' attorneys can collect.[1] Although not enacted into law, broader, more fundamental reforms such as no-fault insurance and mandatory arbitration have been the subject of considerable debate, as the annotations that follow indicate.

Reference

1. Michael G. Macdonald and others (eds.). *Health Care Law: A Practical Guide*. New York: Matthew Bender, 1993; see also Leon I. Jacobson. "Insuring Against Malpractice Liability." In Michael G. Macdonald and others (eds.). *Treatise on Health Care Law*. New York: Matthew Bender, 1995, § 14.

ANNOTATIONS

15.01　LIABILITY FOR PATIENT INJURY

Agency for Health Care Policy and Research. "Compendium of Selected State Laws Governing Medical Injury Claims." Washington, D.C.: AHCPR [AHCPR 96-R058], Mar. 1996, 43 pages.

This report presents a partial update of an earlier Compendium of State Systems for Resolution of Medical Injury Claims. It is very valuable in view of the wide variety of state approaches to this problem that have been enacted by legislatures since the medical malpractice crisis arose in the 1970s. Because of significant changes in both the statutes and the judicial gloss on them, this work has become dated quickly and needs to be updated periodically.

Annot. "Arbitration of Medical Malpractice Claims." *ALR5th*, 1998, *24*, 1.

Cases discussing the validity, scope, and effect of contracts to arbitrate medical malpractice claims, whether or not subject to statutory prescriptions, are collected in this annotation. Because of what has been characterized as a "medical malpractice insurance crisis"—to which have contributed the cost of litigation and large jury verdicts in medical malpractice actions—

attention has focused on arbitration as a less expensive and more efficient method of dispute resolution. Although courts have not objected on principle to contracts providing for arbitration of medical malpractice claims between a patient and a health care provider, issues have been raised as to patients' understanding of such contracts and the potentially coercive circumstances under which the agreements are made.

In *Broemmer* v. *Abortion Servs. of Phoenix, Ltd.* (Ariz. 1992), 840 P2d 1013, 24 *ALR5th* 793, the court refused to enforce a contract to arbitrate because it was presented to the patient as a condition of treatment, contained no explicit waiver of the right to jury trial, and provided that any arbitrator be an obstetrician-gynecologist. However, some jurisdictions have enacted statutes specifically governing medical malpractice arbitration agreements, and a presumption of validity may attach to an agreement conforming to statutory requirements.

Annot. "Medical Malpractice: Who Are 'Health Care Providers,' or the Like, Whose Actions Fall Within Statutes Specifically Governing Actions and Damages for Medical Malpractice?" *ALR5th*, 1998, *12*, 1.

Collects and discusses those cases in which the courts have made a determination as to which individuals or entities are "health care providers" or the like, whose actions fall within medical malpractice code provisions. In response to a perceived medical malpractice crisis, many state legislatures have promulgated a variety of provisions intended to deal with the problems posed by frivolous malpractice actions and exorbitant damage awards. Among the provisions enacted are those that limit the amount of damages recoverable, shorten the limitations period for filing malpractice litigation, or require submitting a malpractice claim to a pretrial screening panel. Medical malpractice statutes are generally limited in that, regardless of their intent, they apply only to particular types of activity engaged in by a specified group of defendants, often labeled "health care providers."

Therefore, one question addressed by the courts is which entities or persons are health care providers whose actions fall within statutes enacted to govern medical malpractice claims. In *Weidig* v. *Crites* (Md. 1991), 593 A2d 1094, 12 *ALR5th* 969, for example, a medical office employee, who was neither a licensed physician nor nurse, was held by the court not to be a health care provider within the meaning of a medical malpractice claims act, and thus could not be compelled to submit to an arbitration proceeding.

Annot. "Nurse's Liability for Her Own Negligence or Malpractice." *ALR2nd*, 1998, *51*, 970.

This brief annotation collects and analyzes cases in which the courts have considered the question of the liability of a nurse for her own negligence or malpractice. It is regularly updated by the publisher.

Annot. "Physicians and Surgeons: Standard of Skill and Care Required of Specialist." *ALR3rd*, 1998, *21*, 953.

Collects and analyzes cases that contain express discussion of the care and skill required of a specialist in treating some particular organ or disease.

Annot. "What Constitutes Physician-Patient Relationship for Malpractice Purposes." *ALR4th*, 1998, *17*, 132.

Collects and analyzes state and federal cases in which the courts have decided what constitutes a physician-patient relationship for purposes of malpractice. Thus, beyond the scope of this annotation are cases in which the courts explicitly or implicitly recognized the relationship but in which the issue was not expressly litigated.

Hal R. Arkes and Cindy A. Schipani. "Medical Malpractice v. The Business Judgment Rule: Differences in Hindsight Bias." *Oregon Law Review*, Fall 1994, *73*, 587–638. Reprinted in *Defense Law Journal*, 1996, *45*, 59–109.

Focuses on hindsight bias, the tendency for people with knowledge of an outcome to exaggerate the extent to which they believe the outcome could have been predicted. The existence of the bias has been documented in a number of studies considering cases of medical malpractice, the authors write. There are, however, numerous legal rules that reduce the probability of biased retrospective evaluation in actions alleging negligent business decisions. This article concludes that although there are several legitimate reasons for courts to treat business decisions differently from medical decisions, there is no legitimate reason to tolerate hindsight bias in medical malpractice actions. The authors then offer a proposal to reduce the effects of the bias in medical malpractice litigation.

Elizabeth J. Armstrong. "Nursing Malpractice in North Carolina: The Standard of Care." (Comment.) *North Carolina Law Review*, 1987, *65*, 579.

Examines North Carolina law relating to the standard of care required of a professional nurse. This comment discusses when and whether expert testimony is necessary to establish the standard, as well as who qualifies as an expert. The author discusses issues of professional vulnerability, including the standard of care for nurses in expanded roles and the latitude of nurses to obey or disobey physicians' orders. Finally, Armstrong analyzes the standard's "same or similar" community requirement. She concludes that various changes should be made in how North Carolina courts determine the nursing standard of care. Such changes are necessary to ensure that nurses are held accountable for their professional expertise and education but shielded from liability for a standard of care they have not assumed.

Jennifer Begel. "Maine Physician Practice Guidelines: Implications for Medical Malpractice Litigation." *Maine Law Review*, 1995, *47*, 68.

Assesses use of physician practice guidelines as a vehicle for medical malpractice tort reform and focuses on Maine's legislation incorporating physician practice parameters into defense of medical malpractice litigation. This article reviews both the practical procedural effects and the constitutional issues triggered by the legislation. It concludes with suggestions regarding how the Maine legislation might be amended to address its procedural and constitutional shortcomings.

"Bibliography of Medical Malpractice Publications and Working Papers Based on Robert Wood Johnson Foundation Grants." Princeton, N.J., Oct. 1, 1993.

This bibliography lists more than ninety publications and unpublished working papers that were based in whole or in significant part on research funded by the Robert Wood Johnson Foundation. Included are articles in journals, conference proceedings, reports, protocols, symposia, books, and book chapters. It is available free of charge from the foundation.

Joseph D. Bloom and others. *Physician Sexual Misconduct.* Washington, D.C.: American Psychiatric Press, 1999, 304 pages.

Examines all the dimensions associated with this occurrence, including legal and ethical aspects. Offers thorough, candid coverage crucial for psychiatrists and other medical professionals, attorneys, and medical board administrators.

James F. Blumstein. "Medical Care Cost Containment and Medical Malpractice." In Elizabeth Rolph (ed.), *Health Care Delivery and Tort: Systems on a Collision Course?* Santa Monica, Calif.: RAND, 1991.

Assesses the intersection of malpractice and cost containment issues.

James F. Blumstein. "A Perspective on Federalism and Medical Malpractice." *Yale Law and Policy Review* (formerly *Yale Journal on Regulation*), 1996, *14*, 411.

Develops a framework by which to assess the appropriate federal role in medical malpractice. Blumstein identifies a set of nonexhaustive criteria for federal involvement: (1) Is there a need for uniformity across states? (2) Are there overriding national interests? (3) Is there consensus on identification of the problem and on the range of potential solutions? (4) Are states actively considering or dealing with the issue? (5) Is there a special federal comparative advantage in addressing the issue?

Blumstein concludes that there is a continuum of potential federal intervention regarding medical malpractice issues. There has been federal intervention on insurance questions and on quality care through peer review. For sound reasons, he adds, there has been relatively little federal initiative on medical malpractice standards, traditionally an arena of state law. The author suggests a federal data-gathering role consistent with the existing medical practice data bank. He also proposes that the federal government develop a pilot program for its own special constituencies: federal employees who participate in the CHAMPUS and FEHBP programs and individuals who participate in the Medicare and Medicaid programs.

Jill Bohannon. "Contractual Liability of Physicians." *Medical Trial Technique Quarterly*, 1994, *40, 499.*

Notes that the vast majority of medical malpractice claims against physicians are grounded in tort, and suggests breach of contract as an alternative theory of recovery against a physician. This article examines case law relating to the types of claim amendable to a contract theory, and the benefits and obstacles to a plaintiff in pursuing a contractual theory. It also discusses damages, malpractice insurance coverage limits, special features of contractual liability, and public policy considerations.

Randall R. Bovbjerg and Frank A. Sloan. "No Fault for Medical Injury: Theory and Evidence." *University of Cincinnati Law Review*, 1998, *67, 53.*

In the late 1980s, Virginia became the first state to introduce no-fault for medical injuries, with Florida following suit a year later. These two Birth-Related Neurological Injury Compensation Acts created targeted administrative systems primarily intended to remove severe neurological injury to a newborn from tort law. This article reports on the experience of these programs and evaluates their performance based on the problems they addressed and their stated objectives. From the evidence of several interrelated analyses, the authors suggest improvements in the existing programs. They also derive key implications for broader approaches, such as those under development in Utah and Colorado, and other approaches that might be used nationwide.

Randall R. Bovbjerg, Frank A. Sloan, and James F. Blumstein. "Valuing Life and Limb in Tort: Scheduling 'Pain and Suffering.'" *Northwestern University Law Review*, 1989, *83, 908.*

Contends that even if juries understand expert testimony presented in a medical malpractice case and do not act out of sympathy, they are still unable to value damages consistently, given the subjectivity of injuries such as pain and suffering. This article proposes three alternative frameworks to perfect valuation of noneconomic damages in the current liability system. Each of these proposed models would constrain the operation of vague and open-ended legal rules and the wide latitude of discretion that has been afforded legal decision makers.

Randall R. Bovbjerg, Frank A. Sloan, Avi Dor, and Chee Ruey Hsieh. "Juries and Justice: Are Malpractice and Other Personal Injuries Created Equal?" *Law and Contemporary Problems*, Winter 1991, *55, 5.*

Documents how jury verdicts for malpractice and other "deep pocket" personal injury defendants (product liability and government cases) compare with ordinary defendants (such as automobile torts) and analyzes possible explanations for observed differences. The dynamics of litigation and the probability of winning are addressed, as well as change over time. The data come from jury verdicts reported in five states, combining data previously computerized by RAND researchers with information similarly compiled by the authors. The authors conclude that the data reveal juries doing better than their critics allege, although the costs of litigation are very high.

Troyen A. Brennan. "Practice Guidelines and Malpractice Litigation: Collision or Cohesion." *Journal of Health Politics, Policy, and Law,* 1991, *16, 67.*

Discusses the implications of practice guidelines on malpractice litigation. Practice guidelines are standardized specifications for managing particular clinical problems and are intended to improve the outcomes of medical care by increasing adherence to standards of care. They are also meant to make medicine more cost-effective by eliminating unnecessary procedures. A relatively recent phenomenon, the practice guidelines now emerging will have implications for malpractice, which also intends to bring about better care. They will probably not revolutionize the procedures that courts use to determine negligence, but judges will integrate guidelines into their decision-making process. This development should be welcomed, the author contends. Guidelines should prove to be useful as either inculpatory or exculpatory evidence of negligence. They are unlikely to generate much new litigation, although there is some potential for suits against those who issue guidelines, especially if guidelines are not revised as the technology of medical care changes.

Robert D. Brussack. "Georgia's Professional Malpractice Affidavit Requirement." *Georgia Law Review,* 1997, *31,* 1031–1091.

Critiques Georgia's procedural statute providing that professional malpractice claims ordinarily must be accompanied by an affidavit executed by an expert. In the affidavit, the expert must substantiate the claim by attesting that some act or omission alleged in the claim was negligent. The author discusses the scope of the affidavit requirement, making the case that the courts and the legislature have rejected the most straightforward, principled approach to the applicability of the requirement.

Fillmore Buckner and Marvin Firestone. "Where the Public Peril Begins: 25 Years After *Tarasoff.*" *Journal of Legal Medicine,* 2000, *21,* 187.

Assesses the consequences of this California Supreme Court decision holding that psychotherapists have a duty to warn third parties of potentially dangerous patients, a ruling adopted in many other jurisdictions that has been expanded to include a variety of health care practitioners.

California Medical Association. *The MICRA Manual.* San Francisco: CMA, 1996.

Designed for attorneys, this law practice manual analyzes the Medical Injury Compensation Reform Act of 1975, California's medical malpractice litigation statute. It includes case law interpreting the statute, sample motions, a sample periodic payments judgment, present value tables, and the Model Periodic Payment of Judgments Act.

California Physician's Legal Handbook (CPLH). Sacramento: California Medical Association, 1999, *2,* 100 pages.

This three-volume text, by the legal staff of the California Medical Association, is written in plain English for physicians and their advisors and discusses malpractice issues, among other topics.

Frank J. Cavico and Nancy M. Cavico. "Nursing Profession in the 1990s: Negligence and Malpractice Liability." *Cleveland State Law Review,* 1995, *43,* 557.

Examines changes in the nursing profession during the last decade, before moving to a general discussion of the topic of negligence, followed by analysis of the concepts of duty, breach, causation, the reasonable person, damages, defenses, and vicarious liability. This article also examines several types of nursing negligence, such as administration of medication; observation and monitoring; assessment and diagnosis; communication, notification, and reporting; following, questioning, and disobeying orders; intervention and advocacy; documentation and charting; and equipment and technology. The authors bring a wealth of citations to case law and other relevant secondary resources.

Maureen E. Corcoran. "Managed Care Liability for Physicians." Washington, D.C.: American Health Lawyers Association [Report No. VMC-0030], 1998, 15 pages.

Examines liability issues for physicians who participate in managed care arrangements, including the liability of physician-owners of PSOs arising from fiduciary duty under ERISA. Also looks at liability for medical directors based on utilization review decisions, for delayed care or denied authorizations or referrals, and for improper financial incentive arrangements. Discusses state laws limiting an MCO's right to require indemnification from providers, and outlines the fundamentals of ERISA fiduciary analysis.

Maureen E. Corcoran. "Managed Care Liability for Physicians." Washington, D.C.: American Health Lawyers Association [Report No. VPH99–0005], 1999, 16 pages.

Examines the liability issues for physicians who participate in managed care arrangements and describes the state law and cases analyzing the practice of medicine by medical directors performing utilization review. Also supplies the fundamentals of ERISA fiduciary analysis.

Douglas Danner, Larry L. Varn, and Susan Mathias. *Medical Malpractice: Checklists and Discovery.* 3 vols. Deerfield, Ill.: Clark, Boardman, Callaghan, 1995.

Written by three seasoned malpractice attorneys, this multivolume, loose-leaf treatise serves as a concise road map for the young attorney who is wary of confronting a medical expert, or for a veteran lawyer who may not find herself in the medical arena often. It will also prove useful for risk managers and for insurance company supervisors and claim representatives.

Jerald J. Director. "Malpractice: Physician's Failure to Advise Patient to Consult Specialist or One Qualified in a Method of Treatment Which Physician Is Not Qualified to Give." (Annot.) *ALR3rd,* 1971, *35,* 349.

Collects the cases in which courts have expressly discussed whether a physician has a duty to advise a patient to consult a specialist or one qualified in a method of treatment that the physician is not qualified to give, and whether a physician can be held liable because of his or her failure to give such advice. This resource is regularly updated.

Sal Fiscina, Marcia Mobilia Boumil, Murdock Head, and David J. Sharpe. *Cases and Materials on Medical Liability.* St. Paul, Minn.: West, 1991.

This short casebook presents issues that are likely to arise in any state; the authors deliberately have not stressed the law of any particular state or region of the United States. Because the facts are so important in medical liability litigation, the authors appear to have selected cases with thorough statements of fact as well as intelligible discussion of law. The authors have avoided including medical and legal horror stories; instead, many cases illustrate commonplace situations in medical practice that lawyers have to discuss with doctors over and over.

Frederic Flach. *A Comprehensive Guide to Malpractice Risk Management in Psychiatry.* Long Island City, N.Y.: Hatherleigh Press, 1997, 384 pages.

Brings together prominent psychiatrists and attorneys to give the practicing psychiatrist a detailed road map through the minefield of malpractice risk management. Subjects discussed include avoiding liability in managed care, how to prevent liability in psychopharmacology, the *Tarasoff* decision and the duty to protect, boundary violation issues, and how to manage the suicidal patient effectively.

G. M. Flick. *Medical Malpractice: Handling Emergency Medicine Cases.* Colorado Springs, Colo.: Shepard's/McGraw-Hill, 1991, 788 pages.

This treatise, regularly updated, arranges in forty chapters the broad range of malpractice topics relevant to the emergency medicine physician. It is supplemented by a table of cases and index.

General Accounting Office. *Medical Malpractice: Maine's Use of Practice Guidelines to Reduce Costs.* (GAO/HRD-94–8.) Washington, D.C.: U.S. Government Printing Office, 1993.

Analyzes the use of medical practice guidelines in Maine as standards in medical malpractice litigation.

Roscoe N. Gray and Louise J. Gordy (eds.). *Attorneys' Textbook of Medicine.* (3rd ed.) New York: Matthew Bender, 1997.

This treatise of twenty-three volumes is designed to provide the attorney with basic medical information, on a wide variety of subjects, that is easy to access and kept up to date. All text is specifically written for the attorney, with technical terms defined and numerous illustrations presented. The material contains information on traumatic injuries and systemic diseases. It is augmented by an index volume, regular supplements, and checklists of questions to be asked in reviewing medical records or in questioning a medical expert about a particular case. It also includes a set of transparencies that can be used on an overheard projector as a courtroom aid or during a pretrial settlement conference.

Paul A. Greve, Jr. "Managing Physician Liability Risk." Washington, D.C.: American Health Lawyers Association [Report No. VPH99–0018], 1999, 9 pages.

Covers topics relating to managing the malpractice risks of physicians or groups, including trends in physician claims, issues in physician practice acquisition, hospital-sponsored malpractice insurance programs, insurance coverage needed for consideration, selection of malpractice carriers, and risk management in the practice setting. The paper is oriented to groups owned or closely affiliated with hospitals.

William P. Gronfein and Eleanor DeArman Kinney. "Controlling Large Malpractice Claims: The Unexpected Impact of Damage Caps." *Journal of Health Politics, Policy and Law,* 1991, *16, 441.*

Compares malpractice compensation in Indiana, Michigan, and Ohio. Indiana's comprehensive malpractice reforms, inaugurated in 1975, include a cap on damages, a mandated medical review before trial, and a state insurance fund to pay claims equal to or greater than $100,000. In this study, the authors found that the amount of compensation going to claimants with such large malpractice claims in Indiana is, on average, substantially higher than in Michigan and Ohio. Indiana's mean claim severity between 1977 and 1988 was $404,832, while the means for Michigan and Ohio were $290,022 and $303,220, respectively, with the difference between these three means being highly significant. Although data on claim and claimant characteristics reveal considerable interstate variation, the results of regression analysis show that claim payment amounts in Indiana are higher than in Michigan or Ohio, independent of the effect of sex, age, severity of injury, allegations of negligence, and year of settlement.

Thomas G. Gutheil. *The Psychiatrist as Expert Witness.* Washington, D.C.: American Psychiatric Press, 1998, 176 pages.

Shares practical, hands-on experience for assuming a role as an expert witness. Describes the ethical, clinical and functional role of the expert witness. The book guides the reader through details of case evaluation, discovery and depositions, and trials.

Thomas G. Gutheil. *The Psychiatrist in Court: A Survival Guide.* Washington, D.C.: American Psychiatric Press, 1998, 150 pages.

Illustrates the basics of the legal process, including the setting, assumptions, personnel, issues, and techniques involved. The author describes the legal process step-by-step, from the subpoena and deposition to the actual trial; he describes the surprises and pitfalls along the way. Gutheil outlines approaches to testifying on the witness stand and discusses the various roles a psychiatrist may play in court procedure.

Mark A. Hall. "The Defensive Effect of Medical Practice Policies in Malpractice Litigation." *Law and Contemporary Problems,* Spring 1991, *54, 119.*

Stresses the value of practice policies in resolving malpractice disputes regarding treatment. By leaving the medical profession free to determine for itself what constitutes proper standards of care, the law strives to be neutral with respect to how medicine should be practiced. The legal system may have major failings in achieving this ambition, the author writes, but formal practice policies have the potential to correct these failings. Whether this potential is large or small depends on two factors: the nature of malpractice allegations and the nature of practice policies. A practice policy, however rigorous, is of no use if the nature of the claimed error is either incorrect performance of the treatment in question or failure to recognize which practice policy applies by virtue of failure in diagnosis. However, where the patient alleges incorrect choice of a treatment plan for a condition or symptom properly diagnosed, a precise and prescriptive practice policy is capable of conclusively resolving disputes over the applicable standard of care.

Clark C. Havighurst. "Practice Guidelines as Legal Standards Governing Physician Liability." *Law and Contemporary Problems*, Spring 1991, 87.

Considers the usefulness of practice guidelines in the law of medical malpractice. "Practice guidelines" are systemic, scientifically derived statements of appropriate measures that physicians should take in diagnosing and treating disease. This article first takes a more or less conventional view of practice guidelines and the tort system, explaining how guidelines will assist in creating legal standards of care that are clearer and more rational than those the courts are currently using to identify professional negligence.

The article then suggests an alternative strategy for using practice guidelines. Instead of visualizing a definitive set of guidelines that would be used to set the general tort law standard for all care, the author suggests encouraging development of competing guidelines that might take different positions on specific issues. Such a strategy, the author writes, would be expressly designed to give health care providers, payers, and consumers new opportunities to choose a particular standard to govern their relationship.

Havighurst argues that if allowed to develop pluralistically, practice guidelines could offer the means for finally "deregulating" the health care field—by greatly expanding consumers' ability to specify what they do and do not wish to purchase in the way of medical services. For the law of medical malpractice, this new understanding of practice guidelines implies a long-overdue shift from tort to contract—from a form of command-and-control regulation to consumer choice.

Carl Horn III, Donald H. Caldwell, Jr., and D. Christopher Osborn. *Law for Physicians: An Overview of Medical Legal Issues*. Chicago: American Medical Association, 1999, 246 pages.

This handbook focuses on issues that affect physicians, with the aim of arming them with the practical knowledge they need to protect themselves from malpractice claims and other forms of litigation. In a straightforward fashion, the authors allay unwarranted concerns while casting light on potential pitfalls. Topics discussed include fraud and abuse, taxation, medical staff issues, informed consent, employment issues, malpractice prevention and litigation, and organizational options for practice. The hot topic of physician unions is examined to familiarize physicians with the means by which they can voice their concerns and exercise leverage in their service contracts. A thorough glossary offers simple definitions to legal terms, and an annotated index of computer databases and Internet sites describes numerous online resources.

Andrew Hyams, David Shapiro, and Troyen Brennan. "Medical Practice Guidelines in Malpractice Litigation: An Early Retrospective." *Journal of Health Politics, Policy, and Law*, 1996, *21*, 289.

Reviews the treatment of practice guidelines and standards in all published medical malpractice decisions reported from Jan. 1, 1980, through May 31, 1994. The results show a definite "two-way street" for guideline use, but plaintiffs have thus far tended to make substantially greater use of guidelines to their advantage than have defendants, at least as reflected in reported decisions. Although the many cases that have used guidelines show that the courts are by and large open to their consideration and use, these cases serve as a reminder that courts are often willing to look at guidelines critically, and they can carefully assess the guideline to ensure that it fits the facts of the case. The authors of this study estimate that more than fourteen hundred sets of practice guidelines are being developed.

Kirk B. Johnson, Carter G. Phillips, David Orentlicher, and Martin S. Hatlie. "A Fault-Based Administrative Alternative for Resolving Medical Malpractice Claims." *Vanderbilt Law Review*, 1989, *42*, 1365.

Argues that juries cannot evaluate independently the expert testimony almost always introduced in a malpractice case. In response to persistent problems with medical malpractice litigation and the failure of conventional tort reform efforts, the authors (one of whom is chief counsel for the AMA) set forth a proposal developed by the AMA, thirty-one national medical specialty societies, and the Council of Medical Specialty Societies for an administrative hearing process to replace the civil jury system in deciding medical malpractice claims.

Michele B. Kaufman, Cheryl A. Stoukides, and Norman A. Campbell. "Physicians' Liability for Adverse Drug Reactions." *Southern Medical Journal*, Aug. 1994, *87*, 780.

The authors discuss the basis for physician liability and review the standard-of-care concept regarding physicians' liability associated with adverse drug reactions. Although the Food and Drug Administration's spontaneous reporting system for adverse drug reactions has been collecting reports since 1960, the number of adverse drug reactions reported is low. One of the perceived deterrents to reporting is the physician's fear of involvement in litigation. Examination of the elements of a professional negligence case and "informed consent" shows what physicians can do to avoid malpractice related to adverse drug reactions.

Christopher Kerns, Carol J. Gerner, and Ciara R. Ryan (eds.). *Health Care Liability Deskbook.* (4th ed.) St. Paul, Minn.: West Group, 1998.

Written by twenty-two veteran health law practitioners, this one-volume treatise is well-organized and covers a spectrum of topics succinctly. They include medical malpractice, clinical practice guidelines, EMTALA, mandatory reporting requirements, AIDS, reporting requirements under the Safe Medical Devices Act of 1990, environmental liability for medical waste, state privileges credentialing and peer review liability, the National Practitioner Data Bank, antitrust liability issues, managed care organization liability exposures, ERISA; and insurance coverage for liability.

Eleanor D. Kinney. "Malpractice Reforms in the 1990s: Past Disappointments, Future Success?" *Journal of Health Politics, Policy, and Law*, 1995, *20*, 99.

State governments, the federal government, interest groups, and researchers have proposed various approaches to reform the malpractice system. Malpractice reforms fall into two generations, the author contends. First-generation reforms are those adopted by states, beginning in the 1970s, chiefly to reduce claim frequency and severity and thereby improve the malpractice system primarily from the perspective of providers and insurers. Scholars and interested constituencies developed second-generation reforms, such as use of medical practice guidelines to set the standard of care, various no-fault approaches, enterprise liability, mandated alternative dispute resolution, and scheduling damages, to streamline the adjudication and compensation system from the perspective of claimants and providers.

Research indicates that first-generation reforms have not been very effective in achieving the compensation and deterrence goals of tort, whereas second-generation reforms hold greater promise of doing so. This analysis of state and federal legislation indicates that states, and more recently Congress, have been reluctant to adopt second-generation reforms but continue to promote and adopt first-generation reforms. The strength of the provider lobby, concerns of health care reformers about the relationship between defensive medicine and health system costs, and lack of an organized consumer force for second-generation malpractice reform are important explanations as to why the states and Congress have not embraced second-generation reforms.

Eleanor D. Kinney and William P. Gronfein. "Indiana's Malpractice System: No-Fault by Accident." *Law and Contemporary Problems*, Winter 1991, *54*, 169.

Reviews Indiana's first ten years of experience with medical malpractice tort and insurance reforms. The reforms were among the most comprehensive malpractice reforms in the nation and have withstood several constitutional challenges. The authors conclude that the state's reforms are a model for other states and the federal government because medical malpractice premiums have stabilized relative to those in other states. Furthermore, they write, both health care providers and insurers are highly satisfied with the system.

Samuel J. Knapp and Leon Vander Creek. *Treating Patients with Memories of Abuse: Legal Risk Management*. Washington, D.C.: American Psychological Association, 1997, 184 pages.

Examines the kinds of legal challenge psychologists face when patients report memories of abuse while in therapy.

Debra T. Landis. "Measure and Elements of Damages in Action Against Physician for Breach of Contract to Achieve Particular Result or Cure." *ALR3rd*, 1980, *99*, 303.

Collects and analyzes the state and federal cases in which the courts have discussed or decided, in an action against a physician for breach of contract to achieve a particular result or cure, the measure and elements of damages recoverable.

Fred Lane and Scott D. Lane. *Lane Medical Litigation Guide*. Deerfield, Ill.: Clark, Boardman, Callaghan, 1993.

This four-volume treatise focuses on a range of medical litigation matters; the primary emphasis is on medical malpractice.

Bryan A. Liang. "Medical Malpractice: Do Physicians Have Knowledge of Legal Standards and Assess Cases as Juries Do?" *University of Chicago Law School Roundtable*, 1996, *3*, 59.

Assesses physician knowledge of medical malpractice law. From the perspective of law and economics, the judicial system can theoretically create an encompassing incentive structure that results in physicians' providing nonnegligent care so as to avoid malpractice liability at a level that is socially optimal. This assumes, however, that physicians are knowledgeable about the legal system and that they respond appropriately to the incentive structure. This study tests the validity of these assumptions. Liang's empirical study concludes that the physicians examined were ignorant about the common law of tort, and their perceptions regarding the legal definition of negligence were incomplete and incorrect.

Bryan A. Liang. *Health Law and Policy, A Survival Guide to Medicolegal Issues for Practitioners*. Woburn, Mass.: Butterworth-Heinemann Press, 1999, 352 pages.

Takes a supplemented case approach to offer physicians legal guidance. Liang plainly states each rule, illustrates it with one or more cases, and then explains how the rule and the case relate to each other. Includes issues of managed care, malpractice and liability.

Orley H. Lindgren, Ronald Christensen, and Don Harper Mills. "Medical Malpractice Risk Management Early Warning Systems." *Law and Contemporary Problems*, Spring 1991, *54*, 23.

Shows evidence that prompt incident reporting by medical professionals can serve a useful "early warning" function to identify future medical malpractice claims. The reporting system described in this article is designed to capture significant medical injuries before claimants' lawyers do. Physicians have helped to design this new system, which encourages prompt reporting, especially by telephone or face-to-face with risk managers.

David W. Louisell and Harold Williams. *Medical Malpractice.* New York: Matthew Bender, 1997.

In this regularly updated treatise of five volumes, the authors examine a range of topics: theories of liability, defending cases, the plaintiff's case, statutes of limitation, review panels, *res ipsa loquitur,* hospital liability, liability of managed care organizations, vicarious liability, nursing negligence, emergency room malpractice, damages, AIDS and malpractice, medical malpractice insurance, consent to treatment, discovery techniques, expert testimony, and medical records. The treatise concludes with an index, table of cases, table of illustrative awards, and appendix referencing reported medical malpractice cases by diagnosis.

JoAnn E. Macbeth and others. *Legal and Risk Management.* Washington, D.C.: American Psychiatric Press, 1994.

Written by four attorneys, this spiral-bound handbook focuses on liability issues that accompany the practice of psychiatry. Topics discussed include confidentiality and privilege, liability for patient suicide, dangerous behavior, civil commitment, reporting duties, psychiatric records, and managed care.

Gary N. McAbee. "Improper Expert Medical Testimony: Existing and Proposed Mechanisms of Oversight." *Journal of Legal Medicine,* June 1998, *19,* 257.

This article addresses existing mechanisms of oversight of expert witnesses by medical, legal, legislative, and regulatory agencies. It concludes by proposing a procedural mechanism for professional oversight of medical expert witnesses by established medical organizations.

Sam A. McConkey IV. "Simplifying the Law in Medical Malpractice: The Use of Practice Guidelines as the Standard of Care in Medical Malpractice Litigation." *West Virginia Law Review,* 1995, *97,* 491.

Argues that doctors are practicing defensive medicine, paying exorbitant malpractice liability insurance premiums, and blaming it all on the perceived shortcomings of the current system of malpractice litigation. By legislating practice guidelines as clear standards of care in medical negligence litigation, health care providers could rest assured that conformity with an established practice would protect them from liability.

George McDonald. *California Medical Malpractice: Law and Practice.* St. Paul, Minn.: West, 1992, supplemented to date.

This three-volume treatise provides expert advice on litigating medical malpractice cases from a purely California perspective.

Catherine S. Meschievitz. "Mediation and Medical Malpractice: Problems with Definition and Implementation." *Law and Contemporary Problems,* Winter 1991, *54,* 194.

Begins with an overview of traditional mediation and examination of the theoretical benefits of mediation as a procedural response to the problems of resolving medical malpractice claims. The article then explores Wisconsin's efforts to resolve medical malpractice claims by requiring that they be mediated.

Thomas B. Metzloff. "Resolving Malpractice Disputes: Imaging the Jury's Shadow." *Law and Contemporary Problems,* Winter 1991, *54,* 43.

This article, based upon an empirical study of all medical malpractice cases litigated in North Carolina over a three-year period, examines the jury's role in the light of four central criticisms: (1) that lay juries are unable to comprehend complex medical testimony submitted as the issues of liability and causation; (2) that juries overlook the legal standards for imposing tort liability because of sympathy toward a severely injured plaintiff; (3) that even if juries understand the expert testimony and do not act out of sympathy, they are unable to value damages consistently, given the flexibility that exists with amorphous concepts such as pain and suffering; and (4) that the slow pace of a jury trial contributes to high costs and protracted resolution of claims.

Deanne Morgan. "Emergency Room Follow-Up Care and Malpractice Liability." *Journal of Legal Medicine*, 1995, *16*, 373–406. Reprinted in *Defense Law Journal*, 1996, *45*, 297–335.

Examines various attempts to design emergency department follow-up care procedures and legal issues that arise when emergency room physicians fail to assess the need for or adequately instruct patients regarding follow-up care.

Lester F. Murphy. *Indiana Medical Malpractice*. St. Paul, Minn.: West, 1988, updated annually.

This single-volume treatise contains a full review of the Indiana Medical Malpractice Act, forms for practicing under the Act, citations, and explanations of all pertinent cases. Highlights include full discussion of the statute of limitations defense; details of filing the claim; the workings of the "Fund," including how to access it, how to obtain payment from it, and how the issue of damages is defended; strategies; how the act limits attorney's fees; and how to apply the doctrine of informed consent.

D. Christopher Osborn. "Medical Malpractice: Claim Prevention, Protection, and Litigation." In Carl Horn III, Donald H. Caldwell, Jr., and D. Christopher Osborn. *Law for Physicians: An Overview of Medical Legal Issues*. Chicago: American Medical Association, 1999, 246 pages.

This chapter discusses how to work with a malpractice insurer; understanding coverage terms, exclusions, and endorsements; litigating claims; pretrial discovery; dispositive motions; alternative dispute resolution; trial; and posttrial motions and appeals.

Steven E. Pegalis and Harvey F. Wachsman. *American Law of Medical Malpractice*. (2nd ed.) St. Paul, Minn.: West, 1998.

This three-volume treatise supplies strategies, procedural guidelines, and checklists for the practicing attorney. Citing law reviews, medical journals, and specialized medical and legal texts, this resource helps the reader determine whether complex cases should be referred to specialists; evaluate appropriate strategies for plaintiffs or defendants; present complex medical subjects to judges, juries, and opposing counsel; and assess one's course of action before filing a responsive pleading using checklists for statute of limitations, informed consent, and comparative negligence.

John R. Penhallegon. "Emerging Physician and Organization Liabilities under Managed Care." *Defense Counsel Journal*, 1997, *64*, 347.

Notes that the new model for delivering health care has spawned a wave of liability theories seeking deep pockets. Traditional fee-for-service practitioners had to ensure that the care they provided met the relevant standard of care, but they rarely found themselves confronted with allegations that their treatment decisions were motivated by personal gain. With managed care and capitation, where physicians may do better financially by not recommending certain diagnostic tests, physicians may now find themselves defending not only their professional judgment but also their professional motivation. This article examines recent cases asserting new theories of liability against physicians and the managed care organizations with which they are associated.

Carter G. Phillips and Paul E. Kalb. "In Search of Alternatives to the Tort System." *Stanford Law and Policy Review*, 1991, *3*, 210.

Contends that the tort system for resolving medical malpractice claims is in dire need of reform. According to the authors, the system is expensive, inequitable, and inefficient. Although much of the focus for malpractice reform has been on no-fault systems, a fault-based administrative system is more promising, they argue. Phillips and Kalb advocate one such system developed by the

AMA/Specialty Society Medical Liability Project. This system has three components. First, it would adjudicate claims through a state administrative agency. Second, it modifies how liability is determined by redefining the standards of care, causation, and informed consent, as well as the rules governing damages. Finally, the proposed system gives special emphasis to monitoring and disciplining physicians. Compared to the tort system, the plan they describe would compensate more equitably, deter negligent practice more effectively, and control costs more efficiently. Compared to a no-fault system, it would be less expensive while deterring negligent behavior more effectively, they claim.

Barton L. Post. *The Law of Medical Practice in Pennsylvania and New Jersey*. St. Paul, Minn.: West Group, 1984, updated annually.

This comprehensive, one-volume treatise covers the legal and ethical issues confronting physicians, as well as the laws and regulations that apply to medical practice and malpractice. Medical licensure, medical training, accreditation, and the relation of physician to hospital are all covered in detail. The book gives current and in-depth treatment of the terminally ill, cost containment, and medical malpractice issues. It has extensive citations to case law, statutes, regulations, and leading medical articles in both New Jersey and Pennsylvania, along with useful forms.

Edward P. Richards III and Katherine C. Rathbun. *Law and the Physician: A Practical Guide*. Boston: Little Brown, 1993, 571 pages.

Topics addressed in this book are physicians and lawyers; physicians and patients; physicians and other medical personnel; physicians and public health; physicians and the family, and physicians and special practice areas. The authors' objective in writing this book is to assist doctors in avoiding legal conflicts. It includes a helpful glossary and index.

John E. Rolph. "Merit Rating for Physicians' Malpractice Premiums: Only a Modest Deterrent." *Law and Contemporary Problems*, Spring 1991, *54*, 65.

This study finds that (1) although there are malpractice-prone physicians, the potential effect of deterrent policies that target individual physicians using readily available information (that is, paid claims) is modest; (2) it is possible that gathering more detailed information about physicians in addition to claims history and premium class might lead to more accurate prospective identification of those who will incur future paid claims; and (3) the first two conclusions do not preclude the possible efficacy of such policies as targeted education, practice monitoring, and other individual specific interventions.

Mikel A. Rothenberg. *Emergency Medicine Malpractice*. (3rd ed.) Gaithersburg, Md.: Aspen, 2000, 704 pages.

Contains an overview of the emergency department and its operation, legal liability in emergency medicine, defense of emergency medicine malpractice cases, analysis of common cases and lawsuits, and a glossary of medical terms. Annually supplemented.

Michael Rustad and Thomas Koenig. "Reconceptualizing Punitive Damages in Medical Malpractice: Targeting Amoral Corporations, Not Moral Monsters." *Rutgers Law Review*, 1995, *47*, 975.

Based upon the findings of their empirical study, the authors conclude that there is little support for the popular characterization of punitive damages in medical malpractice as being unfair, arbitrary, and unpredictable. The authors observe that punitive damages are rarely awarded, are generally proportionate to the harm, and are difficult to collect. As punitive damage awards in medical malpractice increase in both number and size, the remedy performs new functions, the authors write. The increasing concentration of health care decision making in the hands of the leaders of a small number of managed care organizations requires a remedy powerful enough to protect the public.

J. E. Schmidt. *Attorneys' Dictionary of Medicine.* (28th ed.) New York: Matthew Bender, 1994.

This six-volume loose-leaf treatise contains well over sixty-one thousand entries, two hundred full-page illustrations, and five hundred smaller illustrations.

John A. Siliciano. "Wealth, Equity, and the Unitary Medical Malpractice Standard." *Virginia Law Review,* 1991, *77,* 439.

Contends that tort law's efforts to promote equitable distribution of health care benefits is ineffectual and, as a result, misguided. Concluding that the poor are likely to be disserved by the unitary malpractice standard, the author suggests that tort law should recognize that resource-based distinctions in the quality of health care are to a certain extent inevitable, given the country's persistent refusal to finance full health care for all its citizens. To this end, the article suggests that the malpractice standard be modified to expressly encompass patient economic resources as a factor bearing on the legal adequacy of the care provided.

Theodore Silver. "One Hundred Years of Harmful Error: The Historical Jurisprudence of Medical Malpractice." *Wisconsin Law Review,* 1992, 1193.

A medical malpractice suit is identical in all vital respects to any and every other negligence suit. That simple truth, the author writes, has been lost in a maze of judicial mistakes a century in the making. Consequently, most legal minds identify medical malpractice as a discrete body of law.

Robert I. Simon and Robert L. Sadoff. *Psychiatric Malpractice: Cases and Comments for Clinicians.* Washington, D.C.: American Psychiatric Press, 1992, 309 pages.

Through a general overview and discussion of specific legal cases, this award-winning book presents the primary malpractice traps encountered in everyday practice of psychiatry. This text is modestly priced.

Frank A. Sloan and Stephen S. van Wert. "Cost and Compensation of Injuries in Medical Malpractice." *Law and Contemporary Problems,* Winter 1991, *54,* 131.

This article has two major purposes: to quantify the cost of permanent injuries in birth-related and emergency room cases that lead to medical malpractice claims, and to compare the estimated cost with the compensation received. Some of the intricacies of cost estimation are described, as are some of the major policy issues in deciding which costs are and are not covered.

Frank A. Sloan and others. *Suing for Medical Malpractice.* Chicago: University of Chicago Press, 1993.

This book of essays, primarily by Vanderbilt University faculty members, presents new information on medical malpractice claimants and the claiming process. Its main source of information is the authors' Survey of Medical Malpractice Claimants, conducted in Florida in 1989–90. Topics discussed include doctor-patient relationships, lawyer-client relationships, liability, cost of injuries, the dispute resolution process, compensation, and policy implications. Contributors include Penny B. Githens, Ellen Wright Clayton, Gerald B. Hickson, Douglas A. Gentile, and David F. Partlett.

James B. Stewart. *Blind Eye: How the Medical Establishment Let a Doctor Get Away with Murder.* New York: Simon and Schuster, 334 pages.

This is an account of the macabre professional life of Dr. Michael Swango, whom the author, along with many medical and legal authorities, believes to be guilty of at least thirty-five murders by hypodermic needle in hospitals in the United States and Africa. The book is partly an indignant, muckraking tract—an indictment of the physicians and medical authorities who failed to protect the public from Swango over a period of some fifteen years. It is also a meticulous journalistic reconstruction that has the fascination of an acutely observed and troubling novel. The author focuses the majority of his scorn on the medical officials at Ohio State University, who (with some laudable exceptions) shielded Swango from sanctions, tending to believe a fellow doctor's word over nurses' eyewitness accounts.

Laurence R. Tancredi and Randall R. Bovbjerg. "Rethinking Responsibility for Patient Injury: Accelerated-Compensation Events, a Malpractice and Quality Reform Ripe for a Test." *Law and Contemporary Problems*, Spring 1991, *54*, 147.

Focuses on accelerated-compensation events (ACEs), which are medically caused injuries that should not occur. ACE does not cover all injuries, just classes of adverse outcomes that are usually, although not invariably, avoidable through good medical care. The authors argue that medical malpractice reforms based on ACEs would best address the twin goals of making compensation more equitable and avoiding bad outcomes in medical care. As a payment reform, ACEs would wholly replace much or most malpractice litigation with an insurance system, determining simplified payment amounts for listed events—for example, in obstetrics—without individual fact finding. Conceptually, ACEs fall between a fault-based deterrent system and a full no-fault compensation system such as workers compensation.

Nicholas P. Terry. "Cyber-Malpractice: Legal Exposure for Cybermedecine." *American Journal of Law and Medicine*, 1999, *25*, 327.

Addresses liability issues in the context of health care providers' exposure to claims of negligence, misrepresentation, and product liability in the content of their Websites, or "cybermedicine fact patterns." The author looks at Web-based marketing by health care institutions and pharmaceutical companies, and at the growth in health-oriented advice sites. He then examines tort law theories and suggests potential points of exposure for malpractice.

W. John Thomas. "The Medical Malpractice 'Crisis': A Critical Examination of a Public Debate." *Temple Law Review*, Summer 1992, *65*(2), 459.

The thesis of this article is that the adversarial dialogue between physicians and lawyers, rather than objective data, has informed the political and legislative debate over medical malpractice. The author summarizes the data on issues raised in the adversarial dialogue between the medical and legal communities.

Paul C. Weiler and others. *A Measure of Malpractice: Medical Injury, Malpractice Litigation and Patient Compensation*. Cambridge, Mass.: Harvard University Press, 1993, 175 pages.

The principal focus of this book is on alternative ways in which judges and lawyers can deploy the resources of the law to motivate health care providers to avoid injury to patients. Based upon empirical analysis of thousands of medical records and malpractice claims filed in New York State from 1975 to 1989, this study proposes shifting the focus of legal liability from the personal fault of the individual doctor to the collective responsibility of the health care organization, a shift that is consistent with a new systems-based approach to quality management now emerging within the American health care system. The book includes helpful endnotes and an index.

Miles J. Zaremski and Frank D. Heckman. *Reengineering Healthcare Liability Litigation*. Charlottesville, Va.: Michie, 1997, 487 pages.

This practical book is targeted at medical malpractice defense attorneys, assisting them in responding to the pressures of large-scale, complex medical litigation. The authors offer a set of tools, from strategic planning concepts to jury selection techniques to billing software, aimed at making health care defense litigation more efficient. They offer advice concerning expert witnesses, selecting jurors and crafting arguments with jury appeal, and alternative dispute resolution. The text includes a range of pointers for the courtroom attorney, including use of mock juries as a means of both trial preparation and, through risk analysis techniques, strategic objective setting.

15.02   OBLIGATION TO OBTAIN A PATIENT'S INFORMED CONSENT

Paul S. Applebaum. "Must We Forgo Informed Consent to Control Health Care Costs? A Response to Professor Hall." *Milbank Quarterly*, 1993, *71*, 669.

Contends that disclosure at the time of enrollment of an insurer's limitations on coverage based on economic considerations is unlikely to leave subscribers meaningfully informed about how their doctors' recommendations are being affected by concern over costs. Thus, whether one views their acceptance of enrollment as "prior consent" to rationing or as a "waiver" of consent, it is an action that for almost all persons will be taken in profound ignorance of its implications. For the essay by Hall that prompted this response, see below.

Mary Anne Bobinski. "Autonomy and Privacy: Protecting Patients from Their Physicians." *University of Pittsburgh Law Review*, 1994, *55*, 291.

Jurisdictions with generous disclosure requirements typically rely, at least in part, on fiduciary principles as a basis for the disclosure obligation. Fiduciary law thus presents a possible avenue for future growth of a more vibrant disclosure duty. Tort law and the law governing fiduciary relationships are similar in that they impose extracontractual duties on individuals. The two regulatory schemes, however, differ in conception of those duties. Tort law most often imposes general duties irrespective of the status of the parties. The law of fiduciaries, in contrast, is based on the special character of the relationship between two parties.

California Healthcare Association. *Consent Manual: A Reference for Consent and Related Health Care Law.* Sacramento: California Healthcare Association, 1995, 750 pages.

Addresses legal issues facing hospitals and providers regarding informed consent, statutory, regulatory, and case law requirements. Updated annually, the forms in this manual are available in English and Spanish.

Larry R. Churchill and others. "Genetic Research as Therapy: Implications of 'Gene Therapy' for Informed Consent." *Journal of Law, Medicine and Ethics*, 1998, *26*, 38.

Argues that characterization of gene transfer research as "gene therapy" has compromised informed consent in the current environment of regulatory exceptions, routinized consent, fostered therapeutic misconceptions, and oversold research.

Barbara C. Columbo and Robert P. Webber. "Regulating Risk in a Managed Care Environment. Theory vs. Practice: The Minnesota Experience." *Annals of Health Law*, 1999, 147.

Addresses the challenges that state regulators face in controlling the various forms of managed care as numerous hybrid risk-bearing entities emerge. Also highlights the tensions between consumer protection and market competition and focuses on the experience of Minnesota regulators in this area.

John H. Derrick. "Medical Malpractice: Liability for Failure of Physician to Inform Patient of Alternative Modes of Diagnosis or Treatment." (Annot.) *ALR4th*, 1985, *38*, 900.

Collects and discusses those state and federal cases that have considered whether a physician is or may be held liable for malpractice for failure to obtain a patient's informed consent to a method of diagnosis or treatment by failing to disclose to the patient alternative methods of diagnosis or treatment and thereby denying the patient the right to choose which method should be employed.

Daniel E. Feld. "Necessity and Sufficiency of Expert Evidence to Establish Existence and Extent of Physician's Duty to Inform Patient of Risks of Proposed Treatment." (Annot.) *ALR3rd*, 1973, *52*, 1084.

Collects cases concerning the necessity and sufficiency of expert testimony to establish the existence and extent of a physician's duty to inform a patient of the risks of a proposed treatment.

Laurent B. Frantz. "Modern Status of Views as to General Measure of Physician's Duty to Inform Patient of Risks of Proposed Treatment." (Annot.) *ALR3rd*, 1978, *88*, 1008.

Collects representative modern cases bearing on the status of views as to the general measure of the physician's duty to inform her patient of the risks of a proposed treatment. It considers pertinent cases decided in or after 1966.

Mark A. Hall. "Informed Consent to Rationing Decisions." *Milbank Quarterly,* 1993, *71,* 645.

Sketches a theory of economic informed consent that articulates the conceptual parameters for constructive debate about the circumstances and extent of disclosure. Hall writes that disclosure of rationing decisions can occur at two distinct points. General rationing rules and incentives can be disclosed to HMO subscribers, for example, at the time of enrollment. Alternately, particular and case-specific decisions not to contract for potentially beneficial care owing to excessive costs can be disclosed at the time of (non)treatment. This discussion focuses on the second stage, with the author concluding that disclosure of alternative treatments precluded by the patients' insurance coverage is not required by the law of informed consent. For a response to Hall's views, see Paul S. Applebaum above.

James A. Henderson, Jr., and John A. Siliciano. "Universal Health Care and the Continued Reliance on Custom in Determining Medical Malpractice." *Cornell Law Review,* 1994, *79,* 1382.

The authors write that modern medicine displays few of the features that tend to generate reliable customs in other contexts. The problems it confronts are complex and individualized, the solutions it offers are diverse and ever-changing, and the decision makers often lack the incentive or ability to make appropriate choices among such solutions.

D. A. Herz and others. "Informed Consent: Is It a Myth?" *Neurosurgery,* 1992, *30,* 453.

The authors discuss an experiment in which patients were given a "simple" written test immediately after a training session on a procedure they were about to undergo. The mean patient score was only 43.5 percent. Six weeks later, the mean test score dropped to 38.4 percent. The authors conclude that health care providers "cannot necessarily expect accurate patient or family recall or comprehension. Fulfillment of the doctrine of informed consent by neurosurgeons may very well be mythical."

Jay Katz, M.D. "Informed Consent—Must It Remain a Fairy Tale?" *Journal of Contemporary Health Law and Policy,* 1994, *10,* 69.

Argues that notwithstanding any theories of tort law or cost containment to the contrary, patients must ultimately be given the deciding vote in matters that affect their lives. Katz also suggests that informed consent will remain a fairy tale as long as the concept of joint decision making, based on a commitment to patient autonomy and self-determination, does not become an integral aspect of the ethos of medicine and the law of informed consent.

J. Kindley. "The Fit Between the Elements for an Informed Consent Cause of Action and the Scientific Evidence Linking Induced Abortion with Increased Breast Cancer Risk." (Comment.) *Wisconsin Law Review*, 1998, 1595.

A number of medical studies have found a link between induced abortion and later breast cancer. Despite this link, Planned Parenthood and a number of other abortion providers fail to disclose this information to women considering abortion. This Comment focuses on the elements for a cause of action predicated on negligence, which has replaced battery as a theory of liability most commonly applied to informed consent cases. It concludes that women have been led to believe that abortion is a safety net, when in fact its safety is in serious doubt.

Joan H. Krause. "Reconceptionalizing Informed Consent in an Era of Health Care Cost Containment." *Iowa Law Review*, 1999, 85, 261.

Argues that using health care cost containment strategies has had a detrimental effect on the doctrine of informed consent, particularly on the requirement that, in order to obtain truly informed consent, physicians must disclose the existence of alternatives to the proposed treatment. The author assets that current trends in the health care market give physicians and insurers incentives to withhold information about treatments that are not covered under a patient's insurance policy. Moreover, the effect of these incentives is exacerbated by recent efforts to characterize patients as health care "consumers" who should be held to the benefits of their health care *bargains*. Paradoxically, these efforts give physicians and payers an incentive to withhold information while simultaneously placing a premium on patients' acting as well-educated consumers. In this new market, informed consent may be viewed as an expensive luxury.

According to the author, three broad approaches can be adopted to ensure patient access to information about treatment alternatives in this newly cost-sensitive environment. First the law of informed consent could be altered, either by statute or case law, to clarify that failing to disclose noncovered alternatives is an actionable offense, entitling the patient to compensation. Although this approach is popular among academic commentators, it has not succeeded in the legislative and judicial arenas. Second, consumer-oriented protections, such as "anti–gag clause" laws, could be adopted to address patient's rights to receive medical treatment from their health plans, a strategy that many states have adopted with limited success. The author concludes, however, that a third approach may be most promising: using the professional regulation system to enforce a physician's obligation to disclose.

Alan D. Lieberson. *Advance Medical Directives*. Deerfield, Ill.: Clark, Boardman, Callaghan, 1992, 879 pages.

The law governing advance medical directives has grown rapidly, and it is often difficult to find information. This book is designed to bring to the practitioner all the material he or she will need when dealing with an issue of advance directives. Topics include living wills, the *Cruzan* decision, common law considerations, surrogate decision making, do-not-resuscitate orders, and powers of attorney.

Lawrence E. Lifson and Robert I. Simon (eds.). *The Mental Health Practitioner and the Law: A Comprehensive Handbook*. Cambridge, Mass.: Harvard University Press, 1998, 398 pages.

Presents the major risk management areas and legal pitfalls encountered in current clinical practice. Its twenty-three essays by twenty authors focus on practical knowledge and skills designed to decrease the practitioner's likelihood of being sued, and to increase the likelihood of prevailing if sued. The book emphasizes the practitioner's professional, ethical, and moral duty to provide competent care to every patient. The first section addresses the basic issues important to liability prevention, including informed consent, the expectations of state licensing boards, and suggestions from malpractice insurance carriers. The second section identifies high-risk areas for lawsuits. Topics examined here include management of suicidal patients, violation of treatment boundaries, supervising medical students, minimizing risk in treating violent patients, and terminating treatment with difficult patients. The final section supplies a survival guide for clinicians whose testimony is required in court, whether as a defendant, treating clinician, fact witness, or expert witness.

R. H. Lockwood. "Mental Competency of Patient to Consent to Surgical Operation or Medical Treatment." (Annot.) *ALR3rd,* 1969, *25,* 1439.

Collects cases dealing with the question of the mental competency of a patient to consent to a surgical operation or medical treatment for himself. Regularly updated.

Karine Morin. "The Standard of Disclosure in Human Subject Experimentation." *Journal of Legal Medicine,* June 1998, 157.

This article focuses on the standards of disclosure that investigators ought to follow when soliciting participation. The author contends that the standards that have developed through medical malpractice law have been used erroneously by the courts to interpret the standard of disclosure in human subject experimentation, despite the historically separate evolution of the doctrine in each context. The author then argues that this general failure to recognize the differences between medical treatment and experimentation has undermined protection of subjects' rights.

Stephen E. Ronai. "Physicians and Pharmaceutical Company Clinical Trials: Ethical and Legal Issues in Physician New Drug Experimentation." [Report No. VPH99–0020], 1999, 82 pages.

Reviews the legal and ethical issues presented by physician participation in drug company new drug clinical trials, including basic contract provisions, discussions of informed consent, legal liability of physician investigators, medical records confidentiality, ethical issues and the potential applicability of the antikickback statute and Stark II statute, and regulations on physician participation in drug company clinical trials.

Arnold J. Rosoff. "Informed Consent in the Electronic Age." *American Journal of Law and Medicine,* 1999, *25,* 367.

Focuses on the use of the Internet and CD-ROMS as vehicles to inform patients about specific health conditions. The author also looks at how providing this information to patients alters the traditional physician-patient relationship and thereby the scope and meaning of informed consent. He then considers potential liability issues that arise for providers using such technologies.

Fay A. Rozovsky. *Consent to Treatment: A Practical Guide.* (3rd ed.) Gaithersburg, Md.: Aspen, 1997, 814 pages.

The standard authority in the field, this treatise examines such topics as rules for consent to treatment, exceptions to the rule, human research, women and reproductive matters, organ donation, autopsy, prisoners and detainees, mental illness, mental retardation, the right to refuse treatment, consent to AIDS testing, competency, confidentiality, the elderly and consent, documentation of consent, and practical rules for consent. The book includes checklists, flowcharts, forms, and guidelines. It includes regulations and other information in appendix form. Regularly updated.

Bruce D. Sales and Saleem A. Shah (eds.). *Mental Health and Law.* Durham, N.C.: Carolina Academic Press, 1996, 371 pages.

This books of essays by eighteen authors examines such topics as civil commitment; guardianship; involuntary outpatient commitment; informed consent; sex offenders and the law; and research on law and mental health issues affecting minors, among others.

R. S. Saver. "Critical Care Research and Informed Consent." *North Carolina Law Review,* 1996, *75,* 205.

The doctrine of informed consent severely limits the ability of medical researchers to develop, evaluate, and refine investigational technologies for treating patients suffering from heart attacks, strokes, and other "critical care" conditions. In this article, Saver examines the current doctrine of informed consent as applied to critical care research and its various deficiencies. In addition, he analyzes recent reforms proposed by the Food and Drug Administration, which are intended to remove certain obstacles to critical care research posed by informed consent. Although the proposed reforms address several of the current deficiencies, he asserts that they lack the breadth and scope necessary to advance the progress of critical care research ethically and sensibly. Saver proposes several complementary and alternative reforms that would better accommodate the interest of all affected parties: the patients, their families, the researchers, and the general public.

Peter H. Schuck. "Rethinking Informed Consent." *Yale Law Journal*, 1994, *103*, 899.

The author suggests that informed consent idealists—primarily some judges and medical ethicists—seek to promote individual autonomy, while informed consent realists—primarily practicing physicians—argue that the goals of complete individual autonomy cannot be met, at least not without great cost in terms of time, money, and needless patient anxiety and confusion. He contends that informed consent idealists and realists argue past one another, producing a debate that is oblique and inconclusive rather than pointed and fruitful.

David L. Shriner, M.D., and others. "Informed Consent and Risk Management in Dermatology: To What Extent Do Dermatologists Disclose Alternate Diagnostic and Treatment Options to Their Patients?" *Journal of Contemporary Health Law and Policy*, 1992, *8*, 137.

Disclosure of relevant diagnostic facts and treatment options is essential to the informed consent process by which the doctor and patient both arrive at medical management decisions. Yet the practice of informed consent is compromised if the physician withholds reasonable diagnostic or treatment options. This article summarizes the results of a survey designed to document the extent to which disclosure practices within the specialty of dermatology meet the ideal of shared decision making.

Robert I. Simon. *Concise Guide to Psychiatry and Law for Clinicians*. (2nd ed.) Washington, D.C.: American Psychiatric Press, 1998.

Contents include the doctor-patient relationship, confidentiality and testimonial privilege, informed consent, the right to refuse treatment, seclusion and restraint, involuntary hospitalization, the suicidal patient, the violent patient, and maintaining boundaries.

Christopher Stowell (ed.). *Informed Consent for Blood Transfusion*. Bethesda, Md.: American Association of Blood Banks, 1997.

Explains legal principles of informed consent, the factual information regarding transfusion therapy that forms the core of informed consent, and practical guidance on how to develop informed consent policies and procedures. The text also explains why hospitals, as well as the patient's physician, need to be aware of their responsibilities with regard to consent policies.

Paula Walter. "The Doctrine of Informed Consent: A Tale of Two Cultures and Two Legal Traditions." *Issues in Law and Medicine*, Spring 1999, *14*(4), 357.

Walter compares and contrasts the notion of informed consent in medical decision making in the Western legal system with the traditional Jewish biblical legal system. She critically examines the philosophical underpinnings of disease and medical healing in both legal systems and describes the practical consequences that emanate from the ideologies in terms of the individual's right of choice of treatment. She explains that the Western system is predicated on notions of individual autonomy and self-determination. Patients therefore have the autonomous ability to select and direct their own medical therapy. By contrast the traditional biblical system of law is based on the concept that the body does not belong to the individual. Instead, the body is given to the human being by God as a trust to respect and preserve.

Wendy Woolery. "Informed Consent Issues Throughout the Birthing Process." *Journal of Legal Medicine,* June 2000, *21,* 241.

Examines the informed consent doctrine in the light of the use of forceps or the hormone Pitocin.

15.03   OBLIGATION TO REPORT ABUSE

Danny R. Veilleux. "Validity, Construction, and Application of State Statute Requiring Doctor or other Persons to Report Child Abuse." (Annot.) *ALR4th,* 1989, *73, 782.*

Collects and analyzes the reported state and federal cases in which courts have construed, applied, or determined the validity of state statutes establishing a mandatory duty to report known or suspected child abuse.

16

Liability of Health Care Institutions

Although medical malpractice is often seen as a problem exclusively related to physician performance, the rules that have now developed impose substantial responsibilities on administrators and trustees. Not only are hospitals and other health care institutions liable for the acts of their employees and agents, who are increasingly involved in caring for patients, but under certain circumstances institutions are liable for the malpractice of their nonemployed attending physicians as well. Consequently, malpractice prevention has become a basic management responsibility whose discharge requires familiarity with the substantive rules of negligence.

Charitable Immunity

It has long been established that employers, including corporations, are responsible for the acts of their employees. There are several policy reasons for imposing liability: (1) since a corporation can "act" only through its agents and employees, those are an integral and inseparable part of the corporate enterprise; (2) the corporation is in the best position to control the risks associated with the enterprise; and (3) such losses are an appropriate cost of doing business. This type of liability, where the employer is automatically liable for the negligence of its employees, is known as vicarious liability and is often referred to as *respondeat superior*.[1]

Until the 1940s, however, it was the rule in the United States that charitable health care providers were immune from liability, even for the most obvious negligence of their employees. Several reasons were given to support this exemption from accountability in negligence, but the most important ones from the perspective of modern health care administrators were that physicians and nurses—even though employed by the health care facility—were regarded by the courts as independent contractors rather than employees, and that the health care facility could not effectively supervise and control the professional component of the services it provided.[2]

Whatever the reasons actually assigned to exempt health care institutions from liability, the policy of law to do so persisted into the 1940s and 1950s. However, in the decade following World War II, the character of health care institutions began to change. Through their paid nurses and other staff, hospitals and health care institutions became much more involved in providing care to patients. Courts began to recognize that these institutions, like other enterprises, were very much in a position to control and supervise their professional employees. It also became clear that it was far easier for the health care facility to spread the risks of loss than it was for the patient to absorb the costs of injury; also, insurance was readily available to protect the assets of the institution. In short, the same broadly based policy reasons that justified imposing liability on employers for the acts of their employees in other fields of commerce and industry gained acceptance in the health care arena.

Initially, to circumvent the charitable immunity doctrine, some courts attempted to distinguish between "administrative" acts, which would subject the institution to liability, and "professional" acts, to which the immunity rule would apply.[3] But as courts struggled to find ways to impose greater responsibility on the health care charity, the line between the administrative and the professional blurred.

In a remarkably short time, the doctrine of charitable immunity has all but vanished.[4] Abandoning the doctrine of charitable immunity altogether, the court, in the leading case of *Bing* v. *Thunig,* reflected the modern judicial view of hospitals and other providers of care in what has probably become one of the most widely quoted passages in modern jurisprudence relating to health care institutions:

> The conception that the hospital does not undertake to treat the patient, does not undertake to act through its doctors and nurses, but undertakes instead simply to procure them to act upon their own responsibility, no longer reflects the fact. Present-day hospitals, as their manner of operation plainly demonstrates, do far more than furnish facilities for treatment. They regularly employ on a salary basis a large staff of physicians, nurses and interns, as well as administrative and manual workers, and they charge patients for medical care and treatment, collecting for such services, if necessary, by legal action. Certainly the person who avails himself of "hospital facilities" expects that the hospital will attempt to cure him, not that its nurses or other employees will act on their own responsibility.
>
> Hospitals should, in short, shoulder the responsibilities borne by everyone else. There is no reason to continue their exemption from the universal rule of *respondeat superior.* The test should be, for these institutions, whether charitable or profit-making, as it is for every other employer, was the person who committed the negligent injury-producing act one of its employees and, if he was, was he acting within the scope of his employment.[5]

Thus, as hospitals and other health care facilities entered the modern era of medicine, as they grew in size and in their active participation in caring for patients, and as negligence law began to focus on the broader issues of compensation and risk spreading through insurance, the legal doctrine of vicarious liability or *respondeat superior* was applied with full force to them. In general, private and charitable health care institutions are now legally liable for the acts of all of their employees, whether nurses, house staff, or other paid physicians. Indeed, as discussed below, this new attitude toward health care facilities has continued to evolve to the point where hospitals and other health care institutions are now responsible in a variety of situations for the acts of nonemployees as well.

Governmental Immunity

The doctrine of immunity had also been applied to governmental facilities. This time, however, it was based on the principle of "sovereign immunity," which held that the sovereign or government could not be sued. The policy reasons for eliminating the immunity doctrine with respect to charities apply with full vigor to government-owned health care institutions. In the case of those that are federally owned, immunity from suit has now been eliminated by statute. Although state governments have been much slower to respond, only a few states do not permit recovery against the government for the acts of its employees working in health care institutions.[6]

Exception to Liability for Employees: "Borrowed Servants"

As the courts struggled for many years to circumvent the immunity doctrine and its harsh results for injured patients, some attempted to make the physician in charge responsible for the acts of all persons involved in caring for the patient on the theory that the physician had the right to control the totality of care provided to the patient. This theory came to be known as the "captain of the ship" doctrine and represented a thinly disguised effort to substitute the physician for the employer who was immune from suit. The doctrine was commonly applied to the operating room, where the attending physician would frequently be held liable for everything from providing anesthesia to sponge counts.[7]

With the disappearance of immunity from suit and concomitant recognition that health care facilities owe substantial patient care responsibilities directly to patients, the captain-of-the-ship doctrine has now all but been replaced by the more sensible "borrowed servant" doctrine.[8] In rejecting the former doctrine, the Maryland Court of Special Appeals noted:

From our analysis of how other courts have dealt with the issue at hand, we reject any "captain of the ship" theory of liability. Given the statutory curtailment of a hospital's eleemosynary and governmental immunity in Maryland, there is no socioeconomic need to extend the vicarious liability of a surgeon for the negligence of hospital employees simply to create a fund for victims of malpractice. Nor is there any jurisprudential need to do so. The correct doctrine to apply is the traditional "borrowed servant" rule. Where the evidence suffices to support a finding that the surgeon *in fact* had or exercised the right to control the details of another person's work or conduct in the operating room and the other elements of the rule are satisfied, the trier of fact may find that the surgeon was the "special employer" and is therefore liable for the negligence of the borrowed servant.[9]

Under the borrowed-servant doctrine, if an employee of a hospital or other health care facility is carrying out the specific instructions of a nonemployed attending physician, the employee becomes the borrowed servant or "special employee."[10] It is presumed that the employee is no longer acting on behalf of the facility[11] and the facility will not be subject to liability for the employee's act unless he or she knows the physician's instructions are not in accordance with sound medical practice.[12]

The rule has not been easy to apply. Some courts have attempted to resolve the status of the employee by trying to determine who has the right to control the employee's acts. However, the "control" test has not offered a satisfactory basis for the borrowed-servant rule: although a private physician may have the right to control employees working with him, the employees in fact are very often supervised and acting on behalf of the health care facility. Other courts have distinguished between administrative acts and those that involve professional judgment as a basis for applying the doctrine.[13] For example, a Florida appellate court determined that a nurse's responsibility for sponge counts in the operating room does not "involve professional skill or decision on the part of the surgeon" and accordingly sent the case back to the jury to resolve whether in fact the nurse was acting as agent for the hospital or the surgeon.[14] In general, the task of ferreting out administrative acts from professional acts is not without difficulty, nor has the distinction proved to be an adequate expression of the principle involved.

What the courts in these cases seem to be stating is that the borrowed-servant doctrine will not exempt a health care facility from liability for the acts of its employees if the acts performed by the employee constitute part of, or are in furtherance of, the duties owed by the institution directly to the patient. Often the discharge of such duties will involve, in addition to clearly administrative functions, exercise of professional judgment. Thus, courts have held hospitals responsible for injuries caused by negligent administration of anesthesia by a hospital nurse,[15] improper postoperative care by a hospital resident,[16] failure of a nurse to call a physician when a patient's medical condition worsened,[17] and failure to take proper X rays.[18] In a case involving the negligence of nurses in failing to conduct a proper sponge count in the operating room, the court emphasized, in holding the hospital responsible for the nurses' acts, that they were performing hospital duties:

A theory that the surgeon directly controls *all* activities of whatever nature in the operating room certainly is not realistic in present-day medical care. Today's hospitals hire, fire, train and provide day-to-day supervision of their nurse-employees. Fortunately, hospitals can and do implement standards and regulations governing good surgery practices and techniques and are in the best position to enforce compliance.[19]

Only if the physician gives an order to an employee and the order itself is negligent,[20] or if the physician chooses to have a medical procedure performed by an employee who the physician knows is not qualified to perform the task, will the hospital or health care facility not be responsible.[21]

Sometimes an employee discharges a hospital duty and serves the physician as a borrowed servant. In this situation, the acts of the employee may result in liability for both the health care facility and the physician. The point that should be emphasized, however, is that the health care facility will not be exempt from liability as long as a health care facility responsibility is involved.

As hospitals and other health care institutions become increasingly involved with patient care, it is likely that the borrowed-servant doctrine will receive narrower application.

Liability for Nonemployees Who Provide Special Services

Although a health care facility will now almost uniformly be held liable for the acts of its employees, generally a facility will not be responsible for the acts of its nonemployed attending physicians. The reason most often given to support this distinction is that the attending physicians function autonomously, beyond the effective control of the health care facility, treating patients with whom they, and not the institution, have the primary relationship.[22] However, there are two major exceptions to this principle that are gaining increasing judicial acceptance. The first holds a hospital or other health care facility responsible if it fails to properly review the credentials and monitor the performance of its attending staff. This constitutes a direct duty of the health care facility to the patient and is referred to frequently as the doctrine of "corporate negligence."

The second exception typically involves a situation where the courts have found that the physician, although technically an independent practitioner, is rendering services on behalf of the health care facility and is, in effect, the de facto employee or agent of the institution for such purpose. Thus, the principles of vicarious liability or *respondeat superior* are invoked to make the hospital or health care facility liable. These cases, which are by no means uniform from state to state, almost invariably involve services that the public might normally expect the health care institution to provide as an institutional service, such as radiology, anesthesiology, pathology, or emergency room services.

References and Notes

1. See William L. Prosser and Robert E. Keeton. *Torts.* (5th ed.) St. Paul, Minn.: West, 1984, 499-501 [hereinafter cited as Prosser]. These introductory chapter materials were excerpted, with minor changes, from a chapter entitled "The Law of Medical Malpractice." In Michael G. Macdonald and others. *Health Care Law: A Practical Guide.* New York: Matthew Bender, 1997. Copyright 1998 by Matthew Bender, Reprinted with permission from *The Treatise on Health Care Law.* All rights reserved.
2. See *Bing* v. *Thunig,* 2 N.Y.2d 656, 662-663, 163 N.Y.S.2d 3, 7-8, 143 N.E.2d 3, 6-7, 1957.
3. *Bing,* 143 N.E.2d, at 4-5.
4. See Fairchild. "Tort Immunity of Nongovernmental Charities—Modern Status." (Annot.) *ALR4th,* 1983, *25,* 517; Schopler. "Immunity from Liability for Damages in Tort of State or Governmental Unit or Agency in Operating Hospital." (Annot.) *ALR2nd,* 1952, *25,* 203.
5. *Bing,* 143 N.E.2d, at 8.
6. See D. W. Louisell and H. Williams. *Medical Malpractice.* New York: Matthew Bender, 1992, ¶¶ 17.03-17.07.
7. See *McConnell* v. *Williams,* 361 Pa. 355, 65 A.2d 243, 1949. See also Kemper. "Liability of Hospital for Negligence of Nurse Assisting Operating Surgeon." (Annot.) *ALR3rd,* 1970, *29,* 1065.
8. For recent decisions rejecting the "captain of the ship" doctrine, see *Tappe* v. *Iowa Methodist Medical Center,* 477 N.W.2d 396, 403 (Iowa 1991) (noting that "the majority of courts shun this rigid doctrine of vicarious liability"); and *Franklin* v. *Gupta,* 81 Md. App. 345, 567 A.2d 524, 539, *cert. denied,* 572 A.2d 182 (1990). But cf. *Lanzet* v. *Greenberg,* 126 N.J. 168, 594 A.2d 1309 (1991) (finding surgeons have a duty to evaluate the patient's vital signs independently of the anesthesiologist; suggestive of captain-of-the-ship approach).
9. *Franklin,* #524, at 567 A.2d 539 (citations omitted).
10. As stated in *Killeen* v. *Reinhardt:* "The law is clear that a hospital is protected from liability when it follows the direct and explicit orders of the attending physician unless its staff knows that the doctor's orders are 'so clearly contraindicated by normal practice that ordinary prudence requires inquiry into [this] correctness.'" 71 A.D.2d 851, 419 N.Y.S.2d 175, 177 (1979).
11. For example, *Hoffman* v. *Wells,* 260 Ga. 588, 589, 397 S.E.2d 696, 698 (1990) ("If a master lends his servant to another then the master is not responsible for any negligence of the servant committed within the scope of employment by the other."); *Parker* v. *Hospital Auth. of Bainbridge & Decatur County,* 214 Ga. App. 113, 446 S.E.2d 766, *cert. denied,* 1994 Ga. LEXIS 1158 (Nov. 10, 1994).

12. See note 10. See also *Truhitte* v. *French Hosp.,* 128 Cal. App. 3d 332, 180 Cal. Rptr. 152 (1982); *Hoffman* v. *Wells,* 260 Ga. 588, 397 S.E.2d 696 (1990); *Butler* v. *South Fulton Medical Ctr., Inc.,* 216 Ga. App. 809, 452 S.E.2d 768, 772 (1994), *cert. denied,* 1995 Ga. LEXIS 411 (Mar. 17, 1995); *Franklin* v. *Gupta,* 81 Md. App. 345, 567 A.2d 524, *cert. denied,* 572 A.2d 182 (1990); *Simpson* v. *Sisters of Charity of Providence,* 284 Or. 547, 588 P.2d 4 (1978); and *Tonsic* v. *Wagner,* 458 Pa. 246, 329 A.2d 497 (1974).

13. For a general discussion of this distinction, see *ALR3rd 29,* p. 1065, § 4.

14. *Buzan* v. *Mercy Hosp.,* 203 So. 2d 11 (Fla. Dist. Ct. App. 1967).

15. *Sesselman* v. *Muhlenberg Hospital,* 124 N.J. Super. 285, 306 A.2d 474 (1973); "Mrs. Brownbach [the nurse anesthetist] did not become the legal servant or agent of defendant Hely [the private doctor] merely because she received instructions from him as to the work to be performed," Id., at 290; 306 A.2d, at 476. See also *Franklin* v. *Gupta,* 81 Md. App. 345, 567 A.2d 524, *cert. denied,* 572 A.2d 182 (1990).

16. *Adams* v. *Leidholt,* 195 Colo. 450, 579 P.2d 618 (1978).

17. *Darling* v. *Charlestown Community Memorial Hosp.,* 33 Ill. 2d 326, 211 N.E.2d 253 (1965), *cert. denied,* 383 U.S. 946 (1966). See also *George* v. *LDS Hosp.,* 797 P.2d 1117 (Utah Ct. App. 1990), *cert. denied,* 836 P.2d 1383 (1991).

18. *Simpson* v. *Sisters of Charity of Providence,* 284 Or. 547, 588 P.2d 4 (1978): "The jury could have found that the technicians took the requested x-rays in a negligent manner, leading to the physicians' eventual decision to stop taking x-rays. We do not understand the 'Captain of the Ship' rule to insulate hospitals or their employees from liability for following orders in a negligent manner" (588 P.2d, at 9).

19. *Truhitte* v. *French Hosp.,* 128 Cal. App. 3d 332, 348, 180 Cal. Rptr. 152, 160 (1982); See also *Ross* v. *Chatham County Hosp. Auth.,* 258 Ga. 234, 367 S.E.2d 793 (1988) (counting of sponges, instruments, and other items that could be left in a patient during operation is generally considered an administrative act for which the hospital could be held liable); *Piehl* v. *Dallas Gen. Hosp.,* 280 Or. 613, 571 P.2d 149 (1977).

20. Unless, of course, the staff knows that the order is clearly contraindicated by normal practice. *Killeen* v. *Reinhardt,* 17 A.D.2d 851, 419 N.Y.S.2d 175 (1979). See *Hoffman* v. *Wells,* 260 Ga. 588, 397 S.E.2d 696 (1990) (the borrowed-servant rule applicable in medical malpractice action against a hospital for any acts of the nurse who assisted the physician in an operation on the wrong hand because the nurse could not at the same time loyally be the servant of both the hospital and the physician, and the physician made the decision to proceed with the operation on the wrong hand).

21. See *Stumper* v. *Kimel,* 108 N.J. Super. 209, 260 A.D.2d 526, *cert. denied,* 264 A.2d 63 (1970). See also 1 Louisell and Williams (1992), at ¶ 16.06.

22. See general discussion in *Adamski* v. *Tacoma Gen. Hosp.,* 20 Wash. App. 98, 579 P.2d 970, 973–977 (1978).

ANNOTATIONS

S. Allan Adelman. "Liability and Medical Malpractice Issues." Washington, D.C.: American Health Lawyers Association [Report No. VHH99–0034], 1999, 67 pages.

Examines theories of liability in the health care setting, including direct liability (that is, medical record and patient transfer issues), vicarious liability (*respondeat superior*), product liability, and strict liability. Discusses the role of hospital policies and procedures in avoiding and creating liability, and ERISA preemption issues.

American Association of Blood Banks. *Regulatory Resource Manual.* Bethesda, Md.: AABB, 1998.

This is a compilation of the federal rules, regulations, and guidelines that have an impact on the operation of blood banks. It includes excerpts from the Code of Federal Regulations; the FDA

Compliance Program Guidance Manual; FDA Compliance Policy Guides; FDA guidelines; joint statements; CDC recommendations; and OSHA, HCFA, and DOT requirements, along with vital references.

Annot. "Liability of Nursing Home for Violating Statutory Duty to Notify Third Party Concerning Patient's Medical Condition." *ALR5th, 46*, 821.

Applying statutes regarding third-party notification is the subject of this annotation. Some jurisdictions have enacted statutes placing on the nursing home a duty, in certain circumstances, to notify a third party, such as a physician or next of kin, concerning the patient's medical condition. Thus, in *Staceyville Community Nursing Home* v. *Department of Inspections & Appeals* (Iowa 1995), 528 N.W.2d 557, 46 *ALR5th* 947, it was held that a nursing home was liable where there was proof that in a number of instances the home failed to report a patient's deteriorating medical condition, in violation of a statutory duty to do so, and that this was not affected by the fact that the patients were terminal.

Annot. "Exclusion of, or Discrimination Against, Physician or Surgeon by Hospital." *ALR5th, 1998, 28*, 107.

Examines cases addressing a hospital's exclusion of, or discrimination against, a physician or surgeon. Physicians or surgeons may be excluded from hospital staff privileges in various ways and at various points in time. One of the most common instances is rejecting an initial applicant for staff membership. There are also cases where the hospital refuses to renew a staff membership, or a practitioner is granted staff membership but restricted from performing certain functions such as major surgery or diagnostic radiology. As indicated by this annotation, the applicable rules may vary depending upon whether the hospital is a public or private institution. In *Garrison* v. *Board of Trustees of Memorial Hosp.*, 795 P2.d 190 (Wyo. 1990), 28 *ALR5th* 801, the court determined that a public hospital's refusal to grant a physician staff privileges was not arbitrary, where he incorrectly stated in an application that he had not had his privileges at any hospital suspended, diminished, revoked, or not renewed.

Annot. "Hospital's Liability for Injury Resulting from Failure to Have Sufficient Number of Nurses on Duty." *ALR5th, 1998, 2*, 286.

Collects and analyzes those cases in which the courts have considered a hospital's liability for personal injury to a patient, allegedly resulting from its failure to have on duty a number of nurses sufficient to maintain adequate levels of patient supervision and care.

Many hospitals are understaffed and the available nurses overworked; hospitals face a potential tide of lawsuits claiming patient injury caused by a failure to provide adequate care. In *HCA Health Services of Midwest, Inc.* v. *National Bank of Commerce*, 745 S.W.2d 120 (Ark. 1988), 2 *ALR5th* 1030, for example, the court held that a hospital could be held liable for brain damage to a newborn infant when the nurses in its understaffed nursery failed to discover in a timely manner that the baby had stopped breathing.

Laurent B. Frantz. "Patient Tort Liability of Rest, Convalescent or Nursing Homes." (Annot.) *ALR3rd, 1978, 83*, 871.

Collects and analyzes the cases dealing with the liability of rest, convalescent, or nursing homes for nonintentional torts to their patients. Institutions specializing in the treatment of some particular condition, such as mental illness, epilepsy, drug addiction, or chronic alcoholism, are excluded. When there is doubt or ambiguity about the nature of a particular institution, its characterization in the court's opinion has been treated as controlling. Governmental and charitable institutions have been included, as well as privately owned institutions operated for profit, but no effort is made to examine issues of governmental or charitable immunity. This resource is updated at least annually.

Amy Marie Haddad and Marshall B. Kapp. *Ethical and Legal Issues in Home Health Care.* Old Tappan, N.J.: Appleton & Lange, 1991, 225 pages.

Begins with an overview of ethics terminology, decision making, and law, and then turns to an historical discussion of home health care. The authors next examine regulatory issues that influence and structure home health care practice, including licensure, certification, fraud and abuse, antitrust, and price discrimination. Other topics discussed include malpractice, the role of legal counsel, and legal liability.

Linda Marie Harpster and Margaret S. Veach (eds.). *Risk Management Handbook for Health Care Facilities.* Chicago: American Hospital, 1990, 448 pages.

Well organized, this guide examines the regulatory and legislative setting for risk management before turning to the specific roles to be played in that process by the risk manager, the hospital governing board, the medical staff, and nurses. It then focuses on twelve specific high-risk areas of medicine, including obstetrics, emergency services, surgery, and anesthesia. Finally, it assesses risk identification systems, claims management, contract review, and insurance issues. Highly recommended.

John D. Hodson. "Liability of Hospital or Sanitarium for Negligence of Physician or Surgeon." (Annot.) *ALR4th,* 1987, *51,* 235.

Collects and analyzes cases in which courts have imputed to hospitals or sanitariums liability for the negligence of a physician or surgeon.

Diana L. Nolte Huff. "Liability Issues Arising from Hospitals' Use of Temporary Supplemental Staff Nurses." *Loyola University Law Journal,*1990, *21,* 1141-1172. Reprinted in *Defense Law Journal,* 1991, *40, 663–695.*

Discusses the liability issues arising from hospitals' use of temporary, supplemental staff nurses to fill nursing care vacancies. The article examines the professional responsibilities of the professional registered nurse. Next, it addresses the agency's duty to screen and verify a professional nurse's qualifications and abilities before allowing the nurse to practice within a hospital setting. The article then examines the duty a hospital owes to individual patients for the health care rendered by nursing and medical practitioners within its boundaries. Finally, it turns to the interrelationship among the registered professional nurse, the employing agency, and the hospital that solicits supplemental staffing resources.

John Dwight Ingram. "Liability of Medical Institutions for the Negligence of Independent Contractors Practicing on their Premises." *Journal of Contemporary Health Law and Policy,* 1994, *10,* 221.

Presents a history of hospital liability, examining questions of agency and reliance before concluding that a hospital should not be able to use contractual arrangements to insulate itself from liability for acts of medical malpractice committed upon its premises by doctors who appear to be agents or employees of the hospital.

Michael Jones. "Institutional Liability for Medical Malpractice." In Mark A. Hall (gen. ed.), *Health Care Corporate Law: Financing and Liability.* Boston: Little, Brown, 1994.

This article of ninety-four pages is an excellent introduction to the subject. Topics covered include vicarious liability, direct corporate liability, types of duty owed, duties of managed care organizations, the Health Care Quality Improvement Act, and causes of action against managed care organizations. Other topics discussed are the pertinent standard of care, causation, allocation of damages, defenses, immunity, arbitration, the Good Samaritan doctrine, cost containment as a defense, and defensive use of practice guidelines.

Marshall B. Kapp. "Malpractice Liability in Long-Term Care: A Changing Environment." *Creighton Law Review,* 1991, *24,* 1235.

Examines the legal environment of long-term care and its possible liability consequences. Special emphasis is placed on the nursing home industry. After an introduction to relevant demographics and the structure of long-term care in the United States, the traditional underrepresentation of the elderly in malpractice litigation is discussed. The author pays particular attention to potential ramifications of federal nursing home regulations, as well as the influence of voluntary or private standards of care and the network of resources from which attorneys representing nursing home patients may draw support.

Kerry A. Kearney and Edward L. McCord. "Hospital Management Faces New Liabilities." *Health Lawyer*, Fall 1992, 6(3), 1.

Reviews statutes passed by more than twenty-two state legislatures that alter hospitals' liability for the acts of independent physicians by adopting, in some form, a theory of corporate liability.

C. Kearns, C. J. Gerner, and C. Ryan. *Health Care Liability Deskbook*. (3rd ed.) Deerfield, Ill.: Clark, Boardman, Callaghan, 1996, 788 pages.

Enumerates the broad range of activities that could result in a court's finding of liability. Written by practicing attorneys, the book addresses physician malpractice, clinical practice guidelines, patient dumping, reporting of child abuse, AIDS, and underground storage tank leakage and other environmental liability for medical waste. Other topics addressed include federal and state employment law issues, the ADA, staff privileges and peer review, antitrust issues, health care fraud and abuse, and ERISA. The text is supplemented by more than two hundred pages of tables and appendices further breaking this material down by state. It also features a table of cases, index, and detailed table of contents, making the information presented unusually accessible.

Alan D. Lieberson. *Healthcare Enterprise Liability*. Charlottesville, Va.: Lexis Law, 1997, 1,146 pages.

This unusually well-written treatise is arranged in six sections. Following an initial introduction to enterprise liability, it specifically addresses its relationship to hospitals, nursing homes and the insurance industry, and managed care, with a brief interruption for an examination of ERISA preemption. The author, a medical researcher who holds degrees in law and medicine, discloses early in the book his bias in favor of a two-tier socialized delivery system offering every American a baseline level of medical care without limiting the ability of citizens to purchase additional health insurance if they so choose. The text is supplemented by an index, table of contents, table of cases, numerous checklists, and exhaustive footnotes. Each chapter concludes with a list of relevant journal articles.

Harold S. Luft, Patricia P. Katz, and Douglas G. Pinney. "Risk Factors for Hospital Malpractice Exposure: Implications for Managers and Insurers." *Law and Contemporary Problems*, Spring 1991, *54*, 43.

This study was designed as an initial test of the hypothesis that risk factors for hospital malpractice can be identified that help explain the variability in hospital malpractice claims. The variables considered fall into four groups: (1) the type of hospital, (2) the presence and volume of selected specialized services, (3) staffing and organizational patterns, and (4) objective measures of patient outcomes. The authors conclude, from their analysis of more than two hundred California hospitals linked to readily available objective measures of hospital characteristics and performance, that it is possible to identify significant risk factors with plausible coefficients of reasonable magnitude.

Kay McCurdy (ed.). *CLIA and Transfusion Medicine: A Guide to Total Compliance*. Bethesda, Md.: American Association of Blood Banks, 1996.

A comprehensive guide to the Clinical Laboratory Improvement Amendments of 1988 (CLIA) requirements for patient and donor testing related to test requisitions, sample collection, test and quality control procedures, test reports, and record keeping. This book sifts through more than one hundred pages of regulations, extracts the relevant requirements, and brings practical guidance regarding application of the requirements. Appendices present lists of test procedures by manufacturer, with CLIA specialty and complexity level along with addresses and phone numbers of the state surveying offices. Pertinent sections of Title 42, Code of Federal Regulations, are also included at the end of each chapter.

Frederick Miles. "The Use of Survey/Certification Compliance Data in Malpractice Actions." Washington, D.C.: American Health Lawyers Association [Report No. VLT99–0033], 1999, 29 pages.

Offers an overview of claims using compliance data; analyzes arguments that may be made with respect to the requirements of participation (and survey, postsurvey, and enforcement processes) to refute the appropriateness of using OBRA (Omnibus Budget Reconciliation Act) 1987 as a standard of care.

Timothy J. Moore. "Institutional Liability Insurance and Risk Management." In Mark A. Hall (gen. ed.), *Health Care Corporate Law: Financing and Liability*. Boston: Little, Brown, 1994.

Topics covered in this useful chapter of sixty-four pages include conventional insurance arrangements, institutional insurance alternatives, self-insurance, the Liability Risk Retention Act, risk pooling, captive insurance, operational issues, and combining hospital and medical staff insurance.

Laura L. Morlock and Faye E. Malitz. "Do Hospital Risk Management Programs Make a Difference?: Relationships Between Risk Management Program Activities and Hospital Malpractice Claims Experience." *Law and Contemporary Problems*, Spring 1991, *54*, 1.

Examines data on risk management programs in effect at Maryland hospitals, along with data from a study on the malpractice claims experience of Maryland health care providers, to investigate (1) the types of claim arising out of hospital-based incidents, (2) the frequency with which the hospital is named as a defendant in these incidents, (3) the frequency with which the hospital is found liable, and (4) the relationship between clinical risk management activities and hospital malpractice claims experience.

Note. "The Quality of Mercy: 'Charitable Torts' and Their Continuing Immunity." *Harvard Law Review*, 1987, *100*, 1382.

Argues that charitable immunity burdens the innocent victims of torts with the entire cost of their injuries and is therefore fundamentally unjust. Three reforms will be required to lay this injustice to rest. First, the formal doctrine of charitable immunity, blanket or partial, should be abandoned in any jurisdiction that retains it. Second, both courts and legislatures should take measures to prevent enforcement of charitable waivers of liability. Third, legislatures should require asset-poor charities to carry insurance sufficient to cover their potential liability.

Risk and Insurance Management Society. *Risk Management Glossary*. New York: Risk and Insurance Management Society, 1996, 82 pages.

Supplies a core vocabulary for risk managers and others in related fields. The glossary includes insurance, finance, legal, and statistical terms.

James Walker Smith. *Hospital Liability*. New York: Law Journal Seminars-Press, 1998, approx. 1,100 pages.

Regularly updated, this treatise covers such topics as hospital organizational structure; immunity; tortious liability; standards of care; hospital professional liability insurance; admission and emergency treatment; nosocomial infections; equipment-related patient injuries; discharge, transfer, and referral; nursing; pharmacy; informed consent; refusal of treatment; patient records; accreditation; liability for employment law violations; HMO liability for medical malpractice; environmental hazards; and nonmedical liability.

Jay M. Zitter. "Tort Liability of Medical Society or Professional Association for Failure to Discipline or Investigate Negligent or Otherwise Incompetent Medical Practitioner." (Annot.) *ALR4th*, 1989, *72*, 1148.

Collects and discusses state and federal cases in which courts have considered whether and under what circumstances a statewide, national, local, or specialized medical association or society could be liable in tort for personal injuries resulting from its failure to discipline or investigate a medical practitioner who allegedly was negligent or incompetent. This resource is regularly updated.

Liability of Managed Care Organizations

During the past ten years, the need to reduce costs has transformed many health care insurers from third-party payers into active managers of the treatment patients receive, and sometimes into direct care providers. This shift follows a precedent from earlier in this century when hospitals developed from doctors' workshops into independent providers of medical services. Just as hospitals' enhanced role in providing care increased their accountability for quality of care, managed care organizations' integration of health care delivery and finance has led to new legal responsibilities for payers and other MCOs.[1]

So long as payment and treatment were kept separate, insurers had little to worry about in the way of liability for treatment decisions. Yet utilization review, an integral part of managed care, has thrust payers into the position of making clinical decisions. This has created a new legal environment in which managed care plans can be held liable not only for injuries arising out of physician negligence but also for inappropriate denial of treatment and wrongful exclusion of network providers.[2]

In one major respect, MCOs are exposed to greater direct corporate liability than hospitals. For hospitals, it is doubtful whether the branch of direct liability applies that requires active, contemporaneous supervision of discrete medical decisions as they are made. Many courts and commentators reason that it would be poor public policy for the law to impose liability based on the assumption that hospital administrators routinely second-guess the clinical judgment of treating physicians at the bedside. By contrast, for MCOs, this is often their raison d'être. One of the central ways MCOs control costs is by monitoring the decision making of health care providers.[3] Thus, unlike hospitals, MCOs cannot argue that it is inappropriate to require them to actively supervise the quality of care in their institutions.[4]

References

1. William S. Brewbaker III. "Managed Care Liability." In Mark A. Hall (gen. ed.), *Health Care Corporate Law: Financing and Liability.* Boston: Little, Brown, 1994.
2. Brewbaker (1994).
3. Brewbaker (1994).
4. Brewbaker (1994). See generally C. Kearns and others. *Health Care Liability Deskbook.* Deerfield, Ill.: Clark, Boardman, Callaghan, 1996.

ANNOTATIONS

17.01　　IN GENERAL

Kenneth S. Abraham, Robert L. Rabin, and Paul C. Weiler. "Enterprise Responsibility for Personal Injury: Further Reflections." *San Diego Law Review,* 1993, *30,* 333.

The American Law Institute (ALI) commissioned its study "Enterprise Responsibility for Personal Injury" in the mid-1980s in the midst of widespread concern about skyrocketing insurance premiums charged to people and businesses fortunate enough to find any tort liability coverage. In this article, the project's reporter and two associate reporters advocate adopting a no-fault approach to health care liability. Hospitals or health care organizations should eventually be made responsible for a patient's otherwise uncompensated financial losses from all seriously disabling medical injuries, irrespective of the presence or absence of provider fault. They suggest that this plan be implemented first on a pilot, elective basis. Such a plan would allow observation of the pros and cons of the approach in actual operation.

This pilot phase, the authors propose, should consist of six components. First, express legislative authorization would be given to hospitals and other health care organizations to offer their patients the option of an administrative system of no-fault compensation for all medical injury occurring within the hospital, in return for a waiver of any right to sue the hospital and any other health care providers for malpractice associated with the injury in question. Second, after being informed in an understandable manner of the tort rights to be surrendered and the no-fault rights to be provided, patients would choose between treatment in a no-fault hospital or a tort-fault hospital.

The third component is that compensation would be sufficiently generous to replace the vast majority of the economic losses of patients who are disabled for a minimum period of several months. Such compensation would include full medical and rehabilitation expenses not covered by other sources of insurance, a fairly high percentage of wage loss (for example, 80 percent) up to a multiple of the state's average wage (say, up to twice that level), again offset by payments from other sources. Fourth, the program would include a claims administration procedure that is neutral, fair, and easily accessible to patients. A board of independent arbiters would resolve disputes over coverage and amount.

Fifth, hospitals would be authorized to impose a surcharge on physicians and other health care providers with admitting privileges in exchange for relief from the threat of tort liability. Sixth, the hospital or health care facility offering no-fault benefits would have in place an effective quality assurance program and would receive state-given authority to surcharge or suspend the admitting privileges of accident-prone doctors, along with antitrust immunity for doing so.

Kenneth S. Abraham and Paul C. Weiler. "Enterprise Medical Liability and the Evolution of the American Health Care System." *Harvard Law Review*, 1994, *108*, 381.

Discusses enterprise medical liability, a malpractice reform proposal that has gained prominence in the 1990s. Under this approach, the focus of malpractice litigation would be shifted from individual physicians to the health care organizations under whose auspices patients are treated. In this article, Abraham and Weiler, who originally developed this policy proposal in the late 1980s, analyze how such a change should be made in medical liability law.

The authors first chronicle how, beginning in the 1960s, courts gradually developed a measure of hospital liability for physician negligence, at the same time as other changes in the health care system were motivating hospitals to exercise greater control over both the quantity and quality of medical services that physicians offered to patients. The authors then show why completion of this evolution (by making hospitals liable for all malpractice by their affiliated physicians) would better serve the goals of tort law than does the current individual liability regime. The authors also explain why imposing liability on enterprises such as hospitals engaged in delivering patient care is preferable to imposing liability on health plans that finance patient care.

After detailing how enterprise medical liability could be introduced electively, Abraham and Weiler conclude by explaining why this shift in the target of malpractice litigation might serve as a step on the way to a fundamentally different, no-fault medical liability regime.

Kenneth S. Abraham and Paul C. Weiler. "Enterprise Medical Liability and the Choice of the Responsible Enterprise." *American Journal of Law and Medicine*, 1994, *20*, 29.

Over a period of years, the authors have elaborated an argument for shifting the focus of liability for medical injury from individual physicians to the organizations that deliver health care. The question then arises as to whom precisely liability should be shifted. In this article, Abraham and Weiler explain why liability should be imposed on hospital and similar health care delivery organizations.

The authors contend that delivery-based liability would most effectively promote the goals of medical injury prevention and quality assurance. Additionally, delivery-based enterprise liability would be a superior approach to providing insurance against and compensation for medical injury and would outperform any other form of medical liability in reducing the administrative burdens of the tort system. Their proposal, they write, would mesh closely with the underlying goals of tort liability: promoting optimal prevention, providing reasonable compensation to accident victims, and minimizing the administrative cost of a fault-based liability system. Finally, the authors assert that from the point of view of past and future victims of medical injury, delivery-based enterprise liability would also improve upon the protective benefits of tort liability, rather than merely shrink the burden that this regime imposes on physicians.

American Bar Association. *Managed Care Liability: Examining Risks and Responsibilities in a Changing Health Care System.* Chicago: ABA, 1997, 488 pages.

Brings together some of the leading experts in the field of managed care litigation and supplies a discussion of some of the issues that have faced consumers, health care providers, insurers, attorneys, and courts. Topics examined include negligence claims, regulation of health plan companies and provider-sponsored networks, credentialing liability and the managed care organization, handling consumer grievances and minimizing legal liability, controlling liability in managed care, disasters in managed care (a plaintiff's perspective), defending managed care in jury cases, experimental procedures, gatekeeper liability, and liability of the long-distance health care provider.

American Medical Association. *Liability and Managed Care.* Chicago: AMA, 1997.

Where lines of responsibility were once clearly delineated, the emergence of complicated approval, referral, and gatekeeping systems has created liability gaps that can be pitfalls, especially for physicians in high-risk specialties. This book provides practical advice in simple, easy-to-understand terms, with sections that focus on the basis of physician liability and helpful tips.

Annot. "Liability of Health Maintenance Organizations (HMOs) for Negligence of Member Physicians." *ALR5th,* 1998, *51,* 271.

Collects and analyzes those cases in which courts have considered the liability of HMOs for physician negligence, including cases in which ERISA preemption has been asserted as a defense. The author notes that the development of HMOs within the movement toward managed health care has created new issues of liability in medical malpractice suits. The courts tend to analyze the liability of HMOs according to traditional principles of agency law. In some jurisdictions, the courts have recognized that an HMO can be vicariously liable for the negligence of a physician under the theories of *respondeat superior* or ostensible agency. Additionally, courts have considered HMO liability on the basis of corporate liability, breach of contract or warranty, and various tort theories. In *Dunn* v. *Praiss,* 139 N.J. 564, 656 A.2d 413 (1995), 51 *ALR5th* 799, for example, the Supreme Court of New Jersey held that a state statute did not make HMOs immune from medical malpractice claims and stated that HMOs could be sued under theories of vicarious liability based on *respondeat superior,* negligent selection and control of physicians, breach of contract or warranty, and corporate negligence (such as negligence in managing the HMO).

Diana Joseph Bearden and Bryan J. Maedgen. "Emerging Theories of Liability in the Managed Health Care Industry." *Baylor Law Review,* 1995, *47,* 285.

Discusses the characteristics of managed care organizations that make them particularly vulnerable to the emerging theories of liability being asserted against them in medical malpractice actions. This article, written by two practicing attorneys, also addresses defenses available to managed care organizations in such cases and presents specific suggestions for actions HMOs can take to counter liability claims. These suggestions include (1) establishing prescribed procedures in selecting physicians, supervising them, and reviewing continued eligibility of physicians participating in the HMO; (2) using the IPA model of HMO if possible to limit exposure under a theory of *respondeat superior*; (3) clearly documenting subscriber contracts, physician contracts, and promotional materials to clearly delineate the HMO-physician relationship, the program benefits, and those medical treatments and services that are not covered by the program; (4) implementing a risk management system to resolve internal disputes or as a complaint resolution mechanism (the HMO may also provide for binding arbitration of disputes with subscribers.); (5) taking care to avoid advertising that portrays the HMO as a provider of health care rather than a financier of health care (careful advertising can help shield the HMO from liability under the theory of ostensible agency.); (6) delegating the utilization review function to an outside entity to shield the HMO from liability; (7) broadening the patient's choice of physicians to minimize the HMO's appearance of control, thereby reducing exposure to liability under the theory of ostensible agency; (8) emphasizing the importance of the physician's independent medical judgment in the contract between the HMO and the physician; and (9) having the HMO verify that all physicians carry sufficient malpractice insurance.

Charles G. Benda and Fay A. Rozovsky. *Liability and Risk Management in Managed Care.* Gaithersburg, Md.: Aspen, 1996.

This loose-leaf work aims to guide risk managers and others on how to avoid risk exposures in managed care. Written with a refreshing absence of either legal jargon or "biz-school speak," it covers the following topics: federal legal and regulatory issues, state legal and regulatory issues, standards of care and negligence, crediting liability, consent to treatment issues, health care record information, contracting issues, utilization review, capitation, bad faith, and accreditation. This book also contains a superb appendix with twenty checklists for risk management personnel, a glossary of managed care terms, and an index.

Vickie Yates Brown and Barbara Reid Hartung. "Managed Care at the Crossroads: Can Managed Care Organizations Survive Government Regulation?" *Annals of Health Law,* 1998, *7*, 25.

The authors present a comprehensive overview of the development and structural components of managed health care plans. The article discusses the state-regulated controls affecting managed care, including patient protection acts, mandated benefit provisions, any-willing-provider laws, and consumer access provisions. The article considers liability problems facing MCOs, in particular liabilities arising from utilization and medical review discussions as well as gag clauses and financial incentive arrangements. The authors also review relevant federal regulatory initiatives. The article concludes with an appendix setting forth laws of the any-willing-provider type in the fifty states and an appendix concerning provider access statutes in all states.

Patricia Butler. "Managed Care Plan Liability: An Analysis of Texas and Missouri Legislation." Menlo Park, Calif.: Henry J. Kaiser Family Foundation [Report No. 1343], 1997.

This report analyzes recently enacted laws in Texas and Missouri that expand consumers' ability to sue their HMOs or other managed care plans for inappropriately denied care or similar problems.

William A. Chittenden III and Douglas J. Varga. "Liability of Managed Care Organizations." In David W. Louisell and Harold Williams (eds.), *Medical Malpractice.* New York: Matthew Bender, 1997.

Focuses on the growth in malpractice litigation against MCOs in recent years. In some states, courts have developed various theories of liability, sounding in both tort and contract, including (1) vicarious liability founded on traditional theories of *respondeat superior* and apparent or ostensible agency; (2) direct liability for negligent provider selection and control; (3) direct liability for breach of contract, breach of warranty, fraud, or consumer fraud based on statements contained in subscriber contracts and marketing materials; and (4) direct liability for corporate negligence in designing or implementing quality assurance and cost-containment mechanisms, particularly utilization review systems. In other states, medical malpractice reform legislation may govern the liability of MCOs.

In this article of seventy-three pages, the authors, both practicing attorneys, analyze these arguments along with such defenses as ERISA preemption, immunity based on statute, and mandatory arbitration of medical malpractice claims.

Douglas A. Cifu. "Expanding Legal Malpractice to Nonclient Third Parties—At What Cost?" *Columbia Journal of Law and Social Problems*, 1989, *23*, 1.

Notes that in recent years, American courts have departed from the traditional common law restriction of legal malpractice actions to clients. This article examines the assault on the citadel of privity in legal malpractice actions, arguing that some courts have gone too far in recognizing a right of action belonging to third parties. Attorney liability to third parties imposes hardships on attorneys and strains their relationships with clients. Therefore, Cifu argues that liability to third parties should be limited to instances of intentional wrongdoing.

Barry R. Furrow. "Enterprise Liability and Health Care Reform: Managing Care and Managing Risk." *St. Louis University Law Journal*, 1994, *39*(77), 92.

Focuses on enterprise liability in the era of health care reform. What was once the community hospital has now evolved into a corporate institution. Today hospitals are part of "delivery systems," which also include managed care organizations, group practices, and individual physicians.

Kevin D. Gordon. "Legal Liability for Managed Care Entities and Providers." Washington, D.C.: American Health Lawyers Association [Report No. VMC98–0035], 1998, 29 pages.

Discusses emerging theories of liability to MCO members, including vicarious liability and direct corporate liability based upon allegations concerning utilization review and financial incentives. Also discusses emerging defenses to liability, including changing parameters of ERISA preemption, medical malpractice as a prerequisite to liability, and Federal Employee Health Benefits Act preemption and state regulatory procedures.

Kevin D. Gordon and Eric S. Fisher. "Liability of Managed Care Organizations—Two Sides of the Same Coin: Emerging Liability Theories and Defenses Regarding MCOs." Washington, D.C.: American Health Lawyers Association [Report No. VHL 99–0030], 1999, 39 pages.

Examines emerging liability theories and defenses regarding managed care organizations. Liability topics include vicarious liability, breach of contract, bad faith, misrepresentation, and the ADA. Defense topics include ERISA preemption and arbitration clauses. Includes table of relevant cases.

Richard A. Hinden and Douglas L. Elden. "Liability Issues for Managed Care Entities." *Seton Hall Legislative Journal*, 1990, *14*, 1.

Begins with analysis of agency issues and then turns to the Health Care Quality Improvement Act of 1986, which is examined in detail. Elden is a past chair of the American Association of Preferred Provider Organizations.

Susan R. Huntington. "Managed Care Liability Exposures and Insurance Coverage." Washington, D.C.: American Health Lawyers Association [Report No. VMC98–0042], 1998, 39 pages.

Discusses the risk transfer (insurance) challenges presented by the evolving liability exposures encountered by MCOs. Offers an in-depth primer (including sample policy language) for evaluating and understanding liability coverage for directors and officers and for managed care errors and omissions.

Karen A. Jordan. "Preemption of a State 'Legislatively Created' Right to Sue HMOs for Negligence." *Health Care Monthly*, Apr. 1999, 13.

This article discusses *Corporate Health Ins., Inc.* v. *Texas Dept. of Insurance,* 12 F. Supp. 2d 597 (S.D. Tex 1998), in which a federal district court in Texas held that the liability provisions of the Health Care Liability Act enacted by the Texas legislature were not preempted by ERISA. The author posits that if this district court decision is upheld on appeal to the Fifth Circuit Court of Appeals, many other states may extend malpractice liability to HMOs and other managed care plans.

Michael Kanute. "Evolving Theories of Malpractice Liability for HMOs." *Loyola University of Chicago Law Journal*, 1989, *20,* 841.

Traditional health care providers, such as hospitals, have been subjected to liability on a number of theories, including *respondeat superior,* ostensible agency, and corporate negligence. This note examines the traditional bases on which hospitals have been held liable and will examine whether HMOs should be subject to the same liability.

Gary S. Mogel. "American Jurisprudence Proof of Facts." (Annot.) *Managed Care Organization Professional Malpractice,* 1995, *29,* 1.

Explains and illustrates how to prove that a managed care organization has committed professional malpractice related to forming or administering its network of physicians and hospital care providers. This issue ordinarily arises when a patient of the MCO is a victim of medical malpractice by a network provider, an allegedly negligent utilization review or medical necessity decision, or some other form of negligence committed by the organization.

Corinne P. Parver and Kimberly Alyson Martinez. "Holding Decision Makers Liable: Assessing Liability under a Managed Health Care System." *Administrative Law Review,* 1999, *51,* 199.

Compares traditional approaches to medical care by the medical profession with recent changes created by using managed care principles in health care. Next, it addresses theories of liability to explain how tort principles have been applied to correct for wrongdoing under the managed care system. Finally, it discusses the impact of ERISA on this area of the law, revealing the need for congressional action.

Miles J. Zaremski and Bruce C. Nelson. "Liability Exposure Facing Managed Care Organizations." Washington, D.C.: American Health Lawyers Association [Report No. VHL 99–0031], 1999, 54 pages.

Reviews recent trends and theories within case law and statutory and legislative efforts, all affecting the liability of MCOs arising from medical care and treatment of plan enrollees. Features a chart on proposed legislation to remove the ERISA shield, including bills and their sponsors, relevant provisions, and a summary of the provisions.

17.02   TORT LIABILITY

Allen D. Allred and Terry O. Tottenham. "Liability and Indemnity Issues for Integrated Delivery Systems." *St. Louis Law Journal,* 1996, *40,* 457.

Areas of tort liability traditionally applied to hospitals recently have been extended to managed care entities. In the near future, these areas of liability will likely be extended further to the integrated delivery system. In this analysis of eighty-five pages, the authors, both practicing attorneys, address the following topics: theories of liability, agency theories of liability, COBRA issues, general risk management issues, state and federal regulation of the integrated delivery system, ERISA preemption, contractual and indemnification issues, and liability issues on the horizon.

Aimed at the health care lawyer, this article is highly practical and contains extensive advice that attorneys representing integrated delivery systems should impart to their clients.

Annot. "Right of Contractor with Federal, State, or Local Public Body to Latter's Immunity from Tort Liability." *ALR3rd*, 1998, 9, 382.

The issue of tort liability involves consideration of whether a state agency can be sued for a civil wrong, and if so, under what circumstances. Suits against a state agency are affected by specific state immunity statutes. Each state has its own immunity provisions, which must be referred to prior to bringing a civil suit for negligence against a Medicaid state agency. This annotation summarizes cases in which contractors claim such immunity.

John D. Blum. "An Analysis of Legal Liability in Health Care Utilization Review and Case Management." *Houston Law Review*, 1989, 26, 191.

Examines the legal liability involved in both utilization review and case management. Although government efforts in utilization review are briefly noted, this article stresses liability in the context of private sector programs. The discussion of liability primarily concerns risks faced by corporations engaged in utilization review and case management.

William A. Chittenden III. "Malpractice Liability and Managed Health Care: History and Prognosis." *Tort and Insurance Law Journal*, 1991, 26, 451.

Examines the development of malpractice liability of managed care organizations. This article notes that whether brought under traditional theories of vicarious liability or theories of direct liability for negligent selection or control, malpractice-related claims against MCOs have met with some success.

Patricia J. Cummings. "Third-Party Payor Tort Liability for Utilization-Review Decisions." *Medical Trial Technique Quarterly*, 1995, 41, 432.

Extending tort liability to third-party payers for negligent utilization review decisions is an unsettled and relatively new area of the law. This article examines two California cases in this area, *Wickline* v. *State*, 192 Cal. App. 3d 1630, 1633, 239 Cal. Rptr. 810 (1986); and *Wilson* v. *Blue Cross of Southern California*, 222 Cal. App. 3d 660, 271 Cal. Rptr. 876 (1990).

Michael A. Dowell. "Avoiding HMO Liability for Utilization Review." *University of Toledo Law Review*, 1991, 23, 117.

Describes the potential liability of HMOs for utilization review programs. In this unusually well-written article, the author, a practicing attorney, analyzes a number of decided cases and examines a range of liability theories applicable to utilization review claims, including malpractice and negligence, breach of contract, breach of implied covenant of good faith and fair dealing, intentional or negligent infliction of emotional distress, wrongful death, unfair business practices, defamation, interference with contractual relations between physician and patient, and antitrust. The author then offers practical approaches for preventing and defending suits brought against HMOs for utilization review decisions.

Sharon M. Glenn. "Tort Liability of Integrated Health Care Delivery Systems: Beyond Enterprise Liability." (Comment.) *Wake Forest Law Review*, 1994, 29, 305.

Not only will integrated health networks be subject to vicarious liability in the future, the author predicts, but they may also be subject to direct liability. Based on common law duties that are assumed by hospitals and HMOs, it is likely that integrated networks must fulfill a duty of care when selecting network providers. In addition, cases discussing HMO methods of cost containment indicate that the networks may also be subject to direct liability for improper utilization review decisions and inadequate plan design.

Richard A. Hinden and Douglas L. Elden. "Liability Issues for Managed Care Entities." *Seton Hall Legislative Journal,* 1990, *14,* 1.

The introductory essay in a symposium issue titled "The Dark Side of Health Care Containment: Emerging Legal Issues in Managed Care." This article, written by two practicing attorneys, examines a variety of doctrines that may be used to impose liability upon managed care organizations, including ostensible agency, corporate negligence, and abuse of utilization review. As to the latter, the authors offer a detailed analysis of *Wickline* v. *State,* 192 Cal. App. 3d 1630, 239 Cal. Rptr. 810 (Ct. App.), *cert. granted,* 727 P.2d 753, 231 Cal. Rptr. 560 (1986), *review dismissed, case remanded,* 741 P.2d 613, 239 Cal. Rptr. 805 (1987), the first case addressing the issue of whether a third-party payer may be held liable to a plaintiff/patient in a medical malpractice case by virtue of performing utilization management functions.

Edward B. Hirshfeld. "Should Third-Party Payors of Health Care Services Disclose Cost Control Mechanisms to Potential Beneficiaries?" *Seton Hall Legislative Journal,* 1990, *14,* 115.

Written by the associate general counsel of the American Medical Association, this article answers the question posed in its title in the affirmative. The author extrapolates the need for such disclosure from, among other things, a fiduciary's responsibility to avoid conflict of interest.

David H. Johnson. "Managed Care and Financial Incentives to Physicians: Should There Be Limits?" Washington, D.C.: American Health Lawyers Association [Report No. VMC98–0017], 1998, 36 pages.

Examines the ethical, regulatory, and liability issues related to the array of financial incentives offered to physicians and medical groups by managed care organizations. Includes a list of tort cases against MCOs and physicians based on claims relating to financial incentives or breach of fiduciary duty.

Jack K. Kilcullen. "Groping for the Reins: ERISA, HMO Malpractice, and Enterprise Liability." *American Journal of Law and Medicine,* 1996, *1,* 7–50.

Argues that the individual physician and the HMO that dictates the parameters of medical practice are locked in a single enterprise affecting patient care. Therefore, enterprise liability should be an essential component of any form of managed care liability. The article concludes with a proposal to incorporate enterprise liability into ERISA to fairly reflect a true private sector approach to health care reform.

Robin W. Milner. "Enterprise Liability: Channeling Liability with or Without the Health Security Act of 1993." (Comment.) *St. Louis Law Journal,* 1994, *38,* 1009.

Examines the notion of applying principles of enterprise liability to the area of health care delivery. As a system of compensation, enterprise liability is espoused by scholars as a strict liability or no-fault regime analogous to the workers compensation system, where economic recompense is not contingent upon the existence of negligence or the assignment of negligence to a particular party.

Gabriel J. Minc. "ERISA Preemption of Medical Negligence Claims Against Managed Care Providers: The Search for an Effective Theory and an Appropriate Remedy." *Journal of Health and Hospital Law,* 1996, *29,* 97.

Examines the circumstances under which ERISA preempts state law medical negligence causes of action against a managed care provider. When a managed care provider offers health care services through an employee benefit plan, issues arise regarding whether state or federal law applies to medical negligence claims brought against the provider. Managed care providers often assert that ERISA preempts such actions because they are directed to the structure and operation of the employee benefit plan. In resolving the issue of ERISA preemption, courts are forced to construe the function of the provider relative to the ERISA plan. This task becomes more difficult, and the court decisions more inconsistent, as managed care providers increasingly integrate payer, administrator, utilization review, and health care provider functions, the author writes.

This article, written by a practicing attorney, first presents a brief summary of the ERISA preemption doctrine. Next, it offers analysis of recent decisions regarding ERISA preemption of medical negligence claims against managed care providers. Finally, the article summarizes the current state of the law and discusses legal trends and some of the problems facing the courts, providers, and plan participants. This article is supplemented by copious endnotes.

Saul J. Morse. "Ethical Concerns for Physicians and Other Health Care Providers in the Brave New World of Managed Care." Washington, D.C.: American Health Lawyers Association [Report No. VMC98–0018], 1998, 19 pages.

Examines how ethical concerns for health providers in the managed care arena have evolved. Reviews how to counsel clients to minimize the chance that conflicting duties will result in a negative outcome for a patient and potential liability or loss of licensure for the physician and the MCO.

David W. O'Brien. "Procedural Considerations for the Use of ERISA Provisions in the Defense of an HMO against Claims Arising from Medical Malpractice." Health Lawyer, Early Spring 1996, 8, 13.

Discusses tactical issues such as removal to federal court, strategy upon remand to state court, and issues to be adjudicated in a motion to dismiss.

Helene L. Parise. "The Proper Extension of Tort Liability Principles in the Managed Care Industry." (Comment.) Temple Law Quarterly, 1991, 64, 977.

In reviewing recent court decisions, the author concludes that managed care exposure to tort liability is rising. Two decisions in particular—Boyd v. Albert Einstein Medical Center, 547 A.2d 1229 (Pa. Super. 1988), and Schleier v. Kaiser Foundation Health Plan, 876 F.2d 174 (D.C. Cir. 1989)—recognize that managed care plans have begun to place a duty on plans to ensure safe delivery of health services to their enrollees. One way a plan can ensure safe, high-quality health care is to associate with competent health care providers and employ appropriate medical standards when assessing medically necessary treatment. Another way to minimize liability and to ensure the quality of care would be for the plan to receive accreditation.

Barbara A. Quinn. "Tort Liability of Third-Party Payors: Wilson v. Blue Cross of Southern California." (Comment.) Creighton Law Review, 1991, 24, 1399.

Examines case law pertinent to the issue of whether tort liability should be extended to third-party payers such as managed care organizations. The author concludes that policy reasons exist for not holding some government third-party payers liable for their decisions. However, there are no policy reasons for exempting private insurance companies from tort liability for arbitrary and unreasonable actions that are a substantial factor in causing harm to one of their plan participants.

William T. Robinson III. "New Deep Pocket: Managed Care Entity Liability for Alleged Improper Denial of Access." Defense Counsel Journal, 1997, 64, 357.

Analyzes recent cases in which plaintiffs have sought damage awards against health care entities based on a range of theories, which include vicarious liability, denial of access to care, and denial of coverage. The author discusses the denial-of-coverage topic in detail, focusing on care that is not medically necessary, exclusions for desired treatment, utilization review, and tortious interference with the doctor-patient relationship.

Elizabeth N. Rogers. "Risk Management Strategies to Respond to Emerging Trends in Managed Care Liability." Washington, D.C.: American Health Lawyers Association [Report No. VMC98–0019], 1998, 75 pages.

Discusses emerging trends in managed care liability and risk management strategies to deal with them, direct liability for utilization review decisions, capitation payment and financial incentives, direct liability of MCOs under the ADA, fee-splitting issues, vicarious liability of MCOs for medical malpractice, shifting managed care liability through indemnification provisions, and shielding and spreading managed care liability. Includes a sample request for production of documents list, suggested areas to cover in discovery in a managed care setting, the Texas Department of Insurance proposed financial incentive guidelines, commentary on defensive use of the physician incentive plan rules, and sample contract language for existing and future contractual relationships with payors.

William M. Sage, Kathleen E. Hastings, and Robert A. Berenson. "Enterprise Liability for Medical Malpractice and Health Care Quality Improvement." *American Journal of Law and Medicine*, 1994, *20*, 1.

In this article, the authors join "a growing chorus of voices that proposes to refocus liability for medical malpractice on the organizations that will increasingly bear practical responsibility for providing health care services using a system of 'enterprise liability.'" In so doing, they point out that a system of enterprise liability requires two major changes in the American view of medical malpractice. First, medical injuries must come to be regarded as violations of a health care contract rather than tortious offenses against the person. Traditional tort law, they note, is designed primarily to address injuries inflicted by strangers. In contrast, medical malpractice law, particularly the doctrine of informed consent, has always included contractual elements based on the doctor-patient relationship. Second, the role of the physician as patient advocate must be protected in the future by means other than the threat of malpractice litigation. The authors advocate transferring certain legal duties to health plans, furnishing health plans with incentives for providing good medical care and dispute resolution, and reducing the burden on individual practitioners.

Tayebe Shah-Mirany. "Malpractice Liability of Health Maintenance Organizations: Evolving Contract and Tort Theories." *Medical Trial Technique Quarterly*, 1993, *39*, 357.

After a brief introduction to the structure of HMOs, the author discusses case law relating to two theories of liability: breach of contract and negligence.

Joanne B. Stern. "Malpractice in the Managed Care Industry." *Creighton Law Review*, 1991, *24*, 1285.

Attempts to elucidate and explain some of the basic theories pertaining to emerging areas of managed care organization liability. These include vicarious liability, corporate negligence, medical malpractice, quality of care, interference with the physician-patient relationship, and negligent misrepresentation.

Linda V. Tiano. "The Legal Implications of HMO Cost Containment Measures." *Seton Hall Legislative Journal*, 1990, *14*, 79.

By intruding into the traditional physician-patient relationship, utilization review raises a variety of liability issues. This article, written by a practicing attorney, addresses these issues and gives suggestions to HMOs that wish to maximize cost-containment efforts while minimizing liability exposure. The author analyzes a number of leading decisions in this area, reviewing theories plaintiffs have used to seek damages.

Paul C. Weiler. "The Case for No-Fault Medical Liability." *Maryland Law Review,* 1993, *52,* 908.

> Traces the history of proposals for no-fault medical liability as a prelude to setting forth his case. This is a summarized version of his book *Medical Malpractice on Trial* (see the next entry).

Paul C. Weiler. *Medical Malpractice on Trial.* Cambridge, Mass.: Harvard University Press, 1991, 256 pages.

> Contends that because doctors now practice in an environment in which health care enterprises have become increasingly dominant, shifting liability from the physician to the enterprise is a more plausible direction for malpractice reform. Written by a Harvard Law School professor who also served as the chief reporter for the American Law Institute's 1991 study of enterprise liability for personal injury, this book documents the failings of the current individual liability model of malpractice litigation.

Earlene P. Weiner. "Managed Health Care: HMO Corporate Liability, Independent Contractors, and the Ostensible Agency Doctrine." *Journal of Corporation Law,* Spring 1990, *15,* 535.

> In this incisive article, the author examines in detail two decisions, *Boyd* v. *Albert Einstein Medical Center,* 377 Pa. Super. 609, 547 A.2d 1229 (1988), and *Williams* v. *Good Health Plus, Inc.,* 743 S.W.2d 373 (Tex. Ct. App. 1987), which demonstrate that courts are now willing to hold HMOs liable for negligent medical care rendered by independent contractor physicians if the HMO misrepresented, through appearances, that an independent contractor was an employee. *Boyd* and *Williams* represent not only application of the ostensible agency doctrine to a new type of defendant—an HMO—but also circumvention of the independent-contractor doctrine of tort law. The author concludes with a recommended approach to managed care systems in ostensible-agency lawsuits. First, the HMO should make sure that all physicians who provide medical care for the HMO carry adequate malpractice insurance. Second, the HMO should seek to have itself named as an additional insured on the physician's malpractice insurance policy. Third, the HMO should obtain an indemnification agreement from the physician. Finally, the HMO could implement procedures for screening physicians to determine whether any have been previously sued or disciplined.

17.03 LIABILITY FOR PROVIDER EXCLUSION

H. Lee Barfield II and James W. Berry, Jr. "Unique Liability Concerns of Managed Care Organizations." Washington, D.C.: American Health Lawyers Association [Report No. VHL98–0060], 1998, 43 pages.

> Discusses federal and state developments involving liability of managed care organizations, and case law concerning malpractice and utilization review liability, liability for exclusion or termination of participating providers, contract liability, ERISA preemption issues, and any-willing-provider laws.

William G. Kopit and Alexandre B. Bouton. "Antitrust Implications of Provider Exclusion." In Peter R. Kongstvedt (ed.), *The Managed Health Care Handbook.* (4th ed.) Gaithersburg, Md.: Aspen, 2000.

> This chapter of twenty-three pages surveys and offers a framework for analysis of the antitrust issues raised by provider exclusion by MCOs. In addition, the chapter discusses the impact that state any-willing-provider laws have on the ability of MCOs to limit physician participation. Written by two practicing attorneys, this analysis presents a framework setting forth the legal bases upon which judicial and statutory attempts to restrict the ability of MCOs to limit their provider networks can be resisted.

18

Obligations to Provide Medical Care and Access

Despite the failure of Congress to enact President Clinton's health care reform proposal, which included among its key components the guaranty of universal access to basic health care benefits, legislators across the political spectrum agree that making health care more widely available to the poor, to the unemployed, and to children remains a goal that will be advanced, if not by broad federal reform then by market reform, state regulation, and incremental change in Washington. For the moment, however, consumers still collide with one or more barriers in obtaining adequate medical care: financial, cultural, geographic, or physical. Legal reforms can remove these obstacles only in part.

The materials that follow summarize recent writing on statutory and case law that have been imposed on health care organizations to provide health care services, and the rights and ability of individuals to avail themselves of that care.

ANNOTATIONS

18.01   IN GENERAL

"Access to Care: Is Health Insurance Enough?" Menlo Park, Calif.: Henry J. Kaiser Family Foundation [Report No. 2007], 1995.

> This policy brief focuses on access issues facing the low-income population generally and Medicaid beneficiaries specifically. It also examines how well Medicaid beneficiaries have fared in obtaining access to care, the types of access barrier that confront Medicaid beneficiaries, and the issues and options for addressing these barriers.

Alexander Abbe. "'Meaningful Access' to Health Care and the Remedies Available to Medicaid Managed Care Recipients under the ADA and the Rehabilitation Act." (Comment.) *University of Pennsylvania Law Review*, 1999, *147*, 1161.

> This Comment explores the potential causes of action a disabled Medicaid managed care patient has under the Americans with Disabilities Act or the Rehabilitation Act and whether denying care, under recent federal court interpretations, constitutes lack of meaningful access. In his analysis, the author focuses primarily on the state of Pennsylvania.

David W. Baker et al. "Use and Effectiveness of Interpreters in an Emergency Department." *Journal of the American Medical Association*, Mar. 13, 1996, *275*, 10, 783.

E. Richard Brown and others. "The Uninsured in California: Causes, Consequences, and Solutions." Los Angeles: UCLA Center for Health Policy Research, 1997, 46 pages.

Lack of health insurance has risen among all nonelderly Californians and other Americans for nearly two decades, according to this report. In 1995, approximately 6.5 million Californians—22.7 percent of the population under age sixty-five—had no public or private health insurance coverage. One-fourth of the population between the ages of eighteen and sixty-four and 17 percent of all children under age eighteen were uninsured. This report examines such options as expansion of Medi-Cal; use of the section 1115 waiver; expansion of the Health Insurance Plan of California; and increased subsidies for clinics, community and migrant health centers, homeless health centers, and hospitals, especially their emergency rooms. This highly detailed report is buttressed by forty-four exhibits and two appendices.

Center for Health Economics Research. "Access to Health Care: Key Indicators for Policy." Princeton, N.J.: Robert Wood Johnson Foundation, 1993.

A series of health indicators reveal that blacks and the poor suffer substantial disadvantages because they cannot obtain early and preventive care. Caring for the poor is needlessly expensive because it is delivered in expensive hospital settings rather than in a physician's office.

Deborah J. Chollet and Adele M. Kirk. *Understanding Individual Health Insurance Markets.* Menlo Park, Calif.: Henry J. Kaiser Family Foundation, 1998.

This study reviews the individual health insurance markets in ten states: California, Florida, Iowa, Louisiana, Montana, New York, North Dakota, Pennsylvania, Utah, and Washington. These states represent the variation of circumstances and regulation across all states. The study draws on a number of information sources: the Current Population Survey; the Alpha Center's Health Insurance Database; policy and rate information obtained from a stratified sample of major medical insurers in each state; and conversations with regulatory officials, health policy officials, and insurance agents and brokers from each state.

Mim Dixon. *Managed Care in American Indian and Alaska Native Communities.* Washington, D.C.: American Public Health Association, 1998, 189 pages.

Managed care is touching the lives of some of the most culturally distinct people living in both the remotest rural areas and the most impoverished inner cities: American Indians and Alaska Natives. This book presents the unique federal health system provided by the Indian Health Service, with emphasis on public health. It supplies information on the delivery of this health system and the challenges it presents.

Margaret Edmunds and Molly Joel Coye (eds.). *America's Children: Health Insurance and Access to Care.* Washington, D.C.: National Academy Press, 1998, 180 pages.

Today, more than eleven million American children lack health insurance, and the number increases each year. This book is a comprehensive, easy-to-read analysis of the relationship between health insurance and access to care. It addresses three broad questions: How is children's health care currently financed? Does insurance equal access to care? How should the nation address the health needs of this vulnerable population? Topics explored include the changing role of Medicaid under managed care; state-initiated and private sector children's insurance programs; specific effects of insurance status on the care children receive; the impact of chronic medical conditions and special health needs; the status of safety-net providers such as community health centers, children's hospitals, school-based health centers, and others; and finally the changing patterns of coverage, and tax policy options to increase coverage.

David Falcone and Robert Broyles. "Access to Long-Term Care: Race as a Barrier." *Journal of Health Politics, Policy, and Law,* 1994, 19, 583.

This study presents evidence that race affects access to long-term care in North Carolina. The data showed that nonwhite patients experienced much longer discharge delays than did white patients, regardless of the patients' age, sex, condition, or special care requirements; or of the cooperativeness of their families; their behavioral state; how they would pay for long-term care; or whether there were financial preparedness problems involved in the discharge. The authors note that the scant evidence available suggests that the problem of discrimination is not confined to North Carolina and that elsewhere the problem is not attributable to economic factors.

Judith Feder. *Medicare/Medicaid Dual Eligibles: Fiscal and Social Responsibilities for Vulnerable Populations.* Washington, D.C.: Institute for Health Care Research and Policy, Georgetown University, 1997.

This report assesses the implications of policy changes that would affect dual eligibles, focusing on the issues of which program or level of government will have primary control over program expenditures and whether dual eligibles will remain primarily Medicare beneficiaries, entitled to the same choice and access to care as those with higher incomes, or primarily Medicaid beneficiaries, entitled only to care available to the nonelderly poor.

General Accounting Office. "Low Income Medicare Beneficiaries: Further Outreach and Administrative Simplification Could Increase Enrollment." (GAO/HEHS-99-61.) Apr. 9, 1999, 29 pages.

In 1995, premiums, deductibles, and coinsurance cost single persons at the federal poverty level 10 percent of income, married couples 15 percent. State Medicaid programs helped them bear their costs through the congressionally enacted Qualified Medicare Beneficiary (QMB) program, the Specified Low-Income Medicare Beneficiary (SLMB) program, and the Qualifying Individuals Program. In 1996, about 43 percent of the potentially eligible Medicare beneficiaries were not enrolled in either QMB or SLMB. Enrollment in these programs is relatively low for Medicare beneficiaries who are white, widowed or married, or have Medicare coverage because of age rather than disability. Many potential recipients do not enroll because they do not know the programs exist, believe they are only for poor people, fear that the state will try to recover payments made to them from a surviving spouse or children, or are unwilling to accept what they think of as welfare. Moreover, the application process is burdensome and complex, and the states' cost-sharing obligations limit the incentive to notify and enroll eligible individuals. Efforts to increase enrollment include a Social Security Administration demonstration project, state outreach and enrollment efforts through the Children's Health Insurance Program (CHIP), and efforts by the HCFA under the Government Performance and Results Act.

General Accounting Office. "Medicaid: Demographics of Nonenrolled Children Suggest State Outreach Strategies." (GAO/HEHS-98-93.) Mar. 20, 1998, 44 pages.

Health insurance was an increasingly important way to provide children with access to adequate health care, yet in 1996 10.6 million children were uninsured. Congress has sought to insure more children by committing more than $20 billion to fund state expansions of children's health insurance, either through the Medicaid program or through insurance programs developed by the states. However, many uninsured children who are eligible for Medicaid are not enrolled. This report (1) examines the demographic and socioeconomic characteristics of children who qualify for Medicaid and identifies groups in which uninsured children are concentrated and to whom outreach efforts might be targeted, (2) determines the reasons these children are not enrolled in Medicaid, and (3) identifies strategies that states and communities are using to boost enrollment.

Clark C. Havighurst. "Contract Failure in the Market for Health Services." *Wake Forest Law Review*, 1994, 29, 47–70.

Examines the claim that the United States is overspending on health care. Finding much of the evidence inconclusive, Havighurst nevertheless finds one clear cause of allocative inefficiency to be unwise tax subsidies for the purchase of private health insurance. He contends, however, that a more serious problem is the market's failure to offer consumers a full range of health care choices, specifically low-cost options. Here, he asserts that overspending on health care is attributable to the failure of private contracts to specify the precise character and scope of the health services to be provided and the particular rights and obligations of the various parties to the transaction. This contract failure, he writes, is in large part the fault of a legal system that has effectively displaced private contract as the ultimate source of entitlements and rights.

Marianne L. Engleman Lado. "Breaking the Barriers of Access to Health Care: A Discussion of the Role of Civil Rights Litigation and the Relationship Between Burdens of Proof and the Experience of Denial." *Brooklyn Law Review*, Spring 1994, *60*, 239.

Debra J. Lipson and others. "Approaches for Providing/Financing Health Care for the Uninsured: An Assessment of State Options and Experiences." Washington, D.C.: Alpha Center, 1997, 64 pages.

The purpose of this paper is to offer a framework for considering the major alternatives that states might choose for providing and financing health care and health coverage for their uninsured populations. A set of matrices are developed to illustrate how well-known programs in various states fit into this framework. It was designed to assist the California HealthCare Foundation to examine alternatives for that state, but this will be useful for other states. It first presents the framework of alternative approaches, along with an explanation of the distinctions among them. Then the paper examines for each approach (1) background and explanation of the approach, (2) state experience in terms of prevalence and variability in each approach across the states, (3) impact of the approach on expanding access to care or coverage based on research or other evidence on the effects, and (4) implementation problems and issues that states have encountered. The text is supplemented by a number of tables.

Ruth E. Malone. "Whither the Almshouse? Overutilization and the Role of the Emergency Department." *Journal of Health Politics, Policy, and Law*, Oct. 1998, *23*, 795.

The problem of emergency department (ED) overutilization or "inappropriate" utilization is commonly conceptualized in terms of inadequate access to appropriate medical care. Although medical care access is a critical issue, a focus on increased access to medical care as the sole solution to inappropriate ED utilization may obscure other, perhaps equally relevant, issues from consideration. This article reports findings from an ethnographic study focusing on heavy users of EDs in two inner-city hospitals. Drawing on fieldwork and on interviews with clinicians, the author argues that emerging heavy utilization of the ED as both a clinical and a policy problem is a function not merely of unmet medical care needs for individuals but of "almshouse" needs in a changing health care context. This emergence as a problem occurs in the context of market forces that are contributing to shifts in the role of EDs and in the moral boundaries of accepted ED practice. If the problem of heavy ED use is more broadly conceptualized in terms of this role shift, not solely in terms of medical care access, a different set of issues and priorities for research, policy, and clinical practice emerge.

Mathematica Policy Research. *Managed Care and Low Income Populations: A Case Study in Florida*. Washington, D.C.: Mathematica Policy Research, 1997.

This report examines Florida's experience in implementing a Medicaid managed care program and spotlights the implications of this change on numerous stakeholders, including Medicaid beneficiaries, health plans, providers, and other indigent populations.

Mathematica Policy Research. *Managed Care and Low Income Populations: A Case Study in Managed Care in Texas*. Washington, D.C.: Mathematica Policy Research, 1997.

This case study examines the goals of Medicaid managed care initiatives in Texas, program design and the early implementation experience, and the care patterns and access issues that are prominent in moving forward with the initiative. Also considered are the ways that the health care safety net for the poor may have been affected and what spillover effects to other sectors may be relevant.

Mathematica Policy Research. *Managed Care and Low Income Populations: A Case Study of Managed Care in New York.* Washington, D.C.: Mathematica Policy Research, 1996.

This case study examines New York State's early experience in moving Medicaid beneficiaries into managed care and describes the state's early efforts to meet its goal of enrolling half of the 2.4 million Medicaid beneficiaries into managed care by the year 2000.

Michael Millman (ed.). *Access to Health Care in America.* Washington, D.C.: National Academy Press, 1993, 229 pages.

Examines the structural, financial, and personal barriers to health care. This report defines a set of national objectives and identifies indicators, such as measures of utilization and outcome, that can reveal when and where problems occur in accessing specific health care services. Based on these indicators, the panel presents significant conclusions about the situation today, examining the relationships between access to care and factors such as race, ethnic origin, income, and location. The panel proposes recommendations to DHHS; the National Center for Health Statistics; and other local, state, and federal agencies for improving monitoring and data collection. The text is supplemented by four appendices and an index.

National Health Law Program. *Ombudsman: Sample Legislation.* Los Angeles, NHeLP, Jan. 1996.

Sample legislation sets up a statewide managed care "ombudsprogram" to protect consumers enrolled in managed care plans.

Patricia B. Nemore. "Variations in State Medicaid Buy-in Practices for Low-Income Medicare Beneficiaries." Menlo Park, Calif.: Henry J. Kaiser Family Foundation [Report No. 1329], 1997.

This report, based on a fifty-state survey of Medicaid directors and advocates, describes state practices with respect to qualified Medicare beneficiary and specified low-income Medicare beneficiary eligibility, enrollment, cost sharing, and managed care. It identifies areas where changes in administration and outreach at the state level help extend financial protection to more low-income Medicare beneficiaries.

Mary Anne Bobinski. "Unhealthy Federalism: Barriers to Increasing Health Care Access for the Uninsured." *University of California Davis Law Review,* 1990, *24,* 255.

Presents analysis of ERISA and its effect on state-level solutions to the problems of the uninsured. After reviewing the scope of the health care system's cost and access problems, Bobinski examines the appropriate role of federal and state governments in formulating law and policy. The author particularly focuses here on the perverse obstacles to health care access created by ERISA, which preempts many state attempts to regulate health care plans. After examining alternative state-level solutions for the uninsured, the author concludes that specific statutory action is required, through either amendment of ERISA or adoption of a comprehensive federal action plan.

Marc A. Redwing. "Consumer Protection and Managed Care: Issues, Reform Proposals, and Trade-Offs." *Houston Law Review,* 1996, *32,* 1319.

Examines various ways to protect consumers in managed care. This article delineates proposals for consumer protection and discusses their limitations and implications for further reform. It concludes by exploring policy approaches for protecting consumers and analyzing trade-off in consumer protection policy.

Marilyn Werner Serafini. "Oh, Yeah, the Uninsured." *National Journal*, Nov. 15, 1997, 2300.

This article examines the political and legislative obstacles that prevent many Americans from obtaining affordable health insurance.

Southern Institute on Children and Families. "Uninsured Children in the South." Columbia, S.C.: Southern Institute on Children and Families, 1996.

This report, sponsored by the Henry J. Kaiser Family Foundation, offers updated information about the number of uninsured children in the seventeen southern states and the District of Columbia. The report finds that although the number of uninsured children in the nation as a whole was increasing between 1989 and 1993, the number of children without health insurance in the South actually decreased by 3 percent. However, the South still has a disproportionately large share of America's uninsured children.

Steffie Woolhandler and David U. Himmelstein. "The Deteriorating Administrative Efficiency of the U.S. Health Care System." *New England Journal of Medicine*, 1991, *324*, 1253.

U.S. health policies have increased bureaucratic burdens and curtailed access to care, the authors write. Yet they have failed to contain costs. The proportion of health care spending consumed by administration is at least 117 percent higher in the United States than in Canada, which accounts for at least half the total difference in health care spending between the two nations. In addition, the overhead of private insurance consumes 11.9 percent of premiums compared to 3.2 percent of U.S. public programs. The authors conclude that the existence of multiple payers and the administrative structure of the U.S. health system are increasingly inefficient as compared to Canada's national health program.

18.02   EMERGENCY MEDICAL TREATMENT AND ACTIVE LABOR ACT (EMTALA)

American Health Lawyers Association. *Healthcare Model Compliance Manual*. Washington, D.C.: AHLA, 2000.

This binder supplies sample forms, implementation plans, and audits, all material on disk. Specific sections focus on civil sanctions, managed care compliance, and industry guidance, which include guidelines for durable medical equipment, hospices, third-party billing, Medicare+Choice organizations, skilled nursing facilities, EMTALA, research compliance, medical necessity, and environmental compliance. The materials were written by twelve health care attorneys.

Annot. "Construction and Application of [the] Emergency Medical Treatment and Active Labor Act." *ALR Federal*, 1998, *104*, 166.

Collects and analyzes the federal cases in which the courts have construed and applied the Emergency Medical Treatment and Active Labor Act (42 U.S.C.S. § 1395dd), which stipulates that federally funded hospitals are required to give emergency aid to stabilize a patient suffering from an "emergency medical condition" or "active labor" before discharging or transferring that patient to another facility.

Constance H. Baker. "Recent Developments in EMTALA." Washington, D.C.: American Health Lawyers Association [Report No. VMM99–0048], 1999, 34 pages.

Includes an overview of the act, and reviews selected regulatory provisions and proposals, recent EMTALA case law, and the U.S. Supreme Court's decision in *Roberts* v. *Galen of Virginia, Inc.*

Constance H. Baker and Jessica Bowman. "Recent Developments in EMTALA Enforcement." Washington, D.C.: American Health Lawyers Association [Report No. VHL 99–0005], 1999, 26 pages.

Overview of the statute. Includes select regulatory provisions, proposed rules for a prospective payment system for hospital outpatient services, proposed rules for hospital conditions of participation regarding emergency services, practice tips, summaries of recent EMTALA cases, and a review of the Supreme Court's decision in *Roberts* v. *Galen of Va., Inc.*

Jessica Bowman. "Recent Developments in EMTALA Enforcement." Washington, D.C.: American Health Lawyers Association [Report No. VHL-0006], 1999, 36 pages.

Charts demonstrate OIG patient dumping case activity for fiscal year 1999 and for fiscal years 1986 to 1998. Includes a copy of the Supreme Court's opinion in *Roberts* v. *Galen of Va.*

Jane Reister Conard. "Granny Dumping: The Hospital's Duty of Care to Patients Who Have Nowhere to Go." *Yale Law and Policy Review,* 1992, *10,* 463.

COBRA imposes on hospitals an affirmative duty to provide, at a minimum and without regard to ability to pay, a medical screening examination to every individual who enters an emergency room seeking care. Because of problems in the definition, scope, and application of COBRA, hospitals stand in the unenviable position of assuming a duty without a clear end point. The author argues that the COBRA definition of "stable to transfer or discharge" should be changed to include objective, time-limited, medical criteria that would minimize potential liability to hospitals. Then hospitals would be relieved of the legal jeopardy posed by "granny dumping" and left only with the practical social problem of finding appropriate placement. The author also argues that in the long run an effective solution must be fashioned as part of a comprehensive national health policy that incorporates a goal of funding some level of universal care.

Lauren A. Dame. "The Emergency Medical Treatment and Active Labor Act: The Anomalous Right to Health Care." *Health Matrix,* Winter 1998, *8,* 3.

The author, an attorney for the Public Citizen's Health Research Group, looks at EMTALA from the patient's perspective. She contends that although EMTALA provides a private right of action, the population that has historically been most vulnerable to patient dumping is the poor and the uninsured, a group of people often unlikely to have a lawyer to turn to when their rights are violated. Thus, if the government does not enforce EMTALA, or enforces it poorly, then given the strong economic incentives of hospitals to dump patients EMTALA's guarantees will prove illusory.

Lauren Dame and Sidney M. Wolfe. "Hospital Violations of the Emergency Medical Treatment and Labor Act: A Detailed Look at 'Patient Dumping.'" Washington, D.C.: Public Citizen Health Research Group, Dec. 1997, 58 pages.

This report documents 264 incidents in forty-one states in which 256 hospitals violated the patient dumping prohibitions of EMTALA. It is based on data that Public Citizen, a Washington-based consumers' lobby, obtained from the government through Freedom of Information Act requests. It notes that in spite of HHS's ability to terminate hospitals from Medicare or to fine them for violations of EMTALA, the department rarely uses this sanctioning authority. From 1986, when the act first became effective, until the end of the fiscal year 1996, HHS confirmed more than eight hundred patient dumping violations by hospitals but has terminated only nine hospitals from Medicare and has fined only fifty-eight.

    The report observes that hospitals are flouting the law because it is less expensive to refuse service and run the risk of a federal fine than to incur unreimbursed costs. The report concludes with a table breaking down violations by hospital, state, and provision(s) violated; a table setting forth settlement terms with specific hospitals; a bar chart indicating the annual number of monetary settlements between hospitals and the OIG for EMTALA violations; and a lengthy appendix excerpting records of particular violations.

Judith L. Dobbertin. "Eliminating Patient Dumping: A Proposal for Model Legislation." *Valparaiso University Law Review,* 1993, *28,* 291.

Concludes that EMTALA and the Hill-Burton Act have failed to prevent patient dumping. Dobbertin argues that the state level, where physician licensing and hospital regulation are conducted, is the proper place to confront the patient dumping problem. To prevent excessive fines against hospitals, resulting in closure of emergency room facilities, states should adopt legislation clearly stating that patient dumping is not an alternative route to collect more money for what is essentially a state medical malpractice claim.

Michael J. Frank. "Tailoring EMTALA to Better Protect the Indigent: The Supreme Court Precludes One Method of Salvaging a Statute Gone Awry." *DePaul Journal of Health Care Law*, 2000, *3*, 195.

Examines recent Supreme Court jurisprudence interpreting the statute.

David A. Hyman. "Drive-Through Deliveries: Is Consumer Protection Just What the Doctor Ordered?" *North Carolina Law Review*, 1999, *78*, 5.

Although consumer protection against managed care has become extraordinarily popular in recent years, the author contends that there are good reasons to be skeptical about the merits of legislative and regulatory efforts in this area. He analyzes one of the most popular consumer protection initiatives to date: legislation limiting or eliminating the economic incentive for "early" postpartum discharges, commonly known as "drive-through deliveries." The author argues that the case for extended postpartum stays was based on unrepresentative horror stories and reluctance to make explicit cost-benefit tradeoffs in matters of public health and safety.

Louise M. Joy. "EMTALA: An Old Law Gets New Fangs." Washington, D.C.: American Health Lawyers Association [Report No. VHH99–0019], 1999, 32 pages.

Discusses HCFA's proposed revision to the definition of "comes to the emergency department" under new interpretive guidelines, the OIG's advisory bulletin concerning the act and managed care patients, and the Supreme Court's *per curiam* decision in *Roberts* v. *Galen of Virginia*. Also discusses frequent mistakes by surveyors and hospitals and the OIG settlement process. Includes a sample hospital policy for reporting EMTALA violations and a sample transfer form.

Louise M. Joy. *EMTALA: Interpreting and Complying with the Federal Transfer Law.* Washington, D.C.: American Health Lawyers Association, 1999 [Book No. WAA99–0002].

This 275-page book delineates the meaning and scope of the statute by addressing the differing interpretations of the statutory definitions and offers additional information about regulations related to EMTALA from the local, state, and federal levels. Among other topics, this manual examines EMTALA's legislative history, requirements imposed by the statute, mandatory reporting, the survey process and terminations, practical tips for dealing with surveyors and surviving the survey, surveyor's authority, fast-track termination, OIG imposition of sanctions, and pertinent state laws. Additionally, Joy reviews the private causes of action authorized by EMTALA and administrative sanctions that may be imposed, and discusses the appeals process hospitals or doctors may pursue if a penalty has been imposed on them. The author supplies numerous exhibits, with sample documents and applicable statutes relevant to transferring patients.

Louise M. Joy. "Sample Patient Transfer Policy." *Journal of Health Law*, 2000, *33*, 157.

This seven-page policy will be helpful to hospital in-house counsel.

Brian E. Kamoie. "EMTALA: Reaching Beyond the Emergency Room to Expand Hospital Liability." *Journal of Health Law*, 2000, *33*, 25.

The OIG and private plaintiffs are vigorously pursuing EMTALA violations. These efforts are particularly troubling to hospitals, which face difficult statutory interpretation and application questions, especially in light of managed care reimbursement requirements. Two cases, one of them from the U.S. Supreme Court, expand hospital liability under EMTALA. This article reviews current EMTALA standards and regulations; it analyzes how the decisions, in the absence of congressional action, are likely to impose substantial burdens on hospitals. The article concludes with a sample OIG EMTALA Settlement Agreement.

Charity Kenyon and Jeanne L. Vance. "The Obligation to Provide Futile Care: When the Buck Doesn't Stop." *California Health Law News*, Summer 1997, *17, 74.*

This brief article examines the limitations of EMTALA and other statutes, both federal and state, when a patient is not a U.S. citizen and is in a persistent vegetative state. The authors, both practicing attorneys, conclude that medicine has advanced beyond society's ability to equitably control access to its potential for cure. Technology offers more than society can afford, and the only solution will be found in the political arena, they write.

Marilou M. King and Hemi Tewarson. "The Emergency Medical Treatment and Active Labor Act: The Practical Realities." Washington, D.C.: American Health Lawyers Association [Report No. VPH99–0024], 1999, 35 pages.

Reviews the principal provisions of the act and its regulations and agency guidelines, as well as proposed regulations. Reviews the U.S. Supreme Court decision in January 1999 on proof of improper motive in EMTALA cases (*Roberts* v. *Galen of Virginia, Inc.*). Also highlights current controversies on definition of hospital property, disparate treatment of managed care beneficiaries, and physician on-call and peer review exposure.

Julia Krebs-Markrich and others. "EMTALA: The Next Generation." *Health Lawyer*, Early Spring 1995, *8*, 1.

This article questions *In re Baby K*, 16 F.3d 590 (4th Cir. 1994), *cert. denied,* the Fourth Circuit Court of Appeal decision under which EMTALA requires doctors and hospitals to provide to a dying patient medical interventions that serve little therapeutic or palliative purpose and that are contrary to widely accepted standards of medical care.

Gregory M. Luce. "Defending the Hospital under EMTALA: New Requirements/New Liabilities." Washington, D.C.: American Health Lawyers Association, 1995, 31 pages.

Discusses enforcement regulations, enforcement activity, and inconsistencies in findings of the courts. This monograph addresses administrative review of EMTALA violations, deadlines, sanctions, record-keeping requirements, whistle-blower protection, defense of EMTALA claims in court, and jury instructions.

Theodore R. Marmor. *The Politics of Medicare.* (2nd ed.) Hawthorne, N.Y.: Aldine de Gruyter, 2000, 228 pages.

The first half of this book reprints without significant change the original 1970 text of the first edition of this popular and groundbreaking text. The second part deals with three major topics. First, it brings the political history up to date, paying special attention to the Reagan era and the 1990s—times in which the economic significance of Medicare grew dramatically and in which institutional factors such as divided government and the politics of deficit reduction shaped Medicare policy.

Second, concluding chapters set forth some theoretical guidance for those especially concerned about the future of Medicare politics. One deals with the displacement of the social insurance philosophy animating Medicare with procompetitive ideas and microeconomic policies. A subsequent chapter shows how tools of political analysis can be used to explain three puzzling changes in Medicare policy, such as Presidents Reagan and Bush supporting administered pricing and President Clinton's acceptance of Republican procompetition provisions in the Balanced Budget Act of 1997.

Third, in an essay review a final chapter comments on some of the scholarship on Medicare politics.

Maureen D. Mudron. "Provider-Based Entities: Application of EMTALA." Washington, D.C.: American Health Lawyers Association [Report No. VMM99–0021], 1999, 13 pages.

Discusses the American Hospital Association position on potential application of EMTALA beyond the emergency department, as stated in proposed outpatient PPS regulations.

Normand F. Pizza. "Patient Transfers—COBRA as Amended." *Health Lawyer*, Summer 1992, 6(2), 1.

This brief, practical article examines COBRA liability for patient dumping. It is written primarily for the benefit of attorneys who represent hospitals and doctors.

Lawrence Singer. "Look What They've Done to My Law, Ma: COBRA's Implosion." *Houston Law Review*, 1996, 33, 113.

Argues that, although well intentioned, COBRA was hopelessly flawed from the start. By inherently raising concepts of malpractice, COBRA protections invite overuse by plaintiffs and misuse by the courts, Singer contends. Because by its very terms COBRA requires a negligence-like analysis though at the same time holding itself out as a strict liability measure, it invites judicial confusion as courts attempt to define COBRA's obligations away from concepts with which they are inextricably linked.

Symposium on EMTALA. "The Emergency Medical Treatment and Active Labor Act." *Health Matrix: Journal of Law-Medicine*, Winter 1998, 8.

This symposium issue includes three articles published on the tenth anniversary of the enactment of this federal law.

18.03   OBLIGATIONS TO PROVIDE CARE UNDER STATE LAW

Timothy Curley, Robin Omata, and John Luehrs. "State Progress in Health Care Reform." Washington, D.C.: National Governors' Association, 1992, 70 pages.

Skeptical that Washington would implement health reform, a number of states in the early 1990s moved ahead on their own. Governors made health care reform a top priority, with at least thirteen states enacting significant health care reform legislation and even more states considering legislative or gubernatorial health care initiatives. This report describes how states focused their efforts on extending coverage to vulnerable populations, ensuring access to basic benefits, implementing cost controls, reforming the insurance industry, developing financing alternatives, improving delivery systems, and establishing data requirements and resource centers.

Shelly Gehshan. "State Options for Expanding Children's Health Insurance." Denver, Colo.: National Conference of State Legislatures, 1997, 20 pages.

This report examines several state options for providing universal health insurance for children.

Kala Ladenheim. "Patching the Safety Net: Shifting Health Care Costs and State Policies." Denver, Colo.: National Conference of State Legislatures, 1997, 32 pages.

This report presents an overview of how states have handled the issue of shifting costs to cover uncompensated care. The four areas discussed are state efforts to gather information about uncompensated care, state requirements for providers to give care, uncompensated care funds and provider reimbursement rates, and managed care.

National Conference of State Legislatures. *State Programs for Providing Children's Health Insurance: A Resource Notebook.* Denver, Colo.: National Conference of State Legislatures, 1997, 236 pages.

This manual is a compendium of information about state children's health insurance programs. Each description begins with a cover sheet summarizing key facts, including contact name, sponsoring agency, eligibility, benefits, current enrollment, financing, and legal citations. Authorizing legislation and brochures from programs are included. There are sections devoted to Medicaid expansions, state-financed programs, public-private programs, and private programs.

Jane Perkins. "Maintaining Health Services for Children amid Welfare Confusion: The Importance of Early and Periodic Screening, Diagnosis, and Treatment." *Clearinghouse Review,* Jan.-Feb. 1999.

Under the Medicaid Act, poor children and youths are entitled to receive comprehensive medical and behavioral screening and treatment services through the Early and Periodic Screening, Diagnosis and Treatment program (EPSDT). Although the program was not directly affected by welfare reform, many children who lost cash assistance benefits because of the Personal Responsibility and Work Opportunity Reconciliation Act are not applying for Medicaid and as a consequence are losing access to the program. The author writes that advocates can assist their clients by enhancing their own understanding of how the program works and realizing that it is itself a fragile benefit.

18.04   OBLIGATIONS UNDER THE HILL-BURTON ACT

James F. Blumstein. "Court Action, Agency Reaction: The Hill-Burton Act as a Case Study." *Iowa Law Review,* 1984, 69, 1227.

This seminal article begins with an overview of the Hill-Burton Act, while the remainder examines the evolution of its implementation. That evolution illustrates the widespread phenomenon of legislative schizophrenia in enacting health legislation. The article sets forth a theory of political inertia or stalemate in the administrative agency responsible for enforcing the legislation and shows how the agency responded, through inadequate defenses and after unappealed district court fiat, to the stimulus brought by legislation. The author then discusses the complex interaction between litigation, agency response, and legislative enactment. He focuses specifically on the proper role of the courts in stimulating this type of agency response and what he terms "the staggering consequences of district court decisions in effectuating administrative change."

Michael Dowell. *An Advocate's Guide to Auditing the Compliance of Hill-Burton Facilities.* Los Angeles: National Health Law Program, 1996.

This resource includes sample letters, checklists, technical assistance, and other explanatory information useful in assuring compliance with Hill-Burton.

Alan Seltzer and Michael Dowell. "An Advocate's Guide to Hill-Burton Collection Defense." Los Angeles: National Health Law Program, 1996.

This report suggests defenses to hospital collections where the collecting hospital is not in compliance with Hill-Burton regulations.

Donald L. Westerfield. *National Health Care: Law, Policy, Strategy.* Westport, Conn.: Praeger, 1993, 204 pages.

Although the first part of this book is now out of date, the section on special interests, the law, and political posturing remains helpful. This section covers such topics as labor unions and the AMA as lobbyists, the Hill-Burton Act, and obstacles faced by small business.

18.05 NONDISCRIMINATION OBLIGATIONS UNDER TITLE VI OF THE CIVIL RIGHTS ACT OF 1964

Peter Cunningham. "Access to Care in the Indian Health Service." *Health Affairs,* Fall 1993, 224–233.

Presents findings from the 1987 Survey of American Indians and Alaska Natives (SAIAN) about external sources of health care and financing for IHS-eligible people. This article includes findings on the rates of public and private health coverage among IHS-eligible population and patterns of health care use.

David Falcone and Robert Broyles. "Access to Long-Term Care: Race as a Barrier." *Journal of Health Politics, Policy, and Law,* 1994, *19,* 583.

Discusses the extent to which race continues to impede access to health services, for acute as well as long-term care. White patients, for example, use disproportionately more days of nursing home care than do nonwhite patients, not simply because they are more likely to be private payers and therefore preferred over others; the difference in utilization persists even among those whose nursing home stays are covered by Medicare. Using data from a study of patients awaiting alternative placement in North Carolina acute care general hospitals in 1991, this article examines racial differences in discharge delay—that is, in the time between when a patient is medically ready for discharge to another form of care and when he or she actually is discharged. The authors identify patient characteristics associated with delay, and two-way analyses of variance are used to document the independent effect of race.

The results indicate that race has substantial independent explanatory power. This finding is reinforced by analyses of variance with controls for the patient's payment source for long-term care, chronic condition or special care requirements, demographic attributes, family cooperativeness, whether the patient had a behavior problem that impeded the discharge planning process, and whether there was a financial problem in arranging for the patient's discharge. The inescapable conclusion is that nursing homes discriminate on the basis of race in admitting patients. This practice is patently objectionable; it also is costly to hospitals, thus to society, since hospitals bear the direct costs of delayed discharges and do not keep costs to themselves. Although research is needed to determine whether the North Carolina findings are replicable in other states, past research suggests that the problem is not confined to this state.

Jane Perkins. *Ensuring Linguistic Access in Health Care Settings: Legal Rights and Responsibilities.* Los Angeles: National Health Law Program, 1998, 190 pages.

This manual shows advocates how to overcome language barriers and obtain appropriate medical care for their clients. It outlines language access responsibilities under federal and state law, as well as in the private sector, and offers recommendations for addressing specific problems. This text discusses federal requirements for linguistic access: Title VI of the Civil Rights Act of 1964, Hill-Burton obligations, Medicare and Medicaid requirements, EMTALA, and U.S. constitutional provisions. It also describes the growing body of state requirements, including statutes that require translation services in health care settings, along with a state-by-state description of laws. Finally, the book examines activities by managed care and private accreditation organizations.

Jane Perkins. "Race Discrimination in America's Health Care System." *Clearinghouse Review*, 1993, Special Issue, *27*, 371.

David Barton Smith. "Addressing Racial Inequalities in Health Care: Civil Rights Monitoring and Report Cards." *Journal of Health Politics, Policy, and Law*, Feb. 1998, *23*, 75.

> Large racial inequities in health care use continue to be reported, raising concerns about discrimination. Historically, the health system, with its professionally dominated, autonomous, voluntary organizational structure, has presented special challenges to civil rights efforts, the author writes. *De jure* racial segregation in the United States gave way to a period of aggressive litigation and enforcement from 1954 until 1968, and then to the current period of relative inactivity. A combination of factors—declining federal resources and organizational capacity to address more subtle forms of discriminatory practices in health care settings, increasingly restrictive interpretations by the courts, and the lack of any systematic mechanisms for statistical monitoring of providers— offers little assurance that discrimination does not continue to play a role in accounting for discrepancies in use. The current rapid transformation of health care into integrated delivery systems driven by risk-based financing presents both new opportunities and new threats. The author concludes by illustrating how "report card" approaches to monitoring performance of such systems could be used to monitor, correct, and build trust in equitable treatment.

18.06 DISCRIMINATION AGAINST PERSONS BASED ON MEDICAL CONDITION

[Reserved]

18.07 FINANCIAL CRITERIA

18.07(1) Denial of Nonemergency Treatment for Financial Reasons

Stuart H. Altman, Uwe R. Reinhardt, and Alexandra E. Shields. *The Future U.S. Healthcare System: Who Will Pay for the Poor and Uninsured?* Chicago: Health Administration Press, 1997, 430 pages.

> In this text, the authors, veteran health care analysts, examine the role of individual citizens, private charities, employers, and government in providing health care access and service for those unable to pay.

Bridget A. Burke. "Using Good Samaritan Acts to Provide Access to Health Care for the Poor: A Modest Proposal." *Annals of Health Law*, 1992, *1*, 139.

> Some states are providing immunity to those willing to voluntarily offer health care for the poor. The proposal is a false step toward the laudable goal of solving the health care access dilemma, the author contends.

General Accounting Office. *Health Insurance: Coverage Leads to Increased Health Care Access for Children.* Washington, D.C.: GAO, 1997.

> Children covered by health insurance have greater access to health care, including primary and preventive care, and are more likely to obtain acute care when ill and needing more complex care. Insurance, however, does not guarantee entry into the health care system. Poverty, lack of neighborhood clinics, limited transportation, and language barriers are obstacles to care, even for children covered by Medicaid. To ensure access to high-quality care, children need a stable source of

health insurance that covers their care needs, a relationship with a primary care provider who helps them obtain more complex care as needed, primary care facilities that are conveniently located, and outreach and education for their families.

Jane Horvath. "Improving Health Care for Children in Foster Care: Alternative Delivery Models." Portland, Maine: National Academy for State Health Policy, 1997, 19 pages.

This report describes ways of structuring outreach and service delivery targeted to children in foster care under both fee-for-service and managed care systems with the goal of improving utilization and outcomes.

Bernice Steinhardt. "Health Care Access: Opportunities to Target Programs and Improve Accountability." Speech by Bernice Steinhardt, [GAO's] director of health services quality and public health issues, before the Subcommittee on Human Resources, House Committee on Government Reform and Oversight. (GAO/T-HEHS-97-204.) Sep. 11, 1997, 12 pages.

Discusses the Rural Health Clinic Program and other federal programs that often provide aid to communities without ensuring that this assistance has been used to improve access to primary care. In some cases, programs have extended more than enough assistance to eliminate the defined shortage, while needs in other communities have gone unaddressed. In this report, the GAO has identified a pervasive cause for this problem: reliance on flawed systems for measuring health care shortages. These systems often fall short in identifying which programs would work best in a particular setting or how well a program meets the needs of the underserved once it is in place. For several years, the Department of Health and Human Services has tried unsuccessfully to overcome these problems. The goal-setting and performance measurement discipline prescribed by the Government Performance and Results Act should help make programs more accountable for improving access to primary care, according to Steinhardt.

18.07(2) Termination of Nonemergency Treatment for Financial Reasons

Tamara E. Russell. "Trav'lin Light: Early Retirees and the Availability of Post-Retirement Health Benefits." (Note.) *American Journal of Law and Medicine*, 1996, *22*(4), 537–562.

Focuses on the health benefits of so-called early retirees, those typically between the ages of fifty-five and sixty-four who are ineligible for Medicare and who choose to rely on their former employers for health insurance. After examining various proposals suggested to improve the availability of postretirement health benefits for early retirees, the author concludes that both employers and employees must share the cost of providing postretirement health benefits.

18.08 GRIEVANCE AND APPEAL PROCEDURES

Jane Perkins and Kristi Olson. *Model Managed Care Internal Grievance Procedure*. Los Angeles: National Health Law Program, Nov. 1996.

Model grievance procedure, which was drafted for use in state Medicaid managed care programs but can be adapted to other insurance situations as well.

Mark Reagan and Rene Bowser. "Legislating Access." *Health Systems Review*, Mar.–Apr. 1997, *30*(2), 12.

Written by two practicing attorneys, this article examines California's Friedman Knowles Experimental Treatment Act of 1996, which gives terminally ill patients the right to appeal a payer's decision to deny coverage for experimental or investigational treatments, drugs, or therapy before an independent panel of experts who have no financial or medical connection to the payer, patient, or proposed treatment.

Susan J. Stayn. "Securing Access to Care in Health Maintenance Organizations: Toward a Uniform Model of Grievance and Appeal Procedures." (Note.) *Columbia Law Review,* 1994, *94,* 1674.

Uses the limited data that have been collected, namely through the Medicare program, to probe the access-to-care problems that occur in HMOs and the mechanisms available to help patients obtain covered, necessary health care services. Unfortunately, although the federal Medicare program and state regulations offer patients some hope of adequate care from HMOs, there is currently no uniform recourse system in place for timely and effective patient protection from undertreatment. Well-structured grievance and appeal procedures would facilitate access to treatment by enabling HMO members to dispute denials of coverage, and if successful, secure needed services without prohibitive out-of-pocket costs. The existence of a uniform recourse system also would ensure the integrity of HMO decision-making processes. Holding HMOs directly accountable to their members and to government officials would encourage fair and accurate coverage determinations and inspire trust in these health care systems.

18.09   HEALTH INSURANCE PORTABILITY AND ACCOUNTABILITY ACT OF 1996 (HIPAA OR KENNEDY-KASSEBAUM)

R. M. Coffey, J. K. Ball, and M. Johantgen. "The Case for National Health Data Standards." *Health Affairs,* 1997, *16*(5), 58–72.

Contends that as the varied uses of health care data have grown, so has the need for standards. HIPAA contains groundbreaking provisions to encourage development of a national health information system through establishing standards. This article, written by former staff members of the Agency for Health Care Policy and Research, compares statewide inpatient data systems to one system, the Uniform Bill (UB), to understand how standards have been used and how they can be improved.

Taina Edlund. "HIPAA 'Creditable Coverage' Rules Affect Group Health Plans, Insurers." *Tax Adviser,* July 1997, *28,* 418.

On Apr. 1, 1997, the IRS and the Departments of Labor and Health and Human Services issued temporary/interim regulations (the "interim rules") providing statutorily mandated guidance under HIPAA. That statute (P.L. 104–191) amended the Internal Revenue Code, ERISA, and the Public Service Health Act to impose new requirements on group health plans and insurers.

Among the most significant issues addressed by the interim rules is the requirement that any preexisting condition exclusion period of a group health plan (whether self-insured or insured) must be reduced by an individual's creditable coverage—that is, by certain periods of prior coverage. HIPAA's creditable coverage rules raised employer concerns about certifying periods of prior coverage, crediting of periods, and plan record-keeping obligations. If a plan fails to comply with HIPAA requirements, including those for crediting coverage, a $100-a-day penalty may be imposed under Sec. 4980D. In addition, plan participants may sue to enforce compliance with HIPAA. To avoid potential penalties and lawsuits, an employer must immediately decide how responsibility for compliance with certification requirements is to be allocated between it and service providers.

Temp. Regs. Sec. 54.9806–4T clarifies many of the issues involving creditable coverage. Certificates generally must be supplied automatically when an individual loses coverage under a plan and when the individual has the right to elect COBRA coverage. Certificates also must be given on request if made within twenty-four months after loss of coverage (and must reflect each period of continuous coverage within the twenty-four-month period).

Gary M. Ford and Mary Ann D. Edgar. "The Health Insurance Portability and Accountability Act." *ALI-ABA Course Materials Journal*, Feb. 1998, 22, 27.

This brief, practical article outlines the statute and focuses on enforcement issues and post-HIPAA amendments.

General Accounting Office. "Medical Savings Accounts: Results from Surveys of Insurers." (Report No. GAO/HEHS-99–34.) Dec. 1998, 17 pages.

HIPAA established a demonstration of medical savings accounts and directed GAO to contract for a study of them. The low enrollment in medical savings accounts made it impossible to conduct useful surveys of enrollees, employers, or financial institutions. The information obtained for this study comes only from insurers, limiting the extent to which the evaluation can address the issues in the mandate.

Alan S. Goldberg. "Practical Implications of HIPAA Security Standards and the Internet." Washington, D.C.: American Health Lawyers Association [Report No. VHI99–0002], 1999, 49 pages.

Discusses the security measures and safeguards of HIPAA regarding electronic transmissions. Includes two charts—administrative simplification provisions of HIPAA and administrative procedures to guard data integrity—as well as confidentiality and availability; Internet security policy; and HCFA proposed security and electronic signature standards as published in the Aug. 12, 1998, *Federal Register.*

"Health Insurance Standards: New Federal Law Creates Challenges for Consumers, Insurers, Regulators." (GAO/HEHS-98–67.) Feb. 25, 1998, 48 pages.

HIPAA guarantees people who lose group health insurance, through retirement or other termination of employment, continued access to coverage in the individual market regardless of health status. Yet this report finds that consumers attempting to exercise this right have been hindered by carrier practices and pricing or by their own misunderstanding of the law.

Regina T. Jefferson. "Medical Savings Accounts: Windfalls for the Healthy, Wealthy, and Wise." *Catholic University Law Review*, 1999, 48, 685.

Creation of the Medical Savings Account was one of the most contested provisions of HIPAA. This article reviews the development, general structure, and operation of the MSA program. It compares and contrasts the MSA to other tax-preferred retirement savings plans and explores the applicability of pension law to these arrangements. The author contends that the program disproportionately benefits the wealthiest, healthiest, and most informed members of society. It identifies various deficiencies in the MSA model that may undermine significantly its marketability as a viable health care savings program. The article ultimately concludes that the focus and design of the MSA presents serious doubts concerning its ability to accomplish its goals in the manner contemplated by Congress.

Colleen E. Medill. "HIPAA and Its Related Legislation: A New Role for ERISA in the Regulation of Private Health Care Plans?" *Tennessee Law Review*, 1998, 65, 485.

HIPAA and its related legislation represent a broadening, in the private health care context, of ERISA's Title I protective provisions from disclosure and fiduciary administration requirements to substantive benefit and coverage requirements in targeted areas. HIPAA and related legislation also potentially signal a new approach by Congress to the issue of ERISA preemption of state insurance laws, again in the private health care context, for those targeted areas where Congress has created new federal requirements. These changes may foreshadow a new willingness to use ERISA increasingly in the future to establish and enforce minimum federal standards, in specific areas, for private health care plan coverage and benefits.

Elizabeth Mitchell and Cynthia Pernice. *State Perspectives on the Health Insurance Portability and Accountability Act.* Portland, Maine: National Academy for State Health Policy, 1997.

> This guide to HIPAA, intended primarily for a legislative audience, is a basic primer analysis of implications for states and a look at the most pressing issues remaining for states to address. It also includes survey responses from insurance commissioners and legislative leaders about priority future reform efforts.

Jack A. Rovner. "Federal Regulation Comes to Private Health Care Financing: The Group Health Insurance Provisions of the Health Insurance Portability and Accountability Act of 1996." *Annals of Health Law*, 1998, *7*, 183.

> Presents a detailed accounting of the consequences of HIPAA as it relates to group health insurance, including provisions that concern preexisting conditions, special enrollment rights, premium discrimination, maternity lengths of stay, parity for mental health benefits, and small-group coverage.

William J. Scanlon. "Retiree Health Insurance: Erosion in Retiree Health Benefits Offered by Larger Employers." (GAO/T-HEHS-98-110.) Mar. 10, 1998, 12 pages.

> Rising health costs have spurred companies to find ways to control their benefit expenditures, including eliminating retiree coverage and increasing cost sharing. HIPAA (Kennedy-Kassebaum) mandates continued access to persons losing group coverage, but it does not guarantee that the continued coverage will be affordable. This congressional testimony by the GAO's director of health financing and systems issues notes that because state laws governing the operation of the individual market vary, the premiums faced by early retirees vary substantially. He then discusses administration and congressional proposals to address this potential gap in coverage.

Justin D. Simon and Jodi Trulove. "Reliance on Government Advice to Preclude Criminal Enforcement Actions Under the Health Insurance Portability and Accountability Act." *Administrative Law Review*, *51*, 237.

> Analyzes the new advisory opinion procedure under HIPAA, specifically focusing on the preclusive effect an advisory opinion issued by HHS should have with respect to subsequent criminal prosecution by the Justice Department. Also describes the HHS advisory opinion procedure and compares it to other established federal agency advisory opinion regimes to ascertain the likely preclusive effect that should be accorded by law enforcers. Finally, the analysis includes discussion of potential constitutional principles that might be invoked to prevent prosecution in cases where a favorable advisory opinion has been issued and relied upon.

18.10   BALANCED BUDGET ACT OF 1997 (BBA)

Donna Clark and others. "Providers Face a Multitude of Payment Reductions." *Health Law Digest*, Nov. 1997, *25*(11), 3–20.

> Presents an abbreviated summary of the most relevant payment issues associated with Medicare and Medicaid that are affected by the Balanced Budget Act of 1997. Key reductions affected by the BBA include payment cuts for prospective payment system (PPS) hospitals, PPS-exempt hospitals subject to the Tax Equity and Fiscal Responsibility Act of 1982 (TEFRA) and teaching hospitals; the transfer of most home health care spending to Medicare part B; and mandating PPS for skilled nursing facilities, home health, rehabilitation, and hospital outpatient services.

Lisa W. Clark. "The Demise of the Boren Amendment: What Comes Next in the Struggle over Hospital Payment Standards under the Medicaid Act." *Health Law Digest*, Jan. 1998, *26*(1), 11–18.

> Examines the consequences of the BBA's repeal of the so-called Boren Amendment. Until Oct. 1, 1997, when the repeal became effective, the Boren Amendment required that states participating

in Medicaid pay rates to hospitals that take into account a disproportionate number of low-income patients with special needs. The new language replacing the Boren Amendment, the author explains, eliminates the requirement that rates be reasonable and adequate based on state findings and only requires that states engage in a public notice-and-comment process when making rate changes.

H. Guy Collier and Catherine Colyer. "Balanced Budget Act of 1997 Enhances Government's Arsenal in the War on Fraud Abuse and Waste." *Health Law Digest*, Oct. 1997, *25*(10), 3–6.

This article discusses program exclusion provisions, civil monetary penalties, Stark II advisory opinions, surety bonds, disclosure of ownership, and employee information.

Abigail English. "The New Children's Health Insurance Program: Early Implementation and Issues for Special Populations." *Clearinghouse Review*, Jan.–Feb. 1999.

The BBA gave states options to provide essential health care to children and adolescents from low-income families without health insurance. Although almost every state has submitted a children's health insurance program (CHIP) plan, advocates may find significant opportunities for developing the plans to make them more effective and perhaps to help fill some gaps left by welfare reform.

Thomas C. Fox and Joel M. Hamme. "Legislative Update: The Balanced Budget Act of 1997." Washington, D.C.: American Health Lawyers Association [Report No. VLT98–0001], 1998, 80 pages.

Presents an overview of the BBA and its implications for long-term care providers, including Medicare prospective payment rates for skilled nursing facilities, consolidated billing requirements, repeal of the Medicaid rate standard for nursing facilities (Boren Amendment), and the fraud and abuse provisions of the BBA. Attachments include answers to frequently asked questions about the long-term care provisions of the BBA, a client memorandum outlining the BBA provisions applying to provider-sponsored organizations and the new Medicare Part C Program (Medicare+Choice), and two letters from Sally K. Richardson, the director of the HCFA Center for Medicaid and State Operations, to state Medicaid directors, providing guidance on implications of the BBA.

Alice G. Gosfield. "Private Contracting by Medicare Physicians: The Pit and the Pendulum." *Health Law Digest*, Jan. 1998, *26*(1), 3–9.

Considers certain problems in the Balanced Budget Act as enacted. Gosfield notes that throughout the history of Medicare physician payment, potential government intrusion in private financial relationships between physicians and patients has been at issue. Congressional action on this subject has gone from an affirmative avoidance policy to one of increasing involvement in private activity, and now back in the other direction. The BBA enacted a provision to liberalize the restrictions imposed by Medicare law on private financial arrangements between physicians and their Medicare patients, by lifting the imposition of limiting charges in some situations. However, as a result of a controversial conference committee modification, the statute is confusing at best, is internally inconsistent, and in the final analysis eviscerates the whole point of the provision in the first place, the author writes.

Mary R. Grealy. "Explanation of Health Care Provisions in the Balanced Budget Act of 1997." Washington, D.C.: American Health Lawyers Association [Report No. AM97–0015], 1997, 82 pages.

Examines the act's implications for Medicare and Medicaid provisions, children's health insurance initiatives, legal immigrant issues, and health-related tax issues. This seminar paper is supplemented with useful charts and tables.

Mark S. Joffe. "Initiatives in Medicaid Managed Care: Medicaid and Children's Health Provisions of the Balanced Budget Act of 1997." Washington, D.C.: American Health Lawyers Association [Report No. MC97–0020], 1997, 78 pages.

> Discusses new developments in Medicaid managed care as a result of enactment of the BBA, including new requirements and elimination of waivers. This report also reviews the new Children's Health Insurance Program (CHIP) and contains HCFA publications on CHIP and the Medicaid managed care portions of the BBA Conference Report.

Charles N. Kahn III and Hanns Kuttner. "Budget Bills and Medicare Policy: The Politics of the BBA." *Health Affairs*, Jan./Feb. 1999, *18*(1), 37–47.

> With the BBA and a balanced federal budget, the link may be broken between the budget and Medicare's policy's timing and direction. However, despite a balanced budget, Medicare's eventual financial crisis must be addressed. The BBAs of 1995 and 1997 present two models of Medicare legislation: one based on conflict and another on consensus. Because the 1997 act became law and the 1995 act did not, the consensus model has proved to be politically feasible. However, this model appears to be inadequate for devising a solution to Medicare's long-term financial problems.

National Health Law Program. Los Angeles. "The Balanced Budget Act of 1997: Reshaping the Health Safety Net for America's Poor." *Health Advocate*, Fall 1997, 1, 60 pages.

> With the Balanced Budget Act, Congress and the president achieved a mutual objective to cut federal spending and balance the federal budget. This article supplies an extensive, practical analysis of the BBA as it affects Medicare and Medicaid. Discusses consumer protections, quality assurance, protections against fraud and abuse, sanctions for noncompliance, eligibility, expanded health insurance for children and adolescents, accountability, and reporting. Part I focuses on changes in Medicaid. Part II focuses on the Children's Health Insurance Program, and Part III examines changes in the Medicare program. Presents extensive citations to specific provisions of the act. This article is available online at www.healthlaw.org.

AIDS Issues

AIDS is an acronym coined in 1982 for a number of illnesses occurring in persons whose immune systems have been weakened by the presence of the human immunodeficiency virus, or HIV.[1] The U.S. Centers for Disease Control began tracking the extent of the disease before it was well understood.[2] Subcategories of persons at particular risk for infection include homosexual or bisexual males and intravenous drug users.[3] Now well into its second decade, the epidemic remains dynamic and unstable, and its "major impact is yet to come."[4] Moreover, new issues are emerging that call for immediate consideration and action, in the view of some commentators.[5]

Writing on AIDS law and policy has focused on a number of topics in recent years: confidentiality, duty to warn, contact tracing, partner notification, the occupational duties of health care workers, routine testing, duty to treat, medical malpractice in the context of treating AIDS-infected patients, the effect of AIDS on health care facility personnel policy, and obligations of health care facilities to offer a safe working environment.

References

1. Glen A. Reed and S. Wade Malone. "Acquired Immunodeficiency Syndrome." In Anne Dellinger (ed.), *Healthcare Facilities Law: Critical Issues for Hospitals, HMOs, and Extended Care Facilities.* Boston: Little, Brown, 1991, p. 845.
2. Reed and Malone (1991).
3. Reed and Malone (1991).
4. Jonathan Mann, Daniel J. Tarantola, and Thomas W. Netter (eds.). *AIDS in the World.* Cambridge, Mass.: Harvard University Press, 1992, p. 18.
5. Committee on AIDS Research. *AIDS: The Second Decade.* (Heather G. Miller, Charles F. Turner, and Lincoln E. Moses, eds.) Washington, D.C.: National Academy Press, 1990. See generally Lawrence O. Gostin (ed.). *AIDS and the Health Care System.* New Haven, Conn.: Yale University Press, 1990.

ANNOTATIONS

19.01   IN GENERAL

American Bar Association. *Directory of Legal Resources for People with AIDS and HIV.* Washington: ABA AIDS Coordination Project, 1997, 231 pages.

Provides handy access to organizations and groups that supply legal help on a range of AIDS-related issues.

Peter S. Arno and Karyn L. Feiden. *Against the Odds: The Story of AIDS Drug Development, Politics, and Profits.* New York: HarperCollins, 1992, 314 pages.

Highly emotional account of the development of AIDS policy in the United States.

Aspen Communications Data Group. *Infectious Disease Resource Manual.* Gaithersburg, Md.: Aspen, 1999.

This loose-leaf manual is a compilation of guidelines designed to educate health care workers about infectious diseases. Includes discussion of HIV/AIDS education, among other topics.

Atlantic Information Services. *AIDS Reference Guide.* Washington, D.C.: Atlantic Information Services, 1998.

This two-volume, loose-leaf service, updated monthly, is written for lecturers in health law and researchers in medicine, government, business, and education. Chapters include testing issues; employment issues; implications of treatment advances and vaccines; legal issues; impact on health care providers; and legislative, regulatory, and governance issues.

Paul Barron, Sara J. Goldstein, and Karen L. Wishner. "State Statutes Dealing with HIV and AIDS: A Comprehensive State-by-State Summary." *Law and Sexuality: A Review of Lesbian and Gay Legal Issues,* 1995, *5,* 1.

This 512-page project compiles all relevant state statutes concerning HIV and AIDS. This journal is published annually by Tulane University Law School.

Robert J. Buchanan and Scott R. Smith. "State Implementation of AIDS Drug Assistance Programs." *Health Care Financing Review,* Spring 1998, *19,* 39.

AIDS drug assistance programs (ADAPs) allow access to medication for people who lack other health coverage. In this article, the authors present the result of a survey identifying how forty-eight states implemented ADAPs, focusing on the number of beneficiaries; medical and financial eligibility criteria; administration of waiting lists; and coverage of drugs, including protease inhibitors. They conclude that increased funding for ADAPs is necessary to maintain this part of the public sector of the safety net for HIV care. This article is part of a special issue devoted to changing environments of AIDS/HIV service delivery and financing.

Mary E. Clark. "AIDS Prevention: Legislative Options." *American Journal of Law and Medicine,* 1990, *16,* 107.

This article, written by the associate counsel of the Massachusetts Medical Society, examines legislative options to control the HIV epidemic. Part One identifies education as the key component of a comprehensive prevention program and examines options for preexposure education programs designed to avoid or minimize exposure. Part Two details postexposure prevention measures, focusing on reporting and contact-tracing provisions. The author opposes as counterproductive any mandatory reporting by name of individuals testing positive or mandatory contact tracing; she supports voluntary partner notification. Part Three examines a variety of prevention efforts in specific settings, including schools; prisons; and other custodial facilities, hospitals, and dental offices.

Patricia G. Court and Linda Karr O'Connor. "A Selected Bibliography on AIDS and Health Insurance." *Cornell Journal of Law and Public Policy,* 1993, *3,* 109–120.

Collects and organizes citations of books, journal articles, and cases that contribute to legal analysis of the issues involved in providing health insurance to persons with AIDS. The authors also include guidance for identifying legislation and regulations affecting the area so researchers can update this bibliography.

Paul Hampton Crockett. *HIV Law.* New York: Three Rivers Press, 1997, 280 pages.

Written by a Miami attorney who specializes in AIDS litigation, this is a 280-page guide to a broad range of issues, including estate planning, discrimination, Social Security, viatical settlements, planning for incapacity, and dealing with creditors. Modestly priced, it also covers in detail the Kennedy-Kassebaum Health Insurance Portability and Accountability Act of 1996 (HIPAA).

Norman Daniels. *Seeking Fair Treatment: From the AIDS Epidemic to National Health Care Reform.* New York: Oxford University Press, 1995, 204 pages.

This book explores the issues of justice that underlie central controversies about how we should treat one another in the HIV epidemic: the duty of physicians and other health care personnel to treat AIDS patients, the conflicting rights of patients and infected health care workers, insurability of those at high risk, access to unproven drugs, rationing expensive treatments to HIV patients, and sex education in the schools. The needs of HIV patients are similar to those of many other patients, the author writes, because there is little that is unique about HIV, even if the seriousness of the AIDS epidemic has brought every aspect of the health system as it affects HIV patients into sharp relief. He concludes that how we treat one another in our health care system is a metaphor for how we treat one another in all the dimensions of our social life.

Nicholas Freudenberg and Marc A. Zimmerman. *AIDS Prevention in the Community: Lessons from the First Decade.* Washington, D.C.: American Public Health Association, 1995, 225 pages.

This book describes in detail a variety of community-based AIDS prevention programs and synthesizes the experience with such programs in the United States during the late 1980s and early 1990s. It offers AIDS educators and policy makers a summary of the lessons learned about planning, implementing, and managing AIDS prevention programs for the diverse populations that can be reached in community settings. The book differs from other recent works in that it is written primarily for practitioners and program planners and presents practical advice in the broader framework of what is known about changing health behavior and social environments.

Lawrence O. Gostin and David Webber. "The AIDS Litigation Project: HIV/AIDS in the Courts in the 1990s." *AIDS and Public Policy Journal,* Winter 1997, *12*(4); and *AIDS and Public Policy Journal,* Spring 1998, *13*(1).

This two-part article presents a survey of more than 550 cases reported in the federal and state courts in the United States between 1991 and 1997. The first part discusses the duties of government and individuals in the HIV epidemic, while the second part discusses the rights of individuals. Cases sited are divided into those dealing with the topics of AIDS education; protection of the blood supply; governmental regulation of products, consumer protection, and fraud; tort actions; duty to protect workers; administration of justice; privacy and confidentiality; the "right to know"; discrimination; insurance; rights of vulnerable persons: disability, homelessness, and indigence; prisoners; and immigration and international travel.

General Accounting Office. "HIV/AIDS Drugs: Funding Implications of New Combination Therapies for Federal and State Programs." (GAO/HEHS-99–2.) Oct. 14, 1998, 36 pages.

Although state governments and private payers, such as private health insurance and charitable groups, share in financing medical care for people with HIV and AIDS, the federal government picks up the tab for more than half the cost of this care. Much of the more than $5 billion in estimated federal spending for treatment in fiscal year 1998 will go for prescription drugs. Recent developments in HIV and AIDS treatment, especially the new combination drug therapies, are expected to increase demand for state and federal funding. Combination drug therapy costs about $10,000 per patient annually. More than half of the 240,000 people with AIDS in the United States are believed to be receiving combination drug therapies that include a protease inhibitor and other drugs. GAO estimates that at least 67,500 AIDS patients on Medicaid have been receiving combination drug therapy in 1998.

Data are meager on individuals who are HIV-positive but do not have AIDS, but state ADAPs reported that a great majority of their clients were receiving combination therapy in 1998. To stretch available funds and maximize the number of clients they are able to serve, these drug assistance programs are buying drugs at a discount and trying to ensure that clients who are eligible for Medicaid are, in fact, in the program. Nonetheless, some ADAPs have had to restrict enrollment or limit benefits. Other factors, such as evolving standards of care, the long-term effectiveness of current therapies, and new research developments, also influence projections of the impact of new drug therapies on federal and state government programs. The effect of the demand for the new combination therapies is difficult to estimate, but ADAPs will likely experience greater financial pressure than Medicare in caring for people with AIDS or HIV who seek assistance.

General Accounting Office. "'Blood Plasma Safety' Plasma Product Risks Are Low If Good Manufacturing Practices Are Followed." (Report No. GAO/HEHS-98–205.) Sept. 9, 1998, 45 pages.

Limiting the number of donors whose plasma is pooled for production into plasma products helps to lower the risk of viral transmission. Significantly, viral clearance techniques have made the risk of receiving an infected blood plasma product extremely low if manufacturers follow procedures to ensure safety. Viral removal and inactivation procedures can virtually eliminate enveloped viruses, such as those responsible for AIDS, hepatitis B, and hepatitis C. However, recent FDA reports have cited many instances of noncompliance with good manufacturing practices, which could pose a risk to those who rely on plasma products.

Lawrence O. Gostin and others. "The Law and the Public's Health: A Study of Infectious Disease Law in the United States." *Columbia Law Review*, Jan. 1999, 99, 59–128.

Law plays a crucial role in the field of public health, from defining the power and jurisdiction of health agencies to influencing the social norms that shape individual behavior. Despite its importance, public health law has been neglected. More than a decade ago, the Institute of Medicine issued a report lamenting the state of public health administration generally, calling in particular for revision of public health statutes. This article examines the current state of public health law, particularly in the context of contemporary health problems such as AIDS, cancer, heart disease, and hepatitis C.

To help create the conditions in which people can be healthy, public health law must reflect an understanding of how public health agencies work to promote health, as well as the political and social contexts in which these agencies operate. The authors first discuss three prevailing ways in which the determinants of health are conceptualized, and the political and social problems each model tends to create for public health efforts. The analysis then turns to the core functions of public health, emphasizing how laws further public health work. The article reports the results of a fifty-state survey of laws on communicable disease control, revealing that few states have systematically reformed their laws to reflect contemporary medical and legal developments. The article concludes with specific guidelines for law reform.

Lawrence O. Gostin (ed.). *AIDS and the Health Care System.* New Haven, Conn.: Yale University Press, 1990, 299 pages.

Contains sixteen essays focusing on a range of AIDS-related issues. Topics examined include patients' rights and public health, confidentiality, duty to warn, discrimination, the threat to health care workers, routine testing, duty to treat AIDS patients, drug trials, and institutional and professional liability.

Lawrence O. Gostin. "Public Health Strategies for Confronting AIDS." *Journal of the American Medical Association,* 1989, 261, 1621.

Piecing together legislation from states across the country, the author, an attorney, finds that it is possible to discern an overall strategy to confront AIDS. This article contends that legislation can make a critical contribution to health efforts by promoting professional standards through reasoned guidelines; by mandating appropriate health care services and public education, particularly in sensitive areas such as sex education in schools, condom advertising, and outreach programs for drug dependent people; by funding research and policy development; and by safeguarding confidentiality and protecting against discrimination. The article categorizes and reports on AIDS-related legislative and regulatory policy in the United States. It also assesses the likely impact of law in promoting or impeding public health efforts in combating AIDS. It analyzes treatment and education; blood supply protection; screening, reporting and contact tracing; isolation and criminalization; and confidentiality, the power to warn, and antidiscrimination.

Frank P. Grad. *The Public Health Law Manual.* Washington, D.C.: American Public Health Association 1990, 337 pages.

This manual is specifically geared to public health professionals who enforce, administer, and provide health services. Contents include recognizing and managing legal problems; effective communication with lawyers; legal sources of public health powers; protection of individual rights, including equal protection, due process, and privacy rights; laws relating to communicable diseases, including AIDS, permits, licenses, and registrations; searches and inspections; embargo and seizures; correcting nuisance and dangerous conditions; injunctions; civil and penal sanctions; responsibilities and liabilities of public health officers; and developing public health laws.

Joni N. Gray, Phillip M. Lyons, Jr., and Gary B. Melton. *Ethical and Legal Issues in AIDS Research.* Baltimore: Johns Hopkins University Press, 1995, 200 pages.

There are two broad levels of analysis and discussion in this book. It begins and ends with consideration of overarching ethical problems, the dilemmas that permeate psychosocial research on AIDS, and a presentation of arguments about the interests that should be paramount. At the same time, however, resolving these grand dilemmas is contingent on understanding the nuts and bolts of the law. Thus the focus of much of the book is on technical problems of law, such as the problem of preserving confidentiality, informed consent and debriefing, and duties to protect third parties.

Guides for Living. *HIV/AIDS Resources.* (3rd ed.) Longmont, Colo.: Guides for Living, 1997, 887 pages.

Lists 29,500 AIDS service providers, government agencies, and national organizations. Listings are organized by state, county, and type of service. Each listing gives a description of services offered as well as phone and fax numbers and a mailing address.

Amy L. Hansen. "Establishing Uniformity in HIV-Fear Cases: A Modification of the Distinct Event Approach." (Note.) *Valparaiso University Law Review,* 1995, 29, 1251.

Analyzes the general history of negligent infliction of emotional distress in the courts and in the psychological community, and illustrates how the courts have increasingly recognized mental injury claims as legitimate. Hansen then analyzes trends in these cases and the problems courts face in defining an appropriate standard of recovery. Finally, she proposes a judicial approach to gain uniformity in HIV-fear cases.

Donald H. J. Hermann. "AIDS and the Law." In Frederic G. Reamer (ed.), *AIDS and Ethics.* New York: Columbia University Press, 1991.

The goal of Hermann's chapter is to alert readers to the broad range of legal issues raised by the AIDS epidemic. The author emphasizes identifying areas where there have been significant legal developments.

Donald H. J. Hermann and William P. Schurgin. *Legal Aspects of AIDS*. Deerfield, Ill.: Clark, Boardman, Callaghan, 1995.

This regularly updated treatise addresses issues such as access to care, HIV testing, informed consent, required reporting, providing information about patient HIV status, testing, and refusal to care for HIV-infected patients. It also discusses in detail such liability issues as failure to diagnose, incorrect diagnosis, treatment decisions, infection of a patient, and institutional liability. Other chapters examine confidentiality, accidental exposure, control measures, and duties to employees with AIDS. An underlying premise of the discussion is that both interests of individual liberty and social needs will be best met by applying sound legal decisions and legislation based on medical and scientific knowledge about HIV. The volume includes an appendix of state statutes prohibiting discrimination in public accommodations and an appendix of statutes providing protection of physician-patient communications. This one-volume work concludes with a detailed legal bibliography, tables, a table of cases, and an index.

Tracey Hooker. "HIV/AIDS Facts to Consider." Denver: National Conference of State Legislatures, 1996, 64 pages.

This policy guide presents information on affected populations, caseload trends, and state policies. Modestly priced, the book is a compendium of facts—from statistics to a review of state policies—about the current state of the AIDS epidemic in the United States. Highly readable, this text will be helpful for policy makers.

Robert M. Jarvis and others. *AIDS Law in a Nutshell*. (2nd ed.) St. Paul, Minn.: West, 1996.

This book offers a general overview of such topics as access to care, patient testing, required reporting, warning third parties, testing patients to protect health care personnel, employment discrimination, public accommodations, housing, estate planning, insurance, tort liability, transmission, defamation and immigration.

D. C. Jayasuriya. *AIDS: The Public Health and Legal Dimensions*. Boston: Kluwer Law International, 1988, 154 pages.

This paperback manual surveys the public health and legal ramifications of the AIDS epidemic.

Robert K. Jenner. *Transfusion-Associated AIDS*. Phoenix: Lawyers and Judges Publishing Company, 1995, 364 pages.

This manual is written for tort lawyers litigating claims arising from HIV-contaminated blood transfusions. The author, an attorney, examines inconsistent case law, offers tips on fact finding, and supplies citations from medical literature.

Lawrence Lavin. "AIDS, Medicaid, and Women." *Duke Journal of Gender Law and Policy*, Spring 1998, *5*, 193.

Although the overall death rate from AIDS is decreasing in the United States, the number of women with AIDS is increasing. This article examines gaps in the health care system facing women with AIDS and examines alternative sources of health care insurance coverage, focusing on coverage through the Medicaid program, which is the primary insurance program for persons with AIDS. The article examines access and quality in rapid enrollment of Medicaid beneficiaries in managed care plans. It concludes with recommendations to improve women's access to health care through Medicaid.

Arthur S. Leonard and others. *AIDS Law and Policy: Cases and Materials*. (2nd ed.) Houston: John Marshall, 1995, 565 pages.

This law school casebook examines AIDS from a range of perspectives: public health, politicization, testing, confidentiality, tort law, criminal law, disability rights law, paying for care, AIDS in institutions, AIDS and the family, legal issues associated with death and dying, and international human rights law, among others.

LRP Publications. *The AIDS Directory*. Horsham, Pa.: LRP Publications, 1996, 800 pages.

This guide is a reference work for libraries, attorneys, and health organizations; provides contact information on more than fifteen hundred professionals in the field.

Ellen L. Luepke. "HIV Misdiagnosis: Negligent Infliction of Emotional Distress and the False-Positive." (Note.) *Iowa Law Review*, 1996, *81*, 1229.

Addresses the issues involved in a negligent false-positive misdiagnosis of HIV, and focuses on whether a person who alleges negligent misdiagnosis should recover damages for negligent infliction of emotional distress. The author concludes that courts should not allow compensation for negligent infliction of emotional distress in HIV misdiagnosis cases unless the plaintiff shows an attendant physical injury.

Katherine Marconi and others. "The Paradigm Shift in Medicaid: Women with HIV under Managed Care." *Duke Journal of Gender Law, and Policy*, Spring 1998, *5*, 211.

This article addresses three issues of importance to the HIV/AIDS care of women under Medicaid managed care systems: changes concerning access to services women will face, how coordinated quality services will be delivered, and whether reimbursement rates will be sufficient to cover the costs of care.

Robert A. Padgug and others. "AIDS and Private Health Insurance: A Crisis of Risk Sharing." *Cornell Journal of Law and Public Policy*, 1993, *3*, 55.

Explores the nature of American risk-sharing arrangements and the problems they generate, as exemplified by the dual crisis of health financing and AIDS. This article concludes that the only principle upon which a workable and fair system of health care financing can be constructed is that of "social solidarity," whereby all citizens share equitably in the risks of incurring health care expenses.

T. J. Philipson and R. A. Posner. *Private Choices and Public Health: The AIDS Epidemic in an Economic Perspective*. Cambridge, Mass.: Harvard University Press, 1993.

The authors apply economic theory to the AIDS epidemic and conclude that the federal government "has no, or even a negative, stake in the development of treatments, such as the drug AZT, that merely prolong the lives of persons [with HIV because AZT] may increase the total medical costs by extending the period during which infected persons demand and receive treatment."

Abby R. Rubenfeld (ed.). *AIDS Legal Guide*. (2nd ed.) New York: Lambda Legal Defense and Education Fund, 1987.

Topics addressed in this book include employment discrimination, access to health-related services, confidentiality, insurance, and public benefits. The numerous appendices have information on medical aspects of AIDS-related litigation, a sample insurance discrimination complaint, a COBRA memorandum, and various forms.

William B. Rubenstein, Ruth Eisenberg, and Lawrence O. Gostin. *Rights of People Who Are HIV Positive*. (Norman Dorsen, ed.) Carbondale: Southern Illinois Press, 1996, 384 pages.

Prepared in conjunction with the American Civil Liberties Union, this modestly priced handbook supplies helpful information to the layperson, service provider, and policy advocate. It is also a solid point of departure for attorneys beginning work in this field. Written in clear question-and-answer format, the book examines topics such as discrimination in health care, the workplace, and public accommodations; and HIV in special settings such as prisons and schools.

Gerald Schochetman and J. Richard George (eds.). *AIDS Testing: A Comprehensive Guide to Technical, Medical, Social, Legal, and Management Issues.* (3rd ed.) New York: Springer-Verlag, 1994, 410 pages.

Contains twenty-four chapters on a variety of AIDS testing topics. Most of the book is written by medical researchers at the Centers for Disease Control, with only one brief chapter addressing legal concerns.

Mark S. Senak. *HIV, AIDS, and the Law: A Guide to Our Rights and Challenges.* New York: Insight Books, 1996, 249 pages.

This is a self-help guide for individuals and families of those affected by HIV. It discusses such matters as child custody, federal and state entitlements, discrimination, insurance, confidentiality, and the ADA. Appendices include a medical power of attorney, an appointment of guardian, a state-by-state breakdown of living wills and health care agent laws, state positions on forced feeding and hydration, and states that require HIV name reporting.

Siobhan Spillane. "AIDS: Establishing a Physician's Duty to Warn." (Note.) *Rutgers Law Journal,* 1990, 21, 645.

Proposes that physicians have a duty to warn foreseeable third parties who may contract the AIDS virus from the physician's patient.

Theodore J. Stein. *The Social Welfare of Women and Children with HIV and AIDS: Legal Protections, Policy, and Programs.* New York: Oxford University Press, 1998, 258 pages.

The framework that the author uses for analysis is derived from the federal statutes that protect the civil rights of women and children with HIV and AIDS and that identify the financial, medical, and social services that are available to them. Selected state statutes illustrate matters such as child custody, testing for HIV, and confidentiality of medical records. The book includes an extensive bibliography and index.

U.S. Congress, Office of Technology Assessment. *Adverse Reactions to HIV Vaccines: Medical, Ethical, and Legal Issues.* (OTA-BP-H-163.) Washington, D.C.: U.S. Government Printing Office, 1995, 197 pages.

Examines such topics as responsibility for injury and compensation, potential deterrents to HIV vaccine development, tort liability as well as potential liability for adverse reactions to vaccines, tort liability reform, and elements of a no-fault compensation program. It is supplemented by numerous tables, charts, and an index of references.

U.S. Sentencing Commission. "Report to Congress: Adequacy of Penalties for the Intentional Exposure of Others, Through Sexual Activity, to Human Immunodeficiency Virus." Washington, D.C.: U.S. Sentencing Commission, 1995.

In this report, the commission considers whether revisions to the sentencing guidelines were needed to accommodate offenses involving willful exposure to HIV. The report examines (1) operation of the guidelines given the absence of a specific federal statute punishing intentional transmission of HIV, (2) cases sentenced in fiscal year 1993 to determine the frequency with which HIV exposure was an issue at sentencing, and (3) pertinent case law.

Richard K. Vanik. "Emotional Distress for Fear of Exposure to AIDS: An Infection Headed for Texas." (Comment.) *Houston Law Review,* 1996, *32,* 1451.

Examines reported cases in which plaintiffs have sought to recover damages for emotional distress associated with exposure to AIDS. The author concludes that for a plaintiff to recover, he or she should be required to prove that (1) the defendant breached his duty to avoid exposure of the plaintiff to HIV, (2) the plaintiff had a reasonable likelihood of exposure to HIV from defendant, (3) the plaintiff's fear was based on an objective standard of reasonableness that considers the medical probability of contracting the disease, and (4) the plaintiff had himself or herself tested to disprove the presence of infection as soon as practical but no later than six months after the alleged exposure.

Roderick Wallace and Deborah Wallace. "U.S. Apartheid and the Spread of AIDS to the Suburbs: A Multi-City Analysis of the Political Economy of Spacial Epidemic Threshold." *Social Science and Medicine,* 1995, *41,* 333.

The authors present data to show that in many U.S. central cities AIDS diffuses into the suburbs as a single, spatially extended disease ecosystem. These empirical results contradict the conclusions of a National Research Counsel report that AIDS will be largely confined within marginalized urban populations.

David W. Webber (ed.). *AIDS and the Law.* (3rd ed.) New York: Wiley, 1997, 624 pages.

Prepared by Webber and eleven other specialists on HIV and disability law, this treatise is significantly expanded from the earlier edition published in 1992. Although it is primarily intended as a resource for attorneys, the book will also be helpful for AIDS service providers and health care professionals who serve as advocates for their clients and patients. This edition contains a new chapter on sorting through the complexities of public benefits programs. This chapter includes basic examples of how the system works and, helpfully, reprints the Social Security Administration's standards for determining eligibility and disability based on HIV.

Karen L. Wells. "Why the Capping of AIDS Benefits by Self-Funded Employer Welfare Benefit Plans Should Be Actionable Under Section 510 of ERISA." *Health Care Law Monthly,* June 1999, at 17.

Self-funded employer plans continue to look for ways to streamline the cost of administering their benefits. As a result, they have looked at the cost of treating AIDS. However, singling out individuals because of their HIV status and reducing (often only a single beneficiary's) benefits is arguably prohibited conduct within the context of Section 510 of ERISA. Consequently, a Section 510 claim is a potential avenue of recourse against self-funded employer welfare benefits plans that cap only AIDS benefits.

Wiley Law Publications, editorial staff. *AIDS and the Law.* (3rd ed.) New York: Wiley, 1992.

This treatise comprehensively surveys a range of legal topics as they relate to AIDS. Particularly relevant is the chapter on health care issues such as duty to treat, duty to AIDS patients, duty to other patients, duty to hospital employees, and confidentiality versus duty to inform. Other topics addressed are care in an outpatient setting; blood products and tissue transplantation; and the impact of AIDS on health insurance, life insurance, and disability insurance. The book concludes with six appendices covering such useful material as a summary of state statutes on antidiscrimination in the workplace, a similar summary relating to antidiscrimination in insurance underwriting, and another by jurisdiction regarding consent for testing.

World Health Organization (ed.). *Legislative Responses to AIDS.* Boston: Kluwer Law International, 1989, 344 pages.

This hardbound text surveys AIDS-related statutes from around the world.

19.02   LEGAL ISSUES RELATING TO TREATMENT OF PATIENTS WITH AIDS OR HIV INFECTION

Adele A. Waller. "Confidentiality and Data Rights." Washington, D.C.: American Health Lawyers Association [Report No. VPH99–0025], 1999, 49 pages.

Details developments in federal health information privacy law, protecting confidentiality in the interim and data rights. Includes a chart with comparison of key proposals for federal health information privacy legislation.

19.02(1)   Duty to Treat

American Bar Association, Individual Rights and Responsibilities Section. "Calming AIDS Phobia: Legal Implications of the Low Risk of Transmitting HIV in the Health Care Setting." Chicago: ABA, 1995, 66 pages.

This text is published by the ABA AIDS Coordinating Committee of this section.

Mary A. Crossley. "Of Diagnoses and Discrimination: Discriminatory Non-Treatment of Infants with HIV Infection." *Columbia Law Review*, 1993, *93*, 1581.

Although this article focuses primarily on examining the legality of withholding needed medical treatment from an infant with HIV infection, it ultimately concerns itself with the more fundamental question of how medical decision makers may legitimately take into account HIV infection or other disability in making treatment decisions and recommendations. It concludes that disability discrimination law should be interpreted to apply to medical treatment decision making and, as so interpreted, offers a vehicle for addressing treatment of HIV-infected infants in a fashion that is consistently developed in the ethical ferment prompted by the 1982 "Baby Doe" case.

Richard DeNatale and Shawn D. Parrish. "Health Care Workers' Ability to Recover in Tort for Transmission or Fear of Transmission of HIV from a Patient." *Santa Clara Law Review*, 1996, *36*, 751–792.

Examines whether there should be a tort for a patient's failure to disclose HIV infection that results in infection or fear of infection by a health care worker. This article concludes that such a duty does not and should not exist under tort law principles. Furthermore, such a duty would impede the policies adopted by the government and the health care establishment to prevent transmission of HIV.

Michelle Kaemmerling. "*Bragdon v. Abbott*: ADA Protection for Individuals with Asymptomatic HIV." (Note.) *North Carolina Law Review*, 1999, *77*, 1266.

This Note discusses the facts of *Bragdon* v. *Abbott*, its treatment in the lower court, and the Supreme Court's holding that the plaintiff was protected under the ADA because the infection substantially limited her major life activity of reproduction. In an expansive reading of the statutory definition of disability, the Court rejected the argument that whether a life activity is considered major under the statute depends upon its daily character.

Samuel Oddi. "Reverse Informed Consent: The Unreasonably Dangerous Patient." *Vanderbilt Law Review*, 1993, *46*, 1417.

Argues that a patient has a duty to warn health care professionals of material risks (in particular, HIV infection) associated with the patient's care. Oddi advances his thesis in a two-step comparative analysis. First, he shows that the doctrine of informed consent imposes on health care providers a duty to disclose their infectious status prior to treatment. Second, he compares this duty with its converse: imposing a duty on the patient to inform the health care provider of the patient's infectious status. On the basis of analogy, risk utility, and economic analyses, he concludes that placing a duty on patients to disclose is justified when a comparable duty is imposed on health care providers to secure informed consent by disclosing their infectious status to their patients.

Christopher C. White. "Health Care Professionals and Treatment of HIV-Positive Patients: Is There an Affirmative Duty to Treat under Common Law, the Rehabilitation Act, or the Americans with Disabilities Act?" *Journal of Legal Medicine*, Mar. 1999, 20(1), 67–113.

The issue of whether a health care professional may refuse treatment to HIV-positive patients has engendered significant debate in the scholarly literature and the courts. Patient advocates decry the conduct as unethical and increasingly have turned to the courts and argued existing laws obligate health care professionals to offer care. Physicians and others counter that principles of professional autonomy and risk to themselves should allow selective treatment decisions based upon HIV status. This article examines common law, federal statutory enactments, and regulations promulgated pursuant to these enactments and then analyzes the U.S. Supreme Court opinion in *Bragdon* v. *Abbott*, 118 S.Ct. 2196 (1998). This article concludes that, although the U.S. Supreme Court correctly determined that asymptomatic HIV can be a disability entitled to protection under the ADA, the Court incorrectly focused on generalities rather than on conducting an individualized inquiry. Moreover, the Court's ruling on the issue of whether HIV-positive patients pose a direct threat leaves health care providers in a quandary. Because the Court gave instructions to the lower courts to conduct a factual inquiry based on available medical evidence, health care professionals are deprived of guidance as to whether their actions may subject them to liability. Refusal to give health care to HIV-positive patients will result in liability unless the health care provider is able to demonstrate that a direct threat exists owing to the particular patient contact involved.

19.02(2)   HIV Testing of Patients

American Medical Association. *Medicolegal Forms with Legal Analysis*. Chicago: AMA, 1991, 199 pages.

Along with a range of legal consent forms for doctors and health care providers (including one for withdrawal of blood for autologous transfusion for high-risk patients), this book has a chapter devoted to AIDS and informed consent for an HIV antibody test. The book also addresses patient confidentiality and reporting requirements.

Gilbert M. Clark (ed.). *Legal Issues in Transfusion Medicine*. Arlington, Va.: American Association of Blood Banks, 1986, 265 pages.

This text consists of a series of presentations offered at a Washington, D.C., conference on blood bank issues. In addition to AIDS, this series of essays addresses other important issues, such as informed consent, the right to refuse transfusion, and directed donations. The eight appendices contain full case citations, detailed outlines, charts, and graphs.

Ruth R. Faden, Gail Geller, and Madison Powers (eds.). *AIDS, Women, and the Next Generation: Towards a Morally Acceptable Public Policy for HIV Testing of Pregnant Women and Newborns*. New York: Oxford University Press, 1991, 374 pages.

Offers a comprehensive analysis of the complex medical, public health, legal, ethical, and social issues raised by HIV screening and testing of pregnant women and newborns. Specific legal issues addressed include state legislative approaches to prenatal and newborn screening, constitutional and state law constraints on screening, a physician's legal obligation to discuss HIV testing with pregnant women, the legal liability of a physician for failure to advise a woman about her health risks, and existing and proposed laws for protection against breaches of medical confidentiality. The text concludes with a list of ten recommendations and an index.

Martha A. Field. "Testing for AIDS: Uses and Abuses." *American Journal of Law and Medicine,* 1990, *16,* 34.

Responds to the public outcry for mandatory AIDS testing by exploring the major issues concerning identification of persons with AIDS in society. The article reviews testing procedures and rationales behind them to determine if a call for mandatory testing of the general populace would better achieve societal objectives for identifying persons with AIDS. The article concludes that testing should be required neither of the general population nor of subpopulations that society perceives as likely to have or spread the disease. Funds proposed for mandatory testing would be put to better use in education and universal precautions to prevent AIDS, she writes.

Karen Shoos Lipton and Edward L. Wolf (eds.). *Emerging Legal Issues in Blood Banking and Transfusion Medicine.* Bethesda, Md.: American Association of Blood Banks, 1998.

Written by attorneys and targeted at both attorneys and lay readers, this book provides complete information in concise form. Part One explores liability issues facing blood banks, hospitals, and physicians. It examines the changing standard of care with the advent of AIDS-related cases, transfusion-transmitted disease litigation, testing and notification issues, alternative services and products, emerging technologies and blood shield statutes, and alternative dispute resolution. Part Two concentrates on economic and regulatory issues, including antitrust law and provision of blood services, employee obligations, the impact of congressional and agency investigations and reports, and regulation of computer software.

Kay McCurdy (ed.). *Blood Bank Regulations A-Z.* Bethesda, Md.: American Association of Blood Banks, 1997.

This reference work features an alphabetical presentation of more than one hundred pertinent topics in blood banking, with citations for each. It offers readers with applicable sections of the Code of Federal Regulations and interpretive documents that represent current thinking at the FDA, the HCFA, and other regulatory agencies.

Andre A. Panossian and others. "Criminalization of Perinatal HIV Transmission." *Journal of Legal Medicine,* June 1998, *19,* 223.

In the absence of a universally accepted AIDS-specific statute, and forced to apply current case law and statutory mandate, the authors write, it appears feasible to construe perinatal transmission of HIV, in the setting of an informed party who is aware of the potential of transmitting HIV, as criminal assault. Assuming that the elements of this criminal offense are satisfied, such an individual may then be subjected to sanctions warranted by law.

Dennis J. Purtell. "Patient Care." Washington, D.C.: American Health Lawyers Association [Report No. FH97–0009], 1997, 64 pages.

Addresses informed consent issues, HIV/AIDS, OSHA's blood-borne pathogens standards, request and consent for HIV testing, and hospital policy and informed consent release for blood transfusion and blood component administration.

Caitlin A. Schmid. "Protecting the Physician in HIV Misdiagnosis Cases." (Note.) *Duke Law Journal,* 1996, *46,* 431.

In cases of HIV misdiagnosis, the author contends, a balance must be struck between recognizing genuine emotional distress and protecting physicians from unlimited liability. Courts should apply a good faith immunity standard, which would recognize the difficulty of caring for patients with certain illnesses and protect physicians from liability where the physician acts in good faith.

Leo Uzych. "HIV Testing: The Legal Balance Between Individual and Societal Rights." *Southern Medical Journal*, Mar. 1990, *83*, 303.

Contends that testing for the presence of HIV antibodies creates a legal conflict between the individual's right to autonomy and privacy and society's right to control the public health. A body of laws exists to address these conflicting rights. These laws, however, must evolve so as to strike a better balance between what society has a right to know and the individual's right to personal autonomy and privacy. Appropriate statutes should recognize that a legitimate need may arise for a physician to disclose otherwise confidential testing data to the spouse and other intimate sexual partners of the HIV-infected patient. The author holds a law degree and a master's degree in public health.

19.02(3)   Duty to Provide a Safe Workplace

G. W. Rutherford and J. M. Woo. "Contact Tracing to Control the Spread of HIV." *Journal of the American Medical Association*, 1988, *260*, 3275.

The authors, both physicians, encourage public health officials to consider using contact tracing in the context of HIV.

19.02(4)   Privacy

American Bar Association, Committee on Mental and Physical Disability Law. *AIDS/HIV and Confidentiality*. Chicago: ABA, 1991, 132 pages.

This pamphlet sets forth policy, procedures, and sample forms regarding handling confidentiality questions with HIV/AIDS information. The text presents examples for various types of settings.

Annot. "State Statutes or Regulations Expressly Governing Disclosure of Fact That Person Has Tested Positive for Human Immunodeficiency Virus (HIV) or Acquired Immunodeficiency Syndrome (AIDS)." *ALR5th*, 1998, *12*, 149.

As the problem of AIDS grows, more states have passed statutes and regulations governing disclosure of the fact that a person has tested positive for HIV or AIDS. In adjudicating such statutes and like the legislatures enacting them, courts have had to deal with two competing policies: protecting the privacy of the person testing positive for these illnesses, thus encouraging voluntary testing; and disseminating information to the public. In *Hillman v. Columbia County* (Wis. Ct. App.1991), 474 N.W.2d 913, 12 ALR 5th 997, the court attempted to balance these concerns. This lengthy annotation explores a number of issues examined by the court in this case. These include persons or entities subject to the nondisclosure requirement, what constitutes disclosure, hospital patient identification policies, court order for blood samples in criminal prosecution, exceptions to the nondisclosure requirement, including physicians performing invasive surgery, and waiver. It also discusses application of AIDS disclosure statutes to deceased persons, use of pseudonyms, and retroactive application.

Bobbi Bernstein. "Solving the Physician's Dilemma: An HIV Partner-Notification Plan." *Stanford Law and Policy Review*, 1995, *6*, 127.

Argues that the social costs of AIDS partner-notification statutes outweigh the benefits. The implicit breach of confidentiality involved in the statutes deters people who have engaged in high-risk behavior from seeking testing and denies medical professionals critical information about AIDS. After discussing and analyzing the various state statutes, the author proposes a solution in the form of a model statute that minimizes damage to confidentiality and encourages frank disclosure of AIDS information to affected parties.

B. M. Dickens. "Legal Limits to AIDS Confidentiality." *Journal of the American Medical Association*, 1988, *259*, 3449.

The author, a law professor, contends that the law's protection of medical confidence is often illusory. Although some laws appear to require and allow secrecy of medical data, others compel disclosure. The writer concludes that the most effective thrust for new legislation should not be simply seeking to enact further protections on confidentiality of data, which would be subject to the same exceptions, but reinforcing laws against discrimination on grounds of an individual's affliction with HIV.

Roger Doughty. "The Confidentiality of HIV-Related Information: Responding to the Resurgence of Aggressive Public Health Interventions in the AIDS Epidemic." *California Law Review*, 1994, *82*, 111.

During the 1980s, a confluence of opinion among public health officials, elected officials, and AIDS advocates led to creation of protections to ensure confidential treatment of AIDS and HIV-related information. This consensus is now being strained by the emergence of intrusive public health disease control measures, and by revision of the case surveillance definition of AIDS. Doughty examines these new threats to confidentiality in light of three current levels of confidentiality protection: statutory protection for HIV-specific information, constitutional privacy rights, and common law privacy rights. He contends that, given the rapid pace of change in government policies surrounding HIV-related information, legal protections for confidentiality are inadequate to serve the dual function of preserving civil liberties and promoting public health. The author concludes by suggesting several ways of bolstering protection against potential breaches of confidentiality.

Harold Edgar and Hazel Sandomire. "Medical Privacy in the Age of AIDS: Legislative Options." *American Journal of Law and Medicine*, 1990, *16*, 157.

To encourage voluntary HIV testing, state legislatures have promised confidentiality of HIV-related medical records along with protection from discrimination based on HIV seropositivity. However, neither can be granted without affecting others, whose interests range from those of a sexual partner to those of an insurer. Politics and practicality prevent absolute protection of records from unauthorized disclosure and of individuals from discrimination, the authors write. This lengthy article, part of a symposium on the Harvard Model AIDS Legislation Project, surveys the state legislation enacted at the time of its writing. In analyzing the state statutes, they agree that individual rights to medical privacy must be given maximum protection and that discrimination against those with AIDS should be prohibited. Yet, they write, these broad policy views fail to address the hundreds of issues that much of the legal literature ignores.

Lawrence O. Gostin and others. *Legislative Survey of State Confidentiality Laws, with Specific Emphasis on HIV and Immunization.* Washington, D.C.: U.S. Centers for Disease Control and Prevention, 1997, 346 pages.

This report examines state and federal law protecting the confidentiality of health information. It focuses on four areas: public information held by the government, privately held health care information, HIV and AIDS-related information, and immunization information. The report reviews privacy safeguards under both federal and state law to determine whether they are consistent with effective health policy.

Lawrence O. Gostin and James G. Hodge, Jr. "Piercing the Veil of Secrecy in HIV/AIDS and Other Sexually Transmitted Diseases: Theories of Privacy and Disclosure in Partner Notification." *Duke Journal of Gender Law and Policy*, Spring 1998, *5*, 9.

The lead article in a symposium issue entitled HIV Law and Policy: Ensuring Gender-Equitable Reform, this lengthy essay examines the legal interests involved with partner notification, particularly contact tracing. The governmental interests in contact tracing are discussed by framing the constitutional and statutory justifications for contact tracing from the state and federal perspectives. Arguments concerning the infected individual's constitutional, statutory, and common law interests in privacy are discussed along with antidiscrimination protections for persons infected with sexually transmitted diseases—particularly those infected with HIV. The authors propose alternative models for partner notification.

Joni N. Gray and others. *Ethical and Legal Issues in AIDS Research*. Baltimore: Johns Hopkins University Press, 1995, 200 pages.

Summarizes relevant federal regulations and case law that are a resource for attorneys wishing to give advice in this area. The concepts advanced by the authors—for example, that a researcher must consciously seek ways to minimize the intrusiveness of his or her research and plan the research to avoid possible threats to confidentiality—are applicable to psychosocial research generally.

Martin Gunderson, David J. Mayo, and Frank S. Rhame. *AIDS: Testing and Privacy*. Salt Lake City: University of Utah Press, 1989, 241 pages.

This book is the second in a series analyzing ethical issues in technology and science. Part one of the book provides the background of AIDS testing and evaluates four features of testing proposals: voluntariness, distribution of results, uses of testing, and target groups. The authors then discuss those features as they impinge on privacy laws and related doctrines, particularly the Thirteenth and Fourteenth Amendments. The authors conclude with an examination of a number of practical situations in which privacy concerns arise, such as reporting laws, contact tracing, and state- or employer-mandated testing.

Kenneth E. Labowitz. "Beyond Tarasoff: AIDS and the Obligation to Breach Confidentiality." *St. Louis University Public Law Review*, 1990, *9*, 495.

This article develops a legal foundation upon which claims may be advanced for medical negligence against health care providers who, learning of a patient's HIV diagnosis, fail to warn foreseeable persons who are at high risk of being infected through patient contacts.

J. Stryker. "The Legal Limits of AIDS Confidentiality." *Journal of the American Medical Association*, 1988, *260*, 3273.

The author writes that if the legal protections of confidentiality are illusory, they should be shored up, not abandoned. Most third parties, he writes, have no "right to know" about an AIDS diagnosis, other than members of the patient's health care team or the spouse or sexual partner of the infected individual.

David M. Studdert. "Direct Contracts, Data Sharing, and Employee Risk Selection: New Stakes for Patient Privacy in Tomorrow's Health Insurance Markets." *American Journal of Law and Medicine*, 1999, *25*, 233.

Examines potential contracting arrangements in health care systems. The author analyzes how direct contracting arrangements between employer-purchasers of health insurance and provider-sponsored organizations could affect the transfer of medical information, and the kinds of privacy concern such information exchanges could entail.

19.03   **ISSUES RELATING TO HEALTH CARE PROFESSIONALS WITH AIDS OR HIV INFECTION**

19.03(1)   **Risk of Transmission**

Annot. "Transmission or Risk of Transmission of Human Immunodeficiency Virus (HIV) or Acquired Immunodeficiency Syndrome (AIDS) as Basis for Prosecution or Sentencing in Criminal or Military Discipline Case." *ALR5th*, 1998, *13*, 628.

> Criminal liability and punishment based on infecting another with the AIDS virus, or on the risk of doing so, is the subject of this annotation. In *State* v. *Farmer*, 805 P.2d 200 (Wash. 1991), 13 *ALR5th* 1070, the court decided that although the defendant was erroneously required to undergo an HIV blood test prior to his sentencing for offenses involving sexual conduct with juvenile prostitutes, other evidence that he knew he had AIDS at the time of the offenses was properly relied on by the trial judge as an aggravating circumstance in determining the sentence.
>
> Other state and federal cases have considered issues relating to HIV blood testing and using test results in criminal prosecutions, the various criminal offenses under which conduct allegedly threatening to transmit HIV has been prosecuted, and sentencing issues involving AIDS. The annotation also discusses disciplinary cases from the military courts, which fall into many of the same general categories as the criminal court cases but differ from them in the application of military standards of conduct, the prevalence of HIV testing among military personnel, and the fact that most of the cases have involved consensual sexual conduct.

Michael L. Closen. "A Call for Mandatory HIV Testing and Restriction of Certain Health Care Professionals." *St. Louis University Public Law Review*, 1990, *9*, 421.

> Argues that physicians, nurses, emergency medical technicians, and other health care professionals who wish to continue to engage in direct patient contact of a physically invasive nature—which is defined here as involving the risk of transmission of blood from the professional to the patient—should be required to submit to HIV testing.

Michelle Wilcox DeBarge. "The Performance of Invasive Procedures by HIV-Infected Doctors: The Duty to Disclose under the Informed Consent Doctrine." (Note.) *Connecticut Law Review*, 1993, *25*, 991.

> Contends that performance of invasive procedures by HIV-infected physicians poses a risk of HIV infection to the patient; therefore, under the doctrine of informed consent, doctors should be required to disclose their HIV status.

Jody B. Gabel. "Liability for 'Knowing' Transmission of HIV: The Evolution of a Duty to Disclose." (Comment.) *Florida State University Law Review*, 1994, *21*, 981.

> This article argues that a duty to disclose applies to HIV-positive health professionals who perform exposure-prone procedures.

Carol J. Gerner. "AIDS in the Healthcare Workplace: Rights and Responsibilities." *Annals of Health Law*, 1992, *1*, 119.

> This article states that with the increasing spread of AIDS and HIV, courts are confronted with the task of balancing the need of public disclosure of a health care worker's HIV status against that individual's right to privacy.

Donald H. J. Hermann. "Criminalizing Conduct Related to HIV Transmission." *St. Louis University Public Law Review*, 1990, *9*, 351.

Examines the arguments for and against using criminal sanctions as a means of reducing transmission of HIV by those who, with a culpable state of mind, engage in conduct likely to transmit the virus. This article suggests that traditional notions of crime are ineffective and inappropriate in dealing with culpable conduct likely to transmit HIV, and that HIV-specific criminal statutes will best serve the objectives of those who see merit in criminalizing conduct related to HIV transmission.

Scott H. Isaacman. "The Other Side of the Coin: HIV-Infected Health Care Workers." *St. Louis University Public Law Review,* 1990, 9, 439.

Concludes that a review of policies from numerous sources fails to indicate a clear hazard to patients posed by health care workers infected with HIV/AIDS. The policies reveal legitimate concern that a transmission risk might exist where health care workers perform invasive procedures. Little basis exists to formulate a definitive approach to health care workers with HIV/AIDS, Isaacman writes. A blanket policy for all health care workers is unwarranted under any analysis.

Mark Carl Rom. *Fatal Extraction: The Story Behind the Florida Dentist Accused of Infecting His Patients with HIV and Poisoning Public Health.* San Francisco: Jossey-Bass, 1997, 226 pages.

The author, the principal investigator of the GAO's investigation of the case, presents an account of the CDC's study of the matter and of the brief and inglorious career of iatrogenic HIV infection as a major national issue.

19.03(2) Employment Laws: Legal Protections for Employees with HIV

19.03(2)(a) Prohibition Based on Handicap

Scott Burris, Harlon L. Dalton, and Judith L. Miller. *AIDS Law Today: A New Guide for the Public.* New Haven: Yale University Press, 1993.

Covers testing, disclosure and right to privacy, HIV screening and discrimination, private sector responses to HIV, and HIV in the health care and insurance systems. The book concludes with a list of contributors and an index.

Walter B. Connolly, Jr., and Alison B. Marshall. "An Employer's Legal Guide to AIDS in the Workplace." *St. Louis University Public Law Review,* 1990, 9, 561.

Addresses some of the legal issues confronting employers as a result of the spread of AIDS; attempts to offer guidance for employers. This article focuses primarily on federal statutes and case law.

Wendy E. Parmet. "The Supreme Court Confronts HIV: Reflections on *Bragdon* v. *Abbott.*" *Journal of Law, Medicine, and Ethics,* 1998, 26, 205.

Examines in depth the Supreme Court's decision concerning the application of the Americans With Disabilities Act to HIV; explains why the ruling was even necessary, and what the decision says about the relationship between law and public health.

19.03(2)(b) General Duty of Employer to Deal Fairly

Norman Daniels. "HIV-infected Health Care Professionals: Public Threat or Public Sacrifice." *Milbank Quarterly,* 1992, 70, 3–42.

The ethical controversy surrounding the CDC and AMA guidelines for restricting the practice of HIV-infected health professionals appears to hinge on whether we give priority to the rights of infected workers or those of patients. We cannot simply dismiss the concerns of patients as irrational, despite the low risks of transmission, the author writes. Nor can we avoid the dispute about rights by claiming with the AMA that professionals have obligations to refrain from imposing "identifiable risks," however low, on patients. Nevertheless, allowing the full exercise of patient rights, either by giving patients the opportunity to know the risks they face and to switch providers or by removing infected providers (compulsory switching), would make each of us worse off. This gives us adequate reason to reject these guidelines and to emphasize other infection control measures.

John F. Dudley. "The Medical Costs of AIDS: Abandoning the HIV-Infected Employee." (Comment.) *Duquesne Law Review*, 1992, *30*, 915.

This student-written article examines *McGann* v. *H&H Music Co.*, 946 F.2d 401 (5th Cir. 1991), in the context of the preemptive effect of ERISA.

Leonard H. Glantz, Wendy K. Mariner, and George J. Annas. "Risky Business: Setting Public Health Policy for HIV-infected Health Care Professionals." *Milbank Quarterly*, 1992, *70*, 43–80.

Analysis of the restrictive proposals provoked by the case of Kimberly Bergalis and four other patients apparently infected with HIV during the course of dental treatment reveals that they resulted from inability to evaluate appropriately the infinitesimal risk of HIV transmission from practitioner to patient. The proposals also resulted from an effort to create risk prevention policy without appreciating the distinction between regulating things or procedures, which have no human rights, and regulating people, who have rights that should not be infringed without serious justification. This analysis demonstrates, the authors contend, that the proposed restrictive policies are not justified because they do nothing to prevent the spread of HIV, and they cause unnecessary and substantial harm to health care practitioners.

Irwin R. Karassik and Susan V. Kayser. "AIDS and the Health Care Provider." *Health Lawyer*, Spring 1992, *6*, 15.

Examines trends and developments concerning patients' rights of privacy and confidentiality, the duty to warn third parties of the potential danger, the employment rights of those testing HIV-positive, and the rights of patients and health care workers who come into contact with those with AIDS.

19.03(2)(c)   Other Sources of Employment Rights

Annot. "Rescission or Cancellation of Insurance Policy for Insured's Misrepresentation or Concealment of Information Concerning Human Immunodeficiency Virus (HIV), Acquired Immunodeficiency Syndrome (AIDS), or Related Health Problems." *ALR5th*, 1998, *15*, 92.

Insurers may avoid coverage when an insured has made material misrepresentation in applying for insurance. The question turns on whether a particular response to an application question was indeed misrepresentation; if so, was it material to the risk assumed by the insurer? The problem may arise in numerous circumstances, but this annotation focuses on responses made by insured people with regard to their having AIDS, HIV, or similar conditions. Although in some cases it has been found that coverage was voided because the insured concealed or misrepresented the true state of his health with regard to such conditions and that the insurer would not have issued the policy had it been aware of the insured's actual condition, under other circumstances rescission or cancellation of the policy has not been permitted, as in *Waxse* v. *Reserve Life Ins. Co.*, 809 P.2d 533 (Kan. 1991), 15 ALR5th 996, where it was found that the response to the pertinent question, as propounded, did not constitute material misrepresentation warranting rescission of the policy.

Sean C. Doyle. "HIV-Positive, Equal Protection Negative." (Note.) *Georgetown Law Journal*, 1992, *81*, 375.

Examines the extent to which traditional equal protection jurisprudence and the Supreme Court will protect individual rights when policy makers attempt to control the spread of AIDS by restricting the duties of HIV-positive health care workers posing no actual threat to their patients. The author concludes that, because the Court is likely to afford substantial deference to the classifications developed by state actors, the equal protection clause will do little to protect individual rights in most cases.

Jennifer Hertz. "Physicians with AIDS: A Proposal for Efficient Disclosure." (Comment.) *University of Chicago Law Review,* 1992, *59, 749.*

Argues that economic analysis suggests courts should require hospitals to disclose their physician-employees' HIV status only if the benefit in reducing expected accident costs is greater than the costs of notification. In other words, hospitals should be allowed or required to perform look-backs when the cost of accidents prevented by look-back, multiplied by the probability of an accident occurring, exceeds the costs incurred as a result of the look-backs. Hertz concludes that each look-back decision should balance all costs to the individual and society against the benefits of disclosure.

Ryan J. Rohlfsen. "HIV-Infected Surgical Personnel under the ADA: Do They Pose a Direct Threat or Are Reasonable Accommodations Possible?" *Journal of Contemporary Health Law and Policy,* 1999, *16, 127.*

Environmental Concerns Affecting Health Care Facilities

Environmental laws have subdivided the universe of waste into a variety of categories for purposes of regulation: hazardous waste, infectious waste, municipal solid waste, and radioactive waste. In theory, the categories denote differing degrees of risk to the environment and public health and consequently necessitate different treatment and disposal. It is essential to appropriately identify and categorize waste to achieve regulatory compliance.

The annotations that follow examine these various subtypes of waste along with treatment and disposal options.

ANNOTATIONS

20.01 IN GENERAL

American Bar Association, Natural Resources, Energy, and Environmental Law Section. *Environmental Law Manual.* Chicago: ABA, 1992, 520 pages.

> Offers a comprehensive guide to working effectively with the EPA, current developments in regulatory areas, business transactions and compliance, enforcement actions, and citizen suits.

American Bar Association, Natural Resources, Energy, and Environmental Law Section. *The RCRA Practice Manual.* Chicago: ABA, 1994, 272 pages.

> This manual is designed to make the Resource Conservation and Recovery Act more comprehensible to the practitioner. Its chapters are written by experts in the field to give attorneys and environmental managers better understanding of the meaning and practical implications of the law.

Annot. "Tort Liability for Pollution from Underground Storage Tanks." *ALR5th,* 1998, *5,* 1.

> Collects and analyzes cases in which tort liability was alleged because of contamination caused by leaking underground storage tanks. Chemical substances, such as gasoline, leaking from underground storage tanks can migrate through underground geological formations and contaminate water supplies used for agricultural, household, or other purposes. As demonstrated in *Cornell* v. *Exxon Corp.,* 558 N.Y.S.2d 647 (N.Y. App. Div., 3d Dept. 1990), 5 *ALR5th* 1053, which involved contamination of a household water well by leakage of gasoline from underground storage tanks at a nearby service station, there can be tort liability for injuries to persons or property. In that case, the plaintiffs had causes of action based on negligence and nuisance because of alleged personal injuries caused by exposure to contaminated well water and because of alleged injuries to property.

Center for Healthcare Environmental Management. *Healthcare Environmental Management System.* Plymouth Meeting, Pa.: CHEM, 1998.

This is a three-volume reference and management resource that offers guidance for all aspects of health care safety and environmental compliance issues. It contains complete compliance plans and sample policies, analyses, the full text of pertinent regulations, self-assessment question-naires, procedures, and forms. It also supplies information on handling waste management issues, managing hazardous substances and situations, reducing occupational health risks, organizing a compliance program, and regulatory interpretation. This manual of approximately fifteen hundred pages is continuously updated.

Lydia B. Duff. "Environmental Concerns Affecting Health Care Facilities." In Michael G. Macdonald and others (ed.), *Treatise on Health Care Law, Vol. 2.* New York: Matthew Bender, 1995.

Presents a succinct, highly organized examination of the subject. Topics include regulated med-ical waste, dispersal technologies, water supply, air toxics, and the Emergency Planning and Com-munity Right-to-Know Act. The seventy-one-page article concludes with a glossary of relevant environmental terminology and a list of pertinent state statutes.

Health Care Facilities Guide. Washington, D.C.: Bureau of National Affairs, 1997.

This is a three-volume reference work that explains environmental and worker safety and health regulations affecting health care facilities. It discusses such aspects of these fields as safety and health programs, safety hazards, chemical hazards, infectious disease, laboratory standards, waste and hazardous materials, record keeping, and reporting. Updates are issued monthly and include a summary of changes in updated material and a newsletter reviewing current developments. This exhaustive work includes chapters describing federal requirements along with those of each of the fifty states. It concludes with a chart comparing state program requirements.

Jennifer Hernandez. *Environmental Health and Safety Compliance: A Practical Guide for Health Care, Medical, and Laboratory Facilities.* Sacramento: California Healthcare Associ-ation, 1996.

Begins by explaining the most common statutory and regulatory mechanisms associated with spe-cific legal standards: permits, registrations, formal plans, personal safety, operational mandates, record keeping, reporting, fees and taxes, and penalties. Written by an environmental attorney, this guide then turns to more specific areas of concern, including hazardous waste, radioactive mate-rials, biohazardous materials, pharmaceuticals, and medical facility siting and design. The text also includes environmental, health, and safety audit performance standards adopted by the Joint Commission.

Mark Latham. "Maintaining Confidentiality of Environmental Audits: Legal Protections." *Journal of Health and Hospital Law,* 1996, *29,* 20–26.

Presents an overview of the legally recognized measures available to protect environmental audits from compelled disclosure, including review of emerging state statutes that have specifically been enacted to prevent disclosure. In addition, this article explores federal developments that may pro-vide a recognized privilege for environmental audits. Practical steps are also presented to assist a health care facility in protecting, to the extent possible, the confidentiality of its environmental audits.

Because of the many environmental concerns associated with daily operation of health care facilities and the potential for associated liabilities, health care facilities are increasingly the focus of environmental audits. Given the wave of mergers, acquisitions, and affiliations currently sweep-ing through the health care industry, the author writes, perhaps the greatest use of environmental audits is in exercising due diligence, which is routinely a part of these transactions.

An environmental audit will generally contain a full and frank discussion of any environmental concerns identified, including compliance with all applicable federal, state, and local environmental statutes, regulations, and ordinances. It is therefore imperative that findings remain confidential to the maximum extent allowed by law. Disclosing highly sensitive information about the environmental compliance status of a health care facility can have significant adverse ramifications on the facility, by (1) giving state and federal regulators a valuable source of evidence in a civil suit or criminal prosecution, (2) providing information for suits initiated by citizens groups or toxic-tort plaintiffs, and (3) generating embarrassing publicity about violations that may be a threat to human health or the environment. This type of negative publicity can be particularly damaging to the reputation of health care facilities that are devoted to, among other things, maintaining and promoting human health. For health care facilities that choose to conduct environmental audits, there are fortunately a number of measures available to protect confidentiality and to minimize the risk of compelled disclosure.

Karen J. Nardi and others. "Environmental Issues and Health Care." *Whittier Law Review,* 1995, *16,* 1069–1084.

Reviews the many aspects of what "waste" is composed of, how it is handled, and some of the federal and California state regulations applicable to it.

C. Elizabeth O'Keeffe. "Health Care Institutional Planning for Civil and Criminal Enforcement of Environmental Law in the 1990s." *Journal of Health and Hospital Law,* 1996, *29,* 1–6.

Although health care organizations face exposure to civil liability under a variety of environmental laws, this article focuses primarily on liability under the Comprehensive Environmental Response, Compensation and Liability Act of 1980 (CERCLA), better known as Superfund. It then addresses how corporate executives, including health care managers, are increasingly vulnerable to criminal prosecution for violating other environmental laws.

John-Mark Stensvaag. *Hazardous Waste Law and Practice.* Gaithersburg, Md.: Aspen, 1999.

This two-volume treatise has become a standard work in the field. Regularly updated, it is organized (and the material presented) for the user rather than the academic. Frequent cross-references, an extensive index, and user guides to specific sections make it an efficient and usable resource. In readable prose, accompanied where necessary by helpful diagrams and flowcharts, Stensvaag lays out category by category and element by element the numerous components of statutory and regulatory definitions of hazardous waste. He also discusses nuances of the evolving definitions and traces the implications of minor changes in meaning or interpretation.

Norman G. Tabler, Jr. "Implementing Environmental Compliance: The Role of Attorney-Client Privilege." *Journal of Health and Hospital Law,* 1996, *28,* 27–29.

Examines attorney-client privilege in the context of the environmental audit. The author, a practicing attorney, presents a practical overview of the privilege and then supplies a list of suggestions for maximizing its value. These include having the hospital board formally authorize the self-audit, staffing the audit with outside counsel, using a form audit instruction sheet, instructing an attorney to prepare the audit report, and restricting distribution of the report.

Mark S. Zemelman. "Environmental Compliance for Hospitals: A Practical Guide." *Journal of Health and Hospital Law,* 1996, *29,* 7–13.

Written by an attorney for Kaiser Permanente, this article details the wide range of environmental, health, and safety risks present in hospitals and the statutes and regulations that govern their management. The author notes that, in his experience, compliance with these rules requires more than common sense because many of these risks, as defined in federal and state law, are not intuitively obvious. He divides his discussion among the topics of hazardous waste management, medical waste management, underground storage tanks, asbestos, ethylene oxide, and pesticides.

20.02 WASTE

Clark, Boardman, Callaghan. *Medical Waste Handbook*. Deerfield, Ill.: Clark, Boardman, Callaghan, 1993, 700 pages.

Supplies an in-depth review of the various federal statutes and regulations that govern medical waste, including OSHA, the Clean Air Act, and Department of Transportation regulations. The work covers the business and financial issues that affect operations within the medical waste industry. This text offers a detailed summary of the various methods used by individual states to regulate handling, treating, transporting, and disposing of medical waste. It also contains valuable appendices, including complete texts of significant federal and state regulations, as well as a list of state regulatory agencies, contact persons, addresses, and phone numbers. This is an excellent resource.

Patricia A. Younger and Cynthia Conner. *Hospital Waste Management*. Gaithersburg, Md.: Aspen, 1993.

Classifies solid waste into four subcategories: hazardous waste, medical waste, infectious waste, and radioactive waste. It then examines each through the requirements of the relevant statutes, including the Resource Conservation and Recovery Act (RCRA); the Hazardous and Solid Waste Amendments of 1984 (HSWA); the Comprehensive Environmental Response, Compensation, and Liability Act (CERCLA); the Clean Air Act; the Clean Water Act; the Toxic Substances Control Act (TSCA); and the Medical Waste Tracking Act of 1988 (MWTA). Regularly updated.

20.02(1) In General

American Bar Association, Natural Resources, Energy, and Environmental Law Section. *RCRA Policy Documents: Finding Your Way Through the Maze of EPA Guidance on Solid and Hazardous Wastes*. Chicago: ABA, 1993, 520 pages.

Assembles for the first time in one volume recent EPA listings of its unpublished internal RCRA-related guidance documents, and explains how to locate and obtain needed documents.

Michael B. Gerrard. "Fear and Loathing in the Siting of Hazardous and Radioactive Waste Facilities: A Comprehensive Approach to a Misperceived Crisis." *Tulane Law Review*, 1994, 68, 1047.

Examines the failure of federal and state statutes designed to create new facilities for disposing of hazardous waste, including medical waste. In this 170-page article, the author, a practicing attorney and professor of law, argues that siting laws are based on a fundamental conceptual error as well as several factual mistakes and policy blunders.

20.02(2) Regulated Medical Waste

20.02(2)(a) Terminology

David S. Freeman, Gregory H. Siskind, and Sharon O. Jacobs. *Medical Waste Handbook*. Deerfield, Ill.: Clark, Boardman, Callaghan, 1999, 1,830 pages.

Describes legal aspects that govern handling, transporting, treating, and disposing of regulated medical waste, along with business and financial issues that affect operations within the industry and potential regulatory developments. It assists the reader in fully understanding the diverse federal regulatory and agency structures, reviews relevant provisions of key federal statutes (especially RCRA and the Clean Air Act), and includes coverage of state statutory and regulatory material.

Michael L. Garvin. *Infectious Waste Management: A Practical Guide.* Ann Arbor, Mich.: Lewis, 1995, 166 pages.

Aims at assisting hospitals in establishing or revising infectious waste management programs. Topics addressed include defining infectious waste; administration committees; the role of department directors; and educating administration, department directors, and staff. The book, which is written by a hospital administrator, concludes with fifteen helpful appendices and an index.

Kamrin T. MacKnight. "The Problems of Medical and Infectious Waste." *Environmental Law,* 1993, *23,* 785.

The author, an attorney with a doctorate in microbiology, contends that the problem of medical waste must be viewed as only one part of the crisis in waste management. Although regulating hospital waste is appropriate, attention should focus on larger sources of improperly disposed infectious waste: homes, illegal drug users, and smaller clinics. Further, the public should realize that the victims of improper waste management and disposal are primarily health care workers rather than the public at large.

William A. Rutala and David J. Weber. "Infectious Waste—Mismatch Between Science and Policy." *New England Journal of Medicine,* Aug. 22, 1991, *325,* 578–582.

Defines and characterizes medical waste, assesses its public health implications, evaluates waste management practices, and examines federal legislation in this area that could have an impact on health care providers. The authors conclude by criticizing the Medical Waste Tracking Act because of what they view as extraordinary increases in cost associated with the act, with no environmental or public health benefit.

20.02(2)(b)   Regulating Agencies

Laura Carlan Battle. "Regulation of Medical Waste in the United States." *Pace Environmental Law Review,* 1994, *11,* 517.

Discusses varied laws and policies governing treatment, handling, and disposal of medical waste in the United States. When wash-ups of syringes and medical vials closed northeastern beaches in the early 1990s, public outcry galvanized Congress to pass the Medical Waste Treatment Act. Congress directed the EPA to investigate whether medical waste should be treated as hazardous or solid waste and whether a federal regulatory scheme is warranted. In this article, the author explores the ongoing debate about risks associated with exposure to medical waste and the ramifications of our current fragmented regulatory approach.

John J. O'Connell. "Reconstructive Surgery on Medical Waste Management." (Comment.) *Iowa Law Review,* 1992, *77,* 1855.

Addresses the benefits and shortcomings of governmental regulation of medical waste, and offers possible methods to resolve these shortcomings. This comment begins with review of the substantive requirements of current governmental regulations regarding medical waste. It then analyzes problems arising under these regulations and appraises some of the suggested solutions to the problems. Finally, it offers suggestions for future regulations that would curb the hazards of medical waste.

Michael R. Shumaker. "Infectious Waste: A Guide to State Regulation and a Cry for Federal Intervention." (Comment.) *Notre Dame Law Review,* 1990, *66,* 555.

Examines the variation, in state definitions, of the term *infectious waste.* Shumaker then reviews the consequences of this inconsistency and concludes that federal regulation of infectious waste management, establishing minimum regulations and a set definition of infectious waste, would bring uniformity to the industry. Federal regulation in the areas of packaging, storage, treatment, and disposal would result in all state generators and infectious waste handlers being in national conformity, he argues, thereby increasing protection for the public and for health care workers. The regulation that the author advocates would permit states to enforce more rigorous regulations if they so choose.

20.02(2)(c) Medical Waste Tracking Act

Susan Onel. "The Medical Waste Tracking Act of 1988: Will It Protect Our Beaches?" (Comment.) *Virginia Environmental Law Journal*, 1989, 9, 225.

Examines whether the MWTA was an effective response to the problem of medical waste. This comment focuses on the debate over the bill, which was dominated by three often contradictory views. The Natural Resources Defense Council, the American Hospital Association, and private parties engaged in the waste disposal industry each expressed conflicting views over defining the term *infectious waste,* the role of the EPA, and the degree of federal involvement; and over the need for a tracking system to analyze the overall effectiveness of the MWTA. Onel analyzes the arguments propounded by each group, using their divergent positions to illustrate the shortcomings of the act, which resulted from political expedience and hasty passage.

20.02(2)(d) Segregation, Packaging, and Labeling of Medical Waste

Occupational Safety and Health Administration. "Bloodborne Pathogens Rules and Regulations." 29 CFR 1910.1030 (set forth in *Federal Register*, Oct. 6, 1991, *58*, 235).

These rules were promulgated to reduce the spread of hepatitis B virus and HIV. They mandate use of protective equipment, housekeeping procedures, and training requirements for laboratory and other personnel.

William Tutala and others. "Management of Infectious Waste by U.S. Hospitals." *Journal of the American Medical Association*, 1991, *262*, 1639.

This article analyzes the responses of randomly selected U.S. hospitals to a questionnaire intended to identify their waste disposal practices. Responses were received from hospitals in forty-eight states. U.S. hospitals generated a median of 6.93 kg of hospital waste per patient per day, and infectious waste made up 15 percent of the total hospital waste. Approximately 82 percent of the surveyed hospitals are discarding waste in accordance with CDC recommendations; the compliance rate for the EPA's recommendations is 75 percent.

20.02(2)(e) Disposal Techniques

Michael L. Garvin. "Waste Disposal Costs Show Wide Variations from State to State." *Modern Healthcare's Facilities Operations and Management*, Mar. 18, 1991.

Surveys five states with widely varying degrees of air quality regulations to determine the equipment needed to meet the state's air quality standards.

Michael L. Garvin. "Which Waste Treatment Option Is Best for You?" *Health Facilities Management*, Apr. 1991.

Examines the various merits and problems associated with incineration, steam sterilization, microwaving, chemical disinfection, and off-site disposal of medical wastes.

Michael G. Malloy. "Medical Waste Comes of Age." *Waste Age*, July 1997, 55.

Maintains that the business of managing medical waste changed significantly in just one year's time. With the EPA having put in place a rule that curtails 50–80 percent of on-site burning of medical waste at hospitals and a number of maturing technologies coming to market, the medical waste industry has evolved into a mature market. The medical waste industry is concerned about final implementation of the U.S. Transportation Department Hazardous Materials (HM) 181 rule, which took effect in 1996, extending it to intrastate as well as interstate waste movement. HM-181 requires Packaging Group II standards for cultures and stocks, which results in using more expensive containers than those ordinarily required. This is a helpful overview of the medical waste industry at present.

Michael G. Malloy. "Medical Waste. Part II: Alternative Medical Waste Technologies Poised for Takeoff." *Waste Age*, Aug. 1997, 85.

Asserts that for so-called "alternative" medical waste treatment technologies—those that do not burn medical waste but treat it by a variety of systems—the EPA's scheduled implementation of a new rule to curtail nine key incineration-related pollutants could not have come at a better time. The implementation has been the key point of growth for most alternative systems because it will require hospitals to invest as much as $500,000 if they seek to retrofit aging incinerators with enough pollution controls to meet the standard. The article is supplemented by a helpful table setting forth vendors in the field, the number of years of medical waste experience, waste type, and treatment cost.

Eric Weissenstein. "Hospitals Likely to Shift Disposal Approach." *Modern Healthcare*, Feb. 24, 1992.

Reports that rising costs and the heavy burden of the Clean Air Act of 1991 will result in a shift away from incineration and toward alternative technologies.

20.02(2)(e)(i)   Incineration

Committee on Health Effects of Waste Incineration of the National Research Council. *Waste Incineration and Public Health*. Washington, D.C.: National Academy Press, 1998, 315 pages.

Incineration has been used widely for disposal of medical, household, and hazardous waste, but there is increasing public concern over the benefits of combusting the waste versus the health risk from pollutants emitted during combustion. This book informed the debate, with the most up-to-date information available on incineration, pollution, and human health—along with expert conclusions and recommendations for further research and improvement in such areas as risk communication. The committee gives details on processes involved in incineration and how contaminants are released, environmental dynamics of contaminants and routes to human exposure, tools and approaches for assessing possible human health effects, and scientific concerns pertinent to future regulatory actions. The book also examines some of the social, psychological, and economic factors that affect the communities where incineration takes place and addresses the problem of uncertainty and variation in predicting the health effects of incineration processes.

"Health Care Without Harm, Model State Regulations for Medical Waste Incinerators." Apr. 1998. (Available at www.noharm.org)

Nationally, medical waste incinerators (MWIs) are the third leading source of dioxin and the fourth leading source of mercury, according to the EPA. Dioxin is a known human carcinogen that has been linked to reproductive and developmental disorders as well as immune system damage. Mercury is a neurotoxin that interferes with brain development of unborn children and infants. This lengthy report details state plans to implement new federal rules for MWIs. In summary, it contends that the EPA's standards and guidelines should be strengthened. Health Care Without Harm, an organization comprising more than 170 health and environmental groups, maintains that more stringent emissions standards are feasible, and that the standards can be attained through reducing the volume and toxicity of the hospital waste stream, in addition to requiring more pollution control equipment.

Mary Chris Jaklevic. "Incinerator Emissions Rules Cause Dispute over Methodology and Risk." *Modern Healthcare*, Feb. 13, 1995, 18.

This brief article examines the dispute between the EPA and the AHA over the EPA's proposed incinerator regulations.

Leslie Anderson Morales. *Managing Medical Wastes: A Bibliography of the Periodical Literature, 1987-1989.* Monticello, Ill.: Vance Bibliographies, 1990.

Compiles articles from medical, technical, and business literature on the topic.

A. W. Reitze, Jr. and M. K. Stagg. "Air Emissions Standards and Guidelines under the Clean Air Act for the Incineration of Hospital, Medical, and Infectious Waste." *Environmental Lawyer*, Winter 1998, *28*, 791.

"Standards of Performance for New Stationary Sources and Emission Guidelines for Existing Sources: Medical Waste Incinerators." 60 Fed. Reg. 10,654–10,655 (1995) (codified at 40 C.F.R. Part 60).

In February 1995, under court order the EPA promulgated proposed emission standards governing medical waste incineration. Facilities were afforded three months to comply with its tighter standards. As projected by the EPA in the preamble to the medical waste incinerator standards, the proposed incinerator standards and guidelines, in addition to reducing air pollution from medical waste incinerators by more than 95 percent, will cost the health care industry's existing medical waste incinerators $351 million per year in addition to the $265 million spent annually prior to 1995.

20.02(2)(e)(ii) *Autoclaving*

[Reserved]

20.02(2)(e)(iii) *Landfilling*

[Reserved]

20.02(2)(e)(iv) *Microwaving, Irradiation, and Chemical Disinfection*

Howard J. Young. "Medical Waste Disposal: New Technologies on the Horizon." *Journal of Health and Hospital Law*, Jan.–Feb. 1996, *29*, 14–19.

Contends that as medical waste incineration costs increase thanks to the Environmental Protection Agency's proposed new source performance standards implementing the Clean Air Act Amendments of 1990, and as landfill space decreases, new medical waste disposal technology will become more prevalent. Microwaving, dry heat sterilization, chlorination, and other alternative medical waste disposal technologies may be commonplace within a matter of years. This article, written by a practicing attorney, discusses handling, packaging, and transporting medical waste and the associated health risks. It also explores prevalent medical waste disposal technologies and recent technological advances.

20.03 EMERGENCY PLANNING AND COMMUNITY RIGHT-TO-KNOW ACT (EPCRA)

Allyn Finegold. "Emergency Planning and Community Right-to-Know Act: A Status of State Actions." Washington, D.C.: National Governors' Association, 1997.

Examines the progress of state emergency response commissions (SERCs) in educating the public about chemical risks. This report of approximately one hundred pages supplies examples of state outreach programs and discusses problems facing SERCs in implementing the community right-to-know portion of the law. It also includes a profile of each state's emergency response commission.

James M. Kuszaj. *The EPCRA Compliance Manual: Interpreting and Implementing the Emergency Planning and Community Right-to-Know Act of 1986*. Chicago: American Bar Association, 1997, 880 pages.

Presents a comprehensive review of how the EPA has interpreted and implemented the law and regulations. It sets forth a thorough examination of reporting requirements, including hotline answers, administrative decisions, judicial opinions, EPA correspondence, EPA guidance documents, and personal opinions relating to the EPCRA. Includes a five-step analysis for determining if EPCRA notification and reporting requirements apply to a particular facility.

Krista Green. "An Analysis of the Supreme Court's Resolution of the Emergency Planning and Community Right-To-Know Act Citizen Suit Debate." (Comment.) *Boston College Environmental Affairs Law Review*, 1999, 26, 387.

EPCRA mandates that companies using and storing certain hazardous chemicals file reports with specified local and state groups, disclosing the quantity, type, and location of those chemicals. Those groups use the reports to draft an emergency plan to deal with hazardous chemical releases. EPCRA permits citizens to sue the owners or operators of facilities that fail to file the requisite reports. In interpreting the citizen suit provision, the courts have struggled with whether to permit suits to continue if the alleged violator has cured the violation by filing the reports prior to commencement of the suit. The Supreme Court, in *Steel Co.* v. *Citizens for a Better Environment*, 118 S.Ct. 1003 (1998), resolved a split among the circuit courts of appeals on the issue of "historical" violations in EPCRA citizen suits, holding that the plaintiffs, alleging only historical violations under EPCRA, lacked standing to sue. This Comment argues that the Supreme Court's disposal of the historical violation issue through standing doctrine is potentially far-reaching in consequence and therefore misguided. Nonetheless, because of the policies underlying EPCRA and its current construction, the author agrees with the result, if not the rationale, of the Court.

Michael J. Vahey. "Hazardous Chemical Reporting under EPCRA: The Seventh Circuit Eliminates the 'Better Late Than Never' Excuse from Citizen Suits." (Note.) *Loyola University Chicago Law Journal*, Fall 1997, 29, 225.

This Note addresses the enforcement authority granted to private citizens under EPCRA. It begins with a statutory overview of EPCRA, focusing on its goals and objectives. It then reviews the origins of the citizen suit as a means of environmental regulatory enforcement, exploring how the U.S. Supreme Court has treated such legislation. This background offers perspective for discussion of citizen suits under EPCRA and the conflicting interpretations of the Sixth and Seventh Circuits on this issue.

21

Medical Records and Privacy Issues

The requirement that health care organizations maintain records on each patient is imposed by federal and state statutes and regulations, municipal codes, and the Joint Commission on Accreditation of Healthcare Organizations. Record keeping is also a condition of participation in federal reimbursement programs. Another critical legal function of medical records is to provide essential evidence in defending professional malpractice actions. These actions have statutes of limitation of two to five years depending upon the state, and the hospital record is often the only detailed, contemporaneous account of what occurred during treatment. It is critical, therefore, that documentation set forth in a health care organization's records be as complete and accurate as possible.

Like the regulations that govern their creation, record retention requirements vary widely from state to state. A health care organization should consider a variety of factors in developing a retention policy: statutory and regulatory requirements, statutes of limitation, requirements of the organization's malpractice carrier, the need for the information in teaching and research, storage capabilities, cost of transferring to microfilm or microfiche, computerization and other long-term storage methods, and guidelines issued by this and other health care organizations. The organization must first comply with applicable governmental requirements; it should then examine the other factors set forth here to determine if it should exceed these requirements for some or all records.

The annotations that follow examine recent writing on topics of record generation and retention, as well as privacy issues.

ANNOTATIONS

21.01   IN GENERAL

Mervat Abdelhak and others (eds.). *Health Information: Management of a Strategic Resource.* Philadelphia: Saunders, 1996, 753 pages.

> Focuses on the computer-based patient record in the context of managed care. It includes nineteen chapters by more than thirty contributors. In addition to an introduction to health information management, the book focuses on four areas: health care data, information management and use, management, and health information systems. Among the specific topics addressed are registries, risk management, and legal issues. The book includes a large number of figures and tables, lists of references, bibliographies at the conclusion of each chapter, an index, a glossary, and a table of abbreviations.

American Medical Association and Health Care Financing Administration. "Documentation Guidelines for Evaluation and Management Services." Washington, D.C.: American Health Lawyers Association [Report No. VMM98–0002], 1998, 51 pages.

Offers physicians and claims reviewers advice about preparing and reviewing documentation for evaluation and management services (that is, history, examination, medical decision making, counseling, and coordination of care). Includes examples of documentation and a risk chart.

Briggs W. Andrews. "Medical Records Liability." *Health Lawyer*, Summer 1992, 6(2), 11.

This brief practical article examines risks involving medical records, especially those relating to confidentiality and disclosure issues. Other topics addressed are special problems created by medical record computerization, alteration of medical records, retention and destruction requirements, and transmission of medical records by facsimile machine.

Kristyn S. Appleby and Joanne Tarver. *Medical Records Review.* (2nd ed.) Gaithersburg, Md.: Aspen, 1998, 392 pages.

Discusses medical terminology, common components of medical records, confidentiality issues surrounding medical records, and procedures for obtaining records.

California Healthcare Association. *Records Retention Guide.* Sacramento: California Healthcare Association, 1997.

This reference manual begins with an overview of legal considerations, focusing on such issues as the potential for litigation, computerized records, and microfilm. The second section is a retention index that lists the statutory and regulatory retention requirements unique to each type of health care provider. Recommendations for retention are provided where no laws exist. All records commonly used by health care providers are listed—from administrative personnel and engineering records to laboratory, medical, and pharmaceutical records.

John R. Christiansen. "Fundamentals of the Electronic Medical Record." Washington, D.C.: American Health Lawyers Association [Report No. VHI99–0004], 1999, 31 pages.

Presents the basic concepts behind and the legal environment of the electronic medical record. Includes extensive discussion of and references for applicable federal regulatory materials and recommendations for EMR legal compliance and acquisitions.

Anne M. Dellinger and Joan G. Brannon. "The Law of Health Records in North Carolina." Chapel Hill: University of North Carolina Institute of Government, 1987, 86 pages.

Describes the law that North Carolina health providers must consider when handling medical information. This book is addressed to physicians, clinics, hospitals, health departments, and attorneys who advise health care providers. Section I, "Medical Records," covers most treatment records. Section II, "Mental Health Records," covers the particularly sensitive records generated by treatment of mental illness and substance abuse.

Richard S. Dick, Elaine B. Steen, and Don E. Detmer (eds.). *The Computer-Based Patient Record: An Essential Technology for Health Care.* (3rd ed.) Washington, D.C.: National Academy Press, 1997, 234 pages.

Many industries have aggressively automated data collection, but health care organizations have lagged in moving patients' medical records from paper to computers. In its first edition, this report offered a blueprint for introducing the computer-based patient record nationwide. This revised edition adds new information to the original text, including an appendix examining legal aspects of computer-based patient records and record systems, such as state licensure laws, Medicare regulations, hospital accreditation requirements, patient rights issues, evidentiary issues, confidentiality, and unauthorized access. The book concludes by calling for uniform national standards for patient records maintained by health care institutions, either by federal legislation or, preferably, by developing a uniform state act.

Molla S. Donaldson and Kathleen N. Lohr (eds.). *Health Data in the Information Age: Use, Disclosure, and Privacy.* Washington, D.C.: National Academy Press, 1994, 257 pages.

This Institute of Medicine study advances a number of recommendations related to public disclosure of quality-of-care information and protection of confidentiality of personal health information. Specifically, it recommends that the U.S. Congress move to enact preemptive legislation that will (1) establish a uniform requirement for the assurance of confidentiality and protection of privacy rights for health data; (2) impose penalties for violations of the act, including civil damages, equitable remedies, and attorney's fees where appropriate; (3) provide for enforcement by the government and permit private aggrieved parties to sue; (4) establish that compliance with the act's requirements would be a defense to legal actions based on charges of improper disclosure; and (5) exempt health database organizations from public health reporting laws and compulsory process with respect to person-identifiable health data except for compulsory process initiated by record subjects.

Sabra K. Engelbrecht. "The Importance of Clarifying North Carolina's Corporate Practice of Medicine Doctrine." *Wake Forest Law Review, 33,* 1093–1123.

The corporate practice of medicine doctrine originated to protect against the perceived ills of corporate involvement in health care, including lay control, divided loyalty, and commercialization. Although most states prohibit the corporate practice of medicine, several states have created various exceptions to the doctrine. This lack of uniformity has created uncertainty in the current health care environment. The doctrine renders several cost-reducing organizational reforms unworkable, and therefore its utility should be carefully evaluated, the author writes. She contends that the North Carolina legislature should revise the law, allowing approved corporate practice arrangements, while creating legal safeguards to protect against lay interference in medical decision making.

Steven J. Fox. "Advanced Healthcare Information Systems ('HIS') Licensing Issues." Washington, D.C.: American Health Lawyers Association [Report No. VHI99–0006], 1999, 5 pages.

Briefly outlines health care information licensing issues, including system conflicts, payment terms, and confidentiality and proprietary rights.

James L. Gilbert and others. "Evidence Destruction—Legal Consequences of Spoilation of Records." In Cyril H. Wecht (ed.), *Legal Medicine 1994.* Salem, N.H.: Butterworth Legal, 1995.

Discusses consequences of destruction of records in the context of medical litigation, including court sanctions, professional disciplinary action, criminal penalties, and torts.

Phyllis Forrester Granade. "Electronic Medical Records." Washington, D.C.: American Health Lawyers Association [Report No. VHI98–0011], 1998, 21 pages.

Offers an introduction to electronic medical records and the legal issues associated with their creation, storage, use, and destruction, including discussion of pertinent state and federal law. Also discusses risk management recommendations for electronic medical records.

Karen Shedd Guarino. "Developing a Comprehensive Records Management Plan." *Health Lawyer,* Fall 1994, *7,* 15.

Discusses record creation, distribution, duplication, storage, response to subpoenas, surveillance, and destruction.

Harold L. Hirsh. "Medical Records." In *Legal Medicine.* (3rd ed.) St. Louis: Mosby-Year Book, 1995.

This article addresses the purpose of medical records, standards of record keeping, ownership, access, retention requirements, and auto-authentication of medical records.

Lisa I. Iezzoni (ed.). *Risk Adjustment for Measuring Health Care Outcomes.* Chicago: Health Administration Press, 1994, 422 pages.

Examines the conceptual and methodological issues raised in risk adjustment for studies of medical effectiveness and the outcomes of care. Topics addressed include administrative databases, medical records, validity of risk-adjustment methods, and reliability of risk-adjustment methods.

Karla Kinderman. *Medicolegal Forms with Legal Analysis: Documenting Issues in the Patient-Physician Relationship.* Chicago: American Medical Association, 1999, 223 pages.

Designed to offer physicians guidance and model documentation for the difficult legal issues that they may face in the course of medical practice. Topics covered include patient records, appealing utilization review decisions, protecting patient confidentiality, informed consent, end-of-life issues, and organ donation.

Kathleen Knepper. "The Medical Records Maze: A Construct of Federal Inaction and State Inconsistency." *Journal of Health and Hospital Law,* June 1998, *31,* 114.

Examines the federal and state statutory protections available for medical records. It reviews judicial decisions that have sought to protect those rights in the absence of specific statutory protections. It then considers more directly how and to what extent these rights are protected within the Medicare program and the various Medicaid programs. Next to be analyzed is the manner in which public record statutes affect the disclosure requirements for records that are maintained by public agencies administering the Medicaid and Medicare programs. Finally, the author considers how adding HMOs as third-party payers through government health insurance programs may have implications with respect to these disclosure decisions. In particular, the author posits that the records of Medicaid HMOs should be subject to the open record statutes of the various states.

Robert Mittman and Mary Cain. "The Future of the Internet in Health Care." Oakland: California HealthCare Foundation, 1999, 41 pages.

This study forecasts the following: (1) the driving forces that are pushing use of the Internet in health care are strong and inevitable; (2) like the Internet itself, health care on the Internet will be advanced by the needs of consumers who are hungry for information about their health and for control over the health services they receive; (3) the health care sector, however, is not ready to accommodate the Internet; (4) information systems, organizational structures, incentives, and training will restrain use of the Internet; (5) consumer applications of the Internet—seeking information about health and health care and communicating and creating support groups—will develop fastest, but health care professionals will resist direct electronic connection to patients (for example, through electronic mail); (6) health care organizations will use the Internet as a communications channel and for transmitting information such as computer claims; and (7) Internet use in electronic medical records will attract much attention but will not bring a fundamental breakthrough in medical record keeping.

National Research Council. *For the Record: Protecting Electronic Health Information.* Washington, D.C.: National Academy Press, 1997, 288 pages.

Written by the National Research Council's Committee on Maintaining Privacy and Security in Healthcare Applications of the National Information Infrastructure, this report responds to the health care industry's need for greater guidance in protecting health information that increasingly flows through the national information infrastructure—from patient to provider, payer, analyst, employer, government agency, medical product manufacturer, and beyond. This book makes practical, detailed recommendations for technical and organizational solutions and national-level initiatives.

The report describes two principal kinds of privacy and security concern that stem from the availability of health information in electronic form: the increased potential for inappropriate release of information held by individual organizations (whether by those with access to computerized records or those who break into them) and systemic concerns derived from open and widespread sharing of data among various parties.

The committee reports on the organizational and technological aspects of security management, including basic aspects of security; the effectiveness of technologies for user authentication; access control and encryption; obstacles and incentives in adopting new technologies; and mechanisms for training, monitoring, and enforcement. The book notes the growing interest in electronic medical records; the increased value of health information to providers, payers, researchers, and administrators; and the current legal and regulatory environment for protecting health data.

William H. Roach, Jr., and others. *Medical Records and the Law.* (3rd ed.) Gaithersburg, Md.: Aspen, 1998, 352 pages.

Addresses the fundamental legal issues associated with medical records, including contents, retention, authentication, corrections, and destruction, with a focus on current regulatory requirements, case law, and practical advice. Other chapters discuss access to medical record information, liability for improper disclosure of medical record information, and use of medical records as evidence. Particular legal problems are examined in depth, including documentation of advance directives, inclusion of outside test reports in a medical record, compliance with the Emergency Medical Treatment and Active Labor Act (contained in COBRA), child abuse reporting legislation, and disposition of medical records in a change of ownership or closure.

The authors, practicing attorneys in Chicago, analyze the complex issues regarding AIDS patients' records, among them specific statutory reporting and confidentiality requirements. Likewise, a new chapter devoted to the legal aspects of computerized medical records has been added to keep pace with the evolution of information management in the health care industry. The volume concludes with appendices listing statutes concerning medical records and the discoverability and admissibility of medical staff committee records. This is a well-organized, highly useful resource.

Ronald W. Scott. *Legal Aspects of Documenting Patient Care.* Gaithersburg, Md.: Aspen, 1994, 272 pages.

Discusses using the patient treatment record in a legal proceeding; informed consent; and documenting important aspects of patient care.

Marian E. Silber and Maria Elyse Rabar. "Access to Medical Records." *Health Lawyer,* Midwinter 1996, 8, 10.

Examines case law construing when access may be denied to medical records, reasonable copying charges, and other topics in the context of medical malpractice cases.

Paul V. Stearns. "Access to and Cost of Reproduction of Patient Medical Records: A Comparison of State Laws." *Journal of Legal Medicine,* 2000, 21, 79.

This article examines state statutes and case law regarding the costs of obtaining a copy of, or access to, a patient's medical records. It then examines the concepts of ownership and a right of access in regard to patient records, and whether the patient, the physician, or the hospital retains ownership of a patient's medical records.

Jonathan P. Tomes. *Healthcare Records: A Practical Legal Guide.* Westchester, Ill.: Healthcare Financial Management Association, 1990, 321 pages.

This treatise is a legal guide based on federal and state laws and regulations. The purpose of the book is to assist chief financial officers, hospital administrators, medical professionals, and record managers in coping with the complex requirements of proper record management. This book discusses the major topics in record management from the first question—what constitutes a record—

through the last—how to dispose of it. Each topic begins with an introduction to that area of record management and ends with a compilation of state and federal laws covering the particular aspect of record keeping. Appendices provide supplemental information on such topics as state statutes of limitation, recommended retention periods for hospital records, and the American Medical Association's Confidentiality Statement.

Jonathan P. Tomes. *Healthcare Records Management, Disclosure and Retention: The Complete Legal Guide*. Westchester, Ill.: Healthcare Financial Management Association, 1994, 636 pages.

This manual, written by an attorney, supplies a thorough definition of the types of record kept by a health care facility (including both medical and business records), and gives a state-by-state description of the requirements for maintenance, disclosure, and disposal.

Peter H. W. Van Der Goes, Jr. "Opportunity Lost: Why and How to Improve the HHS-Proposed Legislation Governing Law Enforcement of Medical Records." *Pennsylvania Law Review*, Apr. 1999, *147*, 1009–1067.

Societal, technological, legal, and moral justifications exist for Congress to enact legislation governing law enforcement use of individually identifiable medical information, the author writes. Changes in delivery of health care—combined with changes in collecting, using, and sharing health information—drive the need for changes in how law enforcement obtains access to and uses citizens' health records. Effective law enforcement is essential to a well-ordered and beneficial society, and this role requires law enforcement personnel to use medical information. At the same time, moral and legal principles demand meaningful privacy protection of health information, not just for the benefit of society but for each individual's betterment as well.

The author contends that the DHHS report to Congress "Confidentiality of Individually-Identifiable Health Information" fails to recognize that these two competing issues must be considered jointly when Congress debates privacy legislation for medical records. Although the report acknowledges that changes in health care and technology drive the need for change in many areas of medical record privacy law, and that law enforcement must be able to perform its role as investigator and prosecutor, the report does not adequately address the conflicts between the two aims. Instead, the recommendations on this subject indicate abdication by HHS of its duty to weigh these conflicting aims and create potential reconciliation between them. Rather than getting the balance wrong, HHS simply returned this controversy to Congress, wherein ultimate responsibility for the form and content of future law in this area lies.

21.02   PRIVACY ISSUES

Bartley L. Barefoot. "Enacting a Health Information Confidentiality Law: Can Congress Beat the Deadline?" (Comment.) *North Carolina Law Review*, 1998, *77*, 283.

This comment analyzes the current state of the health information confidentiality debate, identifying areas of consensus as well as points of disagreement that must be resolved if Congress is to enact a comprehensive federal health information law.

David W. Bates. "Commentary: Quality, Costs, Privacy, and Electronic Medical Data." *Journal of Law, Medicine, and Ethics*, Summer/Fall 1997, *25*(2 and 3), 111–112.

Although agreeing that proper confidentiality measures are necessary when handling patient records, the author discusses finding a balance between privacy and the benefits of using patient data to improve quality and control costs.

Elisabeth Belmont. "Re-Engineering for Electronic Medical Record Systems." Washington, D.C.: National Health Lawyers Association [Report No. AM97–0012], 1997, 117 pages.

Examines the legal issues raised by using an electronic medical record system (EMRS) including regulatory compliance, identification of media acceptable for storing patient records, the validity of electronic signatures, ensuring accuracy and reliability of patient records, maintaining confidentiality and security of patient records accessible by computer, ownership of patient data, and contracting with vendors. Belmont also discusses practical strategies for implementing an EMRS and analyzes the corresponding legal issues. The appendix includes the National Research Council's report *For the Record: Protecting Electronic Health Information* and a summary of DHHS recommendations regarding the confidentiality of individually identifiable health information.

Bernadette M. Broccolo. "Ownership of Health Data in the Information Age." Washington, D.C.: American Health Lawyers Association [Report No. VHI98–0008], 1998, 44 pages.

Discusses the electronic future of health care, managing legal and business risks, ownership of data, allocation of ownership, and control of data in contractual relationships. Provides an overview of federal and state regulation of the confidentiality and security of individuals' health information.

Fred H. Cate. *Privacy in the Information Age.* Washington, D.C.: Brookings Institution, 1997.

Examines privacy law in the United States and a number of other countries, finding it fragmented, inconsistent, and offering little privacy regarding health information. In this book of approximately two hundred pages, Cate, a law professor at the University of Indiana at Bloomington, addresses these issues in the context of computerized information. He supplies an overview of the technologies that are provoking the current privacy debate and examines the range of legal issues that these technologies raise.

Carolyn Peddy Courville. "Rationales for the Confidentiality of Psychotherapist-Patient Communications: Testimonial Privilege and the Constitution." (Comment.) *Houston Law Review,* 1998, *35*, 187.

All fifty states have some form of psychotherapist-patient privilege, but no such privilege existed uniformly in federal courts until 1996. This Comment analyzes the U.S. Supreme Court case of *Jaffee* v. *Redmond,* 116 S. Ct. 1923, 1932 (1996), in which the Court created such a privilege. It discusses the rationales, both extraconstitutional and constitutional, used by the Court in reaching its conclusion. It describes the state of federal privilege law after *Jaffee* and summarizes variations in treatment of civil litigants and criminal defendants in state and federal courts. Finally, it concludes that rationales for inadmissibility of psychotherapist-patient communications will continue to be relevant as exceptions to the new federal psychotherapist-patient privilege inevitably develop, and some of the alternative rationales discussed may cover cases falling within the exceptions.

Lisa L. Dahm. *Fifty-State Survey on Patient Health Care Record Confidentiality.* Washington, D.C.: American Health Lawyers Association, 1999 [Book No. WM99–0007]).

This comprehensive survey examines the statutes and recently proposed federal legislation relating to patient health care information; also discusses the potential impact of HIPAA on health care providers.

Lisa L. Dahm. "Fundamentals of Confidentiality and Security." Washington, D.C.: American Health Lawyers Association [Report No. VHI99–0001], 1999, 31 pages.

Presents a working definition of the term "patient health care information," discusses the status of state and federal law and proposed federal legislation, and offers practice tips for advising clients on the importance of protecting patient health care information.

Jill Callahan Dennis. *Privacy and Confidentiality of Health Information.* San Francisco: Jossey-Bass, 2000, 106 pages.

Explores emerging risks to confidentiality and privacy. It describes potential solutions to the most common risks, along with the underlying laws, regulations, ethical codes, and case law that form a legal framework for information—handling and dissemination practices. Also discusses common breaches of confidentiality and why they occur, guidelines for developing policies, and procedures to prevent confidentiality breach. Appendix includes a sample protocol for conducting an internal risk assessment of health information systems, print materials, videos, computer-based training, and Internet-based resources.

Janlori Goldman and Zoe Hudson. *Promoting Health/Protecting Privacy: A Primer.* Oakland: California HealthCare Foundation, 1999, 36 pages.

Health privacy is not yet widely regarded as a core part of the health care reform agenda, which centers on efforts to improve quality of care and access to care. At the same time, medical privacy is a leading concern of consumers, and strong emphasis on quality—coming from purchasers, government, and consumers—continues to drive the demand for patient data. Given these competing priorities, protecting the privacy of personal health information is emerging both as a core issue in information privacy as well as a critical one in health policy. This report recommends that providers (1) review existing policies, (2) review and update existing safeguards, (3) determine when identifiable information is necessary, (4) emphasize confidentiality policies and procedures in employee training, and (5) provide clear notice of confidentiality policies along with the contact information for employees who can answer questions.

Lawrence O. Gostin. "Health Information Privacy." *Cornell Law Review,* 1995, *80,* 515.

Argues that there is no easy resolution of the conflict between the need for information and the need for privacy. Powerful reasons exist for broad collection and use of health data, the author writes. High-quality data are needed to help consumers make informed choices among health plans and providers; to provide more effective clinical care; to assess the quality and cost-effectiveness of health services; to monitor fraud and abuse; to track and evaluate access to health services and patterns of morbidity and mortality among underserved populations; and to research determinants, prevention, and treatment of disease. The law at present neither adequately protects privacy nor ensures fair information practices. Moreover, substantial variability in the law probably impedes developing the kind of information systems envisaged; such systems require access to data in many jurisdictions, each of which has its own legal standards. Gostin concludes by calling for a national health information policy that encourages collecting vast amounts of electronic data while creating uniform rules for handling these data.

Lawrence O. Gostin and others. "Privacy and Security of Personal Information in a New Health Care System." *Journal of the American Medical Association,* 1993, *270,* 2487.

Examines the privacy and security goals for collecting, storing, and using health care information in a changing health care system and the means to attain those goals. The goals are to ensure (1) the integrity of health care data so that information is accurate, complete, and trustworthy; (2) the availability of health data so that authorized persons who need the information for legitimate health purposes have ready access to it; and (3) the privacy of patients so that they can be assured that personal information remains private and will not be disclosed without their knowledge or permission.

The authors conclude by calling for (1) establishment, through preemptive federal legislation, of national privacy safeguards based on fair information practices; (2) establishment of a system of universal identifiers for the health care system, probably other than use of Social Security numbers; (3) issuance of effective security standards and guidance for health care information; (4) establishment of a national data protection and security panel for health information; and (5) establishment of a comprehensive program fostering privacy education and awareness.

Janet Hagey. "Privacy and Confidentiality Practices for Research with Health Information in Canada." *Journal of Law, Medicine, and Ethics,* Summer/Fall 1997, *25*(2 and 3), 130–138.

Presents a structural outline of the Canadian statutes and policies governing access to health information for research purposes at the federal level and in three selected provinces.

Harold L. Hirsh. "Disclosure about Patients." In *Legal Medicine*. (3rd ed.) St. Louis: Mosby-Year Book, 1995, 312–342.

Topics addressed in this article include educational use of patient information; privileged communication; testimonial disclosures; statutory duty to disclose, report, or record; duty to warn; limitations of disclosure; discovery, reasonable, and "legitimate interest" disclosures; torts; professional and hospital licensing laws; and defenses.

James G. Hodge, Jr. "The Intersection of Federal Health Information Privacy and State Administrative Law: The Protection of Individual Health Data and Workers' Compensation." *Administrative Law Review*, 1999, *51*, 117.

Examines issues of health information privacy implicated by workers compensation systems. Explores the privacy implications of health information in workers compensation. The purposes, design, and administration of workers compensation claims are further discussed. Legal protections of personal privacy of health-related information are analyzed through examination of existing federal and state constitutional, statutory, and judicial law, and proposed federal health information privacy regulations.

Marie C. Infante. "Confidentiality of Health Information: 1998 Issues, Approaches, and Applications." Washington, D.C.: American Health Lawyers Association [Report No. VLT98–0012], 1998, 73 pages.

Federally mandated use of the Resident Assessment Instrument (RAI), including the Minimum Data Set (MDS) triggers and Resident Assessment Protocols (RAPS), has propelled federally certified nursing homes to the forefront of policy issues and controversies surrounding the privacy and confidentiality of medical records. Discusses the legal requirements and recommendations regarding health information privacy and security of electronic records. Among the attachments are explanation of implementing the administrative simplification provision of HIPAA; testimony of the HHS secretary before the Senate Committee on Labor and Human Resources, recommending standards on privacy and protection of health information pursuant to HIPAA Section 264; Senator Patrick Leahy's statement introducing the Medical Information Privacy and Security Act and a summary of the bill; and Senator Robert Bennett's proposed Medical Records Confidentiality Act of 1998. Also discusses the nursing home quality assurance privilege. Other attachments include the Pennsylvania Department of Health Long-Term Care Provider Bulletin No. 49, copies of *Commonwealth* v. *Slazinsky,* No. 423 M.D. (Pa. Commw. Ct. May 9, 1997) and *State ex rel. Boone Retirement Ctr., Inc.,* No. 79728 (Mo. June 17, 1997).

Medicode. *Patient Confidentiality: Alphabetized Guide to the Release of Medical Information.* Salt Lake City: Medicode, 1998, 107 pages.

Presents information on a range of issues concerning release of confidential records. Topics discussed include requests from government agencies, releasing information by fax, subpoenas, media inquiries, and requests from other physicians.

Robyn A. Meinhardt and Michael R. Overly. "*Treasure* Trove or Pandora's Box? Defining, Using, and Protecting Rights and Obligations in Health Information and Data." Washington, D.C.: American Health Lawyers Association [Report No. VHI99–0003], 1999, 36 pages.

Discusses "health information" versus "health data" as they pertain to patient rights, and examines protecting databases. Outlines a transaction checklist and examples.

Jon F. Merz and others. "Hospital Consent for Disclosure of Medical Records. *Journal of Law, Medicine, and Ethics,* 1998, 26, 241.

Disclosure-of-information clauses in general consent-to-treatment forms used by 202 large hospitals nationwide are described and mapped into a taxonomy to distinguish types of disclosure and to help structure consent documents.

Hugh Miller III. "DNA Blueprints, Personhood, and Genetic Privacy." *Health Matrix*, Summer 1998, *8*, 253.

Argues that advances in genetic science cannot warrant any transformation of the traditional idea of personal identity into essentially genetic terms. Miller's view is that personal identity bears internal relations to the concepts of free will and moral responsibility. Genetic science may shed new light upon factors that causally condition the development through the power of free choice. But future advances in genetic science cannot displace the traditional idea of personal identity without nullifying our customary notions of free will.

William H. Minor. "Identity Cards and Databases in Health Care: The Need for Federal Privacy Protections." *Columbia Journal of Law and Social Problems*, 1995, *28*, 253.

Recommends that Congress act promptly to establish sufficient privacy protections to safeguard the confidentiality of personal medical information and to guard against the emergence of another national identity card. In recent years, health care in America has moved squarely into the information age, with new efforts to computerize and link medical records and other health care data. The Health Security Card, which was proposed together with President Clinton's health reform plan, is a symbol of the changes in the medical information infrastructure. The author chronicles the history of the leading national identifier, the Social Security card and number, and describes recent efforts to introduce a national identity card to fight illegal immigration. He examines legislative efforts, by the Clinton administration and others in the 103rd Congress, designed to protect the privacy of medical data.

Deborah Pergament. "Internet Psychotherapy: Current Status and Future Regulation." (Comment.) *Health Matrix*, Summer 1988, *8*, 233.

Examines the legal implications of Internet psychotherapy and argues for regulations that protect the consumer but permit psychotherapists to explore the advantages, disadvantages, and efficacy of Internet-based treatments.

Helena Gail Rubenstein. "If I Am Only for Myself, What Am I? A Communitarian Look at the Privacy Stalemate." *American Journal of Law and Medicine*, 1999, *25*, 203.

Addresses the debate on health privacy legislation, offering a communitarian perspective on how Congress should view any privacy regulation designed to safeguard patient medical records. Responds to the arguments of privacy advocates by suggesting that legislators consider the public health policy interests in medical data seriously, to ensure that beneficial medical research will not be impeded.

Paul M. Schwartz. "Privacy and the Economics of Personal Health Care Information." *Texas Law Review*, 1997, *76*, 1.

Contends that a strong economic argument can be made in favor of informational privacy. In so doing, Schwartz challenges the current law and economics analysis advanced by Judge Richard Posner and Professor Richard Epstein, who argue against regulation and in favor of unconstrained access to information about individuals. This article considers the nature of an economically efficient regulation for health care information and argues that optimal distribution of personal health information requires rules that are tied to and follow the data through various uses. Once identifiable health information is created, the author argues, it should remain protected health information that is subject to fair information practices. This article develops the necessary elements of optimal legal regulation of health care data. It identifies the core principles essential for health care privacy legislation and offers an explicit economic argument for this statutory approach.

Paul M. Schwartz. "The Protection of Privacy in Health Care Reform." *Vanderbilt Law Review*, 1995, *48*, 294.

Assesses current regulations protecting the privacy of patient medical information. Proposals for health care reform seek to control medical costs while also improving the quality of medical services. Each proposal depends, at least in part, on increasing access to personal medical information for a host of interested parties—including doctors, insurers, employers, and government agencies. Although increased informational flow may have substantial benefits, the author argues that any such changes in using patient data should be accompanied by improvements in legal protection of the privacy of health care information.

Current regulations are inadequate to protect the privacy of patient data, the author contends. First, the regulations permit medical information to be used improperly by both direct market mailers and employers. Additionally, weaknesses in U.S. data protection threaten the nation's access to international data flows: European law prohibits transferring certain personal information to states with insufficient data protection. Finally, these existing problems will be exacerbated by the inevitable increase in the demand for personal medical information.

Accordingly, the United States must develop appropriate federal fair information practices for use of health care data in this country. These information practices must include (1) creating a statutory fabric that defines obligations with respect to the uses of personal information, (2) maintaining transparent processing systems, (3) assigning limited procedural and substantive rights to the individual, and (4) establishing effective governmental oversight of data use. Only by incorporating these four principles into a data protection law can the United States combat existing weaknesses in regulating medical privacy and address the privacy concerns that will inevitably arise as the health care delivery system evolves.

Secretary of Health and Human Services. "Confidentiality of Individually Identifiable Health Information." Washington, D.C.: Department of Health and Human Services, 1997.

Recommendations for federal legislation to establish national confidentiality standards for protecting patients' privacy, issued by DHHS in response to concerns that health information is not adequately safeguarded in the face of interstate transactions and computerized data. The suggested legislation would not supersede existing federal and state laws with stronger privacy protections but instead protect access to data for researchers, public health officials, and policy makers engaged in projects for the public good. It would also ensure that service organizations (such as claims processors and pharmacy benefit managers) and providers and payers (including employers who provide on-site health care or have a self-funded plan) use information only for health purposes. Civil and criminal penalties would be levied on those who misuse information. In addition to imposing a legal duty of confidentiality on payers, providers, and service organizations, the legislation would prohibit them from making treatment or coverage contingent on a patient's agreement to disclose health information. Consumers would have the right to find out who has access to their information and how the information would be used, as well as to obtain copies of their records and make corrections.

Alissa R. Spielberg. "Online Without a Net: Physician-Patient Communication by Electronic Mail." *American Journal of Law and Medicine*, 1999, 25, 267.

Looks at privacy concerns in the context of the physician-patient relationship, specifically evolving use of e-mail as a communication medium. Examines a range of legal issues arising from transfer and storage of, and access to, e-mail exchanges. Because current laws offer little in the way of privacy protection, Spielberg suggests procedures for limiting access to such personal information in the workplace.

Paul Starr. "Health and the Right to Privacy." *American Journal of Law and Medicine*, 1999, 25, 193.

Offers a broad overview of the ongoing congressional debate over health privacy information to control access to medical records and health data. The author acknowledges the need to restrict access to personal medical information but advocates legislation that will not limit access for legitimate research intended to improve public health. He suggests that a federal privacy statute is, in the long run, the preferred choice but believes that the current political landscape may preclude such sweeping legislation and leave most protection up to state legislatures.

Latanya Sweeney. "Weaving Technology and Policy Together to Maintain Confidentiality." *Journal of Law, Medicine and Ethics*, Summer and Fall 1997, *25*(2 and 3), 98–110.

Demonstrates that removing all explicit identifiers from medical data does not guarantee medical record confidentiality. Sweeney examines three new software systems that do help maintain anonymity, but warns that the systems' limitations demand complementary policies.

Richard C. Turkington. "Medical Record Confidentiality Law, Scientific Research, and Data Collection in the Information Age." *Journal of Law, Medicine and Ethics*, Summer and Fall 1997, *25*(2 and 3), 113–129.

Reviews federal and state laws on privacy and confidentiality on access and disclosure of health records concerning government and private sector databases. Turkington also examines legislative proposals and recommendations for privacy and confidentiality.

Adele A. Waller. "Electronic Communication in the Healthcare Industry." Washington, D.C.: American Health Lawyers Association [Report No. VHL99–0022], 1999, 46 pages.

Presents overview of privacy and security issues, including the proposed HIPAA security standard. Reviews important cyberlaw and health law issues related to health care Websites and provides guidance on developing policies, contracts, notices, and disclaimers that give practical protection to health care organizations. Appendix lists e-mail policy considerations for health care organizations.

Adele A. Waller. "Healthcare Web Sites." Washington, D.C.: American Health Lawyers Association [Report No. VHI99–0011], 1999, 23 pages.

Discusses opportunities and pitfalls in health care Websites; Internet security risks and solutions; Web development policies and agreements to minimize liability exposure, protecting rights in domain names and Websites; and the impact of proposed HIPAA security standards and HCFA Internet policy.

Adele Waller. "Emerging Regulation of Health Information Technology." Washington, D.C.: American Health Lawyers Association [Report No. VHL98–0048], 1998, 41 pages.

Discusses the impact of emerging federal and state regulation on health information technology, including regulation by the FDA and under the administrative simplification provisions of HIPAA, as well as the standards for health care electronic data exchange and electronic signatures, federal health information security requirements and health identifiers, and the new felony offense of wrongful disclosure of individually identifiable health information. Also discusses law concerning ownership of health care data and offers practical tips on how to protect valuable rights in health data.

Adele A. Waller. "Hard Choices and Difficult Tradeoffs: The [HHS] Secretary's Health Information Privacy Recommendations to Congress." *Health Law Digest*, Dec. 1997, *25*, 3–12.

Examines Secretary Donna Shalala's proposed guidelines for a federal health information privacy statute. Two of these recommendations have proved particularly controversial: (1) the recommendation that disclosure of health information be permitted without patient authorization for health care and payment purposes, and (2) omission of any proposed requirement for additional legal process prior to disclosure of individually identifiable health information to law enforcement agencies.

Erin D. Williams. "Confidentiality and Security." Washington, D.C.: American Health Lawyers Association [Report No. VHI98–0005], 1998, 26 pages.

Gives an overview of the significant differences among the states as to health information confidentiality laws; compares and highlights significant issues regarding health information confidentiality; lists and summarizes legislation introduced in twenty-five states in 1997 concerning confidentiality of patient medical information.

Beverly Woodward. "Medical Record Confidentiality and Data Collection: Current Dilemmas." *Journal of Law, Medicine, and Ethics,* Summer and Fall 1997, *25*(2 and 3), 88.

Discusses data collection and data disclosure practices that threaten medical record confidentiality. Woodward raises concerns about reidentifying ostensibly deidentified patient information, and discusses measures for protecting confidentiality in a research setting.

21.03 INFORMATION GARNERED FROM GENETIC TESTING

Kenneth S. Abraham. "Understanding Prohibitions Against Genetic Discrimination in Insurance." *Jurimetrics,* 1999, *40,* 123.

The justification for laws prohibiting genetic discrimination in health insurance is not clear, the author contends. It is not to be found in privacy protection, the distinctive features of health insurance, or the distinction between presymptomatic genetic tendencies and actually manifested disease, although certain practical considerations may justify these laws.

American Nurses Association. *Managing Genetic Information: Implications for Nursing Practice.* Washington, D.C.: American Nurses Association, 1995, 60 pages.

Supplies a summary of the ANA's research study on nurse management of genetic information, funded by the National Center for Human Genome Research at the National Institutes of Health. This text includes an overview of genetic advances, guidelines for nursing practice, discussion of future trends and recommendations, and complete results of the survey.

Lori B. Andrews. "Legal Aspects of Genetic Information." *Yale Journal of Biology and Medicine,* 1991, *64,* 29.

Discusses the effect of existing statutes and case law on three pivotal questions: To what sort of information are people entitled? What control should people have over their genetic information? Do people have a right to refuse genetic information? Andrews emphasizes that the law protects a patient's right to obtain or refuse genetic information about oneself, as well as the right to control dissemination of that information to others.

Lori B. Andrews. "Public Choices and Private Choices: Legal Regulation of Genetic Testing." In Timothy F. Murphy and Marc A. Lappé (eds.), *Justice and the Human Genome Project.* Berkeley: University of California Press, 1994.

This essay discusses such topics as restrictions on use of genetic testing bans on certain prenatal testing and mandatory genetic screening.

Lori B. Andrews. "Torts and the Double Helix: Liability for Failure to Disclose Genetic Risks." *University of Houston Law Review,* 1992, *29,* 143.

Explores the legal precedents that may be used to impose upon health care professionals a duty to disclose genetic risks. Andrews also addresses critical questions regarding health care professionals' liability for failure to provide genetic information. This article suggests that the range of available genetic information—and the number of people interested in that information—may be so great that health care providers are not the appropriate source.

Lori B. Andrews and Nanette Elster. "Adoption, Reproductive Technologies, and Genetic Information." *Health Matrix,* Summer 1998, *8,* 125.

Examines state policies requiring collection of genetic information and access to identifying information.

Lori B. Andrews and Ami S. Jaeger. "Confidentiality of Genetic Information in the Work-place." *American Journal of Law and Medicine,* 1991, *17, 75.*

Analyzes existing legal protections for confidentiality of information collected through genetic screening or genetic monitoring in the workplace. This article notes that there are a variety of protections, such as ethical codes for physicians; statutes protecting health care information in the hands of employers; and tort, contract, and constitutional principles. It describes defenses to a suit based on improper disclosure of medical information. It then analyzes legal bases for employee and third-party access to an employee's genetic information. In response to gaps in existing legal protections, the article suggests parameters for a model law protecting the confidentiality of genetic information collected in the workplace.

Lori B. Andrews, Jane E. Fullarton, Neil A. Holtzman, and Arno G. Motulsky. *Assessing Genetic Risks.* Washington, D.C.: National Academy Press, 1994, 338 pages.

Discusses the legal, social, and ethical implications of genetic testing. Because assessment of genetic risks by genetic testing is expanding rapidly, the Institute of Medicine of the National Academy of Sciences undertook this study to determine the current status and future implications of such testing. This report by the institute's committee on assessing genetic risks sets forth a range of recommendations regarding the confidentiality of genetic information, use of genetic disease registries, patient control of medical records, discrimination in insurance and employment, and pricing of insurance.

George J. Annas. "Rules for Gene Banks." In Timothy F. Murphy and Marc A. Lappé (eds.), *Justice and the Human Genome Project.* Berkeley: University of California Press, 1994.

Discusses such topics as current law and practice regarding medical records, rules for medical information systems, and privacy rules for gene banks.

George J. Annas. "Privacy Rules for DNA Databanks: Protecting Coded Future Diaries." *Journal of the American Medical Association,* 1993, *270,* 2346.

Reviews the legal and public policy rationales for protecting genetic privacy and suggests that specific enforceable privacy rules for DNA databanks are needed. In privacy terms, genetic information is similar to medical information. However, the information contained in the DNA molecule itself is more sensitive because it contains an individual's probable "future diary"; is written in a code that has been only partially broken; and contains information about an individual's parents, siblings, and children. Current rules are insufficient for protecting either genetic information or identifiable DNA samples stored in DNA databanks. The author proposes four preliminary rules to govern creation of DNA databanks, collection of DNA samples for storage, limits on using information derived from the samples, and continuing obligations to those whose DNA samples are in the databanks.

George J. Annas and Sherman Elias (eds.). *Gene Mapping: Using Law and Ethics as Guides.* New York: Oxford University Press, 1992, 291 pages.

This book is predicated on the editors' view that law and ethics will add little to the Human Genome Project as a public enterprise unless the legal and ethical issues involved in the project are carefully defined and ranked early. Accordingly, they have assembled this collection of essays by health lawyers, geneticists, and historians and philosophers of science. The underlying theme of the text is that there has been insufficient discussion of the drawbacks of the project, given the tragic history of the misuse of genetic information in the United States and abroad. Topics discussed include privacy, procreation, and patient rights. It concludes by focusing on issues the writers have collectively identified as being priorities for further research. The text is supplemented by an index and glossary.

George J. Annas and Michael A. Grodin (eds.). *The Nazi Doctors and the Nuremberg Code: Human Rights in Human Experimentation*. New York: Oxford University Press, 1992, 371 pages.

Discusses the sources and ramifications of the Nuremberg Code. The atrocities committed by Nazi physicians and researchers during the Second World War prompted development of this seminal document to define the ethics of modern medical experimentation using human subjects. Since its promulgation, the code has been viewed as one of the cornerstones of modern bioethical thought. Contributors to the volume include professionals from the disciplines of history, philosophy, law, and medicine as well as the chief prosecutor of the Nuremberg Military Tribunal and a survivor of the Mengele twin experiments.

This book sheds light on keenly debated issues of both science and jurisprudence, including the ethics of human experimentation, the doctrine of informed consent, and the code's impact on the contemporary human rights agenda. The historical setting of the code's creation, some modern parallels, and the current attitude of German physicians toward the crimes of the Hitler era are discussed in the early chapters. The book progresses to a powerful account of the doctors' trial at Nuremberg, its resulting verdict, and development of the code. The editors conclude with a chapter on foreseeable future developments and a proposal for an international covenant on human experimentation enforced by an international court.

Roberta M. Berry. "The Genetic Revolution and the Physician's Duty of Confidentiality." *Journal of Legal Medicine*, Dec. 1997, *18*(4), 401–441.

Identifies possible responses to genetic disclosure issues. As the genetic revolution proceeds, more genetic information will be produced, and patients and their physicians will face more occasions when disclosure of genetic information is at issue. Legislation and litigation will begin to explore the complex tensions between the physician's traditional duty of confidentiality and the duty of more recent vintage to disclose patient information to third parties against the wishes of the patient under some circumstances. This article compares two approaches that lawmakers might take in answering these questions. The first, which the author describes as the "external approach," entails lawmaking from outside and above the practice of medicine. This approach consists of applying regulatory principles—of welfare maximization, autonomy, and social responsibility—to resolving these issues. The second approach that lawmakers might take instead looks within the practice of medicine to discover the reasons physicians should keep or disclose patient secrets on particular occasions, looking particularly at the "caring virtues" of sympathy, kindness, and loyalty embodied in the Hippocratic tradition.

The article concludes that the Hippocratic virtues can and should inform legal regulation of genetic disclosure issues. Lawmakers must resort to the external principles, however, when the demands of the practice of medicine and of other social institutions—including insurers, employers, and educational institutions—are irreconcilable. This article also concludes that the Hippocratic virtues are in danger of regulatory neglect and that this neglect would be unfortunate for two reasons. First, lawmakers would lose the benefits of the contextually and ethically rich problem-solving capacity of the virtues. Second, physicians and their patients would suffer the consequences of erosion of the regulatory support system necessary to the Hippocratic practice of medicine and its caring purpose.

Katherine Brokaw. "Genetic Screening in the Workplace and Employers' Liability." *Columbia Journal of Law and Social Problems*, 1990, *23*, 317.

Discusses the potential legal liability of employers who misuse genetic screening tests to discriminate against classes of workers. The blossoming science of genetics offers hope for solving problems as diverse as world hunger and water pollution. However, as geneticists map the human chromosome and discover which genes make some people vulnerable to illness, the temptation for employers to use genetic screening tests will increase, especially in the face of pressure from insurers and management to cut costs.

Barry Brown. "Genetic Testing, Access to Genetic Data, and Discrimination: Conceptual Legislative Models." *Suffolk University Law Review*, 1995, *27*, 1573.

Offers a range of legislative models (1) to encourage discussion of the appropriate limits to be placed on genetic screening and testing, and (2) as a guide to developing similar legislation in the future. The statutory models are drawn from existing state statutes, particularly those of California, Maryland, and Wisconsin. Brown writes that he intends the conceptual models drawn from state statutes to be controversial, both as to defined terms and application of public health concepts. Each model statute raises questions regarding informed consent, confidentiality, and proper application of genetic data to employment and insurance matters.

Ellen Wright Clayton. "Problems Posed by Genetics for Law and Ethics: American Policies." In *Jahrbuch für Recht und Ethik (Yearbook of Law and Ethics)*, Vol. 4. Berlin: Duncker und Humblot, 1996.

Focuses on the use of genetic tests to provide information about the present, and particularly the future, health of the individual who is receiving genetic testing. These tests range from metabolic assays that have been used for years to diagnose genetic diseases such as phenylketonuria, to newer techniques such as linkage and direct mutation analysis that can be used both to diagnose current illnesses as well as detect mutations in genes that predispose the individual to develop diseases such as cancer. The purpose of this paper is to explore the forces in the United States that govern development and dispersion of these tests and to ask what role personal choice will have in how those tests are made available and used.

Ellen Wright Clayton. "Screening and Treatment of Newborns." *Houston Law Review*, 1992, *29*, 85.

Argues that society should resist efforts to require that newborns be tested for an ever-increasing number of conditions. Clayton, a professor at Vanderbilt's medical and law schools, presents an overview of the screening process by describing not only what screening can and cannot do but also the general organization of current programs. She then turns to the large body of empirical research that demonstrates that newborn screening causes psychological and other harm to infants and their families. She suggests that diagnosis of disease in the neonatal period, regardless of accuracy, can have adverse social and legal consequences for families and children.

Clayton then argues that state intervention, under the guise of public health, in domains traditionally reserved for the family is not justifiable under constitutional principles. Her analysis of the economic and political forces motivating the state's decision to undertake newborn screening raises questions about the desirability of the state as a major participant in these programs. She concludes that society should screen neonates only when children can derive substantial benefit from early detection and that legislatures should amend existing laws to ensure that parents can participate in the screening process.

Ellen Wright Clayton. "What the Law Says about Reproductive Genetic Testing and What It Doesn't." In Rima D. Apple and Janet Golden (eds.), *Women and Prenatal Testing: Facing the Challenges of Genetic Technology*. Columbus: Ohio State University Press, 1994.

Discusses the large body of statutory, regulatory, and case law that deals directly and indirectly with providing genetic services. Many of these laws have evolved through state legislation, although the federal government has played an important role, Clayton observes. A close look reveals that there is wide variation among the states in their approaches to reproductive genetic testing, with many states also having internal inconsistencies in their policies regarding genetics. These differences and conflicts demonstrate that there is little agreement about appropriate use of prenatal genetic technologies. The article analyzes the state of the law and concludes with extensive endnotes, a bibliography, and four tables examining a variety of state statutes.

Ellen Wright Clayton and others. "Genetic Testing for Cancer Susceptibility." *Journal of Clinical Oncology,* 1996, *14,* 1730–1736.

This is a statement adopted by the American Society of Clinical Oncology taking the position that any physician who offers genetic testing should be aware of, and able to communicate, the benefits and limits of current testing procedures and the range of prevention and treatment options available to patients and their families. The society also endorses the following principles: (1) to the greatest extent possible, genetic testing for cancer susceptibility should be performed in the setting of long-term outcome studies; (2) oncologists must ensure that informed consent has been given by the patient; (3) cancer predisposition testing should be offered only when (a) the person has a strong family history of cancer or very early age of onset of disease; (b) the test can be adequately interpreted; and (c) the results will influence medical management of the patient or family member; and (4) all efforts, including legislation, should be invoked to prohibit discrimination by insurance companies or employers based on an individual's inherited susceptibility to cancer.

Helen R. Davis and Janice V. Mitrius. "Recent Legislation on Genetics and Insurance." (Note.) *Jurimetrics,* 1996, *37,* 69.

Catalogs and describes state and federal legislation regulating use of genetic information by insurance companies. This note is supplemented by four excellent tables analyzing prohibited acts and penalties by state.

A. de Gorgey. "The Advent of DNA Databanks: Implications for Information Privacy." *American Journal of Law and Medicine,* 1990, *16,* 381.

Explores the privacy concerns arising out of collecting and retaining extremely personal information in a central database. Genetic identification tests—better known as DNA profiling—currently allow criminal investigators to connect suspects to physical samples retrieved from a victim or the scene of a crime. A controversial yet acclaimed expansion of DNA analysis is the creation of a massive databank of genetic codes. The potential for unauthorized access by those not investigating a particular crime compels implementation of national standards and stringent security measures.

G. M. Doot. "The Secrets of the Genome Revealed: Threats to Genetic Privacy." (Comment.) *Wayne Law Review,* 1991, *37,* 1615.

Begins with an overview of the Human Genome Project: its goals, progress, and legal implications. As a forerunner to genome applications, DNA fingerprinting illustrates the existing and emergent privacy issues emanating from genetic breakthroughs. DNA fingerprinting raises issues that the author extrapolates to the Human Genome Project. This Comment addresses potential privacy invasions, information abuses, and discrimination problems within the contexts of employment and health insurance. The dearth of safeguards to effectively address legal issues raised by the emerging technology is of grave concern, the author finds. After discussing development and maintenance of databanks as repositories of genetic data, the author proposes recommendations for preserving the rights of the new "biologic underclass."

Rochelle Cooper Dreyfuss and Dorothy Nelkin. "The Jurisprudence of Genetics." *Vanderbilt Law Review,* 1992, *45,* 313.

Argues that genetic assumptions must be examined skeptically before they are allowed to alter concepts such as personhood, normality, responsibility, and culpability, which are fundamental to the law. This skepticism will become more and more important as work on the Human Genome Project progresses, its results become disseminated, and lawmakers are attracted to the apparent certainty and predictions promised by a genetic map. The authors, both law professors, caution that in the rush to incorporate new scholarship, the highly complex and poorly understood relationship between genetics and environment—that is, between nature and nurture—may be grossly oversimplified. With the desire to find unambiguous solutions, more traditional values—

such as equal opportunity, personal privacy, and individual and family autonomy—may be obscured.

Richard A. Epstein. "The Legal Regulation of Genetic Discrimination: Old Responses to New Technology." *Boston University Law Review*, 1994, *74*, 1.

Addresses the question of whether genetic information should be used—and if so by whom—to make decisions in the context of jobs, insurance, and health. Consistent with his earlier criticism of employment discrimination laws, Epstein adopts a libertarian position; although he admits that whatever its quiet virtues, benign nonintervention may not weather the political abuse it is likely to invite.

J. C. Fletcher and D. C. Wertz. "Ethics, Law, and Medical Genetics: After the Human Genome Is Mapped." *Emory Law Journal*, 1990, *39*, 747.

Discusses the results of an international survey, performed by the authors and conducted among medical geneticists, designed to evaluate the ethical and legal framework in which clinical counseling decisions are made.

Mark S. Frankel and Albert H. Teich (eds.). *The Genetic Frontier: Ethics, Law and Policy.* Washington, D.C.: American Association for the Advancement of Science, 1994, 240 pages.

The product of a joint conference between the American Association for the Advancement of Science and the American Bar Association, this book examines a range of topics, including collection and disclosure of genetic information as well as privacy and the control of genetic information. The text is supplemented by ample notes and references, along with an index.

Lawrence O. Gostin. "Genetic Discrimination: The Use of Genetically Based Diagnostic and Prognostic Tests by Employers and Insurers." *American Journal of Law and Medicine*, 1991, *17*, 109.

Maintains that genetic discrimination is detrimental to public health programs, as well as to society generally. Advances in genetic testing and screening, accelerated and prompted by the Human Genome Initiative, increase society's ability to detect and monitor chromosomal differences. These technologies and their resulting genomic data will enhance medical science but may also encourage discrimination. Although few employers or insurers currently use genetic screening, testing, or data, rising employee benefit costs and market forces create powerful incentives for usage.

Current municipal, state, and federal laws, including the ADA, may not sufficiently protect employees and insureds from genetic discrimination. Although municipal and state protections should not be overlooked, the ADA's sweeping scope may currently offer the most comprehensive safeguard. Federal laws banning discrimination on the basis of race or sex might also successfully redress some forms of genetic discrimination. The advent of genetic technologies necessitates efforts to rectify state and federal statutory coverage gaps, strictly regulate employers, and produce comprehensive guidelines.

Lawrence O. Gostin and James G. Hodge, Jr. "Genetic Privacy and the Law: An End to Genetics Exceptionalism." *Jurimetrics*, 1999, *40*, 21.

Although the proliferation of human genetic information promises to achieve many public benefits, acquiring, using, retaining, and disclosing genetic data threaten individual liberties. States (and, to a lesser degree, the federal government) have responded to the anticipated and actual threats of privacy invasion and discrimination by enacting several types of genetic-specific legislation. These laws emphasize the differences between genetic information and other health information. By articulating theses differences, governments afford genetic data an "exceptional" status. The authors argue that genetic exceptionalism is flawed for two reasons: (1) strict protections of autonomy, privacy, and equal treatment of persons with genetic conditions threaten the accomplishment of public goods; and (2) there is no clear demarcation separating genetic data from other health data.

Mark A. Hall. "Legal Rules and Industry Norms: The Impact of Laws Restricting Health Insurers' Use of Genetic Information." *Jurimetrics*, 1999, 40, 93.

Since 1991, twenty-eight states have enacted laws that prohibit insurers' use of genetic information in pricing, issuing, or structuring health insurance. This article evaluates whether those laws reduce the extent of genetic discrimination by health insurers. Using multiple data sources, it concludes that there are almost no well-documented cases of health insurers asking for or using presymptomatic genetic test results in their underwriting decisions either before or after these laws, or in states with or without the laws.

At present, health insurers are not thinking about or interested in using genetic information of this sort. Using this information is not cost effective and is not seen as contributing significantly to underwriting accuracy. However, if genetic testing information were easily available, some health insurers would consider using it in some fashion if it were legal. In the future, such information could become much more relevant to health insurers than it is now. Therefore, the major effect of these laws is to make it less likely that insurers will use genetic information in the future. Although insurers and their agents are only vaguely aware of these laws, the laws have helped convince the industry that it is not appropriate or socially legitimate to use this information. Thus, the laws have caused the insurance industry to embrace more socially oriented norms and attitudes.

Mark A. Hall. "Insurers' Use of Genetic Information." *Jurimetrics*, 1996, 37, 13.

Surveys the arguments for and against allowing insurers to use genetic information in setting premiums or determining coverage. Noting that access to this information raises issues of discrimination and privacy, the article discusses the fit between the various rationales for prohibiting this use of genetic information and the actual statutes that have been enacted and proposed. Hall concludes with a call for more empirical research into the actual impact of the statutes and the magnitude of the social problems that led to their enactment.

Kathy L. Hudson and others. "Genetic Discrimination and Health Insurance: An Urgent Need for Reform." *Science*, 1995, 270, 391.

Observes that a number of states have enacted laws to protect individuals from being denied health insurance on the basis of genetic information. The first wave of laws, the authors write, were limited in scope and focused exclusively on discrimination against people with a single genetic trait (such as sickle cell anemia). Since the Human Genome Project was launched in 1990, however, eight states have enacted some form of protection against genetic discrimination in health insurance. These recently enacted state laws are not limited to a specific genetic trait but apply potentially to an unlimited number of genetic conditions. The state laws prohibit insurers from denying coverage on the basis of genetic test results and prohibit using this information to establish premiums, charge differential rates, or limit benefits. The authors note that a few of these states, including Oregon and California, integrate protection against discrimination in insurance practices with privacy protections that prohibit insurers from requesting genetic information and from disclosing genetic information without authorization.

The authors, officials of the National Institutes of Health and the National Action Plan on Breast Cancer, discuss the weaknesses of current state laws, including ERISA preemption and the narrow focus of the state laws on genetic tests rather than more broadly on genetic information generated by family history, physical examination, or medical record. They conclude with the following recommendations for state and federal lawmakers:

1. Insurance providers should be prohibited from using genetic information, or an individual's request for genetic services, to deny or limit any coverage or establish eligibility, continuation, enrollment, or contribution requirements.

2. Insurance providers should be prohibited from establishing differential rates or premium payments based on genetic information or an individual's request for genetic services.

3. Insurance providers should be prohibited from requesting or requiring collection or disclosure of genetic information.

4. Insurance providers and other holders of genetic information should be prohibited from releasing genetic information without prior written authorization of the individual.

Bartha Maria Knoppers, Claude M. Laberge, and Marie Hirtie (eds.). *Human DNA: Law and Policy: International and Comparative Perspectives.* Boston: Kluwer Law International, 1997, 476 pages.

Presents one of the first international debates on a matter of universal concern. This book focuses on issues of DNA sampling and testing, consent and confidentiality, banking policies, genetic epidemiology, and diversity. Because financial and technological pressures are inextricably linked to human genetics research, commercialization and patents are also examined. This book will be valuable to academic researchers, policy makers, and industry.

Michael J. M. Lin. "Conferring a Federal Property Right in Genetic Material: Stepping into the Future with the Genetic Privacy Act." *American Journal of Law and Medicine,* 1996, *22,* 109.

Asserts that the protections surrounding genetic information that are afforded by current and even proposed state statutes, and the slowly developing case law regarding excised bodily materials for research and experimentation purposes are inadequate and uncertain. The biotechnology and pharmaceutical industries require greater certainty to foster increased investment and experimentation. If Congress adopts the Genetic Privacy and Nondiscrimination Act (GPNA), it will advance the protections available to prevent unauthorized disclosure of genetic information about individuals, but it will fail to clarify issues regarding use and rights to genetic materials themselves. The Genetic Privacy Act (GPA), Lin argues, offers a better solution by advancing all the goals of the GPNA while further granting a property right in one's own genetic materials.

Abby Lippman. "Prenatal Genetic Testing and Screening: Constructing Needs and Reinforcing Inequities." *American Journal of Law and Medicine,* 1991, *17,* 15.

Considers the influence and implications of applying genetic technologies to definitions of disease and to treatment of illness. The author introduces the concept of "geneticization" to emphasize the dominant discourse in today's stories of health and disease. The reassurance, choice, and control supposedly afforded by prenatal genetic testing and screening are critically examined, and their role in constructing the need for such technology is addressed. Using stories told about prenatal diagnosis as a focus, the author explores the consequences of a genetic perspective for and on women and their health care needs.

Brett Lockwood. "Bibliography: Genetics and the Law." (Note.) *Emory Law Journal,* 1990, *39,* 875.

Assembles a significant portion of the literature detailing the relationship between the law and developments in genetic science as of the date of its compilation. This bibliography of sixty-one pages includes references to materials appearing in both article and book form, focusing on leading books, treatises, and law journals.

Roberta B. Meyer. "Justification for Permitting Life Insurers to Continue to Underwrite on the Basis of Genetic Information and Genetic Test Results." *Suffolk University Law Review,* 1995, *27,* 1271.

The author, senior counsel for the American Council of Life Insurance, contends that if life insurers are prohibited from underwriting on the basis of genetic information or genetic tests, medical underwriting will essentially be prohibited and the process of risk classification will be jeopardized, if not totally eliminated. It is unlikely that the current life insurance market could continue to exist in its current form under these circumstances, she writes. Opponents of insurers' use of genetic information or test results have not established the need for—nor has the public sought such a fundamental restructuring of—the current system of life insurance, she says.

William F. Mulholland II and Ami S. Jaeger. "Genetic Privacy and Discrimination: A Survey of State Legislation." *Jurimetrics*, 1999, *39*, 317.

Presents a summary of legislation enacted by forty-four states concerning genetic privacy or discrimination.

Timothy F. Murphy and Marc A. Lappé (eds.), *Justice and the Human Genome Project.* Berkeley: University of California Press, 1994, 178 pages.

The essays gathered in this volume address theoretical and practical concerns relative to the meaning of genomic research and were among those presented at a conference titled Justice and the Human Genome, held in Chicago in November 1991. The goal of that conference, sponsored by the U.S. Department of Energy and the University of Illinois at Chicago, was to consider questions of justice as they are and will be raised by the Human Genome Project. To achieve its goal of identifying and elucidating the challenges of justice inherent in genomic research and its social applications, the conference drew together in one forum members from academia, medicine, and industry to sketch out central questions that will follow the emergence of genomic profiling capabilities.

Whether the authors are concerned with the history of eugenics, the meaning of individual differences, or access to health care, they are all united in their concern about the impact of genomic research on individual persons and their place in specific ethnic and cultural groups. If there is a common goal underlying the analyses here, it is protection of individual persons and cultural groups from unjust social prejudices and arrangements that would burden individual choice or degrade the worth of certain groups defined in invidious ways. It is perhaps a measure of the age that we express as much anxiety as hope with regard to the Human Genome Project.

Thomas H. Murray, Mark A. Rothstein, and Robert F. Murray, Jr. (eds.). *The Human Genome Project and the Future of Health Care.* Bloomington: Indiana University Press, 1996, 248 pages.

This book of twelve essays examines the impact of mapping the human genome on such matters as the physician-patient relationship, health services for minority populations, reproductive decision making, access to health insurance, disability discrimination, distribution of scarce medical resources, access to health care, and health care reform.

Dorothy Nelkin and Laurence Tancredi. "Classify and Control: Genetic Information in the Schools." *American Journal of Law and Medicine*, 1991, *17*, 51.

Reviews genetic advances bearing on educational issues and their implementation through biological tests. Recent advances in molecular and behavioral genetics are providing theoretical models to explain complex behavior—learning disabilities and behavioral problems—in simple biological terms. There are intrinsic difficulties in interpreting genetic information. Yet genetic explanations are particularly appealing in school systems pressed by demands for efficiency and accountability. Thus, genetic explanations are affecting how children are categorized in the schools. The authors suggest the social consequences and legal implications of the growing prevalence of genetic assumptions.

NIH Working Group on the Ethical, Legal, and Social Implications of Human Genome Research. *Genetic Information and Health Insurance: Report of the Task Force on Genetic Information and Insurance.* Bethesda, Md.: NIH, 1993.

Recommends a return to the risk-spreading goal of insurance. The working group suggests that individuals be given access to health care insurance irrespective of information, including genetic information about their past, current, or future health status.

Robert J. Pokorski. "Use of Genetic Information by Private Insurers." In Timothy F. Murphy and Marc A. Lappé (eds.), *Justice and the Human Genome Project.* Berkeley: University of California Press, 1994.

Argues that information garnered from genetic testing must be made available to insurers as a matter of equity.

John A. Robertson. "Privacy Issues in Second Stage Genomics." Jurimetrics, 1999, *40*(1), 59.

Research that identifies genes useful in preventing and treating disease will require access to biologic samples and medical records protected by traditional notions of privacy and confidentiality. Resolving conflicts between privacy and genomic research will require articulating the ethical rules that should govern such practices and then implementing those rules in the national, regional, or local health systems in which the data of interest exist. As consensus develops about the ethical rules that should govern such research, attention will shift to the practical and political problems of installing and implementing those rules in the agencies and institutions where such research will occur.

Patricia A. Roch, Leonard H. Glantz, and George J. Annas. "The Genetic Privacy Act: A Proposal for National Legislation." *Jurimetrics,* 1996, *37,* 1.

Describes the primary features and development of the proposed Genetic Privacy Act.

Mark A. Rothstein. "Genetic Privacy and Confidentiality: Why They Are So Hard to Protect." *Journal of Law, Medicine, and Ethics,* 1998, *26,* 198.

Review of insurance and employment illustrates why it is difficult to protect genetic privacy and confidentiality. Procedural safeguards, such as strict application of informed consent and limits on disclosure by health care providers, are necessary.

Mark A. Rothstein and others. "Protecting Genetic Privacy by Permitting Employer Access Only to Job-Related Employee Medical Information: Analysis of a Unique Minnesota Law." *American Journal of Law and Medicine,* 1998, *24,* 399.

This article examines a different approach to the problem of employer access to and use of genetic information. Instead of advocating another law prohibiting genetic discrimination in employment, arguably already prohibited by the ADA, this article analyzes a Minnesota statute that prohibits employers from performing any tests or gaining access to any medical information that is not job-related. The statute's approach avoids the two main problems of current laws and proposals: (1) defining what is "genetic" and (2) preventing employer access to medical records containing genetic information.

Mark A. Rothstein (ed.). *Genetic Secrets: Protecting Privacy and Confidentiality in the Genetic Era.* New Haven, Conn.: Yale University Press, 1997, 511 pages.

This book consists of twenty-three essays on the effect of new technology, confidentiality in the clinical setting, nonmedical uses of genetic information, and ethics and law; concludes with a set of recommendations. It is based on papers presented at a workshop on Medical Information and the Right to Privacy at the Academy of Sciences, in Washington, D.C., in 1994.

Mark A. Rothstein. "Preventing the Discovery of Plaintiff Genetic Profiles by Defendants Seeking to Limit Damages in Personal Injury Litigation." *Indiana Law Journal,* 1996, *71,* 877.

Considers the scientific, legal, and policy issues giving rise to use of genetic information to determine damages in personal injury litigation. After reviewing the Human Genome Project and discussing the general law of damages for lost future earnings in personal injury, Rothstein considers the circumstances under which a defendant may obtain discovery of a plaintiff's medical records pursuant to Rule 26 of the Federal Rules of Civil Procedure and its state analogs. Following analysis of the public policy implications of using a personal injury plaintiff's genetic profile to assess damages, he proposes three alternatives designed to promote, first, the plaintiff's interest in privacy and confidentiality and the defendant's interest in avoiding overcompensation; second, the judiciary's interest in avoiding complexity in litigation; and the public's interest in conserving health resources.

Mark A. Rothstein and Sharona Hoffman. "Genetic Testing, Genetic Medicine and Managed Care." *Wake Forest Law Review*, 1999, *34*, 849.

As modern human genetics moves from a research setting to a clinical one, it will encounter the managed care system. Issues of cost, access, and quality of care will affect the availability and nature of genetic testing, genetic counseling, and genetic therapies. This article explores such issues as professional education, coverage of genetic services, privacy and confidentiality, and liability.

M. Serafini. "Double Trouble." *National Journal*, Sept. 20, 1997, *29*, 1830.

Considers the challenge facing state and federal lawmakers in determining how to encourage genetic research that offers hope to persons with Alzheimer's disease, cystic fibrosis, cancer, and other serious diseases, while discouraging human cloning and protecting patient privacy. Congress has introduced twelve bills concerning the privacy of medical records and cloning regulation, and state legislatures have fifty-nine to consider. The Biotechnology Industry Association (BIO) and the Pharmaceutical Research Manufacturers of America (PhRMA) have mobilized to protect legitimate gene research from the sometimes heavy hand of regulators and policy makers. They contend that legislation similar to that enacted in New Jersey, giving patients ownership of their genetic information, would destroy clinical research trials and devastate biomedical research. They further argue that poorly worded legislation might result in civil and criminal prosecution of scientists engaged in legitimate research. PhRMA and BIO have their own critics, however, who argue that in an era of integrated health systems the organizations' campaign to protect access to research data is actually a means of holding on to information that will be used for marketing.

Natalie Anne Stepanuk. "Genetic Information and Third-Party Access to Information: New Jersey's Pioneering Legislation as a Model for Federal Privacy Protection of Genetic Information." (Comment.) *Catholic University Law Review*, 1998, *47*, 1105.

This article examines classification of genetic information as a property and a privacy right under New Jersey's Privacy Act of 1996. It discusses whether and to what extent New Jersey's legislation is a model for national policy.

Sonia M. Suter. "Whose Genes Are These Anyway? Familial Conflicts over Access to Genetic Information." (Note.) *Michigan Law Review*, 1993, *91*, 1854.

This Note argues first that courts and legislatures should follow a presumption against mandating disclosure of a person's genetic information to third parties. Second, genetic testing for the benefit of a third party should not, and constitutionally cannot, be compelled. The author concludes by offering legislative and judicial guidelines that prohibit mandatory genetic testing for the benefit of another family member and allow disclosure of test results only when the harm in failing to disclose significantly outweighs the harm from disclosure.

Robert Wachbroit. "Rethinking Medical Confidentiality: The Impact of Genetics." *Suffolk University Law Review*, 1993, *27*, 1391.

Examines the individualistic assumptions in framing confidentiality dilemmas and justifications for medical confidentiality, and considers the nonindividualistic character of genetic information. Wachbroit considers how a standard account of confidentiality, and one without the assumption of individualism, would respond to examples where genetic information, though taken from an individual, is nevertheless not uniquely about that individual.

Tom Wilkie. *Perilous Knowledge: The Human Genome Project and Its Implications*. Berkeley: University of California Press, 1993, 191 pages.

Addresses the potential legal and moral consequences of the Human Genome Project.

21.04   TELEMEDICINE

Judith F. Daar and Spencer Koerner. "Telemedicine: Legal and Practical Implications." *Whittier Law Review*, 1997, 19, 3.

Offers a brief history of the development of telemedicine, as well as a discussion of its current and potential future uses.

Phyllis Forrester. "Telemedicine: Liability and Regulatory Issues." Washington, D.C.: American Health Lawyers Association [Report No. VHI99–0005], 1999, 49 pages.

Discusses medical malpractice and liability issues, FDA regulation of medical devices, reimbursement by public and private payers, fraud and abuse issues for telemedicine networks, and risk management.

Alan S. Goldberg. "Health Care and Telecommunications Technology." Washington, D.C.: American Health Lawyers Association [Report No. VMC-0031], 1998, 73 pages.

Discusses issues in telemedicine involving licensure, reimbursement, liability, privacy, and confidentiality. Examines selected case law, state telemedicine laws, and proposed laws to regulate the practice of medicine across state lines. Includes a copy of *Shannon* v. *McNulty*, No. 940, Pittsburgh 1997 (Pa. Super. Ct. Oct. 5, 1998), holding that HMOs are subject to corporate liability when the HMO is acting like a hospital.

Alan S. Goldberg. "Telemedicine and the Law: An Interim Report." Washington, D.C.: American Health Lawyers Association [Report No. VHL98–0012], 1998, 15 pages.

Telemedicine continues to affect how and where health care is delivered, but legal constraints remain. With examples of success and analysis of failures, these materials present immersion into the current law and lore of telemedicine.

Alan S. Goldberg and Jocelyn F. Gordon. "Telemedicine: Emerging Legal Issues." (2nd ed.) Washington, D.C.: American Health Lawyers Association [Item No. WM990003], 1999, 159 pages.

Topics examined in this spiral-bound monograph include licensing and telemedicine, HCFA policy regarding future reimbursement for telemedicine, Medicare, Medicaid, private payers, telemedicine and the antikickback statute, liability and telemedicine, informed consent, privacy and confidentiality, FDA regulation, and FCC funding.

Alan S. Goldberg and Jocelyn F. Gordon. *Telemedicine: Emerging Legal Issues.* (2nd ed.) Washington, D.C.: American Health Lawyers Association [Book No. WM98–0002], 1999.

This book includes more than thirty pages of tables and exhibits that list existing federal and state law and pending legislation, making this a quick and easy-to-use reference. The authors offer insight into, and a strategic overview of, the primary issues surrounding telemedicine, including questions about licensing, reimbursement, liability, informed consent, privacy, and confidentiality. In addition, they discuss FDA regulation and Federal Communications Commission funding for telemedicine.

Alan S. Goldberg and Jocelyn F. Gordon. "Telemedicine: Emerging Legal Issues." Washington, D.C.: National Health Lawyers Association [Report No. MC97–0021], 1997, 104 pages.

Describes the emerging legal issues involved with the practice of telemedicine, including licensing, reimbursement, liability, informed consent, privacy, and confidentiality. It also discusses the FDA's regulatory policies and new FCC support for emerging telemedical technology. Appendices include a table of existing and pending federal and state legislation concerning telemedicine, and HCFA's list of states reimbursing services using telemedicine.

Alice G. Gosfield. "Disease and Demand Management: State of the Art and Legal Concerns." Washington, D.C.: American Health Lawyers Association [Report No. VMC98–0038], 1998, 21 pages.

Discusses disease management, demand management, and telemedicine, including the motivation for these programs, controversies associated with them, their prevalence, contracting issues, and general legal issues. Contains new case law and new prevalence data.

Alice G. Gosfield. "Disease Management, Demand Management, and Telemedicine: The Leading Edge of Managed Care." In Alice G. Gosfield (ed.), *Health Law Handbook*, St. Paul, Minn.: West, Group, 1998. (Formerly published by Clark, Boardman, Callaghan in earlier editions.)

This article examines the foundations for disease management, demand management, and telemedicine as techniques to influence appropriate health care delivery; presents typical features of these programs; considers some of the controversies they generate; and explores the developing and speculative legal issues they raise.

Lisa I. Iezzoni. *The Potential of Telemedicine: A Guide to Assessing Telecommunications in Health Care.* Washington, D.C.: National Academy Press, 1996, 271 pages.

Presents a framework for evaluating patient-care applications of information and telecommunications technologies to provide and support health care when the participants are separated by distance. Identifies the managerial, technical, policy, legal, and human factors that must be added to the cost-benefit equation. Addresses issues of professional licensure, malpractice liability, privacy, confidentiality, security, and payment policies, among others. Also looks at evaluating specific aspects, such as transmitting images and remote consulting. The text, prepared by the Institute's Committee on Evaluating Clinical Applications of Telemedicine, is supplemented by an exhaustive list of references; glossary and explanation of acronyms; index; and bibliography; as well as a large number of tables, figures, and boxes.

Patricia C. Kuszler. "Telemedicine and Integrated Health Care Delivery: Compounding Malpractice Liability." *American Journal of Law and Medicine*, 1999, *25*, 297.

Analyzes use of communications technology as applied to telemedicine. The author's particular interest concerns how theories of medical negligence might be applied in telemedicine and integrated delivery health plans. She focuses on shared liability among health professionals involved in delivering telemedicine services, either as primary providers or as consultants.

Arti K. Rai. "Reflective Choice in Health Care: Using Information Technology to Present Allocation Options." *American Journal of Law and Medicine*, 1999, *25*, 387.

Examines using the Internet as a means through which health care consumers can obtain information on health care plans and on specific coverage options. The author's interest lies in exploring whether subscriber use of the Internet for information about health care plans will give consumers what they need to make sound choices about competing plans and coverage.

Stephen J. Schanz. *1999 Compendium of Telemedicine Laws.* Raleigh, N.C.: Legamed, 1999, 229 pages.

This annually published book presents an in-depth description of the various requirements of state and federal laws. It is logically arranged in four sections highlighting state statutes, codes, and opinions; federal laws, opinions, and reports; relevant medical journal articles and telemedicine-related Websites; and a listing of law review articles. The book also offers an excellent reference source of addresses and contact information for state licensing and regulatory authorities, as well as definitions of state laws governing the practice of medicine that have been modified to better define issues affected by the advent of telemedicine. It also highlights an advisory opinion rendered by the OIG regarding telemedicine consultation arrangements and the HCFA Internet Security Policy.

Kathryn F. Twiddy. "Fundamentals of Healthcare Computer Contracting." Washington, D.C.: American Health Lawyers Association [Report No. VHI99–0010], 1999, 39 pages.

Discusses software license and development agreements, related information technology agreements, confidentiality, records and data management, and corporate changes. Also discusses unique aspects of health care law and practice in the areas of fraud and abuse, system security, and telemedicine issues.

Robert J. Waters. "Telemedicine, Healthcare, and Technology: The Coming Revolution in Healthcare Delivery." Washington, D.C.: American Health Lawyers Association [Report No VHL99–0008], 1999.

Examines legal and regulatory issues in the emerging field of telemedicine, including licensing, fraud and abuse, malpractice, electronic misappropriation of health information, and payment considerations. Footnotes cite relevant regulations and case law.

Part Four

Selected Health Care Policy Topics

Health Care Reform

In the twentieth century, Americans have been witnesses to a revolution in the medical sciences and technology that continues to accelerate at breathtaking speed as new advances are announced daily. Yet the debate over health policy has been remarkably constant since President Harry S. Truman, in the aftermath of World War II, proposed establishing a comprehensive medical system financed through Social Security taxes. Truman's plan for a national health insurance system immediately ran into opposition from the American Medical Association and a Congress that concluded the program would be too political, too expensive, too administratively burdensome, and too detrimental to the nation's economic health. Such complaints would resound in the halls of power once again nearly fifty years later, when President Clinton offered a new national health insurance scheme in 1993. Today, at the beginning of a new century, health policy remains a perplexing problem for a nation so diverse in its population—ethnically, socially, and regionally.

ANNOTATIONS

Henry J. Aaron. "End of an Era: The New Debate Over Health Care Financing." *Brookings Review*, 1996, *14*(1), 34.

> The nature of the debate over health care financing after the demise of the Clinton health care plan will be transformed by the rise in the number of companies that have hired organizations to manage the health care of their employees. Most insured working-age Americans now receive care through an organization that uses at least some practices associated with managed care. Nearly everyone is expected to be under such arrangements within the next few years. In addition, the flow of cross-subsidies to pay for care for the uninsured has been drying up, and the number of uninsured has increased.
>
> The number of surviving managed care plans is expected to fall. As this happens, the issue of whether the government should regulate an industry in which only a small number of companies control the market will emerge. The process will have three stages: (1) the number of uninsured will rise; (2) popular discontent will grow as the security of insurance coverage for middle-income households is undermined; and (3) health care delivery organizations will be viewed as a kind of public utility, and government will assume responsibility to ensure delivery of care to the uninsured.

Henry J. Aaron. "The Oregon Experiment." In M. A. Strosberg and others (eds.), *Rationing America's Medical Care: The Oregon Plan and Beyond*. Washington, D.C.: Brookings Institution, 1992.

> A group of essays using the Oregon rationing plan as an opportunity to discuss health care rationing.

Henry J. Aaron. *Serious and Unstable Condition: Financing America's Health Care.* Washington, D.C.: Brookings Institution, 1991, 158 pages.

A lay reader's guide to the debate over how to reform the U.S. health financing system. The author, the director of the Brookings economic studies program, reviews the problems confronting the government, private insurers, business, labor, physicians, hospital administrators, and the general population.

Henry J. Aaron (ed.). *The Problem That Won't Go Away: Reforming U.S. Health Care Financing.* Washington, D.C.: Brookings Institution, 1996, 298 pages.

Essay collection constituting a postmortem on the Clinton health care plan. It poses and attempts to answer a number of questions: Why did the plan fail so totally? Did it ever stand a chance of passage? Has the Clinton plan's defeat removed health care reform from the national agenda? Or will it reappear, in a new or a familiar guise, in a few years? Meanwhile, what changes in health care financing deserve immediate consideration because they could move the financing system incrementally in a desirable direction in the long run? Particularly praiseworthy is Graham K. Wilson's essay on interest groups in the health care debate, in which he identifies the most significant players and their agendas and strategies.

Laurie Kaye Abraham. *Mama Might Be Better Off Dead: The Failure of Health Care in Urban America.* Chicago: University of Chicago Press, 1993, 289 pages.

The author, who has degrees in law and journalism, follows four generations of a black family that lives in one of Chicago's poorest neighborhoods, North Lawndale. The book presents a qualitative description of the much-discussed problem of access to care. By following this family, Abraham is able to go behind the one-time tragedies and endless flow of health statistics that make the news and make sense of the oft-uttered phrase "lack of access to care." The writer does a superb job of balancing her admiration for the family and (most of) the health care personnel with outrage at the chronic underfunding of the Medicaid and Medicare programs, which have failed not only their patients but also the institutions that serve them.

Stuart H. Altman and Uwe R. Reinhardt (eds.). *Improving Health Policy and Management. Nine Critical Issues for the 1990s: The Baxter Health Policy Review,* Vol. 1. Chicago: Health Administration Press, 1992, 505 pages.

This award-winning book analyzes a number of key forces to explain the nature of our health care system and to offer a framework for evaluating health policy.

Stuart H. Altman and Uwe R. Reinhardt (eds.). *Strategic Choices for a Changing Health Care System.* Chicago: Health Administration Press, 1996, 413 pages.

Consists of a series of eleven essays, written in the wake of the defeat of the Clinton health care plan, on HMOs and other methods of reducing health care. The second volume in the Baxter Health Policy Series, underwritten by the Baxter Foundation of Deerfield, Illinois, this is one of the first books to help "front-line decision makers understand the evolution and implications of the new structure of the health care enterprise."

George Anders. *Health Against Wealth: HMOs and the Breakdown of Medical Trust.* Boston: Houghton Mifflin, 1996, 299 pages.

This thoroughly researched jeremiad against managed care, written by a reporter for the *Wall Street Journal,* exposes and explains what is unpalatable and even threatening about HMOs. In making his case that HMOs pose dangers to patient care, Anders traces the evolution of health care delivery in the United States since World War II. He then sets forth his thesis: (1) HMOs are too powerful; (2) they can and do commit abuses; and (3) patients must demand the care they need despite HMO resistance. Anders punctuates his arguments with anecdotes of tragedy and frustration that appeal to the reader's sympathy.

Richard J. Arnould and others (eds.). *Competitive Approaches to Health Care Reform.* Washington, D.C.: Urban Institute Press, 1993, 361 pages.

Presents a series of essays arising from a seminar at the University of Illinois. The contributors, overwhelmingly economists or professors of management, discuss a range of issues concerning development of health care markets, the consequences of new technology, the cases for and against competitive reform in health care, and an empirical test of competition in the Medicare HMO market.

Stephen M. Ayres. *Health Care in the United States: The Facts and the Choices.* Chicago: American Library Association, 1996, 277 pages.

This well-written book, targeted at the general reader, imparts (1) what is wrong with the American health care system, (2) what is right about it, (3) how we got where we are today, and (4) how we can provide high-quality health care to all Americans at an affordable price. Each chapter concludes with a helpful bibliography.

James F. Blumstein. "Health Care Reform: The Policy Context." *Wake Forest Law Review,* 1994, 29, 15.

Presents an overview of the policy considerations involved in efforts to reform health care delivery. Blumstein, a professor at Vanderbilt Law School, begins by analyzing what he sees as the two principal sets of health policy issues. The first, efficiency issues, concern the functioning of the medical marketplace. The second set is issues of equity, concerning primarily differing policy views regarding government's obligation to ensure access to health care. Blumstein next turns to discussion of the policy issues in the institutional design of health care mechanisms. He analyzes health care as both an entitlement and an obligation and discusses health care delivery systems that incorporate these principles. Finally, he discusses the issue of comprehensive reform, concluding that current, publicly articulated rationales for government determination of private medical expenditures are neither straightforward nor persuasive.

James F. Blumstein and Frank A. Sloan. "Redefining Government's Role in Health Care: Is a Dose of Competition What the Doctor Should Order?" *Vanderbilt Law Review,* 1981, 34, 849.

This introductory essay to a Vanderbilt Law School symposium on competition in health care advocates a change in policy orientation toward market-oriented alternatives to health care delivery. There is a role for the state in ensuring that patients have ready access to truthful information about the array of choices they face in the medical marketplace. Government action may be necessary to be certain that competitive efforts are not forestalled by collective actions of entrenched provider groups. There should be experimentation with a variety of market-oriented approaches on a small scale. The authors conclude by calling for a gradualist approach toward market-oriented reform.

Harvey Bograd and others. "Extending Health Maintenance Organization Insurance to the Uninsured." *Journal of the American Medical Association,* Apr. 2, 1997, 277, 1067.

Investigates the utilization of health services of low-income patients after they became insured by an HMO by means of a retrospective study of utilization in a previously uninsured group compared with an age- and sex-matched randomly selected control group of commercial HMO enrollees. With the increased prevalence of HMOs, it is likely that future efforts to extend services to the uninsured will take place within managed care settings. The authors conclude that compared with a commercial group of the same age and sex, the patterns of utilization were similar and the financial costs of care were only moderately more for a previously uninsured group offered comprehensive HMO insurance.

Mollyann Brodie and Robert J. Blendon. "The Public's Contribution to Congressional Gridlock on Health Care Reform." *Journal of Health Politics, Policy, and Law*, 1995, *20*, 403.

Although surveys indicated strong public support for universal health insurance coverage, there was never any consensus on how to achieve it. When given a choice of plans that promised universal coverage, such as employer mandate, single payer, and tax-credit arrangement, no alternative received majority support. The public was generally divided into thirds across the options. Although employer mandate garnered somewhat greater public approval, support for it decreased during the debate over health care reform. An in-depth look at public attitudes as early as 1993 showed that for most Americans the critical question was whether their families would fare better or worse under a given reform plan. Media coverage and advertising campaigns sponsored by the key interest groups pointed to potential negative outcomes of comprehensive reform for individuals, particularly those who already had health insurance and enjoyed a wide choice of physicians and hospitals.

By the end of the debate, the middle class became more worried about the possible negative effect of health care reform than they were about the problem itself. Concurrently, the national recession subsided, easing the economic threat to the middle class of losing their health insurance. These factors, combined with signs of a dramatic restructuring within the health care industry, indicated to some that the health care system could transform itself without government intervention. Although divergent currents of public opinion may not have been the only cause of Congressional gridlock during the summer of 1994, it clearly made it easier for the Congress to enter the 1994 elections without having voted on major health reform legislation.

Lawrence D. Brown. "Dogmatic Slumbers: American Business and Health Policy." *Journal of Health Politics, Policy, and Law*, 1993, *18*, 339.

The reluctance of U.S. corporations to enter the battle to reform health care is a tantalizing political mystery, because political engagement usually occurs where there are strong economic incentives. Brown argues that the political diffidence of business in the sphere of health care derives from sectoral fragmentation that anesthetizes three key political motives for political action: economics, organization, and ideology. Lower spending on health services might reduce income growth and economic activities in some communities and thereby depress demand for corporate products. It is not business that swallows rising health care prices; rather, employees pay the bulk of that price in the form of lower real cash income, in the long run.

Despite the oddities of the health care market and problems in slowing the growth of costs, many business leaders retain faith in private, market, voluntary, and communitarian correctives and remain chary of regulatory intervention. The CEOs who could form strong leadership for reform are rarely prepared to commit much time and effort to these struggles, beyond managing benefits within the corporation itself. Additionally, the kinds of reform that a business leader would advocate depend on whether his business faces tough foreign competition and strong unions, whether health insurance is currently extended to employees, and whether the business self-insures and thereby escapes state regulation (included mandated benefits). Even if corporate leaders agreed in detail on what they wanted from health policy reform, they might choose to save their political capital for battles that count more heavily.

Catholic Health Association of the United States. *With Justice for All? The Ethics of Health Care Rationing*. St. Louis, Mo.: Catholic Health Association, 1991.

Although many associate Catholic medical ethics with strong positions on abortion and contraception, its equally strong position on access to health care is not well known. It defines rationing as "withholding of potentially beneficial health care services because policies and practices limit resources available for health care." This work asserts that access to health care services necessary for developing and maintaining life is a human right.

Jeffrey F. Chase-Lubitz. "The Corporate Practice of Medicine Doctrine: An Anachronism in the Modern Health Care Industry." (Comment.) *Vanderbilt Law Review,* 1987, *40,* 445.

Highlights the need to revisit corporate-practice-of-medicine prohibitions, which arose in response to fears that corporate involvement in medicine would restrict physicians' independence and commercialize medical practice. The AMA, the medical profession's organizing body, enacted ethical restrictions against corporate practice. Courts applied the prohibition against corporate practice based on broad interpretations of state medical practice acts and for reasons of public policy.

In recent years, few cases have arisen concerning the doctrine. As corporate involvement in health care intensifies, however, invocation of the corporate-practice prohibitions becomes more likely. These prohibitions threaten the development of nontraditional health care delivery systems in many states. For innovation of delivery systems to continue, the author contends, state courts and legislatures should modify corporate-practice prohibitions to reflect current views on physician autonomy and the role of commercialism in medicine.

Michael H. Cohen. *Complementary and Alternative Medicine: Legal Boundaries and Regulatory Perspectives.* Baltimore: Johns Hopkins University Press, 1998, 180 pages.

Legal authority, the author writes, is slowly becoming more tolerant of patients' autonomy and more supportive of freedom of access to nonorthodox medical providers and treatments. In this book, he describes that shift by analyzing the present legal status of complementary and alternative medicine. He also suggests how regulatory structures might evolve further to support a comprehensive, holistic, and balanced approach to health, one that permits deeper integration of biomedicine and complementary and alternative medicine while continuing to protect patients from fraudulent and dangerous treatments.

John M. Eisenberg, M.D. *Doctors' Decisions and the Cost of Medical Care.* Chicago: Health Administration Press Perspectives, 1986, 190 pages.

Concludes that when HMO physicians are involved in administrative roles related to cost containment, reduced use of diagnostic testing results. The author, a professor of general internal medicine at the University of Pennsylvania, further notes that doctors in these organizations who report greater participation in managing their practices are also more satisfied with their work.

Paul M. Ellwood and Alain C. Enthoven. "'Responsible Choices': The Jackson Hole Group Plan for Health Care Reform." *Health Affairs,* 1995, *14,* 24.

The authors update earlier recommendations of the Jackson Hole Group, which invented the concept of managed care. This proposal has five objectives: (1) to bring Medicare and Medicaid costs into line with their funding, (2) to make tax benefits of health care more equitable, (3) to allow small purchasers to have the same advantages as large groups of purchasers, (4) to ensure that consumers know what various health plans offer, and (5) to set timely and realistic targets and measure results as reform proceeds.

Paul Elwood and others. "Health Maintenance Strategy." *Medical Care,* 1971, *92,* 91.

This early article was written by the original proponents of the HMO concept.

Alain Enthoven. "Why Not the Clinton Health Plan?" *Inquiry,* 1994, *31,* 129.

The author contends that the Clinton plan was based on price controls, which have unintended consequences and will not work, and would have been a complete government takeover of the health care industry.

Alain C. Enthoven. "The History and Principles of Managed Competition." *Health Affairs*, 1993, *12*, 24.

One of the striking features of the U.S. health care economy is how little value-for-money competition there is. Well into the 1980s, the principles of the traditional fee-for-service system (guild free choice) dominated the system. They were enforced by legislation, professional ostracism, denial of staff privileges, and harassment. Blue Cross and Blue Shield were created by hospital associations and medical societies to apply guild principles to health care financing, and only recently have providers been forced to yield controlling positions on their boards. Likewise, commercial insurance companies offered coverage based on the casualty model. Open-ended, cost-unconscious demands of insured patients, combined with large increases in federal funding for biomedical research, led to a huge outpouring of costly medical technologies.

The origins of today's competitors, who have survived strong opposition by organized medicine, are multispecialty group practices that contracted with employment groups and individuals to provide a comprehensive set of health care services to exchange for a periodic per capita payment that was established in advance. The author defines the term *managed competition* and explains how he thinks it should function.

Alain Enthoven. "The Competition Strategy: Status and Prospects." *New England Journal of Medicine*, 1981, *304*, 109.

In this article, Enthoven describes a variety of proposals that would break the link between jobs and health insurance. The link is an important barrier to new health plans' entering the market, he writes, and it greatly complicates the problems of insuring people who are not regular members of employment groups.

Alain Enthoven. "Consumer-Centered Versus Job-Centered Health Insurance." *Harvard Business Review*, 1979, *57*, 141.

Argues that the primary barrier to developing alternative delivery systems is the prevalence of employer provision of a single health insurance plan to all employees.

Alain Enthoven. "Consumer-Choice Health Plan: A National Health Insurance Proposal Based on Regulated Competition in the Private Sector." *New England Journal of Medicine*, 1978, *298*, 650.

This is an early articulation of managed competition as an approach to health care reform, written by a Stanford Business School economist.

Alain Enthoven. *Health Plan: The Only Practical Solution to the Soaring Cost of Medical Care*. Reading, Mass.: Addison-Wesley, 1980.

In this seminal early work, Enthoven proposes competition among health care providers.

Richard A. Epstein. *Mortal Peril: Our Inalienable Right to Health Care?* Reading, Mass.: Addison-Wesley, 1997, 503 pages.

The first half of this book attacks the notion that there exists any right to universal access to health care; in doing so it examines such topics as community rating, preexisting conditions, Medicare, and President Clinton's proposed Health Security Act. The second part examines various aspects of patient self-determination, including organ transplantation, death and dying, and liability issues. The book concludes with an extensive table of cases, index, and endnotes.

Judith Feder and Larry Levitt. "Steps Toward Universal Coverage." *Health Affairs*, 1995, *14*, 140.

The fundamental goal of universal coverage does not need to be implemented all at once in a single reform; instead it can be effected by incremental changes in insurance reform, expanding coverage for working families, and support for long-term care. Changes in insurance coverage could include guaranteeing access regardless of health status, phasing out experience rating, and making sure that individual purchasers are covered and everyone is pooled in the same coverage, so that some will not be charged too much. Regulation would be necessary to guarantee access to all, and that would not be politically easy. It would be easier to guarantee access for children. Some steps would be difficult to enact, but not as difficult as attempting to pass a single overall reform such as the Clinton Plan.

Peter D. Fox and others. *Managed Care and Chronic Illnesses: Challenges and Opportunities.* Gaithersburg, Md.: Aspen, 1996, 304 pages.

Discusses such topics as meeting the needs of chronically ill patients in an HMO, the role of HMOs in integrating care for persons with special health care needs, Kaiser Colorado's cooperative health care clinic, enhancing preventive and primary care for children with chronic or disabling conditions served in HMOs, and a consumer's perspective on caring for children with special needs in HMOs.

Donald K. Freeborn and Clyde R. Pope. *Promise and Performance in Managed Care: The Prepaid Group Practice Model.* Baltimore: Johns Hopkins University Press, 1994, 169 pages.

Examines the potential for HMOs of the group practice variety to deliver managed care, and some of the consequences. Written by two researchers at the Kaiser Permanente (Northwest) Center for Health Research, this monograph opens with a brief history of managed care and describes its major types. It then focuses on why people choose alternative plans, and the characteristics that differentiate people who choose the Kaiser Permanente (KP) prepaid group practice plan from those who do not.

The book's next section examines factors influencing access to and use of services at KP, and the relationship between people's perceived need for care and their actual use of services. The authors then turn to how consumers evaluate their experiences with the KP managed care system and their level of satisfaction with access, costs, and the quality of care and service. Other topics addressed include physicians' views of the KP managed care system, factors influencing physician satisfaction, and the implications of managed care for national health policy. The book is amply supplemented with graphs, tables, an index, and an extensive list of references.

Victor R. Fuchs. *The Future of Health Policy.* Cambridge, Mass.: Harvard University Press, 1993, 246 pages.

Focuses, by way of an attempt at a dispassionate approach, on such topics as poverty and health, how the Canadian health care system functions, cost containment, rationing, and technology assessment. A health care economist at Stanford, Fuchs concludes that although the prospects for some form of national health insurance are poor in the short run, in the long run national health insurance is far from dead. He specifically predicts that national health insurance will come to the United States in the wake of a major change in the political climate, the kind of change that most often accompanies a war, depression, or large-scale civil unrest.

Victor Fuchs and others. "Health Care for the Elderly: How Much? Who Will Pay for It?" In "The Future of Medicare" (Symposium Issue). *Health Affairs,* Jan.–Feb. 1999, *18*(1), 11.

Health care expenditures on the elderly tend to grow about 4 percent per year more rapidly than the gross domestic product. This could plunge the nation into a severe economic and social crisis within two decades. This paper describes recent growth in age- and sex-specific health care utilization by the elderly and discusses the important role of technology in that growth. It also explores the potential for the elderly to pay for additional care through increases in work and savings. Efforts to "save Medicare" will prove to be "too little, too late" unless they are embedded in broader policy initiatives that slow the rate of growth of health care spending and increase the income of the elderly.

E. Preston Gee and Allan Fine. *Dealing Direct: A Strategy for Business-Provider Partnership.* Chicago: AHA Press, 1997, 112 pages.

Examines the environmental forces that make direct contracting attractive, and offers an introduction to direct contracting, along with the "correct" reasons to contract with employers. Health care organizations attempting to improve care while reducing costs and becoming more competitive in the marketplace have found direct contracting to be a viable strategic option. This book also addresses such vital legal and regulatory issues as antitrust, fraud, liability, and self-referral laws; Medicare secondary payer issues; and other important rules. The authors supply an overview of timing issues, responsibilities of employers and providers, contract structures, and regulatory obstacles.

Basil S. Georgopoulos (ed.). *Organizational Research on Health Institutions.* Ann Arbor, Mich.: Institute for Social Research, University of Michigan, 1972.

Original research summarizing the then-current state of thinking on health organizations.

Basil S. Georgopoulos (ed.). *Profession of Medicine: A Study of the Sociology of Applied Knowledge.* New York: Dodd, Mead, 1970.

An insightful early study of the social organization of the medical profession.

S. M. Gerson and J. E. Gladieux. "Advice of Counsel: Eroding Confidentiality in Federal Health Care Law." *Alabama Law Review,* 1999, *51,* 163.

Where once advice given by lawyers was essentially immune from disclosure under the attorney-client privilege and the related attorney work product doctrine and self-evaluation privilege, that advice is now being ordered disclosed by the courts or voluntarily disclosed by the parties in federal health care matters, and the privilege surrounding it is eroding in a manner that is affecting the quality of the attorney-client relationship and also placing attorneys at personal risk. This article is an alarm for preparedness, not a prescription for legal change.

Sherry Glied. *Chronic Condition: Why Health Reform Fails.* Cambridge, Mass.: Harvard University Press, 1997, 288 pages.

Analyzes the causes of the current health care crisis and the shortcomings of reform proposals. A professor of economics at Columbia University who served in both the Bush and Clinton administrations, Glied contends that rising health care expenditures are consistent with a rising standard of living. Because we can, as a nation, afford more health care, reform must address not the overall level of health care costs but the distribution of health care spending. Glied argues that prior reform proposals have failed to account for the tension between the public's interest in improving health care quality and the equally widespread interest in ensuring that the less fortunate share in those improvements. After a detailed evaluation of the Clinton administration's failed proposal, she suggests a new solution that would make the willingness to pay for innovation the means of financing health care improvements for the less affluent. The book's text is supplemented by a variety of illustrations and six tables.

Mark A. Goldberg and others. "The Relation Between Universal Health Insurance and Cost Control." *New England Journal of Medicine,* 1995, *332,* 742.

Cost control and universal coverage not only *can* be combined in a single health care system but *should* be. Americans could reduce costs by abolishing health insurance. If third-party payment is to be the norm, then costs could be controlled by systemwide bargaining and rule making substituting for individual price bargaining (for example, standard fee schedules). Overhead would be reduced, because providers and payers would engage in one round of wholesale price negotiations rather than multiple rounds of retail bargaining. More of the health funds would go to the care providers, and less to the administrative staff or outside managers and consultants. Because they provide care for everyone, universal systems are able to develop ways of managing the capacity of the system as a whole, thus preventing an expensive medical arms race and "cost shifting."

Jacob S. Hacker. *The Road to Nowhere: The Genesis of President Clinton's Plan for Health Security.* Princeton, N.J.: Princeton University Press, 1997, 240 pages.

Calling the defeat of President Clinton's proposal for comprehensive health care reform "one of the most dramatic reversals of political fortune since President Woodrow Wilson's ill-fated campaign on behalf of the League of Nations," the author focuses on why Clinton made the attempt in the first place and why it took the direction that it did. Specifically, Hacker focuses on why the notion of "managed care" came to dominate policy discussions instead of the more widely discussed proposals known as "single payer" or "pay or play" that had been considered more credible by policy analysts earlier in the debate.

Robert B. Hackey. *Rethinking Health Care Policy: The New Politics of State Regulation.* Washington, D.C.: Georgetown University Press, 1998, 272 pages.

The author analyzes the varied routes states have taken in reformulating health care policy and provides a road map of which specific strategies work and why. In this comparative case study, Hackey focuses on four states—Massachusetts, New Hampshire, New York, and Rhode Island—that have had markedly different experiences with regulating health care over the past two decades. Hackey's detailed comparisons show how the states' policies changed over time, moving from regulatory to market-oriented solutions, and examines which policy programs appear best poised to meet the future.

Hackey uses regime theory to explain how the states' policy choices concerning cost control and entry regulation were shaped by the prevailing political culture and institutions of each state. He concludes that the autonomy of state government from special interests is vital to successful adoption, implementation, and outcomes of state initiatives.

Mark A. Hall. "The Individual Health Insurance Market: An Evaluation of New York's Reform." *Journal of Health Politics, Policy, and Law,* 2000, 25, 71.

Examines New York State's comprehensive reforms, prompted by mounting losses at Empire Blue Cross Blue Shield.

Mark A. Hall. "The Individual Health Insurance Market, An Evaluation of Vermont's Reform." *Journal of Health Policy, Politics, and Law,* 2000, 25, 101.

Analyzes the state's reform law, implementing nearly pure community rating, which eliminates most conventional rating factors, such as health status, age, gender, and even geographic location. The author brings health policy reform down out of the clouds by including transcripts of interviews he conducted with insurance agents in the state, who discuss in frank terms the impact of the legislation on their work and their unvarnished view of the individual health insurance market ["a pain in the ass," says one]. Concludes that Vermont's reforms stand out as a qualified success.

Mark A. Hall. *Making Medical Spending Decisions: The Law, Ethics, and Economics of Rationing Mechanisms.* New York: Oxford University Press, 1997, 300 pages.

Hall begins with the premise that rationing of health care services is inevitable in some form—and indeed already exists in irrational and unjust ways in the United States. He then engages in analysis of social institutions that seeks to assess the relative strengths, weaknesses, and characteristics of alternative mechanisms for allocating health care resources, drawing from both political economics and social theory.

Mark A. Hall. "Rationing Health Care at the Bedside." *New York University Law Review*, 1995, *69*, 693.

Advocates physician health care rationing. The collapse of the Clinton administration's national health care reform proposal left unresolved how best to limit rising costs and allocate limited resources within medicine. The rise of HMOs and other cost-conscious providers underscores the inevitability of health care rationing. Hall argues that although scholars and practitioners debate the fine points of various rationing criteria, they ignore the more fundamental question of who should be empowered to make rationing decisions. In this article, Hall calls for lifting the ethical taboo against physician bedside rationing. He argues that the prohibition is justified neither by actual practice nor by broad ethical principles. Physician rationing need not inject cost considerations into dramatic life-or-death medical decision making, since most rationing entails marginal decisions in day-to-day practice.

With this in mind, Hall demonstrates that neither the beneficence nor the autonomy principle of medical ethics dictates a blanket prohibition on physician rationing. He argues further that financial incentives for physician rationing should be permitted if reasonable and disclosed. Hall concludes by calling for an end to the debate over whether bedside rationing is ever justified so that we can proceed with the important task of developing a new ethical framework that incorporates physician rationing.

Mark A. Hall and Robert A. Berenson. "The Ethics of Managed Care: A Dose of Realism." *Cumberland Law Review*, 1998, *28*, 287.

This article examines the ethics of medical practice under managed care from a pragmatic perspective that gives physicians more useful guidance than existing ethical statements. The authors' starting premises and framework for constructing a realistic set of ethical principles are as follows: that bedside rationing in some form is permissible; that medical ethics derive from the physician's role as healer; that actual agreements usually trump hypothetical ones; that ethical statements are primarily aspirational, not regulatory; and that preserving patient trust is the primary objective.

The authors then articulate the following concrete ethical guides: financial incentives should influence physicians to maximize the health of the group of patients under their care; physicians should not enter into incentive arrangements that they would be embarrassed to describe accurately to their patients or that are not in common use in the market; physicians should treat each patient impartially, without regard to source of payment, and in a manner consistent with the physician's own treatment style; if physicians depart from this ideal, they must tell their patients honestly; and it is desirable, although not mandatory, to differentiate medical treatment recommendations from insurance coverage decisions by clearly assigning authority over these different roles and by having physicians advocate for recommended treatment that is not covered.

John W. Hardin. "An In-Depth Look at Congressional Committee Jurisdictions Surrounding Health Issues." *Journal of Health Politics, Policy, and Law*, June 1998, *23*, 517.

Congress plays an important role in shaping U.S. health care policy, and within Congress, committees play the lead policy-making role. To determine the range and extent of committee involvement on health issues, the author examines nine health issue categories over a fifteen-year period (1979–1993) to discover how both "legislative" and "nonlegislative" committee jurisdictions differ across three dimensions: congressional chambers, committees within those chambers, and specific health issue categories. He finds that differences in jurisdiction across each dimension follow general patterns resulting from issue-specific factors.

Clark C. Havighurst. "Competition in Health Services: Overview, Issues, and Answers." *Vanderbilt Law Review*, 1981, *34*, 1117.

Argues that the empirical evidence supporting market-based competitive strategy, although still highly anecdotal, is increasingly compelling. Havighurst concludes that if care is taken about details of implementation, the market reform strategy of removing demand distortions and restraints on innovation would do just what it sets out to do—that is, facilitate efficient allocation of private resources in providing health care services.

Clark C. Havighurst. *Deregulating the Health Care Industry: Planning for Competition.* Cambridge, Mass.: Ballinger, 1982, 500 pages.

Contends that health policy makers—including the system's planners and regulators—would do well to begin viewing competition as a vehicle for turning the health care industry's fragmentation into a virtue. A major proponent of market-based health care reform, Havighurst contends that if properly nurtured, competition could supply the impetus for restructuring the industry not into a single centrally controlled system but into a variety of competing systems. Competing health care plans and financing mechanisms could take a variety of forms. Havighurst's views have effectively prevailed since the collapse of the Clinton health care reform proposal in 1994.

Clark C. Havighurst. *Health Care Choices: Private Contracts as Instruments of Health Reform.* Washington, D.C.: American Enterprise Institute Press, 1995, 341 pages.

Contends that private contracts can be used far more innovatively and effectively than they have been to date to accomplish consumer-driven health care reform. Havighurst argues that the private market fails to offer consumers a range of options that would be offered if private contracts were used to specify the legal rights of patients faced with financing entities and health care providers. He argues that the American health care sector has long been dominated by providers, government, and the legal system. Private contracts could serve to put those important, highly personal decisions back into the hands of consumers—the people who rely on it for their well-being.

Clark C. Havighurst. "Prospective Self-Denial: Can Consumers Contract Today to Accept Health Care Rationing Tomorrow?" *University of Pennsylvania Law Review,* 1992, *140,* 1755.

Explores whether "prospective self-denial"—that is, voluntary decisions by consumers to economize by accepting substantial restrictions on their freedom to draw upon a common fund for future medical needs—can be useful in rationalizing societal spending on health care services. The author concludes that it would be extremely helpful in advancing the needed rethinking of medical care if private agreements for health care financing could be conceptualized and implemented as contracts of prospective self-denial.

Because radical public health reform has been stymied by political gridlock, there is a need to improve the market's ability to control cost and to offer affordable options to those currently without any coverage at all. This, the author argues, can only be done by letting consumers (and public health care programs as well) exercise more control over what they spend. Health care contracts should be viewed as promising tools for achieving this goal. The author concludes that if society can find the will and the skills needed to use these tools well, it should be possible by private action to end the medical profession's dominance and to restore to consumers their customary sovereignty.

Clark C. Havighurst and James F. Blumstein. "Coping with Quality/Cost Tradeoffs in Medical Care: The Role of PSROs." *Northwestern University Law Review,* 1975, *70,* 6.

This article laid some of the early groundwork for applying market theory to health care law and public policy.

Institute of Medicine. *Managing Managed Care: Quality Improvement in Behavioral Health.* Washington, D.C.: National Academy Press, 1997, 370 pages.

Discusses key areas related to the rapid movement into managed care of treatment for mental health and substance abuse problems, also known as behavioral health. This report makes findings and proposes recommendations in twelve areas: structure and financing, accreditation, consumer involvement, cultural competence, special populations, research, workplace, wraparound services, children and adolescents, clinical practice guidelines, primary care, and ethical concerns. The text is supplemented by abundant tables, figures, illustrations, and a glossary.

Haynes Johnson and David S. Broder. *The System: The American Way of Politics at the Breaking Point.* Boston, Mass.: Little, Brown, 1996, 669 pages.

Written by two Washington newspaper columnists, this book chronicles, in a sometimes breathless fashion, the attempt to enact the Clinton Administration health reform package, which they characterize as the largest proposed set of domestic reforms in sixty years.

Timothy S. Jost. "The American Difference in Health Care Costs: Is There a Problem? Is Medical Necessity the Solution?" *Saint Louis Law Journal*, 1999, *43*, 1.

This article seeks to identify the real causes of high American health care costs by contrasting our health care spending patterns with those of other nations. It then considers what effect, if any, limiting coverage of unnecessary care might have on American health care costs. It concludes that our most serious problem is not so much excessive provision of unnecessary care as it is the denial to many of necessary care.

Timothy S. Jost. "German Health Care Reform." *Journal of Health Politics, Policy, and Law*, Aug. 1998, *23*, 697.

From the U.S. perspective, the German health care system offers much to be desired: universal access, moderate costs, and freedom of choice. The Germans consider their health care system to be in crisis, however, because the mechanisms on which they currently rely for financing and paying for health care, as well as the structures through which health care is delivered, seem increasingly less viable. Germany has recently adopted modest reforms to partially address these problems. For longer-term solutions, however, some in Germany are looking to U.S. managed care models, for better or worse.

Timothy S. Jost. "Health System Reform: Forward or Backward with Quality Oversight?" *JAMA*, 1994, *271*, 1508.

The author, a professor of law at Ohio State University, is skeptical of reform efforts that focus their efforts to assure quality on consumer choice and education, with minimal attention to quality regulation. It is questionable whether consumers are sufficiently equipped to evaluate the quality of goods and services. Further, the idea of comparison shopping for health care is relatively new and raises methodological questions regarding data collection and presentation. Outcomes data are meaningless and misleading unless they are adjusted for severity of illness, presence of comorbidities, documentation of advance directives, and other factors not under the control of providers. Significant incentives may exist for plans and providers to manipulate, or even misrepresent, data. One potential result of an information-rich environment is that consumers may be overwhelmed and make choices randomly related to their optimal choice.

Jerome P. Kassirer. "The Next Transformation of the Delivery of Health Care." *New England Journal of Medicine*, 1995, *332*, 52.

The following trends are likely to induce cultural changes in delivery of health care that are even more revolutionary than any restructuring that was occurring in the 1990s: (1) rapid growth of computer-based electronic communication; (2) a new generation increasingly comfortable with electronic transfer of information; and (3) a shift toward giving patients more responsibility for their medical care. Hospitals, medical centers, and HMOs will probably become more integrated to an electronic network, see their expertise, and link their capitated populations on-line with their own providers. Physicians will be expected to interpret more information, but how they will be able to interpret symptoms and results of home laboratory tests they receive on-line from patients is unclear.

Eleanor D. Kinney. "Behind the Veil Where the Action Is: Private Policy Making and American Health Care." *Administrative Law Review*, 1999, *51*, 145.

This article analyzes the private processes for coverage and quality policy for public and private health plans in the United States. It also reviews the development of coverage and quality since the advent of widespread health insurance coverage in the middle of the twentieth century. Additionally, it explores the process by which sponsors of public and private health plans make decisions concerning coverage and quality policy. Finally, it concludes with recommendations for policy-making procedures for private coverage and quality policy, as well as recommendations for the standard of care used to develop these policies.

Adele M. Kirk. "Riding the Bull: Reform in Washington, Kentucky, and Massachusetts." *Journal of Health Policy, Politics, and Law*, 2000, *25*, 133.

Describes the events leading up to reform in each of these states and traces the often troubled history of reform in these states from legislation through implementation (and in two cases, through partial repeal).

J. D. Kleinke. *Bleeding Edge: The Business of Health Care in the New Century.* Gaithersburg, Md.: Aspen, 1998, 338 pages.

This book offers a review of how managed care has transformed the management of patient care. It begins by discussing the issues that led to a need for health care reform, and continues by discussing the health care of today, with its focus on patient health management. Using tools of traditional business analysis, the author presents an enlightening analysis of how the factors that shaped our current system will also affect managed care in the next decade. This text helps make sense of a chaotic system by seeing it along an historical continuum, from past to future, with an understandable evolution and predictable outcome.

R. Korobkin. "The Efficiency of Managed Care 'Patient Protection' Laws: Incomplete Contracts, Bounded Rationality, and Market Failure." *Cornell Law Review*, 1999, *85*, 1.

Contends that policy makers need not naïvely believe that they can legislate away some of the problems of scarcity to support benefit mandates in some circumstances. For two primary reasons, market incentives are likely to encourage managed care organizations and other providers of health insurance to offer an inefficiently low level of benefits. First a game theoretic model suggests that, because it is impossible to completely specify the terms of a health insurance contract, managed care organizations have an incentive to provide a lower level of coverage than consumers might wish to purchase. Second, psychological research on consumer decision making suggests that purchasers of a product as complicated as health care coverage are likely to adopt selective, noncompensatory choice strategies. Such strategies will systematically reward suppliers that offer a low-price service rather than a high-quality one. Because of these market imperfections, mandated benefits can enhance rather than reduce efficiency.

Jennie Jacobs Kronenfeld. *The Changing Federal Role in U.S. Health Care Policy.* Westport, Conn.: Praeger, 1997, 187 pages.

Focuses on changes during the Reagan and Bush administrations and the failed attempt at reform during the first term of the Clinton administration.

David M. Lawrence, Patrick H. Mattingly, and John M. Ludden. "Trusting in the Future: The Distinct Advantage of Nonprofit HMOs." *Milbank Quarterly*, 1997, *75*, 5.

Asserts that managed care's success in improving the health status of communities can be directly attributed to the not-for-profits. Three of the major organizations—Harvard Community Health Plan, Kaiser Permanente, and Group Health Cooperative of Puget Sound—in this category have participated in the critical public policy debates of the past thirty years, have conducted and funded data-based research, and have trained numerous U.S. primary care physicians for practice.

Emphasis on health, rather than profits, has led them to favor community rating. Not-for-profits have created an environment that encourages good relationships between patients and professional caregivers. They have discovered that delivering superior care is the most effective way to control costs, and they have done this while fostering partnerships with organized labor. It is critical for the not-for-profits to communicate their obvious advantages to the general public to ensure their survival.

Harold S. Luft and Merwyn R. Greenlick. "The Role and Contributions of Managed Care." *Milbank Quarterly*, 1996, *74*, 445.

Discusses the influence of group- and staff-model HMOs in developing alternative delivery of health care. Although group- and staff-model prepaid health plans were the original model of HMOs, they now represent a minority of HMOs and their enrollees. Nevertheless, these models made, and continue to make, important public contributions through their demonstration of alternative methods of delivering care and their support of population-based research on specific diseases, utilization of services, and styles of medical practice. The limited number of such plans, however, makes it difficult to ascertain whether these contributions are attributable to the type of HMO per se, with their largely nonprofit ownership, their unique organizational histories, and their key leaders, among other factors. A more comprehensive understanding of this question is crucial to ensuring continuation of the public benefits that have accrued from these models in the past.

Thomas E. Mann and Norman J. Ornstein (eds.). *Intensive Care: How Congress Shapes Health Policy*. Washington, D.C.: Brookings Institution, 1995, 316 pages.

This book, copublished with the American Enterprise Institute, presents a helpful guide to understanding the political process as it relates to health care legislation.

Part One examines how Congress has organized and equipped itself to make health care policy. This part discusses the committees and health jurisdictions in Congress, budgeting and health policy making, how health policy information is used in Congress, and congressional oversight of health policy. Part Two, on health policy making, analyzes two specific episodes in forging health policy: the 1988–89 adoption and repeal of Medicare catastrophic coverage and the 1993–94 failure to pass national health reform.

Theodore R. Marmor. "Forecasting American Health Care: How We Got Here and Where We Might Be Going." *Journal of Health Politics, Policy, and Law*, June 1998, *23*, 551.

This article briefly examines the enormous changes in American medicine since World War II before attempting to foresee some possible medical futures in the America of the early twenty-first century.

Theodore R. Marmor, Richard Boyer, and Julie Greenberg. "Medical Care and Procompetitive Reform." *Vanderbilt Law Review*, 1981, *34*, 966.

Surveys various alternative forms of health care delivery, including HMOs, and concludes that as an approach to universal health care reform competition alone is inadequate.

Mark McClellan and Jonathan Skinner. "Medicare Reform: Who Pays and Who Benefits?" *Health Affairs*, Jan.–Feb. 1999, *18*(1), 48.

As Medicare's share of federal spending and gross domestic product rises, the program may have increasingly important consequences not only for the health of Americans but also for their net income and financial well-being. The authors use incidence analysis to study payments and benefits in Medicare to various generations and income groups. They find that Medicare actually provides larger net dollar transfers to wealthier beneficiaries, although the "insurance value" of these dollars is greater for low-income households. They then evaluate a range of proposed Medicare reforms with regard to their impact on the distribution of both health care and disposable income.

Medi-Cal Policy Institute. "Implementing Continuous Eligibility: Costs and Considerations." Oakland, Calif.: Medi-Cal Policy Institute, May 1999, 19 pages.

The federal government granted permission to states via the Balanced Budget Act of 1997 to offer up to twelve months' "continuous eligibility" to children covered by Medicaid. Under the BBA provisions, continuous eligibility allows children who are determined to be eligible for Medicaid to remain enrolled for a specified period of time regardless of changes in income or resources. States can elect to offer continuous eligibility for specific age groups or for all children under nineteen years old. This report discusses how continuous eligibility can help Medi-Cal reduce money spent each year on outreach efforts to reach uninsured children, including those eligible but not enrolled in Medi-Cal.

Robert H. Miller and Harold S. Luft. "Managed Care Plan Performance Since 1980." *Journal of the American Medical Association,* 1994, *271,* 1512.

Evaluates whether managed care plans can contain utilization and expenses, while maintaining or improving quality of care. This study, written by two veteran health policy analysts, compares study results for key dimensions of managed care and indemnity plan performance, including health care utilization and expenditures; level of premiums; level of preventive tests, examinations, and procedures; quality of care; and enrollee satisfaction.

Miller and Luft conclude that compared with indemnity plans, HMO plans exhibit significantly lower utilization of hospital services and of more expensive or discretionary procedures and tests, likely more physician office visits, increased preventive services use, and mixed results on health outcomes. The HMOs may have reduced system-level hospital costs, according to the sole well-designed study with recent data. Although generally satisfied with their care, some HMO enrollees accepted the trade-off of less satisfaction with their care in return for lower out-of-pocket premium and service costs. The authors found no evidence that staff-model HMO plans performed better than IPA or network HMO plans. There were too few observations on PPO plans to determine performance differences compared with indemnity insurance plans.

Marilyn Moon. "Will the Care Be There? Vulnerable Beneficiaries and Medicare Reform." *Health Affairs,* Jan.–Feb. 1999, *18*(1), 107.

The Medicare program is on the verge of major change. The proof of the value of reforms will not rest in how well the program meets the needs of the healthy and the wealthy, but rather in whether the reforms preserve or improve upon protections for those who would not be well served by an unregulated private sector—people with low income or substantial health problems. This paper examines four key issues: which beneficiaries will likely be best served by a system oriented around choice, what role traditional Medicare should continue to play and what changes will be needed, what protections are necessary for people with low and moderate income, and how these reforms could be incorporated into broader changes to make Medicare more viable over time.

Len N. Nichols. "State Regulation: What Have We Learned So Far?" *Journal of Health Policy, Politics, and Law,* 2000, *25,* 175.

Concludes, among other things, that it is crucial to create a political consensus before reform is passed.

"The Impact of Managed Care on Doctors Who Serve Poor and Minority Patients." (Note.) *Harvard Law Review,* 1995, *108,* 1625.

Argues that the HMO mission to minimize health care costs will compel managed care groups to recruit physicians based on selection criteria that underestimate the value of work of doctors who serve large numbers of poor and minority patients—patients who generally require costlier health care. Furthermore, minority physicians, who already suffer from racial discrimination under traditional medical delivery systems, may be particularly vulnerable to mistreatment as the nation's health care system moves toward managed care, the author contends. This note concludes with a call for legislation to monitor the relationship between HMOs and physicians in ways that respect the legitimate presence of managed care and, at the same time, ensure adequate representation of minority physicians and other physicians who serve poor and minority communities.

"The Role of Prepaid Group Practice in Relieving the Health Care Crisis." (Note.) *Harvard Law Review*, 1971, *84*, 887.

A study of the historical origins and performance of prepaid group practices up to 1971.

John F. O'Malley. *Managed Care Referral: How to Develop a Systematic Sales Approach for Building Your Referral Business in Today's Healthcare Environment.* Chicago: Irwin, 1996, 358 pages.

Includes discussion of such topics as marketing in a managed health care environment, health care sales, referral tracking, referral acquisition, competitor analysis capitation, and panel lockout.

George D. Pozgar, Nina Santucci Pozgar, and Richard B. Wallace. *Long-Term Care and the Law: A Legal Guide for Health Care Professionals.* Gaithersburg, Md.: Aspen, 1992, 510 pages.

Examines a wide range of issues concerning the legal environment of long-term care administration. Topics discussed include liability, consent, the medical staff, nursing and the law, long-term records, death and dying, autopsy, financing, malpractice, and labor relations.

Uwe Reinhardt. "Turning Our Gaze from Bread and Circus Games." *Health Affairs*, 1995, *14*, 33.

Reinhardt discusses Daniel Yankelovich's 1995 analysis on the "debate that wasn't." (See annotation below in this section.) Yankelovich makes three assumptions that can be questioned: that the leadership itself has deliberated health care proposals adequately, that there exist good channels for public debate, and that the public will be predisposed to carry out lengthy debate on complex issues such as health care.

As regards deliberation by the experts, there are deep ideological differences about the goals of health care. Some experts view it as a right, while others see it as a commodity, like food, in which access is conditioned on ability to pay. The "food people" won the 1993–94 debate, and congressional sanction for a three-tier system: the poor and uninsured will have to resort to underfunded public clinics and hospitals. The middle class are being forced into capitated health plans such as HMOs. The rich will be able to get open-ended fee-for-service care.

As for the second assumption, that good channels exist for public debate, Reinhardt finds television inadequate except for top-down presentations. Regarding the third assumption, that the public is ready for complex debate, Reinhardt quotes Juvenal's remark that the public prefers bread and circuses, and there is evidence in Yankelovich's paper that not much has changed since Roman times. The only occasions where effective change has occurred recently were when the experts were united and told the public what was good for it, he writes.

Arnold Relman. "Shattuck Lecture—The Health Care Industry: Where Is It Taking Us?" *New England Journal of Medicine*, 1991, *325*, 854–859.

The former editor of the *New England Journal of Medicine* was one of the first influential physicians to warn about what he called, in 1980, the new medical-industrial complex. The present article emphasizes the threat of rapidly developing technology to the practice of medicine and explains how harmful the effect is on the individual person. The bibliography lists several of his previous writings, outlining his view of the current danger.

Charles E. Rosenberg. *The Care of Strangers.* New York: Basic Books, 1987.

Offers an historical view of health care organizations in the United States.

Rand Rosenblatt. "Health Care, Markets, and Democratic Values." *Vanderbilt Law Review,* 1981, *34,* 1067.

Concludes that when one considers the long traditions of professional dominance; consumer passivity; and class, race, and gender inequality in medical care, the likelihood of successful marketplace reform of health care is slim.

Rand Rosenblatt. "Rationing 'Normal' Health Care: The Hidden Legal Issues." *Texas Law Review,* 1981, *59,* 1401.

Rosenblatt, a Rutgers University critic of market-based approaches to health care reform, argues that the only defensible basis to allocate scarce medical resources is the criterion of medical need.

Irwin M. Rubin and C. Raymond Fernandez. *My Pulse Is Not What It Used to Be: The Leadership Challenges in Healthcare.* Honolulu: Temenos Foundation, 1991, 100 pages.

Offers a candid account of Fernandez's experiences as the first CEO of the Nalle Clinic, a seventy-year-old multispecialty clinic located in Charlotte, North Carolina. His and the clinic's experiences reflect the massive developmental changes confronting the entire health care sector. The core of the book is an observation by Rubin that all organizations have to "grow up"; he describes the stages of growth through which all health care organizations, the Nalle Clinic being a single clinical example, must progress as they mature.

Written in the form of "chart entries" by a physician-CEO about his clinic-patient, the book details the clinic's problems and supplies commentaries by physician executives elsewhere in the country, the clinic's attorney, a clinic consultant, and a member of the board.

W. M. Sage. "Regulating Through Information: Disclosure Laws and American Health Care." *Columbia Law Review,* 1999, *99,* 1701.

Efforts to reform the American health care system through direct government action have failed repeatedly. Nonetheless, an alternative strategy has emerged from these experiences: requiring insurance organizations and health care providers to disclose information to the public. The author assesses the justifications for this type of regulation and its prospects. In particular, he finds that the most commonly stated goal of mandatory disclosure laws—improving the efficiency of private purchasing decision by giving purchasers complete information about price and quality—is the most complicated operationally. The other justifications—which he respectively terms the *agency, performance,* and *democratic rationales*—hold greater promise, but make different, sometimes conflicting assumptions about the sources and uses of information. These insights have implications not only for health care but also for other regulated practices and industries.

Gordon D. Schiff, Andrew B. Bindman, and Troyen A. Brennan. "A Better-Quality Alternative: Single-Payer National Health System Reform." *JAMA,* 1994, *272,* 803.

Opponents of health care reform appeal to fears of diminished quality, warning of waiting lists, rationing, and government control. However, the authors contend that the current system is by no means of the "highest quality," given such problems as denial of care, discrimination, disparities, geographic maldistribution, lack of continuity, lack of primary care, inadequate prenatal care, failure to provide beneficial prevention, substandard providers, declining patient satisfaction and impersonal care, iatrogenesis, diagnostic errors, unnecessary procedures, suboptimal medication prescribing, and neglect of quality-of-life psychological issues. A single-payer national health care program constitutes a better framework for improving quality than the managed competition strategy, they argue, because systems based on trust and common purpose achieve far more than those based on barriers and competition.

Theda Skocpol. *Boomerang: Clinton's Health Security Effort and the Turn Against Government in U.S. Politics.* New York: Norton, 1996, 230 pages.

The author's thesis is that "the presentation and decisive defeat of the Clinton plan in 1993–94 was a pivotal moment in the history of the U.S. government and political system." She argues that the Clinton administration, and the Democratic Party at large, made enactment more difficult through insufficient attention to political strategy in an environment where it was more difficult to mobilize interest groups and parties on behalf of a major reform effort. Additionally, the proposal was "marketed" in an intermittent manner and without adequate effort to explain to the public the plan's key components.

Frank A. Sloan, James F. Blumstein, and James M. Perrin (eds.). *Cost, Quality, and Access in Health Care.* San Francisco: Jossey-Bass, 1988, 293 pages.

Aims to demonstrate how new forms of planning may contribute to attaining health policy objectives of access, cost containment, and quality assurance. Originating in a 1986 Vanderbilt University symposium on the role of health planning in a competitive environment, this volume addresses such topics as lessons learned from certificate-of-need programs, evaluating quality of care, and resolving the tension between health planning and the antitrust laws.

David G. Smith. *Paying for Medicare: The Politics of Reform.* Hawthorne, N.Y.: Aldine de Gruyter, 1992, 277 pages.

This book fills a gap in the health policy literature, by providing an account of the policy developments associated with the hospital prospective payment system and the Medicare fee schedule.

Paul Starr. *The Social Transformation of American Medicine.* New York: Basic Books, 1982.

Pulitzer Prize–winning history of the development of American medicine. The first part of the book concerns the rise of professional sovereignty. The second addresses the transformation of medicine into an industry and the growing, though still unsettled, role of corporations and the state. This is the definitive social history of the medical profession in the United States.

Sven Steinmo and Jon Watts. "It's the Institutions, Stupid! Why Comprehensive National Health Insurance Always Fails in America." *Journal of Health Politics, Policy, and Law,* 1995, 20, 329.

The U.S. Congress did not enact health care reform in 1994 for the same reason it could not pass it in 1948, 1965, 1974, and 1978: American political institutions are structurally biased against this kind of comprehensive reform. The founding fathers explicitly devised a political structure to pit faction against faction in order to protect minority groups from the majority. James Madison's system of checks and balances, the size and diversity of the nation, and the reforms that undermined strong and programmatic parties have worked to fragment political power in America. Subsequently, several generations of Congressional reforms unwittingly turned national politicians into political entrepreneurs.

In 1974, Congressional reforms undermined the controlling power of conservative Southern Democratic committee chairmen and redistributed power to party elites and more junior members. Participation in the House Ways and Means Committee was expanded, making it more difficult to build consensus within the committee. So many congressional actors have some degree of significant authority that the role of central leaders is difficult.

Rosemary Stevens. *In Sickness and in Health: American Hospitals in the Twentieth Century.* New York: Basic Books, 1989.

An historical account of health care delivery in the United States.

Katherine Swartz and Deborah Garnick. "The Individual Health Insurance Market: Lessons from New Jersey." *Journal of Health Politics, Policy, and Law,* 2000, *25,* 45.

Discusses the state's Individual Health Coverage Program, passed in 1993.

Maria R. Traska. *Managed Care Strategies 1996.* New York: Faulkner and Gray, 1995, 267 pages.

Describes eight strategies or issues of concern for managed care. Each strategy or issue gives managed care organizations a path to further growth or renewal. Topics discussed include performance, modified payment in health care, covering the uninsured, connecting public health goals to managed care, finding better ways to gauge patient satisfaction, accountability, workers compensation, and uncoupling Medicaid from welfare. Two helpful appendices supplement the text.

Louise G. Trubek. "Informing, Claiming, Contracting: Enforcement in the Managed Care Era." *Annals of Health Law,* 1999, *8,* 133.

Describes the role of the states in patient and consumer protection in managed care. Focuses on the mechanisms used in Wisconsin: informing consumers, encouraging dispute resolution, and influencing contracts. Includes analysis of the effects of these mechanisms on the actors in the health care regulatory area and concludes with an assessment of the actors' adaptations.

Bruce C. Vladeck. "The Political Economy of Medicare." *Health Affairs,* Jan.–Feb. 1999, *18*(1), 22.

Medicare spends more than $200 billion per year. The politics surrounding the Medicare program cannot be fully understood without adequate appreciation of that fact. Understanding the political economy of Medicare is perhaps best achieved by thinking along three dimensions, the author contends: (1) Medicare as redistributionist politics; (2) Medicare as special interest politics; and (3) Medicare as distributionist politics. Seeing the extent to which Medicare policies flow from these political processes makes clear that Medicare reform and broader political reform are, at some level, inseparable and indistinguishable.

David Willsford. *Doctors and the State: The Politics of Health Care in France and the United States.* Durham, N.C.: Duke University Press, 1991, 355 pages.

Focuses on the relations between organized medicine and the public and private payers of that health care. It compares this relationship between physicians and payers in France and the United States, concentrating on the post–World War II era. The author argues that the two countries are suited for comparison because the French system is a public insurance system while the American health care sector is animated by free enterprise goals.

Furthermore, France and the United States exemplify strong versus weak state traditions in the health care sector. Equally important, each country also permits free and abundant medical association activity. Physician organizations are numerous and active in organizing health care delivery systems and in the politics that affect their health care system interests. Moreover, the author writes, in both countries the medical profession succeeded in using the rise of science and technology at the close of the nineteenth century to establish hegemony over legitimate health care delivery. Most striking, orthodox medicine succeeded in both nations in defining which treatments are legitimate.

Daniel Yankelovich. "The Debate That Wasn't: The Public and the Clinton Health Plan." *Health Affairs,* 1995, *14,* 7.

American elites communicate well with each other but do not seem to be able to communicate with the public, so there is a disconnect between society and its leaders. The experts who designed and promoted the Clinton health plan never adequately explained it to the public, while other experts and special interests attacked it. An informed debate between the experts and the public never took place, which left the public siding by default with the status quo.

Before President Clinton presented the plan to the public, there was general approval for some sorts of change in health care; after his speech before Congress, two-thirds of Americans polled were still in favor of it. Less than a year later, approval had dropped to 37 percent, and those polled expressed confusion over what the Clinton plan involved. Prior to Clinton's speech, polls had found several trends in public opinion: Americans saw health care as a right, were generally pleased with their own coverage, were concerned about rising costs, and felt that the cost increases were unreasonable. In the public mind, the cost increases were believed to stem from waste, fraud, high profits, and abuses by lawyers, health care companies, and health professionals. The public believed that monitoring these factors could control costs. Experts, on the other hand, saw the costs as procedures. The experts never persuaded the public to accept their position.

As time passed, it became clear that Americans were worried about the security of their own health care arrangements and believed in universal coverage, but they were not willing to risk their own coverage to achieve it. Additionally, Americans are more skeptical of their government than they were, and they doubt that the government would be successful in carrying out reforms efficiently and cheaply. Opponents were very successful in portraying the Clinton plan as a big-government operation. The author proposes a model of public communication that might avoid such policy debacles in the future.

Appendix A

Health Law Periodicals, Digests, and Newsletters

AAPPO Journal

American Association of Preferred Provider
    Organizations
601 13th St. NW, Suite 370 S
Washington, DC 20005
202-463-2002

This bimonthly journal is an official publication of the
trade organization representing PPOs and their partners in
managed care.

Abstracts of Clinical Care Guidelines

Joint Commission on Accreditation of Healthcare
    Organizations
One Renaissance Blvd.
Oakbrook Terrace, IL 60181
800-346-0085
www.jcaho.org

Published 10 times annually, this journal features summaries of selected practice guidelines and review articles
with commentary from experts in the field; it is valuable
to health care policy makers.

Academic Medicine

2450 North St. NW
Washington, DC 20037-1126

This monthly journal publishes policy papers, analyses,
and research reports covering issues facing medical
schools, teaching hospitals, and health policy agencies.

Action

Texas Medical Association
401 West 15th St.
Austin, TX 78701-1680
800-880-1300
www.texmed.org

Published monthly, this newsletter monitors federal and
Texas regulatory, legislative, and judicial events.

Action for Universal Health Care

2800 Euclid Ave., Suite 520
Cleveland, OH 44115-2418
216-241-8422
uhcan@uhcan.org

This newsletter is published by Universal Health Care
Action Network, which advocates a single payer universal
health care system.

Action Kit for Hospital Trustees

Action Kit Publications
4614 Fifth Ave.
Pittsburgh, PA 15213
800-245-1205
www.hortyspringer.com

Published since 1971, this bimonthly newsletter helps hospital management and governing board members understand the legal and regulatory changes that affect hospitals.

Administrative Science Quarterly

Christine Oliver, Editor
Editorial Office ASQ
Malott Hall, Cornell University
Johnson Graduate School of Management
Ithaca, NY 14853
607-254-7143
www.gsm.cornell.edu.asq/asq.html

ASQ publishes theoretical and empirical papers based on
selected dissertations across a range of disciplines, including strategic management and industrial relations. ASQ
focuses on identifying new work from young scholars
with fresh views, opening new areas of inquiry.

Advances

Robert Wood Johnson Foundation
College Road
P.O. Box 2316
Princeton, NJ 08543-2316

609-452-8701
www.rwjf.org

This foundation designs, funds, and evaluates health policy research projects.

AHCA Notes

American Health Care Association
1201 L. St. NW
Washington, DC 20005-4014
202-842-4444
www.ahca.org

This is the biweekly newsletter of this organization, a national federation of long-term care providers.

AIDS & Public Policy Journal

University Publishing Group, Inc.
17100 Cole Road
Hagerstown, MD 21740
800-654-8188

This journal is published quarterly.

AIDS Law and Litigation Reporter

University Publishing Group, Inc.
17100 Cole Road
Hagerstown, MD 21740
800-654-8188

This monthly reporter presents complete, retrospective, full-text decisions from federal, state, and local courts, and surveys proposed and enacted legislation. It also supplies analysis of current thinking on crucial issues.

AIDS Litigation Reporter

Andrews Publications
1646 West Chester Pike
P.O. Box 1000
Westtown, PA 19395
610-399-6600

Published semimonthly, this loose-leaf format newsletter has been published since 1987.

AIDS Policy and Law

LRP Publications
747 Dresher Rd.
P.O. Box 980
Horsham, PA 19044-0980
215-784-0860; 800-341-7874
www.lrp.com

This biweekly newsletter monitors legislation, regulation, and litigation concerning AIDS on the federal, state, and local levels, along with fair employment practices, litigation legislation and regulation, policy guidelines, case studies, and interviews.

Alabama Managed Care

Harkey and Associates, Inc.
P.O. Box 159025
Nashville, TN 37215
615-385-4131
www.harkeyreport.com

This quarterly newsletter provides HMO and PPO updates and covers Medicaid, legislation, hospital networks, and physician managed care organizations.

Allan Fine's Trends in Integrated Health Care

(formerly *Hospital Managed Care and Direct Contracting*)

Allan Fine, Editor
Aspen Publishers, Inc.
7201 McKinney Circle
Frederick, MD 21705-9727
800-638-8437
www.aspenpub.com

This monthly newsletter is aimed at guiding hospitals in expanding their managed care contracts. Topics addressed include techniques on approaching employers and business coalitions, regional variations in direct employer contracting, steps to take to avoid future legal risks, and risk-sharing options.

American Academy of Psychiatry and the Law Newsletter

American Academy of Psychiatry and the Law
One Regency Dr.
P.O. Box 30
Bloomfield, CT 06002
860-242-5450
www.aapl.org

This journal is published three times annually and examines recent legal cases and legislation.

American Association of Nurse Anesthetists Journal

American Association of Nurse Anesthetists
222 South Prospect Ave.
Park Ridge, IL 60068
847-692-7050
www.aana.com

This journal is published six times annually and addresses health policy and regulatory issues as they relate to AANA members.

American Journal of Integrated Healthcare

Association Services, Inc.
4435 Waterfront Dr., Suite 101
Glen Allen, VA 23060
804-527-1905

This quarterly journal, inaugurated in 1997, is written for physician executives, medical directors, pharmacy directors, nursing directors, and administrative executives in hospital networks and other integrated networks.

American Journal of Law and Medicine

Boston University
765 Commonwealth Ave., Suite 1634
Boston, MA 02215
617-262-4990
www.aslme.org

This law review, produced jointly by the American Society of Law, Medicine, and Ethics and Boston University Law School, is published quarterly. Each issue contains scholarly articles written by national authorities, book reviews, and annotations of recent health care–related court decisions and legislative enactments.

American Journal of Public Health

American Public Health Association
1015 18th St., NW
Washington, DC 20005
202-789-5600
www.apha.org

This monthly peer-reviewed publication examines health policy issues, among others. Each issue features a theme of vital current interest. Examples are women's health, children's health, HIV/AIDS, and smoking.

American Medical News

American Medical Association
515 North State St.
Chicago, IL 60610
312-464-5000
www.ama-assn.org

This weekly publication addresses professional, social, economic, and policy issues in medicine.

Annals of Health Law

Institute for Health Law
Loyola University Chicago School of Law
One East Pearson St.
Chicago, IL 60611
312-915-7174
www.health-law@luc.edu

This annual publication is a forum for scholarly writing on health law and policy.

AORN Journal

Association of Operating Room Nurses
2170 South Parker Rd., Suite 300
Denver, CO 80231-5711
303-755-6300

This monthly publication is a refereed journal providing professional perioperative nurses with original, practical information.

Arizona Managed Care

HealthCare Computer Corporation of America
655 Broadway, Suite 875
Denver, CO 80203
888-466-2329
www.hmo-info.com

This newsletter is published twice monthly and covers managed care trends in the state.

Arthur Andersen Washington Healthcare Newsletter

Arthur Andersen and Co.
1666 K St. NW
Washington, DC 20006
202-862-6732

This free newsletter is published eleven times annually.

ASHES

American Society for Healthcare Environmental Services
American Hospital Association
One North Franklin
Chicago, IL 60606
312-422-3863
www.aha.org

Formerly known as *Healthcare Environmental Services,* this bimonthly journal, first published in 1986, features articles on trends and developments in environmental services, recycling, and waste management provided by health care institutions.

Aspen's Advisor for Nurse Executives

Aspen Publishers, Inc.
7201 McKinney Circle
Frederick, MD 21705
800-447-1717
www.aspenpub.com

This eight-page service is published in newsletter format each month. Topics addressed include new ventures, human resources, and legislative matters.

Aspen's Health Care Law Bulletin

Aspen Publishers, Inc.
7201 McKinney Circle
Frederick, MD 21705
800-447-1717
www.aspenpub.com

This monthly peer-reviewed journal evaluates critical issues of the past year and has focused on legal aspects of fraud and abuse, tax, managed care, and physician practice management companies.

ATLA Professional Negligence Law Reporter

Association of Trial Lawyers of America
1050 31st St. NW
Washington, DC 20007
202-965-3500

Published ten times annually, this was formerly known as the *Professional Negligence Law Reporter.*

BNA Health Care Daily Report

Bureau of National Affairs, Inc.
1231 25th St. NW
Washington, DC 20037
202-452-4200; 800-372-1033
www.bna.com

Available by fax or electronically, this daily service covers health care providers, insurance companies, managed care organizations, pharmaceutical and medical device manufacturers, and business and labor groups.

BNA Health Care Facilities Guide

Bureau of National Affairs, Inc.
1231 25th St. NW
Washington, DC 20037
202-452-4200; 800-372-1033
www.bna.com

Updated bimonthly newsletter, this resource provides JCAHO, OSHA, EPA, DOT, and NRC compliance information on all environmental and infectious-waste aspects of accreditation. Topics addressed include chemical hazards, inspections and enforcement, laboratory standards, record keeping, and state regulatory requirements.

BNA Health Care Policy Report

Bureau of National Affairs, Inc.
1231 25th St. NW
Washington, DC 20037
202-452-4200; 800-372-1033
www.bna.com

Available either in print or electronically, this weekly report monitors policy proposals, debates, and responses in federal, state, private sector, and public arenas.

BNA Health Law and Business Series

Bureau of National Affairs, Inc.
1231 25th St. NW
Washington, DC 20037
202-452-4200; 800-372-1033
www.bna.com

This service consists of fifteen portfolios supplemented with regular monthly updates and focuses on transactional, contracting, structural, and operational issues.

BNA Health Law Reporter

Bureau of National Affairs, Inc.
1231 25th St. NW
Washington, DC 20037
202-452-4200; 800-372-1033
www.bna.com

This service is a weekly review of legislative, regulatory, and legal developments.

BNA Managed Care Reporter

Bureau of National Affairs, Inc.
1231 25th St. NW
Washington, DC 20037
202-452-4200; 800-372-1033
www.bna.com

This weekly newsletter focuses on new alliances, contracts, and competition. It is available in print or electronic format.

BNA Medicare Report

Bureau of National Affairs, Inc.
1231 25th St. NW
Washington, DC 20037
202-452-4200; 800-372-1033
www.bna.com

Published weekly, this newsletter examines such topics as reimbursement, finance, fraud, and abuse.

BNA Pension and Benefit Reporter

Bureau of National Affairs, Inc.
1231 25th St. NW
Washington, DC 20037
202-452-4200; 800-372-1033
www.bna.com

Published weekly since ERISA was enacted in 1974, this resource covers IRS and Labor Department regulation enforcement issues affecting pension and health benefit plans.

BNA State Health Care Regulatory Developments

Bureau of National Affairs, Inc.
1231 25th St. NW
Washington, DC 20037
202-452-4200; 800-372-1033
www.bna.com

Published biweekly and available in electronic, diskette, and paper formats, this service provides detailed summaries of health care regulatory developments in all fifty states and the District of Columbia.

Business and Health

Medical Economics Co.
5 Paragon Dr.

Montvale, NJ 07645-1742
800-432-4570
www.medec.com

This monthly magazine was inaugurated in 1983 by the Washington Business Group on Health, a national non-profit health policy and research organization. Founded in 1974, WBGH published the magazine until 1988. Working with policy makers and its members, which are large U.S. corporations, WBGH addresses a broad range of health issues. This magazine is now published independently of WBGH.

California Health Law Monitor

M. Lee Smith Publishers LLC
P.O. Box 5094
Brentwood, TN 37024-5094
800-274-6774
www.mleesmith.com

This biweekly update addresses health care law and industry regulation in California.

California Health Law News

Tallien R. Perry, Editor
California Society for Healthcare Attorneys
1215 K St., Suite 800
Sacramento, CA 95814
916-552-7615
www.csha.calhealth.org

This is the quarterly newsletter of the CSHA. It includes articles on California and federal health law issues.

California Medicine

Healthcare Business Media, Inc.
450 Sansome St.
Suite 1100
San Francisco, CA 94111
415-956-8242

This health care business magazine, published bimonthly, includes roundtable discussions; interviews with physicians and industry executives; and regular columns on such topics as HMOs, Medicare, and legal issues as they affect physicians. The magazine is now in its tenth year.

California Physician

California Medical Association
221 Main St.
P.O. Box 7690
San Francisco, CA 94120-7690
800-882-1262
www.cmanet.org

This monthly magazine features articles on legislative, managed care, legal, and other issues affecting medical

practice in California. Specific topics examined in recent issues include the future of for-profit, publicly held HMOs, Medi-Cal managed care, and the effect of megamergers on medical practice.

Capitation and Medical Practice

Aspen Publishers, Inc.
7201 McKinney Circle
Frederick, MD 21704
800-638-8437
www.aspenpub.com

Written for health care providers, this eight-page monthly newsletter guides its readers in controlling costs, assuming risk safely, and seeking financial stability under capitated reimbursement.

Capitol Update

American Nurses Association
600 Maryland Ave. SW
Washington, DC 20024-2571
800-274-4262
www.nursingworld.org

Published twenty times annually, this newsletter provides legislative updates, campaign information, and federal agency and regulatory developments as they relate to nursing and health care at the federal level.

Caring Magazine

National Association for Home Care (NAHC)
228 7th St. SE
Washington, DC 20003
202-547-7424
www.nahc.org

Published by a national trade association for providers of home health and hospice care services, this monthly publication provides regular legislative and policy updates.

Carolina Managed Care

Harkey and Associates, Inc.
P.O. Box 159025
Nashville, TN 37215
615-385-4131
www.harkeyreport.com

This quarterly newsletter covers managed care trends, Medicaid, legislation, hospital networks, and physician managed care organizations. Separate North Carolina and South Carolina editions.

Case Manager

Case Management Society of America
8201 Cantrell, Suite 230
Little Rock, AR 72227

501-225-2229
www.cmsa.org

This is a bimonthly national magazine exclusively focused on case management, providing health care news from all fifty states.

Case Report

Case Management Society of America
8201 Cantrell, Suite 230
Little Rock, AR 72227
501-225-2229
www.cmsa.org

This newsletter highlights local and national case management issues.

Catholic Health World

Catholic Health Association of the United States
4455 Woodson Rd.
St. Louis, MO 63134-3797
314-427-2500
www.chausa.org

Published twice monthly, this newspaper features late-breaking news about legislative and advocacy affairs and operational changes.

CCH California Medi-Cal Guide

CCH Incorporated
4025 W. Peterson Ave.
Chicago, IL 60646-6085
800-435-8878
www.cch.com

This one-volume loose-leaf service contains explanatory, nontechnical information on the California Medicaid program. It monitors eligibility, covered services, provider reimbursement, prepaid plans, and administration. The guide includes the full text of relevant state laws, DHHS regulations, and a list of contract drugs.

CCH Health Care Fraud and Abuse Guide

CCH Incorporated
Healthcare Group
4025 W. Peterson Ave.
Chicago, IL 60646-6085

This guide has combined federal and state legislative and case law developments, current trial and appellate court decisions, and definitive information on settlements, together in one CD-ROM. It is designed to meet the needs of attorneys in firm practice, in-house counsel of managed care and provider organizations, and risk managers. This CD-ROM is updated monthly, while its accompanying Internet site is updated daily.

CCH Health Care Law and Management Guide on CD-ROM

CCH Incorporated
4025 W. Peterson Ave.
Chicago, IL 60646-6085
800-835-5224
www.cch.com

This monthly service assists hospital and nursing home administrators, medical staff directors, and their counsel in understanding the issues and finding solutions to problems encountered in day-to-day operation of health care facilities. It provides all-state comprehensive coverage.

CCH Health Law and Policy Reporter

CCH Incorporated
4025 W. Peterson Ave.
Chicago, IL 60646-6085
800-835-5224
www.cch.com

This twice-monthly newsletter offers full-text materials and provides an analysis of issues and reports covered in the CCH state and federal newsletters. The topical organization covers background, in-depth analysis, reports, studies on federal and state issues, and developments regarding reform of the American health care system, for health care policy makers, academics, attorneys, and researchers.

CCH Healthcare Compliance Letter

CCH Incorporated
Healthcare Group
4025 W. Peterson Ave.
Chicago, IL 60646-6085

Published every two weeks, this newsletter follows legislative and regulatory developments, court decisions, policy and procedure guidelines, proven success guidelines, tips and techniques, and interviews.

CCH Healthcare Compliance Reporter

CCH Incorporated
Healthcare Group
4025 W. Peterson Ave.
Chicago, IL 60646-6085

This full-text, electronic, CD-ROM based tool provides access to relevant laws, regulations, cases, and advisory opinions on the federal level and for all fifty states, the District of Columbia, and Puerto Rico.

CCH Home Care Provider's Guide

CCH Incorporated
4025 W. Peterson Ave.
Chicago, IL 60646-6085

800-835-5224
www.cch.com

Supplemented monthly, this guide provides analysis of federal and state laws, regulations, and administrative and court decisions, explaining how they apply to home health care and hospices. Also covered are Medicare and Medicaid by states, patients' rights, employment issues, certificate of need, certification and accreditation, advance medical directives, and job safety.

CCH Medical Devices Reports

CCH Incorporated
4025 W. Peterson Ave.
Chicago, IL 60646-6085
800-835-5224
www.cch.com

This monthly newsletter monitors the rules controlling the manufacture and marketing of medical, diagnostic, and radiological devices—classification, standards, inspection, seizures, and bans. Requirements for efficacy, performance characteristics, premarket approval, and notification are treated.

CCH Medicare and Medicaid Guide

CCH Incorporated
4025 W. Peterson Ave.
Chicago, IL 60646-6085
800-835-5224
www.cch.com

This weekly service provides complex reimbursement, prospective payment, eligibility, and coverage rules—federal law, regulations, manuals, forms and cost information, accounting procedures, interpretations, rulings, and decisions of the Health Care Financing Administration and Provider Reimbursement Review Board and court decisions.

CCH Monitor: The Newsletter of Managed Care

CCH Incorporated
4025 W. Peterson Ave.
Chicago, IL 60646-6085
800-835-5224
www.cch.com

Published biweekly, this newsletter provides coverage of issues facing employers and managed care providers, particularly legislative and judicial topics.

CCH Physicians' Medicare Guide

CCH Incorporated
4025 W. Peterson Ave.
Chicago, IL 60646-6085
800-835-5224
www.cch.com

This guide and accompanying newsletter, published six times annually, provides guidance to Medicare Part B and is published in cooperation with the AMA. It features full-text reproductions of the Medicare fee schedule with medical service codes and complete descriptions from the AMA's *Current Procedural Terminology Manual.*

CCH State Pulse: The State Health System Report

CCH Incorporated
4025 W. Peterson Ave.
Chicago, IL 60646-6085
800-835-5224
www.cch.com

This twelve-to-sixteen-page monthly report provides state health care reform information and contains in-depth articles on key states.

CCH's Understanding CHAMPUS

CCH Incorporated
4025 W. Peterson Ave.
Chicago, IL 60646-6085
800-835-5224
www.cch.com

This service contains statutory revisions and regulations governing the Civilian Health and Medical Program of the Uniformed Services. In addition, it contains an explanatory division covering eligibility, scope of coverage, reimbursement, fraud and abuse, and peer review. Updates reflect changes to the laws or regulations and any policy changes necessitated by enactment of health care reform legislation.

CHA News

California Healthcare Association
1215 K St., Suite 800
Sacramento, CA 95814
916-443-7401
www.cahhs.org

This weekly publication recaps major news of interest to hospital and health system leaders in California.

Checklist

States Information Center
Council of State Governments
P.O. Box 11910
Lexington, KY 40578-1910
606-244-8253
www.csg.org

This is a bimonthly newspaper with listings of new reference materials on state issues with comparative data on all fifty states. The organization provides access to more than twenty thousand documents available on a thirty-day loan basis and an online retrieval system to the council's database of more than twenty thousand titles, abstracts, and full-text records. These services are free to state government officials and employees.

College Review

American College of Medical Group
    Administrators
1355 South Colorado Blvd., Suite 900
Denver, CO 80222
303-397-7869
www.mgma.com

This is the biannual professional journal of the American College of Medical Practice Executives. Its articles include a range of contemporary issues pertinent to medical practice management.

Colorado Managed Care

HealthCare Computer Corporation of America
655 Broadway, Suite 875
Denver, CO 80203
888-466-2329
www.hmo-info.com

Published twice monthly, this newsletter monitors managed care developments in the state.

Colorado Managed Care Review

Allan Baumgarten
4800 West 27th St.
Minneapolis, MN 55416
612-925-9121

This annual survey of managed care trends covers a state that is the competitive battleground for the largest HMO companies in the nation.

Contemporary Long-Term Care

Bill Communications, Inc.
355 Park Ave. South, 5th Floor
New York, NY 10010-1789
212-592-6200
www.billcom.com/citcmag

Formerly known as *Contemporary Administrator*, this monthly trade publication is targeted at administrators, directors of nursing, medical directors, and other professionals responsible for management at nursing facilities, residential care centers, and hospitals with long-term care.

Continuum

American Hospital Association
Society for Social Work Administrators in Health Care
One North Franklin
Chicago, IL 60606

312-445-3616
www.aha.org

Formerly known as *Discharge Planning*, this interdisciplinary journal is published bimonthly and examines issues related to delivery of posthospital care.

Defense Counsel Journal

International Association of Defense Counsel
One North Franklin, Suite 2400
Chicago, IL 60606
312-368-1494
www.iadclaw.org

This law review is a quarterly forum for publishing topical and scholarly writings on the law, particularly from the viewpoint of the litigator in the civil defense and insurance fields.

Defense Law Journal

Michie Company
P.O. Box 7587
Charlottesville, VA 22906-7587
800-562-1215

This quarterly journal reprints articles of interest for defense, insurance, and corporate counsel.

Dennis Barry's Reimbursement Advisor

Aspen Publishers, Inc.
7201 McKinney Circle
Frederick, MD 21705
800-447-1717
www.aspenpub.com

This monthly newsletter provides practical up-to-date information, analyses of developments in prospective payments, recommended courses of action, legislative updates, and management strategies.

DePaul Journal of Health Care Law

DePaul University Law School
25 East Jackson Boulevard
Chicago, IL 60604-2287
312-362-6831

This new quarterly law review addresses both health law and policy issues.

DES Litigation Reporter

Andrews Publications
1646 West Chester Pike
Box 1000
Westtown, PA 19395
610-399-6600

This newsletter monitors litigation concerning diethylstilbestrol.

EBRI Benefit Outlook

Employee Benefit Research Institute
2121 K St. NW, Suite 600
Washington, DC 20037-1896
202-659-0670
www.ebri.org

Published three times annually, this newsletter provides a comprehensive legislative bill chart, along with observations on the likelihood of passage of employee benefits–related legislation. Established in 1978, EBRI is a nonprofit, nonpartisan organization that prepares analyses on employee benefits. EBRI does not lobby or endorse specific approaches. EBRI's membership includes businesses, pension funds, trade associations, labor unions, health care providers, insurers, government organizations, and service firms (including those in actuarial science, accounting, law, consulting, and investment management).

EBRI Issue Brief

Employee Benefit Research Institute
2121 K St. NW, Suite 600
Washington, DC 20037-1896
202-659-0670
www.ebri.org

Each issue of this topical monthly periodical evaluates a single employee benefit issue or trend. Recent topics have included the changing health care delivery system and hospital pricing.

EBRI Notes

Employee Benefit Research Institute
2121 K St. NW, Suite 600
Washington, DC 20037-1896
202-659-0670
www.ebri.org

This monthly periodical provides up-to-date information on a variety of employee benefit topics. Each issue includes a feature article on an important benefit topic, a statistical article highlighting new benefits data, a review of findings from the most recent EBRI Gallup survey, highlights of Washington employee benefits activities, and a list of selected new publications.

EBRI Washington Bulletin

Employee Benefit Research Institute
2121 K St. NW, Suite 600
Washington, DC 20037-1896
202-659-0670
www.ebri.org

Published twice monthly, this newsletter provides updates on major employee benefits developments in Washington, including important legislative, executive, and regulatory activities.

Elder Law Forum

Legal Counsel for the Elderly
American Association of Retired Persons
601 E St. NW, Dept. A9
Washington, DC 20049
202-434-2560
www.aarp.org

This bimonthly newsletter provides current information for advocates serving older persons. This reference monitors recent law changes, court decisions, and practice pointers.

Employee Benefits Digest

International Foundation of Employee Benefit Plans
P.O. Box 69
18700 West Bluemound Rd.
Brookfield, WI 53008-0069
414-786-6710
www.ifebp.org

This monthly publication includes articles on timely topics and legislative developments, and a review of the current employee benefits literature.

Employee Benefits Journal

International Foundation of Employee Benefit Plans
P.O. Box 69
18700 West Bluemound Rd.
Brookfield, WI 53008-0069
414-786-6710
www.ifebp.org

This quarterly magazine covers employee benefit trends and issues.

EOTR [Exempt Organization Tax Review] Weekly

Tax Analysts
6830 North Fairfax Dr.
Arlington, VA 22213
800-955-3444
www.tax.org

This weekly newsletter monitors IRS regulation of tax-exempt organizations, including health facilities. Tax Analysts operates twenty-one Internet discussion groups focusing on specialized issues of taxation.

European Journal of Health Law

Kluwer Law International
675 Massachusetts Ave.
Cambridge, MA 02139
617-354-0140; 800-577-8118
www.kluwerlaw.com

Published in the Netherlands, this quarterly journal focuses on the development of health law in Europe: national, comparative, and international. It addresses legislation, court decisions, and other relevant material nation by nation. Each issue contains articles (with abstracts), selected legislation, judicial decisions, a chronicle of events, and book reviews.

Executive Report on Managed Care

American Business Publishing
3100 Hwy. 138, P.O. Box 1442
Wall Township, NJ 07719-1442
908-681-1133

Published since 1988, this monthly newsletter focuses on how major employers are implementing managed care programs. It aims to help companies evaluate and monitor various managed care proposals in terms of cost-effectiveness, quality, and liability to the employer.

Florida Healthtrac

M. Lee Smith Publishers LLC
P.O. Box 5094
Brentwood, TN 37024-5094
800-274-6774
www.mleesmith.com

This monthly update monitors health policy developments in Florida.

Florida Managed Care

Harkey and Associates, Inc.
P.O. Box 159025
Nashville, TN 37215
615-385-4131
www.harkeyreport.com

This quarterly newsletter covers such topics as managed care, market-level enrollment, health care networks, Medicare and Medicaid, and pertinent state and federal legislation.

Focus on Change

National Business Coalition on Health
1015 18th St. NW, Suite 450
Washington, DC 20036
202-775-9300
www.nbch.org/nbch/

This newsletter is published two to six times annually. The NBCH has a membership of more than one hundred employer-led coalitions nationwide, composed of mostly medium and large-size employers in both the private and public sectors in a particular city, county, or region.

Food and Drug Law Journal

Food and Drug Law Institute
1000 Vermont Ave., NW, Suite 1200
Washington, DC 20005-4903

This quarterly journal is devoted to scholarly and practical analysis of legislation, regulations, court decisions, and public policies that affect development, manufacture, distribution, and use of foods, drugs, biologics, cosmetics, and medical devices.

Forum News

Forum on Health Care Planning
314 Vista del Valle
Mill Valley, CA 94941
415-381-1846

This quarterly newsletter focuses on health care delivery issues and public policy. It contains proceedings of programs, editorials, and member letters.

Frontiers of Health Services Management

American College of Health Care Executives
Health Administration Press
One North Franklin, Suite 1700
Chicago, IL 60606
312-424-2800
www.ache.org.

This quarterly journal examines a variety of issues faced by health care executives, including legal matters. Each issue focuses on a single topic in depth.

Georgia Health Law Update

M. Lee Smith Publishers LLC
P.O. Box 5094
Brentwood, TN 37024-5094
800-274-6774
www.mleesmith.com

This service provides a monthly survey of Georgia and federal health law developments.

Georgia Hospitals Today

Georgia Hospital Association
1675 Terrell Mill Road
Marietta, GA 30067
770-955-0324

This monthly magazine is published for members of the association.

Georgia Managed Care

Harkey and Associates, Inc.
P.O. Box 159025
Nashville, TN 37215
615-385-4131
www.harkeyreport.com

This quarterly newsletter provides information on managed care developments. Topics covered include HMOs and PPOs, market-level enrollment, hospital networks, physician networks, managed care contracts, Medicaid, and legislation.

Hastings Center Report

Hastings Center
Route 9D
Garrison, NY 10524-5555
914-424-4040

This bimonthly publication prints research reports on ethical issues in medicine, health care, technology, and the environment.

Hazardous Waste Litigation Reporter

Andrews Publications
1646 West Chester Pike, Box 1000
Westtown, PA 19395
610-399-6600

This semimonthly newsletter monitors hazardous waste–related litigation.

Hazardous Waste News

Business Publishers, Inc.
951 Pershing Dr.
Silver Spring, MD 20910-4464
800-274-6737
www.bpinews.com

This weekly newsletter focuses on Superfund and environmental remediation issues.

Health Advocate

National Health Law Program, Inc. (NHeLP)
2639 South La Cienega Blvd.
Los Angeles, CA 90034-2675
310-204-6010
www.healthlaw.org

This is the newsletter of NHeLP, a nonprofit organization representing the poor, minorities, and the aged in obtaining equity and nondiscrimination in federal, state, local, and private health care programs.

Health Affairs

Project Hope
7500 Old Georgetown Rd., Suite 600
Bethesda, MD 20814
301-656-7401
www.projhope.org

This quarterly is a multidisciplinary, peer-reviewed journal dedicated to serious exploration of domestic and international health policy issues. It is partially underwritten by the Robert Wood Johnson Foundation.

Health and Welfare Benefit Plans

Butterworth Legal Publishers
8 Industrial Way, Bldg. C
Salem, NH 03079
800-548-4001

This service covers all aspects of health and welfare benefits regulations.

Health Care Almanac and Yearbook

Faulkner and Gray, Inc.
11 Penn Plaza
New York, NY 10001
212-631-1400; 800-535-8403
www.faulknergray.com

This annual text supplies a statistical profile of the health care sector, with a year-in-review and other information.

Health Care Annual

United Hospital Fund of New York
350 Fifth Ave., 23rd Floor
New York, NY 10118-2399
212-645-2500

This academic publication examines use of health care facilities in New York City, Long Island, and the northern metropolitan area.

Healthcare Business

Healthcare Business Media, Inc.
450 Sansome St., Suite 1100
San Francisco, CA 94111
415-956-8242

This new magazine, published bimonthly, includes round-table discussions, interviews with physicians and industry executives from around the country, along with regular columns on such topics as HMOs, Medicare, and legal issues as they affect physicians.

Health Care Business News

567 Seminole Drive
Marietta, GA 30060
770-499-1220
www.healthcarebusinessnews.com

This newspaper is published monthly in seven state-specific editions: Alabama, Florida, Georgia, North Carolina, South Carolina, Tennessee, and Virginia. It monitors such topics as state health planning agencies, certificates of need, insurance commission activity, utilization review, and managed care.

Health Care Compliance Association Newsletter

Health Care Compliance Association
c/o Debbie Troklus
School of Medicine
University of Louisville
Louisville, KY 40292
502-852-0758

This quarterly newsletter is designed to be a forum for health care professionals involved in compliance.

Healthcare Executive

American College of Healthcare Executives
Publications Center
1951 Cornell Ave.
Melrose Park, IL 60160-1001
312-424-2800
www.ache.org.

This is the official magazine of the ACHE. This bimonthly journal is targeted at health care managers in diverse health care management settings, including managed care, long-term care, and physician and nurse executives.

Healthcare Financial Management

Two Westbrook Corporate Center, Suite 700
Westchester, IL 60154
708-531-9600
www.hfma.org

This monthly trade publication has been published since 1947. It monitors management and finance of health care organizations, application of new procedures and accounting systems, financial reporting, information systems, patient records management, reimbursement issues, and legislation.

Healthcare Forum Journal

Healthcare Forum
425 Market St., 16th Floor
San Francisco, CA 94105
415-356-4300
www.thfnet.org

This publication offers information regarding applied research in health care leadership. It has been published since 1958.

Health Care Fraud & Abuse Newsletter

Leader Publications
345 Park Ave. South
New York, NY 10010
800-888-8300

This monthly newsletter monitors health care fraud enforcement from the DHHS, OIG, Justice Department, FBI, and state and local authorities. It also provides analysis of rulings and judicial opinions, reviews of health care fraud Websites, and Internet resources. It is written by current and former prosecutors, defense attorneys, doctors, and industry professionals.

Healthcare Fund Raising Newsletter

Health Resources Publishing
Brinley Professional Plaza
3100 Hwy. 138
P.O. Box 1442

Wall Township, NJ 07719-1442
908-681-1133

Published since 1979, this bimonthly newsletter aims to foster exchange of information among hospitals, summarizing how they are raising funds to meet competitive pressures and demands for services. It was formerly known as *Hospital Fund Raising Newsletter.*

Healthcare Hazardous Materials Management

ECRI
5200 Butler Pike
Plymouth Meeting, PA 19462-1298
610-825-6000

This monthly newsletter monitors developments in relevant regulatory agencies and is written for the health care environmental and occupational safety manager.

Health Care Innovations

Association of Managed Healthcare Organizations
c/o Health Care Communications, Inc.
One Bridge Plaza, Suite 350
Fort Lee, NJ 07024
201-947-5545

This bimonthly magazine is the official journal of the association. It provides regular updates on legislation.

Health Care Labor Manual

Aspen Publishers, Inc.
7201 McKinney Circle
Frederick, MD 21705
800-447-1717

Published since 1974, this bimonthly loose-leaf service keeps up with new rulings, regulations, and court decisions.

Health Care Law Monthly

Matthew Bender and Co., Inc.
1275 Broadway
Albany, NY 12204-2694
800-252-9257

Each issue of this journal is devoted to a specific health care law topic.

Health Care Law Newsletter

Matthew Bender & Co., Inc.
2 Park Ave.
New York, NY 10016
518-487-3000

This loose-leaf newsletter is published monthly.

Healthcare Leadership Review

COR Healthcare Resources
Box 40959
Santa Barbara, CA 93140

805-564-2177
www.mednet-i.com

Published monthly except for July, this newsletter summarizes articles selected from more than 140 health care management periodicals. Founded in 1982, it was known until 1995 as *Hospital Management Review.*

Health Care M & A Monthly

Irving Levin Associates, Inc.
72 Park St.
New Canaan, CT 06840
800-248-1668
www.levinassoc.com

This is a monthly newsletter setting forth summaries of health care merger and acquisition activity nationwide. It is an adjunct to *Health Care M & A Report,* a quarterly publication.

Health Care M & A Report

Irving Levin Associates, Inc.
72 Park St.
New Canaan, CT 06840
800-248-1668
www.levinassoc.com

This quarterly report provides summaries of health care merger and acquisition activity nationwide. Each issue is approximately 175 pages in length. The information provided is culled from SEC filings and interviews with company management.

Health Care Management Review

Aspen Publishers, Inc.
7201 McKinney Circle
Frederick, MD 21705
800-447-1717
www.aspenpub.com

Published quarterly, this journal is peer-reviewed, with the primary objective being to provide health care administration with useful information regarding application of management principles to the structure and systems of the health care facility.

Healthcare Management Team Letter

Health Resources Publishing
Brinley Professional Plaza
3100 Hwy. 138
P.O. Box 1442
Wall Township, NJ 07719-1442
908-681-1133

This monthly newsletter monitors grants, fundraising techniques, marketing, capital, reimbursement, hospice, capital equipment, hospital restructuring, financing, and hospital energy issues.

Health Care on the Internet
A Journal of Methods and Applications

Eric P. Delozier and M. Sandra Woods, Editors
Haworth Press
10 Alice St.
Binghamton, NY 13904-1580
607-722-5857, 800-429-6784
www.haworthpressinc.com

This publication, inaugurated in 1997, provides helpful evaluations of relevant Websites along with information about Website development.

Health Care Strategic Management

Business Word, Inc.
5350 S. Roslyn St., Suite 400
Englewood, CO 80111-2125
303-290-8500
www.businessword.com

This monthly newsletter focuses primarily on issues of health care business and finance.

Healthcare Supervisor

Aspen Publishers, Inc.
7201 McKinney Circle
Frederick, MD 21705
800-447-1717
www.aspenpub.com

Published quarterly, this journal is peer-reviewed and provides practical, applied management information for supervisors in institutional health care settings.

Healthcare Trends Report

Health Trends
4405 East-West Hwy., Suite 406
Bethesda, MD 20814
301-652-8937, 800-945-8816
www.htrinc.com

This monthly sixteen-page newsletter digests articles from more than one hundred pertinent journals, government documents, industry publications, and research reports. It focuses particularly on managed care, health reform, Medicare, Medicaid, costs, access, and outcomes. The publication provides an annual index, an annual health industry outlook, and a source book.

Health Facilities Management

Health Forum, Inc.
One North Franklin
Chicago, IL 60606
312-893-6800
www.healthforum.com

This journal is published monthly for facilities managers.

Health Fraud Monitor

Millin Publications, Inc.
714 Church St.
Alexandria, VA 22314-4202
703-739-8500

Inaugurated in January 1998, this newsletter monitors litigation, enforcement, investigations, compliance, legislation, and regulation at both the state and federal levels.

Health Freedom News

National Health Federation
212 West Foothill Blvd.
Monrovia, CA 91016
818-357-2181

This bimonthly consumer publication monitors educational, legislative, and legal topics related to health. Its former titles include *Public Scrutiny* (until 1982) and *National Health Federation Bulletin.*

Health Insurance Litigation Reporter

Strafford Publications, Inc.
590 Dutch Valley Rd. NE
P.O. Drawer 13729
Atlanta, GA 30324-0729
404-881-1141
www.straffordpub.com

This monthly case digest service focuses on decisions of national significance selected from a review of cases published by virtually all courts of record in the United States.

Health Labor Relations Reports

Interwood Publications
P.O. Box 20241
Cincinnati, OH 45220
513-221-3715

Published twice monthly, this newsletter monitors judicial and National Labor Review Board decisions, including wrongful discharge, employment at will, contract settlements, arbitration awards, and discrimination.

Health Law Bulletin

Institute of Government
University of North Carolina
C.B. No. 3330, Knapp Bldg.
Chapel Hill, NC 27599-3330
919-966-5381
http:ncinfo.iog.unc.edu

This service is published on an occasional basis to address issues of special interest to local and state government and employees.

Health Law Digest

American Health Lawyers Association
1120 Connecticut Ave. NW, Suite 600

Washington, DC 20036-5405
202-833-1100
www.healthlawyers.org

This monthly digest supplies abstracts of the most recent federal and state court decisions on the subject of health law. It also includes synopses of IRS Revenue and Private Letter Rulings, the Provider Reimbursement Review Board's decisions, and other administrative rulings.

Health Law News

Mary Ann Jauer, Editor
Center for Health Law Studies
St. Louis University School of Law
3700 Lindell Blvd.
St. Louis, MO 63108
314-977-3067
www.lawlib.slu.edu

This six-page newsletter focuses on health law activities occurring at this law school.

Health Law Week

Strafford Publications, Inc.
590 Dutch Valley Rd. NE
P.O. Drawer 13729
Atlanta, GA 30324-0729
404-881-1141
www.straffordpub.com

This newsletter summarizes judicial decisions that concern or affect the health care industry. It provides a concise and comprehensive research tool for attorneys along with health care administrators and practitioners concerned about trends in health care law.

Health Lawyer

American Bar Association
750 Lake Shore Dr.
Chicago, IL 60611
312-988-5000
www.abanet.org

Published six to eight times annually, this is the official newsletter of the ABA's Health Law Section.

Health Lawyers News

American Health Lawyers Association
1120 Connecticut Ave., NW, Suite 600
Washington, DC 20036-3902
202-833-1100
www.healthlawyers.org

Published monthly, this magazine addresses current legislative and regulatory activity.

Health Legislation & Regulation

Faulkner and Gray, Inc.
11 Penn Plaza
New York, NY 10001

212-631-1400, 800-535-8403
www.faulknergray.com

This weekly newsletter covers the White House, Capitol Hill, and agencies relevant to health care.

Health Letter

Public Citizen Health Research Group
Sidney M. Wolfe, M.D., Editor
1600 20th St. NW
Washington, DC 20009-1001
202-588-1000, 800-289-3787
www.citizen.org

Since its founding by Ralph Nader in 1971, Public Citizen has advocated consumer rights in the marketplace. This monthly newsletter examines such issues as patient records confidentiality, product safety, drug recalls, pitfalls of managed care, patient dumping, and physician licensing.

Health Matrix: Journal of Law-Medicine

Case Western Reserve Law School
11075 East Blvd.
Cleveland, OH 44106-7148
216-368-2099

This law journal is published twice annually by the students of Case Western Reserve Law School.

Health PAC Bulletin

Health Policy Advisory Center
237 Thompson St.
New York, NY 10012-1017
212-614-1660

This quarterly newsletter provides analysis and commentary on health care and health policy advocating decent, accessible health care for all.

Healthplan

American Association of Health Plans
1129 20th St. NW, Suite 600
Washington, DC 20036-3421
202-778-3247
www.aahp.org

Published every two months, this magazine focuses on issues of concern to those involved in HMOs and managed care.

Health Policy

Elsevier Science
Box 945
New York, NY 10159-0945
212-633-3730

This monthly journal is a forum for discussion of health policy issues among health policy researchers, legislators, decision makers, and other professionals.

Health Policy, Economics & Management Abstracts

Elsevier Science, B.V.
Secondary Publishing Division
Molenwerf 1
1014 AG Amsterdam, Netherlands
31-20-485-3229
www.elsevier.nl/locate/SPD

This service presents abstracts of the current literature, selected by specialists who scan thirty-six hundred journals published in seventy countries. It is published six times annually.

Health Policy Issue Brief

Catholic Health Association of the United States
4455 Woodson Rd.
St. Louis, MO 63134-3797
314-427-2500
www.chausa.org

This is a monthly backgrounder for advocacy coordinators in Catholic-sponsored health care organizations.

Health Policy Week

United Communications Group
11300 Rockville Pike, Suite 1100
Rockville, MD 20852-3030
301-816-8950

This newsletter offers an inside look at state and federal government actions affecting financing and delivery of health care services.

Health Progress

Catholic Health Association of the United States
4455 Woodson Rd.
St. Louis, MO 63134-3797
314-427-2500
www.chausa.org

Published six times annually, this excellent refereed journal covers a variety of health care management issues, including corporate structure, ethics, mission, sponsorship, and finance.

Health Services Management Research

Longman Group
Fourth Ave.
Harlow Essex, CM19 5AA United Kingdom

Health Span

Prentice Hall Law and Business, Inc.
270 Sylvan Ave.
Englewood Cliffs, NJ 07632

This newsletter, published eleven times annually, provides in-depth information on the legal and regulatory events that are shaping the health care industry. It was formerly known as *Healthscan*.

Health Systems Review

Federation of American Health Systems
1111 19th St. NW, Suite 402
Washington, DC 20036
202-833-3090
www.fahs.com

This is the bimonthly magazine of the FAHS, a trade group representing the investor-owned health systems industry, consisting of more than fourteen hundred institutions in fifty states, Puerto Rico, and eleven foreign countries. FAHS advocates market-based health care reform through managed competition instead of global budget or price caps.

Health Texas

Texas Hospital Association
6225 U.S. Hwy. 290 East
Box 15587
Austin, TX 78761-5587
512-465-1050
www.thaonline.org

Published monthly since 1944, this trade publication was formerly known as *Texas Hospitals*.

HIT News

American Health Lawyers Association
1120 Connecticut Ave. NW, Suite 600
Washington, DC 20036-3902
202-833-1100
www.healthlawyers.org

This is the quarterly newsletter of the AHLA's Health Information and Technology Substantive Law Committee.

HMO Managers Letter

American Association of Health Plans
1129 20th St. NW, Suite 600
Washington, DC 20036
202-778-3200
www.aahp.org

HMO Practice

Health Care Plan
3980 Sheridan Dr.
Amherst, NY 14226
716-839-4877

This monthly magazine is the journal of the HMO Group, a national alliance of twenty-one nonprofit, federally qualified independent group- and staff-model HMOs, formed in 1984 with the goal of defining and strengthening HMO quality and performance. The HMO Group participated in developing the Health Plan Employer Data

and Information Set (HEDIS), a standardized data collection and reporting system for assuring purchasers of the quality of HMO services.

HMOs & Health Plans

American Health Lawyers Association
1120 Connecticut Ave. NW, Suite 600
Washington, DC 20036-3902
202-833-1100

This is the newsletter of the AHLA's HMOs and Health Plans Substantive Law Committee.

Home Health Care Acquisition Report

Irving Levin Associates, Inc.
72 Park St.
New Canaan, CT 06840
800-248-1668
www.levinassociates.com

This annual report of approximately 140 pages provides verified fact sheets on each of one hundred transactions for the year ending June 30. It also supplies analysis of trends in this segment of the health services industry.

Hospice Journal

Haworth Press, Inc.
10 Alice St.
Binghamton, New York 13904-1580
800-429-6784

This quarterly journal is the official publication of the National Hospice Organization, the professional independent nonprofit national association devoted exclusively to hospice care.

Hospice Letter

Health Resources Publishing
Brinley Professional Plaza
3100 Hwy. 138
P.O. Box 1442
Wall Township, NJ 07719-1442
908-681-1133

This monthly newsletter, published since 1979, is targeted at administrators and directors who follow Medicare reimbursement and hospice accreditation issues.

Hospital Acquisition Report

Irving Levin Associates, Inc.
72 Park St.
New Canaan, CT 06840
800-248-1668
www.levinassoc.com

This annual research report supplies financial analyses on per bed prices, revenue multipliers, and consolidation strategies. The text, running approximately 125 pages, supplies fact sheets on each year's 170 or so hospital mergers and acquisitions.

Hospital & Health Services Administration

Foundation of the American College of Health Care Executives
Publications Service Center
1951 Cornell Ave.
Melrose Park, IL 60160-1001
708-450-9952
www.ache.org/hap.html

The official journal of the American College of Healthcare Executives, this quarterly publication explores varied facets of health care management, from policy to finances. Issues also contain reviews of current, relevant health care management books. It has been published since 1956.

Hospital & Healthcare News

Robert Jacobs Publishing Co., Inc.
2022 East Allegheny Ave.
Philadelphia, PA 19134
215-739-2033

Formerly known as *Hospital News Delaware Valley,* this general interest health care journal is published monthly and focuses on hospital-based regional health care issues and practitioners.

Hospital Blue Book

Billian Publishing, Inc.
2100 Powers Ferry Rd., Suite 300
Atlanta, GA 30339
404-955-5656

This annual guide lists some 7,175 U.S. hospitals with more than 118,800 key personnel.

Hospital Fundraising

American Health Consultants, Inc.
3525 Piedmont Rd. NE
Bldg. 6, Suite 400
Atlanta, GA 30305

This monthly newsletter provides advice on researching and writing grant proposals; it monitors changing regulations and tax rulings.

Hospital Law Newsletter

Nathan Hershey, Editor
Aspen Publishers, Inc.
7201 McKinney Circle
Frederick, MD 27105
800-447-1717
www.aspenpub.com

This monthly newsletter examines changes and trends in hospital law. Topics discussed include mergers, physician staff appointments, incident reports, exclusive hospital-physician contracts, and confidentiality protection.

Hospital Litigation Reporter

Strafford Publications, Inc.
590 Dutch Valley Rd. NE
P.O. Drawer 13729
Atlanta, GA 30324-0729
404-881-1141
www.straffordpub.com

This is a monthly service that screens and selects approximately forty cases representing current issues facing hospitals; it then provides a brief summary of each.

Hospital Risk Management

American Health Consultants, Inc.
3525 Piedmont Rd. NE, Bldg. 6, Suite 400
Atlanta, GA 30305
404-262-7436, 800-688-2421
www.ahcpub.com

This monthly newsletter has been published since 1979.

Hospitals & Health Networks

Health Forum, Inc.
One North Franklin
Chicago, IL 60606
312-893-6800
www.healthforum.org

This magazine is published twice monthly and spotlights health care business issues.

Hospital Topics

Heldref Publications
1319 18th St., NW
Washington, DC 20036-1802
202-296-6267
www.heldref.org

This quarterly journal focuses on planning, organizing, staffing, and decision making. It is written primarily for health care administrators.

Houston Law Review

University of Houston Law Center
4800 Calhoun, Room 25 BLB
Houston, TX 77204-6370
713-743-2247
www.law.uh.edu/publications/hlr/

This journal publishes a significant number of articles on health care law and policy.

HSR: Health Services Research

Foundation of the American College of Healthcare Executives

Publications Service Center
1951 Cornell Ave.
Melrose Park, IL 60160-1001
708-450-9952
www.ache.org/hap.html

The official journal of the Association for Health Services Research, this multidisciplinary review provides those engaged in research, public policy formulation, health care administration education, and practice with advance information on new trends and the latest techniques of research and evaluation. Published six times annually, it is edited by Stephen M. Shortell of Northwestern University.

Illinois Managed Care Review

Allan Baumgarten
4800 West 27th St.
Minneapolis, MN 55416
612-925-9121

This detailed annual report examines trends in Illinois's managed care markets.

In Confidence

American Health Information Management
  Association
919 North Michigan Ave., Suite 1400
Chicago, IL 60611-1683
800-335-5535

This bimonthly newsletter examines health information security, privacy, and confidentiality.

Infectious Waste News

Environmental Industry Associations
4301 Connecticut Ave. NW
Washington, DC 20008
202-364-3777
www.wasteage.com

This newsletter is published biweekly for generators and handlers of biohazardous wastes.

*Information Technology Report for Doctors
and Health Networks*

Atlantic Information Services, Inc.
1100 17th St. NW, Suite 300
Washington, DC 20036
800-521-4323
www.aispub.com

Published twenty times annually, this newsletter supplies advice on developing long-term IT strategies and analysis on new products, trends, and strategies in health care information technology. It also monitors which technology is working best and includes details of IT inventories of the nation's leading hospitals.

In-House Counselor

American Health Lawyers Association
1120 Connecticut Ave. NW, Suite 600
Washington, DC 20036-2902
202-833-1100
www.healthlawyers.org

This is the newsletter of the AHLA's In-House Counsel Special Interest Committee.

Inquiry

Blue Cross and Blue Shield Association
840 North Lake Shore Dr.
Chicago, IL 60611
312-297-6000
www.bluecares.com

Inquiry seeks to improve the nation's health care system by providing a thoughtful forum for communicating and discussing relevant public policy issues, innovative concepts, and original research and demonstrations in the areas of health care organization, provision, and financing. Collectively, Blue Cross and Blue Shield member plans make up the nation's largest provider of managed care services.

Inside HCFA

P.O. Box 7167, Ben Franklin Station
Washington, DC 20044
800-424-9068

Published every other Thursday, this newsletter covers such topics as the State Children's Health Insurance Program, development of new policies for clinical labs, and development of quality policy for Medicare/Medicaid managed care, as well as broad payment policy issues such as risk adjustment, practice expenses, ambulatory care prospective payment, and support for graduate medical education.

Inside Health Law

Judy Solomon, Editor
Aspen Publishers, Inc.
7201 McKinney Circle
Frederick, MD 21705
800-447-1717
www.aspenpub.com

This monthly newsletter is written for both lawyers and lay readers. It covers such issues as tax exemption, managed care, fraud and abuse, antitrust, health care reform, Medicare, integrated delivery systems, and risk management.

Inside Medicaid Managed Care

Sarah E. Mooney, Editor
Aspen Publishers, Inc.
7201 McKinney Circle

Frederick, MD 21705
800-447-1717
www.aspenpub.com

This monthly newsletter is written for contractors, insurers, and providers.

Inside PPMCs

Atlantic Information Services, Inc.
1100 17th St. NW, Suite 300
Washington, DC 20036
800-521-4323
www.aispub.com

Published twenty-four times annually, this business newsletter focuses on physician practice management companies. Topics covered include upcoming M & A action, market expansion plans, new sources of capital, contracting trends, and integration strategies.

Insider

American Federation of Home Health Agencies
1320 Fenwick Lane, Suite 100
Silver Spring, MD 20910
301-588-1454
www.his.com/afhha/usa.html

This newsletter presents the views of Medicare-certified home health care agencies and provides updates of legislative and regulatory issues.

Institute News

Institute for Health Care Research and Policy
Georgetown University Medical Center
2233 Wisconsin Ave. NW, Suite 525
Washington, DC 20007
202-687-0880

This monthly newsletter describes new projects, publications, and seminars at the center.

Integrated Delivery Systems Newsletter

American Association of Physician-Hospital
    Organizations/Integrated Healthcare Delivery
    Systems
4435 Waterfront Dr., Suite 101
P.O. Box 4913
Glen Allen, VA 23060
804-747-5823
www.aaihds.org

This quarterly newsletter addresses marketing, management, legal, information systems, and physician development issues.

International Journal of Health Services

Vincent Navarro, Editor
Baywood Publishing Co., Inc.

26 Austin Ave.
P.O. Box 337
Amityville, NY 11701
516-691-1270
www./baywood.com

This quarterly journal is a multidisciplinary publication devoted to health and social policy, political economy and sociology, and ethics and law.

Issue Brief

Center for Studying Health System Change
600 Maryland Ave. SW, Suite 550
Washington, DC 20024-2512
202-554-7549

These four-page monographs are published irregularly by the center, which is supported by the Robert Wood Johnson Foundation as part of its health tracking initiative and affiliated with Mathematica Policy Research, Inc.

Issues in Law and Medicine

National Legal Center for the Mentally Dependent
    and Disabled, Inc.
7 South 6th St., Suite 208
Terre Haute, IN 47807
812-238-0769

This quarterly peer-reviewed journal is copublished by the National Legal Center for the Mentally Dependent and Disabled, the Horatio R. Storer Foundation, and the American Academy of Medical Ethics. It focuses on providing technical and informational assistance to attorneys, health care professionals, bioethicists, educators, and administrators concerned with a broad range of legal, medical, and ethical issues that arise from providing health care services.

Jahrbuch für Recht und Ethik
(Annual Review of Law and Ethics)

Duncker & Humblot
Jahrbuch Institut für Strafecht und Rechtsphilosophie
    Schiller
Strabel D-91054
Erlangen, Germany

This annual journal examines bioethics and medical law, among other topics. It is published in both German and English.

Jenks Healthcare Business Report

Strafford Publications, Inc.
590 Dutch Valley Rd. NE
P.O. Drawer 13729
Atlanta, GA 30324-0729
404-881-1141
www.straffordpub.com

Published twice monthly, this service focuses on business developments in the health care sector. Its target audience includes managed care providers, hospitals, physician practice management groups, drug companies, and medical device manufacturers.

Joint Commission Journal on Quality Improvement

JCAHO
One Renaissance Blvd.
Oakbrook Terrace, IL 60181
800-346-0085
www.jcaho.org

This monthly, peer-reviewed journal, prepared by the Joint Commission on Accreditation of Healthcare Organizations—the major national private accrediting body for hospitals and other health care organizations—is devoted to quality improvement. Articles are often presented in special single-topic issues.

Joint Commission Perspectives

JCAHO
One Renaissance Blvd.
Oakbrook Terrace, IL 60181
800-346-0085
www.jcaho.org

Published six times annually, this is the commission's official newsletter. It addresses issues related to the accreditation process, performance measurement, and other Joint Commission developments.

Journal of Ambulatory Care Management

Aspen Publishing, Inc.
7201 McKinney Circle
Frederick, MD 21705
800-447-1717
www.aspenpub.com

Published quarterly, this is a peer-reviewed journal that supplies timely, applied information on the most important developments in ambulatory care management.

Journal of the American Health Information Management Association

AHIMA
919 North Michigan Ave., Suite 1400
Chicago, IL 60611
312-787-2672
www.ahima.org

This monthly publication examines evolving issues relating to health care records.

Journal of the American Medical Association (JAMA)

515 North State St.
Chicago, IL 60610
www.ama-assn.org/jama

This weekly peer-reviewed journal is an official publication of the AMA and addresses clinical and health policy topics.

Journal of the American Pharmaceutical Association

American Pharmaceutical Association
2215 Constitution Ave. NW
Washington, DC 20037-2985
202-628-4410
www.aphanet.org

This is the JAPhA's official bimonthly magazine (formerly *American Pharmacy*). It contains articles on a variety of clinical and policy issues.

Journal of the Association for Healthcare Philanthropy

Association for Healthcare Philanthropy
313 Park Ave., Suite 400
Falls Church, VA 22046
703-532-6243
www.go-ahp.org

This journal is published twice annually for association members and others who share an interest in health care philanthropy.

Journal of Care Management

8201 Cantrell, Suite 230
Little Rock, AR 72227
501-225-2229
www.cmsa.org

This is a peer-reviewed bimonthly publication of the Case Management Society of America. Its editorial content focuses on managed care trends and legislative issues.

Journal of Contemporary Health Law and Policy

Catholic University of America
Columbus School of Law
Washington, DC 20064
202-319-5732

Published semiannually, this journal examines topics in health law, bioethics, and legal aspects of the delivery of health care services. It also treats such subjects as public and environmental health.

Journal of Health Administration Education

Association of University Programs in Health
  Administration
1911 North Fort Myer Dr., Suite 503
Arlington, VA 22205
703-524-5500
www.aupha.com

A quarterly publication of the association, this journal has, since its inception in 1983, provided a forum for the interdisciplinary world of health administration.

Journal of Health Care Compliance

Aspen Publishers, Inc.
7201 McKinney Circle
Frederick, MD 21705
800-447-1717

This bimonthly journal, inaugurated in January 1999, includes columns that subdivide compliance by profession (physicians, coders, auditors, and so on) and by settings (managed care organizations, physician practices, home health). Specialists in each area of compliance submit articles that seek to assist hospitals in communicating with physicians, physicians in communicating with labs, labs in communicating with billing offices, and so forth.

Journal of Health Care Law & Policy

University of Maryland School of Law
500 West Baltimore St.
Baltimore, MD 21201-1786
410-706-2115

This law review, inaugurated in 1999, is a semiannual publication of the University of Maryland School of Law.

Journal of Health Economics

c/o Joseph P. Newhouse, Editor
Division of Health Policy, Research, and Education
Harvard University
25 Shattuck St., Parcel B 1st Floor
Boston, MA 02115

This journal, published six times annually, addresses efficiency and distributional aspects of health policy, among other subjects.

Journal of Health and Hospital Law

Jesse Goldner and Tim Greaney, Coeditors
One North Franklin
Chicago, IL 60606
312-422-3700
www.aaha.org

A quarterly publication of the American Academy of Healthcare Attorneys of the American Hospital Association in association with the St. Louis University School of Law.

Journal of Health and Social Behavior

American Sociological Association
1722 N St. NW
Washington, DC 20036
202-833-3410
www.asanet.org

This quarterly journal is written for those interested in sociological aspects of illness.

Journal of Health Law

American Health Lawyers Association
1120 Connecticut Ave. NW, Suite 950
Washington, DC 20036
202-833-0766
www.healthlawyers.org

This quarterly journal is jointly produced by the AHLA and the St. Louis University School of Law. Prior to 1998, it was known as the *Journal of Health and Hospital Law*.

Journal of Health Politics, Policy, and Law

Duke University Press
6697 College Station
Durham, NC 27708
919-687-3653
www.duke.edu/web/dupress/

Published bimonthly, this journal publishes articles and commentary primarily from academic writers.

Journal of Healthcare Risk Management

American Hospital Association
One North Franklin
Chicago, IL 60606
312-422-3989
www.aha.org

Founded in 1981, this quarterly refereed journal supplies information on quality assurance, professional liability claims management, loss prevention, risk financing, risk management program development, workers compensation, and risk management legislation and legal issues.

Journal of Insurance Regulation

National Association of Insurance Commissioners
2301 McGee, Suite 800
Kansas City, MO 64108-2604
816-842-3600
www.naic.org

Published four times annually, this publication is a forum for discussion of regulatory and public policy issues in insurance.

Journal of Insurance Regulation

2301 McGee, Suite 800
Kansas City, MO 64108-2604
816-842-3600

This newsletter examines the insurance industry as it affects health care, along with other insurance topics.

Journal of Law and Health

Cleveland-Marshall College of Law
Cleveland State University
Cleveland, OH 44115

216-687-2344
www.law.csuohio.edu

This journal is published twice annually by the students of Cleveland-Marshall College of Law.

Journal of Law, Medicine and Ethics

American Society of Law, Medicine, and Ethics
765 Commonwealth Ave.
Boston, MA 02215
617-262-4990
www.aslme.org

This journal publishes scholarly articles on such issues as access to health care, AIDS, ethics committees, and assisted dying. It is a peer-reviewed quarterly read by more than five thousand health care professionals.

Journal of Legal Medicine

Taylor and Francis
1101 Vermont Ave. NW, Suite 200
Washington, DC 20005-3521
202-289-2174
www.tandfdc.com

This is the official quarterly publication of the American College of Legal Medicine.

Journal of Legal Nurse Consulting

American Association of Legal Nurse Consultants
4700 W. Lake Ave.
Glenview, IL 60025-1485
877-402-2562

This quarterly refereed journal seeks to promote legal nurse consulting within the medical-legal community.

Journal of Long-Term Care Administration

American College of Health Care Administrators
8120 Woodmont Ave., Suite 200
Bethesda, MD 20814

Journal of Long-Term Home Health Care

Springer Publishing Co.
536 Broadway, 11th Floor
New York, NY 10012-3955
212-431-4370
www.springer-ny.com

Journal of Mental Health Administration

Association of Behavioral Healthcare Management (ABHM)
840 North Lake Shore Dr.
Chicago, IL 60611
847-480-9626
www.abhm@abhm.org

This quarterly journal circulates to more than one thousand subscribers and examines, among other topics, federal and state policy as they relate to mental health issues.

Journal of the National Cancer Institute

Oxford University Press
2001 Evans Rd.
Cary, NC 27513
800-852-7323
www.oup.co.uk/jnci/

Published semimonthly, this journal publishes original research papers in oncology along with news, editorials, commentary, and articles relating to health policy issues, including health care delivery systems and quality of care.

Journal of Nursing Administration

J. B. Lippincott Co.
East Washington Square
Philadelphia, PA 19105
215-238-4200
www.lrpub.com

This monthly publication addresses a range of managed care issues, among others.

Journal of Public Health Policy

23 Pleasant Way
Burlington, VT 05401
800-464-4343

This journal is published quarterly and addresses public health issues.

Journal of Rural Health

National Rural Health Association
One West Armour Blvd., Suite 301
Kansas City, MO 64111
816-756-3140
www.NRHArural.org

Published quarterly, this is the official journal of the association.

Journal of Taxation of Exempt Organizations

RIA Group
31 St. James Ave.
Boston, MA 02116-4112

This bimonthly magazine contains a wealth of information about health care tax issues.

Jurimetrics

American Bar Association, Science and Technology Section
750 North Lake Shore Dr.
Chicago, IL 60611
312-988-5000

Cosponsored by the Arizona State University Center for the Study of Law, Science, and Technology, this quarterly journal focuses on legal issues in science and technology, including medicine.

Kentucky Managed Care

Harkey and Associates
P.O. Box 159025
Nashville, TN 37215
615-385-4131
www.harkeyreport.com

This newsletter provides information on state managed care developments. Topics covered include HMOs, PPOs, market-level enrollment, hospital networks, physician networks, and legislation.

Law Reports

Catholic Health Association of the United States
4455 Woodson Rd.
St. Louis, MO 63134-3797
314-427-2500
www.chausa.org

Published quarterly, this service keeps CHA members and their attorneys apprised of legal issues affecting Catholic health care entities.

Law & Sexuality: A Review of Lesbian and Gay Legal Issues

Tulane University Law School
John Giffen Weinmann Hall
6329 Freret St.
New Orleans, LA 70118
504-865-5835
www.law.tulane.edu/journals.htm

This journal is published annually by Tulane Law School and focuses on AIDS law, among other topics.

Legal-Legislative Reporter

International Foundation of Employee Benefit Plans
18700 West Bluemound Rd.
P.O. Box 69
Brookfield, WI 53008-0069
414-786-6710
www.ifebp.org

This is a monthly review of legislative developments, court cases, arbitration awards, and administrative decisions of importance in the employee benefits area.

Legal Medicine Perspectives

American College of Legal Medicine
1111 North Plaza Dr., Suite 550
Schaumburg, IL 60173

800-433-9137
www.aclm.org

This newsletter is a quarterly review of medical-legal developments, including summaries of prominent cases and discussions of recent statutes.

Legisbrief

National Conference of State Legislatures
1560 Broadway, Suite 700
Denver, CO 80202-9883
303-830-2054
www.ncsl.org

This service provides an overview of critical state issues, multistate information, analysis of alternative courses of action, and successful approaches and resources.

LTC Advisor

American Health Lawyers Association
1120 Connecticut Ave. NW, Suite 600
Washington, DC 20036-3902
202-833-1100

This is the newsletter of the AHLA's Long-Term Care Substantive Law Committee.

McKnight's Long-Term Care News

Medical Economics Co.
Five Paragon Dr.
Montvale, NJ 07645
www.medec.com

This monthly newsletter is written for nursing facility administrators and directors, retirement housing directors, and their attorneys. It is a source of industry news and monitors Medicare and related topics.

Managed Behavioral Health News

Atlantic Information Services, Inc.
1100 17th St. NW, Suite 300
Washington, DC 20036
800-521-4323
www.aispub.com

Published forty-five times annually, this business newsletter examines such topics as capitation, integration models, Medicaid and risk contracting, contracting strategies, quality initiatives, strategic alliances, and performance measures.

Managed Care Careers

American Association of Health Plans
1129 20th St. NW, Suite 600
Washington, DC 20036-3421
202-778-3247
www.aahp.org

Published twenty-two times annually, this service lists job opportunities in managed care.

Managed Care Compliance Alert

Eli Research, Inc.
P.O. Box 9132
Chapel Hill, NC 27515
800-874-9180
www.eliresearch.com

This biweekly newsletter provides news and analysis on regulatory compliance and quality assurance for managed care readers.

Managed Care Contract Negotiator

Brownstone Publishers, Inc.
149 Fifth Ave.
New York, NY 10010-6801
800-643-8095
www.brownstone.com

This practical monthly newsletter is written to assist providers in negotiating less risky, more profitable managed care contracts. Topics covered include hold-harmless clauses, indemnification clauses, credentialing, peer review, model schedules of covered services, volume enrollment guarantees, applicability of rates clauses, arbitration, and mediation.

Managed Care Magazine

Stezzi Communications
301 Oxford Valley Rd., Suite 1105A
Yardley, PA 19067
215-321-6663

This is an independent monthly guide for physicians and health plan executives on capitation, contracting physician compensation, and other health insurance and delivery services.

Managed Care Outlook

Aspen Publications, Inc.
7201 McKinney Circle
Frederick, MD 21705-9782

This biweekly newsletter includes reports on new business, industry trends, regional happenings, and legal and policy news.

Managed Care Quarterly

Allan Fine, Editor
Aspen Publishers, Inc.
7201 McKinney Circle
Frederick, MD 21705
800-447-1717
www.aspenpub.com

Written for attorneys, managed care executives, utilization review managers, CFOs, actuaries, and physician

executives, this journal examines such topics as risk sharing, capitation, and integrated networks.

Managed Care Update

Faulkner and Gray, Inc.
11 Penn Plaza
New York, NY 10001
212-631-1400, 800-535-8403
www.faulknergray.com

Provides bimonthly briefings on managed care, health care costs, and Medicare and Medicaid.

Managed Care Week

Atlantic Information Services, Inc.
1100 17th St. NW, Suite 300
Washington, DC 20036
800-521-4323
www.aispub.com

This eight-page journal, published forty-five times annually, focuses on compliance with federal insurance mandates, evaluating Medicare managed care opportunities, monitoring new employer purchasing strategies, tracking state reforms, meeting new quality-related data collection rules, and keeping up with merger and acquisition strategy.

Managed Healthcare

Advanstar Communications, Inc.
7500 Old Oak Blvd.
Cleveland, OH 44130
216-826-2839

This monthly trade publication is directed toward health care benefits managers, managed health care organizations, and providers of health services. It monitors issues of concern for managers responsible for controlling employee health care costs and quality, including regulatory and legislative trends.

Managed Medicare and Medicaid

Atlantic Information Services, Inc.
1100 17th St. NW, Suite 300
Washington, DC 20036
800-521-4323
www.aispub.com

Published forty-five times annually, this newsletter focuses on new payment methods, market trends, administrative developments, and financing opportunities.

Maryland Managed Care

Harkey and Associates
P.O. Box 159025
Nashville, TN 37215
615-385-4131
www.harkeyreport.com

This quarterly newsletter monitors managed care trends, Medicaid, legislation, hospital networks, and physician managed care organizations.

Medical Benefits

Aspen Publishers, Inc.
P.O. Box 990
Frederick, MD 21705

Twice monthly, this newsletter supplies current data, news, and corporate policies shaping the future of health care. Includes abundant charts and graphs. Focuses on where savings are to be found, which strategies work, which have failed, and why. Discusses the impact of managed care trends and developments, new methods of provider contracting, changing reimbursement structures, cost-containment strategies, new quality measurement methods and standards, state and federal reform measures, and important court rulings affecting health benefits.

Medical Care

J. B. Lippincott Co.
East Washington Square
Philadelphia, PA 19105
215-238-4200
www.lrpub.com

This monthly publication is the official journal of the medical care section of the American Public Health Association.

Medical Care Research and Review

Sage Publications
2455 Teller Rd.
Thousand Oaks, CA 91320
805-499-0721
www.sagetub.com

Formerly *Medical Care Review,* this quarterly journal publishes peer-reviewed articles synthesizing empirical and theoretical research on health services, focusing on issues of organization, quality of care, and patient-provider relationships.

Medical Economics

Five Paragon Dr.
Montvale, NJ 07645
800-432-4570
www.medec.com

This twice-monthly magazine covers medical office management, health legislation, health insurance, and other nonclinical topics.

Medical Group Management Journal

Medical Group Management Association
104 Inverness Terrace East
Englewood, CO 80112-5306

303-799-1111
www.mgma.com

Published since 1953, this bimonthly journal targets physicians, administrators, CEOs, office managers, and other professionals involved in medical group practices.

Medical Group Management Update

Medical Group Management Association
104 Inverness Terrace East
Englewood, CO 80112-5306
303-799-1111
www.mgma.com

This newspaper, published twelve times annually, is an account of the association's activities, services, and news, as well as current legislative information and trends in the health care community that are pertinent to group practice management.

Medical Law Review

Oxford University Press
2001 Evans Rd.
Cary, NC 27513
919-677-0977

This journal, inaugurated in 1993, provides information for academics, lawyers, legal practitioners, and all others interested in health care and law.

Medical Legal Aspects of Breast Implants

Stephanie McEvily, Editor
Leader Publications
345 Park Ave. South
New York, NY 10010
800-888-8300 ext. 6170
www.ljx.com

This is a monthly newsletter focused on breast implant litigation.

Medical Legal Lessons

American College of Legal Medicine
611 East Wells St.
Milwaukee, WI 53202-3816
201-916-1000
www.aclm.org

This bimonthly publication addresses day-to-day medical-legal concerns.

Medical Litigation Alert

Jury Verdict Review Publications, Inc.
24 Commerce St., Suite 1722
Newark, NJ 07102
201-624-1665

This is a monthly nationwide review of medical litigation for physicians, hospitals, and health care administrators.

Medical Malpractice Law & Strategy

New York Law Publishing Co.
345 Park Ave. South
New York, NY 10010
800-888-8300
www.nylj.com

This monthly newsletter monitors judicial, legislative, and medical developments and discusses how physician clients can obtain the best malpractice insurance, as well as new legal concerns raised by telemedicine, legislative restrictions on managed care incentives and penalties, state versus federal doctrines of HMO liability, and other issues.

Medical Network Strategy Report

Edward Larkin, Editor
COR Research Resources
P.O. Box 40959
Santa Barbara, CA 93140-0959
805-564-2177

This monthly newsletter offers integration strategy case studies, interviews with those developing and implementing integration strategies, and reports on issues affecting integration.

Medical Staff Advocate

California Medical Association
221 Main St.
P.O. Box 7690
San Francisco, CA 94120-7690
800-882-1262
www.cmanet.org

This quarterly journal addresses legal, economic, quality-of-care, and organizational issues facing medical staffs.

Medical Staff Counselor

Matthew Bender & Co., Inc.
136 Carlin Rd.
Conklin, NY 13748-1531
800-252-9257

This quarterly journal is written for the independent physician, not the hospital or organized medicine. It focuses on such topics as medical staff governance, hospital and medical staff relations, changing payment systems, credentialing, quality assurance, peer review activities, malpractice and risk management, managed care and its implications for physicians, and tax changes involving medical practice.

Medical Trial Technique Quarterly

Clark Boardman Callaghan
50 Broad St. East
Rochester, NY 14694

This journal is designed for the attorney and doctor interested in the medicolegal field.

Medical Waste News

Business Publishers, Inc.
951 Pershing Dr.
Silver Spring, MD 20910-4432
301-587-6300
www.bpinews.com

This monthly newsletter monitors legislation and regulation concerning identification, handling, transportation, treatment, and disposal of medical waste.

Medicare Compliance

Atlantic Information Services, Inc.
1100 17th St. NW, Suite 300
Washington, DC 20036
800-521-4323
www.aispub.com

Published forty-five times annually, this business newsletter aims to assist management in complying with current federal rules. This resource is copublished by the Healthcare Financial Management Association.

Medicare and Medicaid Law Bulletin

LRP Publications
747 Dresher Rd.
P.O. Box 980
Horsham, PA 19044-0980
215-784-0860, 800-341-7874
www.lrp.com

This biweekly newsletter provides updates on all federal and state decisions regarding Medicare and Medicaid. It also supplies summaries of all Provider Reimbursement Review Board and HCFA Administrator decisions and summaries of all Departmental Appeals Board decisions, including both civil remedies and appellate decisions.

Medicine & Health

Faulkner and Gray, Inc.
11 Penn Plaza
New York, NY 10001
212-631-1400, 800-535-8403
www.faulknergray.com

This newsletter is published fifty times annually and focuses on issues of health care quality, managed care, capitation, and other policy issues.

Medicine and Law

World Association for Medical Law
Yozmot Ltd.
P.O. Box 56055
Tel-Aviv 61560, Israel
972-3-5284851

This quarterly journal covers medicolegal issues in both developed and emerging countries. Topics covered include nursing law, dentistry law, pharmaceutical law, child abuse, medical experimentation, genetic engineering, and AIDS, among others.

Michigan Health and Hospitals

Michigan Health and Hospital Association
6215 West St. Joseph Hwy.
Lansing, MI 48917
517-323-3443
www.mha.org

This magazine is published bimonthly and focuses on current trends. Its readership includes health care executives, physicians, and insurers.

Michigan Managed Care Review

Allan Baumgarten
4800 West 27th St.
Minneapolis, MN 55416
612-925-9121

Written by a veteran health care observer, this detailed annual survey examines reform initiatives that affect the market: integrated provider networks, employer purchasing initiatives, Medicaid managed care, and others.

Milbank Quarterly

Cambridge University Press
1 East 75th St.
New York, NY 10021
212-924-3900
www.cup.org

Published since 1923, this journal provides a forum for discussing public health and health care policy issues.

Millin's Health Fraud Monitor

Millin Publications, Inc.
714 Church St.
Alexandria, VA 22314-4202
703-739-8500

This newsletter, published twice monthly, is written by attorneys and for attorneys and health care executives. It monitors compliance programs, investigative trends, new government negotiating tactics, and new legislation and regulation.

Minnesota Managed Care Review

Allan Baumgarten
4800 West 27th St.
Minneapolis, MN 55416
612-925-9121

Written by a veteran health care observer, this detailed annual survey examines reform initiatives that affect the market: integrated provider networks, employer purchasing initiatives, Medicaid managed care, and others.

Modern Healthcare

Crain Communications, Inc.
740 Rush St.
Chicago, IL 60611
312-649-5350
www.modernhealthcare.com

This weekly magazine covers breaking news in the health care industry.

NAIC News

National Association of Insurance Commissioners
2301 McGee, Suite 800
Kansas City, MO 64108-2604
816-374-7259
www.naic.org

Published monthly, this newsletter provides summaries of current insurance regulatory activity. It includes articles about salient federal regulations along with model legislation reports.

Nation's Health

American Public Health Association
1015 15th St. NW
Washington, DC 20005-2605
202-789-5600
www.apha.org

This monthly newspaper monitors federal and state legislation and government-related proposals.

National Journal

National Journal Group, Inc.
1501 M St. NW
Washington, DC 20005
202-739-8531
www.cloakroom.com

This weekly magazine covers politics and government and includes frequent articles on health care policy.

New England Journal of Medicine

Massachusetts Medical Society
10 Shattuck St.
Boston, MA 02115-6094
617-893-3800
www.massmed.org

This journal is published weekly and frequently addresses health care policy issues.

New York Health Law Update

M. Lee Smith Publishers LLC
P.O. Box 5094

Brentwood, TN 37024-5094
800-274-6774
www.mleesmith.com

This service provides a monthly survey of New York State and federal health law developments.

North Carolina Healthcare News

567 Seminole Dr.
Marietta, GA 30060
770-499-1220

This monthly newsletter covers legislation, managed care, and other topics.

North Carolina Legislative Health Watch

Harkey and Associates, Inc.
P.O. Box 159025
Nashville, TN 37215
615-385-4131
www.harkeyreport.com

This weekly newsletter, inaugurated in January 1999, covers legislative and regulatory developments in the health care and health insurance sector in North Carolina.

Nuclear Waste News

Business Publishers, Inc.
8737 Colesville Road, Suite 1100
Silver Spring, MD 20910
800-274-6737
www.bpinews.com

This weekly newsletter monitors generation, packaging, transportation, processing, and disposal of nuclear waste.

Nurses Notes

American Association of Managed Care Nurses, Inc.
4435 Waterfront Dr., Suite 101
P.O. Box 4975
Glen Allen, VA 23058-4975
804-747-9698
www.aamcn.org

Published by a managed care professional organization dedicated to career development, this newsletter is targeted at nurses who are employed by HMOs, IPAs, or PPO networks, military health care settings, and other managed care programs.

Nursing Administration Quarterly

Aspen Publishing, Inc.
7201 McKinney Circle
Frederick, MD 21705
800-447-1717
www.aspenpub.com

This journal, published for more than twenty years, focuses on strategies for improving quality and cutting costs.

Nursing Home Law Letter

National Senior Citizens Law Center
1101 14th St. NW, Suite 400
Washington, DC 20005
202-289-6976
www.nsclc.org/

This quarterly publication provides in-depth information on a specific nursing home law topic in each issue.

Nursing Trends and Issues

American Nurses Association
600 Maryland Ave. SW, Suite 100 W
Washington, DC 20024-2571
202-651-7000, 800-637-0323
www.nursingworld.org

Published sixteen times annually, this newsletter provides commentary and analysis on issues, policies, research, and trends affecting nurses, the nursing profession, and the future of health care.

Ohio Health Law Update

M. Lee Smith Publishers LLC
P.O. Box 5094
Brentwood, TN 37024-5094
800-274-6774
www.mleesmith.com

This newsletter provides a monthly survey of Ohio and federal health law developments.

Ohio Managed Care

Harkey and Associates, Inc.
P.O. Box 159025
Nashville, TN 37215
615-385-4131
www.harkeyreport.com

This newsletter provides a quarterly survey of Ohio and federal health law developments as they relate to HMOs, PPOs, Medicaid, legislation, hospital networks, and physician managed care organizations.

Ohio Managed Care Review

Allan Baumgarten
4800 West 27th St.
Minneapolis, MN 55416
612-925-9121

Consultant Baumgarten analyzes managed care events and trends in Ohio's medical markets in this concise annual report.

Patient Care Law

Action Kit Publications
1614 Fifth Ave.
Pittsburgh, PA 15213
800-245-1205
www.hortyspringer.com

This bimonthly newsletter serves as a resource for nurse management and provides current legal analyses.

Pennsylvania Managed Care

Harkey and Associates, Inc.
P.O. Box 159025
Nashville, TN 37215
615-385-4131
www.harkeyreport.com

This quarterly newsletter provides research on managed care developments. Topics covered include HMOs and PPOs, market-level enrollment, hospital networks, physician networks, managed care contracts, Medicaid, and legislation.

Physician Manager

Atlantic Information Services, Inc.
1100 17th St. NW, Suite 300
Washington, DC 20036
800-521-4323
www.aispub.com

Published twenty-four times annually, this newsletter assesses managed care markets and trends, provides guidance in designing partnerships and alliances, and evaluates capitation strategies. It also helps physician executives track clinical performance, manage medical utilization, monitor risk-sharing arrangements, select appropriate information systems, and understand Medicare compliance issues.

Physician Medical Group Acquisition Report

Irving Levin Associates, Inc.
72 Park St.
New Canaan, CT 06840
800-248-1668
www.levinassociates.com

This annual report of approximately 150 pages provides verified fact sheets on each of the past year's 225 or so acquisitions, along with analyses of activity during the last three years, bringing this rapidly consolidating field into focus.

Physician Organizations

American Health Lawyers Association
1120 Connecticut Ave. NW, Suite 600
Washington, DC 20036-3902
202-833-1100

This is the newsletter of the AHLA's Physician Organizations Substantive Law Committee.

Provider

American Health Care Association
1201 L St. NW
Washington, DC 20005-4014
202-842-4444
www.ahca.org

This organization, a federation of fifty-one associations representing eleven thousand nonprofit and for-profit long-term care providers, publishes this monthly newsletter to keep its members abreast of legislative and regulatory policy, facility administration issues, and management questions.

Psychology, Public Policy, and Law

American Psychological Association
750 First St. NE
Washington, DC 20002-4242
800-374-2721
www.apa.org/journals/law.html

This quarterly peer-reviewed journal evaluates the contributions of psychology and related disciplines to public policy and legal issues, assesses policy alternatives in light of the knowledge base in psychology, and points out research needs that address policy and legal issues for which there is currently insufficient theoretical or empirical knowledge.

RAP Sheet

American Health Lawyers Association
Suite 950, 1120 Connecticut Ave. NW
Washington, DC 20036-3902
202-833-1100

This is the newsletter of the AHLA's Regulation, Accreditation and Payment Substantive Law Committee.

RN

Medical Economics Co.
Five Paragon Dr.
Montvale, NJ 07645
800-432-4570
www.medec.com

This monthly magazine covers a range of legal, professional, and career issues.

Refusal of Treatment Legislation

Choice in Dying, Inc.
200 Varick St.
New York, NY 10014
212-366-5540

This loose-leaf binder is periodically updated to reflect new legislation.

Regan Report on Hospital Law

Medica Press, Inc.
Westminster Sq. Bldg., Suite 500
10 Dorrance St.
Providence, RI 02903-2018
401-421-4747

This monthly newsletter reports on the latest appellate court decisions on hospital law in a case-and-comment format.

Regan Report on Medical Law

Medica Press, Inc.
Westminster Square Bldg., Suite 500
10 Dorrance St.
Providence, RI 02903-2018
401-421-4747

This monthly newsletter provides appellate court decisions on medical law.

Regan Report on Nursing Law

Medica Press, Inc.
Westminster Square Bldg., Suite 500
10 Dorrance St.
Providence, RI 02903-2018
401-421-4747

This monthly newsletter reports on the latest appellate court decisions on nursing law in a case-and-comment format.

Regulatory Update

American Association of Blood Banks
8101 Glenbrook Rd.
Bethesda, MD 20814-2749
888-223-7329
www.aabb.org

This monthly newsletter focuses on regulatory issues that affect blood bank operations. Also included are legislative issues that will ultimately have regulatory impact. Issues contain a question-and-answer column, relevant *Federal Register* notices, updates on federal requirements, and articles from guest writers on regulatory issues. Regular topics include FDA, CBER (Center for Biologics Evaluation and Research), and CDRH (Center for Devices and Radiological Health) activities; CLIA updates; and safety issues.

Report on Medicare Compliance

Nina Youngstrom, Editor
Atlantic Information Services, Inc.
1100 17th St. NW, Suite 300

Washington, DC 20036
800-521-4323
www.aispub.com

This weekly newsletter is published jointly by the Health Care Compliance Association and Atlantic Information Services. It monitors Medicare fraud, false claims, billing issues, and self-referral.

Research and Policy Briefs

Maine Rural Health Research Center
Edmund S. Muskie Institute of Public Affairs
96 Falmouth St.
Portland, ME 04103
207-780-4430
www.muskie.usm.maine.edu/research/healthpol

This newsletter is published on an occasional basis by the center.

Risk Management Magazine

Risk and Insurance Management Society, Inc.
655 Third Ave.
New York, NY 10017-5367
800-713-7467
www.rims.org

This monthly magazine provides risk managers and other professionals with articles on legal, regulatory, and liability issues.

Risk Management News

Risk and Insurance Management Society, Inc.
655 Third Ave.
New York, NY 10017-5367
800-713-7467
www.rims.org

This biweekly newsletter provides analysis of management trends, case studies, and legal and legislative trends.

St. Anthony's Medicare Billing Compliance Monitor

11410 Isaac Newton Square
Reston, VA 20190
800-632-0123
www.st.anthony.com

This company publishes a range of coding, compliance, and reimbursement newsletters, of which this is one.

St. Louis University Law Journal

3700 Lindell Blvd.
St. Louis, MO 63108
314-977-2766
www.lawlib.slu.edu/

This law review publishes an annual health law symposium issue.

Science

American Association for the Advancement of Science
1200 New York Ave.
Washington, DC 20005
www.sciencemag.org

This weekly magazine is the official organ of the AAAS. It examines policy as well as technical issues.

Self-Insurer

Self-Insurance Institute of America, Inc. (SIIA)
P.O. Box 15466
Santa Ana, CA 92735-5466
800-851-7789
www.siia.org

This monthly magazine provides information on legislation and regulatory issues of interest to companies that self-insure to meet their health care liabilities.

Senior Care Acquisition Report

Irving Levin Associates, Inc.
72 Park St.
New Canaan, CT 06840
800-248-1668
www.levinassoc.com

This annual research report provides fact sheets on more than 120 publicly announced transactions that occur over the preceding year, with prices, deal terms, and key contacts. The text, with approximately 150 pages, supplies comprehensive five-year analyses on per bed prices, capitalization rates, geographic breakdowns, and IPOs on a range of senior care options, including retirement, assisted, nursing, and subacute care.

Senior Care Investor

Irving Levin Associates, Inc.
72 Park St.
New Canaan, CT 06840
800-248-1668
www.levinassoc.com

Published since 1967, this eight-page monthly newsletter monitors recent initial public offerings, acquisitions, and divestitures. It also supplies stock forecasts on publicly traded companies and REITs.

Southern Medical Journal

Southern Medical Association
35 Lakeshore Dr.
P.O. Box 190088
Birmingham, AL 35219-0088
205-945-1840, 800-423-4992
www.sma.org

This monthly publication provides occasional articles on health care policy and law along with its articles on clinical issues.

Spectrum

Council of State Governments
3760 Research Park Dr.
P.O. Box 11910
Lexington, KY 40578-1910
606-244-8000
www.csg.org

This journal is published quarterly by the Council of State Governments and often addresses health policy issues.

State Health Monitor

Atlantic Information Services, Inc.
1100 17th St. NW, Suite 300
Washington, DC 20036
202-775-9008

This newsletter is published twenty-four times annually. It examines health law and policy activity at the state level.

State Health Notes

National Conference of State Legislatures
1560 Broadway, Suite 700
Denver, CO 80202
303-830-2200
www.ncsl.org

This biweekly newsletter is devoted to health issues, legislation, and current trends from the states' perspective. It focuses on such topics as cost containment, state policy issues, and options for expanding children's health insurance.

State Health Watch

American Health Consultants
3525 Piedmont Road
Suite 400
Atlanta, GA 30304
800688-2421

This monthly newsletter focuses on state health care reform.

Strategies for Healthcare Excellence

COR Research
P.O. Box 40959
Santa Barbara, CA 93410-0959
805-564-2177
www.mednet-i.com

This monthly newsletter features case studies highlighting efforts by health care organization to streamline and improve health care delivery.

Telehealth Magazine

600 Harrison St.
San Francisco, CA 94107
415-905-2134
www.telehealthmag.com

This bimonthly magazine focuses on telemedicine and other electronic information topics.

Telemedicine

Miller-Freeman, Inc.
600 Harrison St.
San Francisco, CA 94107
415-905-2550

This monthly newsletter monitors the growing telemedicine sector for implementers, end users, strategic planners, and vendors.

Telemedicine Today

5101 College Boulevard
Suite 206
Overland Park, KS 66211
913-338-3631

This bimonthly magazine includes breaking news along with discussions of legal aspects of telemedicine.

TennCare News

Harkey and Associates, Inc.
P.O. Box 159025
Nashville, TN 37215
615-385-4131
www.harkeyreport.com

This monthly newsletter monitors Tennessee's Medicaid managed care program.

Tennessee Health Law Update

M. Lee Smith Publishers LLC
P.O. Box 5094
Brentwood, TN 37024-5094
800-274-6774
www.mleesmith.com

This newsletter provides a monthly survey of Tennessee and federal health law developments.

Tennessee Managed Care

Harkey and Associates, Inc.
P.O. Box 159025
Nashville, TN 37215
615-385-4131
www.harkeyreport.com

This quarterly newsletter monitors the state's managed care trends, Medicaid, legislation, hospital networks, and physician managed care organizations.

Texas Health Law Reporter

Butterworth Legal Publishers
8 Industrial Way, No. C
Salem, NH 03079-2837

This bimonthly loose-leaf newsletter covers Texas litigation, regulation, and legislation regarding health issues.

Texas Hospital Law

Butterworth Legal Publishers
8 Industrial Way, No. C
Salem, NH 03079-2837

This service provides case analysis and examination of legal and administrative issues affecting the medical community in Texas.

Texas Managed Care

Harkey and Associates, Inc.
P.O. Box 159025
Nashville, TN 37215
615-385-4131
www.harkeyreport.com

This state-level publication includes a directory updated quarterly, with information on HMO and PPO enrollment (for the state and metro areas), hospital networks, physician networks, financial and utilization data for HMOs, and managed care contracts. The twelve-to-sixteen-page newsletter that accompanies the directory is published three or four times yearly.

Texas Medicine

Texas Medical Association
401 West 15th St.
Austin, TX 78701-1680
800-880-1300
www.texmed.org

This monthly magazine regularly publishes articles on legislative affairs, tort reform, and a range of other medicolegal issues, as well as presenting the views of the state's physicians.

Today's Corporate Compliance

Health Care Compliance Association
1211 Locust St.
Philadelphia, PA 19107
888-580-8373
www.hcca-info.org

This newsletter includes articles and valuable Websites.

Topics in Health Care Financing

Aspen Publishers, Inc.
7201 McKinney Circle
Frederick, MD 21704

800-638-8437
www.aspenpub.com

This quarterly journal is targeted at health information professionals.

Tort & Insurance Law Journal

American Bar Association
Section of Tort and Insurance Practice
750 North Lake Shore Dr.
Chicago, IL 60611
312-988-5000
www.abanet.org

This journal is published quarterly as a service to lawyers and laypersons involved in practicing tort law and insurance. It was formerly known as *Forum*.

Trustee

Health Forum, Inc.
One North Franklin
Chicago, IL 60606
312-893-6800
www.healthforum.com

This monthly magazine is targeted at members of the governing boards of health care organizations.

Vanderbilt Law Review

Vanderbilt Law School
Vanderbilt University
Nashville, TN 37240
615-322-4766
www.vanderbilt.edu

Published six times annually, this student-edited law review is a significant forum for discussing health care law and policy issues.

Virginia Healthcare News

567 Seminole Dr.
Marietta, GA 30060
770-499-1220

This monthly newspaper covers legislation, managed care, and related topics.

Virginia Managed Care

Harkey and Associates, Inc.
P.O. Box 159025
Nashville, TN 37215
615-385-4131
www.harkeyreport.com

This quarterly newsletter monitors Virginia's managed care trends, Medicaid, legislation, hospital networks, and physician managed care organizations.

Washington Health Week

Atlantic Information Services, Inc.
1100 17th St. NW, Suite 300
Washington, DC 20036
800-521-4323
www.aispub.com

Published forty-five times annually, this business newsletter examines topics such as insurance reform, Medicare and Medicaid payment innovations, antitrust rules, and federal insurance mandates.

Washington Highlights

American Association of Medical Colleges
Office of Governmental Relations
2450 N St. NW
Washington, DC 20037-1126
202-828-0525
www.aamc.org

This weekly newsletter provides a summary of the major legislative and regulatory issues of importance to medical schools and teaching hospitals. It focuses particularly on legislation and regulations on budget and appropriations and on physicians, biomedical and behavioral research, health professions education, and student aid. It also tracks the activities of the Prospective Payment Assessment Commission and the Council on Graduate Medical Education.

Washington Update

Catholic Health Association of the United States
4455 Woodson Rd.
St. Louis, MO 63134-3797
314-427-2500
www.chausa.org

This is a semimonthly briefing on health care policy and legislation.

Waste Age

4301 Connecticut Ave. NW
Washington, DC 20008
202-364-3777
www.wasteage.com

This magazine is published monthly by the Environmental Industry Associations. It monitors business and legal issues pertinent to the industry, including medical waste topics.

Western Journal of Medicine

Carden Jennings Publishing Co., Ltd.
1224 West Main St., Suite 200
Charlottesville, VA 22903-2858
804-979-8034

This monthly publication is an official journal of the Alaska State Medical Association, the Arizona Medical Association, the California Medical Association, the Denver Medical Society, the Idaho Medical Association, the Nevada State Medical Association, the New Mexico Medical Association, the Utah Medical Association, the Washington State Medical Association, and the Wyoming Medical Society.

West Virginia Managed Care

Harkey and Associates, Inc.
P.O. Box 159025
Nashville, TN 37215
615-385-4131
www.harkeyreport.com

This quarterly newsletter monitors HMOs and PPOs, Medicaid, legislation, hospital networks, and physician managed care organizations.

Whittier Law Review

3333 Harbor Blvd.
Costa Mesa, CA 92626
714-444-4141
www.whittier.edu

This journal publishes an annual symposium issue on health law.

Appendix B

Reference Sources and Government Serials

California State Health Plans

Office of Statewide Health Planning and Development
1600 Ninth St., Room 440
Sacramento, CA 95814
916-654-2080
www.oshpd.cahwnet.gov/default.htm

This government publication contains an overview of the health care industry in California, assessment of the current financial condition of hospitals, and identification of health care planning issues facing the state over the long-term planning horizon.

Code of Federal Regulations

Government Printing Office
Washington, DC 20402

Excerpts Medical: Health Economics and Hospital Management

E.M.
Box 211
1000 AE Amsterdam, Netherlands

Federal Register

Office of the Federal Register
National Archives and Record Service
Washington, DC 20402

GAO Reports

General Accounting Office
441 G St. NW
Washington, DC 20548
202-512-6000
www.gao.gov

These government investigative reports are now available on the Internet.

Harvard Business School (Case Studies)

Publishing Division
Operations Department

Boston, MA 02163
617-495-6700
www.hbs.harvard.edu/

Health Care Financing Review

Linda F. Wolf, Editor-in-Chief
Health Care Financing Administration
Department of Health and Human Services
Office of Strategic Planning
7500 Security Blvd.
Mailstop C-3-11-07
Baltimore, MD 21244-1850
410-786-6572
www.lwolf@hcfa.gov

Published monthly on CD-ROM only, this service provides the policies and procedures developed by HCFA for providers of health care services, including information regarding processing Medicare and Medicaid claims.

Health Law and Policy Abstracts

www.SSRN.com
Timothy S. Jost, Editor
Ohio State University Law School

This online journal is published by the Legal Scholarship Network, a division of Social Science Electronic Publishing (SSEP) and Social Science Research Network (SSRN). The journal lists recent and forthcoming articles on health law and policy; it appears every two weeks. During the startup phase, subscriptions are free and may be obtained by e-mailing either Sherry_Beauchamp@ssrn.com or Jost at jost.1@osu.edu.

Hospital Abstracts

HMSO
P.O. Box 569
London SE1 9NH, England

Hospital and Health Administration Index

American Hospital Association Resource Center
One North Franklin

Chicago, IL 60606-9537
312-422-3000
www.aha.org

Published continuously by the AHA since 1945, this reference work is a primary guide to literature on organizing hospitals and other health care providers, financing and delivering health care, developing and implementing health policy and reform, and health planning and research. It is published three times annually, with the third issue being a hardbound cumulative volume. Since 1978, the AHA and the National Library of Medicine (NLM) have collaborated on producing this resource from NLM's Health Planning and Administration database and its successor, HealthSTAR.

NTIS Newsline

National Technical Information Service
5285 Port Royal Rd.
Springfield, VA 22161
703-487-4650
www.ntis.gov

The National Technical Information Service serves as the nation's largest central resource and primary disseminator of information produced by the U.S. government, non-U.S. government departments, universities, and corporate research organizations in the United States and around the world. This service is produced by the federal Commerce Department.

NTIS Weekly Abstract: Health Planning and Health Services Research

National Technical Information Service
5285 Port Royal Rd.
Springfield, VA 22161
703-487-4650
www.ntis.gov

This summary of articles is now available on the Internet.

Public Health Reports

Government Printing Office
Superintendent of Documents
Washington, DC 20402

Research Activities

Agency for Health Care Policy and Research (AHCPR)
Public Health Service

U.S. Department of Health and Human Services
2101 East Jefferson St., Suite 501
Rockville, MD 20852
800-358-9295
www.ahcpr.gov/

This newsletter is a monthly digest of research findings that have been produced with support from the AHCPR. The information in this digest is intended to contribute to the policy-making process, not to make policy. Topics addressed include health insurance, access to care, children's health, managed care, market forces, outcomes research, quality of care, and women's health.

Social Security Bulletin

Social Security Administration
5401 Security Blvd.
Baltimore, MD 21235

This service supplies information on the administration's positions and rulings.

Specialty Law Digest: Health Care Law

Specialty Digest Publications, Inc.
P.O. Box 24439
Minneapolis, MN 55424
612-823-4220
www.specialtylaw.com

This monthly publication is targeted at attorneys, hospital trustees, law libraries, medical libraries, physicians, hospital administrators, and medical educators. It is designed to provide general-interest updating on significant issues and trends in the law and to facilitate in-depth research on particular legal issues. Each issue supplies a case survey arranged state by state, along with an outline of health care law designed to organize the field for easy location of legal rulings by subject matter.

Vital and Health Statistics

National Center for Health Statistics
Public Health Service
Government Printing Office
Washington, DC 20402
301-436-8500
www.cdc.gov/nchswww/nchshome.htm

The center serves as the government's primary health statistics agency. It is part of the Centers for Disease Control.

Appendix C

Computer Databases and Internet Sites

INTERNET SITES

Agency for Health Care Policy and Research
www.ahcpr.gov
AHCPR, part of the U.S. Department of Health and Human Services, is the lead agency charged with supporting research designed to improve the quality of health care, reduce its cost, and broaden access to essential services. AHCPR's broad programs of research are aimed at bringing practical, science-based information to medical practitioners, consumers, and other health care purchasers. The agency comprises eleven major functional components, which are described in detail in this Website.

AIDS Action
www.aidsaction.org
Promotes and monitors legislation on AIDS research and education and on related public policy issues.

AIDS Virtual Library
www.planetq.com/aidsvl/index.htlm
This site addresses social, political, and medical aspects of AIDS, HIV, and related issues.

Alpha Center
www.ac.org
Established in 1976, this nonprofit and nonpartisan health policy center, based in Washington, D.C., helps public and private sector clients obtain necessary information on health care issues. The Website includes a glossary of terms commonly used in health care.

American Academy of Physician Assistants
www.aapa.org
This superb site includes subfiles addressing a vast range of issues, including the State Children's Health Insurance Program (SCHIP), model state legislation for physician assistants, and a summary of state laws concerning physician assistants.

American Accreditation HealthCare Commission/URAC
www.urac.org
Founded in 1990, this organization establishes standards for the managed care industry. This site includes information about the group, accreditation information, a list of accredited organizations, and a list of publications. Also includes a valuable set of links to other managed care sites.

American Association of Critical Care Nurses
www.aacn.org
This Website includes a wealth of information about policy and politics in nursing and health care, along with an online resource catalog.

American Bar Association Health Law Section
www.abanet.org/health/home.html
Contains free access to BNA's Health Care Daily electronic resource, among other features.

American Board of Medical Specialties
www.abms.org
This is an umbrella organization for the twenty-four approved medical specialty boards in the United States. Established in 1933, the ABMS coordinates the activities of its member boards and provides information to the public, the government, the profession, and its members concerning issues involving specialization and certification in medicine. The Website provides information about the organization's numerous publications.

American College of Surgeons
www.facs.org
This site features a list of the organization's recently published articles on health policy. It also includes transcripts of testimony by officials of the organization before Congress, along with e-mail addresses of individuals within the organization who are able to provide the group's position on specific issues.

American Compliance Institute

www.compliance.com

ACI is a national membership organization of individuals and organizations involved in health care compliance. Established in 1995, it seeks to promote principles of compliance with all applicable laws, regulations, standards and ethics in health care. Members include hospitals and hospital systems, managed care, nursing homes, home health agencies, and other health care businesses. Also represented are law firms, accounting firms, insurance companies, academia, consulting firms, and law enforcement.

American Federation of State, County, and Municipal Employees Union

www.afscme.org

Affiliated with the AFL-CIO, this union represents physicians who work for hospitals owned by state or local units of government.

American Foundation for AIDS Research

www.amFAR.org

This site provides information about the organization's public policy publications.

American Health Care Association

www.ahca.org

Washington, D.C.-based federation of associations representing assisted-living nursing facilities and subacute care providers. Library is open to public by appointment.

American Health Information Management Association

www.ahima.org

This site includes an online version of the *Journal of AHIMA* and *In Confidence*, a newsletter on health care privacy.

American Health Quality Association

www.ahqa.org

Seeks to improve physicians' ability to assess the quality of medical care services; assists in developing methods to monitor the appropriateness of medical care.

American Medical Association

www.ama-assn.org

This extensive Website includes a number of subfiles on policy and advocacy issues, including access to insurance coverage, Medicare+Choice, utilization management, HIV/AIDS, and end-of-life care, among others. It also includes an online version of *JAMA,* the *Archives of Internal Medicine,* and nine other specialist journals. Additionally, it includes the full text of the AMA's congressional testimony on everything from Medicare reform to gag clauses, and summaries and analyses of state and federal health insurance reforms. Finally, it includes information about the AMA's 1999 decision to form a physicians' bargaining unit to advocate on behalf of the profession.

American Nurses Association

www.nursingworld.org

This site includes significant amounts of health care policy information and useful hypertext links to other relevant sites.

American Public Health Association

www.apha.org

This organization is concerned with a broad set of issues affecting personal and environmental health, including federal and state funding for health programs, pollution control, programs and policies related to chronic and infectious diseases, a smoke-free society, and professional education in public health.

American Public Human Services Association

www.aphsa.org

Founded in 1930, APHSA is a nonprofit, bipartisan organization of individuals and agencies concerned with human services. Based in Washington, D.C., its members include all state and many territorial human services organizations. APHSA educates members of Congress, the media, and the broad public on what is happening in states concerning health care and other issues involving families and the elderly. This site provides links to state and territorial health agencies.

American Social Health Association

www.ashastd.org

Based in Research Triangle Park, N.C., this organization advocates for eradication of sexually transmitted diseases.

American Telemedicine Association

www.atmeda.org

Focusing on promoting "professional, ethical, and equitable improvement in health care delivery through the application of telecommunications technology," this Washington, D.C.–based group offers a site that presents an organizational overview as well as background on issues such as state telemedicine policy initiatives. Website includes recent seminar abstracts. It also includes an excellent set of links on the subject, including telemedicine-specific search engines.

Americans for Free Choice in Medicine

www.afcm.org

This organization promotes a philosophy of individual rights, personal responsibility, and free market economics in health care. It advocates medical savings accounts, among other goals.

Antitrust Policy

www.antitrust.org/index.htm

This site is an online resource linking economic research, policy, and cases. It contains subfiles on mergers, price fixing, and vertical restraints, along with a merger simulation and a discussion area. Make sure not to miss the antitrust humor subfile.

Association for Healthcare Philanthropy

www.go-ahp.org

This site includes information about many of the organization's publications on fundraising for health care organizations.

Association for Healthcare Philanthropy

www.go-ahp.org

With headquarters in Falls Church, Virginia, this is a not-for-profit organization of more than twenty-eight hundred hospital and health care fundraisers.

Association of Academic Health Centers

www.ahcnet.org

Group consisting of academic health centers. Participates in studies and public debates on health professional training and education, patient care, and biomedical research.

Association of American Medical Colleges

www.aamc.org

The AAMC is a nonprofit association comprising the 125 accredited U.S. medical schools, the 16 accredited Canadian medical schools, more than 400 major teaching hospitals and health systems, nearly 90 academic and professional societies representing 75,000 faculty members, and the nation's medical students and residents.

Association of State Medical Board Executive Directors

www.docboard.org

This is a health professional licensing database that provides hypertext links to participating state licensing authorities.

Association of University Programs in Health Administration

www.aupha.com

This organization promotes graduate and undergraduate curriculum reforms and faculty development responding to the changing needs of the health services delivery system.

Bazelon Center for Mental Health Law

www.bazelon.org

Contains legislative alerts, advocacy materials, publications, and links to other mental health law sites.

Behavioural Management, Alaska, Inc.

www.behmgmt.com

This organization provides counseling and therapy services throughout Alaska. The superb Website includes a valuable description of its confidentiality policies. It also includes more than one thousand links to other health sites.

BenefitsLink

www.benefitslink.com

Developed by a health care attorney, this site targets managers of employee benefits and human resources and offers a variety of news services. A guide to online benefits resources is linked to some twenty newsletters and magazines. There's also a frequently updated compendium of legal decisions related to employee benefits, especially ERISA.

Beth Israel Deaconess Hospital

www.bih.harvard.edu

This is the site for the Boston hospital, which is one of the Harvard teaching facilities.

Blue Cross and Blue Shield Association

www.bcbs.com

This site includes a helpful glossary of health insurance terms.

Brookings Institution

www.brookings.org

Studies federal health care issues and health programs, including Medicare, Medicaid, and long term care.

Bureau of Primary Health Care

www.bphc.hrsa.dhhs.gov

BPHC is one of four bureaus of the Health Resources and Services Administration, an agency of DHHS.

California Consumer Health Care Counsel

www.cchcc.org

This is a grassroots, volunteer-run organization offering assistance with consumer problems with HMOs, insurers, or other health plans.

California Department of Health Services

www.dhs.cahwnet.gov

This site includes subfiles on audits and investigations, health information, strategic planning, and legislative and governmental affairs.

California HealthCare Foundation

www.chcf.org

This organization was established in May 1996 as a result of the conversion of Blue Cross of California from a nonprofit plan to WellPoint Health Networks, a for-profit organization. The foundation is one of two philanthropies created by the conversion; the other is the California Endowment, the principal charitable entity. The California Healthcare Foundation was vested with the majority of outstanding WellPoint stock and is charged with responsibility for (1) gradually divesting the foundation of WellPoint stock and transferring 80 percent of the proceeds to the California Endowment for its philanthropic efforts, and (2) developing the foundation's own independent grantmaking program with the remaining 20 percent of the funds from stock sales. This Website supplies a cornucopia of pertinent information, along with a list of publications available from the foundation.

California Medical Association

www.cmanet.org

This is a superb website, providing valuable information for researchers and consumers on topics such as access to health care, HIV/AIDS, and tobacco. It also provides extensive hyperlinks to other relevant sites, including ones containing the full text of California legislation, regulations, and laws.

California Nurses Association

www.califnurses.org

Contains a large amount of breaking news, particularly on legislative and labor issues. The site has subfiles on each of the larger California hospital groups. It also boasts an enormous number of hyperlinks to related sites.

California Telehealth and Telemedicine

telemed.calhealth.org

This site provides information on relevant California statutes and regulations, newsletters, resource guides, and links.

Catalaw

www.catalaw.com

This is a metaindex of law and government sites. This catalogue of catalogues is designed to ease the difficulty of finding law on the Internet. It speeds research by arranging more than one hundred indexes on the Internet into a single, intuitive index. Each page within Catalaw lists hyperlinks to all subpages within all other indexes pertinent to a single legal subject. Also included are links to additional sites that, although not comprehensive, provide focused links to subject-specific information. Highly recommended.

Catholic Healthcare West

www.catholichealthwest.org

Contains information about this organization of forty-eight hospitals in California, Nevada, and Arizona.

Cecil G. Sheps Center for Health Services Research

www.schsr.unc.edu

Located at the University of North Carolina at Chapel Hill, the center encompasses an interdisciplinary program of research, consultation, technical assistance, and training focused on accessibility, adequacy, organization, cost, and effectiveness of health care services.

Center for Budget and Policy Priorities

www.cbpp.org

This is a policy institute conducting research on government programs and policies that affect low- and moderate-income people.

Center for Democracy and Technology

www.cdt.org/privacy

This is the center's privacy issues page.

Center for Health Program Development and Management

www.research.umbc.edu/chpdm

Located at the University of Maryland, this site provides expertise in health care policy analysis and research, and health program design, implementation, and evaluation.

Center for Patient Advocacy

www.patientadvocacy.org

This McLean, Virginia, advocacy organization, founded in 1995, focuses on securing patient access to health care. In particular, the group focuses on access to treatment for cancer patients.

Center for Rural Health and Social Service Development

www.siu.edu/%7Ecrhssd/rhres.htm

This site, provided by Southern Illinois University at Carbondale, offers a superb list of links to other pertinent sites on rural health.

Children's Defense Fund

www.childrensdefense.org

This site includes a series of reports on innovative approaches to outreach and enrollment in the State Children's Health Insurance Program (SCHIP) and Medicaid.

State Children's Health Insurance Program (SCHIP)

www.insurekidsnow.gov

www.ed.gov/chip

These sites address the State Children's Health Insurance Program, enacted by Congress in 1997. This program provides the states with $39 billion over a period of ten years, along with considerable flexibility in how the money may be used. Although some states—notably, South Carolina, Nebraska, and Ohio—have aggressively implemented the program, others have been chided by the Clinton Administration for their slow progress in enrolling eligible children. States have a financial incentive to enroll children in the SCHIP program, rather than in Medicaid, because the federal government pays a larger share of the costs. wwwinsurekidsnow.gov contains a subfile on each of the fifty states. Anyone seeking additional information can do so by calling 877-543–7669 toll-free.

Civil False Claims Act Decisions

www.ffhsj.com./quitam/cfcdecs

Developed by the law firm of Fried Frank, Harris, Shriver & Jacobson, this extensive site includes subfiles providing the text of the statute, legislative history, amendments to the statute, recent decisions under the act, recent case filings under the act, recent settlements under the act, and the Justice Department's latest statistics on *qui tam* cases filed and FCA recoveries.

Cleveland Clinic
www.ccf.org

Coalition Against Insurance Fraud
www.insurancefraud.org
This is an independent, nonprofit organization of consumers, government agencies, and insurers focused on combating all forms of insurance fraud through public information and advocacy.

Coalition for Patient Rights
www.nationalcpr.org
This Lexington, Massachusetts, organization advocates protection of patient privacy, including the privacy of medical records.

Code of Federal Regulations
www.access.gpo.gov/nara/cfr/index.html
Contains the CFR, *Federal Register,* Privacy Act Issuances, U.S. Government Manual, and a weekly compilation of presidential documents.

Committee on Interns and Residents
www.cirdocs.org
The largest union of residents is CIR. Based in New York City, it represents almost ten thousand residents in about fifty hospitals. It has led strikes and engaged in collective bargaining and grew by nearly 40 percent in 1996–97. In 1975, CIR led a strike of New York City interns and residents that resulted in eliminating every other night call. In 1996, CIR voted to affiliate with the Service Employees International Union of the AFL-CIO.

Commonwealth Fund
www.cmwf.org
Founded in 1918, this organization focuses on improving health care services, bettering the health of minority Americans, advancing the well-being of elderly Americans, and developing the capacities of children and young people. This site provides information on fellowships and grant guidelines, among other information.

Community Health and Counseling of Maine
www.chcs-me.org
This site includes the confidentiality policies of this organization.

Computer-Based Patient Record Institute
www.cpri.org
This site includes information on confidentiality of patient records.

Consumers Union
www.consunion.org
This nonprofit membership organization was chartered in 1936 to provide consumers with information and education about goods and services, including health care. The organization has established three regional advocacy offices to represent consumer interests in such areas as Medicaid reform, implementation of SCHIP, the Healthy Families Program, legislation protecting consumers enrolled in managed health care plans, and conversion of nonprofit health care institutions into for-profit companies.

Council for Affordable Health Insurance
www.cahi.org
Consists of insurance carriers in the small-group, individual, and senior markets; business groups; doctors; actuaries; and insurance brokers. Research and advocacy organization promoting free-market solutions to health care problems.

Dartmouth Atlas of Healthcare
www.dartmouth.edu/dms/atlas
Contains a list of publications, tables of contents, and a limited number of graphics.

Department of Labor Pension and Welfare Benefits Administration
www.dol.gov/dol/pwba/
Contains pertinent laws and regulations. Also contains amicus briefs on ERISA preemption of medical malpractice claims against HMOs.

Directory of State Offices of Rural Health
www.nal.usda.gov/orhp/50sorh.htm#stateoffices
This site contains a directory of state offices of rural health and state rural health associations.

Doctors Council
www.doctorscouncil.com
Founded in 1961, Doctors Council is a union of approximately three thousand attending physicians, dentists, optometrists, podiatrists, and veterinarians employed by New York City agencies, hospitals, private health care facilities, and the New York Transit Authority.

Duke Health Policy Cyberexchange
www.hpolicy.duke.edu
Provides information on policy research organizations, universities, foundations, and relevant government agencies.

Duke University Medical Center Information and Record Services
hirs.mc.duke.edu
This site includes the center's confidentiality policy and confidentiality agreement for employees.

Electronic Policy Network
www.epn.org
This virtual magazine includes a subfile on health policy.

Emergency Medical Treatment and Active Labor Act Site

www.emtala.com/emtala

This site provides updates on cases interpreting EMTALA.

Employee Benefit Research Institute

www.ebri.org

Like EBRI itself—billed as the "only nonprofit, non-partisan organization committed to original public policy research" in its field—the site is a valuable resource. One of its most useful offerings is a solid list of other Websites dealing with employee benefits, neatly divided into categories such as pension, labor, and government. Another is a list of EBRI's briefs—analytical, fact-laden reports examining major health benefit and pension issues of the day. EBRI publishes twelve to twenty briefs a year, on topics ranging from ERISA to mental health parity. Most are accompanied by press releases that can be downloaded; the issue briefs themselves can be ordered online. A digest of the organization's twice-monthly *Washington Bulletin,* a mininewsletter on the latest churnings in the nation's capital, is another key feature.

Eskind Biomedical Library

www.mc.vanderbilt.edu/biolib

Located at Vanderbilt University Medical School, the Annette and Irwin Eskind Biomedical Library site provides access to a range of online journals along with books and other references to health legislation, regulation, and standards.

Families USA

www.familiesusa.org

Families USA is a national nonprofit, nonpartisan organization dedicated to achieving high-quality, affordable health and long-term care for all Americans. It is a voice for health care consumers. This Website provides a list of publications dealing with health care consumer protection issues.

Family Voices

www.familyvoices.org

This site provides policy information and publications concerning children with special health needs.

FDA MedWatch News

www.fda.gov

Provides new alerts related to the FDA's medical products reporting program.

Federal Register

www.access.gpo.gov/su_docs/aces/aces140.html

The *Federal Register* is the official publication for rules, proposed rules, and notices of federal agencies and organizations, as well as executive orders and other presidential documents.

Federal Telemedicine Gateway

www.tmgateway.org/

This site provides information on federally funded telemedicine projects.

Federal Trade Commission

www.ftc.gov/

This excellent site provides an overview of the FTC's investigative and law enforcement authority. It also contains amicus briefs, statutes enforced or administered by the commission, rules of practice, a litigation status report, and FTC regulations and guides.

Federation of State Medical Boards of the United States

www.fsmb.org

The federation is composed of sixty-nine member boards whose primary responsibilities and obligations are to protect the public through regulation of physicians and other health care providers. This Website describes the federation's publications and services.

Findlaw

www.findlaw.com

This expansive site embraces subfiles on a range of legal subjects, including one on health law.

Florida AIDS Health Fraud Task Force

www.applicom.com/tcrs/AIDSline.htm

This site provides information and guidance on how to stop the selling or advertising of fraudulent health products and services.

Francis A. Countway Library of Medicine

www.countway.harvard.edu

This library serves the Harvard School of Medicine, Harvard School of Public Health, Harvard School of Dental Medicine, Boston Medical Library, and Massachusetts Medical Society.

Galen II

www.library.ucsf.edu/journals

Named after the ancient Greek anatomist, physiologist, and physician, this is the Webpage of the library of the University of California at San Francisco. It provides access to more than one hundred academic medical journals.

General Accounting Office

www.gao.gov

Electronic files are available for most GAO reports and testimonies from 1995 to the present. In addition, the agency posts special publications (for instance, GAO's annual report), annual indexes, comptroller general decisions and opinions, reports on federal agency rules, selected numbered correspondence, GAO policy and guideline publications, and a daily listing of released GAO reports and testimony. This Website is well organized and highly accessible.

GovBot
www.business.gov/Search_Online.html
This site contains more than 535,000 pages from government sites around the country. Like much of the Internet, this site requires the user to formulate queries in a Boolean format.

Harvard Medical School
www.med.harvard.edu

Health Administration Responsibility Project (HARP)
www.harp.org
This site is a resource for patients, doctors, and attorneys seeking to establish the tort liability of managed care organizations. It provides practical information on how to fight denial of coverage by managed care plans. It contains links to pertinent sections of the federal, New York, and California Codes; relevant cases; and other helpful sites. It also provides a summary of New York's new External Review and Coverage Denials Act, which took effect July 1, 1999. HARP plans to organize a legal aid society for patients injured by HMOs.

Health Care Financing Administration
www.hcfa.gov
This is the site for the federal agency that administers Medicare, Medicaid, and State Children's Health Insurance Program.

Health Care Without Harm
www.noharm.org
This Washington, D.C.–based environmental health organization is made up of health care professionals, hospitals, environmental advocates, organizations of individuals with illnesses such as breast cancer and endometriosis, and religious organizations. Its goal is to transform the health care industry so it no longer is a source of environmental harm by eliminating pollution in health care practices without compromising safety or care. Health care practices, especially medical waste incineration, are a leading source of dioxin and mercury emissions. Dioxin has been linked to endometriosis, learning disabilities, birth defects, infertility, nervous system disorders, and cancer. Mercury is a potent neurotoxin and reproductive toxin. This impressive site makes reports available in French, Spanish, and English.

Health Hippo
www.hippl.findlaw.com
Health Hippo is a collection of policy and regulatory materials related to health care. Its whimsical name notwithstanding, this is an impressive compendium of cases, legislation, regulations, and hypertext links on such issues as advanced directives, antitrust, the Balanced Budget Act, fraud and abuse, labs, long term care, Medicaid, Medicare,

mental health, public health, and rural health, along with such topics as "Hipponews" and "Hippotalk."

Health Law News
www.ljx.com/practice/health/health/index.html
This site focuses on events reported in such publications as the *New York Law Journal* and the *New Jersey Law Journal.*

Health Law Update
www.mwe.com/news/indexhlu.htm
This law firm newsletter provides summaries of OIG advisory bulletins, HCFA actions, relevant IRS activities, and other agency actions of interest to health care practitioners.

Health Privacy Project
www.healthprivacy.org
This organization seeks to raise public awareness of the importance of health privacy to improved health care, both on an individual and a community level. Founded in 1997, this project is part of Georgetown University Medical Center's Institute for Health Care Research and Policy.

Healthcare Financial Management Association
www.hfma.org
Originally formed as the American Association of Hospital Accountants, this organization seeks to influence health policy on behalf of its members.

Healthcare Integrity and Protection Data Bank
www.npdb.com/HIPDB/h
This is a national fraud and abuse data collection program for reporting and disclosing certain final adverse actions taken against health care providers, suppliers, or practitioners.

Healthcare Journal
www.amcity.com/journals/health_care/
Mostly concerned with business dealings, this site allows the researcher to check local health care business news for dozens of major cities.

Healthcare Leadership Counsel
www.hlc.org
The organization consists of health care leaders who examine major health care issues, including access and affordability. Works to implement new public policies.

HealthGrades
www.healthgrades.com
This Internet-based consumer information service has devised its own formula for rating all U.S. hospitals' performance by product line. The service, which debuted in August 1999, also claims to have a method for determining who among the nation's 640,000 physicians should be judged better than the rest. Data for all areas (except obstetrics) are taken from clinical outcome reports that hospitals regularly submit to Medicare.

Henry J. Kaiser Family Foundation
www.kff.org
Based in Menlo Park, California, this is an independent health care philanthropy focusing on four main areas: health policy, reproductive health, HIV policy, and health and development in South Africa. This site offers information about the foundation's publications and provides links to other pertinent sites.

HIV/AIDS Bureau, Health Resources and Services Administration, DHHS
www.hrsa.dhhs.gov/hab
This federal government site includes publications, bureau staff papers, journal articles, and information on obtaining government contracts.

HIV/AIDS Information Center
www.ama-assn.org/special/hiv/hivhome.htm
This highly focused site, prepared and maintained by the AMA, includes information on health policy issues.

HIV Law Today
www.hivlawtoday.com
This site bills itself as a survival guide to the legal system for persons living with AIDS.

HIVPositive.com
www.hivpositive.com/index
This site includes valuable links to other AIDS policy sites.

How to Fight Your HMO
www.bright.net/~ewp/fight_your_hmo.html
This site was designed by an Ohio woman whose surgery for endometriosis was not covered by her managed care plan. It provides practical (and feisty) advice along with information about HMO reform.

Idea Central: Health Policy
epn.org/idea/health.html
Bimonthly virtual journal on health care policy issues.

Impact of Managed Care on Clinical Research (National Center for Research Resources)
www.ncrr.nih.gov/newspub/mancare.htm
This report was originally prepared in January 1996; is subdivided into chapters; and is heavily illustrated with charts, tables, and graphs. The document concludes with a glossary of managed care terms.

Indian Health Service
www.tucson.ihs.gov
This is an agency within DHHS, responsible for providing federal health services to American Indians and Alaska Natives.

Inside Health Care
www.insidehealthcare.com
This supersite supplies links to more than one hundred other sites relating to health care policy, news, search engines, publications, reference works, directories, government information, and vendors. If you can't find it here, you won't find it anywhere. Its only weakness is that it does not provide the Web address of particular subfiles one is seeking, making navigation more difficult.

Institute for Medical Quality
www.imq.org
This nonprofit organization seeks to improve the quality of care provided to patients across the continuum of care.

Internal Revenue Service
www.irs.gov
Curiously, this site opens with an invitation for the reader to pour herself a cup of coffee and enjoy the service's warm and fuzzy online publication, *The Digital Daily.* Once past the thicket of bonhomie, however, there are subfiles on rules, regulations, forms, publications, IRS bulletins, a tax deadline table, and a keyword search engine to locate more specific information.

Joint Commission on Accreditation of Healthcare Organizations
www.jcaho.org
The Joint Commission accredits more than nineteen thousand health care organizations in the United States and in other nations. This Website allows the user to report (in English or Spanish) a complaint about a health care organization by phone, fax, e-mail, or letter.

Journal of the American Medical Association
www.jama.com
Tables of contents, abstracts, and full text of selected articles online.

Kaiser Permanente
www.kaiserpermanente.org
Founded in 1945, Kaiser Permanente is the largest non-profit HMO in the United States, with 8.6 million members in eighteen states and the District of Columbia.

Lambda Letters
www.lambdaletters.org
This is a California-based, nonprofit organization focused on HIV/AIDS advocacy. This site provides information and links concerning California and federal legislation.

Law Links Legal Resource Center
www.lawlinks.com
Provides links to sites on regulations, codes, legislation, judicial and administrative decisions, governmental agencies, and law school libraries.

Lawcrawler
www.lawcrawler.findlaw.com
Provides a legal subject index, cases and codes, law schools, law journals, and legal associations.

Legal Action Center

www.lac.org

This law and policy organization combats discrimination against persons with AIDS, among others.

Legislative Survey of State Confidentiality Laws, with Emphasis on HIV and Immunization

www.critpath.org/msphpa/ctse.txt

This is a report prepared by Lawrence O. Gostin, Zita Lazzarini, and Kathleen M. Flaherty and presented to the U.S. Centers for Disease Control and Prevention. It examines current state and federal law protecting confidentiality of health care information. This lengthy report is followed by an appendix summarizing each state's laws.

Library of Congress Internet Resource Page

www.cweb.loc.gov/global/legislative/congress

This site contains addresses, calendars, legislation, and the U.S. Code. The Library of Congress is the largest library in the world, with more than 115 million items catalogued.

List of Excluded Individuals/Entities (LEIE)

www.hhs.gov/progorg/oig/cumsan/index.htm

The OIG's list provides information to health care providers, patients, and others regarding more than fifteen thousand persons and entities that are excluded from participation in Medicare, Medicaid, and other federal health care programs.

Mayo Clinic

www.mayohealth.org

This site, directed by a team of physicians and researchers from the clinic, includes a journal link.

Managed Care Information

www.managedcareinfo.com

This vast site is a managed care reference library, resource, and information center. It explains managed care accreditation organizations, managed care contracting, marketing, planning, financial management, terminology, and history.

Managed Care Information Center

www.themcic.com

Contains reports and market news. Provides helpful links to insurance company and health plan sites.

Medi-Cal Policy Institute

www.medi-cal.org

Medi-Cal is a source of health care insurance for low-income, elderly, and disabled Californians. The Medi-Cal Policy Institute's goal is to bring clear, concise data and analysis to the people who develop Medi-Cal policy, those who provide health care services, and those who care about the program. The institute was founded in 1997 by a grant from the California Healthcare Foundation. This Website supplies valuable resources and publications.

The organization, established in 1997 by a grant from the California HealthCare Foundation, is an independent source of information on the Medi-Cal program. The institute seeks to facilitate and enhance development of effective policy solutions with the interests of Medi-Cal recipients guiding this work. It conducts and commissions research, distributes information about the program and its recipients, highlights its successes, and identifies its weaknesses.

Medicaid and Telemedicine

www.hcfa.gov/medicaid/telemed.htm

HCFA has not formally defined telemedicine for purposes of the Medicaid program, and federal Medicaid law does not recognize telemedicine as a distinct service. Nevertheless, Medicaid reimbursement for services furnished through telemedicine applications is available, at the state's option, as an alternative to more traditional ways of providing care. This site includes a list of states that permit use of telemedicine in their Medicaid program.

Medicaid Consumer Network of Massachusetts

pw1.netcom.com/~rcauchi/mdg/intro.html

This organization, which is affiliated with the Medicaid Defense Group network, has a goal of preserving the positive features and benefits of MassHealth, the Massachusetts Medicaid program. Contains links to sites providing status of Medicaid legislation in the U.S. Congress and in other states.

Medical Malpractice, Professional Liability, and Health Care

www.afss.com/medical/medmal.htm

Medical Malpractice Resource Page

webs.soltec.net/fish/medmal.htm

Contains a range of subfiles on the topic.

Medicare and Managed Care

www.hcfa.gov/medicare/mgdcar1.htm

This site contains managed care information for an audience of current and future HCFA-contracting managed care (including Medicare+Choice) organizations and other parties interested in the operational and regulatory aspects of the Medicare managed care program. It includes links to more beneficiary-oriented sites that are also managed by HCFA.

Medsite Navigator's List of Electronic Medical Journals

www.medsitenavigator.com/med/Journals

Contains a comprehensive list of electronic medical journals, including some on policy issues.

Meta-Subject Index to Government Information

www.isu.edu/~woodstep/Subjects_1.html

This site, maintained by Idaho State University, is intended to direct the user to subject indexes that have been created for the purpose of identifying government Internet resources in a given subject area. This index contains more than 1,630 entries.

Mining Company—Health Care Industry

www.about.com

The core of this supersite is a topical directory, which leads to a range of articles on pertinent legislation, with links to text and commentary from both supporters and opponents; critiques of software; as well as hot issues and Websites that address them.

Minnesota Health Data Institute

www.mhdi.org

This organization was created by the Minnesota state legislature in 1993 to foster a competitive health care system. This site includes the institute's reports to the legislature and other publications.

Model State Public Health Privacy Project

www.critpath.org/msphpa/privacy.htm

Under the direction of Lawrence O. Gostin and James G. Hodge, Jr., both of Georgetown University Law Center, this project seeks to develop a blueprint for a model privacy statute. The site includes drafts of the document along with links to other pertinent Websites, notably to those of all state health departments.

Modern Healthcare

www.modernhealthcare.com

Site contains full-length articles from the magazine, which focuses on health care business news.

National Academy for State Health Policy

www.nashp.org

This Portland, Maine, organization is a nonprofit forum of state health policy leaders from the executive and legislative branches. Its staff conducts policy analysis, provides training and technical assistance to states, produces informational resources, and convenes forums for policy makers. The organization focuses on five areas of health reform: access for the uninsured, family and community care, the health care marketplace, long-term and chronic care, and managed care and purchasing strategies.

National AIDS Fund

www.aidsfund.org

Provides grants to support state HIV/AIDS programs. Assists public health agencies in developing new models of community-based care and prevention. Supports community leadership with financial, program, and technical assistance. Administers the Workplace Resource Center, which works with businesses to create AIDS policies, guidelines, and educational programs.

National Association of Public Hospitals

www.naph.org

Among the interests here are Medicaid patients and vulnerable populations, including persons with AIDS, the homeless, the mentally ill, and non-English speaking patients.

National Association of State Medicaid Directors

www.medicaid.aphsa.org

National Center for Health Statistics

www.cdc.gov/nchs

NCHS is the primary federal organization responsible for collecting, analyzing, and disseminating health statistics. This site provides access to publications, statistical tables, and data files.

National Center on Poverty Law

www.povertylaw.org

Formerly known as the National Clearinghouse for Legal Services, this is a Chicago-based nonprofit communications, advocacy, and policy organization that fosters and develops creative approaches to policy research, development, analysis, and advocacy affecting low-income communities. This site includes articles on health policy issues from the bimonthly journal *Clearinghouse Review.*

National Clearinghouse on Managed Care

www.mcare.net

Somewhat misnamed, this site focuses on managed care and individuals with developmental disabilities. It includes a number of position papers and policy briefs. The site is maintained by the University of New Hampshire.

National Coalition for Patient Rights

www.nationalcpr.org

This site includes articles and legislative alerts.

National Committee on Vital and Health Statistics

aspe.os.dhhs.gov/ncvhs/privrecs.htm

Site includes health privacy recommendations of the committee.

National Committee to Preserve Social Security and Medicare

www.ncpssm.org

Interests include retirement income protection, health care reform, and quality of life for seniors.

National Conference of State Legislators

www.ncsl.org

This site includes a forum on state health policy leadership.

National Governors' Association

www.nga.org

This association's goal is to provide a forum for state governors to exchange views and experiences among themselves and to supply information on state innovations and practices. This site supplies information about a number of health issues and publications, including those on topics such as ERISA reform and Medicaid.

National Health Care Anti-Fraud Association

www.nhcaa.org

Founded in 1985 by several private health insurers and federal and state law enforcement official, this group seeks to improve detection, investigation, civil and criminal prosecution, and prevention of health care fraud.

National Health Information Center

nhicnt.health.org

Established in 1979 by the Office of Disease Prevention and Health Promotion, the NHIC provides online access to its database, publications, and Partnerships for Networked Consumer Health Information conferences. In the database, one can find well over a thousand organizations and government offices that provide health information upon request. Click on an organization and get contact information, Internet address—including a link to its home page—an organizational abstract, publication information, and a list of keywords for further searches.

National Health Law Program

www.healthlaw.org

This is a Los Angeles-based organization of attorneys representing the poor, minorities, the disadvantaged, and the elderly in issues concerning federal, state, and local health care programs. It offers technical assistance and training for health law specialists.

National HIV/AIDS Update Conference

www.nauc.org

Maintained by the American Foundation for AIDS Research, this site includes valuable links to other sites.

National Information Center on Health Services Research and Health Care Technology

www.nlm.nih.gov

This government organization seeks to make the results of health care research, including practice guidelines and technology assessments, readily available to health practitioners, health care administrators, health policy makers, and payers, and to contribute to the information infrastructure needed to foster patient record systems that can produce useful health services research data as a by-product of providing health care.

National Institute for Mental Health

www.nimh.gov

This site includes news and publications information.

National Journal of Sexual Orientation Law

metalab.unc.edu/gaylaw

This is an online journal focused on legal issues affecting lesbians, gay men, and bisexuals, including AIDS.

National Library of Medicine NGI & Telemedicine Project

www.nlm.nih.gov/research/telfront.html

Among other things, this site provides information on the NLM telemedicine initiative.

National Practitioner Data Bank

www.npdb.com

This is the central repository for information on physicians and dentists. It contains reports on medical malpractice payments, adverse licensure actions, adverse clinical privilege actions, and adverse professional society membership actions.

National Reference Center for Bioethics Literature

www.georgetown.edu/research/nrcbl

This site includes a link to Bioethicsline.

National Rural Health Association

www.nrharural.org/

This site contains abstracts of articles contained in the *Journal of Rural Health*. This organization's position papers are available in their entirety here.

New York Academy of Medicine

www.nyam.org

This nonprofit organization has been engaged in policy development and advocacy since 1847.

New York University School of Law

www.law.nyu.edu/library

This site provides a portal to such search tools as Lawcrawler, Excite, Galaxy, Google, Govbot, Infoseek, Netscape Search, Northern Light, Snap, WebCrawler, Yahoo, and many others.

Next Generation Internet Initiative

www.ngi.gov/apps/#nih_apps

This site showcases six breakthrough projects, including real-time telemedicine, high-resolution imaging telemedicine, remote control telemedicine, and medical image reference libraries.

North Carolina Rural Health Research and Policy Analysis Cartographic Archive

www.schsr.unc.edu/research_programs/Rural_Program/maps/maps.html

Includes subfiles on demographics of rural America, health status indicators, rural hospitals, health manpower supply, services, and programs.

Office for the Advancement of Telehealth

telehealth.hrsa.gov/hometxt.htm

DHHS created OAT to promote wider adoption of effective telecommunications and information technologies in providing health services to the nation's underserved population.

Office of the Inspector General Anti-Kickback Advisory Opinions

www.hhs.gov/progorg/oig/advopn/index.htm

Provides opinions from the Department of Health and Human Services OIG.

Office Professionals and Employees International Union

www.opieu.org

Of the largest nonphysician based unions that seek to represent physicians, OPEIU has had the most reported success to date. It has formed an affiliation with the American Podiatric Medical Association and has formed the first National Guild for Providers of the Lower Extremities. State chapters have been formed in Pennsylvania, California, Michigan, and New Hampshire; as of the end of 1999, the union reports that chapters are being formed in at least three other states. OPIEU expects to enroll ten thousand out of the nation's fourteen thousand podiatrists. However, there have been no published reports of unions of allopathic physicians formed by the OPEIU.

Pam Pohly's Net Guide—Links to Numerous Health Care Sites

www.pohly.com

This site includes an extensive glossary of managed health care terms, along with a guide to managed care, hospital and health care companies, and relevant professional associations.

Physician's Guide to Medical Liability Litigation

www.afss.com/medical/physguid.htm

This guide is intended as a reference for physicians practicing in Michigan. Some of the information it provides is Michigan-specific and does not apply to other states. This guide offers general information on the subject matter.

Policy.com

www.policy.com

Contains a subfile on health care policy issues and links to public policy organizations and issues.

Project Inform

www.ProjectInform.org

Project Inform's policy department's priorities include treatment access and funding for AIDS treatment, research, care, prevention, and housing. It works on a range of legislative and funding issues that affect access to health care and services, with particular emphasis on treatment access through state, federal, and industry-sponsored programs.

Project on Government Oversight

www.pogo.org

Since 1981, POGO has worked to investigate, expose, and remedy abuses of power, mismanagement, and subservience to special interests by the federal government. This site has a subfile on the False Claims Act as it relates to health care.

Qui Tam Information Center

www.quitam.com

This is a how-to site for whistle-blowers and attorneys to gain information and help in pursuing *qui tam* actions.

Reuters Health Information

www.reutershealth.com

Contains regularly updated medical news and health information.

Roswell and Alistair: Mismanaged Care (a Forum)

www.roswellandalistair.com/mismanaged_care.htm

This absolutely hilarious site consists of a sustained attack on managed care and "bloodsucking insurance companies." A must-visit.

Rural Policy Research Institute

www.rupri.org

A joint effort of the University of Nebraska, the University of Missouri, and Iowa State University, this organization produces policy papers on rural health issues.

Security in Healthcare Systems

afis.colstate.edu/stephens/cis425/moorbib.html

This site is an annotated bibliography on security and confidentiality in health care.

Self-Insurance Institute of America, Inc.

www.siia.org

This is a lobbying organization for self-insured employers. Among other things, it supports federal preemption, opposes legal liability for its members, and supports access to medical records for claims management purposes.

Service Employees International Union

www.sieu.org

The fastest-growing union in the AFL-CIO, the SEIU claims 1.3 million members nationwide, among whom about 600,000 are health care workers, including nurses, medical technicians, and other hospital employees. Following an eleven-year struggle, in February 1999 the SEIU won a vote to represent 74,000 Los Angeles home care workers, organized labor's biggest victory in sixty years, according to the *New York Times*. The following month, the union's high-profile president, Andrew Stern, announced a major push to unionize doctors around the country.

Stanford Medical School

www-med .stanford.edu [or www.smi.stanford.edu]

Stark Advisory Opinions

www.hcfa.gov/regs/aop/

These opinions are issued by the Health Care Financing Administration.

Stateline.org

www.stateline.org

A project of the Pew Center on the States, this site includes newspaper articles from around the country on breaking health news, health care data, and background information.

Taxpayers Against Fraud

www.taf.org

This is a nonprofit public interest organization focused on combating fraud against the federal government through promoting the *qui tam* provisions of the False Claims Act and filing whistle-blower lawsuits. This site contains a detailed description of the act, a description of amicus submissions, statistics concerning the act, library resources, and a subfile on proposed congressional amendments to the act.

Telemedicine and the Law

www.arentfox.com/telemedicine.html

This site deals with the legal issues surrounding health information systems, computerized decision support technologies, and telemedicine. This excellent site includes a range of links to related sites.

Telemedicine Information Exchange

www.telemed.org

This site was created and is maintained by the Telemedicine Research Center with major support from the National Library of Medicine. It includes a subfile on legal issues, links, publications, and state and federal legislation.

Thomas

thomas.loc.gov/

Updated several times daily, this valuable site provides the status on legislation in the U.S. House and the U.S. Senate. Includes congressional calendars and information on committee activities. One can search by keyword or bill number for major legislation.

UC Berkeley Public Health Library

www.lib.berkeley.edu/PUB/internet.html

This helpful site, which provides information on a variety of health policy issues, is regularly updated.

United Hospital Fund of New York

www.uhfnyc.org

Founded in 1879, this philanthropic organization undertakes research, policy development, program analysis, and educational activities. This site includes a list of books, papers, newsletters, and practical guides based on the organization's research activities, conference proceedings, and grantmaking.

U.S. Attorneys' Manual

www.usdoj.gov/usao/eousa/foia_reading_room/usam/

This site includes sections on civil, tax, criminal, and antitrust law, among other topics.

U.S. Department of Health and Human Services

www.dhhs.gov

This is the DHHS home page.

U.S. Department of Health and Human Services, Health Resources and Services Administration

www.hrsa.dhhs.gov

Directs national health programs targeted at the underserved and vulnerable.

U.S. Department of Health and Human Services, Office of Inspector General

www.dhhs.gov/progorg/oig/

Contains advisory opinions, audit reports, antikickback information, compliance guidance, OIG exclusions, fraud alerts, inspection reports, and other information. Also contains the OIG hotline number (800-447–8477).

U.S. Department of Health and Human Services, Office of Rural Health Care Policy

www.nal.usda.gov/orhp

This comprehensive site focuses on health care service in rural America. It provides hypertext links to a vast number of related sites and provides a directory of state offices of rural health.

U.S. Justice Department Antitrust Division

www.usdoj.gov/atr

This site is a true gold mine, including such information as the Joint Statements of Policy Regarding the Health Care Industry, selected documents filed by the Antitrust Division since December 1994, amicus curae briefs, the Antitrust Division manual, the 1997 Horizontal Merger Guidelines, and a range of other policy documents. It also contains news on ongoing cases, the division's phone directory, and additional contact information for the division.

U.S. Public Health Service

phs.os.dhhs.gov/phs/phs.html

This site includes reports on such topics as HIV/AIDS, tobacco use, and suicide prevention.

U.S. Supreme Court Decisions

www.law.cornell.edu/

This site includes U.S. Supreme Court decisions since 1990, along with decisions of U.S. appellate courts and those of the New York Court of Appeals, with full text of opinions.

U.S. Tax Code on Line

www.fourmilab.ch/ustax/ustax.html

U.S. Tax Court

www.ustaxcourt.gov

This site includes information about the court along with full-text versions of court opinions.

Universal Health Care Action Network (UHCAN!)

www.uhcan@uhcan.org

This Cleveland, Ohio, organization advocates a single-payer, Canadian-style health care system. Through its networking, publications, workshops, and national conferences, UHCAN! serves to stimulate development of strategies that will strengthen local activists' efforts to organize effectively around health care justice issues. In October 1997, UHCAN! organized a public demonstration in Washington targeting the Federation of American Health Systems, the trade association of for-profit hospitals.

University of Arkansas for Medical Sciences

www.uams.edu/infotech/confdntl.htm

This site contains the medical information confidentiality policy of the University of Arkansas for Medical Sciences.

University of California Association of Interns and Residents

www.igc.apc.org

This group is affiliated with the California Association of Interns and Residents, which has between one thousand and two thousand members and is affiliated with Hospital and Health Care Workers Union Local 250 in Oakland.

University of Houston Health Law and Policy Institute

www.law.uh.edu/healthlaw

Contains a listing of recently published articles and documents.

University of Maine (Muskie School) Institute for Health Policy

www.muskie.usm.maine.edu/research/healthpol

The institute focuses its work in four primary areas: rural health, long-term care, organization and financing of health services, and mental health. Its publication *Rural Health News* is available in full text on this site.

University of Michigan Documents Center—Federal Government Resources on the Web

www.lib.umich.edu/libhome/Documents.center/federal.html

This huge, yet well-organized, site provides information on all three branches of government along with agency directories and Websites, bibliographies, regulations, executive orders, and related resources.

Washburn University Law School

www.washlaw.edu

This eclectic site includes a valuable subfile on health care issues.

Webdoctor

www.gretmar.com/webdoctor/journals.html

Contains online medical journal articles.

WebTaxi

www.webtaxi.com

This is a navigational service designed to help Internet users conveniently search the World Wide Web. This free service was developed to offer efficient access to search engines, newsgroups, and thousands of hard-to-reach databases.

Western Journal of Medicine

www.ewjm.com

This is an electronic version of the publication, which is the official journal of the Alaska State Medical Association, the Arizona Medical Association, the California Medical Association, the Denver Medical Society, the Idaho Medical Association, the Nevada State Medical Association, the New Mexico Medical Association, the Utah Medical Association, the Washington State Medical Association and the Wyoming Medical Society.

White House

www.whitehouse.gov

This site includes health policy proposals and documents.

Yale Medical School Library

www.med.yale.edu/library/sir

This site makes available a large number of electronic resources on health policy from the Cushing/Whitney Medical Library at Yale.

Appendix D

State-by-State Synopsis of Selected Statutes of Limitation Laws

State	Malpractice/ Tort Action	Contract Action	Death Action	Date of Negligence	Date of Last Treatment	Date of Discovery	Foreign Object Exception	Overall Limitations Period
Alabama	2 yrs	2 yrs	2 yrs	2 yrs	—	6 mos	—	4 yrs
Alaska	2 yrs	—	2 yrs	2 yrs	—	—	—	2 yrs
Arizona	2 yrs	2 yrs	2 yrs	2 yrs	—	—	—	2 yrs
Arkansas	2 yrs	2 yrs	3 yrs	2 yrs	—	—	1 yr	—
California	3 yrs	—	1 yr	3 yrs	—	1 yr	3 yrs	3 yrs
Colorado	2 yrs	2 yrs	2 yrs	—	—	2 yrs	2 yrs	3 yrs
Connecticut	2 yrs	—	2 yrs	3 yrs	—	2 yrs	—	3 yrs injury, 5 yrs death
Delaware	2 yrs	2 yrs	2 yrs	2 yrs	—	3 yrs	—	—
District of Columbia	3 yrs	3 yrs	1 yr	—	3 yrs	3 yrs	—	—
Florida	2 yrs	2 yrs	2 yrs	2 yrs	—	2 yrs	—	7 yrs
Georgia	2 yrs	—	2 yrs	2 yrs	—	—	1 yr	5 yrs
Hawaii	2 yrs	—	2 yrs	—	—	2 yrs	—	6 yrs
Idaho	2 yrs	2 yrs	2 yrs	2 yrs	—	2 yrs	1 yr	2 yrs
Illinois	2 yrs	2 yrs	2 yrs	—	—	2 yrs	—	4 yrs
Indiana	2 yrs	2 yrs	2 yrs	2 yrs	—	—	—	2 yrs
Iowa	2 yrs	—	2 yrs	—	—	2 yrs	2 yrs	6 yrs
Kansas	2 yrs	2 yrs	2 yrs	2 yrs	—	2 yrs	—	10 yrs tort, 4 yrs contract
Kentucky	1 yr	1 yr	1 yr	1 yr	—	1 yr	—	1 yr
Louisiana	1 yr	1 yr	1 yr	1 yr	—	1 yr	—	3 yrs
Maine	3 yrs	—	3 yrs	3 yrs	—	—	3 yrs	—
Maryland	5 yrs	—	3 yrs	5 yrs	—	3 yrs	—	—
Massachusetts	3 yrs	3 yrs	3 yrs	3 yrs[1]	3 yrs	7 yrs	—	—
Michigan	2 yrs	—	3 yrs	2 yrs	—	6 mos	6 mos	6 yrs
Minnesota	2 yrs	2 yrs	2 yrs	—	—	—	—	2 yrs
Mississippi	2 yrs	—	2 yrs	—	—	2 yrs	—	2 yrs
Missouri	2 yrs	—	3 yrs	2 yrs	—	—	2 yrs	10 yrs
Montana	3 yrs	3 yrs	3 yrs	3 yrs	—	3 yrs	—	5 yrs
Nebraska	2 yrs	2 yrs	2 yrs	2 yrs	—	1 yr	—	10 yrs
Nevada	4 yrs	—	4 yrs	4 yrs	—	2 yrs	—	4 yrs
New Hampshire	2 yrs	2 yrs	5 yrs	2 yrs	—	—	2 yrs	—

State	Malpractice/ Tort Action	Contract Action	Death Action	Date of Negligence	Date of Last Treatment	Date of Discovery	Foreign Object Exception	Overall Limitations Period
New Jersey	2 yrs	2 yrs	2 yrs	—	—	2 yrs	2 yrs	—
New Mexico	3 yrs	3 yrs	3 yrs	3 yrs	—	—	—	3 yrs
New York	2½ yrs	—	2 yrs	2½ yrs	2½ yrs	—	1 yr	—
North Carolina	3 yrs	—	2 yrs	3 yrs	—	—	—	—
North Dakota	2 yrs	—	2 yrs	2 yrs	—	2 yrs	—	5 yrs
Ohio	1 yr	—	2 yrs	1 yr	1 yr	—	1 yr	4 yrs
Oklahoma	2 yrs	2 yrs	2 yrs	—	—	2 yrs	—	3 yrs[2]
Oregon	2 yrs	—	3 yrs	—	—	2 yrs	—	3 yrs[3]
Pennsylvania	2 yrs	—	2 yrs	2 yrs	—	2 yrs	—	2 yrs
Rhode Island	3 yrs	—	3 yrs	3 yrs	—	3 yrs	—	—
South Carolina	3 yrs	—	6 yrs	3 yrs	—	3 yrs	2 yrs	6 yrs
South Dakota	2 yrs	2 yrs	3 yrs	2 yrs	—	—	—	2 yrs
Tennessee	1 yr	1 yr	1 yr	—	—	1 yr	1 yr	3 yrs
Texas	2 yrs	—	2 yrs	2 yrs	—	—	—	2 yrs
Utah	2 yrs	2 yrs	2 yrs	—	—	2 yrs	1 yr	4 yrs
Vermont	3 yrs	—	2 yrs	3 yrs	—	2 yrs	2 yrs	7 yrs
Virginia	2 yrs	2 yrs	2 yrs	2 yrs	—	—	1 yr	10 yrs
Washington	3 yrs	—	3 yrs	3 yrs	—	1 yr	3 yrs	67 yrs[4]
W. Virginia	2 yrs	2 yrs	2 yrs	2 yrs	—	2 yrs	—	10 yrs
Wisconsin	3 yrs	3 yrs	3 yrs	3 yrs	—	1 yr	1 yr	5 yrs
Wyoming	2 yrs	2 yrs	2 yrs	2 yrs	—	2 yrs	—	2 yrs

Notes

1. Accrual not specified by statute, but statute implies that accrual is three years from date of negligence and three years from date of discovery.

2. Actions brought more than three years from the date of injury are limited to actual medical and surgical expenses incurred as a direct result of the injury.

3. If not within five years because of fraud, deceit, or misleading representation, then within two years of discovery of fraud and so forth, or of the date that fraud and so forth should have been discovered.

4. Tolled for foreign object exception.

Appendix E

Table of Acronyms and Abbreviations

AAAHC	Accreditation Association for Ambulatory Health Care
AABB	American Association of Blood Banks
AAFP	American Academy of Family Physicians
AAHP	American Association of Health Plans
AAMCN	American Association of Managed Care Nurses
AAPCC	adjusted average per capita cost
AAPHO/IHDS	American Association of Physician-Hospital Organizations/Integrated Healthcare Delivery Systems
AAPI	American Accreditation Program, Inc.
AAPPO	American Association of Preferred Provider Organizations
ABA	American Bar Association
ACG	ambulatory care group
ACHE	American College of Healthcare Executives
ACP	American College of Physicians
ACR	adjusted community rating
ACS	American College of Surgeons
ADA	Americans with Disabilities Act
ADC	average daily census
ADG	ambulatory diagnostic group
ADL	activities of daily living
ADS	alternative delivery systems
AFHHA	American Federation of Home Health Agencies
AHA	American Hospital Association
AHCA	American Health Care Association
AHCPR	Agency for Health Care Policy and Research
AHLA	American Health Lawyers Association
AHP	accountable health partnership
ALJ	administrative law judge
ALOS	average length of stay
AMA	American Medical Association
AMCP	Academy of Managed Care Pharmacy
AMCRA	American Managed Care and Review Association
AMPRA	American Medical Peer Review Association

ANA	American Nurses Association
AOB	assignment of benefits
APG	ambulatory patient group
APN	advance practice nurse
APR	average payment rate
ASHRM	American Society for Healthcare Risk Management
ASO	administrative-services-only contract
AWP	any willing provider
BBA	Balanced Budget Act of 1997
BC/BS	Blue Cross/Blue Shield Plans
CAM	catchment area management project
CAP	capitation
CARF	Commission on Accreditation of Rehabilitation Facilities
CAT	computerized axial tomography
CCN	community care network
CCP	coordinated care program
CCRC	continuing care retirement community program
CERCLA	Comprehensive Environmental Response, Compensation, and Liability Act; also known as SARA or Superfund
CHAMPUS	Civilian Health and Medical Program of the Uniformed Services
CHC	community health center
CHMIS	Community Health Management Information System
CLIA	Clinical Laboratory Improvement Amendments of 1988
CM	case management; case manager
CMP	competitive medical plan
CMSA	Case Management Society of America
CNM	certified nurse midwife
COA	certificate of authority
COB	coordination of benefits
COBRA	Consolidated Omnibus Budget Reconciliation Act of 1985
COC	certificate of coverage
COI	certificate of insurance
CON	certificate of need
Copay	copayment
COPC	community-oriented primary care
CPI	consumer price index
CPI-MCS	consumer price index-medical care services
CPR	customary, prevailing, and reasonable
CPT-4	Physician's Current Procedural Terminology, 4th Edition
CQI	continuous quality improvement
CRC	community rating by class
CRF	comprehensive referral fund
CRI	CHAMPUS Reform Initiative
CSR	continued stay review
CTD	cumulative trauma disorder
CVO	credential/central verification organization

CWW	clinic without walls
DC	dual choice
DCI	duplicate coverage inquiry
DHHS	Department of Health and Human Services
DME	durable medical equipment
DMO	dental maintenance organization
DMS	demand management services
DOS	date of service
DPR	drug price review
DRG	diagnosis-related group
DSM	disease state management
DUM	drug utilization management
DUR	drug utilization review
E of I	evidence of insurability
EAP	employee assistance program
EAPA	Employee Assistance Professionals Association
EASNA	Employee Assistance Society of North America
EBIS	employee benefits information system
EBR	employee benefits representative
EBRI	Employee Benefits Research Institute
ECF	extended care facility
EDI	electronic data interchange
EMO	exclusive multiple option
EMS	emergency medical services
EMTALA	Emergency Medical Treatment and Active Labor Act
EOB	explanation of benefits
EPA	Environmental Protection Agency
EPCRA	Emergency Planning and Community Right-to-Know Act
EPO	exclusive provider organization
EPSDT	early and periodic screening, diagnosis, and treatment
ERISA	Employee Retirement Income Security Act of 1974
ESOP	employee stock ownership plan
ESRD	end-stage renal disease
FAHS	Federation of American Health Systems
FAR	Federal Acquisition Regulations
FAS-106	Financial Accounting Standards, Rule 106
Fee max	fee maximum
FEHBP	Federal Employee Health Benefits Program
FFS	fee-for-service reimbursement
FI	fiscal intermediary
FMC	Foundation for Medical Care
FP	family practice
FPP	faculty practice plan
FQHMO	federally qualified HMO
FSMB	Federation of State Medical Boards
FTC	Federal Trade Commission

FTE	full-time equivalent
FWPCA	Federal Water Pollution Control Act
GAO	Government Accounting Office
GCM	General Counsel Memorandum
GDP	gross domestic product
GHAA	Group Health Association of America
GP	general practitioner
GPC	geographic practice cost (index)
GPWW	group practice without walls
HCFA	Health Care Financing Administration
HCPCS	HCFA Common Procedural Coding System
HCPP	health care prepayment plan
HCQIA	Health Care Quality Improvement Act of 1986
HEDIS	Health Plan Employer Data and Information Set
HFMA	Healthcare Financial Management Association
HHA	home health care agency
HHS	Health and Human Services (DHHS)
HI	horizontal integration
HIAA	Health Insurance Association of America
HIN	health insurance network
HIO	health insuring organization
HIPAA	Health Insurance Portability and Accountability Act of 1996 (also known as Kennedy-Kassebaum)
HIPC	health insurance purchasing cooperative
HISB	Health Insurance Standards Board
HMO	health maintenance organization
HOI	Health Outcomes Institute
HPA	hospital-physician alliance
HPNS	Healthcare Provider Networks Section of the AHA
HRA	health risk appraisal
HRSA	Health Resources and Services Administration
HSA	health services agreement
HSB	health standards board
IAF	industry adjustment factor
IBNR	incurred but not reported
ICD-9	International Classification of Disease, 9th Edition
ICF	intermediate care facility
ICMA	Individual Case Management Association
ICU	intensive care unit
IDS	integrated delivery system
IFEBP	International Foundation of Employee Benefit Plans
IHPS	Institute for Health Policy Solutions
IP	inpatient
IPA	independent practice association
IRB	institutional review board
IRC	Internal Revenue Code

IRS	Internal Revenue Service
ISHA	International Subacute Healthcare Association
JCAHO	Joint Commission on Accreditation of Healthcare Organizations
JHG	Jackson Hole Group
JPA	joint powers authority
LCAH	life care at home program
LCM	large case management
LLC	limited liability company
LOB	line of business
LOS	length of stay
LPN	licensed practical nurse
LTC	long-term care
LVN	licensed vocational nurse
MA	medical assistant
MAC	maximum allowable charge
MAP	maximum allowable payment
MaxLOS	maximum length of stay
MCE	medical care evaluation
MCM	medical case management
MCO	managed care organization
MCP	managed care plan
MDC	major diagnostic categories
MERP	medical expense reimbursement plan
MET	multiple employer trust
MEWA	multiple employer welfare association
MGMA	medical group management association
MH/SA	mental health/substance abuse
MHCA	managed health care association
MHSS	military health services system
MIB	Medical Information Bureau
MIC	maternal and infant care
MIG	Medicare-insured group
MIP	managed indemnity plan
MIS	management information system
MLP	midlevel practitioner
MLR	medical loss ratio
MM	member months
MOB	maintenance of benefits plan
MOR	monthly operating report
MPP	minimum premium plan
MRI	magnetic resonance imaging
MSA	medical savings account
MSA	metropolitan statistical area
MSO	management service organization
MTS	Medicare transaction system
NAEBA	National Association of Employee Benefit Administrators

NAHC	National Association for Home Care
NAHDO	National Association of Health Data Organizations
NAHMOR	National Association of HMO Regulators
NAIC	National Association of Insurance Commissioners
NAMCP	National Association of Managed Care Physicians
NBCH	National Business Coalition on Health
NCCH	National Council of Community Hospitals
NCI	nursing care institution
NCPA	National Center for Policy Analysis
NCQA	National Committee for Quality Assurance
NDC	national drug code
NDG	network design group
NHB	National Health Board
NIH	National Institutes of Health
NLR	net loss ratio
NMHCC	National Managed Health Care Congress
NonPar	nonparticipatory provider
NP	nurse practitioner
NPDB	National Practitioner Data Bank
NTIS	National Technical Information Service
OBRA	Omnibus Budget Reconciliation Act
OGE	Office of Governmental Ethics
OHMO	Office of Health Maintenance Organizations
OIG	Office of Inspector General
OMC	Office of Managed Care
OMSB	Outcomes Management Standards Board
OOA	out-of-area services
OON	out-of-network services
OOP	out-of-pocket payments
OP	outpatient
OPHCOO	Office of Prepaid Health Care Operations and Oversight
OPL	other party liability
OPM	office of personnel management
OSC	organized system of care
OSCR	on-site concurrent review
OSHA	Occupational Safety and Health Act (or Administration)
OT	occupational therapist
OTC	over-the-counter drug
OWA	other weird arrangement
P&T	pharmacy and therapeutics committee
PA	physician's assistant
PAS	preadmission screening program
PAS	Professional Activities Survey
PAT	preadmission testing
PBM	pharmacy benefit manager
PCCM	primary care case manager

PCLR	paid claims loss ratio
PCN	primary care network
PCP	primary care physician (or practitioner)
PCPM	per contract per month
PCR	physician contingency reserve
PET	positron emission tomography
PHCO	physician-hospital-community organization
PHO	physician-hospital organization
PLI	professional liability insurance
PMA	Pharmaceutical Manufacturers Association
PMPM	per member per month
POP	premium-only plan
POS	point-of-service plan
PPI-H	producer price index-hospital
PPO	preferred provider organization
PPP	private practice partnership
PPS	prospective payment system
PRF	pooled risk fund
PRO	peer review organization
ProPAC	Prospective Payment Assessment Commission
PSA	professional services agreement
PSAO	pharmacy services administration organization
PSN	provider-sponsored network
PSRO	Professional Standards Review Organization
PSV	primary source verification
PTMPY	per thousand members per year
QA	quality assurance
QIP	quality improvement program
QM	quality management
QMB	qualified Medicare beneficiary
QRC	quality review committee
R&C	reasonable and customary charge
RAP	radiologists, anesthesiologists, and pathologists
RBPG	risk-bearing provider group
RBRVS	resource-based relative value scale
RCF	residential care facility
RCRA	Resource Conservation and Recovery Act
Retro	retrospective rate derivation
RFI	request for information
RFP	request for proposal
RICO	Racketeer Influenced and Corrupt Organizations Act
RIMS	Risk and Insurance Management Society
RN	registered nurse
RVS	relative value of services
SAP	service assessment program
SCP	specialty care physician

SCR	standard class rate
SDU	step-down unit
SEC	Securities and Exchange Commission
SHP	state health plan
SHPDA	State Health Planning and Development Agency
SHPM	Society for Healthcare Planning and Marketing
SIC	standard industry code
SIIA	Self-Insurance Institute of America
SIW	service intensity weights
SMG	specialty medical group
SMI	supplementary medical insurance program
SNF	skilled nursing facility
SOBRA	Sixth Omnibus Reconciliation Act
SPBA	Society of Professional Benefit Administrators
SSO	second surgical opinion
SSSG	similarly sized subscriber group
STD	sexually transmitted disease
SUR	statistical utilization review
TEFRA	Tax Equity and Fiscal Responsibility Act of 1982
TPA	third-party administrator
TPL	third-party liability
TQM	total quality management
TSCA	Toxic Substances Disposal Act
UB-92	Uniform Billing Code of 1992
UCR	usual, customary, and reasonable fees
UHDDS	uniform hospital discharge data set
UM	utilization management
UNAC	universal access
UPR	unitary pricing rule
UR	utilization review
URAC	Utilization Review Accreditation Commission
URO	utilization review organization
VNAA	Visiting Nurse Associations of America
VPS	volume performance standards
WBGH	Washington Business Group on Health
WDC	weighted daily census
WEDI	Workgroup for Electronic Data Interchange
ZEBRA	zero-balanced reimbursement account

Appendix F

Glossary

AAHP: American Association of Health Plans. The trade organization that represents all forms of MCOs. Created in 1996 by the merger of GHAA and AMCRA. Based in Washington, D.C., the AAHP has a heavy focus on lobbying, educational activities, and service to member plans.

AAPCC: Adjusted average per capita cost. The HCFA's best estimate of the amount of money it costs to care for Medicare recipients under fee-for-service Medicare in a given area. The AAPCC is made up of 142 rate cells; 140 of them are factored for age, sex, Medicaid eligibility, institutional status, working aged, and whether a person has both Part A and Part B Medicare. The two remaining cells are for individuals with end-stage renal disease.

AAPPO: American Association of Preferred Provider Organizations. A trade organization for PPOs.

Abuse: A manner of operation that results in excessive or unreasonable costs to the Medicare or Medicaid programs.

Accelerated benefits option: Life insurance provision under which terminally ill persons with a life expectancy of less than a year, or persons confined to a nursing home, can choose to have a certain portion of life insurance proceeds paid out before death to use as they deem appropriate.

Accreditation: Granting of approval or credentials to an agency or facility, based on the agency or facility's demonstrating (usually by passing a specific survey or inspection) that standards prescribed by the accrediting body have been met.

Accrete: The term used by the HCFA for the process of adding new Medicare enrollees to a plan.

Accrual: The amount of money that is set aside to cover expenses. The accrual is the plan's best estimate of what those expenses are; for medical expenses, it is based on a combination of data from the authorization system, the claims system, the lag studies, and the plan's history.

ACEs: Accelerated-compensation events. These are medically caused injuries that should not occur. ACEs do not cover all injuries, just classes of adverse outcomes that are usually, although not invariably, avoidable through good medical care.

ACG: Ambulatory care group. ACGs are a method of categorizing outpatient episodes. There are fifty-one mutually exclusive ACGs that are based on resource use over time and are modified by principal diagnosis, age, and sex. *See also* ADG and APG.

ACR: Adjusted community rate. Used by HMOs and CMPs with Medicare risk contracts. A calculation of what premium the plan would charge for providing exactly the Medicare-covered benefits to a group account adjusted to allow for greater intensity and frequency of utilization by Medicare recipients. The ACR includes the normal profit of a for-profit HMO or CMP. The ACR may be equal to or lower than the APR but can never exceed it. *See also* APR.

Actuarial assumptions: The assumptions that an actuary uses in calculating the expected costs and revenues of the plan. Examples include utilization rates, age and sex mix of enrollees, and cost of medical services.

ADG: Ambulatory diagnostic group. These offer a method of categorizing outpatient episodes. There are thirty-four possible ADGs.

Administrative law judge (ALJ): An employee of the Department of Health and Human Services who presides over civil fraud and abuse administrative hearings brought by the Office of the Inspector General. The ALJ's decision is final and binding thirty days after it is served on the parties, unless the decision is appealed to the Departmental Appeals Board (DAB) or the DAB grants an extension of time to file an appeal.

Advance directives: Written instructions executed by decisionally capable adults that pertain to the future medical treatment preferences or values of the party executing the document. These directives take effect only if the patient is decisionally incapacitated at the time that specific decisions need to be made.

Adverse selection: The problem of attracting members who are sicker than the general population (specifically, members who are sicker than was anticipated when the budget for medical costs was developed).

AFDC: Aid to Families with Dependent Children. A program administered and funded by federal and state governments that provided financial assistance to needy families. In 1996, welfare reform legislation replaced this entitlement program with Temporary Assistance to Needy Families (TANF).

ALOS: *See* LOS.

Ambulatory surgical center (ASC): A freestanding, self-contained facility providing outpatient surgical services to patients who do not require inpatient hospitalization.

Ambulatory surgical center (ASC): Provides surgical services that do not require a hospital stay. Medicare pays an institutional fee for use of an ambulatory surgical center for certain approved surgical procedures.

AMCRA: American Managed Care and Review Association. A trade association that represented managed indemnity plans, PPOs, MCOs, and HMOs. Merged with GHAA in 1995 to become the AAHP in 1996. *See also* AAHP.

Ancillary services: Auxiliary or supplemental services such as diagnostic, home health, and other services used to support diagnosis and treatment of a patient's condition.

Antikickback statute: A provision of the Social Security Act that forbids any knowing and willful conduct that involves soliciting, receiving, offering, or paying any kind of remuneration in return for referring an individual for any Medicaid- or Medicare-covered item or service, or for recommending or arranging purchase, lease, or order of an item or service that may be wholly or partially paid for through Medicare or Medicaid programs. Violation of the antikickback provision can result in a fine of up to $25,000 for each violation and/or imprisonment for up to five years. The law also mandates exclusion or suspension from government health care programs following a conviction under this statute.

Antisupplementation provision: A provision of the Social Security Act that makes it a criminal offense to charge a higher amount than the Medicaid rate for a covered service provided to a Medicaid beneficiary. Violation of this provision can subject an individual to a fine of up to $25,000 and up to five years imprisonment.

APG: Ambulatory patient group. A reimbursement methodology developed by 3M Health Information Systems for the HCFA. APGs are to outpatient procedures what DRGs are to inpatient days. APGs provide for a fixed reimbursement to an institution for outpatient procedures or visits and incorporate data regarding the reason for the visit and patient data. APGs prevent unbundling of ancillary services. *See also* ACG and ADG.

APR: Average payment rate. The amount of money that the HCFA could conceivably pay an HMO or CMP for services to Medicare recipients under a risk contract. The figure is derived from the AAPCC for the service area adjusted for the enrollment characteristics that the plan would expect to have. The payment to the plan, the ACR, can never be higher than the APR, but it may be less.

ASO: Administrative services only; sometimes referred to as an administrative services contract (ASC). A contract between an insurance company and a self-funded plan where the insurance company performs administrative services only and does not assume any risk. Services usually include claims processing but may include actuarial analysis, utilization review, and so forth. *See also* ERISA.

Assigned claim: A claim for which the physician or supplier agrees to accept the amount approved by Medicare as the total payment. Medicare pays the physician 80 percent of the Medicare approved fee schedule (less any unmet deductible). The doctor or supplier can charge the beneficiary only for the coinsurance, which is the remaining 20 percent of the approved amount. The participating physician or supplier agrees to accept assignment on all claims.

Assignment of benefits: Payment of medical benefits directly to a provider of care rather than to a member. Generally requires either a contract between the health plan and the provider or a written release from the subscriber to the provider allowing the provider to bill the health plan.

AWP: Any willing provider. This is a form of state law that requires an MCO to accept any provider willing to meet the terms and conditions in the MCO's contract, whether the MCO wants or needs that provider or not.

AWP: Average wholesale price. Commonly used in pharmacy contracting, the AWP is generally determined through reference to a common source of information.

Balance billing: The practice of a provider billing a patient for all charges not paid for by the insurance plan, even if those charges are above the plan's UCR or are considered medically unnecessary. Managed care plans and service plans generally prohibit providers from balance billing except for allowed copays, coinsurance, and deductibles. Such prohibition against balance billing may even extend to the plan's failure to pay at all (for example, because of bankruptcy).

Balance billing: A type of cost sharing under Medicare whereby a beneficiary is responsible for the difference between a physician's submitted charge and the Medicare allowed charge on unassigned claims.

Blue Cross: Membership corporation (usually nonprofit) providing protection against the cost of hospital care in a limited geographical area.

Blue Shield: Membership corporation (usually nonprofit) providing protection against the cost of hospital care in a limited geographical area.

Buy-in: A Medicare beneficiary who is also eligible for Medicaid, and for whom Medicare Part B premiums are paid by a state Medicaid program.

California Collaborative Healthcare Reporting Initiative (CCHRI): Sponsored by the Pacific Business Group on Health, this program represents the collective interests of health plans, purchasers, and provider organizations. CCHRI collects, analyzes, and reports performance data; promotes use of accurate and comparable quality measures; and designs and engages in collaborative improvement projects.

Capitation: A method of reimbursement where the provider, hospital, or health plan is paid a fixed per-patient amount and is expected to provide all necessary covered services at no additional charge.

Carrier fraud control unit: A fraud control unit housed within a Medicare carrier that receives referrals of potential fraud and abuse cases and conducts case reviews.

Carve out: Refers to a set of medical services that are carved out of the basic arrangement. In terms of plan benefits, this may refer to a set of benefits that are contracted for separately, for example, mental health or substance abuse services separated from basic medical-surgical services. May also refer to carving out a set of services from a basic capitation rate with a provider (as with capitating for cardiac care but carving out cardiac surgery and paying case rates for that).

Case management: An approach to managing provision of health care to members with high-cost medical conditions. The goal is to coordinate the care to improve both continuity and quality of care and to lower costs. This generally is a dedicated function in the utilization management department. The official definition, according to the Certification of Insurance Rehabilitation Specialists Commission, is as follows: "Case management is a collaborative process which assesses, plans, implements, coordinates, monitors, and evaluates the options and services required to meet an individual's health needs, using communication and available resources to promote quality, cost-effective outcomes" and that "occurs across a continuum of care, addressing ongoing individual needs" rather than being restricted to a single practice setting. When focused solely on high-cost inpatient cases, it may be referred to as large case management or catastrophic case management.

Case mix: Refers to the mix of illness and severity of cases for a provider.

Certificate of coverage: Refers to the document that a plan must provide to a member to show evidence that the member has coverage and to give basic information about that coverage. Required under state regulations.

Certification: Granting of approval or credentials to an individual professional, based upon the professional demonstrating (usually through education, experience, and specific examination performance) that the standard prescribed by the certifying body has been met.

CHAMPUS: Civilian Health and Medical Program of the Uniformed Services. The federal program providing health care coverage to families of military personnel, military retirees, certain spouses and dependents of such personnel, and certain others.

Children's Health Insurance Program (CHIP): A program established in 1997, designed to provide health assistance to uninsured low-income children either through separate programs or through expanded eligibility under state Medicaid programs.

Churning: The practice of a provider seeing a patient more often than is medically necessary, primarily to increase revenue through increased service delivery. Churning may also apply to any performance-based reimbursement system where there is heavy emphasis on productivity (in other words, rewarding a provider for seeing a high volume of patients, whether through fee-for-service or through an appraisal system that pays a bonus for productivity).

Civil investigative demand: The attorney general has the authority to serve a civil investigative demand on a person who may be in possession of any documents or information relating to a false-claim investigation. A demand imposes a broader range of requests than an Office of Inspector General subpoena, including producing documents, providing responses to written interrogatories, or giving oral testimony concerning documentary material.

Civil Monetary Penalty Law (CMPL): Under this law, the OIG may bring administrative actions against providers who submit false or fraudulent claims to the United States or its agent for a medical item or service. The OIG need only demonstrate that the person knew or should have known that the claim was false or fraudulent. The penalty for violation of this law can be a fine of up to $2,000 for each item or service that is submitted in violation of the CMPL, an assessment of not more than two times the amount claimed for each item or service, or a fine of $50,000 for violations regarding patient stabilization and appropriate transfers. In addition, the provider can be terminated from Medicare, Medicaid, or other state health care programs.

Civilian Health and Medical Program of the Uniformed Services: *See* CHAMPUS.

Claim fraud: Use of various means (material misrepresentation, exaggeration of an injury, alteration of medical bills, and so on) to obtain benefits to which an insured or a physician is not entitled.

Claim lag: Time incurred between date of a claim and its submission to the insurer for payment; also, the time between claim incurred and payment (check or draft issue or redemption).

Clinical Laboratory Improvement Amendments of 1988 (CLIA): A federal law subjecting nearly all clinical laboratories operating in the United States—whether they are located in hospitals or physicians' offices or are independent—to comprehensive federal quality regulation.

Closed panel: A managed care plan that contracts with physicians exclusively for services and does not allow those physicians to see patients for another managed care organization. Examples include staff- and group-model HMOs. Could apply to a large private medical group that contracts with an HMO.

CMP: Competitive medical plan. A federal designation that allows a health plan to obtain eligibility to receive a Medicare risk contract without having to obtain qualification as an HMO. Requirements for eligibility are somewhat less restrictive than for an HMO.

COA: Certificate of authority. The state-issued operating license for an HMO.

COB: Coordination of benefits. Method of integrating benefits payable under more than one health insurance plan so that the insured's benefits from all sources neither exceed 100 percent of allowable medical expenses nor eliminate appropriate patient incentives to contain costs. For example, a husband may have Blue Cross and Blue Shield through work, and the wife may elect an HMO through her place of employment. The COB agreement gives the order for which organization has primary responsibility for payment and which one has secondary responsibility.

COBRA: Consolidated Omnibus Budget Reconciliation Act. Federal statute requiring employers with more than twenty employees to make group health care coverage available for eighteen months, at employee expense, to employees who leave the employer for any reason other than gross misconduct. Another portion eases a Medicare recipient's ability to disenroll from an HMO or CMP with a Medicare risk contract. *See also* Conversion.

Coinsurance: A provision in a member's coverage that limits the amount of coverage by the plan to a certain percentage, commonly 80 percent. Any additional costs are paid by the member out of pocket.

Coinsurance: The portion of reimbursable hospital and medical expenses, after subtraction of any deductible, that Medicare does not cover and for which the beneficiary is responsible. Under Part A (hospital insurance), there is no coinsurance for the first sixty days of inpatient hospital care; from the sixty-first to ninetieth days of inpatient care, the daily coinsurance amount is equal to one-half of the inpatient hospital deductible. For each of the sixty lifetime reserve days used, the daily coinsurance amount is equal to one-fourth of the inpatient hospital deductible.

Cold claim: A claim for medical services received by the plan for which no authorization has been received; that is, it arrives "cold."

Collective knowledge doctrine: A doctrine attributing liability to a corporation for the separate actions of several employees who are operating independently of one another. The corporation is considered to have acquired the collective knowledge of its employees and is held responsible for their failure to act lawfully.

Commission: The money paid to a sales representative, broker, or other type of sales agent for selling the health plan. May be a flat amount of money or a percentage of the premium.

Commissioner of insurance: Chief state official responsible for matters related to insurance regulation.

Common law: Judge-made or court-made law, as opposed to statutes, which are laws enacted by legislative bodies. *Compare* Statute.

Community rating: The rating methodology required of federally qualified HMOs, HMOs under the laws of many states, and occasionally indemnity plans under certain circumstances. The HMO must obtain the same amount of money per member for all members in the plan. Community rating does permit variability by allowing the HMO to factor in differences for age, sex, mix (average contract size), and industry factors; not all factors are necessarily allowed under state laws, however. Such techniques are referred to as community rating by class and adjusted community rating. *See also* Experience rating.

Competitive medical plan (CMP): A federal designation that allows a health plan to contract for a Medicare risk contract without becoming a federally qualified health maintenance organization (HMO). Like an HMO, a CMP provides health care on a prepaid basis. However, a CMP differs from a federally qualified HMO because services must be provided primarily through the CMP, the CMP may be able to limit the scope of some of the services it is required to offer, and the CMP can require higher copayments and deductibles.

CON: Certificate of need. The requirement that a health care organization obtain permission from an oversight agency before making changes. Generally applies only to facilities or facility-based services.

Concurrent review: Refers to utilization management that takes place during provision of services. Almost exclusively applied to inpatient hospital stays.

Consolidated Omnibus Budget Reconciliation Act: *See* COBRA.

Continuing care retirement community (CCRC): Self-sufficient life care community in which residents, for a substantial entry fee plus a monthly maintenance fee, enter into a contractual relationship with the community that can last a lifetime.

Contract year: The twelve-month period for which a contract for services is in force. Not necessarily tied to a calendar year.

Contributory plan: A group health plan in which the employees must contribute a certain amount toward the premium cost, with the employer paying the rest.

Conversion: Conversion of a member covered under a group master contract to coverage under an individual contract. This is offered to subscribers who lose their group coverage (through job loss, death of a working spouse, and so forth) and who are ineligible for coverage under another group contract. *See also* COBRA.

Coordination of benefits: *See* COB.

Copayment: The portion of a claim or medical expense not covered by insurance that a patient must pay for himself or herself.

Corporate compliance program: A program designed, implemented, and enforced by a corporation to detect and prevent violations of the fraud and abuse laws.

Corporate death sentence: A penalty that may be imposed under the federal Guidelines for Sentencing of Organizations on a corporation that does not take effective measures to prevent wrongdoing among its employees. If a death sentence is imposed on the corporation, the corporation will be fined an amount sufficient to divest it of all net assets.

Corporate-practice-of-medicine acts or statutes: State laws that prohibit a physician from working for a corporation; in other words, a physician can only work for himself or herself or another physician. Put another way, a corporation cannot practice medicine. Often created through the effort on the part of certain members of the medical community to prevent physicians from working directly for managed care plans or hospitals.

Cost sharing: Any form of coverage in which the member pays some portion of the cost of providing services. Usual forms of cost sharing include deductibles, coinsurance, and copayments.

Cost shifting: When a provider cannot cover the cost of providing services under the reimbursement received, the provider raises the prices to other payers to cover that portion of the cost. Some of the costs are shifted to and absorbed by private health insurance.

County Medical Services Program (CMSP): This is a county medical assistance program for smaller California counties. It serves people who are not eligible for Medi-Cal but who are unable to pay for their health services. CMSP programs are funded and administered by the county. CMSP is not a Medi-Cal program.

Credentialing: The most common use of the term refers to obtaining and reviewing the documentation of professional providers. Such documentation includes licensure, certifications, insurance, evidence of malpractice insurance, malpractice history, and so forth. Generally includes both reviewing information offered by the provider and verifying that the information is correct and complete. A less-frequent use of the term applies to closed panels and medical groups and refers to obtaining hospital privileges and other privileges to practice medicine.

Current Procedural Technology Codes (CPT): Used for reporting medical services and procedures performed by physicians.

Current Procedural Terminology, 4th edition (CPT-4) coding: A set of five-digit codes corresponding to medical services that are frequently used for billing purposes.

Custodial care: Care provided to an individual that is primarily the basic activities of living. May be medical or nonmedical, but the care is not meant to be curative or as a form of medical treatment, and it is often lifelong. Rarely covered by any form of group health insurance or HMO.

CVO: Credentialing verification organization. This is an independent organization that performs primary verification of a professional provider's credentials. The managed care organization may then rely on that verification rather than requiring the provider to tender credentials independently. This lowers the cost of credentialing. The NCQA has issued certification standards for CVOs. *See also* NCQA.

CWW: Clinic without walls. *See* GPWW.

Date of service: Refers to the date that medical services were rendered. Usually different from the date a claim is submitted.

DAW: Dispense as written. The instruction from a physician to a pharmacist to dispense a brand-name pharmaceutical rather than a generic substitution.

Days per thousand: A standard unit of measurement of utilization. Refers to annualized use of a hospital or other institutional care. It is the number of hospital days that are used in a year for each thousand covered lives.

DCI: Duplicate coverage inquiry. A document used in COB when one plan contacts another to inquire about dual coverage of medical benefits.

Death spiral: An insurance term that refers to a spiral of high premium rates and adverse selection, generally in a free-choice environment (typically, an insurance company or health plan in an account with multiple plans, or a plan offering coverage to potential members who have alternative choices, such as through an association). One plan, often the indemnity plan competing with managed care plans, ends up having continuously higher premium rates such that the only members who stay with the plan are those whose medical costs are so high (and who cannot change because of provider loyalty or benefit restrictions, such as preexisting conditions) that they far exceed any possible premium revenue. Called the death spiral because the losses from underwriting mount faster than the premiums can ever recover, and the account eventually terminates coverage, leaving the carrier in a permanent loss position.

Deductible: The portion of a subscriber's (or member's) health care expenses that must be paid out of pocket before any insurance coverage applies, commonly $100 to $300. Common in insurance plans and PPOs, uncommon in HMOs. May apply only to the out-of-network portion of a point-of-service plan. May also apply only to one portion of the plan coverage (for example, there may be a deductible for pharmacy services but not for anything else).

Deductible: The amounts paid by enrollees for covered services before Medicare made reimbursements.

Defensive medicine: Physician use of extensive laboratory tests, increased hospital admissions, and extended hospital stays for the principal purpose of reducing the likelihood of malpractice suits by patients or providing a good legal defense in the event of such lawsuits.

Delete: Term used by the HCFA for the process of removing Medicare enrollees from a plan. *See also* Accrete.

Departmental Appeals Board (DAB): In a civil action brought by the Office of the Inspector General, a party may appeal an ALJ's decision to the DAB. The DAB's decision is final and binding sixty days after the parties are notified of the decision. Any petition for review of the DAB's decision must be filed with the appropriate U.S. Court of Appeals before the sixty-day period has expired.

Department of Health and Human Services (DHHS, or HHS): Through the Health Care Financing Administration, this department administers the Medicare and Medicaid programs and is the federal agency primarily concerned with health care fraud.

Department of Justice: The agency responsible for enforcing health care fraud and abuse at the federal level. Health care fraud may be prosecuted by the antitrust, civil, and/or criminal divisions.

Dependent: A person who is covered by virtue of a family relationship with the member who has the health plan coverage. For example, one person has health insurance or an HMO through work, and that individual's spouse and children, the dependents, also have coverage under the contract.

Diagnosis coding: A numerical coding system, such as the International Classification of Diseases, 9th Edition, Clinical Modification (ICD-9-CM), that is used to specify diseases, conditions, injuries, services, and items provided to patients. Medicare and many other insurance programs require use of ICD-9-CM codes on most claims for payment.

Diagnosis-related group: *See* DRG.

Direct contracting: A term describing a provider or integrated health care delivery system contracting directly with employers rather than through an insurance company or managed care organization. A superficially attractive option that occasionally works when the employer is large enough. Not to be confused with direct contract model (see below).

Direct contract model: A managed care health plan that contracts directly with private practice physicians in the community rather than through an intermediary, such as an IPA or a medical group. A common type of model in open-panel HMOs.

Discharge planning: The part of utilization management that is concerned with arranging for care or medical needs to facilitate discharge from the hospital. It includes a system of expediting transfer of a patient to a more cost-effective health care facility.

Disease management: The process of intensively managing a particular disease. This differs from large case management in that it goes well beyond a given case in the hospital or an acute exacerbation of a condition. Disease management encompasses all settings of care and places heavy emphasis on prevention and maintenance. Similar to case management but more focused on a defined set of diseases.

Disenrollment: The process of termination of coverage. Voluntary termination would include a member quitting because he or she simply wants out. Involuntary termination would include a member leaving the plan because of changing jobs. A rare and serious form of involuntary disenrollment is when the plan terminates a member's coverage against the member's will. This is usually only allowed (under state and federal laws) for gross offenses such as fraud, abuse, nonpayment of premium or copayments, or demonstrated inability to comply with recommended treatment plans.

Disproportionate share hospital: One serving a relatively large volume of low-income persons.

DME: Durable medical equipment. Medical equipment that is not disposable (meaning, it is used repeatedly) and is related only to care for a medical condition. Examples are wheelchairs, home hospital beds, and so forth. An area of increasing expense, particularly in conjunction with case management. DME is covered under Medicare Part B.

DMO: Dental health maintenance organization. An HMO organized strictly to provide dental benefits.

Dread disease policy: A type of health insurance that only covers a specific and frightening type of illness, such as cancer.

DRG: Diagnosis-related group. A statistical system of classifying any inpatient stay into groups for the purposes of payment. The DRG classification system divides possible diagnoses into more than twenty major body systems and subdivides them into almost five hundred groups for the purpose of Medicare reimbursement. The groups are clinically coherent and homogeneous with respect to inpatient short-stay hospital resource use. Factors used to determine the DRG payment amount include the diagnosis involved as well as the hospital resources necessary to treat the condition. Also used by a few states for all payers and by many private health plans (usually non-HMO) for contracting purposes. Hospitals are paid a fixed rate for inpatient services corresponding to the DRG group assigned to a given patient.

DRG creep: Placing patients in a higher-value DRG than is warranted by the patient's condition, to receive increased Medicare reimbursement.

DRG payment window: The period of time before a patient's admission to the hospital when the services provided to the patient are eligible for Medicare reimbursement. Between the advent of a prospective payment system in 1983 and 1990, hospitals were eligible for reimbursement for outpatient services performed in the twenty-four hours prior to admission. In 1990, Congress expanded the DRG payment window to include services provided during the three days prior to admission and expanded services to include not only outpatient services but services furnished by any entity wholly owned or operated by the hospital.

DSH: *See* disproportionate share hospital.

DSM-IV: *Diagnostic and Statistical Manual of Mental Disorders,* 4th edition. The manual used to provide a diagnostic coding system for mental and substance abuse disorders. Far different from ICD-9-CM. *See also* ICD-9-CM.

Dual choice: Sometimes referred to as Section 1310 or "mandating." The portion of the federal HMO regulations that required any employer with twenty-five or more employees that resided in an HMO's service area, paid minimum wage, and offered health coverage to offer a federally qualified HMO as well. The HMO had to request it. This provision was "sunsetted" in 1995. Another definition, unrelated to the previous one, pertains to point of service. *See also* POS.

Dual eligible: Elderly and/or disabled persons who qualify for benefits under both Medicaid and Medicare. In such cases, payments for any services covered by Medicare are made before any payments are made by the Medicaid program.

Dual option: Offer of both an HMO and a traditional insurance plan by one carrier.

Duplicate claims: Submission of the same claim more than once, usually because payment has not been received quickly. Can lead to duplicate payments and incorrect data in the claims file.

DUR: Drug utilization review.

Durable medical equipment: *See* DME.

EAP: Employee assistance program. A program that a company puts into effect for its employees to provide them with help in dealing with personal problems, such as alcohol or drug abuse, mental health or stress issues, and so forth.

Effective date: The day that health plan coverage goes into effect or is modified.

Eligibility: When an individual is eligible for coverage under a plan. Also used to determine when an individual is no longer eligible for coverage (for example, a dependent child reaches a certain age and is no longer eligible for coverage under his or her parent's health plan).

ELOS: *See* LOS.

Encounter: An outpatient or ambulatory visit by a member to a provider. Applies primarily to physician office visits but may encompass other types of encounters as well. In fee-for-service plans, an encounter also generates a claim. In capitated plans, the encounter is still the visit, but no claim is generated. *See also* Statistical claim.

Enrollee: An individual enrolled in a managed health care plan. Usually applies to the subscriber or person who has the coverage in the first place rather than to the dependents, but the term is not always used so precisely.

EOB: Explanation of benefits. A statement mailed to a member or covered insured explaining how and why a claim was or was not paid; the Medicare version is called an explanation of Medicare benefits, or EOMB. *See also* ERISA.

EPO: Exclusive provider organization. An EPO is similar to an HMO in that it often uses primary physicians as gatekeepers, often capitates providers, has a limited provider panel, and uses an authorization system. It is referred to as exclusive because the member must remain within the network to receive benefits. The main difference is that EPOs are generally regulated under insurance statutes rather than HMO regulations. Not allowed in many states that maintain that EPOs are really HMOs.

EPSDT: The early and periodic screening, diagnostic, and treatment mandate of the Medicaid Act. It requires states to provide any service that Medicaid offers and a physician has deemed "medically necessary." Treatment is available to Medicaid-eligible children under the age of twenty-one.

Equity model: A term applied to a form of for-profit vertically integrated health care delivery system in which the physicians are owners.

ERISA: Employee Retirement Income Security Act of 1974. One provision of this act allows self-funded plans to avoid paying premium taxes, complying with state-mandated benefits, or otherwise complying with state laws and regulations regarding insurance, even when insurance companies and managed care plans that stand at risk for medical costs must do so. Another provision requires that plans and insurance companies provide an explanation-of-benefits statement to a member or covered insured in the event of a denial of a claim, explaining why the claim was denied and informing the individual of his or her rights of appeal. Numerous other provisions in ERISA are important for a managed care organization to know.

Ethics in Patient Referrals Act: The official name for the laws that have become known as the Stark Laws or Stark I and Stark II. *See* Stark I and Stark II.

Evidence of insurability: The form that documents whether an individual is eligible for health plan coverage when the individual does not enroll through an open enrollment period. For example, if an employee wants to change health plans in the middle of a contract year, the new health plan may require evidence of insurability (often both a questionnaire and a medical examination) to ensure that it will not be accepting adverse risk.

Experience rating: The method of setting premium rates based on the actual health care costs of a group or groups.

Experimental medical procedure: Medical practice, procedure, or treatment still in a trial stage— that is, being tested on humans or animals. *See* Investigational medical procedure for distinction in meaning.

Extracontractual benefits: Health care benefits beyond what the member's policy actually covers. These benefits are provided by a plan to reduce utilization. For example, a plan may not provide coverage for a hospital bed at home, but it is more cost-effective for the plan to provide such a bed than to keep admitting a member to the hospital.

False Claims Act (FCA): The criminal False Claims Act makes it illegal to present a claim upon or against the United States that the claimant knows to be false, fictitious, or fraudulent. The civil False Claims Act provides that any person who knowingly presents, or causes to be presented, to the U.S. government a false or fraudulent claim for payment or approval; knowingly makes, uses, or causes to be made or used, a false record or statement to get a false or fraudulent claim paid or approved by the government; or conspires to defraud the government by getting a false or fraudulent claim allowed or paid violates the act. The act also has *qui tam* provisions. Under the civil provisions of the FCA, a defendant can be assessed a penalty of at least $5,000 and as much as $10,000 per claim, plus three times the damages incurred by the federal government in its prosecution and investigation of the case. The criminal provisions provide for a fine of $25,000 and up to five years' imprisonment upon conviction.

False statements statute: A statute that prohibits any false, fictitious, or fraudulent statement to the United States or any government agency. This statute is often used to prosecute health care providers who make false Medicare or Medicaid claims.

FAR: Federal acquisition regulations. The regulations applied to the federal government's acquisition of services, including health care services. *See also* FEHBARS.

Favored nations discount: A contractual agreement between a provider and a payer stating that the provider will automatically provide the payer the best discount it provides anyone else.

Federal Bureau of Investigation (FBI): As the federal government's law enforcement agency, the FBI investigates federal crimes, including health care fraud.

Federal Employee Health Benefits Program: *See* FEHBP.

Federal qualification: Applies to HMOs and CMPs. It means that the HMO/CMP meets federal standards regarding benefits, financial solvency, rating methods, marketing, member services, health care delivery systems, and other standards. An HMO/CMP must apply for federal qualification and be examined by the OMC, including an on-site review. Federal qualification does place some restrictions on how a plan operates but also allows it expeditious entry into the Medicare and FEHBP markets. Federal qualification is voluntary and not required to enter the market.

Federally qualified health centers (FQHC): An entity that has entered into an agreement with the HCFA to meet Medicare program requirements and is receiving a grant under Sections 329, 330, or 340 of the Public Health Service Act or is receiving funding from such a grant pursuant to a contract with the grant recipient and meets the grant requirements; based on the recommendation of the Public Health Service, is determined by HCFA to meet the requirements for receiving such a grant; was treated by HCFA as a comprehensively federally funded health center as of Jan. 1, 1990; or is an outpatient health program or facility operated by a tribe or tribal organization under the Indian Self-Determination Act or by an urban Native American organization receiving funds under Title V of the Indian Health Care Improvement Act.

Federally qualified health maintenance organization: An HMO that has met federal standards delineated in the federal HMO Act for legal and organizational status, financial viability, marketing, and health service delivery systems. Federally qualified HMOs are required to provide or arrange for basic necessary services with no limitation as to time, cost, frequency, extent, or kind of services actually provided. Federal qualification under the HMO Act is voluntary.

Fee-for-service: Method of charging whereby a physician or other provider bills for each visit or service rendered.

Fee schedule: May also be referred to as fee maximums or a fee allowance schedule. A listing of the maximum fees that a health plan will pay for certain services based on CPT billing codes.

FEHBARS: Federal Employee Health Benefit Acquisition Regulations. The regulations applied to OPM's purchase of health care benefits programs for federal employees.

FEHBP: Federal Employees Health Benefits Program. The health insurance program for federal employees and their families. The FEHBP is administered by the U.S. Office of Personnel Management. *See also* OPM.

Flexible benefit plan: Plan in which an employer allows employees to choose a variety of options in benefits up to a certain total amount. The employee then can tailor the benefit package among health coverage, life insurance, child care, and so forth to optimize benefits for his or her particular needs.

Forensic medicine: Specialty area of medicine concerned with investigating, preparing, preserving, and presenting medical opinion and other evidence in courts and other legal, correctional, or law enforcement settings.

Formulary: A listing of drugs that a physician may prescribe. The physician is requested or required to use only formulary drugs unless there is a valid medical reason to use a nonformulary drug.

Foundation: A not-for-profit form of integrated health care delivery system. The foundation model is usually formed in response to tax laws that affect not-for-profit hospitals or in response to state laws prohibiting the corporate practice of medicine. The foundation purchases the tangible and intangible assets of a physician's practice, and the physicians then form a medical group that contracts with the foundation on an exclusive basis for services to patients seen through the foundation. *See also* Corporate practice-of-medicine acts or statutes.

Foundation for Accountability (FACCT): This nonprofit organization was created in 1995 to bring a consumer perspective to quality assessment of health care. It emphasizes outcome measures but also endorses process measures.

Foundation model: Refers to an integrated health care delivery system in which a not-for-profit foundation is responsible for providing the income to a medical group that is exclusive with the foundation. The foundation is usually, but not necessarily, associated with a not-for-profit hospital and is often found in states with corporate practice of medicine acts.

FPL: Federal poverty level. Federal income guidelines based on family size that are used to determine financial eligibility for public assistance programs such as Medicaid.

FPP: Faculty practice plan. A form of group practice organized around a teaching program. It may be a single group encompassing all the physicians providing services to patients at the teaching hospital and clinics, or it may be multiple groups drawn along specialty lines (psychiatry, cardiology, surgery, and so forth).

FQHC: Federally qualified health center. Health clinics, such as community or migrant health centers, that receive funding under the Public Health Services Act. FQHCs provide important health services to a population that may otherwise be uninsured.

Fragmented claims: Billing separately for procedures rather than using a global billing code covering all of these services, when billing separately results in a higher payment rate.

Fraud: Knowing and willful deception or misrepresentation, or a reckless disregard of the facts, with the intent to receive an unauthorized benefit.

Fraud alerts: During the past few years, the Office of Inspector General has issued fraud alerts as a way of informing the health care industry about prohibited practices. The alerts are generally brief documents that describe conduct that the OIG perceives as violating the fraud and abuse laws.

FTE: Full-time equivalent. The equivalent of one full-time employee. For example, two part-time employees are 0.5 FTE each, for a total of 1 FTE.

Full capitation: A loose term used to refer to a physician group or organization receiving capitation for all professional expenses, not just for the services it provides itself; does not include capitation for institutional services. The group is then responsible for subcapitating or otherwise reimbursing other physicians for services to its members. *See* Global capitation.

Gatekeeper: An informal, although widely used, term that refers to a primary care case management model health plan. In this model, all care from providers other than the primary care physician, except for true emergencies, must be authorized by the primary care physician before being rendered. This is a predominant feature of almost all HMOs.

Generic drug: A drug that is equivalent to a brand-name drug but usually less expensive. Most managed care organizations that provide drug benefits cover generic drugs but may require a member to pay the difference in cost between a generic drug and a brand-name drug or pay a higher copay, unless there is no generic equivalent.

GHAA: Group Health Association of America, now AAHP. A trade association that represented managed care with a focus on HMOs, both open- and closed-panel. Merged with AMCRA in 1995. *See also* AAHP.

Global billing codes: Billing codes used by Medicare to pay for surgical services that cover not only the surgery itself but also the usual preoperative and postoperative services.

Global capitation: A capitation payment that covers all medical expenses, including professional and institutional expenses. May not necessarily cover optional benefits (for example, pharmacy). Sometimes called total capitation.

GPWW: Group practice without walls. A group practice in which the members of the group come together legally but continue to practice in private offices scattered throughout the service area. Sometimes called a clinic without walls (CWW). *See also* CWW.

Group: The members who are covered by virtue of receiving health plan coverage at a single company.

Group-model HMO: An HMO that contracts with a medical group for provision of health care services. The relationship between the HMO and the medical group is generally close, although there are wide variations in the relative independence of the group from the HMO. A form of closed-panel health plan.

Group practice: The American Medical Association defines group practice as three or more physicians who deliver patient care, make joint use of equipment and personnel, and divide income by a prearranged formula.

Group purchasing organization (GPO): An entity authorized to act as a purchasing agent for a group of individuals or entities that are furnishing services payable by Medicare or a state health care program, and that are wholly owned by neither the GPO nor the subsidiaries of a parent corporation that wholly owns the GPO (either directly or through another wholly owned entity).

HCFA: Health Care Financing Administration. A branch of the Department of Health and Human Services that is responsible for administering Medicare and Medicaid programs.

HCFA-1500: A claim form used by professionals to bill for services. Required by Medicare and generally used by private insurance companies and managed care plans.

HCPCS: HCFA Common Procedural Coding System. A set of codes used by Medicare that describe services and procedures. HCPCS includes CPT codes but also has codes for services not included in CPT, such as DME and ambulance. Although HCPCS is nationally defined, there is provision for local use of certain codes.

HCPP: Health care prepayment plan. A form of cost contract between the HCFA and a medical group to provide professional services; does not cover Medicare Part A institutional services.

Health Care Financing Administration: *See* HCFA.

Health Care Quality Improvement Program (HCQIP): In 1992, HCFA established this program, which promotes partnerships between PROs and hospitals, health plans, and physicians. These partnerships profile patterns of medical care, identify areas in which treatment could be improved, assist in developing quality improvement efforts, and measure improvement.

Health Insurance Portability and Accountability Act of 1996 (HIPAA): This statute, often known as Kennedy-Kassebaum after its sponsors in the U.S. Senate, addresses the availability of private insurance to persons with preexisting medical conditions, among other topics.

Health maintenance organization (HMO): A system of health care delivery that not only pays for the care but also arranges for provision of services. For the HMO to pay for the cost of health care, members must receive care from a participating provider who has contracted with the HMO. In most HMOs, members choose a primary care physician from a panel of physicians affiliated with the HMO. The primary care physician serves as a gatekeeper, authorizing all visits to a specialist.

Healthy Families Program: A state and federally funded health insurance program for children with family incomes above the level eligible for no-cost Medicaid and below 200 percent of the federal poverty level.

HEDIS: Health Plan Employer and Data Information Set. Developed by the NCQA with considerable input from the employer community and the managed care community, HEDIS is an ever-evolving set of data reporting standards. HEDIS is designed to provide some standardization in performance reporting for financial, utilization, membership, and clinical data so that employers and others can compare performance among plans and across organizational structures. A voluntary system, HEDIS uses primarily process measures but also includes some outcome and structural measures. It covers preventive care, acute care, and chronic care.

HMO: *See* Health maintenance organization.

Home health services: Items furnished to a patient's home under the care of physicians. These services are supplied under a plan established and periodically reviewed by a physician.

Hospice: Concept of care provided to terminally ill patients and their families that emphasizes emotional and spiritual needs and coping with pain and death rather than cure.

Hospice: A public agency or private organization that is primarily engaged in providing pain relief, symptom management, and supportive services to patients who are certified to be terminally ill. Medicare beneficiaries may elect to receive hospice care instead of standard Medicare benefits for terminal illnesses.

Iatrogenic injuries: Injuries caused by the medical treatment itself, not the underlying disease.

IBNR: Incurred but not reported. The amount of money that the plan should accrue for medical expenses that it knows nothing about yet. These are medical expenses that the authorization system has not captured and for which claims have not yet hit the door. Unexpected IBNRs have torpedoed more managed care plans than any other cause.

ICD-9-CM: International Classification of Diseases, 9th revision, clinical modification. Classification of disease by diagnosis codified into six-digit numbers. The ICD-10 will use alphanumeric codes and is scheduled for publication soon.

IDS: Integrated delivery system; also referred to as an integrated health care delivery system. Other acronyms that mean the same thing include IDN (integrated delivery network), IDFS (integrated delivery and financing system), and IDFN (integrated delivery and financing network). An IDS is a system of health care providers organized to span a broad range of health care services. Although there is no clear definition of an IDS, in its full flower an IDS should be able to access the market broadly, optimize cost and clinical outcomes, accept and manage a full range of financial arrangements to provide a set of defined benefits to a defined population, align financial incentives of the participants (including physicians), and operate under a cohesive management structure. *See also* IHO, IPA, PHO, MSO, equity model, staff model-HMO, and foundation model.

IHO: Integrated health care organization. An IDS that is predominantly owned by physicians.

Illegal drug distribution statute: A federal law that is applicable when a health care scheme is accompanied by a narcotics distribution not in the proper course of medical treatment by a licensed professional.

Illegal remuneration statute: Another term for the antikickback statute. *See* Antikickback statute.

Incurred but unpaid claims: Claims that may not have been paid as of some specific date. May include reported and unreported claims. *See also* Lag study.

Indemnification: Obligation, established by contractual agreement or imposed as a matter of tort law, in which one party is required to reimburse another for losses of a particular type.

Informed consent: Legal right of all adults, with no upper age limit, to make their own decisions regarding medical, financial, and daily living matters.

Institutional review board: Panel that prospectively reviews and approves biomedical or behavioral protocols involving human subjects that are supported with federal funds. Mandated by the National Research Act of 1973.

Integrated (carve-out) plan: Method of combining two or more benefit plans to prevent duplication of benefits or overinsurance.

Investigational medical procedure: Ongoing clinical observation of an approved agent with respect to immediate and long-term effectiveness, complications, consequences, and care. (*See* Experimental medical procedure for distinction in meaning.)

IOM: Institute of Medicine. This organization is part of the National Academy of Sciences in Washington, D.C.

IPA: Independent practice association. An organization that has a contract with a managed care plan to deliver services in return for a single capitation rate. The IPA in turn contracts with individual providers to provide the services either on a capitation basis or on a fee-for-service basis. The typical IPA encompasses all specialties, but an IPA can be solely for primary care, or it may be a single specialty. An IPA may also be the "PO" part of a PHO.

Joint Commission (JCAHO): Joint Commission for the Accreditation of Healthcare Organizations. A not-for-profit organization that performs accreditation reviews primarily on hospitals, other institutional facilities, and outpatient facilities. Most managed care plans require any hospital under contract to be accredited by the Joint Commission.

Lag study: A report that tells managers how old the claims are that are being processed and how much is paid out each month (both for that month and for any earlier months, by month) and compares this with the amount of money that was accrued for expenses each month. A powerful tool used to determine whether the plan's reserves are adequate to meet all expenses.

Licensure: Permission granted by a state, under requirements and conditions established by statute, to an individual or entity to engage in a particular type of activity (for example, practice medicine, nursing, or social work; or operate a hospital, nursing facility, or home health agency).

Life care at home (LCAH): Concept of health care finance and delivery program models that resemble a CCRC while allowing an elderly person to live at home instead of at a centralized location.

Lifetime reserve: A Medicare hospital insurance enrollee has a nonrenewable lifetime reserve of sixty days of inpatient hospital care to draw on if the ninety covered days per benefit period are exhausted.

Line of business: A health plan (for example, an HMO, EPO, or PPO) that is set up as a line of business within another, larger organization, usually an insurance company. This legally differentiates it from a freestanding company or a company set up as a subsidiary. It may also refer to a unique product type (for example, Medicaid) within a health plan.

Loading factor: Amount added to the net premium rate determined for a group insurance plan to cover the possibility that losses will be greater than statistically expected because of older average age, hazardous industry, large percentage of unskilled employees, or adverse experience.

Long-term care: Continuum of maintenance, custodial, and health services to the chronically ill, disabled, or retarded. Services may be provided on an inpatient, outpatient, or at-home basis.

LOS, ELOS, ALOS: Length of stay, estimated length of stay, average length of stay.

Loss ratio: *See* Medical loss ratio.

MAC: Maximum allowable charge (or cost). The maximum, although not the minimum, that a vendor may charge for something. This term is often used in pharmacy contracting; a related term, used in conjunction with professional fees, is fee maximum.

Magnuson-Moss Warranty-Federal Trade Commission Improvement Act: A federal law governing warranties that protects buyers of any consumer product, any person to whom the product is transferred during the duration of the implied or written warranty, and any other person who is entitled under the terms of the warranty or state law to enforce the obligations contained in the warranty.

Mail fraud statute: A federal law prohibiting anyone who has devised a scheme to defraud from using the mails to further that scheme.

Major medical expense insurance: Form of health insurance that provides benefits for most types of medical expense up to a high maximum benefit. Such contracts may contain internal limits and usually are subject to deductibles and coinsurance.

Managed care: A broad term used to describe a system of health care delivery that tries to manage the cost of the health care, the quality of health care, and access to health care. The term encompasses a variety of health care delivery organizations, including HMOs, preferred provider organizations (PPOs), and physician-hospital organizations (PHOs).

Mandated benefits: Benefits that a health plan is required to provide by law. This is generally used to refer to benefits above and beyond routine insurance-type benefits, and it generally applies at the state level (where there is high variability from state to state). Common examples include in-vitro fertilization, defined days of inpatient mental health or substance abuse treatment, and other special-condition treatments. Self-funded plans are exempt from mandated benefits under ERISA.

Master group contract: Also known as a master policy, this is the actual contract between a health plan and a group that purchases coverage. The master group contract provides specific terms of coverage, rights, and responsibilities of both parties.

Material misrepresentation: A false or misleading statement on an application for an insurance policy that influences the insurer's decision as to the prospective insured's insurability. These statements may create the basis for rescinding the policy.

Maximum daily hospital benefit: Maximum amount payable for hospital room and board per day of hospital confinement.

Maximum out-of-pocket cost: The largest amount of money a member will ever need to pay for covered services during a contract year. The maximum out-of-pocket cost includes deductibles and coinsurance. Once this limit is reached, the health plan pays for all services up to the maximum level of coverage. Applies mostly to non-HMO plans such as indemnity plans, PPOs, and POS plans.

McCarren-Ferguson Act (Public Law 15): Legislation stipulating that federal law would apply to the insurance business only to the extent that it was not regulated by state law.

MCE: Medical care evaluation. A component of a quality assurance program that looks at the process of medical care.

MCO: Managed care organization. A generic term applied to a managed care plan. Some people prefer it to the term *HMO* because it encompasses plans that do not conform exactly to the strict definition of an HMO (although that definition has itself loosened considerably). May also apply to a PPO, EPO, IDS, or OWA.

Medicaid: A federal- and state-funded program administered by participating states that finances health care for the poor. States receive federal matching funds and are free to design their programs as long as they cover certain federally mandated services and run their programs within federal parameters. Demonstration projects, especially for managed care, may get waivers from certain requirements imposed by the federal government. Most individuals are eligible for Medicaid because they receive cash assistance through federal or federally assisted welfare programs, such as Aid to Families with Dependent Children (AFDC) or Supplemental Security Income (SSI). Medicaid also covers some low-income children and pregnant women without regard to their eligibility for cash assistance programs.

Medicaid fraud control unit (MFCU): Entities located in forty-two states and funded jointly by state and federal money that are charged with investigating and pursuing convictions against health care providers who defraud the Medicaid program. These units are usually affiliated with the state Attorney General's office and directed by an assistant attorney general. An MFCU's authority is concurrent with the OIG at the HHS.

Medi-Cal: California's Medicaid Program. It provides health care coverage for low-income and disabled individuals who lack health insurance. Jointly funded by the state and federal governments, it is the primary source of health and long-term care coverage for 5.1 million Californians.

Medical Information Bureau (MIB): System for exchange of underwriting information among insurers writing life and health insurance.

Medical loss ratio: The ratio between the cost to deliver medical care and the amount of money that was taken in by a plan. Insurance companies often have a medical loss ratio of 92 percent or more; tightly managed HMOs may have medical loss ratios of 75 percent to 85 percent, although the overhead (or administrative cost ratio) is concomitantly higher. The medical loss ratio is dependent on the amount of money brought in as well as on the cost of delivering care; thus if the rates are too low, the ratio may be high even though the actual cost of delivering care is not really out of line.

Medically Indigent Adult Program (MIA): This is the county medical assistance program in the larger California counties. MIA serves the same population as the County Medical Services Program: people who are not eligible for Medi-Cal but who are unable to pay for their medical care. MIA programs are funded and administered by the county. MIA is not a Medi-Cal Program.

Medically necessary: Term used by insurers to describe medical treatment that is appropriate and rendered in accordance with generally accepted standards of medical practice.

Medical policy: Refers to the policies of a health plan regarding what will be paid for as medical benefits. Routine medical policy is linked to routine claims processing and may even be automated in the claims system; for example, the plan may only pay 50 percent of the fee of a second surgeon or may not pay for two surgical procedures done during one episode of anesthesia. This also refers to how a plan approaches payment policies for experimental or investigational care and payment for noncovered services in lieu of more expensive covered services.

Medical review criteria: Systematically developed statements that can be used to assess the appropriateness of specific health care decisions, services, and outcomes.

Medicare: The federal health insurance program that provides coverage for most Americans over age sixty-five, the permanently disabled, and people with end-stage renal disease. Medicare coverage is divided into two parts. Part A, the Hospital Insurance Program, covers hospital and other institutional health services. Part B, Supplemental Medical Insurance, covers outpatient hospital visits, physician services, other types of outpatient service, DME, and diagnostic tests. Part A is compulsory coverage and is financed by a payroll tax on employers and employees. Part B is optional coverage; most individuals who elect this coverage must pay a monthly premium. State Medicaid programs pay Part B premiums for individuals who are entitled to Medicaid in addition to Medicare.

Medicare and Medicaid Patient and Program Protection Act (MMPPPA): A 1987 federal law that broadened the grounds for excluding health care providers from participation in the Medicare and Medicaid programs. This statute also granted the OIG the authority to exclude from Medicare and state health care program participation individuals or entities who violate the law, even if there has been no criminal conviction.

Medicare-Medicaid antifraud and abuse laws: Federal laws designed to control and punish fraud and abuse in connection with claims for payment under the Medicare and Medicaid programs.

Medicare secondary payer statute: A federal statute providing that when payment sources in addition to Medicare are available, those sources are primary payers and Medicare is a secondary payer.

Medicare SELECT: A fifty-state Medicare demonstration program that permits Medicare supplemental insurance companies (Medigap insurers) to offer a preferred provider organization policy to Medicare recipients. Medicare SELECT policies may waive or reduce deductible and coinsurance payments if the plan participant uses a network provider. Plan participants are free to choose a non-network provider, but the Medicare SELECT policies may restrict or eliminate payment of deductibles and coinsurance that the policy would otherwise cover.

Medicare Supplemental Insurance (MSI) or Medigap: Private insurance that supplements Medicare by paying Medicare deductibles and coinsurance. There are ten nationally standardized policies. Some policies offer coverage not provided by Medicare, such as coverage for outpatient prescription drugs and care outside of the United States.

Medigap: Private insurance designed to supplement Medicare coverage by paying for medical costs that Medicare does not pay, such as deductibles and coinsurance.

Member: An individual covered under a managed care plan. May be either the subscriber or a dependent.

Member months: The total of all months for which each member was covered. For example, if a plan had ten thousand members in January and twelve thousand members in February, the total member months for the year to date as of March 1 would be twenty-two thousand.

MeSH: Medical staff-hospital organization. An archaic term. *See* PHO.

MET: Multiple employer trust. *See* MEWA.

MEWA: Multiple employer welfare association. A group of employers that band together for purposes of purchasing group health insurance, often through a self-funded approach to avoid state mandates and insurance regulation. By virtue of ERISA, such entities are regulated little, if at all. Many MEWAs have enabled small employers to obtain cost-effective health coverage, but some MEWAs have not had the financial resources to withstand the risk of medical costs and have failed, leaving the members without insurance or recourse. In some states, MEWAs and METs are no longer legal.

Military suspension: Interruption of insurance coverage while a covered person is in military service.

MIS: Management information system (or service). The common term for the computer hardware and software that provides the support for managing the plan, or a department or group that administers and maintains such computer hardware and software.

Mixed model: A managed care plan that mixes two or more types of delivery system. This has traditionally been used to describe an HMO that has both closed-panel and open-panel delivery systems.

MLP: Midlevel practitioner. Physician's assistants, clinical nurse practitioners, nurse midwives, and the like. Nonphysicians who deliver medical care, generally under the supervision of a physician but for less cost.

Modified risk: Person who cannot meet the normal health requirements of a standard health insurance policy.

Money laundering statute: A federal statute that prohibits any monetary transaction in excess of $10,000 where the money was obtained from certain specified unlawful activities, including theft of federal funds or mail or wire fraud.

Morbidity: Frequency and severity of sicknesses and accidents in a well-defined class or classes of persons.

Morbidity table: Actuarial statistics showing the expected average frequency and duration of disability, illness, and sometimes accidents.

Mortality: Death rate in a group of people as determined from prior experience.

Mortality table: Exhibit showing the incidence of death in various age groups.

MSO: Management service organization. A form of integrated health delivery system. Sometimes similar to a service bureau, the MSO often actually purchases certain hard assets of a physician's practice and then provides services to that physician at fair market rates. MSOs are usually formed as a means to contract more effectively with managed care organizations, although their simple creation does not guarantee success. *See also* Service bureau.

Multispecialty group: Just what it sounds like; a medical group made up of different specialty physicians. May or may not include primary care.

NAHMOR: National Association of HMO Regulators.

National Association of Insurance Commissioners (NAIC): National organization of state officials charged with regulating insurance. It has no official power but wields tremendous influence. The association was formed to promote national uniformity in insurance regulations.

National Center for Health Statistics: The component of the U.S. Public Health Service that collects and maintains statistics on various aspects of public health.

National Practitioner Databank: Database maintained by the federal government that contains information about physicians and other medical practitioners against whom medical malpractice claims have been settled or other disciplinary actions have been taken.

NCQA: National Committee on Quality Assurance. A not-for-profit organization that performs quality-oriented accreditation reviews of HMOs and similar types of managed care plan. The NCQA also accredits CVOs and produces HEDIS (Health Plan Employer and Data Information Set) standards.

NDC: National drug code. The national classification system for identifying prescription drugs.

Negligence: An unintentional, but legally blameworthy, tort.

Net revenue: For a hospital, total revenue less deductions for bad debts, charity, and contractual adjustments. Net revenue is the amount of money actually received by the hospital resulting from charges for services provided.

Network-based programs: Insurer arrangements with health care providers (such as HMOs, PPOs, and point-of-service programs) under contracts to provide services aimed at managing health care costs.

Network model HMO: A health plan that contracts with multiple physician groups to deliver health care to members. Generally limited to large single-specialty or multispecialty groups. Distinguished from group-model plans that contract with a single medical group. IPAs that contract through an intermediary, and direct contract-model plans that contract with individual physicians in the community.

Newborns' and Mothers' Health Protection Act (NMHPA): Federal statute mandating that coverage for hospital stays for childbirth cannot generally be less than forty-eight hours for normal deliveries or ninety-six hours for cesarean births.

Nonpar: Short for nonparticipating. Refers to a provider that does not have a contract with the health plan.

Nonprofit insurers: Corporations organized under special state laws to provide medical benefits on a not-for-profit basis (for example, Blue Cross Blue Shield, dental service corporations).

OBRA: Omnibus Budget Reconciliation Act. What Congress calls the many annual tax and budget reconciliation acts. Most of these acts contain language important to managed care, generally in the Medicare market segment.

Occupancy rate: Measure of inpatient health facility use, determined by dividing available bed days by patient days. It measures the average percentage of occupied beds in a hospital, either for the entire institution or for one department or service.

Occupational rate: Variation in premium based upon occupational class, due to differences among occupations in the incidence of accidents or illness.

Occupational schedule: Method of insurance listing under which persons are insured for an amount based on their job classifications.

Office of Audit: The branch of the Office of Inspector General that performs audits of large health care entities to ensure that they are filing accurate cost reports. The Office of Audit also identifies specific areas of waste or abuse in HCFA's administration of these programs.

Office of Evaluations and Inspections: The branch of the OIG that analyzes particular reimbursement or systems issues and produces reports on various topics.

Office of Inspector General (OIG): Every federal agency has an Inspector General, who is responsible for ferreting out waste, fraud, and abuse in that agency's programs. The HHS OIG is responsible for enforcing most fraud and abuse civil penalties and programs exclusions. The OIG's office is divided into three sections: (1) the Office of Audit, (2) the Office of Evaluations and Inspections, and (3) the Office of Investigations. The Office of Personnel Management's OIG oversees the FEHB program. The Defense Contracting Investigative Service located in the Department of Defense oversees the CHAMPUS program. Finally, the Railroad Retirement Board's OIG oversees the Medicare program for railroad retirees.

Office of Investigations: The branch of the OIG responsible for investigating health care fraud and abuse cases.

OIG subpoena: One of the primary ways that investigators and prosecutors obtain information in health care fraud and abuse cases. The OIG subpoena power permits the OIG to compel only documentary information and not testimonial information. The OIG subpoena may request documents for use in criminal, civil, or administrative investigations. The OIG may also serve a subpoena on parties that have no immediate connection with the HHS. *See also* Civil investigative demand.

OMC: Office of Managed Care. The latest name for the federal agency that oversees federal qualification and compliance for HMOs and eligibility for CMPs. Old names were HMOS (Health Maintenance Organization Service), OPHC (Office of Prepaid Health Care), and OPHCOO (Office of Prepaid Health Care Operations and Oversight). Once part of the Public Health Service, the OMC and most of its predecessors are now part of the HCFA. This agency could be reorganized yet again as this book is being written, so heaven only knows what its new acronym will be.

Onset of condition: Date an illness or disease first manifested itself—generally when medical treatment and advice were first sought or when symptoms were such that an ordinarily prudent person would seek diagnosis, care, or treatment.

Open enrollment period: The period when an employee may change health plans; usually occurs once per year. A general rule is that most managed care plans will have around half their membership up for open enrollment in the fall for an effective date of January 1. A special form of open enrollment is still law in some states. This yearly open enrollment requires an HMO to accept any individual applicant (that is, one not coming in through an employer group) for coverage, regardless of health status. Such special open enrollments usually occur for one month each year. Many Blue Cross and Blue Shield plans have similar open enrollments for indemnity products.

Open-panel HMO: A managed care plan that contracts (either directly or indirectly) with private physicians to deliver care in their own offices. Examples include direct-contract HMOs and IPAs.

Operating a continuing criminal enterprise: A federal statute that is applicable in the health care fraud area where physicians or pharmacists are involved in repeated drug violations involving numerous people.

Operation Restore Trust: A two-year health care fraud demonstration project instituted by the OIG on May 3, 1995, targeting nursing home, home health, and DME providers in California, Florida, Illinois, New York, and Texas. Under this program, the OIG issued four to eight Special Fraud Alerts in the first six months to let the public know about health care fraud schemes, established a new fraud and waste report hotline, and created a voluntary disclosure program for providers targeted by the initiative.

OPL: Other party liability. *See* COB.

OPM: Office of Personnel Management. The federal agency that administers FEHBP. This is the agency with which a managed care plan contracts to provide coverage for federal employees.

Original source: In *qui tam* actions, the term refers to an individual who has direct and independent knowledge of the information on which the allegations are based and has voluntarily provided the information to the government before filing an action.

Outlier: Something that is well outside an expected range. May refer to a provider who is using medical resources at a much higher rate than his or her peers, or to a case in a hospital that is far more expensive than anticipated.

Out-of-pocket expense: Those medical expenses that an insured must pay that are not covered under the insurance contract.

Outstationing: Placing trained individuals at sites other than the county welfare department to assist individuals in applying for Medicaid.

Overhead expense insurance: Form of health insurance for business owners designed to help offset continuing business expenses during an insured's total disability.

OWA: Other weird arrangement. A general acronym that applies to any novel and bizarre managed care plan that has thought up a new twist.

Pacific Business Group on Health (PBGH): A nonprofit organization of large health care purchasers in California and Arizona created in 1989 to improve the quality of health care and address rising costs. One of its projects is the California Collaborative Healthcare Reporting Initiative, which represents the collective interests of health plans, purchasers, and provider groups.

Package pricing: Also referred to as bundled pricing. An MCO pays an organization a single fee for all inpatient, outpatient, and professional expenses associated with a procedure, including preadmission and postdischarge care. Common procedures that use this form of pricing include cardiac bypass surgery and transplants.

Par provider: Shorthand term for participating provider (that is, one who has signed an agreement with a plan to provide services). May apply to professional or institutional providers.

PAS norms: The common term for professional activity study results of the Commission on Professional and Hospital Activities. Broken out by region; the western region has the lowest average LOS, so that it tends to be used most often to set an estimated LOS. Available as *LOS: Length of Stay by Diagnosis,* published by CPHA Publications, Ann Arbor, Michigan.

Patient Self-Determination Act: Congressional act mandating that all Medicare- and Medicaid-certified provider organizations notify patients of their rights to make decisions concerning medical treatment and the right to formulate advance directives.

Pay and pursue: A term in OPL that refers to a plan paying for a benefit first and then pursuing another source of payment (for example, from another plan). Also referred to as "pay and chase." *See also* Pursue and pay.

PCCM: Primary care case manager. This acronym is used in Medicaid managed care programs and refers to the state designating PCPs as case managers to function as gatekeepers, but reimbursing those PCPs using traditional Medicaid fee-for-service as well as paying them a nominal management fee, such as $2.00–5.00 PMPM.

PCP: Primary care physician. Network physician designated by an employee (and each of his/her dependents) to serve as the employee's entry into the health care system. The PCP often is reimbursed through a different mechanism (such as capitation) than other network providers. This physician sometimes is referred to as the gatekeeper. Generally applies to internists, pediatricians, family physicians, general practitioners, and occasionally to obstetricians/gynecologists.

Peer review: Analysis of a clinician's care by a group of that clinician's professional colleagues.

Peer review organization (PRO): *See* PRO.

Pending claim: Claim that has been reported but on which final action has not been taken.

Per cause deductible: Flat amount that an insured must pay toward the eligible medical expenses resulting from each illness before the insurance company will make any benefit payments.

Percentage participation: *See* Coinsurance.

Per diem reimbursement: Reimbursement of an institution, usually a hospital, based on a set rate per day rather than on charges. Per diem reimbursement can vary by service (for example, medical-surgical, obstetrics, mental health, and intensive care) or be uniform regardless of intensity of services.

PHO: Physician-hospital organization. These are legal (or perhaps informal) organizations that bond hospitals and their attending medical staff. Frequently developed for the purpose of contracting with managed care plans. A PHO may be open to any member of the staff who applies, or it may be closed to staff members who fail to qualify (or who are part of an already overrepresented specialty).

PMG: Primary medical group. A group practice made up of primary care physicians, although some may have obstetrician/gynecologists as well.

PMPM: Per member per month. Specifically applies to a revenue or cost for each enrolled member each month.

PMPY: Per member per year. The same as PMPM, but based on a year.

POD: Pool of doctors. This refers to the plan grouping physicians into units smaller than the entire panel but larger than individual practices. Typical PODs have between ten and thirty physicians. Often used for performance measurement and compensation. The POD is often not a real legal entity but rather a grouping.

Policyholder (also policy owner): The owner of a health insurance policy. In group insurance, the legal entity (employer, union, trustee, creditor) to whom an insurer issues a contract.

Policyholder (self-) administration: Situation whereby a group policyholder maintains all records and assumes responsibility regarding insureds covered under its insurance plan, including preparing the premium statement for each payment date and submitting it with a check to the insurer. The insurance company, in most instances, has the contractual prerogative to audit the policyholder's record.

Portability: Characteristic of an insurance policy that allows an insured to accumulate and transfer insurance benefits from one employer to another, or from an employer to a nongroup or personal policy.

POS: Point-of-service. A plan where members do not have to choose how to receive services until they need them. The most common use of the term applies to a plan that enrolls each member in both an HMO (or HMO-like) system and an indemnity plan. Occasionally referred to as an HMO swingout plan, an out-of-plan benefits rider to an HMO, or a primary care PPO. These plans provide a difference in benefits (for example, 100 percent coverage rather than 70 percent) depending on whether the member chooses to use the plan (including its providers and in compliance with the authorization system) or go outside the plan for services. Dual choice refers to an HMO-like plan with an indemnity plan, and triple choice refers to the addition of a PPO to the dual choice. An archaic but still valid definition applies to a simple PPO where members receive coverage at a greater level if they use preferred providers (albeit without a gatekeeper system) than if they choose not to do so.

PPA: Preferred provider arrangement. Same as a PPO but sometimes used to refer to a somewhat looser type of plan in which the payer (that is, the employer) makes the arrangement rather than the providers. Archaic term.

PPM: Physician practice management company. An organization that manages physicians' practices and in most cases either owns the practices outright or has rights to purchase them in the future. PPMs concentrate only on physicians, not on hospitals, although some PPMs have also branched into joint ventures with hospitals and insurers. Many PPMs are publicly traded.

PPO: Preferred provider organization. A plan that contracts with independent providers at a discount for services. The panel is limited in size and usually has some type of utilization review system associated with it. A PPO may be risk-bearing, as with an insurance company, or nonrisk-bearing, as with a physician-sponsored PPO that markets itself to insurance companies or self-insured companies via an access fee.

PPS: Prospective payment system. A generic term applied to a reimbursement system that pays prospectively rather than on the basis of charges. Generally it is used only to refer to hospital reimbursement and is applied only to DRGs, but it may encompass other methodologies as well.

Practice guidelines: Systematically developed statements to assist practitioner and patient decisions about appropriate health care for specific clinical circumstances.

Precertification: Also known as preadmission certification, preadmission review, and precert. The process of obtaining certification or authorization from the health plan for routine hospital admissions (inpatient or outpatient). Often involves appropriateness review against criteria and assignment of length of stay. Failure to obtain precertification often results in a financial penalty to either the provider or the subscriber.

Preexisting condition: A medical condition for which a member has received treatment during a specified period of time before becoming covered under a health plan. May have an effect on whether treatments for that condition will be covered under certain types of health plan.

Preexisting conditions limitation: Restriction on payments for those charges directly resulting from an accident or illness for which the insured received care or treatment within a specified period of time (for example, three months) prior to the date of insurance.

Preferred provider organization (PPO): Entities that supply networks of health care providers to employer health benefit plans and health insurance carriers. Providers contracting with PPOs typically agree to abide by procedures designed by the PPO to control utilization and cost of health services and to accept the PPO's reimbursement structure and payment levels. PPOs provide incentives for enrollees to use network providers. Individuals may choose a nonparticipating provider and still receive coverage, although they will pay a higher coinsurance or deductible amount.

Primary care: First contact and continuing health care, including basic or initial diagnosis and treatment, health supervision, management of chronic conditions, preventive health services, and appropriate referral.

Primary care physician: *See* PCP.

Private inurement: What happens when a not-for-profit business operates in such a way as to provide more than incidental financial gain to a private individual, for example, if a not-for-profit hospital pays too much money for a physician's practice or fails to charge fair market rates for services provided to a physician. The IRS frowns heavily on this.

PRO: Peer review organization. An independent, private organization generally operating at the state level that reviews medical necessity, as well as quality and cost of care for Medicare and Medicaid programs. PROs conduct reviews primarily in connection with inpatient hospital care. Established under TEFRA.

Procedure coding: Coding services, treatments, and procedures to file an insurance, Medicare, or Medicaid claim for payment.

Professional Standards Review Organization (PSRO): Organization responsible for determining whether care and services provided were medically necessary and meet professional standards regarding eligibility for reimbursement under the Medicare and Medicaid programs.

Profile: Longitudinal or cross-sectional aggregation of medical care data. Patient profiles list all services provided to a particular patient during a specified period of time. Physician, hospital, or population profiles are statistical summaries of the pattern of practice of an individual physician, a specific hospital, or the medical experience of a specific population. Diagnostic profiles are a subcategory of physician, hospital, or population profiles for a specific condition or diagnosis.

Prognosis: Forecast or prediction of the probable course of a disease or injury.

Prospective payment system (PPS): A reimbursement system that pays a predetermined rate, rather than paying an amount that is determined retrospectively based on incurred charges. Prior to 1983, Medicare reimbursed most hospitals for the "reasonable costs" of inpatient services provided to Medicare patients. Beginning in 1983, Medicare began phasing in a PPS designed to reimburse general acute care hospitals for inpatient operating costs provided to Medicare patients.

Prospective rating: Method of renewal rating that adjusts the rates for the coming policy year in accordance with such factors as known credible past experience, insurance industry and insurance company trends, general business trends (inflation, deflation), current manual rates, and so forth.

Prospective review: Reviewing the need for medical care before the care is rendered. *See also* Precertification.

Provider discounts: Element of network-based managed care programs whereby financial arrangements are negotiated with providers to reduce fees for medical services rendered.

PSA: Professional services agreement. A contract between a physician or medical group and an IDS or MCO for provision of medical services.

PSN: Provider-sponsored network; occasionally the acronym stands for provider-service network. Also referred to as a PSO (provider-sponsored organization). A network developed by providers, whether as a vertically integrated IDS with both physicians and hospitals or as a physician-only network. Formed for the purpose of direct contracting with employers and government agencies. A PSN may even end up being an HMO, but its origins are with sponsoring providers rather than nonproviders.

PSO: *See* PSN.

PTMPY: Per thousand members per year. A common way of reporting utilization. The most common example is hospital utilization, expressed as days per thousand members per year.

Pursue and pay: A term used in OPL that refers to a plan not paying for a benefit until alternate sources of payment (for example, another plan) have been pursued. Also referred to as "chase and pay." *See also* Pay and pursue.

QA or QM: Quality assurance (older term) or quality management (newer term).

Quality Assurance Reform Initiative (QARI): This program, created by HCFA in 1991 to improve oversight of Medicaid managed care, has developed a uniform set of guidelines for a comprehensive, state-based system for ensuring and improving quality of care.

***Qui tam* action:** Abbreviation of the Latin phrase "*qui tam pro domino rege quam pro si ipso in hac parte sequitur,*" which means, "He who brings the action for the King as well as for himself." *Qui tam* provisions of a statute allow a private person to bring a civil action on behalf of both the United States and himself or herself and to share in part of the monetary recovery. The individual bringing the *qui tam* action can receive 15–25 percent of whatever is recovered from the lawsuit, with the remainder going to the government.

***Qui tam* relator:** The private person who may bring a lawsuit on behalf of the U.S. government as well as himself or herself based on his or her knowledge of wrongdoing. A relator is often a current or former employee, or an employee of a competitor or subcontractor of the organization accused of wrongdoing.

Racketeer Influenced and Corrupt Organization Act (RICO): A federal statute that prohibits the receipt of any income from a pattern of racketeering activity. To prove a RICO case, the government must show that the activity has an effect on interstate commerce, association of the defendant with the enterprise and participation in its activities, and commission of a predicate act (for example, mail or wire fraud) at least twice within ten years.

Rate: The amount of money that a group or individual must pay to the health plan for coverage. Usually a monthly fee.

Rating: Determining the cost of a given unit of insurance for a given year.

Reasonable and customary charges (R and C): Amounts charged by health care providers that are consistent with charges from similar providers for identical or similar services in a given locale.

Reinsurance: Insurance purchased by a health plan to protect it against extremely high-cost cases. *See also* Stop-loss insurance.

Relative value study (RVS): Guide (not a fee schedule) that attempts to show in a general way by a unit or point designation the relationship among the time, competency, experience, severity, and other factors required to perform services under usual conditions. Such a study becomes a schedule when dollar conversion factors are applied.

Renewal rating: Insurer's review of the premium rates and claim experience for a group plan from which the necessity of rate changes is determined.

Renewal underwriting: Review of the financial experience of a group case and establishment of the renewal premium rates and terms under which the insurance may be continued.

Rescission: Voiding of an insurance contract from its date of issue by the insurer because of material misrepresentation on the application for insurance. The act of rescission must take place within the contestable period or time limit on certain defenses. The policy is treated as never having been issued, and the sum of all premiums paid plus interest, less any claims paid, is refunded.

Reserves: The amount of money that a health plan puts aside to cover health care costs. May apply to anticipated costs, such as IBNRs, or to money that the plan does not expect to have to use to pay for current medical claims but keeps as a cushion against future adverse health care costs.

Resource-based relative value scale (RBRVS): A fee schedule that uses a complex formula to determine the payment due a physician for patient services. Factors that are considered in determining the payment due include the resources used, practice expenses, malpractice expenses, geographic location, and whether the services were outpatient or inpatient. Medicare began phasing in this PPS in 1992. The practical effect has been to diminish reimbursement for procedures such as cardiac surgery and raise reimbursement for primary care office visits.

Responsible-corporate-officer doctrine: A doctrine holding that an officer, even without criminal intent or actual knowledge of an offense, can be convicted for the criminal acts of lower-level company employees merely because of his or her responsible share in overseeing the company's business activities and failure to correct or prevent the criminal violations.

Retrospective rating: Method of experience rating that adjusts the final premium of a risk in accordance with the experience of that risk during the term of the policy for which the premium is paid.

Retrospective reimbursement: Method of payment to providers by a third party after costs or charges have actually been incurred by insureds.

Retrospective review: Reviewing health care costs after the care has been rendered. There are several forms of retrospective review. One looks at individual claims for medical necessity, billing errors, or fraud. Another form looks at patterns of costs rather than individual cases.

Risk contract: Also known as a Medicare risk contract. A contract between an HMO or CMP and the HCFA to provide services to Medicare beneficiaries under which the health plan receives a fixed monthly payment for enrolled Medicare members and then must provide all services on an at-risk basis.

Risk management: Management activities aimed at lowering an organization's legal and financial exposures, especially to lawsuits.

Risk pools: Method operating in some states through which persons who can afford private health insurance but who are uninsurable for medical reasons can obtain access to health insurance.

Safe harbor: Regulatory or statutory provisions that shield certain designated payment arrangements from criminal prosecution or program exclusion. Safe harbor provisions are contained in the Stark Laws and the antikickback statute.

Schedule H: Accident and Health Exhibit of an insurer's annual statement. Its purpose is to show the profitability of various categories of health insurance business.

SCP: Specialty care physician. A physician who is not a PCP.

Second opinion: An opinion obtained from a physician regarding the necessity for a treatment that has been recommended by another physician. May be required by some health plans for certain high-costs cases, such as cardiac surgery.

Section 1931(b): A new category of Medicaid coverage created by the federal welfare reform legislation in 1996. Section 1931(b) was designed to ensure that the states did not decrease families' access to Medicaid when the historical link between Medicaid and cash assistance programs was severed.

Self-insured or self-funded plan: A health plan where the risk for medical cost is assumed by the company rather than an insurance company or managed care plan. Under ERISA, self-funded plans are exempt from state laws and regulations, such as premium taxes and mandatory benefits. Self-funded plans often contract with insurance companies or third-party administrators to administer the benefits. *See also* ASO.

Sentinel effect: The phenomenon that when it is known that behavior is being observed, the particular behavior changes, often in the direction the observer is looking for. Applies to the fact that utilization management systems and profiling systems often lead to reduction in utilization before much intervention even takes place, simply because the providers know that someone is watching.

Service area: The geographic area in which an HMO provides access to primary care. The service area is usually specifically designated by the regulators (state or federal), and the HMO is prohibited from marketing outside the service area. May be defined by county or by ZIP code. It is possible for an HMO to have more than one service area and for the service areas to be either contiguous (that is, they actually border each other) or noncontiguous (there is a geographic gap between the service areas).

Service bureau: A weak form of integrated delivery system in which a hospital (or other organization) provides services to a physician's practice in return for a fair market price. May also try to negotiate with managed care plans, but generally is not considered an effective negotiating mechanism.

Service plan: A health insurance plan that has direct contracts with providers but is not necessarily a managed care plan. The archetypes are Blue Cross and Blue Shield plans. The contract applies to direct billing of the plan by providers (rather than billing of the member), a provision for direct payment of the provider (rather than reimbursement of the member), a requirement that the provider accept the plan's determination of UCR and not balance-bill the member in excess of that amount, and a range of other terms. May or may not address issues of utilization and quality.

Shadow pricing: The practice of setting premium rates at a level just below the competition's, whether or not those rates can be justified. In other words, the premium rates could actually be lower, but to maximize profit the rates are raised to a level that will remain attractive but result in greater revenue. This practice is generally considered unethical and, in the case of community rating, possibly illegal.

SHMO: Social health maintenance organization. An HMO that goes beyond the medical care needs of its membership to include their social needs as well. A relatively rare form of HMO.

Shoe box effect: When an indemnity-type benefit plan has a deductible, there may be beneficiaries who save up their receipts to file for reimbursement at a later time (that is, they save them in a shoe box). It is likely the receipts get lost or the beneficiary never sends them in, so the insurance company never has to pay.

Shortfall: Difference between the cost for a service charged by a hospital and the actual portion of such charges a hospital will receive as payment from a payor.

Sickness insurance: Form of health insurance providing benefits only for loss resulting from illness or disease, but excluding loss resulting from accident or injury.

Single point of entry: A relatively new term that means an individual uses the same system to access both group health medical benefits and benefits for work-related medical conditions.

Skilled nursing facility (SNF): Institution providing the step in progressive care during which a patient receives the degree of medical care required from, or under the supervision of, registered nursing personnel or a physician.

Skilled nursing facility (SNF): An institution that has a transfer agreement with one or more Medicare participating hospitals, is primarily engaged in providing skilled nursing care and rehabilitative services to inpatients, and meets specific regulatory certification requirements.

SMG: Specialty medical group. A medical group made up predominantly of specialty physicians. May be a single-specialty group or a multispecialty group.

Social Security Act: Federal law under which the federal government operates the Old Age, Survivors, Disability, and Health Insurance Program (OASDHI). Includes Medicare and Medicaid.

Specialty network manager: A term used to describe a single specialist (or perhaps a specialist organization) that accepts capitation to manage a single specialty. Specialty services are supplied by many specialty physicians, but the network manager has the responsibility for managing access and cost and is at economic risk. A relatively uncommon model as this book is being written.

Spending down: Gradual depletion of one's assets until indigent, thus qualifying for Medicaid benefits. Usually associated with nursing home or long-term care.

Staff-model HMO: An HMO that employs providers directly; those providers see members in the HMO's own facilities. A form of closed-panel HMO. A different use of this term is sometimes applied to vertically integrated health care delivery systems that employ physicians but in which the system is not licensed as an HMO.

Standard provisions: Policy provisions setting forth certain rights and obligations of insureds and insurers under health insurance policies. Originally introduced in 1912, these provisions were replaced by the Uniform Policy Provisions Law (UPPL).

Standards of quality: Authoritative statements of (1) minimum levels of acceptable performance or results, (2) excellent levels of performance or results, or (3) the range of acceptable performance or results.

Stark I: Colloquial name for the physician self-referral prohibitions introduced to Congress in 1988 by California representative Fortney "Pete" Stark. The initial Stark Law became effective Jan. 1, 1992, and provides that a physician or an immediate family member who has a financial relationship with an entity may not refer a Medicare patient to that entity for clinical laboratory services, unless an applicable exception exists. In addition, the law prevents an entity with which a physician has a financial relationship from billing Medicare or a beneficiary for clinical laboratory services furnished pursuant to a prohibited referral.

Stark II: The 1993 amendments to Stark I that extend the physician self-referral restrictions to Medicaid services and beneficiaries and expand the referral and billing prohibitions to ten additional designated health services reimbursable by Medicare or Medicaid: (1) physical therapy; (2) occupational therapy; (3) radiology services, including magnetic resonance imaging, computerized axial tomography scans, and ultrasound services; (4) radiation therapy services and supplies; (5) DME and supplies; (6) parenteral and enteral nutrients, equipment, and supplies; (7) prosthetics, orthotics, and prosthetic devices; (8) home health services and supplies; (9) outpatient prescription drugs; and (10) inpatient and outpatient hospital services. Stark II became effective on Jan. 1, 1995. The statute contains many exceptions, which can be grouped into categories applicable to all financial relationships, to ownership and investment interests, and to compensation arrangements.

Statistical claim: Another term for an encounter whereby data are entered by an MCO's claims department but no FFS payment is made. Occurs in a capitated environment.

Statute: A law enacted by an elected legislature. Compare *Common law.*

Step-rate premium: Rating structure in which the premiums increase periodically at predetermined times, such as policy years or attained ages.

Stockholder derivative lawsuits: An action brought by a stockholder on behalf of a corporation because the corporation was caused to suffer damage but refuses to redress the act causing the damage.

Stop-loss insurance: A form of reinsurance that provides protection for medical expenses above a certain limit, generally year by year. This may apply to an entire health plan or to any single component. For example, the health plan may have stop-loss reinsurance for cases that exceed $100,000. After a case hits $100,000, the plan receives 80 percent of expenses in excess of $100,000 back from the reinsurance company for the rest of the year. Another example would be the plan providing a stop-loss to participating physicians for referral expenses greater than $2,500. When a case exceeds that amount in a single year, the plan no longer deducts those costs from the physician's referral pool for the remainder of the year.

Subacute care facility: A health facility that is a step down from an acute care hospital. May be a nursing home or a facility that provides medical care but not surgical or emergency care.

Subrogation: The contractual right of a health plan to recover payments made to a member for health care costs after that member has received such payment for damages in a legal action.

Subscriber: The individual or member who has health plan coverage by virtue of being eligible on his or her own behalf rather than as a dependent.

Supplemental medical insurance: Another term for Medicare Part B coverage.

Supplemental Security Income: SSI is a cash payment designed to increase the monthly income of the elderly and disabled to a minimum amount deemed necessary to live. The federal government sets a minimum amount for SSI payments, and each state may choose to increase this limit based on cost-of-living adjustments.

Surplus: Amount by which the value of an insurer's assets exceeds its liabilities.

TANF: Temporary Assistance to Needy Families. The federal welfare program formerly known as AFDC that provides cash benefits to low-income families. The specific name of the program varies from state to state. CalWORKs is the name of California's TANF program.

TAT: Turnaround time. The amount of time it takes a health plan to process and pay a claim from the time it arrives.

TEFRA: Tax Equity and Fiscal Responsibility Act. One key provision of this act prohibits employers and health plans from requiring full-time employees between the ages of sixty-five and sixty-nine to use Medicare rather than the group health plan. Another key provision codifies Medicare risk contracts for HMOs and CMPs.

Ten-day free look: Right of the insured to examine a policy for ten days and return it for a refund of premium if not satisfied with it. A notice of this right is required to appear on the first page of health insurance policies.

Termination date: The day that health plan coverage is no longer in effect.

Third-party administration (or administrator; TPA): Method by which an outside person or firm, not a party to a contract, maintains all records regarding the persons covered under the insurance plan. Entity also may pay claims using the draft book system.

Third-party payer: Any organization, public or private, that pays or insures health or medical expenses on behalf of beneficiaries or recipients, such as Blue Cross and Blue Shield, commercial insurance companies, Medicare, and Medicaid. A person generally pays a premium for coverage in all such private (and in some public) programs. The organization then pays bills on the insured's behalf. These payments, called third-party payments, are distinguished by the separation between the individual receiving the service (the first party), the individual or institution providing it (the second party), and the organization paying for it (the third party).

Time-loss management: Application of managed care techniques to workers compensation treatments for injuries or illnesses to reduce the amount of time on the job that the affected employee loses.

Tort: A civil wrong, leading to imposition of liability, based on violation of an obligation other than a breach of contract.

Total capitation: The term used when an organization receives capitation for all medical services, including institutional and professional. The more common term is global capitation.

TPA: Third-party administrator. A firm that performs administrative functions (for example, claims processing, membership, and the like) for a self-funded plan or a start-up managed care plan. *See also* ASO.

TPL: Third-party liability. Also called OPL. *See* COB.

Triage: In health plans, this refers to the process of sorting out requests for services by members into those who need to be seen right away, those who can wait a little while, and those whose problems can be handled with advice over the phone.

TRICARE: A health care plan, available to more than six million military personnel and their families, which is administered by private contractors.

Triple option: One carrier's offering an HMO, a PPO, and a traditional insurance plan.

Twenty-four-hour care: An ill-defined term that essentially means that health care is provided twenty-four hours per day regardless of the financing mechanism. Applies primarily to the convergence of group health, workers compensation, and industrial health all under managed care.

Twisting: An agent or broker inducing a policyholder to drop an existing policy in order to take a similar policy from him or her.

UB-92: The common claim form used by hospitals to bill for services. Some managed care plans demand greater detail than is available on the UB-92, requiring hospitals to send additional itemized bills.

UCR: Usual, customary, or reasonable. A method of profiling prevailing fees in an area and reimbursing providers on the basis of that profile. One common technology is to average all fees and choose the 80th or 90th percentile, although a plan may use other technologies to determine what is reasonable. Sometimes this term is used synonymously with a fee allowance schedule when the schedule is set relatively high.

Unbundling: The practice of a provider billing for multiple components of service that were previously included in a single fee. For example, if dressings and instruments were included in a fee for a minor procedure, the fee for the procedure remains the same, but there are now additional charges for the dressings and instruments.

Uncompensated care: Health care rendered by providers to persons unable to pay and not covered by private or governmental health insurance plans.

Underwriting: In one definition, this refers to bearing the risk for something (for example, a policy is underwritten by an insurance company). In another definition, it refers to analysis of a group done to determine rates and benefits or to determine whether the group should be offered coverage at all. A related definition refers to screening the health of each individual applicant for insurance and refusing to provide coverage for preexisting conditions.

Underwriting profit: Insurer's profit from its insurance operations as distinguished from its investment earnings.

Unfair Trade Practices Act (NAIC Model): NAIC regulatory model that sets certain standards for prompt and efficient handling of claims. Used by many states as the basis for similar legislation.

Uniform Policy Provisions Law (UPPL): Statutory policy provisions of health insurance policies that specify some of the rights and obligations of the insured and the insurer. These provisions, with some modifications, are part of the insurance laws of all fifty states and the District of Columbia.

Uninsurables: High-risk persons who do not have health care coverage through private insurance and who fall outside the parameters of risks covered as a result of standard health underwriting practices.

Upcoding: Using improper billing codes to charge Medicare or Medicaid for an item or service to receive higher payments than would ordinarily be due for treatment of a patient.

URAC: Utilization Review Accreditation Commission. A not-for-profit organization that performs reviews of external utilization review agencies (freestanding companies, utilization management departments of insurance companies, or utilization management departments of managed care plans). Its sole focus is managed indemnity plans and PPOs, not HMOs or similar types. States often require certification by URAC for a utilization management organization to operate.

URO: Utilization review organization. A freestanding organization that does nothing but utilization review, usually remotely using the telephone and paper correspondence. It may be independent or part of another company, such as an insurance company that sells utilization review services on a stand-alone basis.

Utilization: Patterns of usage for a single medical service or type of service (hospital care, prescription drugs, physician visits). Measurement of utilization of all medical services in combination usually is done in terms of dollar expenditures. Use is expressed in rates per unit of population at risk for a given period, such as number of annual admissions to a hospital per thousand persons over age sixty-five.

Utilization review: Program designed to reduce unnecessary hospital admissions and to control the length of stay for inpatients through using preliminary evaluations, concurrent inpatient evaluations, or discharge preplanning.

Variable deductible: Deductible amount applied to a particular sickness or injury that is the greater of either the minimum deductible stated in the policy or an amount equal to all benefit payments received from any other medical expense coverage for the same eligible expenses.

Volume discount: Premium rate reduction application to new group case coverages that is based on total case premium (for specific coverages) or total premium and premium per certificate (employee).

Volume loading: Premium rate increase applicable to new group case coverages that is based on the total case premium (for specified coverages) or total premium and premium per certificate (employee).

Voluntary disclosure program: A component of the OIG's Operation Restore Trust, which provides DME suppliers, nursing facilities, or home health companies located in California, Florida, Illinois, New York, and Texas with the opportunity to self-disclose any potentially fraudulent acts. Self-disclosure may reduce the possibility that the OIG will subject the corporation to a complete audit and investigation or bring an exclusion action against the provider. In addition, the corporation might be liable for a lower amount of fines and penalties thanks to its cooperation with the government.

Waiver: An exception to the usual requirements of Medicaid granted to a state by HCFA, authorized through the following sections of the Social Security Act:

- 1915(a) Allows states to waive provisions of the Medicaid law to test new concepts that are congruent with the goals of the Medicaid Program. Radical, systemwide changes are possible under this provision.
- 1915(b) Allows states to waive freedom of choice. States may require that beneficiaries enroll in HMOs or other managed care programs, or select a physician to serve as their primary care case manager.
- 1915(c) Allows states to waive various Medicaid requirements to establish alternative, community-based services for individuals with developmental disabilities who quality for services in a nursing home, institution for mental disease, or inpatient hospital.
- 1929 Allows states to provide a broad range of home and community care to functionally disabled individuals as an optional state plan benefit.

Well-baby care: Those medical services, physician visits, and immunizations that are recommended by the American Pediatric Association as appropriate and routine care for a normal child from birth to one year of age.

Wellness programs: Employer programs provided to employees to lessen health risks and thus avoid more serious health problems.

Whistle-blower: An employee who reports the illegal or wrongful actions of his or her coworkers.

Wholesale HMO: A term occasionally used when a licensed HMO does not market itself directly, but rather contracts with another licensed HMO and accepts capitation in return. This most commonly occurs when an IDS wants to accept global capitation from an HMO and in turn capitate other providers, since many states will only allow an HMO to capitate providers. Therefore, the IDS obtains an HMO license but does not go directly to market to the public, and thus does not disrupt existing relationships with other MCOs.

Wire fraud statute: A federal statute that prohibits use of wire, radio, or television communication in interstate or foreign commerce for the purpose of executing a scheme to defraud.

Workers compensation: A form of social insurance provided through property-casualty insurers. Workers compensation provides medical benefits and replacement of lost wages that result from injuries or illnesses that arise from the workplace; in turn, the employee cannot normally sue the employer unless true negligence exists. Workers compensation has undergone dramatic increases in cost as group health has shifted into managed care, resulting in workers compensation carriers adopting managed care approaches. Workers compensation is often heavily regulated under state laws that are significantly different from those used for group health insurance and is often the subject of intense negotiation between management and organized labor.

Wraparound plan: Commonly used to refer to insurance or health plan coverage for copays and deductibles that are not covered under a member's base plan. This is often used for Medicare.

Zero down: The practice of a medical group or provider system distributing all the capital surplus in a health plan or group to the members of the group rather than retaining any capital or reinvesting it in the group or plan.

Appendix G

Relevant Federal Agencies

Agency for Health Care Policy and Research (AHCPR)
(Health and Human Services Department)

Formed in December 1989 by combining two predecessor agencies, this organization is a component of the Public Health Service. The purpose of the AHCPR is to increase access to health care; to improve the way health services are organized, delivered, and financed; and to enhance quality and effectiveness of health care services, which begins with defining and measuring quality. AHCPR produces clinical practice guidelines for important diseases or conditions. The guidelines describe provider and organizational practice deemed most likely to be associated with good health outcomes; guidelines and other studies make up what is also known as medical effectiveness research.

John M. Eisenberg
2101 East Jefferson St., #600
Rockville, MD 20852
301-594-6662
www.ahcpr.gov

Centers for Disease Control and Prevention
(Health and Human Services Department)

Surveys national disease trends and epidemics and environmental health problems; administers block grants to states for preventive health services; promotes national health education program; administers foreign quarantine program and occupational safety and health programs; assists state and local health departments and programs with control of sexually transmitted diseases, treatment of tuberculosis, childhood immunization, and health promotion regarding chronic diseases and injury. Headquarters:

1600 Clifton Rd. NE
Atlanta, GA 30333
404-639-3534

Washington office:

Donald E. Shriber, Associate Director
200 Independence Ave. SW
Washington, DC 20201
202-690-8598
www.cdc.gov

Department of Defense (DOD)

The Defense Department includes the U.S. Army, Navy, and Air Force. The department maintains a health services delivery system for eight million actual or potential beneficiaries, including children and other dependents of active duty members of the services, as well as retirees and their dependents.

Department of Labor (DOL)

The DOL administers a variety of federal labor laws created to address employees' rights to safe and healthful working conditions, a minimum hourly wage and overtime pay, freedom from employment discrimination, unemployment insurance, and workers compensation. DOL also addresses employee pension issues, administers job training programs, and manages issues related to collective bargaining.

Disease Prevention and Health Promotion
(Health and Human Services Department)

Develops national policies for disease prevention, clinical preventive services, and health promotion; coordinates health promotion; assists the private sector and agencies with disease prevention, clinical preventive services, and health promotion activities.

Dr. Claude Earl Fox, Deputy Assistant Secretary for Health
200 Independence Ave. SW, #738G
Washington, DC 20201
202-401-6295
800-336-4797
odphp.osophs.dhhs.gov.

Division of Nursing

The Division of Nursing administers the Nurse Education Act (NEA), which in turn administers training support for nursing schools, programs, and projects, as well as some direct nursing student support. The division's structure corresponds with sections of the NEA, professional nurse traineeships, scholarships for disadvantaged students, advanced nurse training, nurse anesthetist programs and student support, special projects, and others.

Drug Enforcement Administration (DEA)

The Drug Enforcement Administration coordinates the drug enforcement activities of other federal agencies and works with them to control the supply of illicit drugs.

Environmental Protection Agency

EPA's purpose is to ensure that all Americans are protected from significant risks to human health and to provide accurate information sufficient to effectively participate in managing human health and environmental risks.

401 M Street SW
Washington, D.C. 20460-0003
(202) 260-2675
www.epa.gov

Food and Drug Administration (FDA)
(Health and Human Services Department)

The focus of the Food and Drug Administration, a Public Health Service agency, is to ensure the safety and effectiveness of consumer goods sold in the United States. This includes the safety, purity, and nutritive value of foods; the safety of drugs, biologics, and vaccines; and the safety of cosmetics and radiological products. In addition, FDA enforces labeling laws to ensure information useful to the public. (See Figure G.1.)

Michael Friedman, Acting Commissioner
5600 Fishers Lane
Rockville, MD 20857
301-827-2410
301-443-3170 (information)
301-443-3285 (press)
www.fda.gov

General Accounting Office (GAO)
(Health, Education, and Human Services)

The General Accounting Office is the investigative arm of Congress and is charged with examining all matters relating to use of public funds. GAO performs significant research on health and human services issues as well as the performance of federal agencies.

Richard L. Hembra, Assistant Comptroller General
1 Massachusetts Ave. NW, #550
P.O. Box 37050
Washington, DC 20013
202-512-6000

Health Care Financing Administration (HCFA)

The Health Care Financing Administration administers Medicare and federal participation in state Medicaid programs. It was established to combine health financing and quality assurance programs within a single agency. It is responsible for policies regarding payment, reimbursement, and benefits. HCFA's Office of Research and Demonstrations directs a large number of projects that examine the impact of federal programs on beneficiary health status, access, utilization, and out-of-pocket expenditures. This office also funds, manages, and evaluates pilot programs that test new ways of delivering and financing Medicare and Medicaid services. HCFA establishes and enforces quality of care regulations for hospitals and other institutions and providers, ensures state compliance with federal requirements for the Medicaid program, and grants waivers to the states to exempt them from those requirements when appropriate.

202-727-0735
410-966-6674 (research office)
410-597-3855 (Office of Statistics and Data Management)
www.hcfa.gov

Health Resources and Services Administration (HRSA)
(Health and Human Services Department)

A federal agency of the Public Health Service within the Department of Health and Human Services (HHS) that is responsible for developing primary health care services and resources; protecting and improving the health of mothers, infants, and children; improving access to care for the medically underserved and those with special needs; and maintaining high-quality health care nationally. The HRSA has five major operating components: Office of the Administrator; Bureau of Health Professions, which administers the National Practitioner Data Bank (NPDB); Bureau of Health Resources Development; Bureau of Primary Health Care; Maternal and Child Health Bureau.

Dr. Ciro V. Sumaya, Administrator
5600 Fishers Lane, #1405
Rockville, MD 20857
301-443-2216
301-443-3376 (information)
301-443-2086 (press)

Health Resources and Services Administration Rural Health Policy
(Health and Human Services Department)

Works with federal agencies, states, and the private sector to develop solutions to health care problems in rural communities. Administers grants to rural communities and supports rural health services research. Studies the effects of Medicare and Medicaid programs on rural access to health care. Oversees the joint working group on telemedicine. Provides the National Advisory Committee on Rural Health with staff support.

Dena Puskin, Acting Director
5600 Fishers Lane, #905
Rockville, MD 20857
301-443-0835
www.nal.usda.gov/ric/richs/orhp.htm

Indian Health Service (IHS)

The Indian Health Service provides a comprehensive health services delivery system for Native Americans and Alaska Natives with opportunity for maximum tribal involvement in developing and managing programs to meet their health needs. The IHS goal is to raise the health status of the Native American and Alaska Native people to the highest possible level.

National Center for Health Statistics
(Health and Human Services Department)

Compiles, analyzes, and disseminates national health statistics on population health characteristics, health facilities and human resources, health costs and expenditures, and health hazards.

Edward J. Sondik, Director
6525 Belcrest Rd., #1140
Hyattsville, MD 20782
301-436-7016
301-436-8500 (information)
301-436-7551 (press)
www.cdc.gov/nchswww/nchshome.htm

National Clearinghouse for Primary Care Information
(Health and Human Services Department)

Supports planning, development, and delivery of ambulatory health care to urban and rural areas in need of medical personnel and services; gives information to health care providers, administrators, and other interested persons.

Judy A. Cramer, Project Director
2070 Chain Bridge Rd., #450
Vienna, VA 22182
703-821-8955

National Institute of Nursing Research (NINR)

Originally called the National Center for Nursing Research, the NINR is the federal focal point for nursing research and nursing research training. NINR administers grants to prepare nurse researchers and to support the work of nurse researchers. A strategic process ensures that grant applications are relevant to the health of the nation and to nursing.

National Institutes of Health
(Health and Human Services Department)

Supports and conducts biomedical research into the causes and prevention of disease and furnishes information to health professionals and the public. Comprises seventeen research institutes and seven components: the National Library of Medicine, the Warren Grant Magnuson Clinical Center, the National Center for Research Resources, the John E. Fogarty International Center, the National Center for Human Genome Research, the Division of Research Grants, and the Division of Computer Research and Technology. (See Figure G.2.) All institutes are located in Bethesda except the National Institute of Environmental Health Sciences:

P.O. Box 12233
Research Triangle Park, NC 27709

Harold Varmus, Director
1 Center Dr., Bldg. 1, #126
Bethesda, MD 20892-0148
301-496-2433
301-496-4461 (press)
www.nih.gov

National Library of Medicine
(Health and Human Services Department)

Offers medical library services and computer-based reference service to the public, health professionals, libraries in medical schools and hospitals, and research institutions; operates a toxicology information service for the scientific community, industry, and federal agencies; assists medical libraries through the National Network of Libraries of Medicines with research in medical library science; and assists in improving basic library resources.

Dr. Donald A. B. Lindberg, Director
8600 Rockville Pike
Bethesda, MD 20894
301-496-6221
www.nlm.nih.gov

National Practitioner Data Bank (NPDB)

A repository for certain information related to the professional competence and conduct of physicians, dentists, and other health care practitioners. The NPDB was established by the Health Care Quality Improvement Act of 1986 (HCQIA) to serve as a background reference for health care organizations to check practice records of physicians and practitioners being considered for employment. The HCQIA requires hospitals, health plans, malpractice insurers, state licensing boards, and professional societies to report malpractice claims settlements, licensure sanctions, and restrictions against practice privileges of a practitioner. NPDB information is confidential, and access is restricted to certain eligible entities. NPDB is administered by the Health Resources and Services Administration, a federal agency in the DHHS.

NPDB
P.O. Box 10832
Chantilly, VA 22021
800-767-6732

National Technical Information Service (NTIS)

A division of the U.S. Department of Commerce that maintains the database for the Drug Enforcement Agency (DEA), which monitors legal and disciplinary actions taken against physicians for illegal or inappropriate use of certain drugs. NTIS has been designated a primary source verification (PSV) agency for credentialing and recredentialing by the National Committee for Quality Assurance (NCQA), the leading independent HMO accrediting organization.

NTIS
Springfield, VA 22161
800-553-6847
www.ntis.gov

Office of Health Maintenance Organizations (OHMO)

The former name for the federal agency within the Department of Health and Human Services that oversees federal activity relating to HMOs. OHMO has been reorganized, initially as the Office of Prepaid Health Care (OPHC), and now as the Office of Prepaid Health Care Operations and Oversight (OPHCOO).

Office of Personnel Management (OPM)

The federal agency authorized to offer certain choices of health benefit plan to federal employees. OPM can offer both experience-rated plans and comprehensive community-rated plans (mostly HMOs). OPM does not engage in a competitive-bidding process. Instead, it relies on rates set by other managed care contractors and compares OPM rates with other HMO groups of similar size and benefits. HMOs participating in FEHBP are subject to periodic audit by the OPM, which involves reviews of state and federal rate filings, actual billings to commercial accounts, and rate worksheets used in developing the HMO's premium.

Office of Prepaid Health Care Operations and Oversight (OPHCOO)

A division of the HCFA that is responsible for overseeing federal HMO qualification, CMP eligibility, ongoing HMO and CMP regulation, and employer compliance efforts. OPHCOO also administers Medicare risk contracts, determines the capitation formula and reimbursement policies, and oversees operation of the prepaid health information system. HMO qualification and CMP eligibility review processes are complex and can take six months to a year, or longer. Review areas include legal, financial viability, health services delivery, and marketing. The OPHCOO was once a part of the Public Health Service and was called the Office of Health Maintenance Organizations (OHMO).

OPHCOO
Cohen Building, Room 4406
330 Independence Ave. SW
Washington, DC 20201
202-619-0845

Physician Payment Review Commission (PPRC)

This commission advises Congress on issues related to Medicare reimbursement of health care practitioners. These often include far-reaching proposals such as the resource-based relative value scale (RBRVS), which is affecting higher reimbursement for primary care services provided by advanced practice nurses as a result of its examination of utilization and payment policies.

Planning and Evaluation
(Health and Human Services Department)

Provides policy advice and makes recommendations to the secretary on the full range of department planning, including Medicare, Medicaid, health care services, human resources, health care facilities development and financing, biomedical research, and health care planning.

David Garrison, Acting Assistant Secretary
200 Independence Ave. SW, #415S
Washington, DC 20201
202-690-7858
www.osape.ssw.dhhs.gov

Prospective Payment Assessment Commission (ProPAC)

A government agency established under the Social Security Act Amendments of 1983 to advise Congress and the DHHS on maintaining and updating Medicare payments to hospitals and other provider facilities. Because ProPAC is an appointed advisory body, it has no regulatory or appeals authority. ProPAC's responsibilities include Medicare inpatient and outpatient hospital payment policies, prospective payment policies for skilled nursing facilities and home health services, and payment for services furnished in end-stage renal disease (ESRD) facilities. ProPAC also is required to examine uncompensated care and Medicaid payments and their relationship to the financial condition of hospitals.

ProPAC
300 7th St. SW, Suite 301-B
Washington, DC 20024
202-401-8986

Public Health and Science
(Health and Human Services Department)

Promotes protection and advancement of physical and mental health; establishes national health policy; maintains cooperative international health-related agreements and programs; administers programs to develop health resources and improve delivery of health services; works to prevent and control communicable diseases; conducts and supports research in medicine and related sciences; and provides scientific information. Protects against impure or unsafe foods, drugs, and cosmetics; develops education for the health professions.

Dr. Philip R. Lee, Assistant Secretary for Health
200 Independence Ave. SW, #716G
Washington, DC 20201
202-690-7694
www.osophs.dhhs.gov

U.S. Public Health Service (USPHS)

The mission of the Public Health Service is to protect and advance the nation's health; to support and conduct research; to prevent and control diseases; and to enforce laws that ensure the safety and efficacy of drugs, foods, cosmetics, medical devices, and so on. The chief nurse officer maintains a communication network with all other PHS agencies including FDA, the surgeon general, AHCPR, the Centers for Disease Control and Prevention (CDC), and the National Institutes of Health. Other PHS agencies include IHS, the Substance Abuse and Mental Health Services Administration, the Health Resources and Services Administration, and the Agency for Toxic Substances and Disease Registry.

FIGURE G.1. Food and Drug Administration.

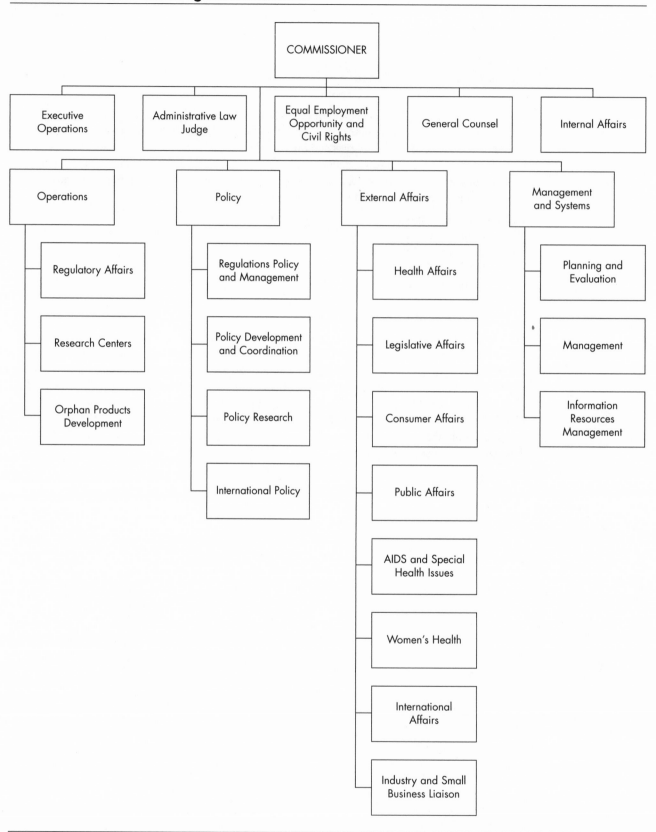

FIGURE G.2. National Institutes of Health.

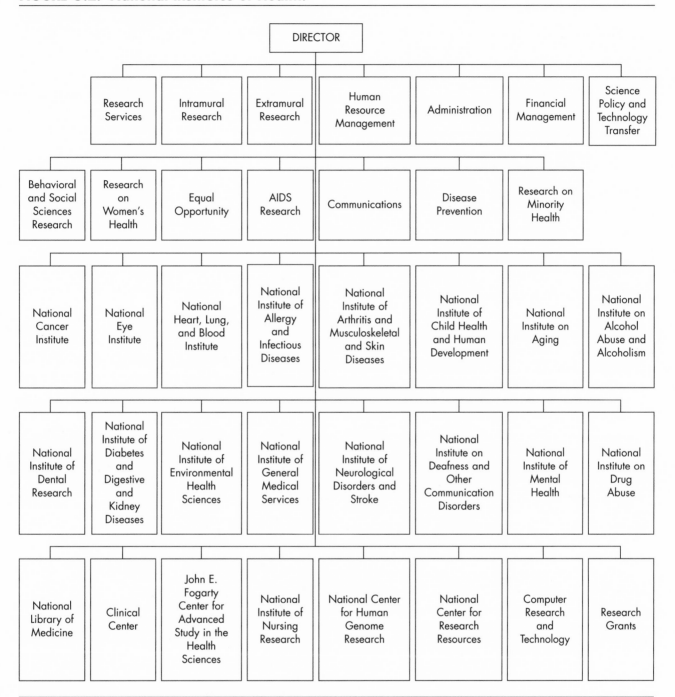

Reprinted with permission from *Washington Information Directory* (1997–1998), p. 387. Copyright © 1997 Congressional Quarterly, Inc.

Appendix H

Selected Nongovernmental Associations

AIDS Action Council

Promotes and monitors legislation on AIDS research and education and on related public policy issues.

1875 Connecticut Ave. NW, #700
Washington, DC 20009
202-986-1300

Alliance for Health Reform

Nonpartisan organization that advocates health care reform, including cost containment and universal coverage. Sponsors conferences and seminars for journalists, business leaders, policy makers, and the public.

1900 L St. NW, #512
Washington, DC 20036
202-466-5626

American Association of Health Plans

Membership: managed health care plans and organizations. Provides legal counsel and conducts educational programs; conducts research and analysis of managed care issues; produces publications; monitors legislation and regulations.

1129 20th St. NW, #600
Washington, DC 20036
202-778-3200
202-778-3245 (press)

American Association of Homes and Services for the Aging

Membership: nonprofit homes, housing, and health-related facilities for the elderly, sponsored by religious, fraternal, labor, private, and governmental organizations. Conducts research on long-term care for the elderly; sponsors institutes and workshops on accreditation, financing, and institutional life; monitors legislation and regulations.

901 E St. NW, #500
Washington, DC 20004
202-783-2242
www.aahsa.org

American Brain Tumor Association

This organization raises awareness of the problem of brain tumors and advocates increased funding of brain tumor research.

2720 River Road
Des Plaines, IL 60018
847-827-9910
www.abta.org

American Cancer Society

The American Cancer Society is a nationwide community-based voluntary health organization dedicated to eliminating cancer as a major health problem by preventing cancer; saving lives; and diminishing suffering from cancer through research, education, advocacy and service.

1599 Clifton Road NE
Atlanta, GA 30329
800-227-2345
www.cancer.org

American Clinical Laboratory Association

Membership: laboratories and laboratory service companies. Advocates laws and regulations that recognize the role of laboratory services in cost-effective health care; works to ensure the confidentiality of patient results; provides education, information, and research materials to members.

1250 H St. NW, #880
Washington, DC 20005
202-637-9466

American College of Health Care Administrators

Membership: administrators of long-term health care organizations and facilities, including home health care programs, hospices, day care centers for the elderly, nursing and hospital facilities, retirement communities, and mental health care centers. Conducts research on statistical characteristics of nursing home and other medical administrators; conducts seminars; offers education courses; provides certification for administrators. Library open to the public by appointment.

325 South Patrick St.
Alexandria, VA 22314-3571
703-549-5822
www.achca.org

American Health Lawyers Association

Membership: corporate, institutional, and government lawyers interested in the health field; law students; and health professionals. Serves as an information clearinghouse on health law; sponsors health law educational programs and seminars. Known until March 1998 as the NHLA/AAHA, a merger of the Washington, D.C.-based National Health Lawyers Association and the Chicago-based American Academy of Health Attorneys.

1120 Connecticut Ave. NW, #600
Washington, DC 20036
202-833-1100
www.healthlawyers.org

American Heart Association

The American Heart Association is a nationwide voluntary health organization dedicated to providing individuals with information on fighting heart disease and stroke.

National Center
7272 Greenville Avenue
Dallas, TX 75231
800-242-8721
www.americanheart.org

American Hospital Association

Membership: hospitals, other inpatient care facilities, outpatient centers, Blue Cross plans, area-wide planning agencies, regional medical programs, hospital schools of nursing, and individuals. Conducts research and education projects in such areas as provision of comprehensive care, hospital economics, hospital facilities and design, and community relations; monitors legislation and regulations; participates with other health care associations in establishing hospital care standards.

325 7th St. NW
Washington, DC 20004
202-638-1100

American Lung Association

This organization fights lung disease through education, community service, advocacy and research.

1740 Broadway
New York, NY 10019
212-315-8700
www.lungusa.org

American Medical Association

Membership: physicians, residents, and medical students. Monitors legislation and regulations on health matters and malpractice insurance; provides information on health care. Headquarters in Chicago.

1101 Vermont Ave. NW, 12th Floor
Washington, DC 20005
202-789-7400
www.ama-assn.org

American Nurses Association

Membership: registered nurses. Sponsors the American Nurses Foundation; monitors legislation and regulations.

600 Maryland Ave. SW, #100W
Washington, DC 20024-2571
202-651-7000

American Public Health Association

Membership: health care professionals, educators, environmentalists, social workers, industrial hygienists, and individuals. Interests include all aspects of health care and education. Establishes standards for scientific procedures in public health; conducts research on the causes and origin of communicable diseases; produces data on the number of women and minority workers in public health and on their health status.

800 I St. NW
Washington, DC 20001-3710
202-777-2742
www.apha.org

American Red Cross

The Red Cross is the nation's largest supplier of blood, plasma, and tissue products in the United States. It works with more than 4.5 million donors and three thousand hospitals through its national network of thirty-eight blood regions. It supplies one-quarter of the nation's tissue for transplantation through its network of fifteen tissue centers nationwide. Its Website is excellent.

11th Floor
1621 North Kent St.
Arlington, VA 22209

703-206-6000
www.redcross.org

Association for Healthcare Philanthropy

Membership: hospital and health care executives who manage fundraising activities.

313 Park Ave., #400
Falls Church, VA 22046
703-532-6243
www.go-ahp.org

Association of State and Territorial Health Officials

Membership: executive officers of state and territorial health departments. Serves as legislative review agency and information source for members.

1275 K St. NW, #800
Washington, DC 20002
202-546-5400
www.astho.org

Blue Cross and Blue Shield Association

Membership: Blue Cross and Blue Shield insurance plans that operate autonomously at the local level. Certifies member plans; acts as consultant to plans in evaluating new medical technologies and contracting with doctors and hospitals; operates a national telecommunications network to collect, analyze, and disseminate data. Headquarters in Chicago.

1310 G St. NW
Washington, DC 20005
202-626-4780
www.bluecares.com

Brain Tumor Society

This organization works to educate the medical community about brain tumors, to raise public awareness, to facilitate early diagnosis and treatment, and to effect a cure. It also advocates for federal funding for brain tumor research.

84 Seattle St.
Boston, MA 02134-1245
617-783-0340
www.tbts.org

Brookings Institution, Economic Studies Program

Studies federal health care issues and health programs, including Medicare, Medicaid, and long-term care.

1775 Massachusetts Ave. NW
Washington, DC 20036
202-797-6111
202-797-6302 (information)

Catholic Health Association of the United States

Concerned with the health care needs of the poor and disadvantaged. Promotes health care reform, including universal insurance coverage and more cost-effective, affordable health care.

1875 Eye St. NW, #1000
Washington, DC 20006
202-296-3993
www.chausa.org

Center for Patient Advocacy

Supports the right of patients to receive state-of-the-art medical care in a timely manner. Monitors the Food and Drug Administration's regulation of drugs and medical devices; works to preserve the doctor-patient relationship and establish universal clinical practice guidelines; monitors legislation and regulations.

1350 Beverly Rd., #108
McLean, VA 22101
703-748-0400
800-846-7444
www.patientadvocacy.org

Council for Affordable Health Insurance

Membership: small and midsize insurance companies that favor free-market health care financing reform. Promotes reform measures, including establishment of medical savings accounts, tax equity, limited rating bands (rates that vary with age, physical condition, or geography), universal access, medical price disclosure prior to treatment, and caps on malpractice awards; serves as liaison with businesses, provider organizations, and public interest groups; monitors legislation and regulations.

112 South West St.
Alexandria, VA 22314
703-836-6200
www.worldweb.net/~cahi

Employee Benefit Research Institute

Conducts research on health insurance coverage, health care utilization, and health care cost containment; studies health care delivery and financing alternatives, including long-term care, flexible benefits, and retiree health financing options.

Jack Van Derhei, Research Associate
2121 K St. NW, #600
Washington, DC 20037-1896
202-659-0670
www.ebri.org

Federation of American Health Systems

Membership: investor-owned, for-profit hospitals and health care systems. Studies Medicaid and Medicare reforms; maintains speakers bureau; compiles statistics on investor-owned hospitals; monitors legislation and regulations.

1111 19th St. NW, #402
Washington, DC 20036
202-833-3090
www.fahs.com

Food and Drug Law Institute

Membership: providers of products and services to the food, drug, medical device, and cosmetics industries, including major food and drug companies and lawyers working in food and drug law. Arranges conferences on technological and legal developments in the industry; sponsors law courses, fellowships, and legal writing. Library open to the public.

1000 Vermont Ave. NW, #200
Washington, DC 20005-4903
202-371-1420
www.fdli.org

Grantmakers in Health

Seeks to increase the capacity of private sector grant makers to enhance public health; fosters information exchange among grant makers. Publications include a bulletin on current news in health and human services and the *Directory of Health Philanthropy.*

1130 Connecticut Ave. NW, #700
Washington, DC 20036
202-452-8331

Healthcare Leadership Council

Membership: health care leaders who examine major health issues, including access and affordability. Works to implement new public policies.

1800 Massachusetts Ave. NW, #401
Washington, DC 20036
202-452-8700

Hospice Foundation of America

Promotes hospice care for terminally ill people, disseminates information, conducts education and training, awards small grants. Headquarters in Miami Beach.

2001 S St. NW, #300
Washington, DC 20009
202-638-5419
800-854-3402 (Miami Beach)
www.hospicefoundation.org

Institute for Health Care Research and Policy

Research branch of Georgetown University School of Medicine. Interests include quality of care, cost-effectiveness, outcomes research, structure and impact of managed care, and access to care.

2233 Wisconsin Ave. NW, #525
Washington, DC 20007
202-687-0880

Institute of Medicine

Independent research organization chartered by the National Academy of Sciences. Conducts studies of policy issues related to health and medicine; issues position statements. National Academy of Sciences library open to the public by appointment.

2101 Constitution Ave. NW
Washington, DC 20418
202-334-3300
202-334-2169 (information)
202-334-2138 (press)
202-334-2125 (library)
www.nas.edu

Intergovernmental Health Policy Project

Researches state health laws and programs; provides health policy makers, administrators, and others with information on state health programs and policies. Affiliated with the National Conference of State Legislatures.

444 North Capitol St. NW, #515
Washington, DC 20001
202-624-5400
www.ncsl.org

Managed Health Care Association

Organization of public and private sector employers that promotes expanding and improving managed health care. Provides health care management professionals with education and training; supports innovation in designing and operating managed care programs; provides a forum for information exchange among employers, managed care organizations, and health care providers; serves as a technical resource on managed health care systems.

1401 Eye St. NW, #900
Washington, DC 20005
202-371-8232

National Association of City and County Health Officials

Represents local health departments; promotes partnership among local, state, and federal health agencies; works to improve the capacity of local health departments to assess health needs, develop public health policies, and ensure delivery of community services; submits health policy proposals to the federal government.

440 1st St. NW, #450
Washington, DC 20001
202-783-5550
www.naccho.org

National Association for Homecare

Promotes high-quality hospice, home care, and other community services for those with chronic health problems or life-threatening illness; conducts research and provides information on related issues; works to educate the public concerning health and social policy matters; monitors legislation and regulations; oversees the National Home Caring Council, which provides training, education, accreditation, and certification in the field.

228 7th St. SE
Washington, DC 20003
202-547-6586

National Brain Tumor Foundation

Among other things, this organization advocates for public funding for brain tumor research.

414 Thirteenth St., #700
Oakland, CA 94612-2603
415-284-0208
www.braintumor.org

National Citizens' Coalition for Nursing Home Reform

Seeks to improve the long-term care system and quality of life for residents in nursing homes and other facilities for the elderly; promotes citizen participation in all aspects of nursing homes; acts as a clearinghouse for nursing home advocacy; coordinates the Campaign for Quality Care, concerned with implementing the Nursing Home Reform Law of 1987.

1424 16th St. NW, #202
Washington, DC 20036-2211
202-332-2275

National Coalition for Cancer Survivorship

Membership: survivors of cancer (from newly diagnosed to long-term), their families and friends, health care providers, and support organizations. Disseminates information about living with cancer; works to reduce cancer-based discrimination in employment and insurance; operates Cansearch, a guide to cancer resources on the Internet.

1010 Wayne Ave., #505
Silver Spring, MD 20910
301-650-8868
www.access.digex.net/~mkragen/cansearch.html

National Coalition of Hispanic Health and Human Services Organizations

Assists agencies and groups serving the Hispanic community in general health care and in targeting health and psychosocial problems; provides information, technical assistance, health care provider training, and policy analysis; coordinates and supports research. Interests include mental health, chronic diseases, substance abuse, maternal and child health, youth issues, juvenile delinquency, and access to care.

1501 16th St. NW
Washington, DC 20036
202-387-5000

National Governors' Association

Monitors state health issues, including health care reform. Medicaid, primary care, maternal and child health care, and managed care.

444 North Capitol St. NW
Washington, DC 20001
202-624-5319
202-624-5300 (information)
www.nga.org

National Health Care Anti-Fraud Association

Membership: health insurance companies and regulatory and law enforcement agencies. Members work to identify, investigate, and prosecute individuals defrauding health care reimbursement systems.

1255 23rd St. NW, #850
Washington, DC 20037-1174
202-659-5955
www.nhcaa.org

National Health Council

Membership: voluntary health agencies; associations; and business, insurance, and government groups interested in health. Conducts research on health and health-related issues; serves as an information clearinghouse on health careers; monitors legislation and regulations.

1730 M St. NW, #500
Washington, DC 20036-4505
202-785-3913
www.housecall.com/sponsors/nhc/index.html

National Health Law Program

Organization of lawyers representing the economically disadvantaged, minorities, and the elderly in issues concerning federal, state, and local health care programs. Offers technical assistance and training for health law specialists. Headquarters in Los Angeles.

1815 H St. NW, #705
Washington, DC 20006-3604
202-887-5310
www.healthlaw.org

National Health Policy Forum

Nonpartisan policy analysis and research organization that provides state agencies and congressional staff with information on financing and delivery of health care services. Affiliated with George Washington University.

2021 K St. NW, #800
Washington, DC 20006
202-872-1390

National Hospice Organization

Membership: institutions and individuals providing hospice care and other interested organizations and individuals. Promotes supportive care for the terminally ill and their families; sets hospice program standards; provides information on hospices; monitors legislation and regulations.

1901 North Moore St., #901
Arlington, VA 22209
703-243-5900
800-658-8898
www.nho.org

Public Citizen, Health Research Group

Citizens' interest group that conducts policy-oriented research on health care issues. Interests include hospital quality and costs, doctors' fees, physician discipline and malpractice, state administration of Medicare programs, workplace safety and health, unnecessary surgery, comprehensive health planning, dangerous drugs, carcinogens, and medical devices. Favors a single-payer (Canadian-style) comprehensive health program.

1600 20th St. NW
Washington, DC 20009
202-588-1000
www.citizen.org

Rand Corporation, Health Sciences Program

Research organization that assesses health issues, including alternative reimbursement schemes for health care. Headquarters in Santa Monica, California.

1333 H St. NW, #800
Washington, DC 20005
202-296-5000
www.rand.org

Washington Business Group on Health

Membership: large corporations with an interest in health. Monitors health care legislation and regulations of interest to large corporations. Interests include reimbursement policies, Medicare, retiree medical cost, hospital cost containment, health planning, and corporate health education.

777 North Capitol St. NW, #800
Washington, DC 20002
202-408-9320

Appendix I

State Laws Governing Medical Records[1]

Federal, state, and local governments are responsible for protecting and safeguarding the public health and welfare. Accordingly, during terms of various epidemics, the state has required registration of infected persons in order to treat or quarantine them and to study the spread of the disease to ultimately control and eradicate it. Thus access to medical records is highly guarded but reporting of diseases is widely practiced at all levels of government. The Centers for Disease Control, for example, publishes the *Morbidity and Mortality Weekly Report,* containing a comprehensive list of all reported illnesses by both state and region that benefits the family practice doctor as well as the epidemiologist. The cases that are reported, from the flu to various venereal diseases to AIDS, are given in confidence, and access to the records is forbidden for most other purposes.

The outbreak of AIDS has sparked controversy over the confidentiality of medical records and diagnoses. Some employers and insurance companies have sought to have individuals tested for the HIV virus (which can lead to AIDS) before hiring, to prevent considerable expense in the future as the employee's health fails. Often these same parties argue for access to medical records for background checks as part of the interview process. The great tension regarding the rights of individuals with the HIV virus or AIDS; the public's interest in controlling and fighting the epidemic; and the interest of employers, insurers, and health officials in providing adequate and affordable medical care has created a dynamic ethical and legal dilemma that will not soon be resolved.

The laws controlling and regulating access to medical records vary greatly from state to state, although the basic protection is always there: a person's medical records are personal and private. As is historically the case, Congress has become increasingly involved in the area of individual rights and has enacted a number of pieces of privacy legislation. For example, the Federal Privacy Act of 1974 requires release of information in federal files to the subject individual upon request, although some government agencies have established regulations allowing release of information to a physician chosen by the requesting individual (5 U.S.C. 552a(f)(3)). Federally funded community mental health and mental retardation centers must maintain safeguards to preserve confidentiality and protect the rights of patients (59 U.S.C. 2689(d)(2)), and the Department of Defense may not use for any adverse personnel decision any personal information obtained in interviews with members of the service who are HIV-positive (PL 49–661 §705(c)).

This appendix treats all statutes that could be found concerning privacy and medical records. It must be noted, however, that this emerging field is increasingly subject to revision and new legislative attention. In addition, in certain areas such as AIDS information, the courts may have construed other statutes as protecting or not protecting AIDS victims. In these cases the courts may be awaiting or inviting legislative action. Spaces on the chart that are left blank are those situations where specific laws cannot be found; this does not necessarily mean that an individual is without protection in these areas.

State	Who Has Access	Privilege	Mandatory Reporting	Patient Waiver	Insurance Purposes	AIDS
ALABAMA	Notifiable disease records confidential (§22-11A-2)			Waiver of medical record of persons infected with sexually transmitted disease by written consent of patient (§22-11A-22)		An individual must be notified of a positive test result including face-to-face counseling, information, and health care services related to locating and testing persons who have been in contact with infected individual. Otherwise confidentiality must be maintained.
ALASKA	Any agent authorized by the principal, custodial, or noncustodial parent (§25.20.130; 13.26.344); Dept. of Social Services for financial records of medical assistance beneficiaries (§47.07.074)	In the case of emergency medical services, records of those treated may be disclosed to limited individuals for limited purposes (§18.08.087)		Mental health records may be disclosed only with patient consent or court order or for law enforcement reasons (§47.30.845)		
ARIZONA	Communicable disease related information confidential; release of information by consent or according to §36-664	Physicians and surgeons in most cases (§12-2235)	Nonaccidental injuries, malnourishment, physical neglect, sexual abuse, or other deprivation with intent to cause or allow death of minor child are confidential and may only be used judicially (§13-3620); abused incapacitated adult may only be used judicially (§46-454)			Any release of information must specifically authorize HIV-related information. Person with confidential HIV-related information may not be compelled to disclose information by subpoena, search warrant, or other judicial process, but may report if there is an identifiable third party at risk; no prohibition from listing in death certificate (§36-664)

State	Who Has Access	Privilege	Mandatory Reporting	Patient Waiver	Insurance Purposes	AIDS
ARKANSAS	Not open to public (§25-19-105); patient (§23-76-129); or through patient's attorney (§16-46-106)	Doctors may deny giving patients or their attorneys or guardians records on adequate showing of detrimentality (§16-46-106)		Express consent (§23-76-129)		Reporting required to Arkansas Dept. of Health by physicians and other medical and lab directors (§20-15-906); all information and reporting confidential (§20-15-904)
CALIFORNIA	Patient, but mental health professional may refuse if disclosure would have adverse effect on patient; in that case, patient may designate another professional to inspect records; minor may inspect records only for health care for which he or she is lawfully authorized to consent (H&S §1795.12 and .14)	Doctors, including psychotherapists and psychiatrists (Ev. §1010); patient must waive doctor-patient confidentiality when plaintiff in civil suit (Ev. §1016)		Patient must waive doctor-patient confidentiality when plaintiff in civil suit (Ev. 1016); other: Civ. Code §56.	Insurer may obtain to the extent noted in (Civ. Code §56.10(c)(2))	Blood testing must be anonymous and test results may not disclose identities of persons tested even through subpoena (H&S §199.20 and 199.42)
COLORADO	Patient or designated representative with written authority, except for psychiatric records that would have significant negative psychological impact, in which case patient is entitled to summary (§25-1-801); both parents in joint custody (§14-10123.5)		Venereal disease, other communicable diseases, HIV infections, AIDS, and other diseases required by the state board of health (§25-1-122)			Confidential counseling and testing preferred; anonymous testing conducted for persons with high risk (§25-4-1405.5)
CONNECTICUT	Patient may see and copy (§4-105); state law limits disclosure of mental health data about a patient by name or other identifier (§52-146h); state departments may release information on patients only to the extent necessary to obtain support or payment for care of patient; all information is confidential (§17b-225)					Confidential HIV-related information disclosed only according to §19a-583.

State	Who Has Access	Privilege	Mandatory Reporting	Patient Waiver	Insurance Purposes	AIDS
DELAWARE	All information and records of known or suspected cases of sexually transmitted disease (STD), including HIV infections, shall be strictly confidential; released only under certain circumstances: Tit. 16 §711	None in child abuse cases except for attorney-client privilege (Tit. 16 §908)	Sexually transmitted diseases reported to Division of Public Health, some reported in number and manner only (Tit. 16 §702)			Strictly confidential (Tit. 16 §711)
DISTRICT OF COLUMBIA	Person of record or his/her legal representative (§14-307); public mental health facility must make patient records available to patient's attorney or personal physician upon that person's written authorization (§21-562)	Physician/ surgeon; mental health professional except in interests of public justice; or other circumstances (§14-307) (§6-2511)				Information and records pertaining to persons with AIDS are confidential (§6-2805)
FLORIDA	Patient or his/her legal representative or health care provider except for psychological or psychiatric records which may be provided as a report instead of copies of records (§455.241); patient's guardian, curator, or personal representative, anyone authorized in writing (§395.3025)	Psychotherapist-patient (§455.241)		Patient must consent to release of records except by subpoena or unless patient consented to a compulsory physical examination pursuant to Rule 1.360, Fla. Rules of Civ. Pro. (§455.241)		Results may be disclosed with specific written consent of person to whom information pertains (§381.004)
GEORGIA	Disclosure of medical records pursuant to laws requiring disclosure or to limited consent to disclosure does not destroy confidential or privileged nature (§24-9-42)	Psychiatrist (§24-9-21); physician (§24-9-40); pharmacist (§24-9-40)	Venereal disease and suspected child abuse (§§19-7-5; 31-17-2)	Patient must make written authorization or waiver (or parents/ guardian in case of minor) except by subpoena or appropriate court order (§24-9-40)		All AIDS information confidential; may be disclosed to that person or in case of minor to parents or guardian and with notice, to reasonably believed spouse/partner (§24-9-47)
HAWAII	Patient or his attorney, but doctor may require patient's authorization to make them available to attorney if detrimental to patient's health (§622-57)		Those with diseases or conditions declared to be communicable or dangerous to the public health (§325-2)	Identity of individuals in Hawaii Tumor Registry and other studies is confidential; no person providing such information is liable for it (§§324-11, et. seq.)		All records of AIDS, HIV, or AIDS-related patients are confidential; release of information under circumstances in §325-101

State	Who Has Access	Privilege	Mandatory Reporting	Patient Waiver	Insurance Purposes	AIDS
IDAHO	Patient or agent by subpoena (§9-420); parent of minor child whether custodial or non (§32-717A); in some civil actions records may be open to discovery (§39-1392(e)); public medical records or records of those with reportable diseases exempt from disclosure (§9-340 (25) and (26))	Physician (§9-203(4))	Child abuse cases within 24 hours (§16-1619); enumerated venereal diseases including AIDS and HIV (§39-601)	Patient or doctor or nurse responsible for entries in hospital record may request protective order to deny or limit access (§9-420)		Confidentiality of patient information maintained; use of information restricted to "public health requirements" and "those with a legitimate need to know" (§39-609)
ILLINOIS			Child abuse (325 ILCS 5/4); sexually transmissible diseases (410 ILCS §325/4)	Right to privacy and confidentiality in health care may be waived in writing by patient or patient's physician (410 ILCS 5013)		AIDS test information must be kept confidential (410 ILCS 305/1, et seq.) No disclosure of AIDS test information without consent, court order, or as listed in 410 ILCS 305/9
INDIANA	Patient, anyone patient authorizes, physicians, anyone by court order, coroner, parent or guardian of minor patient (§34-3-15.5-4)	Doctor-patient information not divulgible (§34-1-14-5)	Child abuse must be reported by physicians and nonphysicians immediately (§31-6-11-3 & 4)		Insurance company may obtain records with written consent (§16-39-5-2)	All HIV cases must be reported (§16-41-2-3)
IOWA	Medical and psychiatric records held by Dept. of Human Services are confidential (§217.30)		Confidential reports of venereal disease must be filed (§140.3 & .4)	Patient may waive so that person in confidence may disclose at trial		All reports and information related to HIV are strictly confidential medical information; released under circumstances in § 141.10
KANSAS		Doctor-patient (with exceptions) (§§60-427); psychologist-patient (§§ 74-5323)	Any physician or lab director with knowledge of AIDS sufferer must report to secretary of health and environment; information shall be confidential and disclosed as per §65-6002 (c)	Mental health records may not be disclosed except with patient's consent or court order or with consent of the head of the treatment facility (§59-2931)		Any physician or lab director with knowledge of AIDS sufferer must report to secretary of health and environment; information shall be confidential and disclosed as per §65-6002 (c)

State	Who Has Access	Privilege	Mandatory Reporting	Patient Waiver	Insurance Purposes	AIDS
KENTUCKY	Patient may make written request for medical record to hospital or provider (§422.317)	Psychiatrist-patient privilege (§422.330)		Patient or physician may ask to prohibit or limit use by protective order (§422.315)		Test results disclosed only to those listed in §214.181
LOUISIANA	Health care providers must provide copies of records upon patient's request (unless injurious to health or welfare of patient) or subject to subpoena (§40: 1299.96)	Health care provider–patient (usually waived in cases of child abuse or molestation) (Art. 510 Louisiana Code of Evidence)				Information related to HIV is confidential; disclosure according to §§1300.14 and 1300.15
MAINE	Patient unless doctor thinks it would be detrimental to his/her health, then to an authorized representative (22 §1711); attorney general in a criminal proceeding although still confidential (5 §200-E)	Doctor-patient; psychologist-patient (both abrogated in child protective activity) (22 §4015)				Blood tests may not be conducted without consent and results must be kept confidential within health community (5§19203)
MARYLAND	Records of Secretary of Health & Mental Hygiene must be kept confidential. It is unlawful to disclose them except for research (Health-Gen §4-101, et seq.)	Psychologist/ psychiatrist–patient (Cts. & Jud. Proc. §9-109)	Medical Advisory Board allowed to report to Motor Vehicle Administration on patients whose driving may be impaired for mental or physical reasons (Transp. §16-118)		When insurance company compiles medical file for health or life policies, they must permit claimant, agent, or applicant to inspect file except information provided by doctor not available for 5 years unless doctor authorizes written release (Art. 48A §490c)	Test results confidential (Health-Gen. §18-334) but if individual refuses to notify sexual or needle-sharing partners, physician may inform local health officer (Health-Gen. §18-337)

State	Who Has Access	Privilege	Mandatory Reporting	Patient Waiver	Insurance Purposes	AIDS
MASSACHUSETTS	Patient has right to confidentiality of all records and communications to extent provided by law and to inspect and receive copy of medical records (psychotherapist may give summary of record if it would adversely affect patient's well-being (Ch. 112 §12CC): employer requiring physical exam of any employee shall upon request furnish copy of medical report (Ch. 149 §19A); mental health records private except for court order, at patient's request, or if mental health commissioner allows for sake of best interest of patient (Ch. 123 §36)		Any injury from discharge of gun or a burn affecting over 5% of the body or a rape or sexual assault (victim's name not included in report) (Ch. 112 §12A and §12A-1/2)			Labs and hospitals that conduct blood test for AIDS must not disclose results without obtaining written informed consent of patients (Ch. 111 §70F)
MICHIGAN	Any review entity (331.531); Dept. of Health shall protect privileged communications and individual's expectation of privacy with regard to Dept.'s activities (§333.2611)	Physician-patient privilege is recognized (§600.2157)	Serious communicable diseases (§333.5117)			All reports of HIV infection and AIDS are confidential; release subject to §333.5131
MINNESOTA	Patient, patient's representative, or minor's parent or guardian has right to copy doctor's and hospital records about themselves (if provider determines that information is detrimental to physical or mental health of patient, may withhold information and supply to third party) (§144.335); mentally committed patients have access (§253B.03)	Physician, nurse, or psychologist may not disclose confidential information acquired in professional capacity (§595-02)				HIV prevention program—some reporting requirements (§214.19); victims can require HIV testing of sex offender and know results (§611A.07); commissioner may subpoena privileged medical information of those exposed by HIV-infected dentist or physician in order to notify patients (§144.054 subdiv. 2)

State	Who Has Access	Privilege	Mandatory Reporting	Patient Waiver	Insurance Purposes	AIDS
MISSISSIPPI	Medical or dental review committee for evaluation of quality of care; patient's identity not divulged (§41-63-1, and 3)	Physician, dentist, nurse, pharmacist, and patient (§13-1-21)	Licensing boards may establish reporting requirements for Hepatitis B virus and HIV (§41-34-1, *et seq.*)	Patient waiver of doctor's privilege implied to comply with state and local health departments and for information regarding communicable diseases (§13-1-21)		Convicted sex offenders shall be tested for HIV; results reported to victims and spouses (§99-19-203)
MISSOURI		Physician and surgeon/ psychologist, or dentist (§491.060)				All information concerning one's HIV status is confidential; disclosure subject to §191.656
MONTANA	Patient may authorize disclosure of health care information (50-16-526); without patient's authorization (50-16-530); all records of Dept. of Public Health and Human Services are confidential; disclosed according to §41-3-205 (3)	Doctor-patient (§26-1-805); psychologist-client (§26-1-807)	Sexually transmitted diseases (§50-18-105); must report if conduct is such that might expose another to infection (50-18-106)			Person may not disclose or be compelled to disclose the identity of a subject of an HIV test or results (50-16-1009); HIV testing: 50-16-1007
NEBRASKA	Counsel for mentally ill patient (§83-1053); mental patient's records available to patient, counsel, parents or guardian if minor or legally incompetent, person authorized by the court, or patient (§83-1068); medical review panel (§44-2892)		Reporting of patients with cancer to Dept. of Health upon its request for Cancer Registry (§81-642); brain injuries for Brain Injury Registry (§81.651); all "reportable diseases" (including sexually transmitted diseases) (§71.503.01)	Privileged communications waived by patient consent and court of record		

State	Who Has Access	Privilege	Mandatory Reporting	Patient Waiver	Insurance Purposes	AIDS
NEVADA	Patient has right to inspect and copy both doctor's and hospital's records; also authorized representative or investigator (§629.061); required to forward record upon transfer to new medical facility (do not need patient's consent) (§§433.332; 449.705)	Doctor/ therapist–patient (§49.235 and 248)	Communicable diseases (§441A.150)	Patient may refuse to disclose or forbid any other person (including family members) from disclosing medical information (§49.225); right does not extend to mental patient; other exceptions (§49.245)		
NEW HAMPSHIRE	Records are deemed property of patient (§332:I-1); anyone with durable power of attorney for health care for patient (§137-J:7); patient and one with his written consent or with written certification of ombudsman (§161-F:14); no employee may be required to bear cost of any medical exam or record required as condition of employment (§275:3)	Doctor-patient (§329:26) and psychologist-patient privilege recognized (330-A:19)	Communicable disease (141-C:7)			All records and information pertaining to person's HIV testing are confidential and protected from unwarranted intrusion (141-F:8) (Disclosures pursuant to 141-F:7 and F:8)
NEW JERSEY	Limited right of access for attorneys and next of kin of mental patients in state institutions and attorneys handling personal injury cases; professional staff of community agency under contract to Division of Mental Health may disclose relevant information to staff of other agencies (§§30:4-24.3; 2A:82-42)	Psychologist-patient (45:14B-28); physician-patient (2A:84A-22.1, .2)	Child abuse (§9:6-8.30); pertussis vaccine (§26:2N-5); venereal disease (§26:4-41); AIDS (26:5C-6)			All records with identifying information are confidential (26:5C-6); disclosure per 26:5C-8, *et seq.*

State	Who Has Access	Privilege	Mandatory Reporting	Patient Waiver	Insurance Purposes	AIDS
NEW YORK	Medical director of prison in reference to inmate (Corrections §601); director of youth facility of a juvenile offender (Exec. §508); records access—no disclosures without patient consent; ombudsman (Exec §544); inspector of a mental facility—all information kept confidential (Men. Hyg. §16.11); physician or hospital must release medical file to another physician or hospital upon written request of parent, guardian, or patient; records concerning venereal disease treatment or abortion for minor may not be released, even to parent (NY Pub. Health §17)	Doctors, nurses, and dentists (Civ. Prac. §4504)				All HIV-related information is confidential and may only be disclosed according to §2782 N.Y. Pub. Health
NORTH CAROLINA	All privileged patient medical records possessed by Dept. of Health or local health department are confidential (§130A-12); pharmacists when necessary to provide services (§90-85.35)		Physicians, lab directors, and local health directors must report communicable diseases; hospitals may report (§130A-133, et seq.)			All AIDS information and records are confidential; subject to release only according to §130A-143
NORTH DAKOTA		Physician/ psychotherapist– patient (§31-01-06) pursuant to North Dakota Rules of Ev., Rule 503	Sexually transmitted diseases, contagious, infectious, or chronic disease that impact the public significantly and child abuse or neglect (§§23-07-01; 50-25.1-01 to 03)			Information regarding HIV infection is strictly confidential; release subject to §23-07-02.2)
OHIO	Employee or designated representative may request records from employer, physician, health care professional, hospital, or lab when they are contracted by employer (§4113.23)	Doctor-patient (§2317-02(B))	Child abuse (§2151-421); occupational diseases (3701.25); cases of cancer for cancer registry (3701.262); contagious or infectious diseases (including AIDS) §3701.24			Disclosure of HIV- or AIDS-related information subject to §3701.243

State	Who Has Access	Privilege	Mandatory Reporting	Patient Waiver	Insurance Purposes	AIDS
OKLAHOMA	Patient to nonpsychiatric files unless court ordered (Tit. 76§19); health professional may inform parents of treatment needed or provided to minor; such disclosure does not breach right to privacy (Tit. 63 §2602; Tit. 43A §1-109)	Physician–psychotherapist–patient (Tit. 12 §2503; Tit. 43A §1-109)	Child abuse (physical, sexual, and/or neglect); communicable or venereal disease (Tit. 21 §846; Tit l. 63 §1-528(b))			HIV tests or records upon written request of person affected, or in cases of certain crimes, test results released to victim (Tit. 63 §1-525)
OREGON	Institutions are encouraged to permit patient to copy doctor and hospital records and prevent unnecessary disclosure (§192.525)		Suspected violence: physical injury with knife, gun, or other deadly weapon (in confidence) (§146-750)			HIV test results confidential (§433.075)
PENNSYLVANIA	Mental health records in state agencies must be kept confidential (Tit. 50 §7111)	Physician privilege limited to civil matters (Tit. 42§5929)				All HIV-related information confidential; limited disclosure under Tit. 35 §7607
RHODE ISLAND	Patient (§5-37-22); holders of medical records must keep them confidential; patient's written consent generally required (§5-37.3-4)		Occupational diseases (§23-5-5); sexually transmitted and communicable diseases (§23-8-1); §23-11-5)			Disclosure of AIDS test result to third parties limited by §23-6-17
SOUTH CAROLINA	Express written consent of patient (§44-115-40)	Mental health provider–patient (19-11-95)	Sexually transmitted diseases (z016744-29-70)			Information and records are strictly confidential except under circumstances in §44-29-135; in minor cases, if attending public school, superintendent and nurse must be notified; court orders: §44-29-136
SOUTH DAKOTA		Physician-patient; waived for criminal proceedings or if physical or mental health of person is at issue (§19-2-3)	Venereal disease (34-23-2); child abuse or neglect (26-8A-3)			Victims of sexual assault may request testing and receive notification of results (23A-35B-1, et seq.)

State	Who Has Access	Privilege	Mandatory Reporting	Patient Waiver	Insurance Purposes	AIDS
TENNESSEE	Hospital records property of hospital, upon court order or written request of patient may see (§68-11-304); medical records of patients in state facilities and those whose care is paid for by state funds are confidential (§10-7-504)	Psychiatrists (§24-1-207); psychologists (§63-11-213)	Communicable diseases (68-5-101); sexually transmitted diseases (68-10-101)			No liability for real estate agent failing to disclose that occupant was HIV infected (66-5-207); law enforcement officer may request arrested person to be tested for Hepatitis B or HIV if exposed to blood (68-10-116); records strictly confidential; released as per 68-10-113
TEXAS	Medical information identifiable as to individuals is to be kept confidential and information used for studies is privileged (Health & Safety §161.022)		Bullet or gunshot wounds (Health & Safety §161.041); certain occupational diseases (Health & Safety §84.003); certain communicable diseases (Health & Safety §81.041)			State law spells out when AIDS blood tests may be conducted, including when employer can show necessity based upon bona fide occupational qualification (unless less discriminating means available); blood donations, etc., results must be kept confidential (Health & Safety §81.102, 103); mandatory testing of person who may have infected law enforcement officials (Health & Safety §81.050)
UTAH	Patient's attorney with patient's written authorization (§78-25-25)	Doctor-patient (§78-24-8(4))	Suspected child abuse (§62A-4A-403); communicable and infectious diseases (including HIV and AIDS) (§26-6-3)			All reports regarding communicable diseases are confidential (§26-6-20.5)

State	Who Has Access	Privilege	Mandatory Reporting	Patient Waiver	Insurance Purposes	AIDS
VERMONT		Physician, dentist, nurse, or mental health professional not allowed to disclose information acquired in attending a patient in a professional capacity (Tit. 12 §1612)	Infectious venereal diseases (Tit. 18 §1093)			HIV-related testing and counseling information disclosed upon court order showing "compelling need" that can't be accommodated "by other means" (pseudonym substituted if possible) (Tit. 12 §1705)
VIRGINIA	Individual medical data in state files exempt from public disclosure (§2.1-342(B)(3)); patient or his/her attorney upon patient's written request to hospital or health care records except for records when doctor declares release would be injurious to patient's health or well-being (§8.01-413)	Duly licensed practitioner of any branch of the healing arts dealing with patient in professional capacity including clinical psychologist (§8.01-399)			Insurance company must provide medical information to individual or to medical professional designated by individual; must notify individual that information was released at time of disclosure (38.2-609)	All test results are confidential, released only to that person, his legal representative, Dept. of Health, parents of minor, spouse, by court order, and others authorized by law (§32.1-36.1)
WASHINGTON	Patient may authorize disclosure (70.02.030); situations without patient's authorization: 70.02.050	Psychologist (18.83.11); physician (§5.60.060)	Child abuse (§26.44.030); tuberculosis (70.28.010); sexually transmitted diseases (70.24.105)			Disclosure of identity of person investigated, considered, or requested to test for HIV permitted to those under 70.24.105
WEST VIRGINIA	Patient through written request; summary provided in case of psychiatric or psychological treatment (16-29-1)		Venereal disease; communicable diseases; tuberculosis (§§16-4-6; 16-2A-5; 26-5A-4); suspected child abuse (§49-6A-2); gunshot and other wounds; burns (§§61-2-27 and 27A)	Physician-patient (except for W.V. Board of Medicine) (§30-3-9)		Disclosure of identity of person tested for HIV according to §16-3C-3

State	Who Has Access	Privilege	Mandatory Reporting	Patient Waiver	Insurance Purposes	AIDS
WISCONSIN	Patient may inspect and copy upon submitting statement of informed consent (§146.83); records must be kept confidential except for use in health care, processing payments and claims, and research (§146.82)	Physician, nurse, psychologist–patient (§905.04)	Sexually transmitted diseases (§252.11); tuberculosis (§252.07); child abuse (§48.981); communicable diseases (§252.05)			AIDS/HIV test results must remain confidential except as released per §252.15 (5)
WYOMING	Patient (with written authorization) §35-2-606; without authorization: §35-2-609	Doctor may testify only with patient's express consent or when patient voluntarily testifies on medical matters (§1-12-101)	Child abuse; sexually transmitted diseases; communicable disease (§§14-3-205; 35-4-130; 35-4-103)			

Appendix J

Health Care Financing Administration Regional Offices

For Connecticut, Maine, Massachusetts, New Hampshire, Rhode Island, and Vermont:

John F. Kennedy Federal Building
Room 2375
Boston, MA 02203
617-565-1234

For New Jersey, New York, Puerto Rico, and the Virgin Islands:

26 Federal Plaza
Room 3800
New York, NY 10278
212-264-8522

For Delaware, the District of Columbia, Maryland, Pennsylvania, Virginia, and West Virginia:

3535 Market St.
Room 3100
Philadelphia, PA 19101
215-596-1332

For Alabama, Florida, Georgia, Kentucky, Mississippi, North Carolina, South Carolina, and Tennessee:

101 Marietta Tower
Suite 702
Atlanta, GA 30323
404-730-3782

For Illinois, Indiana, Michigan, Minnesota, Ohio, and Wisconsin:

105 West Adams Street
15th Floor
Chicago, IL 60603
312-353-5737

For Arkansas, Louisiana, New Mexico, Oklahoma, and Texas:

1200 Main Tower Building
Dallas, TX 75202
214-767-4467

For Iowa, Kansas, Missouri, and Nebraska:

New Federal Office Building
601 East 12th Street
Room 220
Kansas City, MO 64106
816-426-2866

For Colorado, Montana, North Dakota, South Dakota, Utah, and Wyoming:

Federal Office Building
1961 Stout St.
Room 522
Denver, CO 80294
303-844-6136

For Arizona, California, Guam, Hawaii, Nevada, and Samoa:

75 Hawthorne St.
4th Floor
San Francisco, CA 94105
415-744-3621

For Alaska, Idaho, Oregon, and Washington:

Mail Stop 44
2201 6th Ave.
Seattle, WA 98121
206-615-2352

Subject Index

A

Name Index

Title Index

P

"The Paradigm Shift in Medicaid: Women with HIV under Managed Care," 349

"Parallel Proceedings: Concurrent *Qui Tam* and Grand Jury Litigation," 209

"Part B Billing Issues in Hospital/ Physician Integration," 182

Partners for the Dance: Forming Strategic Alliances in Health Care, 100

"Patching the Safety Net: Shifting Health Care Costs and State Policies," 332–333

"Patient Care," 354

Patient Confidentiality: Alphabetized Guide to the Release of Medical Information, 381

"Patient Rights and Remedies in Managed Care," 185

"Patient Rights Meets Managed Care: Understanding the Underlying Conflicts," 67

Patient Self-Determination in Long-Term Care: Implementing the PSDA in Medical Decisions, 34

"Patient Tort Liability of Rest, Convalescent or Nursing Homes," 306

"Patient Transfers—COBRA as Amended," 332

Paying for Medicare: The Politics of Reform, 418

"Paying Physicians for Charity Care," 121

Paying Physicians: Options for Controlling Cost, Volume and Intensity of Services, 183

"Payment by Capitation and the Quality of Care," 264

"Paymentfor Services Provided by Health Maintenance Organizations," 65

"Payment Principles Applicable to Mergers and Acquisitions," 181

"Payor Relationships with Providers— Comments from the Government and Private Perspective," 151

"Peer Review Confidentiality," 268

"Peer Review, Disciplining, Hearings and Appeals," 268

Peer Review Law (3rd ed.), 268

"Peer Review: Recent Developments and Future Trends," 268

"The Performance of Invasive Procedures by HIV-Infected Doctors: The Duty to Disclose under the Informed Consent Doctrine," 358

Perilous Knowledge: The Human Genome Project and Its Implications, 396

"Personal Liability for Health Lawyers: *U.S. v. Dan Anderson* and Beyond," 218

"A Perspective on Federalism and Medical Malpractice," 281–282

"The Physicianas Entrepreneur: State and Federal Restrictions on Physician Joint Ventures," 102

Physician Assistant Legal Handbook, 258

"Physician Authority for Unilateral DNR Orders—Federal Patient Self-Determination Act," 35

Physician Capitation Strategies, 97

"Physician Compensation: Exempt Organization Creativity Without IRS Problems," 128

"Physician Contracting," 63

Physician Credentialing and Peer Review Answer Book, 267

"Physician Focus: Fraud and Abuse," 213

"Physician Group Deals," 92

"Physician Group Practice Formation," 96

"Physician Group Practices," 38

"Physician Joint Ventures/Networks," 101

"Physician Managed Care Contracting" (Katz), 89

"Physician Managed Care Contracting" (Rust), 63–64

"Physician Mergers," 98, 99

Physician Organizations and Medical Staff: Contracts, Rights and Liabilities, 262

"Physician Practice Acquisitions: Can They Survive Antitrust?," 156

"Physician Practice Management Companies," 91

Physician Practice Management Companies: What You Need to Know, 90–91

"Physician Practice Mergers: Defining Relevant Markets," 156

"Physician Practice Mergers:1997 Business Review Advice," 155

"Physician Profiling: An Analysis of Inpatient Practice Patterns in Florida and Oregon," 110

"Physician Recruitment after Hermann Hospital," 134

"Physician Satisfaction Under Managed Care," 46–47

Physician Sexual Misconduct, 281

"Physician Unionization: Current Legal Constraints and Future Trends," 277

"Physician Unionization: The Impact on the Medical Profession," 277

"Physiciansand Pharmaceutical Company Clinical Trials: Ethical and Legal Issues in Physician New Drug Experimentation," 297

The Physician's Guide to Managed Care, 62

"Physicians in Managed Care: A Multidimensional Analysis of New Trends in Liability and Business Risk," 220

"Physicians' Liability for Adverse Drug Reactions," 287

"A Physician's Liability for Mistakes of a Physician Assistant," 259

Physician's Managed Care Manual (3rd ed.), 47

"Physicians and Surgeons: Standard of Skill and Care Required of Specialist," 280

"Physicians Unions: Developing Strength in Numbers," 276

"Physicians, Unions, and Antitrust": 1998 report, 277; 1999 journal article, 276–277

"Physicians with AIDS: A Proposal for Efficient Disclosure," 361

"Piercing the Veil of Secrecy of HIV/ AIDS and Other Sexually Transmitted Diseases: Theories of Privacy and Disclosure in Partner Notification," 357

"Planning for and Surviving a CEP Audit," 136

"The Police Power and the Regulation of Medical Practice: An Historical Review and Guide for Medical Board Regulation of Physicians in ERISA–Qualified Managed Care Organizations," 54

"Policy Implications of Recent ERISA Court Decisions," 244

"The Political Economy of Medicare," 419

"Politics and Charity: A Proposal for Peaceful Co-Existence," 121

The Politics of Medicare (2nd ed.), 331–332

Positioning Your Practice for the Managed Care Market, 92

"The Pot of Gold: Monitoring Health Care Conversions Can Yield Billions of Dollars for Health Care," 139

"A Potent Weapon: Federal Peer Review Immunity under HCQIA," 267

"Potential Anticompetitive Effects of Most Favored Nation Contract Clauses in Managed Care and Health Insurance Contracts," 150

The Potential of Telemedicine: A Guide to Assessing Telecommunications in Health Care, 397

"PPMC Contracts: Nuts & Bolts," 64

"A Practical Approach for Analyzing Antitrust Issues Faced by Provider Networks," 163